Human Rights

The United Nations General Assembly adopted the Universal Declaration of Human Rights in 1948. A burgeoning human rights movement followed, yielding many treaties and new international institutions and shaping the constitutions and laws of many states. Yet human rights continue to be contested politically and legally and there is substantial philosophical and theoretical debate over their foundations and implications. In this volume, distinguished philosophers, political scientists, international lawyers, environmentalists and anthropologists discuss some of the most difficult questions of human rights theory and practice: What do human rights require of the global economy? Does it make sense to secure them by force? What do they require in *jus post bellum* contexts of transitional justice? Is global climate change a human rights issue? Is there a human right to democracy? Does the human rights movement constitute moral progress? For students of political philosophy, human rights, peace studies, and international relations.

CINDY HOLDER is Associate Professor of Philosophy at the University of Victoria. She has published extensively on cultural rights and the philosophy of international law.

DAVID REIDY is Professor of Philosophy and Adjunct Professor of Political Science at the University of Tennessee. He works mainly in political and legal philosophy and has published many articles and book chapters on issues related to the philosophical foundations of human rights and international justice.

*To Bird –
Thanks for all the
care during the
rough patch in '12-'13.
love, David*

Human Rights

The Hard Questions

Edited by CINDY HOLDER

AND

DAVID REIDY

CAMBRIDGE UNIVERSITY PRESS
Cambridge, New York, Melbourne, Madrid, Cape Town,
Singapore, São Paulo, Delhi, Mexico City

Cambridge University Press
The Edinburgh Building, Cambridge CB2 8RU, UK

Published in the United States of America by Cambridge University Press, New York

www.cambridge.org
Information on this title: www.cambridge.org/9781107003064

© Cambridge University Press, 2013

First published 2013

Printed and bound in the United Kingdom by the MPG Books Group

A catalogue record for this publication is available from the British Library

Library of Congress Cataloguing in Publication data
  Human rights : the hard questions / edited by Cindy Holder and David Reidy.
    pages   cm
  Includes bibliographical references and index.
  ISBN 978-1-107-00306-4 – ISBN 978-0-521-17626-2 (pbk.)
  1. Human rights.   I. Holder, Cindy, editor of compilation.
  JC571.H84 2013
  323–dc23
  2012048495

ISBN 978-1-107-00306-4 Hardback
ISBN 978-0-521-17626-2 Paperback

Contents

Figure

Table

Contributors

EVELYN AMONY lives in Northern Uganda and is the leader of a women's group that conducts income-generation initiatives, works to empower women through exchange of ideas and experiences, and with the community to minimize stigma against women who have returned from Lord's Resistance Army captivity. She is the mother of four children and is currently completing her primary education.

ERIN BAINES is Assistant Professor at the Liu Institute for Global Issues, an adjunct professor in the Department of Political Science, and a faculty associate at the Institute for Gender, Race and Social Justice at the University of British Columbia. She has authored journal articles in *Security Dialogue* (2012), *African Affairs* (2010), *Third World Quarterly* (2003), the *Journal of Human Rights* (2011), the *Journal of Modern African Studies* (2009) and the *International Journal of Transitional Justice* (2007).

CHRIS BROWN is Professor of International Relations at the London School of Economics and Political Science. He is the author of numerous articles in international political theory and of *Practical Judgement in International Political Theory: Selected Essays* (2010), *Sovereignty, Rights and Justice* (2002), *International Relations Theory: New Normative Approaches* (1992), editor of *Political Restructuring in Europe: Ethical Perspectives* (1994) and co-editor (with Terry Nardin and N.J. Rengger) of *International Relations in Political Thought: Texts from the Greeks to the First World War* (2002). His textbook *Understanding International Relations* (2009) is now in its fourth and final edition and has been translated into Arabic, Turkish and Chinese.

ALLEN BUCHANAN is James B. Duke Professor of Philosophy and Professor of Law, Duke University; Visiting Research Professor, Freedom Center, University of Arizona, Tucson; and Distinguished Research Associate, Oxford Uehiro Centre for Practical Ethics, University of Oxford, UK. His work is mainly in political philosophy, philosophy of international law, and bioethics. His most recent books are *Justice and Healthcare* (2010), *Human Rights, Legitimacy and the Use of Force* (2010), *Beyond Humanity* (2011) and *Better Than Human* (2011).

HILARY CHARLESWORTH is an Australian Research Council Laureate Fellow and a professor of International Law at the Australian National University in Canberra. Her research interests are in human rights law and theories of international law.

THOMAS CHRISTIANO is Professor of Philosophy and Law at the University of Arizona and an editor of *Politics, Philosophy and Economics*. He has written *The Constitution of Equality: Democratic Authority and its Limits* (2008) and *The Rule of the Many* (1996) and many articles in moral and political philosophy on democracy, distributive justice and international institutions. He is currently working on projects on the legitimacy of international institutions, the human right to democracy and the foundations of equality as a principle of distributive justice.

CLAUDIO CORRADETTI is Teaching and Research Fellow at the Norwegian Centre for Human Rights at the University of Oslo. He has been visiting at the University of Oxford, Cornell and McGill. He is the author of *Relativism and Human Rights* (2009) and the editor of *Philosophical Dimensions of Human Rights: Some Contemporary Views* (2012).

ANN E. CUDD is University Distinguished Professor of Philosophy and Associate Dean for Humanities at the University of Kansas. Her work focuses on issues of oppression, inequality and freedom, particularly with regard to gender equity, and seeks to bring empirical economic and psychological theory to bear on normative philosophical questions. Her recent work includes *Analyzing Oppression* (2006) and *Capitalism, For and Against: A Feminist Debate*, co-authored with Nancy Holmstrom (2011).

TONY EVANS is Professor of Global Politics at the University of Winchester. He has researched and published on human rights for many years. His latest book is *Human Rights in the Global Political Economy: Critical Processes* (2011).

STEPHEN M. GARDINER is Professor of Philosophy and Ben Rabinowitz Endowed Professor of Human Dimensions of the Environment at the University of Washington, Seattle. He is the author of *A Perfect Moral Storm: The Ethical Tragedy of Climate Change* (2011), the coordinating co-editor of *Climate Ethics: Essential Readings* (2010) and the editor of *Virtue Ethics: Old and New* (2005).

MARK GOODALE is Associate Professor of Conflict Analysis and Anthropology at George Mason University and Series Editor of Stanford Studies in Human Rights. He is the author or editor of eight books, including, most recently, *Human Rights at the Crossroads* (2012), *Mirrors of Justice: Law and Power in the Post-Cold War Era* (with K. Clarke, 2010), *Surrendering to Utopia: An Anthropology of Human Rights* (2009) and *Human Rights: An Anthropological Reader* (2009). Forthcoming books include *Neoliberalism, Interrupted: Social Change and Contested Governance in Contemporary Latin America* (with N. Postero, 2013) and *The Bolivia Reader* (with Sinclair Thomson *et al.*, 2013).

CAROL C. GOULD is Distinguished Professor of Philosophy at Hunter College and the Graduate Center of the City University of New York, where she is a member of the doctoral faculties in Philosophy and Political Science and Director of the Center for Global Ethics & Politics at the Ralph Bunche Institute. She is the editor of the *Journal of Social Philosophy*. Gould is the author of *Marx's Social Ontology* (1978); *Rethinking Democracy: Freedom and Social Cooperation in Politics, Economy, and Society* (1988, 1990); and *Globalizing Democracy and Human Rights* (2004), which won the 2009 David Easton Best Book Award from the American Political Science Association.

CINDY HOLDER is Associate Professor of Philosophy at the University of Victoria. Her articles have appeared in journals such as *Human Rights Quarterly*, *Human Rights Review*, *Alternatives*, *Public Affairs Quarterly* and *The Monist*. Her research focuses on cultural rights and philosophical issues in international law, including the human rights of indigenous peoples and transitional mechanisms such as truth commissions and international criminal tribunals.

PETER JONES is Emeritus Professor of Political Philosophy at Newcastle University, UK. He is the author and editor of books on rights and has written on rights of various sorts, including human rights, group rights, democratic rights, welfare rights and rights of free expression. His published work has also ranged over a number of other subjects, including toleration, identity, recognition, cultural diversity, democracy, neutrality, international and global justice, and the nature of liberalism.

GAIL KARLSSON is an environmental lawyer and Senior Policy Advisor for ENERGIA, the International Network on Gender and Sustainable Energy. In addition to her work with ENERGIA, she serves as a consultant to the United Nations Development Programme (UNDP) Environment and Energy Group, the UNDP Gender Team, and other international organizations.

ADAM MCBETH is a Deputy Director of the Castan Centre for Human Rights Law and Associate Professor in the Law Faculty at Monash

University, Melbourne, Australia. His research focuses on the relationship between international human rights law and transnational economic activity, including responsibility for human rights in the course of trade, aid, development projects and commercial operations, and he has delivered human rights training to government and civil society representatives from Australia, Indonesia and Iraq. His recent books include *International Economic Actors and Human Rights* (2010) and *The International Law of Human Rights* (with Justine Nolan and Simon Rice, 2011).

REX MARTIN is Professor of Philosophy, Emeritus, at the University of Kansas and Honorary Professor at Cardiff University. His fields of major interest include political and legal philosophy and the history of political thought. Among his books are *A System of Rights* (1997) and *Rawls's Law of Peoples: A Realistic Utopia?* (co-editor, 2006).

LARRY MAY is W. Alton Jones Professor of Philosophy, Professor of Law, and Professor of Political Science at Vanderbilt University. He has published 27 books, 11 of which are single authored monographs, and over 100 articles. These writings have been translated into French, German, Spanish, Italian, Polish, Serbian, Japanese, Chinese and Korean. His work on legal ethics and international law has led to invitations to advise such groups as: the Indiana State Senate, the US State Department, the CIA, as well as members of the Australian High Court. His six most recent books have been published by Cambridge University Press. The most recent books have won awards in international law, philosophy and international relations.

JULIE MERTUS is a Professor and Co-Director of the MA program in Ethics, Peace and Global Affairs at American University. She has over 20 years of experience working for a wide range of non-governmental and governmental human rights organizations in the human rights field. She is the author of numerous books including *Bait and Switch: Human Rights and U.S. Foreign Policy* (2004), which was named human rights book of the year in 2005 by the American Political Science Association Human Rights Section. Her most recent books, *Human Rights Matters* (2009) and *The United Nations and Human Rights* (2005) are required reading on many syllabi throughout the country and her book on Kovoso – *Kosovo: How Myths and Truths Started a War* (1999) – has been influential in Washington, DC policy circles. Professor Mertus has also published in law journals and leading multidisciplinary journals such as: *Ethics and International Affairs, Global Governance, International Studies Perspectives, International Feminist Journal of Politics* and *The Harvard International Review*. As a practitioner she has worked as a field researcher, lawyer, advocate, consultant political analyst and trainer.

LAURA PARISI is Associate Professor of Women's Studies at the University of Victoria, Canada. Her articles have appeared in journals such as *Politics and Gender*, *Journal of Human Rights* and *Canadian Foreign Policy*. Her current research focuses on the gender mainstreaming practices of human rights and development non-governmental organizations.

DAVID REIDY is Professor of Philosophy at the University of Tennessee. He works in political and legal philosophy and has in recent years published widely on the political philosophy of John Rawls and on issues of human rights and global justice, his essays appearing in many journals and anthologies. He is also the editor or co-editor of numerous books and the author of *On the Philosophy of Law* (2006). He has twice been awarded the American Philosophical Association's Berger Prize for his work in the philosophy of law.

ALISON DUNDES RENTELN is Professor of Political Science, with joint appointments in Anthropology, Law and Public Policy, at the University of Southern California where she teaches law and public policy with an emphasis on international law and human rights. She has authored or edited *The Cultural Defense* (2005), *Multicultural Jurisprudence: Comparative Perspectives on the Cultural Defense* (co-edited with Marie-Claire Foblets, 2009), and *Cultural Law: International, National, and Indigenous* (co-authored with James Nafziger and Robert Paterson, 2010). She has worked with the United Nations on the Convention on the Rights of Persons with Disabilities. She served on several California civil rights commissions and the California committee of Human Rights Watch.

AYELET SHACHAR is Professor of Law, Political Science and Global Affairs at the University of Toronto, where she holds the Canada Research Chair in Citizenship and Multiculturalism. She has published and lectured widely on citizenship theory, immigration law, multiculturalism, cultural diversity and women's rights, family law and religion in comparative perspective, highly skilled migration, and global inequality. Shachar is the author of *Multicultural Jurisdictions: Cultural Differences and Women's Rights* (2001) and *The Birthright Lottery: Citizenship and Global Inequality* (2009), and the recipient of several research and excellence awards. She has held visiting professor positions at Stanford Law School and Harvard Law School. Her work has also proven influential in the real world, intervening in actual public policy and legislative debates.

KRISTIN SHRADER-FRECHETTE is O'Neill Professor, Biological Sciences Department and Philosophy Department, University of Notre Dame, USA. Author of nearly 400 articles and 15 books, including *Taking Action, Saving Lives* (2007) and *What Will Work: Fighting Climate Change with Renewable Energy* (2011), Shrader-Frechette has held membership on many US National Academy of Sciences boards/committees, government, and UN committees. The first woman president of three international scholarly/scientific organizations, she works mainly on ethical/methodological issues in science and public health and quantitative risk assessment. Her research, funded by the US National Science Foundation for 28 years, has been translated into 13 languages. In 2004 Shrader-Frechette became the third American to win the World Technology Award in Ethics. In 2007, *Catholic Digest* named her one of 12 "Heroes for the US and the World" for her global, *pro bono* environmental-justice work with minority/poor communities.

NEIL WALKER is the Regius Professor of Public Law and the Law of Nature and Nations at the University of Edinburgh. He was previously Professor of European Law at the European University Institute in Florence between 2000 and 2008. He has published widely on questions of national and transnational constitutional theory, and also on the relationship between law and security.

MARYSIA ZALEWSKI is Professor and Head of School of Social Science at the University of Aberdeen. She has published widely on feminist theory, gender and international relations and masculinities. Her monograph *Feminist International Relations: Exquisite Corpse* will be published in 2013.

Introduction

CINDY HOLDER AND DAVID REIDY

Background

Over recent decades human rights have moved center stage within the theory and practice of international law and politics. This development has drawn the attention of philosophers, lawyers, political scientists, anthropologists, activists, politicians and diplomats, and others eager to understand or shape international law and politics. Whether as cause or effect (perhaps a bit of both) of this attention, there can be little doubt any longer that, as a feature of international law and politics, human rights are here to stay. So, too, then are the many questions, theoretical and practical, they raise.

As a theoretical matter, the most general questions to be raised about human rights concern their nature, function, justification and content. There is considerable overlap in and interaction between these questions, of course. How one thinks about the nature or function of human rights will shape how one thinks about their justification and content, for example. But it is nevertheless illuminating to consider the questions separately, at least initially.

Consider the nature of human rights. There is, first, the question of what it is to be a right. What distinguishes a right from what simply is right? What distinguishes these from what is good? And how are these three notions related? Then there is the question of what distinguishes human rights from other species and subspecies of the general genus "rights." What distinguishes human rights from constitutional or legal rights, for example? What distinguishes human rights from moral rights generally? There was once, and in some quarters is still, extensive skepticism about the very idea or possibility of human rights on any understanding. But such skepticism is increasingly a thing of the past, and rightly so as the arguments adduced for it have proved insufficient to sustain it. This is not to say that more targeted and limited skepticisms about specific understandings of human rights or about particular human rights can be set aside. On the contrary, several of the chapters in this volume examine one or another version of such a targeted skepticism.

However there is today widespread support for the view that human rights are intelligible and really exist as a distinct kind or subspecies of rights. Moreover, while it is not uncommon or undesirable for human rights to achieve institutional embodiment as conventional legal rights, for example, by treaty, the majority view these days is that they are not fundamentally a kind or subspecies of conventional legal rights; rather they are a subspecies of moral rights. But as a subspecies of moral rights, human rights are not easy to understand. Are they simply timeless universal moral rights derived from or ingredient in the one true moral code binding all human persons and discernible by the light of reason? Or are they simply the moral rights that would have to figure, as a practical matter, into any reasonable public justification of specific contemporary historically contingent institutions? In particular, are human rights the moral rights that have to figure in justifications of institutions with a global reach, such as modern states engaged in international relations, the emerging international legal order, and various international and transnational organizations? On the first view, human rights are pre-institutional, pre-political moral rights susceptible perhaps to a purely theoretical justification. On the second view, they are post-institutional, post-political moral rights, the justification of which may be inseparable from the practical interest of people alive today in peacefully and successfully navigating and rendering publicly intelligible and acceptable the institutional and political world that history has bequeathed to us.

Questions such as these about the nature of human rights immediately invite questions about human rights' function and justification. For example, do human rights function mainly as a theoretical pre-institutional constraint on the institutions we might defensibly have? Or do they function mainly as a practical post-institutional criterion for reconciling ourselves to and further improving institutions as we find them? Either way, there are further questions about how human rights discharge their function. Do human rights function mainly by establishing a fairly determinate mandatory moral minimum to be secured universally? Or do they function mainly by establishing a less determinate, more open-ended aspirational ideal to be secured by each and all in their own way and on their own schedule, albeit in conversation with others? Within existing practice, human rights seem to function in both ways to some significant degree. When functioning in the first way, they seem to specify a key necessary condition of political sovereignty and the associated right to non-intervention. When functioning in the second way, they structure and serve as basic currency within an increasingly important domain of global political discourse.

Some particular human rights seem to function more the first way and others more the second. Is this an indication that there are different types of human right? Does it indicate that how human rights function may or should vary?

Functioning either way, there is an important and related question here about human rights and both the universal (that which necessarily is or ought to be common to the moral experience of all) and the particular (that which necessarily is or may be particular to the moral experience of only some) within human moral experience. This question concerns the function of human rights not only in terms of the scope of and permissible means to securing that which is universal but also in terms of the scope and role of human rights in defending that which is particular.

To some observers human rights have long seemed to function in a more insidious way: as a rhetorical or ideological mechanism by which powerful international actors legitimate the use of force, sometimes even the pointing of guns, to impose universally on others what is in the end no more than, at best, their own particular aspirational ideal, and at worst their narrow self-interest masquerading as an ideal. If human rights cannot be made to function otherwise than this third, darkly parochial possibility, then human rights may appear or pretend to be a subspecies of real moral rights when in fact they are not and there is, properly speaking, no justification for them. And even if in theory human rights could be made to function as more than rhetorical or ideological mechanisms of power, it may be that presently they do not. In either case, we ought to approach existing human rights discourse and practice with the aim of critiquing rather than justifying.

However, no critique of contemporary human rights discourse and practice is likely by itself to establish that human rights must or will always function as mere ideological legitimation of the exercise of power on the international stage, or that every corner of contemporary discourse and practice so functions. Significant domains of contemporary discourse and practice seem to function genuinely as morally defensible attempts to secure universally a mandatory moral minimum or to organize voluntary international undertakings around various attractive and widely and potentially universally shared aspirational ideals. And so even if a critical stance is necessary and appropriate with respect to some domains of human rights discourse and practice, in other domains there will be no avoiding the task of, and so questions regarding, substantive justification.

Can we justify human rights without appealing to a robust conception of human nature? Should we try? Can we justify them without asserting the unique truth of a comprehensive moral doctrine? Should we try? Can we publicly justify them as morally essential to the emerging international order when that order is one that includes both liberal democracies and non-liberal and/or non-democratic states? Should we try? These questions lead inexorably into substantive questions about whether certain rights claimed to be human rights can really be justified as such. Here we come to questions about the content of human rights: what goes on the list of human rights? How does that list get settled? Does the list have to be settled to be effective? Human beings have many pressing interests, not all of which will underwrite a specific human right. So which interests do underwrite specific human rights? What's the normative relationship between the interests that do underwrite a right and the ones that don't? If we don't turn to a survey of the most pressing interests widely shared among human persons to answer this question, what do we turn to? And to what extent must we specify and attend to the reasonableness of the duties entailed by a candidate human right when determining whether it is properly included in the list?

Some of the most difficult questions raised by contemporary human rights theory and practice sit at the intersection of the theoretical and practical considerations bearing on content or list questions. Among them: for any given human right, or for human rights generally, how is respect for the universal to be balanced against respect for the particular? And how is respect for the individual to be balanced against respect for the groups in which individuals live and make intelligible their lives? What role can or should human rights play when it comes to the rapidly changing global economy or global environment? Is there a human right to democracy that can be invoked in support of various and highly visible democratization movements, whether national, international or transnational? Which, if any, human rights are properly enforced coercively, whether by unilateral, multilateral or international institutions and initiatives, and when? Is the enthusiasm that so many bring to the human rights project as it has unfolded historically in recent decades justified? Should it be tempered? Reformed? It is these sorts of hard questions, addressed from multiple disciplinary perspectives and with an eye to both theory and practice, that this volume takes up.

Overview of the chapters

What are human rights?

In Part I Chris Brown, Neil Walker and Rex Martin consider the question "what are human rights?" Chris Brown opens with a very basic and controversial question: do human rights require an account of what it is to be human? Claims about what makes for a distinctively human existence have an unsavoury history in the Western intellectual tradition, but Brown argues that the idea of a human right necessarily relies on an account of what is good for all people everywhere. Reluctance to rely on an account of human nature is grounded in a legitimate worry about how such accounts have figured in approaches to otherness that associate difference with inferiority. However, Brown argues that the lesson is not that there are no commonalities across people that may safely be used as grounds for claims about human rights. The lesson is that the specific content of various communities' customs is not a good ground for such claims. That there are commonalities in the subject matter of human communities' customs, on the other hand – that peoples universally treat certain activities or relationships as central to who they are and whether they live well – can be plausible grounds for identifying rights that can be justified in virtue of what it is to exist as a human.

Neil Walker takes up a different question: how can human rights both serve as a common standard that identifies the minimal conditions of equal moral standing and recognize divergences in conclusions about what is normatively significant about and in a particular context? Walker argues that the tension this question points to is inherent to human rights' function as a regulatory architecture and must be explicitly addressed or else risk compromising that function. Pretending that the tension is only apparent and easily resolved does not address the tension and undermines the effectiveness of human rights concepts by leaving unarticulated what is to be accomplished by describing human rights as universal and what human rights are supposed to rule out. Pretending that the tension is a fundamental incoherence that is impossible to resolve does not address the tension and undermines the effectiveness of critical engagement with human rights concepts by leaving unarticulated why commonalities that seem obvious and incontrovertible are either illusory or, if they are real, are not grounds for common cause. Walker describes the tension as between generality and uniformity in standards and particularity and difference in applications. He argues that although resolving it has become both more challenging and more urgent in the context of globalization, the plural configuration of international institutions offers a productive way forward. The key is recognizing the modest reach of the universality proposed by human rights institutions. For example, Walker argues that international human rights institutions do not presuppose a comprehensive political morality, and that increasingly human rights communities are multi-scalar and multiply configured. Human rights themselves are disaggregated, open-ended and locally implemented. In this, human rights concepts and institutions are a complex blend of the universal and the particular.

Rex Martin takes up questions about justification. He examines whether is it possible to justify human rights for and to all people everywhere, and whether human rights must be conceived of as "natural," in the sense of pre-political, for universal justification to work. Martin begins by distinguishing four different dimensions of human rights' universality: that they are rights of all persons, that they establish responsibilities for all persons, that they are justifiable to and for all persons, and that they are feasible in all contexts. Against this background, he considers several common arguments against treating human rights as applying to all people everywhere: that the most plausible candidates for universal rights and duties are moral constraints on individuals rather than claims against societies or governments; that the most commonly named human rights cannot, as a practical matter, be universally implemented and may not, as a matter of justice, be demanded in all contexts; and that some human rights are rights of groups or are rights that apply only to a sub-set of human beings. Martin argues that in all these objections there is a mistaken conflation of the pre-political traits or criteria that figure in universal justification and the justification itself. For Martin, universal justification requires showing that a right is justifiable to and for all people everywhere. This requires establishing that almost all people can reasonably be expected to see a right as being of benefit. Universal justification does not require that it can be shown that a right would benefit every single person; it is enough to show that it is reasonable to expect that almost all people would see the right as being of benefit to a vast number of people. So although organized society and governments are emphasized in human rights, they are not the only addressees. And although the explanation of why some rights are universally justifiable may depend on the empirical fact of the prevalence of the modern state, neither having human rights nor having a specific human right will depend on specific facts about the government to which a human is subject. Finally, that a right is group-specific is not necessarily incompatible with its being universally justifiable, as almost all people may reasonably be expected to see the benefit for vast numbers of people in rights related to circumstances or properties that create special vulnerabilities.

How do human rights relate to groups and culture?

Part II takes up the questions of whether and how human rights might protect the interests of particular and typically minority groups, including religious, ethnic, linguistic, or other groups; and, relatedly, whether human rights can be reconciled with the obvious fact, and to the normative desirability, of cultural diversity. Alison Dundes Renteln begins with the familiar question of whether cultural relativism poses a threat to human rights. Taking note of the distinctions between descriptive and normative relativism, universal and absolute truths, moral pluralism and moral skepticism, and so on, she concludes that the relativism championed by many anthropologists in the mid twentieth century poses no threat to human rights. However, this does not mean that cultural diversity can be ignored or does not render many human rights questions very hard indeed. Taking up a number of cases – female circumcision, corporal punishment for children within the family, certain gendered religious practices, varying conceptions of disability, and so on – and paying attention to the full range of human rights bearing on these cases, Renteln shows just how difficult these questions can be, but also just how morally necessary it is to grapple with these questions and arrive at cross-cultural, shared understandings of what human rights require across diverse cultural contexts.

Peter Jones then takes up the question of whether human rights can be held by groups or can be held only by individuals (even if individuals qua group members) severally. The question arises because it is sometimes said that without human rights held by groups as such the human rights movement threatens the structure, ends and even survival of some groupings. Jones takes the right to political, collective self-determination to be a group right of this sort. In the absence of a right to self-determination of the group as such the human rights movement would constitute a threat to free, independent, self-determining bodies politic. This suggests that there is a good reason to try to make sense of the idea that at least some human rights may be held by a group as such. Jones argues that we can make sense of this idea, but only if we reject what he terms a "corporate" understanding of the group, where the right is held by the group understood as an "it" that transcends and is independent of the individuals whose relations constitute it. Many who reject group human rights do so because they reject the corporate understanding as the only way that a group as such could be a right-holder. But there is an alternative, "collective" understanding of the group in which the group is not an "it" but a "we." On the collective understanding, the members of the group hold the right jointly, as a "plural subject." The right to collective, political self-determination understood in this way is not a right that human beings can hold simply as individuals or as individuals qua group members. And it is not a right that ought to be thought of as held by some reified nation or state that transcends and is independent of the individuals out of whose relations it is constituted. Rather, it is a right properly thought of as held only by a "we," by individuals jointly together as a group. Jones then extends his analysis to show how other putative group rights might be vindicated as human rights by appeal to this collective understanding of the group. Of course, that any group right might, formally speaking, be vindicated as a human right does not establish that it ought, substantively speaking, to be so vindicated. Group rights must not violate the human rights individuals hold as individuals and they must be justified by reference to the compelling interests that the group, that "we" in some sense, have, interests sufficiently weighty to justify the duties the right imposes on others. Still, this clears the way to a meaningful notion of group rights as human rights, one that might well serve the interests of human persons not only as individuals or individuals who happen to belong to groups but as "plural subjects" or a "we" (as in, e.g., "we the people"). To be sure, there are limits to the work that can be done by the collective understanding of groups. For example, it is hard to see how the claimed human right of indigenous groups to reparations for historical injustice could be vindicated by appeal to a collective understanding of the group.

Ayelet Shachar pursues the relationship between human rights and group and cultural diversity by looking to the issue of how minority religious women seek to navigate their way between the apparently competing claims of equality and of respect for diversity, especially in contemporary Western liberal democracies. Shachar examines claims both to be included in the public sphere (e.g., is it permissible legally to prohibit women from wearing the veil in public places?) and to withdraw from the public sphere (e.g., is it permissible for religious groups to establish their own systems for adjudicating disputes, say in the areas of family law?). The latter pose questions especially hard within the context of societies, like contemporary liberal democracies, that have sought to establish a secular rule of law clearly separated from religious authority. Shachar carefully explores the interests of women within a context defined by the intersection of religion, gender, family, the rule of law, liberal democracy, human rights, and increased mobility across borders and so across legal and religious contexts. Seeking a reasoned middle way that avoids a "your rights or your culture" dilemma, and that acknowledges the claims of both religious commitment and gender equality, Shachar urges a form of regulated interaction between religious and secular sources of authority, consistent with maintaining a baseline defined by the rights that must be guaranteed to all.

Claudio Corradetti notes at the outset of his chapter that the Wars of Religion set the historical context for the emergence of the right to freedom of conscience and expression. Human rights and pluralism, cultural, religious, ethnic and so on, have been interacting from the beginning. Engaging critically the complex history of this interaction, Corradetti aims to tease out of our current practices and understandings a conception of the relationship between human rights and cultural pluralism adequate to our current tasks and times. He argues that human rights constitute the conditions of communicative rationality, and so normatively valid social coordination, between persons across diverse but never fully or radically incommensurable or mutually unintelligible cultures, contexts and worldviews. The Wars of Religion put on the table a principle of communicative freedom (freedom of thought and expression) and thus put us on the admittedly crooked path to our current situation within which human rights underwrite and facilitate not only communicative freedom, but also communicative rationality aimed at normatively binding social coordination across all the world's peoples. Properly understood human rights make possible a certain kind conversation, one that need not threaten cultural diversity.

What do human rights require of the global economy?

Some of the most challenging questions that arise in connection with human rights regard the effects and operation of the global economy. Adam McBeth begins Part III by asking about the human rights responsibilities of non-state actors such as intergovernmental organizations and multinational corporations. McBeth observes that from the perspective of the rights-bearer, it is obvious that their rights may be and are violated by non-state actors. But do non-state actors have duties under international legal regimes? Under a purposive approach to international legal interpretation – an approach that emphasizes the purposes or goals of international legal instruments – it is not difficult to establish that non-state actors have duties not directly to violate human rights and not to interfere with the protection and promotion of human rights by governments. However, it is difficult to identify and develop effective mechanisms of accountability for non-state actors. McBeth argues that rule-making intergovernmental organizations, such as the WTO, are accountable for how their rules impact human rights enjoyment, including the impact of the terms under which an organization's rules are negotiated, and the manner in which those rules are interpreted and applied. Intergovernmental organizations that directly engage within communities, such as the World Bank, are accountable for their performance standards and their policies on the choice, structure and conduct of projects. Corporations are accountable for accepting regulation of their activities, for refraining from contributing to human rights violations, for preventing such violations from occurring when they can do so, for mitigating human rights violations when they can, and for supporting and securing access to remedy for rights violations. McBeth notes that as the international legal mechanisms currently operate, the accountability of both international organizations and corporations for their conduct with respect to human rights is primarily normative rather than operational. This means that failure to respect human rights is recognized and accepted by non-state actors themselves as a legitimate basis for criticism; but there are few if any effective mechanisms for converting this criticism into changes in the way such actors operate. Attempts to develop and augment the effectiveness of accountability mechanisms for non-state actors are underway in many parts of the world. As yet, these are primarily located within and focused on municipal, or national, legal systems.

Tony Evans takes up the question of whether human rights empower people with respect to the global economy. He begins with the observation that post-World War II the story of human rights is typically told as a story of arrival and completion of an international moral project with only the practical work of implementing norms still left to do. This story has closed off the rich, explicitly political debate about what human rights ought to be for implementation to be an appropriate and worthwhile international project. Moreover, the typical story about human rights has encouraged the handing over of the task of implementing and assessing the success of human rights to an international political order that is dominated by Western capitalist states. Against this background, the shift away from states and towards international institutions that is associated with globalization has not translated into improved enjoyment of human rights in the sense of improved conditions of life for actual persons. Instead, this shift has exposed a tension between advocating for global forms of governance and advocating for human rights. Historically, human rights discourse has contrasted national and local threats and barriers to human rights with international support and assistance. However, state and local political actors may have interests in health, education, water and nutrition of local populations and local communities that global actors do not. Consequently, in the same way that processes of globalization have challenged the coherence of claims that states are appropriate and effective vehicles for the priorities of local communities, so too have these processes challenged the coherence of claims that global institutions are appropriate and effective vehicles. Evans concludes that the lesson to take from this is not that there is no place for human rights language in projects of resistance. The lesson is rather that if human rights language is to have a place in liberatory projects it must be as non-legal, explicitly political concepts.

Ann Cudd examines an explicitly moral question: does the assumption that all human beings have the same moral importance rule out accepting differences in economic status or economic opportunities between them? Some have argued that it is morally indefensible to accept and support contemporary global political and economic institutions because these generate arbitrary differences in the level of income and degree of economic security that is available to people in different parts of the world. Cudd argues that treating people as moral equals requires that individuals not be deprived of the opportunity to live a decent life and that individuals not be categorically excluded from the bases of social respect; but that this does not in itself rule out differences in economic status or economic opportunities, nor does it necessarily rule out distributing economic status and economic opportunities in ways that operate to the advantage of some and the disadvantage of others. Cudd argues that there is nothing inherently disrespectful in treating people differently because there is nothing inherently disrespectful in competition, so long as the outcomes of the competition do not impact participants' opportunities to live a decent life, and the terms of the competition do not treat some competitors as less worthy than others. Competition and inequality are only disrespectful when they are conducted in such a way as to imply that some people are of lesser moral standing than others, or do not have the same fundamental claim to a decent life as everyone else. Cudd identifies categorical exclusion as the key element in determining whether the structure of a distributive scheme is acceptable. Equality is important not in itself but as an indicator of people having been ruled out as candidates for social respect or participation in collective decision-making on the basis of ascribed features. Insofar as global political and economic institutions are morally indefensible, then, it is because these institutions operate in a way that implies that some people do not have a right to the elements of a decent life, or do not have the same right to a decent life, social respect, the ability to plan, and the ability to participate in collective self-determination as everyone else. When institutions are indifferent to individuals' access to the bases of a healthy life, the bases of social respect, the ability to plan as an individual and/or the ability to determine collectively the laws under which they live, or when institutions categorically exclude individuals from economic opportunities and economic standing on the basis of ascriptive characteristics, these institutions fail to treat all people as of equal moral importance and are morally indefensible.

How do human rights relate to environmental policy?

Part IV takes up the hard question of whether human rights constitute a non-trivial part of the best response to various environmental problems, from global climate change to the health risks associated with various forms of pollution. Human rights obviously contribute trivially to the best response to such problems. The human right to subsistence, for example, expresses the high priority interest of all persons in access to potable water and non-life-threatening food and the correlate high priority duties of all states to secure the same for their members. But this does not take us far. And so the question arises of whether human rights do or should contribute more.

Stephen Gardiner takes up the pressing problem of climate change, a problem global, intergenerational and ecological in nature and arising in a context of some scientific uncertainty. He notes that while the idea of human rights – the idea that institutions that inflict certain sorts of harms on persons ought not to be tolerated – may compel us morally to take on the institutional causes of human effects on climate change, it is less clear what human rights have to contribute beyond this initial moral push. Gardiner considers a number of candidate contributions, including:

1. a shift away from the aggregative cost/benefit analysis so common to economic approaches to the problem and toward a victim-centered, harm to persons, approach;
2. access to institutions, legal and otherwise, through which policies might be implemented and enforced; and
3. a theoretical grounding for assigning such policies a very high moral priority.

It is potential contributions like these that underwrite arguments to the effect that global climate change threatens core human rights to life, subsistence and health and thus demand immediate coordinated international action. Gardiner casts a critical eye on such arguments not so much to debunk them as to reveal just how hard it is to vindicate all their assumptions and inferences. He concludes that it remains a hard question whether human rights have anything non-trivial to contribute to our response to the "perfect moral storm" of global climate change.

Of course, energy production is, according to the scientific consensus, a key factor in global climate change. And yet, as Gail Karlsson notes, access to energy is an ingredient in or condition of any number of human rights, the content of which remains a mere hope for large segments of the human population. Whatever our response to global climate change, it ought not compromise the human rights of those without access to energy, and especially the most vulnerable among them, often women in impoverished countries. Here Karlsson picks up one of the worries Gardiner raises about a human rights approach to global climate change: there are many human rights and they often seem to pull in different directions. Attending to the empirical linkages between poverty, gender inequality and the production of energy, Karlsson addresses herself to the thorny issue of how to advance development and reliable access to energy along with gender equality in the developing world without contributing to, and ideally while making a contribution to solving, the problem of global climate change. She examines a number of case studies drawing out both common themes and the value of avoiding imposed, one-size-fits-all responses and of the potential for creative responses to local conditions. Karlsson concludes that if pursued with careful and serious attention to the rights of women, a human rights approach to global climate change represents a positive opportunity to address together the problems of poverty, gender inequality and climate change.

Of course, energy production, like so many valuable activities, including the production of consumer goods, medicines and much else, generates side effects. These are often discussed in terms of aggregated risks. The production of X amount of a plastic will over time generate Y degree of exposure to a carcinogen or neurotoxin in a human population predictably yielding Z numbers of early deaths or disabilities, often among the most vulnerable within the population. Kristin Shrader-Frechette raises the hard question of whether the risks generated by these activities constitute human rights violations. She shows in illuminating detail why the question is hard ethically, practically and scientifically but also how, with reforms to both our thinking and our practices and institutions, it might ethically, practically and scientifically be less difficult than it currently is or seems to be, leading, she hopes, to a human rights response to the widespread and serious health risks currently generated by industrial pollution.

Is there a human right to democracy?

Democracy and human rights are often rhetorically linked; but can democracy itself be the object of a human right? In Part V Hilary Charlesworth, Carol Gould and Thomas Christiano address this question. Hilary Charlesworth examines the conceptual space that the right to democracy occupies in debates about the role and purpose of international human rights law and in the politics of international governance. Charlesworth begins by pointing out that although there is support for rights of popular control over and political equality with respect to collective decision-making, there is no right to democracy in international human rights law. To the extent that international legal regimes take democracy into account, it is defined narrowly in terms of participation in electoral competition. However, international legal instruments generally treat human rights and democracy in the broader sense of popular control and political equality as closely related. Within discussions of international law, arguments for recognizing a right to democracy have developed it as an international standard by which to measure legitimacy. But Charlesworth notes that this way of thinking about the relationship between democracy and human rights is problematic. For example if, as many have suggested, human rights ideas are most effective when locally adopted and accompanied by institutional teeth, then the right to democracy as an external standard will be of limited effect. Charlesworth argues that the challenge in establishing a human right to democracy is that democracy is not a state of affairs that can be measured or monitored, but rather a process. Democracy is a commitment that societies undertake rather than a property they exhibit. Conceived of as a legal standard, there is not a human right to democracy and probably will not be one. But conceived of as "yeast for social movements," not only can a human right to democracy make sense, but such a right may be an essential element of the project as a whole.

Carol Gould takes up the question of what recognizing a human right to democracy implies for global governance. For Gould, it is obvious that democracy, defined as decision-making under conditions of equal participation, is central to agency and so also that it is a central normative claim that calls for institutions that recognize and protect it. The difficult question is what this right implies. For example, when do individuals have a right to participate in decision-making and what form of participation is required? Do all people affected by a collective decision have rights of participation in it? Do all people affected have the same rights of participation? Gould argues that people have a right to participate on terms of equality whenever a collective decision importantly affects them. People are importantly affected when control over their life activity is implicated. This means that distant others often have a human right to democratic participation in a community's decisions. But it does not necessarily mean that such participation must include equal say in what is decided. What it is to participate on terms of equality depends on how agency is implicated. For example, agency may be implicated by the fact that important interests are affected.

It may also be implicated by the fact that the decision regards a common activity. The different implications for agency may ground legitimate differences in the form and extent of participation that is required by the right to democracy, but it will not necessarily do so. The constellation of participation that is required for specific decisions will depend on how the agency of all those affected is implicated, and that will depend on which interests of whom are impacted and in what way. Gould identifies several implications of this argument for global governance including that all decision-making at the global level ought to have democratic procedures, that there ought to be a global democratic parliament, and that new mechanisms of input and representation at the global level are necessary.

Thomas Christiano asks one of the most difficult questions about the human right to democracy: is using the right to democracy as an international standard of legitimacy compatible with the self-determination of peoples? Christiano argues that public equality is a minimum condition of realizing and respecting individuals' basic interests and treating them as moral equals, and democracy is a minimal empirical condition for effective public equality. Given these facts, there is a strong moral justification for establishing, protecting and promoting a legal right to democracy both within and between states. This moral justification establishes rights: to have the content of international legal regimes determined democratically; and to not have democratic decision-making within one's own state undermined. Christiano argues that these rights imply that states ought not to treat non-democratic states as legitimate parties to treaties or to the negotiations that determine the structure and content of international legal regimes. To apply international legal regimes whose content has been determined by processes that include non-democratic states is to violate the conditions of public equality within states whose decisions have been produced democratically as well as within the non-democratic states. There may be circumstances in which the pragmatic effects of excluding non-democratic states are judged to be so serious that the moral importance of securing public equality ought to give way. But, Christiano notes, to allow the pragmatic effects to trump is to sacrifice the democratic rights of all people who are subject to the international legal regimes that result, both within democratic regimes and outside of them, and this is no small thing.

What are the limits of rights enforcement?

There are many paths to the implementation of human rights, but among the most controversial is that of coercive enforcement. Part VI explores a number of hard questions raised by the prospect of internationally coercively enforcing human rights. The largely state-centric and anti-interventionist structure of international law stands as an often alleged and so familiar obstacle to the international coercive enforcement of human rights. And yet, as Julie Mertus argues, the matter is not so clear-cut, at least as a matter of international law. Mertus draws on the "declaratory tradition" of international law and ethics – a tradition within which non-state international actors seek through various declaratory acts to fill in lacunae and shape the shared understanding among states of their obligations under international law. She offers an account – rooted in the aspirational ideals of numerous significant non-state actors on the international stage – of permissible intervention for the sake of enforcing human rights that is consistent with, though perhaps not already an explicit part of, the aims and structure of existing international law and institutions. Recognizing that so-called humanitarian interventions are ripe for abuse and pose a potential threat to international stability and so to international law and legal institutions, Mertus develops several criteria for states to use in assessing whether a particular intervention ought to be conceived of as permissible under international law. In this she contributes to what might be characterized as the shared moral understandings that inform states, their interpretations of international law, and their activities within international institutions. The emerging "responsibility to protect" doctrine (referred to as R2P), though still controversial and not always clear in its content, might be cited as the anticipated fruit of such labor.

The emerging R2P doctrine authorizes, indeed requires, the international coercive enforcement of human rights in certain cases of grave systematic violation. Such enforcement is often accomplished by military means. State A puts its soldiers to work, risking their lives, for the sake of securing human rights in state B, which, let us assume, poses no immediate threat to state A. As Larry May notes in his chapter, this raises a hard question indeed. What authorizes, or more strongly requires, state A to put the human rights of its soldiers, in particular their right to life, and potentially also the rights of its citizens, in particular their social and economic rights, at risk for the sake of the human rights of persons elsewhere? This question is made especially difficult if we allow what May insists on, which is that states may give some priority or extra weight, even if only slight, to the human rights of their own citizens over and against the human rights of non-citizens. Charged by R2P to protect the human rights of both their own citizens and of non-citizens worldwide, how are particular states, the resources of which are nearly always limited, to fulfill their responsibilities without violating human rights? May explores the structure of the problem and then adduces a number of considerations – the number of rights in jeopardy, the moral character of the rights in jeopardy, the circumstances of the relevant right-holders, and the nature of the act or person causing the rights violation in need of remedy through coercive intervention – to be taken into account in order to adjudicate, case by case, whether a particular state may refuse to put its own resources, including its soldiers, to work, and so at risk, in service of coercively securing the human rights of non-citizens. There is no moral algorithm here, but May does conclude that it is likely that fewer humanitarian interventions will prove fully justified than many proponents of R2P currently seem to suppose.

Humanitarian interventions aim, of course, to initiate a period of transition to fuller compliance with human rights. Periods of significant social transition, whether initiated by a humanitarian intervention or a domestic movement, are often seen and seized upon as special opportunities to improve the situation of women. In her chapter, Marysia Zalewski examines the struggle for women's human rights paying special attention to the need for and difficulty of a conscious and emancipatory restructuring of gender, on the one hand, and the challenges, theoretical and practical, posed by a context of widespread social transition, on the other. She casts a cautiously critical eye on many attempts to secure "human" rights for women, attempts that too often fail to deliver an emancipatory reconstruction of gender. She concludes by looking at two categories familiar in contemporary pop culture with similarly problematic relations to "human," the members of which might, hypothetically, be thought to be in a position to lodge claims to humanity: the intelligent ape (think Caesar in *The Rise of the Planet of the Apes*) and the vampire (think Edward Cullen in "The Twilight Saga"). And she asks: given the apparent intelligibility to people of drawing these categories within the circle of the human, hypothetically speaking, what makes the problem of women's rights as human rights so hard? Perhaps, she suggests, it is precisely this way of framing the problem.

In their chapter, Erin Baines and Evelyn Amony, a survivor of the gross human rights abuses in Northern Uganda, explore by way of Evelyn's diary entries the concrete lived challenges of securing human rights in the context of a transition from systematic violence to peace. What emerges is that these challenges extend well beyond the structural and institutional foci that so often organize the attention and efforts of states, NGOs, international organizations and others aimed at securing human rights in the wake of widespread systematic violations. They extend to the moral psychology of trust, dignity and self-worth. It is not enough to restore the rule of law

or basic health-care services, though these things must be done. The rule of
law, basic health-care services, and economic and political reconstruction
should not be secured in ways that leave survivors of gross human rights
abuses still liable to humiliation, fear and insecurity. The challenge, then, is
to restore not only the institutions, but also the moral psychology, essential
to human rights. How to meet this challenge is among the hardest questions
raised in this volume.

Are human rights progressive?

The language of human rights is often rhetorically positioned as an obvious improvement over other moral languages and normative frameworks.
In Part VII Allen Buchanan, Mark Goodale and Laura Parisi critically
examine this association of human rights and change for the better. Allen
Buchanan begins by asking what it is to say that the modern human rights
project is morally progressive. He argues that to say that the modern human
rights project is morally progressive is to say that it reflects and contributes
to improvement in moral conceptualization, and that the modern human
rights project is progressive in this sense, as it reflects and has contributed to positive conceptual change in the form of better moral principles,
better understandings of and approaches to moral standing, better ways
of bringing moral concepts to bear on relationships and institutions, and
better drawings of the boundary between justice and charity. In particular,
Buchanan argues that the modern human rights project has contributed
to the development and entrenchment of subject-centered conceptions of
justice, which emphasize individuals' standing as subjects to whom justice
is owed, and who may rightly command a response when obligations are
not fulfilled. This is in part due to the concept of a right, which puts the
rights-bearer at center-stage and ties the moral standing of rights-bearers to
acceptance of their being rightly in charge of what is due them. Buchanan
points to disabilities rights and equal rights for women as good illustrations
of how the modern human rights project has given subject-centeredness
more determinate content and expanded conceptions of what justice can
require and of the contexts and relationships to which justice concepts
apply.

Mark Goodale treats the question of moral progress very differently.
Goodale notes that progressiveness is built into the very concept of a human
right, so that to ask whether human rights are progressive is in some ways
tautological and beside the point. Empirical support for the contention
that human rights has been a force for progress is not very good; but then,

empirical measures of human rights outcomes do not do a good job of capturing what people on the ground want human rights to do. For Goodale,
these observations suggest that questions about whether human rights are
moral improvements are not the right ones to ask. A better question, he
suggests, is: how is agency being shaped by human rights and what are the
broader implications of this shift? Human rights constitute a mode of moral
action – a mode of constituting social life through normativity. This entails
transcendence of norms as well as constraint by them and in this respect
human rights are intrinsically creative. Yet as a language of social and
political change, human rights reorients moral relationships, often in ways
that narrow the range of options for people in conditions of conflict, crisis
and despair. Goodale notes that even if human rights is a universal moral
grammar, the effects of this grammar's being deployed by specific people
within specific communities for specific purposes (vernacularization) are
unpredictable. The combination of transcendence and constraint that char-
acterizes human rights enables forms of moral poetry; but this combination
is also a reason to be cautious, and to recognize the limitations of human
rights as a logic. If human rights functions as a universal moral grammar,
then the global forces shaping its content must be acknowledged as a limiting factor on its transformative potential. For Goodale, this suggests that
insofar as the transformative potential of human rights as a project of making humanity can be made concrete, this will be in and through multiple,
local processes of vernacularization and moral innovation, and not through
the logic of the rights themselves.

Laura Parisi asks a question about one strategy that has been pursued to
make the transformative potential of human rights concrete: gender mainstreaming. Gender mainstreaming seeks to incorporate women's concerns
and experience into design, implementation, monitoring and evaluation of
policies and programs. Parisi asks: has this strategy for ensuring that wom-
en's human rights are equally protected and promoted been an improvement
for women's human rights? Her answer is "yes and no." A basic challenge for
improving protection and promotion of human rights for women is that the
idea of progressive realization, which is an entrenched element of human
rights monitoring and interpretation, inevitably involves judgments about
how various aspects of individual and social life should be weighted and
these judgments open up space for discriminatory practices and effects.
Gender mainstreaming could potentially help to address this problem,
as decisions about which aspects of life to prioritize and which delays in
implementation are acceptable must reflect the experiences and interests
of women. Parisi points out, however, that finding appropriate indicators,

identifying dimensions of experience and policy priorities that are important for women generally, and identifying changes in policy, outcomes and experiences that improve women's lives is empirically difficult and conceptually fraught. Parisi argues that some of the challenges of using gender mainstreaming as a tool of transformation may be addressed by focusing on processes and inputs, such as budgeting and decision-making structures. But she notes that the transformative potential of gender mainstreaming depends on whether it is possible to maintain that framework without homogenizing women and men as groups. In this respect, intersectional analysis, which describes subjects as inhabiting a space at which multiple identities intersect and interact, is a promising way forward. Yet although intersectionality may help gender mainstreaming develop a transformative account of progressive realization of human rights, there remains the problem of how realizing human rights in policy measures and statistical indicators relates to realizing human rights enjoyment for actual women.

Human rights and hard questions

The chapters collected in this volume do not offer a comprehensive survey of all the hard questions that can be asked about human rights, nor do they exhaust the range of views on the questions they take up. But they do offer an effective entry point into the complexities and the promise of human rights concepts, theory and practice. The authors in this volume have been drawn from a range of disciplinary backgrounds and they offer important insights about, and illuminating framings and reframings of, the questions taken up. Individually the chapters establish that hard questions in human rights are not always what they seem, and open new and fruitful ways of engaging the existing literature. As a collection, the chapters suggest that there are valuable and interesting conversations to be had across disciplines and perspectives, and between theorists and practitioners. Whether read independently or in juxtaposition with one another, these chapters are evidence of the continuing richness and vibrancy of human rights as a theoretical field and as a basis of practice.

PART I

What are human rights?

1 | Human rights and human nature

CHRIS BROWN

Introduction

Whether a viable account of human rights requires an accompanying account of human nature is a hard question. The assumption made by proponents of the international human rights regime has usually been that an account of human nature is neither desirable in its own terms, nor necessary for the task of promoting human rights. I want to suggest that both elements of this assumption are now highly contestable and contested and that the international human rights regime is under considerable strain as a result. This chapter is devoted to examining why so many people have been reluctant to associate human rights with a theory of human nature, why this reluctance has now become counter-productive and why we should now be prepared to re-examine the issue.

To tell a familiar story very briefly, from relatively modest beginnings in 1948 the international human rights regime now purports to grant very extensive rights to individuals; however, this expansion has been accompanied by criticisms to the effect that the regime represents a specifically Western, and perhaps masculine, vision of the world (Alston *et al.* 2007; Bauer and Bell 1999; Cook 1994). In support of this regime, international criminal law has also developed at high speed in the post-1945 period, and especially post-1989 with the establishment of special Tribunals and, in 2002, of the International Criminal Court (ICC) (Cassese 2008, 2009; Peskin 2009; Schabas 2007). But again, the actions of these courts are criticized because the standards of justice they promote are widely regarded as reflecting Western values and interests.

My aim here is not to justify these criticisms but to make the point that they stem from the fact that the international human rights regime has been established without the employment of a coherent account of human nature. Unlike the rights of the individual in a domestic legal system, which are clearly based in positive law, the international human rights regime appears to rest on an account of the good life for human beings, which is cast in universal terms – yet it is deeply reluctant to admit that this is actually the case, and this reluctance makes it vulnerable to those critics who argue that the advocacy or enforcement of human rights standards (whether in the classroom or in international courts or via "humanitarian interventions") is an act of cultural imperialism. Human rights advocates frequently describe rights as useful notions, perhaps useful fictions, but, of course, this begs the question – to whom are rights useful, and why should those who doubt their utility feel bound by them (Beitz 2009; Donnelly 2002)? Alternatively, the argument is that human rights are actually part of positive law insofar as they are created by created by international treaties – but again, this ignores the obvious fact that many states sign up to obligations they have not the slightest intention to honor, or, to put a better interpretation on such behavior, take on obligations they regard as aspirational rather than compelling in any legal sense.

What human rights advocates very rarely say is that the notion of human rights rests on a developed account of human nature, i.e. that humans have such and such a set of rights simply because that is what they need in order to be truly human – and yet it is difficult to see what other basis for the idea of human rights there could be. Arguments from human nature appear to have been de-legitimized in contemporary discourse. Of course, there are many people in the world today who have – and express – strong views about the nature of the human beings. For example, Islamic thinkers and those Christian theologians who employ an account of natural law in their theology have a clear account of who and what human beings are and what constitutes human flourishing, but both traditions are rejected by most secular Westerners and by adherents to non-theistic religions – and, of course, they contradict each other. Islam and Christianity are universal systems of thought grounded in clear views of human nature, but the claims they make are not recognized by each other or by third parties. Whereas once their kind of account of what it is to be human would have been widely accepted, now they are minority positions even in the lands of the religions of the Book. How did this happen?

How human nature became a myth

Telling the story here is difficult for a number of reasons. In the first place, one has to acknowledge that the story that comes out of the classical world and the religions of the Book is not one that would be recognized by Hindus, Buddhists, adherents of Chinese philosophies such as Confucianism, or of many African religions. For example, while they disagree amongst themselves about much else, common to classical Greece, the Roman heritage,

Jews, Muslims, Christians and modern secularists is the idea that, in this world at least, we have but one life to live, a position that is central to ethical thought in those traditions but is clearly contradicted by Hindu and Buddhist thinking. The implications of this contradiction will not be explored here, which is, of course, a serious omission and is justified, if it is justifiable at all, by the fact that the contemporary international order was shaped by, and still reflects, the "one-life" position. The key point is that it is a little misleading to talk of human nature "becoming a myth." There is a strong sense in which it has always been a myth, if by the term "human nature" one means a universally agreed account of what it is to be human. Still, within the West at least, there was once a fairly coherent account of what it meant to be human, and this account has gradually, over the last century or more, come apart at the seams.

Perhaps more important is a second difficulty, which is that the concept of "human nature" takes on different meanings depending on the broader assumptions about psychology and social theory adhered to by the user of the term. For some thinkers a scientific account of what human nature actually is (if such could be provided) would provide us with an account of how we should live our lives – would be, in effect, a theory of the good life upon which the idea of human rights could be directly based. Others argue that there is no link at all between a scientific account of human nature and a moral account of how we should live. A third position is that there is no direct, but a strong indirect, connection between human nature, the good, and human rights; our rational capacities (themselves part of our nature) allow us to determine how to live our lives but our nature is the starting point for this process. This position – which is broadly the one adopted here – follows the Aristotelian idea that human nature as it actually is needs to be transformed by practical reason and experience into human nature as it could be (MacIntyre 1981, 50).

The medieval Christian church held such a position, with "human nature as it actually is" and "how it could be" encompassed by the idea of "natural law," which was adapted from classical civilization and provided an account of what it meant to be human; this is where the story of how human nature became a myth begins. There were – and, in fact, still are, because this remains Catholic doctrine (Finnis 1979) – two components to this idea, the elements of which can be found in St. Paul's 2nd Epistle to the Romans, and that were developed by St. Augustine, St. Thomas Aquinas and the Scholastics. First, there is the notion that all human beings have an essential nature that dictates that certain kinds of human goods are always and everywhere desired; because of this there are common moral standards that govern all human relations and these common standards can be discerned by the application of reason to human affairs. Many Greek and Roman philosophers would have agreed with this characterization (although not necessarily on the content of these "common moral standards") and some would have agreed that this nature was given to human beings by God, but they would have rejected the second component of Medieval thought on this matter, which fitted this account of human nature into a salvation history revealed to human beings by God, first in His Covenant with the Jews, then in the person of Jesus Christ.

Whereas all human beings were bound by those common standards that can be reached by the application of reason, Christians were held to a higher standard by their knowledge of God's will. In the Medieval worldview, Jews have a place as a group who had rejected Jesus Christ, but who would, eventually, be converted, and Muslims likewise could be seen as heretics and fitted into this narrative. Beyond these three groups, the existence of other human beings – sometimes with outlandish physical characteristics – was posited, and sometimes these groups were also given a place in God's plan, as humans who had not yet been exposed to Revelation, but were equally subject to those common standards referred to above (Cohen 1999; Friedman 2000). It is worth mentioning these latter groups because it is sometimes argued that the Medieval world was thrown off balance by the discovery of peoples in the New World who did not fit into the Christian scheme of things.

Still, the contact with the inhabitants of the New World did reveal something quite important about the worldview of Christian Europe, as Tzvetan Todorov's brilliant book *The Conquest of America: The Question of the Other* (1987) illustrates. Enlightened opinion, represented by some of the Christian theologians and priests who encountered the "Indians," argued that although they seemed alien in so many respects they were, at bottom, people like us, sharing our nature, our needs and our desires, and therefore potential converts to the one true religion. The other possibility (adhered to by most of the Conquistadors) was that they were genuinely different and definitely inferior – there was only one true way of being human, that of the European world, and these people simply did not measure up, weren't really "people" at all in the full sense of the term, and therefore could be subjected to slavery and were unsuitable for Christian proselytizing. The point Todorov drives home is that the available formulations for understanding the Indians were "essentially the same, and equal" or "different and inferior" – crucially, "different but equal" was not an available answer to the question of the Other.

This is a powerful piece of scholarship, which tells us something very important about the Western approach to Otherness ("Alterity") and thereby to human nature, and we can see its implications echoing down over the last half-millennium. Still, before looking a little more closely at how this has played out, it is worth making the point that this blindness to the possibility of "different but equal" is by no means confined to Europeans. The Chinese self-understanding as the "Middle Kingdom" and the Japanese sense of racial superiority are well attested. Tribal peoples generally think of themselves as the norm and everyone else as deviants – such names as "Cheyenne" or "Maori" usually translate as something like "people" or "normal people," as opposed, that is, to everyone else. In short, even the most tolerant of civilizations generally draw a pretty clear distinction between themselves (superior) and others (inferior). European guilt about the sins of colonialism, although certainly justified, should not blind us to the fact that the most distinctive feature of European approaches to the Other was not that the latter were often seen as inferior, but rather that they were sometimes seen as equal – this feature will later be of some significance when it comes to the idea of human rights.

To return to the story, from one perspective, that of "natural law" and universal values, differences were denied or regarded as superficial; if only they knew it, all peoples were really like us, sharing our nature, our needs and our desires. The other possibility was that they were genuinely different but inferior – there was only one true way of being human, ours, and these people simply did not measure up, weren't really "people" at all in the full sense of the term. These two positions can be observed in action in different guises throughout the last 400 years. The first of these strategies accorded best with traditional Christian doctrine (although Christian justifications for slavery suggest that this identification should not be taken too far) and was continued by the dominant strand of Enlightenment thought, and by some powerful strands of post-Enlightenment thought. The second strand could be seen in the casual racism that accompanied European imperial expansion, the institution of slavery and, in the nineteenth century, in Social Darwinism and so-called "scientific racism" (Hawkins 2008).

The point to note here is that while these two positions point in radically different directions when it comes to guiding the behavior of states or individuals, both actually rely on a single account of human nature, in one case using such an account to buttress a superficially generous willingness to incorporate, in the other to support a decidedly ungenerous rejection of those who fail to meet the required standard. This underlying similarity is an important part on the story of the rejection of the idea of human nature in the twentieth century, because the sins of a "different and inferior" conception of Otherness were also laid at the door of the "similar and equal" school. Admittedly, when the scientific racism of the nineteenth century left the classroom and joined the popular racism of the street to create movements such as National Socialism, or when the more genteel, but equally obnoxious, ideas of Social Darwinism and eugenics led to programs of sterilization of the allegedly inferior, the opposition to these trends could have been, and sometimes was, cast in terms that Las Casas and the Enlightenment would have recognized. Thus, many, perhaps most, of those who resisted Nazism and rescued its victims did so because they adhered to universalist positions such as those generated by traditional socialist ideas or Christianity (Geras 1995).

But while a reassertion of natural law and the idea of a universal human nature was one powerful response to the horrors of a "different but inferior" conception of human beings, an alternative approach was to revalue the idea of Otherness, and to oppose the idea of a singular human nature altogether – in other words, to get away from the dichotomy outlined so well by Todorov. Or, in a different context, one might abandon the idea that the social sciences require an account of human nature – rather than challenging or redefining the idea, one could simply regard it as irrelevant.

This latter strategy was adopted by many Marxists, and by Durkheimian sociologists. Even while Marx was alive, many Marxists set aside his early thinking about human "species-being" and developed instead his critique of bourgeois political economists who assumed that the laws of motion of capitalist society were universal – instead they argued that different modes of production did not simply generate different kinds of society; they generated different kinds of people (Cohen 2001). Many twentieth-century Marxists took the view that the very idea of human nature should be regarded as reactionary, a position still held by many on the left (on which see the controversy stirred up by evolutionary psychology (Sagerstrale 2000)).

Emile Durkheim's position, formalized in *The Rules of Sociological Method* (1982 [1895]), is that only social facts could explain other social facts, and the notion of human nature could have no explanatory power for social scientists. Arguments that attempted to explain social behavior in terms of individual characteristics were "reductionist" and to be rejected. Students of International Relations theory will be reminded of Kenneth Waltz's argument in *Theory of International Politics* (1979), reasonably enough because Waltz identifies Durkheim as a major influence on his thinking. In parenthesis, it is often thought that one of the ways in which Waltz differs from the "classical" realists is in his rejection of a basis in human nature for his position, although I have argued elsewhere that the picture is a little more complicated than that (Brown 2009).

If Durkheimian sociology and Marxian political economy were major intellectual opponents of the idea of human nature, at the popular level the influence of the work of social anthropologists was more influential. The role of anthropologists – especially those who were the pupils of Franz Boas – in the first half of the twentieth century seemed to be to produce evidence in support of the view that features of what had been thought of as human nature and universal were in fact the product of modern, Western, industrial societies (Boas 1995). In terms of popular impact, but also as an iconic work within the profession, Margaret Mead's *Coming of Age in Samoa* (1928) is a core text. Her thesis – based, or so it was believed, on extensive fieldwork – was that the kind of traumas associated with sexual awakening and the preservation or loss of virginity that characterized adolescence in the West were absent in Samoa. These traumatic experiences, far from being human universals, were the product of bourgeois society and their alleged absence in Samoa illustrated the dangers of reductionist argument even more dramatically than Durkheim's studies of suicide. This position was later fleshed out and expanded by other writers, who argued that even the most basic notions of "color" and "time" are not constants (Brown 1991, 9–38).

These studies were quite explicitly used to spread a message of tolerance in a world where racism and intolerance were rampant. The aim was to undermine the notion that white, European men and women were in any sense the end result of human evolution; the idea that non-Europeans were different and therefore inferior was to be replaced not by the old idea that all human beings are essentially the same, but by simultaneously acknowledging and revaluing difference. People (and peoples) were not the same – different societies had different mores, different standards of right and wrong, different understandings of the most basic human ideas – but this radical difference was to be welcomed, and in any event there is no basis upon which a judgment of the value of difference could be made. In the Wittgensteinian formulation set out in Peter Winch's *The Idea of a Social Science and its Relation to Philosophy*, "forms of life" simply have to be accepted as a given, there being no standard against which they could be judged (Winch 2007 [1957]). Winch in this very influential book declares that there is no objective reason to believe that Western notions of science are superior to witchcraft beliefs of the Azande in West Africa – to judge the latter against criteria chosen by the former would be as inappropriate as judging the former by criteria chosen by the latter.

The purpose of this work was to combat intolerance and racism, although it might be argued that this project is self-defeating if by undermining the universal account of human nature one simultaneously undermines the reason for thinking that intolerance and racism are unacceptable – paradoxically, the very unwillingness to tolerate intolerance suggested that some universal values are actually, indeed have to be, present in this work. Still, the apparent self-contradiction here seemed not to enter into most people's consciousness, and as European political control of the non-European world receded, post-colonial theorists have demonstrated the ways in which Western "universalism" privileges certain kinds of reasoning, certain mental categories that act to legitimate imperialism and oppression (Williams and Chrisman 1993). And feminist theorists point to the role of traditional concepts of human nature in providing support for an account of traditional and oppressive gender roles as natural rather than as social creations and so for patriarchy (MacKinnon 2007).

In summary, as the social anthropologist Marshall Sahlins put it, in a short but powerful summary of a lifetime's work, the Western notion of human nature is an illusion, and a dangerous and undesirable illusion at that (Sahlins 2008). Those who use the concept are either ignorant or, more likely, involved in throwing a smokescreen over something that would otherwise be recognized as undesirable. Putting all this together, the case against a rigid account of what human beings are seems compelling, and it is quite understandable that human rights advocates have shied away from using such arguments to buttress their position, resorting instead to the idea that human rights are a political construction, a fiction that provides a valuable ethical template for the living of a good life. On this account, human rights are to be seen as, at root, a valuable human construct, similar to the idea of a "social contract"; just as no one nowadays understands the idea of a contract as anything other than a useful thought experiment, so the idea of rights has to be understood in similar terms. The problem with this ungrounded idea of human rights – as noted above – is that it has little to say to those for whom rights are not a useful fiction and who reject the terms of the thought experiment. For this reason it is important to ask whether it is possible to tell a story about human nature that is less rigid, more plastic, less open to manipulation in the interests of the powerful, but still with serious content. I think it is, and a good place to start to construct such a story would be at the very beginning of Western thought on identity and difference.

Darius, the Hellenes and the Kallatiai

As noted above, classical Greek thought did not offer a single conception of the good life or what it meant to be human, but there was one related notion to which nearly all Greeks subscribed, namely that there was a pretty fundamental difference between Greeks and non-Greeks. The latter were described as barbarians (*barbaros*); originally the term was probably onomatopoeic, a reference to the babbling sound that foreign tongues made for the monoglot Greeks, but later it came to be a term that denoted inferiority. Greek was understood to be the language of rational thought, and it did not require much of a leap to assert that those who didn't speak Greek were barely capable of achieving rationality. Unsurprisingly, such an attitude is seen by some post-colonial theorists as the source for many of the worst features of European thought over the last four centuries. Todorov's classification of ways of handling Otherness as oscillating between "the same and equal" and "different and inferior" could, apparently, have been designed for the Greeks rather than the Spanish Conquistadors.

   Still, there is another side to this story. The most interesting way in which the categories of Greek and barbarian play out is evidenced by Greek attitudes to Persia. The Persian Wars were the formative experiences that led to the idea that the Greeks were different from and superior to Asiatics, but for my purposes their importance is that they produced a superb commentator, the so-called Father of History, Herodotus. Soon after the defeat of Xerxes, Herodotus traveled around the then-known world putting together his history of the wars; this involved a great many diversions and the provision of an extraordinary amount of wholly irrelevant, but very interesting, detail. Herodotus was fascinated by the differences between the Greeks and their various others; he was a perceptive and tolerant (albeit occasionally somewhat credulous) observer, fascinated by human nature in all its forms.

   In the course of his history, as part of a long digression on Egypt, he tells of the Persian Great King Cambyses, who openly mocked the religious beliefs of his Egyptian subjects. This is seen by Herodotus as a sign of insanity; Herodotus thinks that all peoples will believe that their own customs are best and in support of this position tells of a thought experiment conducted by one of Cambyses' successors, Darius:

During his reign, Darius summoned the Hellenes at his court and asked them how much money they would accept for eating the bodies of their dead fathers. They answered that they would not do that for any amount of money. Later, Darius summoned some Indians, called Kallatiai, who do eat their dead parents. In the presence of the Hellenes, with an interpreter to inform them of what was said, he asked the Indians how much money they would accept to burn the bodies of their dead fathers. They responded with an outcry, ordering him to shut his mouth lest he offend the gods. Well then, that is how people think, and so it seems to me that Pindar was right when he said in his poetry that custom is king of all. (Herodotus 2008, Book 3: 38, p. 224)

Mary Midgely and Steven Lukes – two of the many commentators who have retold this story – complete the message of the anecdote by noting that Darius the Persian would have been quite sure that the correct way to honor the dead is to expose bodies on high towers to be eaten by vultures, a practice still employed by Parsees (present-day Zoroastrians) in Mumbai in India (Midgely 1991, 78 cited in Lukes 2003, 4ff.).

This is a popular story because it is open to many different interpretations. Herodotus and Darius seem to be suggesting that what we have here is a radical incommensurability – there is nothing we can say about these practices except that custom is king. This is a more tolerant and generous approach to the matter than Cambyses' approach displayed; he mocked those who did not believe as he did, and he did this in the name of nature – he would have regarded non-Persian ways of treating the dead as "unnatural." With the approval of Herodotus, Darius in the story is (or, better, as Great King behaves as if he is) a relativist in the sense that he denies the existence of relevant criteria for distinguishing between these customs; "forms of life" have to be accepted; there is no way to tell which of these behaviors is natural.

However, I want to suggest that a different story can be told using the material Herodotus gives us; the key here is to identify the correct level of generality. Exposing the dead to the elements, eating them and burning them are radically different ways of expressing respect, but it is clear from the story that they actually *are* all ways of expressing respect – if this were not the case then there would be no reason for one group not to accept the customs of the other. The reason why neither the Hellenes nor the Indians will give up their customs is because to do so would be a form of sacrilege, horrifying to the gods and unacceptable to any dutiful son. There is a basic similarity of attitude at work here.

The parallels with twentieth-century debates on human nature are, I hope, obvious; respect for "difference" and a generous tolerance produce a more attractive politics than any attempt to impose one particular "form of life" on all others, but such a desirable outcome need not be arrived at at the expense of any notion of human nature. At the right level of generality, it may still be possible for human nature to do some important work.

The universal people

An anecdote recounted by Herodotus doesn't of course constitute an argument (and wouldn't even if it were a true story, which it probably isn't). Still there is at least a prima facie case for thinking that, if one can get the level of generality right, there is scope for the view that all human beings have a lot more in common than some variants of conventional wisdom would have us believe. Herodotus' story concerns post-mortem customs, which is the sort of issue that social anthropologists focus on, so it may be helpful to look a little more closely at their findings. Certainly in the first half of the twentieth century the environment ("nurture") was stressed at the expense of nature as the key to understanding how humans behave and think. Influential studies, the most famous of which was the aforementioned *Coming of Age in Samoa* by Margaret Mead, portrayed societies that were unworried about adolescent sexual experimenting and other allegedly modern taboos (Mead 1928). The nuclear family was likewise seen as culture-specific; institutions such as the Kibbutz were as effective ways of raising children as male–female pairs. And, reacting to the horrors of twentieth-century warfare, it became a point of principle for many anthropologists to insist that so-called primitive societies were less violent and troubled than industrial societies. In such societies war is largely a symbolic affair; violence had to be seen as learned behavior and learned particularly in modern capitalist states. This latter position was formalized in the so-called "Seville Statement on Violence" in 1986, later adopted as official doctrine by UNESCO (UNESCO 1989). These positions were held to be "scientifically correct," to use the Seville phraseology; the "bad sciences" of Social Darwinism, Eugenics and Scientific Racism were to be driven out not by a "good science" of human nature but by the scientific rejection of essentialism. Like Darius, the anthropologists who produced these propositions wanted to show that custom was king, although the current preferred terminology had a more scientific ring to it.

But well-meaning liberals are as capable of producing bad science as racists, and this anti-essentialist position has been pretty much demolished over the last quarter century. Thus, it now seems clear that Margaret Mead was the victim of what was essentially a practical joke, her informants having made up tall tales that they did not expect to be believed – coming of age in Samoa was every bit as stressful as it was, and still is, in modern industrial societies (Freeman 1983, 1999). The reversal of opinion on violence in pre-modern societies has been equally dramatic; here the issue has been a question of interpreting rather than challenging the data. The central point has been statistical – warfare in "primitive" societies may only lead to the occasional death, but in small societies one death can have an impact greater than tens of thousands in modern mass societies (Keeley 1996). In fact, the probability of violent death for young men in primitive societies is higher than in any civilized society at any time period, including the twentieth century, which experienced the two most destructive wars in human history. Modern industrial societies are actually the least violent of any societies of which we have knowledge.

One could go on; contra one popular misconception, the Hopi have much the same notion of time as Western (and every other) society, and Inuits don't have lots more ways of describing snow than others do – but although this sort of anthropological work is valuable in undermining the naïve anti-essentialist position it doesn't establish a positive account of what human beings are like. Donald Brown does tentatively provide such an account in his description of the "universal people" (UP) synthesizing the work of other anthropologists (Brown 1991, 130–141). He begins with features of language and grammar – including the use of metaphor and metonym – goes on to look at features of human psychology that are universal – distinguishing self and others, recognizing the self as both subject and object – and then describes universal features of social arrangements – including commonalities in child-rearing, the division of labor, social stratification, play, ritual, notions of justice, a theory of mind, and the presence of a worldview. His full account runs to around 6,000 words, packing in far more detail than can be conveyed here.

Interestingly, to a great extent, the features of the UP are discerned in the same way that the commonality behind burial practices can be discerned by a reading of Herodotus, that is by pointing out social customs that are so basic that their similarity is often lost. Similarly, the process involves an ability to get beyond surface meanings; to acknowledge, for example, that the UP "practice magic, and their magic is designed to do such things as to sustain and increase life and to win the attention of the opposite sex" (Brown 1991, 139) requires us to drop the notion that "magic" is something only associated with primitive people, and recognize that our own behavior often rests on beliefs about the world that can only be described as magical, even though we try to dress them up in different clothing.

Brown bases his account of the UP on a synthesis of work by other anthropologists; what is the standing of such a synthesis and what work can it do? One might describe what he has done as establishing by induction a kind of lowest common denominator for cultural arrangements, true by definition but unhelpful for precisely that reason (in the same way, for example, that the biological needs of the human body, although obviously important, tell us little about the social arrangements needed to meet them). If this is simply how things are *and had to be* then there is very little else to be said. But the most interesting fact about the common features of the UP is that they could have been different; the human need for food, water and a breathable environment is a given – a "human being" who did not need sustenance would not actually be a human being – but the features of the UP are not true simply by definition. Given that they could have been different, it makes sense to ask why the UP are as they are.

Conclusion: rethinking human nature

It seems to me to be pretty clear that the answer to this question has to be consistent with, and shaped by, the findings of evolutionary psychology. Admittedly most evolutionary psychologists eschew the notion of a human nature, regarding it as little more than a very crude and rather misleading piece of shorthand; it implies a constant whereas their thinking rests on the idea that while some things are certainly constant they are so at a much more disaggregated level than is implied by the notion of human nature. Instead the product of evolution is seen to take the form of multiple mechanisms – formed *ex hypothesi* in the ancestral environment, the 1.5 to 2 million years of the Pleistocene Era when the human brain is believed to have evolved – which, taken together, and combined with the environment, produce actual human behavior (Dunbar and Barrett 2007).

This is not the place to summarize the findings of this new discourse, which are, in any event, still to be regarded as highly provisional, but there are one or two things we can say with some confidence. To summarize Steven Pinker's summary, it seems that human beings have evolved to be rather selfish and violent animals (Pinker 2002). We are biased in favor of our kin and immediate circle of friends, and are potentially ethnocentric, violent and domineering. Cooperative behavior is kin-based or based on reciprocity; more extended systems of cooperation rely on a degree of coercion to minimize free-riding, and, contrary to the myth of the peaceful "garden," beloved of the counter-culture of the 1960s and perhaps today, the existence of authoritative and coercion-based political institutions is central to minimizing interpersonal violence. Incidentally, Pinker is often seen as a controversial figure, but his account is consistent with Brown's account of the UP, and would only lead to reactionary conclusions if adopted by someone who holds the view that a scientific account of human nature leads directly to a moral account.

This suggests that one good reason to think of humans as rights-bearers is that we need the protection from each other that rights provide, but there is also a less Hobbesian basis for rights; apart from producing the dark side of humanity, there is good evidence that mechanisms have evolved to facilitate cooperation and altruism amongst humans. The most thoroughly researched of such mechanisms focuses on the capacity of human beings to understand social exchanges and, in particular, to spot individuals who "cheat." Since many accounts of altruism stress reciprocity, it seems plausible that the capacity to identify people who do not respect promises they have made would be selected for, and experiments conducted using variants of the Wason Selection Task give evidence that it has been (Cosmides and Tooby 1992). This is a logic problem designed to test how good individuals are at identifying a "material conditional";[1] the answer is, not very, when the Task involves the manipulation of abstract symbols – but when exactly the same Task is described in terms of social relations (a classic example involves spotting whether the age rules on drinking alcohol are being observed) people do much better. The hypothesis is that we have no inherited capacity to solve logic problems, but we are extremely good at spotting whether rules are being followed. This is a mechanism that is selected for, but, conversely, there was no advantage in the ancestral environment associated with being able to spot a "material conditional" in an abstract problem.

Alongside this finding, writers such as Ken Binmore and Herbert Gintis employ game-theoretic reasoning to argue that such mechanisms can be deployed in support of a stable moral theory that argues that humans have evolved to follow rules of "natural justice" (Binmore 2005, 2009; Bowles and Gintis 2011; Gintis 2006). This work is in its infancy, but it does suggest that the idea of "human nature" as the basis for human rights is worth developing – for the time being it is not clear how far this development will go and in what direction, but we already know enough to suggest that there are some elements of the idea of human rights that can be divorced from their Western origins and associated with the nature of the human animal.

The twentieth-century rejection of human nature was a reaction to Social Darwinism and the political implications of notions of scientific racism,

---

[1] In the formal version, four cards are laid on the table. Each has a letter on one side and a number on the other; visible cards show E, G, 3, 4. The rule is that if a card has a vowel on one side, it must have an even number on the other side. Which cards do you have to turn over to see if this rule is being followed?

but there is good reason to think that the genuinely scientific study of the human animal will not lead to such reactionary conclusions. Essentialist accounts of human nature need not be anti-progressive. In short, returning to the initial question posed in this chapter, a viable account of human rights does require a theory of human nature, and such a theory is becoming available.

References

Alston, Philip, Goodman, Ryan and Steiner, Henry J., eds. 2007. *Human Rights in Context: Law, Politics, Morals*, 3rd edn. Oxford University Press.

Bauer, Joanne and Bell, Daniel, eds. 1999. *The East Asian Challenge for Human Rights*. Cambridge University Press.

Beitz, Charles. 2009. *The Idea of Human Rights*. Oxford University Press.

Binmore, Ken. 2005. *Natural Justice*. Oxford University Press.

2009. "Fairness as a Natural Phenomenon." Available at: http://else.econ.ucl.ac.uk/papers/uploaded/332.pdf.

Boas, Franz. 1995. *Race, Language and Culture*. University of Chicago Press.

Bowles, Samuel and Gintis, Herbert. 2011. *A Co-operative Species: Human Reciprocity and its Origins*. Princeton University Press.

Brown, Chris. 2009. "Structural Realism, Classical Realism and Human Nature." *International Relations* 23:2, 257–270.

Brown, Donald E. 1991. *Human Universals*. New York: McGraw-Hill.

Cassese, Antonio. 2008. *International Criminal Law*, 2nd edn. Oxford University Press.

Cassese, Antonio. ed. 2009. *The Oxford Companion to International Criminal Justice*. Oxford University Press.

Cohen, G.A. 2001. *Karl Marx's "Theory of History": A Defence*, 2nd edn. Princeton University Press.

Cohen, Jeffrey Jerome. 1999. *Of Giants: Sex, Monsters and the Middle Ages*. Minneapolis: University of Minnesota Press.

Cook, Rebecca J., ed. 1994. *Human Rights of Women*. Philadelphia: University of Pennsylvania Press.

Cosmides, Leda and Tooby, John. 1992. "Cognitive Adaptions for Social Exchange." In Jerome Barkow *et al.*, eds., *The Adapted Mind*. New York: Oxford University Press, pp. 163–228.

Donnelly, Jack. 2002. *Universal Human Rights in Theory and Practice*. Ithaca: Cornell University Press.

Dunbar, Robin and Barrett, Louise, eds. 2007. *Oxford Handbook of Evolutionary Psychology*. Oxford University Press.

Durkheim, Emile. 1982 [1895]. *The Rules of Sociological Method*. New York: The Free Press.

Finnis, John. 1979. *Natural Law and Natural Rights*. Oxford: Clarendon Press.

Freeman, Dennis. 1983. *Margaret Mead and Samoa*. Cambridge, MA: Harvard University Press.

    1999. *The Fateful Hoaxing of Margaret Mead*. Boulder: Westview Press.

Friedman, John Block. 2000. *The Monstrous Races in Medieval Art and Thought*. Syracuse University Press.

Geras, Norman. 1995. *Solidarity in the Conversation of Humankind*. London: Verso.

Gintis, Herbert. 2006. "Behavioural Ethics Meets Natural Justice." *Politics, Philosophy and Economics* 5, 5–32.

Hawkins, Mike. 2008. *Social Darwinism in European and North American Thought, 1860–1945*. Cambridge University Press.

Herodotus. 2008. *The Histories*. The Landmark Herodotus, translated by Andrea L. Purvis. London: Quercus.

Keeley, L.H. 1996. *War Before Civilization: The Myth of the Peaceful Savage*. New York: Oxford University Press

Lukes, Steven. 2003. *Liberals & Cannibals: The Implications of Diversity*. London: Verso Press.

MacIntyre, Alasdair. 1981. *After Virtue*. University of Notre Dame Press.

MacKinnon, Catherine. 2007. *Are Women Human? And other International Dialogues*. Cambridge, MA: Harvard University Press.

Mead, Margaret. 1928. *Coming of Age in Samoa*. New York: Blue Ribbon Books.

Midgely, Mary. 1991. *Can't We Make Moral Judgements?* Bristol Press.

Peskin, Victor. 2009. *International Justice in Rwanda and the Balkans*. Cambridge University Press.

Pinker, Stephen. 2002. *The Blank Slate: The Modern Denial of Human Nature*. London: Allen Lane.

Sagerstrale, Ullica. 2000. *Defenders of the Truth: The Battle for Science in the Sociobiology Debate and Beyond*. Oxford University Press.

Sahlins, Marshall. 2008. *The Western Illusion of Human Nature*. University of Chicago Press.

Schabas, William A. 2007. *An Introduction to the International Criminal Court*. Cambridge University Press.

Todorov, Tzvetan. 1987. *The Conquest of America*. New York: Harper Torchbooks.

UNESCO. 1989. *The Seville Statement on Violence*. Available at: www.unesco.org/cpp/uk/declarations/seville.pdf.

Waltz, Kenneth. 1979. *Theory of International Politics*. New York: McGraw-Hill.

Williams, Patrick and Chrisman, Laura, eds. 1993. *Colonial Discourse and Post-Colonial Theory: A Reader*. London: Longman.

Winch, Peter. 2007 [1957]. *The Idea of a Social Science and its Relations to Philosophy*. London: Routledge.

2 | Universalism and particularism in human rights

NEIL WALKER

Introduction

The relationship between universal and particular ways of thinking about our ethical commitments has an important bearing on the sustainability, desirability and shape of the global promotion of human rights today. It is a relationship that combines mutual support with mutual tension. On the one hand, most who take human rights seriously, whether as objective moral truth or as socially constructed consensus, believe there is an internal connection between the very idea of human rights, with its strong suggestion of the equal worth of all humans, and a common standard of protection, with all that implies by way of universals (Waldron 1987). On the other hand, and partly due to the same background modernist considerations of equal value and equal respect for all expressions of individual and collective autonomy in contradistinction to the pre-modern emphasis on conformity with a pre-given order, many believe that any rights-regarding regulatory architecture must accommodate difference – and so particularize – in a manner that qualifies or even challenges the underlying universalism (Vincent 2002).

Take first the universalist pole. To believe in rights as something we possess just in virtue of being human implies also believing in the "universality" of rights – whether the "negative" rights of liberty, conscience, expression, privacy, etc., or the "positive" rights of shelter, subsistence, etc. – in the following three respects and stages: first, as to the *general* quality of what is covered (i.e., its terms should not be so qualified that there remains no significant range of situations – of "core" contexts – across which the right is capable of being universally asserted); second, as to the equal and so *uniform* application of the general right to all within the protected category; and, third, as to the extensive, ideally *unlimited* category of persons protected. In short, rights universalism requires of any qualifying right certain basic substantive and structural features, namely that they be available on broadly drawn and equal terms to all in the class of right-holders, which class should be as inclusive as possible.

However, alongside and in part against this universalist stream, particularism makes both normative and practical arguments. Normatively, in a world where moral truth claims are perennially contested, particularism treats divergences between and within different locales in the governing framework of beliefs of what and who is worthy of protection as morally significant. Practically, it calls attention to how variant national or other local circumstances, as well as founding or corroborating a moral claim to respect difference, also impose ideological pressures and feasibility constraints on the development of any viable framework of common norms.

The sense of equality and difference as imperatives in conflict or precarious tandem lies deep in the "global imaginary" (Steger 2009; Walker 2010) of a transnationally connected late modern age. It informs many key contemporary questions of global law and politics, such as humanitarian intervention, universal jurisdiction in criminal law, veto rules in international legislative and executive decision-making, the reach of *ius cogens*, etc., but none more so than the debate between universalism and particularism in human rights.

In practice, however, despite its significance, or in part because of it, the question of the resolution of universal and particular considerations in human rights often lacks focus. It suffers from a confusion of concepts and a polarization of perspectives. Debate is conducted in loaded terms, tending to avoid or mirror – and so reinforce – the very opposition it addresses, and thereby excluding or obscuring more productive lines of thought. The bar for reconciling the universal and the particular is set either too low or, more often, and at a considerably higher political and cultural volume, too high. But in either case the setting fails to do justice to both dimensions simultaneously.

The bar is set too low where the universal and the particular are defined such that the articulation of any human rights norm necessarily combines both, but does so in a way that artificially favors one dimension by asking too little of the other. Here the problem of reconciliation is avoided by conceptual fiat. More commonly, the bar is set too high, universal and particular each understood in such uncompromising terms that the price of one prevailing is the exclusion or marginalization of the other. This frame of reference reflects more closely the deep sense of the global imaginary noted above, but is in equal danger of failing to take reconciliation seriously, albeit from a position of undue pessimism rather than false optimism.

Let us first examine both sets of possibilities so as to identify the dead-ends and dogmas – the false solutions and false oppositions – to be avoided. We will then be in a position to explore what remains crucially at stake in the relationship between the universal and the particular in human rights protection. In particular, what scope is there to address the inescapable tension between them in terms more productive than a stark trade-off?

Setting the bar too low

In what sense can the bar be set too low? How might we define universal and particular dimensions so that human rights norms embrace both, but in a manner that fails to engage the tensions between them? This can be done by developing either a minimal conception of the universal or a minimal conception of the particular.

A minimal conception of the universal addresses the bare *form* of the human rights norm. It holds that human rights norms, just in virtue of being *normative*, possess the quality of universalizability. A species of the genus of normative or "ought" statement, human rights norms are necessarily general in their basic propositional character. As the major premise in a practical syllogism, any human right, abstractly conceived, subsumes and embraces *all* its possible concrete instantiations, or minor premises, as qualifying for protection.

There is nothing trivial about this formal quality of universalizability. An important claim about morally relevant action in the Kantian tradition is that whatever is warranted must be universally warranted. And like most important claims, it is also controversial, with some moral philosophers in disagreement. These skeptics hold, on metaphysical or epistemological grounds, that the basis of moral action lies not in universal precepts – dismissed as illusory or unverifiable – but in the particulars of each case (Dancy 2006). However, for those many non-skeptics who maintain, with Kant, that all morally informed action, or practical reason, is inherently rational and intelligible, and so reducible to universal principles, it follows that the special type of practical reason we call law, and, a fortiori, the special kind of non-sector-specific but generally applicable law we call human right law, is also universalizable (MacCormick 2005, ch. 5).

Even if it stands against strong forms of metaphysical or epistemological skepticism, however, formal universalism provides an insufficient basis for defending the "universal" in universal human rights. If the most that can be said about the universal dimension in human rights is that which can be said about all law, and indeed all practical reason, then this fails to address what might be distinctive, and so of added value, in the universality of universal human rights. As we noted at the outset, any such distinctive value must instead rest in the substance and structure (i.e., generality, uniformity and scope) of the supposedly universal human rights, for which universality of form provides no more than a methodological preliminary.

If we approach the reconciliation of the universal and the particular from the opposite angle, an even stronger point can be made about the dilution of particularism. Stretching the idea of the particular to its limit, we must concede that there is something unavoidably unique and distinctive about any norm at its point of application. Even the most uncompromising exponent of a "covering law universalism" (Walzer 2007) according to which all relevant information about the resolution of particular cases is supplied in advance by the general norm, could hardly deny that the particular remains indispensable to realizing the general norm, however "thick" and directive in content (see e.g., Raz 1998). Yet this involves an even "thinner" claim on behalf of the particular than does formal universalism on behalf of the universal. Indeed, in this highly reductive sense particularism is nothing more than an *expression* of the universal, a trivial claim whose acknowledgment requires even the "thickest" and most uncompromising version of universalism to concede nothing of its tenets.

In summary, there are ways of defining universalism and particularism such that they can be reconciled with either universalism yielding little of significance no matter how "thick" the particularism or particularism yielding little of significance no matter how "thick" the universalism. But neither approach confronts the more interesting or pressing questions about the relationship between universal and particular in human rights, and so need detain us no further than is necessary to warn us off their empty promise of reconciliation. Yet, we should note that this is as much a political as a philosophical warning. So widespread is the rhetorical endorsement of human rights today – a phenomenon explored below – that it is vulnerable to opposite forms of double-speak. Whether in the refusal of staunch supporters of global or regional rights standards to concede that such standards risk anything of value in local autonomy or in the effort of some particularists to dress up the most distinctive of ethical commitments in universalist clothes, the seduction of false reconciliation remains a palpable danger on either side.

Setting the bar too high

If the reconciliation of the universal and the particular is sometimes made too quickly and easily, at other times it becomes too difficult. This opposite danger arises when uncompromisingly "thick" versions of universalism and particularism lock horns.

We referred in passing to a stylized version of an uncompromisingly "thick" universalism – a covering law approach holding that all particulars are subsumed under its terms. But once we leave the deep causalities of the natural world and enter the domain of human relations, covering laws lose much of their purchase. Where we seek to explain patterns of human action, as in the social sciences, then the agency of the subject – the possibility of acting otherwise – militates against unqualified covering laws. And where we are concerned, not with explanation, but with the prescriptions of moral or legal philosophy, as in the present case, the reasons why we might eschew strict covering laws are more complex and controversial. But, whatever their basis, all such reasons tend to express themselves in the impossibility or undesirability of general rules that conclusively *determine* how we should act in every case.

This does not mean, however, that we cannot have strong versions of universalism other than the covering law model in moral or legal philosophy. Short of definitive prescription, universal rules may nevertheless be *relatively determinate* of appropriate conduct in their domain of application. As anticipated in our discussion of substantive and structural universalism, a strong case can be made for contemporary human rights as one species of such rules. Within this more familiar version of human rights universalism, the range of possible actions is shaped and influenced by the general rule. Yet there remains scope for reasoned or reasonable disagreement across that range, with such disagreement based upon an irreducible element of value pluralism or practical contestability not (necessarily) grounded in variation in particular background circumstances or commitments.

For its part, a "thick" particularism, as already noted, may be deeply skeptical on metaphysical or epistemological grounds of the very idea of universals. It may involve a form of intuitivism or subjectivism or anti-rationalism that denies the very basis of universalism even as a formal thesis about the nature of moral justification and practical reasoning (MacCormick 2005, ch. 5; Waldron 1999, ch. 8). However, as also anticipated in our introduction, short of these radical positions there are more common forms of particularism that, on both normative and practical grounds, offer a stern challenge to the kind of substantive and structural claims we associate with a more robust human rights universalism.

Before examining "actually existing" thick universalism and thick particularism in detail, we should say a little more about how their uneasy confluence in the politics of human rights resonates so closely with the coupled concern for equality and diversity we flagged as a key "twin" narrative of the global age. The increasing intensity and scale of transnational relations, movements and processes of an economic, technological and cultural nature under the sign of contemporary globalization has given rise to a "sense of the compression of global time and space, so that the effects of distant events, situations and actions arise more quickly, directly and powerfully than in the past" (Cotterrell 2008). This has two effects. It supplies the conditions under which, culturally, we simultaneously become more aware of both difference and similarity. It also provides the material circumstances under which powerful global actors and structures can exert greater transnational influence, thereby reinforcing existing differences and creating and pursuing new conflicts of interest as well as imposing or facilitating new kinds of commonalities of appetites, experiences and values. In the "compression chamber" of globalization, therefore, our similarities and differences of life experiences and life chances alike are amplified, as are our perceptions of what is valuable or otherwise both in the common standards to which we aspire and the different conceptions of the good life we inherit and develop. These amplifications find a strong echo, but also a reinforcing cause, in the perspectives of universalism and particularism through which the human rights project is addressed and pursued.

The universalist tendency

Let us first consider the universalist side. Never have the languages and structures of universal human rights protection been as broadly and densely articulated as today. The proliferation of human rights regimes in international law and national constitutional law since the end of World War II marks an unprecedented commitment to strong universalism. Globally, we have the International Bill of Rights comprising the UDHR, adopted by the new United Nations in 1948, and the two international covenants on civil and political rights and on economic, social and cultural rights respectively, both concluded in 1966. Alongside these, we have seven other so-called "core" international human rights instruments, covering race and gender discrimination, proclaiming the rights of the child, of disabled persons and of migrant workers, and providing protection against enforced disappearances and against torture. Only the race and gender conventions were concluded before the mid 1980s, indicating exponential rather than incremental growth in the later period. Each regime is supported by a committee monitoring implementation, and in addition to these specialist bodies, there are a number of general UN institutions dedicated to human rights protection. These include the Office of the High Commissioner for Human Rights, the system of universal periodic review and the Human Rights Council, which investigates and reports on human rights issues and violations in particular subject-matter or territories. Additionally, there are an increasing number of supplementary universal instruments in areas as diverse as rights of self-determination and of indigenous people and minorities, rights of older persons and prisoners, of refugees and stateless persons, and rights associated with the administration of justice, social welfare, health, work, association, slavery, war crimes and humanitarian concerns more generally (Steiner *et al.* 2008, chs 2–4).

At the regional level the graph also indicates significant growth. The three most active regional systems are in Europe, America and Africa, with the European Convention system witnessing the most remarkable recent transformation. Embracing the ten original member states of the Council of Europe, the European Convention on Human Rights entered into force in 1953. Today it covers 47 states and over 800 million people. The Court of Human Rights has become central to the enforcement system, culminating in Protocol 11 of 1998, which confers upon it compulsory jurisdiction over all individual petitions once national remedies are exhausted. In the 1970s only 163 individual petitions were raised, rising to 455 in the 1980s. By the turn of the century the court was receiving nearly 10,000 complaints annually, and by 2010 this had grown to 61,300. Judgments tell a similarly spectacular story, with 2,607 in 2010, a tenfold increase on 1999 (250), which in turn was four times as many as the court issued in its first 20 years (60) (Stone Sweet 2012).

Regional rights catalogues lack certain universalizing features of their global counterparts. Their jurisdiction is territorially limited, and so the category of protected persons cannot be unrestricted. Yet as regards the generality of the protected content and equal protection to all within jurisdiction, regional human rights catalogues are just as universal as their global counterparts – except for the African Charter on Human and People's Rights with its heavier qualification in favor of individual duties and collective goods. Even as regards the category of protected persons, the regional catalogues are expressed as the local articulation of what are assumed to be universally appropriate norms – applicable just in virtue of their recipients being "human." Explicit language apart, this orientation reveals itself various different ways, including the applicability of rights to all in the jurisdiction regardless of citizenship; or the identity of the rights claimed with these in other charters; or, as is frequently true of the American Charter vis-à-vis the European system, through explicitly drawing upon the other's jurisprudence in the home court (Steiner *et al.* 2008, chs. 8 and 11).

A similar story can be told of national rights frameworks. Again, the structure of rights protection tends toward the universal as regards generality of content and uniform application to all protected. Again, this universality cannot apply directly to the category of those protected, but once more, through extension to non-citizens, textual identity and recognizing foreign courts "as if" rights were a common jurisdiction – a feature reinforced by the practice, especially in European states, of the domestic incorporation of regional or global charters – national courts assume the mantle of universalism.

This commitment to universalism in national charters is as old as the very idea of constitutionally recognized rights. In the first French republic of 1789, the "rights of (universal) man" precede the rights of Frenchmen. The "self-evident" equality of the independent Americans of the 1776 Declaration of Independence derives from the claim that "all men are created equal." Today, however, the exponential growth of a universally oriented national rights charter matches that at regional and global levels. Prior to World War II, few constitutional frameworks included judicially enforceable fundamental rights provisions. Yet all new European constitutions since 1949 have embraced universal rights and constitutional review, and even systems traditionally skeptical of judicial authority, such as France and Britain, have recently moved in the direction of robust rights universalism. A similar pattern applies in constitutional (re)settlement beyond Europe, with many common law jurisdictions of the old Commonwealth and other post-colonial systems across the globe adopting universal rights frameworks (Gearty 2006).

The particularist tendency

Against this record, the particularist can make two sorts of claim. The impressive textual and institutional edifice of global human right protection may be exposed as ineffective, as lacking the means to realize its ambition. More fundamentally, the very ambition of universalism can be criticized as illegitimate or, at least, ever-inclined to overstep the boundaries of its legitimacy.

We begin with the sheer range of problems of international and domestic compliance with the universal commitments contained in human rights instruments in a world where different states and peoples have different constellations of interests and conceptions of the coordinates of good government. Anne Kent (1999) identifies five sets of problems, progressively dimming the bright picture of human rights universalism painted in the above paragraphs. First, there is the problem of non-universal accession to human rights treaties or of qualified accession – ratifications hedged with significant reservations or followed up by derogations. Second, there is the problem of procedural compliance with reporting and other aspects of the monitoring regime. Third, there is the problem of substantive compliance with the requests or determinations of transnational human rights bodies. Fourth, there is the problem of limited *de jure* domestic endorsement of the universal character of human rights. Finally, there is the problem of limited de facto compliance of domestic governments even when *de jure* regimes are in place, whether due to the incapacity or to the unwillingness of nominally compliant governments to honor their legal commitments.

There is nothing unusual in low levels of compliance with transnational legal norms at any of these stages. However, with transnational human rights, the usual contributory elements of weak or attenuated control mechanisms, imprecision of standards and the low and scattered visibility of the monitored activity are exacerbated by other factors. The vast range and scale of normative ambition of the rights catalogue is an underlying consideration. More specifically, state compliance is tested by the fact that human rights treaties, still unusually amongst international legal instruments, include individuals as their subjects (with states mostly figuring only as the primary addressees of the rights of the individuals subject to their jurisdiction), and do not operate, or at least not primarily so, in terms of reciprocal state interests or a more general associative logic of the common good of states qua states. Indeed, states are themselves the most significant perpetrators of human rights abuse and so assiduous implementation of their binding human rights agreements may have, from the narrow state-centered perspective of state interest, negative-sum consequences. Finally, the gap between interests and ideals is also due to the ideological significance of the ideals. The reputation gains in the international community for states from apparent commitment to universal right standards are significant, as are the reputation deficits of palpable non-commitment. Here, more than in any other international law area, there is a tendency toward "mock" commitment in the drafting phase and "mock" compliance in the implementation phase.

The charge of hypocrisy or cynicism, however, is not reserved exclusively for those responsible for compliance failures. If, for some, universal human rights is a noble dream in danger of frustration, for others it is just a closet particularism, a reified reflection of one way amongst many of thinking about moral and political claims and aspirations (Baxi 2006). Here the concern is not the vulnerability of human rights universalism in the face of state recalcitrance. Rather it is the prospect of its difference-blind success before a genuine multiplicity of conceptions of just social and political order, of the moral costs incurred as it realizes its ambition for uniformity even though uniformity is not morally required.

Skepticism toward such a universalizing claim may be of a radical sort, denying *any* value to the register of universal rights. This may be because the very structure of rights involves an attitude that is self-regarding, pays insufficient heed to responsibilities, leads to an atrophied sense of belonging, gives undue priority to individual over collective agency, or allows agency in general too central a place in the moral world (Twining 2010, ch. 6). These criticisms do not always come from defenders of a pluralism of political orders – and so of difference in general – but sometimes from positions merely committed to another kind of social and political order, as with the proponents of so-called "Asian values" (Bauer and Bell 1999) or the defenders of the mixed approach in the African charter. Likewise, more selective forms of skepticism, while they do not disown the basic structure of a rights-based approach, challenge received standards for filling out that basic structure. The dispute between Western and socialist conceptions of rights around the 1948 UN Declaration and the dominance of "first generation" rights in many subsequent transnational and national charters is only the most prominent example of this (Sen 2004).

From the point of view of an approach that stresses the prevalence or legitimacy of diverse forms of political order, the claim of a global human rights universalism is at best naïve and hubristic, at worst a knowing and misleading conceit. From this perspective, the global architecture of human rights either promises more than it can deliver or delivers something quite different from what it promises.

Reconciling universalism and particularism

Can we avoid the complacency of a stance that reconciles universalism and particularism at the cost of evacuating one or other concept of meaning, or the partiality of a stance that endorses strong universalism or particularism at the expense of the other, or a fatalism which understands something of value may be lost if the two cannot be reconciled but does not know how to achieve that reconciliation? One position seeks to avoid the fatalism that lies beyond complacency and unilateralism by resort to a new type of "substantive minimalism" (Cohen 2010). It acknowledges the value of universal rights standards for a world that takes individual freedom and equality seriously, but understands that such a world will also inevitably produce a diversity of legal and political arrangements. It suggests that the only and inert space between these large possibilities is one where universal rights are modestly affirmed, a residual surface of common cause that may posit general standards and condemn the most egregious and commonly affirmed breaches of rights but that contemplates no dynamic of common development beyond that (Ferrara 2003; Ignatieff 2001).

Can we upgrade the reconciliation of the universal and the particular beyond this minimal baseline? In this final section, I will outline a series of connected arguments showing how this might be possible. These arguments stress and combine the normative flexibility, the trans-cultural attractiveness and the structural reconfigurability of human rights claims.

Normative factors

The modest reach of human rights universalism

In terms of normative reach, human rights universalism is more limited than sometimes credited by critics. Just because human rights universalism asserts generality of standards, uniformity of application and universality of enjoyment does not make it a comprehensive theory of political morality. To the extent that it successfully claims these universal attributes, the human rights approach will supply the dominant template within its sphere of influence – the specification of the basic entitlements that humans individually or collectively can claim against public authorities, or against each other. But that sphere of influence is far from the whole of political morality. As Jeremy Waldron (1987) argues, the object of human rights universalism need be no more than to draw sufficient attention to certain basic interests in the overall elaboration of schemes of political morality. Far from being a colonization of the whole from the perspective of the part, its object is to supply a counterpoint to other powerful themes, to facilitate an equilibrium between consideration of individual entitlements and other more responsibility-based, collective–good-enhancing or otherwise individual–decentering concerns.

So where, for example, the European Court of Human Rights has developed an extensive jurisprudence on the open-textured idea of the "margin of appreciation" allowable to national legislative and executive authorities in the interpretation of universal rights, this should not be quickly dismissed as an unprincipled trimming of universalist ambitions. To recognize, as the court's jurisprudence does, that local political actors can have greater insight into local standards and some independent authority to speak for these standards where rights protection spills over into controversial policy matters, say, of bioethics, sexual mores or religious freedom, is not to deny rights their universal place. Rather, it should be seen as an unavoidable exercise in frontier management – a formula framing the inevitable zone of contestation and negotiation of the terms of the equilibrium between respecting rights and other concerns (Greer 2006).

The disaggregated quality of human rights universalism

This point is reinforced when we consider that, even within its sphere of influence, human rights universalism does not operate holistically. That is to say, the value of the universal protection of some human rights is not *necessarily* undermined by the lesser protection of other rights in the universal catalogue.

This is *not* to claim that human rights do not hang together in important ways. We are more likely to enjoy our freedom of conscience if it is joined with freedom of expression and assembly, and vice versa, for the benefits or interests associated with each, in particular the interest in living in accordance with one's understanding of what constitutes a good life, significantly overlap. To take another example, we are more likely to enjoy our freedom of movement and our freedom from arbitrary deprivation of our liberty if they are joined to a right to respect for family life and privacy, and vice versa. Again, the stake is similar, namely the assurance of a protected sphere within which public authority cannot intrude on our choice of lifestyle. Turning from the moral to the causal relationship between rights, again we observe a web of connection. Because the failure to observe any particular right or set of rights, first, is often symptomatic of a broader deficiency of respect by national governments or other public authorities for the freedom and well-being of their citizens, and, second, tends to undermine citizens' capacity to defend or pursue a broader range of rights, the absence or deterioration of certain rights sometimes indicates or foretells the absence or deterioration of others (Habermas 2001).

But these are tendential rather than necessary relationships. Mostly, the absence of certain rights does not fatally undermine the enjoyment or accessibility of others. Any stronger argument is probably limited to Henry Shue's thesis that only rights to security and subsistence, alongside some measure of basic liberty, are "basic" in supplying indispensable social preconditions for the enjoyment of any other rights (Beitz and Goodin 2009; Shue 1996). Such foundational claims aside, rights are more loosely clustered.

This disaggregated picture has implications for the defensibility of rights universalism alongside more particularistic domains of social organization. For it becomes possible to justify the pursuit of one right

or one set of rights, universally conceived, without there being any pressing moral or practical imperative to pursue all others equally. Universal
human rights protection, notwithstanding the superficial association of
universalism with the contrary thought, becomes a more-or-less rather
than an either–or affair, graduated and selective rather than categorical
and comprehensive.

Cultural factors

The rhetorical commonality and inclusiveness of human rights discourse

As noted earlier, the rhetorical power of universal human rights discourse
can lead to its cynical endorsement for reputational purposes. But there is
another side to this coin. We should attend to what Jon Elster (1998) calls
"the civilizing effect of hypocrisy"; namely, how adopting a public discourse
on reputational grounds may, given the appropriate context of publicity and
enforceability, attract the expectation of behavior verifiably adapted toward
the terms of that discourse and, over time, may even lead to a genuine
acceptance of its underlying normative structure.

We need not understand this in one-sided terms, as gravitation toward
a unilaterally specified norm. Instead, we may understand the evolution of
the relevant universal in more broadly "iterative" terms (Walzer 2007). As
Charles Taylor (2011) argues, once the language of universal human rights
is universally acknowledged, we can begin to contemplate something like
a Gadamerian "fusion of horizons" in which, as a result and reinforcing
cause of the moral worldview of the other gradually becoming less strange,
different parties who invest in the language and institutions of universal
human rights come to find common justificatory ground and to influence
the shared or overlapping meaning attached to human rights.

Other factors weigh in favor of progressive convergence. The basic universalism of scope within human rights – the ideal assumption of unlimited jurisdiction – is crucial. Many human rights treaties have spread
incrementally and unevenly, and that jagged progress continues, but their
in-principle geographical and jurisdictional illimitability, adumbrated in
the all-embracing scope of the original UN Declaration of 1948, means that
all states and *all* other relevant parties have always been putative players
in the modern international human rights arena. Compared to much contemporary international law, therefore, from climate change to food safety,
from drugs control to intellectual property, the conditions of discourse

formation, although framed within a Western tradition of liberal individualism, have been of explicitly global ambition from the outset.

Rhetorical inclusiveness is also encouraged through the national tradition. As already noted, the earlier national catalogues presented themselves as particularizations of a fundamentally universal register. Increasingly, that rhetorical inclusiveness is reflected in the receptiveness of national courts to foreign judgments on human rights (Jacobsohn 2010: ch. 4). The inter-cultural momentum toward human rights universalism, therefore, is as evident in the "bottom-up" spread of comparative emulation as in the growing reach of international treaties and doctrine. Indeed, these processes feed off one another. Arguments for the sympathetic consideration of "foreign" standards are reinforced by evidence of common national reception of international standards. Reciprocally, the development of international treaties as global standard-bearers is encouraged by past and continuing practices of comparative emulation.

The open-endedness of human rights discourse

The continuing global ambition of international human rights is reflected, amongst other things, in the open-ended development of the subject-matter of human rights discourse. The very idea of "second" generation (social) and "third" generation (collective) rights (and the very fact that the language of rights "generations" has become dated!) suggests an expansionary dynamic in which different categories of rights, emphasized by different interests and compatible with different overall frameworks of political morality, are self-consciously linked. Ever since the Vienna Declaration adopted at the World Conference on Human Rights in Vienna in 1993, indeed, the emphasis on human rights as not only universal, but also as "indivisible, interdependent and interrelated" has been routinely stressed in the discourse of transnational human rights.

We should be aware, however, of the limits of the claims of inclusiveness and open-endedness, and also the dangers involved in their pursuit. As noted, there is no compelling moral or sociological argument that all human rights should or must hang together. Yet even if "first generation" forbearance rights and freedoms evidently continue to enjoy greater recognition and protection than their second and third generation counterparts, the narrative of subject-matter open-endedness, by highlighting the transformative possibilities of human rights discourse, remains an important consequence and reinforcing cause of an equally open-ended inclusiveness of rights-holding populations. But this remains a double-edged prospect.

While, on the one hand, it aspires toward a more even-handed and mutually engaged inter-cultural treatment of the relative priority of rights claim, on the other, by promising so much it threatens the anti-utopian modesty that accounts for the broad initial appeal of the universal human rights register (Moyn 2010).

Structural factors

The rescaling of human rights communities

This tension between unduly modest and immodest conceptions of human rights is unavoidable, and knows no single or ideal resolution. However, alongside the ideological momentum created by the rhetorical inclusiveness and open-endedness of human rights discourse, and the counter-current of a continuing particularistic insistence upon a local "margin of appreciation," there are other fluid structural factors that bear upon the pattern of relations between universal human rights institutions and particular political communities, and that suggest additional ways of addressing the basic opposition in question.

Another means by which greater uniformity of general standards – a shared "appreciation" of the core – may be realized over time is the development of new forms of political community *beyond* the state. Whereas the universal dimension of human rights is typically particularized in different ways in different states, we can imagine broader and more inclusive forms of particularization for broader forms of political community. Here, then, we look to new commonalities not by making connections across old jurisdictions, but through the introduction of new jurisdictions.

This is most obviously the case of the development of regional integration in Europe. In 2000 the European Union declared its own Charter of Fundamental Rights, finally legally adopted under the Lisbon Treaty in 2009 (Craig and De Burca 2011, ch. 5). Arguably, the Charter will function more like a domestic Bill of Rights than a variable international standard. Given the distinctive underlying structure of the EU as a community of developing common cause, its rights, rather than reflecting sympathy with the universal "other," may come to form part of a thicker fabric of shared commitment. First, there are new reciprocal obligations arising from the denser network of shared or mutually implicated practices. To make a common market in Europe is to share in a common enterprise in which life chances become interlocked in new ways. The affirmation of common market forms of access and standards *requires* a common floor of understanding of how rights, economic and otherwise, may express, facilitate or qualify the operation of the market. Common rights protection, then, become a matter both of providing for the efficacious design of the overall common enterprise and of underpinning common commitment by ensuring even-handedness in the allocation of benefits and burdens (Besselink 1998). In the second place, moreover, although the evidence for this remains decidedly mixed, the denser framework of common practice may encourage a new community of attachment or solidarity (Williams 2010, ch. 4). For those who live in communities of thicker practice will develop new senses of affinity – and these will make them more likely to contemplate common human rights standards with those who have become "like us."

Beyond the EU, we can see some evidence of other fledgling transnational communities of shared commitment in which rights become part of a wider fabric of common enterprise. The other regional free trade organizations such as NAFTA and Mercosur may be seen in this light, as may the World Trade Organization. In each case the project involves the realization of a common trading bloc and the (often narrow) range of rights involved are interpreted and developed in the light of that common discipline. Here the common project is insufficiently "thick" for new forms of special affinity or attachment to accompany the new enterprise, but a "level playing field" of rights may nevertheless emerge from the thinner framework of mutually implicated practice.

Elsewhere, the sense of mutual implication within a shared community of practice may be reactive rather than proactive – emanating from conditions of proximity and intersection of risk rather than the construction of common enterprises. Take, for example, global climate change, or nuclear peace, or protection from the mobile violence of "new wars" (Kaldor 2007) and non-national terrorism. The elaboration of the rights (environmental, security, humanitarian aid, etc.) implicated in any common response will again tend toward convergence as part of our common interest – here as one particular (if global) community of risk or fate – in responding effectively and even-handedly.

The plural configuration of institutionalized human rights protection

Finally, let us look more specifically at the evolving structure of human rights monitoring and adjudication. Here we briefly consider how the increasing complexity of the global institutional design of human rights protection defies any simple dichotomy between national and transnational, and between the presumptively particular and the presumptively universal.

There has been much discussion in recent years of the value of network analysis of human rights protection (Keck and Sikkink 1998), the concept often invoked to signal new forms of transnational activism in which non-state-centered movements use the language and mechanisms of human rights to strengthen their claims. The emphasis here is not upon abstract universalism of ambition, or inter-state emulation, or post-state political community, but on forms of interest formation and mobilization unconnected to the state, or any particular polity. Yet this remains a tentative line of research, one that risks exaggerating the capacity of transnational movements to address and overcome the power of established state interests (Goodale 2007).

One important way of strengthening the network argument, however, reinforcing the state-decentering societal pluralism that lies at the heart of its analysis, focuses upon the emergent institutional pluralism of human rights courts. Alec Stone Sweet (2012), for example, has suggested the emergence of a "cosmopolitan order" of rights adjudication across Europe. He emphasizes how, today, neither national nor transnational realms describe an institutional (still less cultural) unity of rights protection. Just as the European level of rights adjudication now involves both the ECJ and ECHR, together with a plethora of other international tribunals whose jurisdiction includes Europe, so too at the national level there is typically a diversity of rights-recognizing jurisdictions – constitutional courts, administrative courts, ordinary appellate courts, functionally specialist courts – which do not converge at a single state-sovereign apex. In such a decentered authority system, no one has the last word. System polyarchy is a function both of multi-levelness and of plurality *within* levels, which features reinforce each other. Dialogue between courts, and the search for common ground or, at least, the appeal to common public reason in defense of continued difference, is, on this analysis, not just the echo of a deep moral universalism, or indicative of a growing sense of family resemblance, but a structural inevitability borne of the incomplete and interdependent authority of multiple judicial sites.

This plural institutional configuration has important consequences. It provides more "in-between" space for transnational movements to become involved in right advocacy, and encourages a more cooperative culture between courts absent a clear hierarchy between or within levels. It also decouples human rights orientation from political pedigree. In the unending cycle of rights articulation, neither transnational nor national courts speak with a single voice, and the sense that one (transnational) level defends a strong universalism and the other displays a highly qualified state-particularist bias is lost. This, in turn, means that the call for universalizing human rights protection is less likely to be restricted to judicial voices that challenge (rather than feed off) the higher constitutional and cultural legitimacy of the nation state.

Conclusion

I have concluded by sketching the possible modes and trajectories of an "unforced consensus" (Taylor 2011) in human rights in which the universal and the particular are complexly blended. Much more detail and qualification is needed. However, my aim here has simply been to move beyond either naïve assertion or a pessimistic bias against the possibility of rights universalism. In particular, I have sought to stress that there are various connected ways of moving beyond zero-sum calculation in this field, according to which every invocation of the universal is a denial of the values and interests distinguishing particular communities, or every invocation of the particular is an indictment of any progressive sense of universalism.

References

Bauer, Joanne and Bell, Daniel, eds. 1999. *The East Asian Challenge to Human Rights*. New York: Cambridge University Press.

Baxi, Upendra. 2006. *The Future of Human Rights*, 2nd edn. New Delhi: Oxford University Press.

Beitz, Charles and Goodin, Robert, eds. 2009. *Global Basic Rights*. Oxford University Press.

Besselink, Leonard. 1998. "Entrapped by the Maximum Standard: On Fundamental Rights, Pluralism and Subsidiarity in the European Union." *Common Market Law Review* 35: 629.

Cohen, Joshua. 2010. "Minimalism about Human Rights: The Most We Can Hope For?" In Joshua Cohen, *The Arc of the Moral Universe and other Essays*. Cambridge, MA: Harvard University Press, pp. 319–348.

Cotterrell, Roger. 2008. "Transnational Communities and the Concept of Law." *Ratio Juris* 21: 1–15.

Craig, Paul and De Burca, Grainne. 2011. *EU Law*, 5th edn. Oxford University Press.

Dancy, Jonathan. 2006. *Ethics without Principles*. Oxford University Press.

Elster, Jon. 1998. "A Plea for Mechanisms." In Peter Hedstrom and Richard Swedberg, eds., *Social Mechanisms: An Analytical Approach to Social Theory*. Cambridge University Press, pp. 45–73.

Ferrara, Alessandro. 2003. "Two Notions of Humanity and the Judgment Argument for Human Rights." *Political Theory* 31: 392–420.

Gearty, Conor. 2006. *Can Human Rights Survive?* Cambridge University Press.

Goodale, Mark. 2007. "Introduction." In Mark Goodale and Sally Engle Merry, eds., *The Practice of Human Rights: Tracking Law Between the Global and the Local.* Cambridge University Press, pp. 17–21.

Greer, Steven. 2006. *The European Convention of Human Rights: Achievements, Problems and Prospects.* Cambridge University Press.

Habermas, Jürgen. 2001. "A Paradoxical Union of Contradictory Principles?" *Political Theory* 29: 766–781.

Ignatieff, Michael. 2001. *Human Rights as Politics and Idolatry.* Princeton University Press.

Jacobsohn, Gary. 2010. *Constitutional Identity.* Cambridge, MA: Harvard University Press.

Kaldor, Mary. 2007. *New and Old Wars*, 2nd edn. Cambridge: Polity Press.

Keck, Margaret and Sikkink, Kathryn, eds. 1998. *Activists Beyond Borders: Advocacy Networks in International Politics.* Ithaca: Cornell University Press.

Kent, Anne. 1999. *China, the United Nations and Human Rights: The Limits of Compliance.* Philadelphia: University of Pennsylvania Press.

MacCormick, Neil. 2005. *Rhetoric and the Rule of Law.* Oxford University Press.

Moyn, Samuel. 2010. *The Last Utopia: Human Rights in History.* Cambridge, MA: Harvard University Press

Raz, Joseph. 1998. "Multiculturalism." *Ratio Juris* 11: 193–205.

Sen, Amartya. 2004. "Elements of a Theory of Human Rights." *Philosophy and Public Affairs* 32: 315–356.

Shue, Henry. 1996. *Basic Rights: Subsistence, Affluence and US Foreign Policy*, 2nd edn. Princeton University Press.

Steger, Manfred. 2009. *The Rise of the Global Imaginary and the Persistence of Ideology.* Oxford University Press.

Steiner, Henry, Alston, Philip and Goodman, Ryan. 2008. *International Human Rights in Context*, 3rd edn. Oxford University Press.

Stone Sweet, Alec. 2012. "A Cosmopolitan Legal Order: Constitutional Pluralism and Rights Adjudication in Europe." *Global Constitutionalism* 1: 53–90.

Taylor, Charles. 2011. "Conditions of an Unforced Consensus on Human Rights." In Charles Taylor, *Dilemmas and Connections.* Cambridge, MA: Harvard University Press, pp. 105–123.

Twining, William. 2010. *General Jurisprudence: Understanding Law from a Global Perspective.* Cambridge University Press.

Vincent, Andrew. 2002. *Nationalism and Particularity.* Cambridge University Press.

Waldron, Jeremy. 1987. *Nonsense Upon Stilts: Bentham, Burke and Marx on the Rights of Man.* London: Methuen.

1999. *Law and Disagreement.* Oxford University Press.

Walker, Neil. 2010. "Constitutionalism and the Incompleteness of Democracy: An Iterative Relationship." *Rechtsfilosofie & Rechtstheorie* 39: 206–233.

Walzer, Michael. 2007. "Nation and Universe." In Michael Walzer, *Thinking Politically; Essays in Political Theory, edited by* David Miller. New Haven: Yale University Press, pp. 183–218.

Williams, Andrew. 2010. *The Ethos of Europe: Values, Law and Justice in the EU.* Cambridge University Press.

3 | Are human rights universal?

REX MARTIN

Natural rights and human rights

Natural rights are the ancestor of contemporary human rights; and the idea of natural rights was a doctrine of universal rights, at least of those basic moral rights that were thought to hold good in a state of nature. The UN's Universal Declaration of Human Rights (UDHR, 1948) is the keystone of contemporary human rights thinking, and it proceeds from the view that the human rights enunciated there have a foundation in morality and are universal.

By the last few decades of the nineteenth century, the notion of natural rights had lost or begun to lose its appeal (see Waldron 1987, for excerpts from some of the main critics). After World War II, universal rights made a return to center stage, first in the United Nations Charter (1945) and then in the UN's Universal Declaration of Human Rights (UDHR, 1948) and the various covenants and treaties respecting human rights that came after that. But this return was not simply a revival of old-style natural rights. Indeed, many writers today (e.g., Beitz 2009; Boucher 2009; Darby 2009) stress that there is a considerable discontinuity between natural rights and what are today called human rights.

Natural rights are regarded as independent of society; they are held by human beings simply in virtue of their being human. Focused as they are on the rights of persons as such, natural rights are claimed to hold good in all times and places.

But human rights (as laid out in the UDHR of 1948) are rights of persons in society, specifically in organized societies (which are typically embodied in territorially based states). Human rights represent important interests of such persons (in personal autonomy and in participation in the institutions and practices of self-governance, as well as interests in security, dignity, health and well-being) and these interests are treated as especially worthy of mention on lists of human rights because these interests are vulnerable to specific threats (Beitz 2009; Nickel 2007; Shue 1996) that are characteristic of life in society, in particular, in modern societies.

The human rights of the UDHR assume the conditions of modern life, at the time the UDHR was promulgated (and for the foreseeable future beyond that). This means they are universal with respect to the way people and things are now.

Universal rights: some matters for concern

In the present chapter I want to look at universality under four distinct themes:

1. as concerned with the rights of all (or almost all) persons;
2. as concerned with a responsibility or obligation, on the part of all individual persons (or, again, of almost all persons), to help fulfill and protect these rights;
3. as concerned with the universality – and universal acceptance – of the moral justification provided for these rights; and finally
4. as concerned with universal worldwide feasibility.

I will examine leading criticisms of universality or concerns about it (under one or more of these themes) and suggest, as we reflect on these concerns, where there might be called-for modifications in the notion of the universality of human rights. In trying to determine this matter, I will attempt to assess specific arguments – for or against universality – by looking at sample cases in the light of prominent claims that can be advanced against the universality of human rights.

There are I think at least five such claims, discussed in subsequent sections of the chapter:

1. There is no universal ground for human rights that is accepted by everyone.
2. Human rights should hold strictly between persons, simply as persons.
3. So-called welfare rights (especially the UDHR social and economic rights to such things as adequate income or holidays with pay) can't literally be rights of everybody.
4. The UDHR social and economic rights are not universally practicable or feasible under contemporary conditions.
5. Some rights are rights of a particular class of persons (e.g., rights of women) or they are group rights; such rights cannot literally be rights of everyone.

These claims, these criticisms represent five distinct hard questions that a theory of human rights must address.

Universal moral grounds for human rights

The first criticism can be stated simply enough: there is no single argument or justification for universal human rights that would be accepted as normatively sound by everyone, everywhere. The justifiability of actual human rights, for example, the UDHR rights, is not supportable on a universally recognizable moral ground; such rights are not normatively universal, then, in modern societies.

The authors and initial supporters of the Universal Declaration believed that the rights listed there were morally supportable; however, they identified no single moral ground or justification as the one that did the supporting. Rather, the founders believed that a variety of recognized moral systems and conventional moralities would justify and support these rights either in the sense that they would overlap or converge on the UDHR set of rights (or most of them) or in the sense that each constituent moral system, taken on its own, would morally endorse and support the UDHR set of rights, or most of them (Beitz 2009; UNESCO 1949).

Such an attitude about justification made sense in the culturally and morally pluralistic world that existed in 1948 (and that exists now, and for the foreseeable future). Although we cannot say that the UDHR rights have a single moral justification that would be accepted as normatively sound by absolutely everyone, they do have substantial parallel or convergent moral grounds of support and can be regarded (on that basis) as normatively well grounded. There's no good reason to decry or disparage the UDHR rights, on moral grounds, for lacking a single absolutely universal accepted-by-all moral justification.

The two UN treaties or Covenants (1966, entered into force 1976), one treaty covering the political and civil rights of the UDHR and the other the social and economic rights, have *each* been ratified up to now by over 75 percent of the 200 or so countries in the world (Nickel 2007). These rights reflect important interests of individual persons; they are possible (practicable or enactable) in modern societies; they protect right-holders from many standard threats characteristically found in modern societies. The UDHR rights have enough moral authority worldwide, and in general support, to stand, as they do, as part of international law and to be regarded as morally justified and morally justifiable.

Human rights as rights of persons as such

The second criticism starts from a fairly straightforward claim: *some* universal moral rights do hold strictly between persons, simply as persons. The moral right to be told the truth (or at least not lied to) and, perhaps, the moral right to have promises kept are examples. Such rights, we can assume, have widespread acceptance. These universal moral rights, understood in the way I've described them, are rights against other individuals, but they are in no way claims against the basic institutions of society (including government).

Maurice Cranston does not mention governments at all in his characterization of human rights. On his view human rights are rights of all individuals *against all individuals*: "To say that all men have a right to life is to impose on all men the duty of respecting human life" (1973, 68–69; also 6–7, 21, 67). A similar position is taken by David Raphael (1967a, 65–66; 1967b, 108–110).

Cranston and Raphael claim to be talking about human rights, but the position they hold is characteristic of old-style natural rights. And the background to this traditional view of natural rights was a pre-political state of nature in which individuals, taken one by one, had the rights and duties of persons simply as such.

The Universal Declaration and the other great human rights manifestos of today don't concern rights that hold strictly between individual persons; rather, they are mainly intended to impose restraints upon governments or on organized societies. And the same is true of the natural rights manifestos, once governments were seen to be required and were agreed upon, thus ending the state of nature.

Individuals were involved as beneficiaries of these restraints but, for the most part, they were not the parties to whom the manifestos were addressed. Or, at least, the class of all living individuals, taken one by one, was never the sole addressee of such manifestos, nor was it the primary one.

That governments are an intended addressee (and often the principal addressee) of human rights norms is too deeply embedded historically to be erased (Mayo 1965). This is not to deny, of course, that individuals are often addressed as well (the crucial prohibition invoked in the right not to be killed is addressed *both* to governments and to individual persons, for example). When things go well, it is typically one's *fellow citizens* who do the maintaining of human rights, through conduct that complies with those rights. But government is typically called upon to enforce compliance when individual conduct fails to support a given right.

Sometimes, though, the primary addressee of human rights is neither individual persons, taken one by one within a given body politic, nor governments per se. Rather, it is organized society itself that is being directly addressed, respecting the role and character of its social institutions and practices – for example, its economic arrangements (such as open and competitive markets).

In the end, it is really organized society that is the essential addressee of those moral rights that are singled out under the heading of human rights. Government enters the human rights picture as the organizer, and as one of the major agencies, of the kind of entity (that is, organized society) against which a human rights claim is characteristically lodged. The role of government is not limited simply to formulating laws, thereby making the content of rights more specific and assigning more closely specified duties to second parties, and so on. Governments – popular governments in the favored case – help decide, as legal rights and duties and other arrangements take shape, which rights are truly basic. The idea is that basic civil and constitutional rights, including such of these as are morally based, have a high priority and are not to be superseded or significantly impaired in the normal case by other normative considerations, such as mere aggregate net welfare. This idea represents one of the central understandings of rights in contemporary thought (Dworkin 1978; Rawls 1971, 1993).

Besides formulating rights and duties and deciding on and implementing basic rights, governments need to act so as to harmonize rights, to reduce or eliminate conflict among them. And they need to promote and to enforce, as need be, the rights they have formulated.

Insofar as organized society (government, in particular) is the principal addressee of human rights norms, then recognition and institutional embodiment of rights by such addressees belongs to the conception of human rights (see Beitz 2009; Martin 1993). This emphasis on organized society and on the special role of governments, when they act properly as institutional maintainers of human rights, is another important difference between UDHR rights and state-of-nature natural rights.

The UN's Declaration (of 1948) presupposed, at the time it was written, the idea that organized societies (and their governments, in particular) are the principal addressees of human rights norms. Clearly, the Declaration lays out a set of aspirations; but it does not stop there. Repeatedly, the idea of the recognition of the rights proclaimed and their observation is invoked. Thus, human rights can effectively be regarded as constitutional rights within "Member States" (as they're called in the UDHR preamble). This is, in fact, the case primarily contemplated in the UN's Universal Declaration and in the two UN Covenants mentioned earlier.

In time, human rights have become more of an international concern as well. I have in mind here the appearance of the European Convention on Human Rights (1950) and later of the EU, the appearance of various

UN agencies concerned with international food, health (and so on), of a growing EU and UN court system (including an international court of criminal justice and more specialized tribunals concerned with war crimes in specific countries), and of UN-sponsored treaties ranging over such issues as genocide (1948) and apartheid (1973) and setting out the international responsibilities involved. Accordingly, the dimensions discussed in this and the previous paragraph – both the national constitutional and legislative dimension and the dimension of international concern and responsibility and its growth, just described – are crucial features of the political culture engendered by the UN Charter and the Universal Declaration.

Welfare rights as universal rights

Now we come to a third main criticism. Some have claimed that several of the UDHR rights (such as rights to own private property, rights to self-governance based on periodic elections by a society-wide electorate, and especially the social and economic rights to pensions, adequate income, holidays with pay, free but compulsory schooling, etc.) can't be universal. They cannot literally be rights of everybody.

The institutional thesis

One reason they give for saying this is that these rights assume social or economic arrangements that are not themselves found universally or inevitably among all peoples, or in all times and places (Cranston 1967). John Rawls's argument is on this point similar to Cranston's. Rawls suggests, speaking roughly, that articles 19–30 of the UDHR, including in particular all the so-called social and economic rights, are not "proper" human rights "since they presuppose specific institutions" (Rawls 1999, 80, n23).

Cranston's requirement of a strict universality regarding the institutions named in the various UDHR articles – in order for the rights that subtend these institutions to count as human rights – is off on the wrong foot. The UDHR makes no claims at all to this particular sense of universality. It is concerned, rather, with human rights that assume the conditions of life at the time the UDHR was promulgated. This means they're universal with respect to important interests of persons living in such societies, then and now.

Normative concerns about counterpart obligations under the UDHR

Onora O'Neill's basic analysis starts with what are often called perfect (= complete) obligations, obligations that are held by everyone and owed to everyone (all of whom are understood to be right-holders); other details, including the content of the obligation, are spelled out or well understood. Take for example a universal liberty right: "if A has the liberty right to do x, then everyone will have the obligation to allow A to do x" (O'Neill 1996, 135). Here we know what the obligation-bearer is supposed to do (not interfere with the doing of x) and we know who the obligation-bearer is (everyone).

O'Neill's analysis here can be extended beyond liberties in the sense of things right-holders do or can do (like speaking freely). It can also cover universal rights that serve as proscriptions against injuring the rightholder in certain quite specific ways, as in a right not to be raped or to be tortured (O'Neill 2000, 105). Again we know the content of the injury forbidden, know who is not to be injured in that way (no one is), and we know the relevant obligation-bearers for each type of case (everyone). What these examples of rights have in common is that all obligation-bearers satisfy the relevant obligation in the same way: by *refraining* from doing something.

In the case of the UDHR social and economic rights to the provision of goods and services, unlike the case with rights to refrainings, it is typically unclear (for given rights) what the specific content of the counterpart obligation is and who specifically has that obligation. For example, does everyone, under the social and economic rights listed in the UDHR, have specific and diverse obligations to provide education or work or social security or a "standard of living adequate for health and well-being" (UDHR, Article 25), and to provide these things for literally everyone in the world?

Underlying O'Neill's criticism is a more fundamental point: there are no rights without specific obligations on the part of second parties and, in the ideal case, some spelling out of the relevant obligation-bearers. Where these things are lacking we don't have a proper right (2005, 431).

In order to remedy this problem, one would have to supply the content of the obligations and the identification of the respective obligation-bearers typically through the establishment of appropriate institutions and practices, something largely done by the UN or by the governments or other agencies of organized societies (O'Neill 1996, 132; 2000, 104). One result of such a remedy is that the obligations become institutional or conventional in character, and thus, lose their status as universal.

The fact that the specific obligations and the identification of the obligation-bearers have become institutional or conventional in nature means also that the normative status of these obligations has changed. They are now institutional or positive or positional obligations and not moral ones. In O'Neill's account, the counterpart obligations to the UDHR social and economic rights lack universality in two distinctive respects:

1. they are not specific obligations held by literally everyone; and
2. these particular obligations do not have a normatively universal moral character (2000, 99; 2005, 431–432).

To deal with these problems, one might consider the case of universal "imperfect" obligations. Such duties are owed by all – but as to when they're owed, in what form, by whom and to whom, at given times and in given cases, is not specified. Unlike perfect obligations these obligations are incomplete. And their filling in, at the points where they are unspecified, and ultimately their fulfillment is left to discretion. Classic examples here are obligations of aid (to people in trouble) and obligations of beneficence (for the provision of goods and services to people who need them).

Let us suppose that the UDHR social and economic rights identify important needs of persons, at least at certain points in their lives, to goods and services. Now, if we look just at the *content* of the interests and needs identified in these rights, that content comprises the sort of thing that the universal obligation of beneficence is directed toward, at least where we have regard to the circumstances, worldwide, of the very poorest people, or of people in the very poorest countries. That obligation is concerned with ameliorating (up to a certain level of sufficiency) items that belong within this content and to do so through the provision of goods, services and other benefits by obligation-bearers.

The moral obligation of beneficence is owed by everyone. But it's not part of the *logic* of universal imperfect obligations that fulfilling the obligation is always a discretionary matter to be left *solely* in the hands of the individual obligation-bearer. The normative force of that obligation and its carrying out are not diluted or abrogated in any essential way by reliance on institutional or other agents (especially where we are dealing with the needs of distant others). Thus, we have grounds for rejecting O'Neill's criticism that the obligations that are counterparts to the UDHR social and economic rights do not have a normatively universal moral character.

Concerns about the universal feasibility of the UDHR social and economic rights

This brings us to a fourth main criticism: the practicability of this particular set of rights, universally, under modern conditions. The UN's Covenant on Economic, Social and Cultural Rights (CESCR, 1966, in force as of 1976) lays out several general principles at the start.

(1) Each "State Party" to the treaty undertakes to take appropriate steps "individually and through international assistance and cooperation" to achieve the rights listed.
(2) These steps and the achievement they bring will occur "progressively," gradually until these rights are fully realized.
(3) In particular, among the appropriate steps is the adoption of implementing national legislation intended to extend and refine the content of the obligations involved even further and to lay out in some detail the obligations and responsibilities that fall, but variously, on government and on specific individual citizens (CESCR, Article 2).

The specific rights concerned with social and economic and cultural matters (CESCR, Articles 6–15) are very demanding. Individual articles call for fair wages (for a decent living), social security insurance, an adequate standard of living (in such matters as food, clothing, housing), the wide availability and use of various medical and social services designed to sustain healthy lives, and an elaborate agenda for the provision of education, beginning with an elementary education for all that is both free and compulsory.

But severe poverty is a prevailing feature in the least well-off nations. The World Bank treats a purchasing power equivalent to (or a standard of living appropriate to) $1/day per capita as the base line for calculating *absolute* poverty: the latest figures (from 2004) indicate that there are 969 million persons below this line. A second and higher line is set at $2/day; here the number (excluding those below $1/day) is 1,579 million (that is, 1.5 billion people), with a grand total of 2,548 million for the $2/day line. A recent World Bank paper concludes that "the developing world outside China has seen little or no sustained progress in reducing the number of the poor, with rising poverty counts in some regions." Indeed, using the $2/day line, the paper says that "the count of the poor has been rising over most of the period" – for example as of 2004 when compared with 1981, the first year in which such data was collected (see Chen and Ravallion 2007, 1, 16). And Amartya Sen, drawing on a number of factors (life expectancy, infant mortality, malnutrition, gender bias against women, illiteracy, poor health-care and control of disease), sees a concentration of nations in sub-Saharan Africa and South Asia that are deeply impoverished (Sen 1999, chs. 4, 7; see also Chen and Ravallion 2007, 12; UNDP 2010, 162–163).

These factors (of absolute poverty, etc.) have made it all but impossible for the poorest nations to satisfy, in anything like an adequate or even minimal way, the demanding economic and social rights set forth in the UDHR and in the relevant Covenant. And private assistance, through NGOs, for instance, cannot plausibly be called on to make a significant difference in this matter (Wenar 2003, 291–294).

How have the best-off nations done in providing international assistance and cooperation to meet these problems? The percentage of Gross National Income (GNI) devoted by the most developed nations (in North America, Western Europe, the Pacific Rim) to official development assistance (ODA) stood at roughly 0.33 percent (well less than 1 percent) in 1990, at the very end of the Cold War. In the year 2000 it had dropped to 0.22 percent. (And only a small part of this aid actually goes toward meeting basic needs.)

In 2005 the G8 nations – which are among the wealthiest nations – pledged to increase ODA aid substantially. The most recent G8 Accountability Report from its 2011 meeting in Deauville, France, indicates that the G8 average stood at just 0.28 percent overall. For comparison, Marshall Plan aid, extended by the United States to the devastated economies of Western Europe after World War II, came to about 3 percent per year of the US GDP, for the years it was in place (see also Pogge 2002, chs. 4, 6, 8; Pogge 2005).

The basic record indicates that the UDHR social and economic rights have not and apparently cannot, under existing conditions, be feasibly or practically fulfilled at even a minimal level for millions upon millions of people. James Nickel argues that the list of such rights is "too long," "too expansive" and "excessively grandiose"; it needs scaling down to a "pruned version" (Nickel 2007, 187, 145, 139, 86 respectively).

Nickel advocates a simpler and shorter set of rights – following lines laid down by Cyrus Vance, US Secretary of State, in a 1977 speech – rights to basic subsistence, basic medical services, basic and usable but free and compulsory elementary education; the main idea here is too keep these three things minimal (Nickel 2007, 102, 139–141). We also need, Nickel adds, more specific and determinate obligations to guide the better-off nations in their provision of assistance, with minimum-standard benchmarks to be set and met (and closely monitored) as progressive advance is made by the poorest nations toward achieving a barebones and then a minimally adequate realization of these scaled-down rights. For now we need to think, not in terms of full-scale rights, but of realistic rights-based goals (Nickel 2007, 45, 81).

However, Nickel does not think that the incapacity of the poorest nations, the impracticability for now of their fully achieving the UDHR social and economic rights, means that these rights are not universal. Rather, the test for feasibility is whether an "ample majority" of *all* the nations can satisfy the test of achieving those rights for their citizens. Nickel thinks that test is met now; the social and economic rights are feasible by this test and thus the standard of universality has been met (see Nickel 2007, ch. 9; for the quoted term see pp. 79, 98).

I cannot agree with Nickel's analysis. The UDHR social and economic rights (given their very demanding terms) can't be met now by a whole lot of countries, probably not even by an "ample majority" and certainly not by the poorest countries. These rights cannot cover a huge number of people now alive and at present therefore are not universal (Beetham 1995, 42, 44, 55–60). Nickel's claim that the Vance norms could be met in time, even if true, does not mean they are being met now. Their full achievement is not feasible yet; so the test of universality in any standard sense has not been met at this level either. But the full set of social and economic rights (or some scaled-down version of rights-based goals, as a minimum standard for very poor countries) is still worth trying hard to achieve, in time.

Women's rights and group rights as universal rights

This brings us to the fifth and final main criticism: that, to take one example, rights that single out women in particular or as a group are not universal in character. Rights of women that might be suspect in this regard involve such matters as abortion and maternal leave (with pay) and other benefits/concerns, before and after the child's birth. In both cases important interests, in adequate medical care, health and autonomy, are at issue. But these are not issues distinctive of any one sex. Men too have health-care needs specific to them, needs that are governed by the same interests.

A somewhat different set of examples arises when individual countries consider such issues as the rights of women to vote or to an education (either elementary or advanced). These often take on the coloration in public discussions (as did voting or the right to graduate education or the right to employment in certain professions, in the United States in the late nineteenth and early twentieth centuries) of being issues specific to women. But they are not. They are simply attempts for and by women to have rights, without discrimination, equal to those already enjoyed by men. They are universal rights that are to be had by all (UDHR, Article 2).

Another and even more complex set of issues is raised by what might be called group rights. Let us take the case of group rights for women as found in the UN Convention on the Elimination of all Forms of Discrimination Against Women (CEDAW, adopted 1979, in effect 1981). Article 6 speaks of prejudices and customary practices that are based on ideas of the inferiority of one of the sexes or on "stereotyped roles for men and women." This brief statement covers a multitude of discriminatory beliefs and practices.

Here are a few sample cases. Selective abortion of female fetuses is common in Southern Asia. Sen (1999, ch. 4), to cite a similar example, speaks of the problem of "missing women" – that is, the number of women born and the number who reach adulthood in some of the poorer and less developed regions is far less proportionately than is the case with men. The traditional division of labor in these same places (and in many others) is unfair and even oppressive. In many places in Africa, the Middle East, and elsewhere, girls and young women are subjected to inadequate diets (compared to men) in periods of serious malnutrition. And they are often denied educational opportunities (sometimes violently so).

Many of the things just mentioned are injuries and indignities visited on individual women; they are incompatible with and derogatory of the interests that persons, men and women, have in personal autonomy, political participation, security, dignity, health and well-being. These injuries and indignities violate human rights of the individual women subjected to them.

These examples also bespeak deep ideas of the inferiority of women and of "stereotyped roles for men and women." These notions of inferiority and the stereotyping of roles are pervasive in some societies and constitute a way of life, which for the women there engenders a systemic sense of inferiority and oppression. Even when these same notions are more like background features in other societies (and this background aspect will take in lots of contemporary societies), they still point to a set of systemic attitudes, practices and problems. These systemic problems (whether in aggravated form or as background matters) are problems for women as such, for women as a group.

One might claim then that the rights involved are not merely rights of individuals within the group but also of the group itself – rights of the group as such. It is this latter kind of right that has proven especially controversial.

Some assert flatly that groups as such are not agents and cannot have rights (Wellman 1995). Others claim that group rights cannot be universal, for example, the rights of women as a group; they are not the rights of everyone and hence are not universal in the sense of universality required as a criterion for human rights status. Accordingly, rights of groups cannot be human rights (Nickel 2007, 167).

But is it true that *no* group right can be universal? If we consider a typical run of group rights, rights that necessarily involve the conception of the rights of a group as such, we would list (as examples) genocide and the independence of colonial peoples from subordination to the dominion of another people or state. I would suggest that genocide necessarily identifies a trait (ethnic identity) that can be ascribed universally to persons as individuals or to classes of persons. The crime of genocide, in the central case, is to try to kill off a whole group simply on the basis of some particular shared or supposed ethnic identity. Indeed, UDHR Article 2 (and Article 2 in the civil and political rights covenant) lists the various classifications that might be brought together, singly or in combination, under the rather vague notion of ethnic identity. So we cannot say that no group right can be universal.

Nickel says that the group right not to be subject to genocide is not *described* in the UN Convention on Genocide (1948) as a human right (2007, 157) – even though it could be described as a universal right, or so I have argued. On the other hand, the UN's General Assembly (in 1960) passed a "Declaration on the Granting of Independence to Colonial Countries and Peoples." This Declaration has had a long and influential history and has been reaffirmed on various occasions. It grants human rights status to a group (colonial countries and peoples). But the status of being a colonial people – who seek their independence from subordination – cannot be a universal feature of literally *all* peoples at any given time; for, then, we'd have no dominion by another people or state from which such independence could be sought.

I would conclude that there is not a canonical position, if we regard UN practice as an important consideration, on the precise point at issue. Universality does not appear to be a decisive criterion for when or whether a group right can count as a human right.

I would suggest, then, two other relevant considerations. First, human rights reflect important interests that individuals have in personal autonomy, political participation, security, dignity, health and well-being. A group-directed practice (like genocide or the treatment of colonial peoples by countries that have dominion over them or the oppressive status of women) definitely harms important interests that *individual* persons have and violates their human rights. Second, where this is so, it is not improper to describe as a human right the group status that such people have, when as individuals they are *also* characterized as belonging to an ethnic group (that is harmed by genocide), or as members of a colonized people (that is injured by discriminatory and harmful treatment by the colonizing country that has dominion over them), or as women (that as a group are harmed by a systemic sense of inferiority and oppression). In each case we have a standard threat to human rights that is group-directed or focused; people have human rights, including group rights, against such threats. It need not be a crucial consideration here whether the group in question has a character that is itself universal. So we can conclude, on the basis of these considerations, that the rights that women have as individuals are universal rights and that the rights of women as a group can be characterized as human rights.

Now that we have in hand the various criticisms and concerns canvassed in this chapter against universality, and my responses to these concerns, we can reach a rough conclusion. Human rights, with the possible exception of the UDHR social and economic rights in very poor countries, are universal (under some plausible interpretation). The exception mentioned is called "possible" because it could be removed in principle – that is, removed in time and with concentrated effort.

A general argument for the universality of human rights

One of the main points in the present chapter is that the primary plausibility of worries about the universality of human rights comes from mistakenly conflating the claim that human rights are grounded naturalistically (in some specific trait or criterion, like rationality or purposive agency) with the claim that human rights are universal. Once these claims are separated out, new lines of argument for universality will be required.

My strategy in the present chapter has been to provide a twofold argument for universality. I have first taken up, piecemeal, a set of five distinct concerns and criticisms (hard questions) about universality to which were matched specific (and I think) credible replies to these hard questions. Second, I want now (in this final section) to provide a more general argument for the universality of human rights, as a backstop to these five specific replies.

I'll begin here by sketching out a minimal argument favoring a presumptive case for claims of universality. Let us assume that a human right, understood simply as a moral right, is morally justified by accredited standards. More particularly, a human right is justified by the standard of mutual and general benefit (that is, the benefit of each and all). It would be hard to say, convincingly, that something could be claimed by each and that directives on conduct should be put in place to support that claim unless the thing claimed was widely beneficial. If the right in question is a human right, then the specific way of acting or way of being treated it identifies should (at a *minimum*) be a matter of benefit to a widespread and large number of human beings alive now (and in the foreseeable future).

Where the standard of benefit – the mutually *perceived* benefit of a whole lot of people – is not satisfied (or cannot reasonably be expected to be satisfied), we don't have an adequate moral justification for the *universality* of the right(s) in question. We don't have an adequate *public* justification, one that could be widely discussed and assessed or that could command widespread assent. Thus, the standard of mutual and general benefit has a continuing and essential importance in showing that the requirement of universality has been satisfied in a plausible and sound fashion. Mutual and general benefit is a first-order standard that needs to be met.

It could be met in the following way. Each person can be presumed to focus and to reflect on a single set of considerations: whether an active right to a particular way of acting or a particular way of being treated would on the whole (a) be beneficial for that person (as beneficial in itself or as a reliable means to some other good thing) and (b) that person can see how it would be beneficial to others as well, now and in the foreseeable future. If everyone could say, upon reflection, that these two tests are plausible and that, in their view, it would be reasonable to think these tests would prove true for all or almost all people for the particular right(s) in question, then the standard is satisfied. (Similar tests are deployed in Nickel 2007.)

These tests probably cannot be satisfied in any given case for everyone. This is why the governing standard has to be specified somewhat more loosely, to say these tests could be satisfied if (arguably) the right under consideration, say one of the UDHR rights, could be reasonably seen by almost all people as being of benefit, not literally to everyone, but as being of benefit to a *vast number* of individual human beings alive now (and in the foreseeable future).

The idea that this somewhat relaxed test can be satisfied by the UDHR rights is not implausible. These rights represent important interests in personal autonomy, security, and so on (as described earlier).

The idea of justification – by convergence or by "overlapping consensus" (an idea developed extensively in Rawls 1993) – serves as a second stage of public justification in which a practice or set of principles, for example, the rights on the UDHR list of human rights, already given an appropriate and initial *independent* justification (by the standard of mutual and general benefit), is then endorsed from the respective points of view of a variety of comprehensive ethical and religious doctrines, drawn from around the world.

In sum, the *general* argument for universality has two dimensions. The first dimension is (a) the reasonable presumption that the UDHR rights satisfy the idea of mutual and general benefit; such satisfaction counts as an initial and independent line of justification. The second dimension is (b) the idea of an overlapping consensus that converges on and justifies (on moral grounds, so to speak) the set of human rights that has been independently justified, as in (a). The combination of the general account of universality (as background) and the specific replies to certain hard questions (as foreground) is my positive solution to some of the most conspicuous and recurrent puzzles that universality seems to pose.

References

Beetham, David. 1995. "What Future for Economic and Social Rights?" *Political Studies* 43, 41–60.

Beitz, Charles. 2009. *The Idea of Human Rights*. Oxford University Press.

Boucher, David. 2009. *The Limits of Ethics in International Relations: Natural Law, Natural Rights, and Human Rights in Transition*. Oxford University Press.

Chen, Shaohua and Ravallion, Martin. 2007. "Absolute Poverty Measures for the Developing World." World Bank Policy Research Working Paper 4211.

Cranston, Maurice. 1967. "Human Rights, Real and Supposed." In D.D. Raphael, ed., *Political Theory and the Rights of Man*. Bloomington: Indiana University Press, pp. 43–53.

    1973. *What Are Human Rights?* 2nd edn. London: Bodley Head.

Darby, Derrick. 2009. *Rights, Race, and Recognition*. Cambridge University Press.

Dworkin, Ronald. 1978. *Taking Rights Seriously*. Cambridge, MA: Harvard University Press. (Originally published in 1977; important appendix added in 1978.)

Martin, Rex. 1993. *A System of Rights*. Oxford University Press.

Mayo, Bernard. 1965. "What Are Human Rights?" Symposium on "Human Rights," II. *Proceedings of the Aristotelian Society Supplementary Volume* 39, 219–236.

Nickel, James W. 2007. *Making Sense of Human Rights*, 2nd edn. Oxford: Blackwell.

O'Neill, Onora. 1996. *Toward Justice and Virtue: A Constructive Account of Practical Reasoning*. Cambridge University Press.

2000. *Bounds of Justice*. Cambridge University Press.

2005. "The Dark Side of Human Rights." *International Affairs* 81:2, 427–439.

Pogge, Thomas. 2002. *World Poverty and Human Rights*. Cambridge: Polity Press.

2005. "Severe Poverty as a Human Rights Violation." In Thomas Pogge, ed., *Freedom from Poverty as a Human Right: Who Owes What to the Very Poor?* Oxford University Press, pp. 11–54.

Raphael, David. 1967a. "Human Rights, Old and New." In D.D. Raphael, ed., *Political Theory and the Rights of Man*. Bloomington: Indiana University Press, pp. 54–67.

1967b. "The Rights of Man and the Rights of the Citizen." In D.D. Raphael, ed., *Political Theory and the Rights of Man*. Bloomington: Indiana University Press, pp. 101–118.

Rawls, John. 1971. *A Theory of Justice*, 1st edn. Cambridge, MA: Harvard University Press. (2nd edn., 1999.)

1993. *Political Liberalism*. New York: Columbia University Press. (Enlarged edn., in paperback, 1996.)

1999. *The Law of Peoples with "The Idea of Public Reason Revisited."* Cambridge, MA: Harvard University Press.

Sen, Amartya. 1999. *Development as Freedom*. New York: Anchor Books.

Shue, Henry. 1996. *Basic Rights*, 2nd edn. Princeton University Press.

UNDP (United Nations Development Programme). 2010. *Human Development Report 2010*. New York: Palgrave Macmillan.

UNESCO, ed. 1949. *Human Rights: Comments and Interpretations*. New York: Columbia University Press.

Waldron, Jeremy, ed. 1987. *Nonsense Upon Stilts: Bentham, Burke and Marx on the Rights of Man*. New York and London: Methuen.

Wellman, Carl. 1995. *Real Rights*. New York: Oxford University Press.

Wenar, Leif. 2003. "What We Owe to Distant Others." *Politics, Philosophy, and Economics* 2:3, 283–304.

PART II

___

How do human rights relate to group
rights and culture?

4 | The significance of cultural differences for human rights

ALISON DUNDES RENTELN

Introduction: whether culture represents a challenge to human rights

In the twentieth century, international human rights standards emerged in the global arena. There was tremendous excitement about their potential to protect individuals from atrocities and to help guarantee a decent quality of life for all. From the beginning there were questions about the philosophical foundations of human rights. In particular, there has been considerable attention paid to the challenge culture poses to the validity of international human rights. Because human rights notions were seen as being derived from the Enlightenment tradition, this seemed to imply that human rights are "Western" or "Eurocentric" (Pannikkar 1982).[1] If, in fact, they did reflect a cultural bias, that might undermine the legitimacy of this new regime.

During the drafting of the initial human rights instruments collectively known as "the International Bill of Rights," delegates came together from diverse countries. Insofar as there was representation from different parts of the world at the meetings, one might have thought this would mitigate the impact of such a critique. Nevertheless, the challenge from cultural relativism remained.

Beginning in the 1940s and continuing into the twenty-first century the challenge of culture to human rights recurred. During the drafting of the Universal Declaration of Human Rights (UDHR), there was, for instance, controversy over the formulation of the right to religious freedom. Some countries that followed Islamic law rejected the proposition that the right could include the right to change one's religion as this was apostasy. This led a few states to abstain from voting for the adoption of the UDHR.[2] Decades, later, in 1993 US representative, Warren Christopher, made reference to cultural relativism at the World Conference on Human Rights in Vienna, warning against allowing it become "the last refuge of repression." Since

---

[1] For a contrary view, see Manglapus (1978).
[2] Saudi Arabia abstained, and Egypt objected to the phrasing of the right to religious freedom as including freedom to change one's religion (Tahzib 1996).

then scholars have insisted that we are in an era "post" cultural relativism (Cowan *et al.* 2001). Sometimes this view relies on a post-modern understanding of culture that emphasizes divisions within cultural communities and the deconstruction of culture (Wilson 1997). Despite this sort of assertion on the parts of scholars, the reality is that contemporary debates continue to reflect an underlying preoccupation with cultural relativism. This is true whether one thinks of the debate over "Asian values" or controversies about religious garb or the status of sharia law in North America and Western Europe.

In this chapter I briefly explain the theory of cultural relativism to show how it has been misconstrued and to demonstrate how culture can be rendered compatible with some human rights.[3] Subsequently I discuss some of the hard questions associated with conceptualization and enforcement of human rights in light of cultural differences.

Cultural differences across the globe are regarded as threatening because many have assumed that subscribing to cultural relativism would preclude the possibility of embracing international human rights standards. This reasoning fails to distinguish between absolutism and universalism. While relativism is necessarily diametrically opposed to moral absolutes, it is compatible with universals. Whereas absolutes are immutable principles that, by definition, cannot vary, a universal principle may be shared in all societies at a given point in time, even if the consensus did not exist in prior eras.

Providing evidence of such a global consensus would help establish support for an international standard. Such proof would constitute inter-subjective agreement as to the existence of a shared value, i.e., a type of moral convergence. Thus, acknowledging that culture is consistent with cross-cultural universals (which one may conceptualize as a Venn diagram), means acceptance of human rights is possible. In short, advocating for the adoption of universal human rights standards as well as for their enforcement is feasible, even for cultural relativists.

Although scholarly debates about relativism and human rights may overlook this fact, the right to culture is itself protected as a part of human rights jurisprudence. Insofar as the right to culture is part of the corpus of human rights law, it deserves protection unless the custom in question involves irreparable harm. Of course, this begs the question: determining what constitutes a harm is one of the hardest questions of all.

---

[3] This argument is treated in more detail in my first book (Renteln 1990).

Cultural relativism as a descriptive theory

To understand why cultural differences have been viewed with such suspicion in human rights, it is necessary to consider the early formulations
of cultural relativism. Anthropologists developed the theory of cultural
relativism in the early twentieth century. Franz Boas and his students Ruth
Benedict and Melville Herskovits were the most famous proponents of relativism (Hatch 1983). Elsewhere I have identified some of the difficulties
associated with their versions of it (Renteln 1990).

Cultural relativism is a theory that has been much misunderstood and
unfairly vilified. Clifford Geertz, in his essay "Anti-Anti-Relativism," com-
piled rather extreme characterizations of the theory. In a sardonic tone, he
calls it "the relativist Dracula" and "the anti-hero with a thousand faces"
(Geertz 1984). At first glance, it is not obvious why this theory caused such
consternation.

According to cultural relativism, every society has its own moral code.
Morality is "local," created within a social context. Properly understood it
is a descriptive theory that emphasizes the manner in which individuals
are enculturated to accept the standards of their own society. On the basis
of these standards, they make evaluations about what is right and what is
wrong. Often the debate about cultural relativism is more precisely a debate
about ethical relativism (Westermarck 1932; Wong 1984).

Historically, most of those who have written about cultural relativism cast
the theory as a prescriptive or normative theory. They assume that because
societies have differing value systems this necessarily requires tolerance.
Their view is that because there are differences, we therefore must tolerate
them all. It is this conclusion that most have found repugnant. The common misconception that relativism requires tolerance is largely responsible
for the widespread rejection of the theory.[4] There is, however, no reason to
make this logical jump. Having identified the existence of multiple moral
systems, one need not like or accept them all. As Robert Redfield succinctly
put it: "It cannot be proved from the proposition that values are relative,
that we ought to respect all systems of values. We might just as well hate
them all" (Redfield 1962, 146–147).

Another fallacy is that relativism logically implies that there are no values.
However, noting that moral standards are social constructs does not mean

---

[4] I elaborate on this point in Renteln (1988). There is also the criticism that theory is self-refuting,
which many cite as a basis for dismissing it.

that relativism should be equated with nihilism. Rather, relativism involves a different understanding of morality as local in character.

If relativism is interpreted as a descriptive theory that does not require a moral posture of tolerance, then some wonder why it has been considered an important theory. It is still a powerful theory because it highlights the human tendency to assume the validity of one's own value system, i.e., ethnocentrism. All individuals are subject to the mostly unconscious processes of enculturation by which they acquire the categories of their society. This results inevitably in ethnocentrism, namely the presumption that one's own moral code is the best and only correct one. Theorists dating back to Herodotus (484–425 BC) identified the phenomenon of ethnocentrism, which William Sumner defined:

Ethnocentrism is the technical name for this view of things in which one's own group is the center of everything, and all others are scaled and rated with reference to it … Each group thinks that its own folkways are the only right ones, and if it observes other groups that have other folkways, these excited its scorn. (Sumner 1911, 13)

Cultural relativism is properly understood as a descriptive theory that focuses on the ethnocentric nature of moral perceptions. This does not mean that cultural relativists believe people ought to be ethnocentric. People who claim that relativists believe people ought to act on their ethnocentric values have confused the prescriptive theory of relativism with the descriptive one.[5] Relativists do believe one should guard against the tendency of presuming the validity of one's own moral judgments.

The reality that there are culturally divergent views of human behavior makes decisions about various practices more complicated. This occurs because of possible interpretations of the customs including risk assessments as to whether they pose any threat of harm. Furthermore, the right to culture is itself protected in international human rights law (Francioni and Scheinin 2008; Niec 1998; Stamatopoulou 2007). Consequently, individuals may invoke a right to culture when governments try to prevent them from following traditions important for their way of life (Renteln 2002). Sometimes these claims are raised in the form of cultural defenses in litigation. In some of the cases the government cites the protection of other human rights, such as children's rights or women's rights, as the state interest that justifies regulating the particular custom. In what follows I examine

[5] For example in Rhoda Howard's article "Cultural Relativism as Cultural Absolutism" (1993) she attacks prescriptive relativism, a position she erroneously attributes to me. In all of my scholarship I am careful to defend only the descriptive version of the theory.

highly publicized disputes that illustrate the interplay of competing rights claims. Through the consideration of examples I show that cultural differences do matter for human rights.

Vulnerable groups: conflicting perspectives on cultural traditions

Children's human rights

Many sensational cultural conflicts involve the question of the proper treatment of children. This is because when it comes to child-rearing practices, there are many views about what are the best methods, and there is also disagreement about which are unacceptable from the perspective of international human rights. Insofar as customs are restricted, parents may claim violation of their cultural rights.[6]

One such issue is corporal punishment (Benatar 1998; Coleman and Dodge 2010). Parents often believe they have the right to discipline their children to ensure respect for authority and adherence to rules. Some of the techniques give rise to concern about excessive force that may constitute child abuse. This issue attracts public attention when migrants use physical discipline considered unreasonable in the new home country. For instance, parents from the West Indies have been prosecuted in England and the United States when they used corporal punishment deemed excessive (Fontes 2005; Renteln 2010). In other cases parents using unfamiliar discipline techniques such as putting pepper in the wounds or punishment with sticks found their practices judged unacceptable.[7]

While spanking has been used in many parts of the world, a worldwide movement has emerged questioning its continued usage. Over 100 countries have banned its use as a disciplinary technique in schools and in penal institutions. Over 150 forbid its use as punishment for a crime committed by a child (Durrant *et al.* 2009). Moreover, the committee that enforces the Convention on the Rights of the Child (CRC) has issued a general comment that interprets spanking as clearly in violation of children's rights (Committee on the Rights of the Child 2007, 2011).

---

[6] In a previous essay (Renteln 1994) I dealt with the general question of the cultural defense in child abuse and neglect cases.

[7] For example in one California case the defense attorney wanted to introduce expert testimony to support the argument that a Chinese mother's use of sticks to beat her child was based on culture (*People v. Weili Kao* 2005, 2).

The first challenge for those wishing to end corporal punishment is persuading skeptics that children's rights are human rights. Although most states have ratified the CRC, in some countries like the United States, concern about the empowerment of children contributed to the failure of the United States to ratify the treaty (Renteln 1997). The second is the worry that the state will encroach upon parental decision-making authority if the policy banning spanking is enforced. In those jurisdictions where anti-spanking policies have been implemented, there has been some evidence of a backlash.[8] This suggests that a global social movement to establish children's rights will encounter continuing cultural opposition, even in "developed" countries.

Another illustration of the difficulty culture may pose concerns surgeries that children undergo (Sabatello 2009, especially 67–89). Probably the most sensational of these is female genital cutting, also known variously as female circumcision and female genital mutilation, which millions of girls undergo in Africa and parts of the Middle East. Although the cutting is considered a rite of practice and necessary for girls in order to be able marry in societies that follow this tradition, feminists and health professionals have waged a campaign within countries and in the international community to halt this practice.

For those unfamiliar with this surgery, it is almost incomprehensible because it involves removing parts of the genitalia of young girls.[9] Although I do not defend this custom, I would like to point out a few difficulties with the way the issue is treated in the scholarly literature and the popular press. First, the terminology itself is highly inflammatory. The word "mutilation" conveys the degree to which the cutting is viewed with contempt (Gunning 2002, 118; Obiora 1997). As Leslie Obiora observes:

Describing a vital aspect of African cultural identity as "mutilation" has proven offensive, if not psychically mutilating, to critical African constituencies like the Premier Group des Femmes D'Afrique who prefer to employ the term "female circumcision." This semantic tug-of-war is emblematic of the constellation of misunderstandings that surround the practice. Ironically, the catch-all phrase of "genital mutilation" favored by Westerner-influenced critics is potentially as much a misnomer as "female circumcision" because not all forms of the genital surgeries are impairing. (Obiora 1997, 290)

---

[8] In New Zealand the government implemented a ban to make its domestic law consistent with its CRC obligations. This mobilized a pro-smacking movement, which launched a referendum to repeal the law (Renteln 2010, 276).

[9] In England it was also advocated as a cure for various diseases including hysteria (Favazza 1996).

Second, many types of surgery are subsumed under the single term. Some, like clitoridectomy, are far more extreme than others, but they are often referred to as though they were all identical (Gruenbaum 2001). Although there are those who condemn all forms of genital surgery, some engage in moral criticism entirely unaware of their oversimplification.

Third, the vast literature on the practice has been subject to trenchant criticisms. For instance, African women have campaigned for decades to eradicate the practice, and are insulted when Western feminists give the impression that they were responsible for launching the campaign (Abusharaf 2006; Lane and Rubinstein 1996; Savane 1979). Moreover, the moral condemnation is sometimes regarded as cultural imperialism.[10] Finally, banning the custom outright has simply driven it underground.

For the most part, critics focus on the potentially serious health consequences of the procedure.[11] Yet when parents have their daughters circumcised in hospitals, this can be done without any complications. However there is concern about the "medicalization" of female genital cutting because this may lend an air of legitimacy to the custom. As a UNICEF report put it: "The fact that certain medical professionals or health works are known to be involved in the practice may contribute to a general misconception that FGM/C is somehow acceptable" (Innocenti 2005, 17). Because of this concern, the WHO and the World Medical Association have condemned the practice and any involvement by medical professionals.

The risk of criminalizing the practice is that individuals who cannot go to hospitals may either perform it themselves or take their daughters to countries where the operation is permitted.[12] This policy has the unintended consequence of driving the custom underground where there is even less protection for girls (Jones *et al.* 1997).

Western commentators' primary objection is that the custom is designed to control the purity of women, and surgeons who participate in this reaffirm patriarchal, misogynist values. This was made clear when the Harborview hospital in Seattle considered implementing a policy to allow girls to receive a symbolic cut in lieu of actual removal of tissue (Dugger 1996). Because this compromise was objectionable to feminist legislators,

[10] A leader at Equality Now said: "there is a strong feeling that movement against this must be led by African activists" (Crossette 1998).

[11] The surgery, when performed without antiseptic circumstances, can cause infection, death, problems urinating, difficult pregnancies, pain, and death.

[12] Obiora refers to a Dutch controversy where African immigrants who had been turned away from medical facilities circumcised themselves. Somali immigrants requested a symbolic prick at the Harborview Medical Center in Seattle (Coleman 1998).

the hospital rescinded the policy, even though it could have prevented girls from undergoing the traditional form of the surgery. Doriane Coleman explains poignantly:

> In their Pyrrhic victory … Harborview's opponents probably denied some Somali girls in Seattle the possibility of living a life free of the physical and emotional devastation caused by the traditional circumcision practiced by their community; in the name of ideological purity, they probably sacrificed some of the very girls they claim are the beneficiaries of their efforts … Additionally, Harborview's opponents also squelched what was probably the most successful compromise of a cultural collision that has been publicly contemplated in this country. (Coleman 1998, 737–738)

Ultimately the strongest argument against female genital cutting is that it is performed on minors. Children do not have the legal capacity to consent to surgical procedures, and the removal of a healthy body part should be presumed to be against the best interests of the child.[13] The Convention on the Rights of the Child has a provision, Article 24(3) that was drafted with this in mind. Because of objections that it targeted African states, the language was changed from female genital cutting to "traditional practices prejudicial to the health of children." Not only is this formulation vague, but it also appears either to be in tension with Article 30, which guarantees the right to culture for the children of ethnic minorities and indigenous peoples, or to constitute an exception to this right.

As noted above, many have condemned female genital cutting because it usually results in death or serious adverse health consequences for girls. However, as also noted above, the surgery can be performed in hospitals under antiseptic conditions and so it is possible to avoid these outcomes to a large extent. If the custom does not jeopardize the health of children, then critics have to formulate an alternative criticism of the practice. One might advance the argument that surgery resulting in an irreparable harm should be prohibited insofar as children lack the ability to consent to cultural practices or medical procedures. Following this line of argument consistently might require a presumption against surgery, even though the right to essential surgery is itself an aspect of the right to health.

Another aspect of the debate about surgeries is whether male circumcision constitutes child abuse and a violation of the human rights of boys.

---

[13] Indeed, consent is emphasized in the Testimony on Female Genital Mutilation of Dr. Nahid Toubia, a Sudanese physician, to the House of Representatives, Committee on Foreign Affairs' subcommittee on International Security, International Organizations, and Human Rights: "All professional organizations must pronounce it unethical for any of their members to undertake circumcising a girl under the age of consent" (1993, 6). See also Martin (2009).

Although it is not comparable to female circumcision with regard to the extent of tissue removed, male circumcision is a medical procedure that results in a permanent bodily change and is undertaken without the child's consent. Some have begun to ask whether a presumption against surgery precludes the possibility of male circumcision (Cannold 2006; DeLaet 2009; Fox and Thomson 2006). It arguably does constitute a "traditional practice prejudicial to the health of children." Acting on this interpretation, some campaigned for a ballot measure to ban male circumcision in the boundaries of San Francisco in 2011 (Anonymous 2011; Medina 2011). The logic is that baby boys should be protected against an unnecessary cultural tradition that involves permanent removal of body tissue.[14]

Questions such as these are complex because one must not neglect the parents' human rights. Indeed, some take the view that parents have the right to religious freedom and the right to culture and this should allow them to raise their children in accordance with long-standing traditions. Others contend that children have a right against customs prejudicial to their health, particularly as they have not chosen to be part of particular religious or cultural communities. There is also a claim that surgical procedures violate the right to bodily integrity, though the basis for this right is not explicit in human rights instruments.

The Rights of Persons with Disabilities (PWD)

Cross-cultural understandings of bodily integrity are also central to debates about the rights of persons with disabilities. Disability rights deserve much greater attention in the field of international human rights because at least 650 million persons live with disabilities, roughly 10 percent of the world's population, and they are among the most marginalized of all people.[15] The Convention on the Rights of Persons with Disabilities (CRPD), the first new human rights treaty of the twenty-first century, was ratified more quickly

---

[14] In Cologne, Germany, a court called the practice of male circumcision into question in that region. Although the court did not ban it and acquitted the doctor accused of endangering the health of a boy, it concluded that "the right of parents to raise their children in a religion does not override the right of a child to bodily integrity" (Eddy 2012a). This led to public controversy and united religious minorities, including Jewish and Muslim groups, in their opposition to the ruling (Eddy 2012b). Many Jewish leaders and organizations condemned the court, alleging that this was yet another instance of anti-Semitic action by Germans against the Jewish people. In response, the Prime Minister's office announced that Jewish and Muslim communities could continue to follow this tradition as long as it was "carried out in a responsible manner" (Reuters 2012).

[15] For information about the Convention on the Rights of Persons with Disabilities, see the website of UN World Enable: www.un.org/disabilities/default.asp?navid=14&pid=150.

than any previous instrument. Given the likelihood that it can be applied around the world and the fact that the community is an open minority that anyone can join at any time, the need to address the challenges associated with cross-cultural conceptualization merits further consideration.

The conceptualization of disability varies in different parts of the world. It is noteworthy that not all conditions are considered disabilities in all places (Renteln 2003). Furthermore, even a condition such as visual impairment may not be viewed in the same way. National standards for evaluating who counts as legally blind vary (Lane *et al.* 1993). The definition of who is a person with a disability has been fraught with difficulty and has included questions about what conditions should be classified as disability, e.g., obesity, body-odor, and others.

Some object to the quest for precise definitions because definitions may be used either to stigmatize individuals or to exclude them from receiving government services. While these concerns are certainly legitimate, in the absence of definitions, governments have no basis for distinguishing among those entitled to services. Because governmental agencies have finite resources, they are arguably unable to provide personal assistants and other social benefits to all who might apply for them.[16]

Assuming there is a consensus as to what counts as a disability, there may still be disagreement regarding what action, if any, should be taken. A little boy who was Hmong and born with clubbed feet, lived in Fresno, California (Renteln 2004, 61–63). His pediatrician decided that he should have surgery to correct the disability so as to ensure greater mobility and minimize pain. Despite strong opposition from his family and the entire Hmong community, a court ordered the surgery to be performed. This result was somewhat surprising and contrary to established legal precedents given that the child did not have a life-threatening condition. Ordinarily, courts in the United States do not intervene to order surgery unless there is an imminent threat to the life, health, or well-being of a child.

Cross-cultural differences in conceptualizing disability arise not only in the context of interpreting specific rights, but also in evaluating objections to the implementation of the rights. Countries often claim cost as a reason for non-compliance as did the US Treasury when officials refused to change the size of currency to assist the Blind in counting their change (Savage 2008). Apparently, modifying the size of bills would require redesigning vending machines and other equipment, which would entail an exorbitant

---

[16] The logic behind Principles of Universal Design is that the environmental adaptations benefit everyone, not just individuals with disabilities.

sum estimated at $3.5 billion dollars. Why US currency could not be reissued with some type of embossment was not clear.[17]

Sometimes members of religious minorities maintain they should not have to comply with anti-discrimination laws designed to protect the rights of persons with disabilities. For instance, when some Muslim taxi cab drivers refuse to transport passengers who have guide dogs with them because dogs are considered dirty, the drivers contend that their right to religious freedom should be respected. The question is whether there is a duty to accommodate a religious employee under these circumstances, especially if doing so would put the taxi company out of compliance with civil rights laws. A compromise policy proposed in one Canadian case involved having the religious cab driver call for another taxi and wait until it arrived before he could depart (*Gilmour* v. *North Shore Taxi* 2006). This compromise assumes the passenger has time to wait for another cab, and that it is reasonable for taxi cab drivers to pick and choose among those whom they will take in their vehicles (Renteln and Valladeres 2009).[18]

Women's human rights

Some of the conflicts attracting the greatest public attention focus on religious garb. Increasingly governments around the world, most notably in Canada, France and Italy, have begun to ban the wearing of garments in public such as the burqa or hijab. The rationale is often that the attire symbolizes the inferior position of women and hence should be prohibited. Other times, when the conflict is over the religious dress in court, the claim is that the garb interferes with a defendant's constitutional right to see his accuser. Sometimes the government contends the veil poses a threat to national security because individuals might carry weapons underneath their clothes, or else risks causing an auto accident by impeding a driver's ability to see. While a serious risk to public safety might warrant the adoption of public policies of this sort, the lack of empirical evidence documenting any such threat renders these policies subject to the charge of ethnocentric overreaction.

The scholarship on the subject of "the veil" or "l'affaire des foulards" is vast, and does not always note that women have various motivations for wearing religious garb. There are some who do so under parental pressure

---

[17] This type of redesign was at least briefly under consideration (Mohammed and Mendoza 2006).

[18] Cab drivers have also been known to refuse to pick up passengers carrying bottles of alcohol, even if they are still sealed. There was a public controversy over this at the Minneapolis airport.

or governmental coercion, while others want to convey to the dominant culture that they identify with their countries of origin. Some have suggested that religious dress is correlated with lower rates of sexual assault, and others have indicated that it serves as an effective smog device. The point is that governments should not make simplistic assumptions about motivations for wearing religious garb and should consider that some women might wish to exercise their rights to religious liberty and the right to culture. These debates, unfortunately, tend to reflect "essentialist" or stereotyped views of Muslim women.

Another highly publicized cultural conflict revolves around honor killings. Here again the media present the human rights of women as the central concern without acknowledging the influence of cultural imperatives that lead fathers, uncles, brothers and cousins to kill their own relatives, sometimes with the assistance of the girls' mothers (Aggarwal 2008). Without understanding the role that honor plays in the worldview of these individuals, it will be difficult to find a means by which to stop this extreme violation of women's rights. If severe punishment were sufficient to deter these acts of violence, then the disturbing practice would not persist. Although I do not condone culturally motivated killings, there is no question that culture is relevant to this phenomenon.

Rather than pretending that violence against women is "torture" and not "culture," it would be much better to admit this is a cultural practice but one that should be discarded. It is intellectually dishonest and unhelpful to try to preserve the term culture for only those customs of which we approve.

Other vulnerable groups

There are many other groups that lack protection under both domestic law and international human rights law. For instance, indigenous peoples lobbied for decades before the United Nations even adopted the Declaration on the Rights of Indigenous Peoples. Without adequate representation in the UN system, they have had to raise their cultural rights claims via the Human Rights Committee and the Inter-American Human Rights system.

Raising their claims via Article 27 of the ICCPR minorities rights provision is problematic because many indigenous peoples do not regard themselves as minorities subordinate to the state. Another difficulty they have faced is litigating cases to protect landscapes important to them. In order to prevail in sacred site lawsuits, they may have to reveal to the court land that is of spiritual significance even if divulging this information violates their own customary law. Indigenous attorneys have also had to call non-Indian expert witnesses to explain to courts the value of cultural landscapes rather than tribal elders. They have to present experts with credentials in order to win in the courts of the dominant culture.

Gays and lesbians, known as sexual minorities in international human rights circles, have also encountered tremendous resistance to the recognition of their cultural rights. With regard to this group, some have argued for the cultural rights to their own traditions, e.g., parades. Other more conservative constituencies prefer to argue for the right to participate in more mainstream traditions such as marriage. The movement for Marriage Equality is presented as one of equal protection of the laws rather than cultural rights.

The dead are another group denied cultural rights. Because in Anglo-American jurisdictions, the dead are treated as "quasi-property," it has been hard to object to the desecration of graves, removal of human remains, and theft of cultural objects buried with the dead. If international law had a broader view of personhood that reflected a broader range of cultural views about the legal status of the dead, the human rights of the dead might be recognized to a much greater extent.

Systems of punishment: proportional justice and the right to a fair trial

Culture is clearly relevant to systems of punishment. First, one must grapple with the question of what behaviors are sufficiently egregious to be classified as crimes. Sometimes the newly arrived are taken by surprise when their culturally motivated actions are regarded as criminal offenses. For example, some defendants from Kenya, Somalia and Yemen were astonished to find that the chewing of khat (qat) is considered a serious criminal offense in the United States because it is not proscribed in their countries of origin and many other parts of the world (Anderson *et al.* 2007; Renteln 2004). Because khat has a similar effect to the drinking of a double espresso, some question the fairness of punishing the consumption of this substance, when coffee drinkers can drink as many lattes as they wish without any risk of arrest. The double standards that may operate in the criminal law should give us pause.

Second, there is the question of what constitutes condign punishment, as notions of proportionality vary considerably in different societies (Beirne 1983; Skovron *et al.* 1987). In the past there were debates about whether the use of amputation for theft, at least for recidivists, violated international human rights law (An-Na'im 1992; Souryal and Potts 1994). While many found amputation as a punishment abhorrent, they did not consider whether life imprisonment, especially under repeat offender laws (such as "three strikes"), also violated the prohibition against cruel, inhuman or degrading treatment or punishment. Others were aghast when Michael Fay was sentenced to caning for defacing a car while in Singapore (Lal 1994). Here the objection was not to punishment per se, but to the type of punishment. In China, over a hundred different offenses qualify for the imposition of the death penalty, and these include white-collar crimes such as embezzlement. While some Americans might have wished that Bernard Madoff had received capital punishment, this would be inconceivable in the United States.

Not only are there concerns about the nature of punishment but also the process by which defendants are judged guilty. One of the most fundamental human rights is the right to a fair trial, which is guaranteed in many treaties. According to the International Covenant on Civil and Political Rights, every defendant has the right to due process, which is interpreted to include the right to an attorney, and the right to have proceedings in a language he can understand, and others. The European Convention on Human Rights contains Article 6, which also requires protection of due process rights. Here there is an argument that failure to take culture into account can result in the violation of due process rights. An example should illustrate how some defendants may have experienced a miscarriage of justice because of cross-cultural misunderstandings.

In a number of cases defendants invoke a provocation defense, which, if successful, reduces a charge of murder to manslaughter. In order to prevail, the defendant must show meet two requirements: a subjective part, that he was provoked, and an objective part, that the reasonable person would have been provoked. The difficulty for individuals who come from other cultures is that it can be virtually impossible to prove to a court the magnitude of the insult to which they were exposed. For instance, a Mexican American man, Trujillo-Garcia, refused to give back money to a man who lost it to him in a poker game a few days earlier. The man insisted, saying to Trujillo-Garcia "Chinga tu madre," the worst possible insult in Spanish, after which Trujillo-Garcia pulled out a gun and killed him (Paz 1961; *Trujillo-Garcia* v. *Rowland* 1992). The problem was that the objective reasonable person would not be provoked by a phrase in Spanish that he could not understand. In this and other cases defendants whose cultural background is different from the majority will be effectively unable to raise provocation defenses. The failure to take cultural evidence sufficiently into account arguably violates the defendant's right to equal protection of the law. The trial seems unfair if defendants from the dominant culture receive lesser punishment because they were lucky enough to be provoked by an insult understood by the judge and the jury.

Often courts exclude evidence about culture because they consider it irrelevant. This refusal to allow individuals to explain what motivated them arguably violates the right to a fair trial as well as the right to culture. To ensure due process, courts should admit cultural evidence and the state should subsidize the payment necessary for experts crucial for the maintenance of the cultural defense.

Legal pluralism: two types

Separate courts

Individuals sometimes attempt to have courts consider their customary or religious law in the courts belonging to the dominant legal system. In other contexts ethnic and religious minorities prefer to establish separate tribunals within the new home country to adjudicate commercial and family law matters. The question of whether the state should give its stamp of approval to these institutional arrangements has been fraught with controversy.

While Muslim arbitration boards were condemned in Canada partly because of fears their decisions would deny women their rights, in the UK the tribunals were formally authorized. In the United States, voters in Oklahoma approved a measure prohibiting courts from considering sharia law in their decision-making. As of August 2012, an injunction issued by a federal court judge prevented the policy from coming into effect.

Although motivated by a desire to protect human rights such as women's rights, the policy barring the consideration of religious law would make it impossible for judges to resolve at least some matrimonial questions. For example, when couples have been married in another jurisdiction in accordance with foreign law, and they seek a divorce in the United States, it will be necessary to consult the relevant law of the country where the marriage occurred.

When multiple courts exist in the same geographic area, this is known as legal pluralism. These structural arrangements for customary or religious law represent what might be called applied legal pluralism. In general, it has proven exceedingly difficult for ethnic minorities to establish their own fora for the resolution of conflicts.

The cultural defense policy

In cases in which cultural claims arise within the national courts, they often take the form of a cultural defense. Although such a public policy does not officially exist in any jurisdiction, judges have surreptitiously allowed cultural arguments to figure into legal proceedings in many cases.

The question of the extent to which courts should allow for the consideration of culture is a serious question in multicultural societies. And insofar as states fulfill their obligations under the ICCPR, which includes the right to culture as a human right, they ought, at the very least, to allow litigants the opportunity to introduce evidence regarding their cultural background in a court of law.

While culture should be treated as admissible in all cases, whether it should influence the disposition of the case is a separate question. Such a judgment will have to be made on a case-by-case basis.

If a cultural defense policy were to be adopted as an official public policy, judges would need to ascertain the validity of cultural claims. To verify them, I have proposed a cultural defense test:

1. Is the litigant a member of the ethnic group?
2. Does the group have such a tradition?
3. Was the litigant influenced by the tradition when he or she acted? (Renteln 2004, 207)

This analysis can be used in criminal and civil proceedings.[19] Even if it turns out that the argument meets the requirements of the test, judges might still reject it, if it involves irreparable harm.

The concept of irreparable harm would surely disallow honor killings. It might even result in the rejection of the provocation defense, not simply for defendants from other cultures, but all defendants. Surgeries that result in irreparable harm would also have to come to a halt. As it is not possible to anticipate all circumstances in which cultural arguments may be proposed, it is best to allow cultural defenses in all cases. Judges will then need to assess the arguments on a case-by-case basis.

[19] For a consideration of the possible misuse of the defense, see Renteln (2005).

Conclusion

In this chapter I have argued that the theory of cultural relativism, if construed as a descriptive theory, is compatible with universal human rights. Culture does influence the interpretation of norms, the drafting of international instruments, and the enforcement of human rights standards. Culture affects many aspects of legal processes, as we have seen. Furthermore because there is a right to culture as part of human rights law, it deserves protection in domestic and international courts. Likewise, the exclusion of cultural evidence arguably violates the right to a fair trial and constitutes another reason to consider culture in the courtroom.

In the final analysis one must weigh the relative importance of this right as compared to other human rights such as women's rights and children's rights. Ultimately theorists and policy-makers will need to reconsider the hierarchy of rights to ascertain the proper place of the right to culture vis-à-vis other human rights. Although culture complicates the analysis of human rights, we can no longer afford to avoid these hard questions.

References

Abusharaf, Rogaia Mustafa, ed. 2006. *Female Circumcision*. Philadelphia: University of Pennsylvania Press.

Aggarwal, Archana. 2008. *Crimes of Honor: An International Human Rights Perspective on Violence Against Women in South Asia*. Doctoral dissertation, Political Science, University of Southern California.

Anderson, David, Beckerleg, Susan, Hailu, Degol and Klein, Axel. 2007. *The Khat Controversy: Stimulating the Debate on Drugs*. Oxford: Berg.

Anonymous. 2011. "Against the Cut: The 'Intactivist' Movement Takes on the Oldest Surgery Known to Man." *The Economist* 399:8734 (May 21, 2011), 34.

An-Na'im, Abdullahi Ahmed. 1992. "Toward a Cross-Cultural Approach to Defining International Standards of Human Rights." In Abdullahi Ahmed An-Na'im, ed., *Human Rights in Cross Cultural Perspectives: A Quest for Consensus*. Philadelphia: University of Pennsylvania Press, pp. 19–43.

Beirne, Piers. 1983. "Cultural Relativism and Comparative Criminology." *Contemporary Crises* 7, 371–391.

Benatar, David. 1998. "Corporal Punishment." *Social Theory and Practice* 24, 237–260.

Cannold, Leslie. 2006. "The Ethics of Neonatal Male Circumcision: Helping Parents to Decide." In David Benatar, ed., *Cutting to the Core: Exploring the Ethics of Contested Surgeries*. New York: Rowman & Littlefield, pp. 47–61.

Coleman, Doriane. 1998. "The Seattle Compromise: Multicultural Sensitivity, and Americanization." *Duke Law Journal* 47, 717–783.

Coleman, Doriane and Dodge, Kenneth A., eds. 2010. *Special Issue on Corporal Punishment of Children Law and Contemporary Problems* 73, 1–341.

Committee on the Rights of the Child. 2007. *General Comment No. 8.* UN Doc. CRC/C/GC/ (March 2, 2007).

    2011. *General Comment No. 13.* UN Doc CRC/C/GC/13 (April 18, 2011).

Cowan, Jane, Dembour, Marie-Bénédicte and Wilson, Richard A., eds. 2001. *Culture and Rights: Anthropological Perspectives.* Cambridge University Press.

Crossette, Barbara. 1998. "Mutilation Seen as Risk for the Girls of Immigrants." *New York Times*, March 23.

DeLaet, Debra L. 2009. "Framing Male Circumcision as a Human Rights Issue? Contributions to the Debate over the Universality of Human Rights." *Journal of Human Rights* 8, 405–426.

Dugger, Celia. 1996. "New Law Bans Genital Cutting in the United States: Violators Could Face Five Years in Prison." *New York Times*, October 12, 1 and 6.

Durrant, Joan E., Trocme, Nico, Fallon, Barbara, Milne, Cheryl and Black, Tara. 2009. "Protection of Children from Physical Maltreatment in Canada: An Evaluation of the Supreme Court's Definition of Reasonable Force." *Journal of Aggression, Maltreatment & Trauma* 18:1, 64–87.

Eddy, Melissa. 2012a. "In Germany, Ruling Over Circumcision Sows Anxiety and Confusion." *New York Times*, July 13.

    2012b. "Germany: Circumcision Ruling Opposed." *New York Times*, July 13.

Favazza, Armando R. 1996. *Bodies Under Siege: Self-mutilation and Body Modification in Culture and Psychiatry.* Baltimore: Johns Hopkins University Press.

Fontes, Lisa A. 2005. *Child Abuse and Culture: Working with Diverse Families.* New York: Guildford Press.

Fox, Marie and Thomson, Michael. 2006. "Short Changed? The Law and Ethics of Male Circumcision." In Michael Freeman, ed., *Children's Health and Children's Rights.* Leiden: Martinus Nijhoff, pp. 161–181.

Francioni, Francesco and Scheinin, Martin, eds. 2008. *Cultural Human Rights.* Leiden: Martinus Nijhoff.

Geertz, Clifford. 1984. "Anti-Anti Relativism." *American Anthropologist* 86, 263–277.

Gilmour v. North Shore Taxi and others. 2006. BCHRT 629, October 31, 2006, File 3775.

Gruenbaum, Ellen. 2001. *The Female Circumcision Controversy: An Anthropological Perspective.* Philadelphia: University of Pennsylvania Press.

Gunning, Isabelle R. 2002. "Female Genital Surgeries: Eradication Measures at the Western Local Level—A Cautionary Tale." In Stanlie M. James and Claire C. Robertson, eds., *Genital Cutting and Transnational Sisterhood: Disputing U.S. Polemics.* Urbana: University of Illinois Press, pp. 114–125.

Hatch, Elvin. 1983. *Culture and Morality: The Relativity of Values in Anthropology.* New York: Columbia University Press.

Howard, Rhoda. 1993. "Cultural Relativism as Cultural Absolutism." *Human Rights Quarterly* 15, 315–338.

Innocenti. 2005. *Changing a Harmful Social Convention: Female Genital Mutilation/ Cutting.* Rome: UNICEF.

Jones, Wanda, Smith, Jack, Kieke Jr., Burney and Wilcox, Lynne. 1997. "Female Genital Mutilation/Female Circumcision: Who is at Risk in the United States?" *Public Health Reports* 112, 368–377.

Lal, Vinay. 1994. "The Flogging of Michael Fay." *Economic and Political Weekly* 29 (June 4), 1386–1388.

Lane, Sandra D. and Rubinstein, Robert A. 1996. "Judging the Other: Responding to Traditional Female Genital Surgeries." *Hastings Center Report*, May–June, 31–40.

Lane, Sandra, Mikhail, Blanche I., Reizian, Alice, Courtright, Paul, Marx, Rani and Dawson, Chandler R. 1993. "Sociocultural Aspects of Blindness in an Egyptian Delta Hamlet: Visual Impairment vs. Visual Disability." *Medical Anthropology* 15, 245–260.

Manglapus, Raul S. 1978. "Human Rights Are Not a Western Discovery." *Worldview* 4, 4–6.

Martin, Jean F. 2009. "Article 7: Persons Without the Capacity to Consent." In Henk A.M.J. ten Have and Michele S. Jean, eds., *The UNESCO Universal Declaration on Bioethics and Human Rights: Background, Principles and Application.* Paris: UNESCO, pp. 139–159.

Medina, Jennifer. 2011. "Efforts to Ban Circumcision Gain Traction in California." *New York Times*, June 5, 18.

Mohammed, Mima and Mendoza, Moises. 2006. "Court Orders a Currency Redesign to Aid the Blind." *Los Angeles Times*, November 6, A19.

Niec, Halina, ed. 1998. *Cultural Rights and Wrongs.* Paris: UNESCO & Institute of Art and Law.

Obiora, L. Amede. 1997. "Bridges and Barricades: Rethinking Polemics and Intransigence in the Campaign against Female Circumcision." *Case Western Reserve Law Review* 47, 275–378.

Pannikkar, Raimundo. 1982. "Is the Notion of Human Rights a Western Concept?" *Diogenes* 120, 75–102.

Paz, Octavio. 1961. "The Sons of La Malinche." In *The Labyrinth of Solitude: Life and Thought in Mexico*, translated by Lysander Kemp. New York: Grove Press, pp. 65–89.

People v. *Weili Kao.* 2005. "Points and Authorities, Re: Cultural Expert." Super. Ct. NO. 04F04427 (Cal. Super. Ct. Aug. 8 2005).

Redfield, Robert. 1962. *The Primitive World and Its Transformations.* Ithaca: Cornell University Press.

Renteln, Alison Dundes. 1988. "Relativism and the Search for Human Rights." *American Anthropology* 90, 56–72.

1990. *International Human Rights: Universalism Versus Relativism.* Newbury Park: Sage Publications.

1994. "Is the Cultural Defense Detrimental to the Health of Children?" *Law and Anthropology* 7, 27–106.

1997. "Who's Afraid of the CRC: Objections to the Convention on the Rights of the Child." *ILSA Journal of International and Comparative Law* 3:2, 629–640.

2002. "Cultural Rights." In Paul Baltes and Neil Smelser, eds., *International Encyclopedia of Social and Behavioral Sciences.* London: Elsevier.

2003. "Cross-Cultural Perceptions of Disability: Policy Implications of Divergent Views." In Stan Herr, Lawrence Gostin, and Harold Koh, eds., *The Human Rights of People with Intellectual Disabilities: Different but Equal.* Oxford University Press, pp. 59–81.

2004. *The Cultural Defense.* New York: Oxford University Press.

2005. "The Use and Abuse of the Cultural Defense." *Canadian Journal of Law and Society* 20:1, 47–67.

2010. "Corporal Punishment and the Cultural Defense." *Law and Contemporary Problems* 73: 253–279.

Renteln, Alison Dundes and Valladeres, Rene. 2009. "The Importance of Culture for the Justice System." *Judicature* 92, 193–201.

Reuters. 2012. Anon. "Angela Merkel Intervenes over Court Ban on Circumcision of Young Boys." *Guardian*, July 13.

Sabatello, Maya. 2009. *Children's Bioethics: The International Biopolitical Discourse on Harmful Traditional Practices and the Right of the Child to Cultural Identity.* Leiden: Martinus Nijhoff.

Savage, David. 2008. "Appeals Court Rules U.S. Currency is Discriminating against the Blind." *Los Angeles Times*, May 21, A12.

Savane, Marie-Angelique. 1979. "Why We Are Against the International Campaign." *International Child Welfare Review* 40, 37 and 39.

Skovron, Sandra Evans, Scott, Joseph E. and Rao, Kamalakara Rao. 1987. "Cross-cultural Perceptions of Offense Severity: The United States, India, and Kuwait." *International Journal of Comparative and Applied Criminal Justice* 11, 47–60.

Souryal, Sam and Potts, Dennis W. 1994. "The Penalty of Hand Amputation for Theft in Islamic Justice." *Journal of Criminal Justice* 22, 249–265.

Stamatopoulou, Elsa. 2007. *Cultural Rights in International Law: Article 27 of the Universal Declaration of Human Rights and Beyond.* Leiden: Martinus Nijhoff.

Sumner, William G. 1911. *Folkways: A Study of the Sociological Importance of Usages, Manners, Customs, Mores, and Morals.* Boston: Ginn, Atheneum.

Tahzib, Bahiyyih G. 1996. *Freedom of Religion or Belief: Ensuring Effective International Legal Protection.* The Hague: Martinus Nijhoff.

Toubia, Nahid. 1993. "Testimony on Female Genital Mutilation of Dr. Nahid Toubia," House of Representatives, Committee on Foreign Affairs' subcommittee on International Security, International Organizations, and Human Rights, September 28, 1993.

Trujillo-Garcia v. *Rowland.* 1992. US District Court, Northern District of California (1993), US Court of the Appeals, 9th Circuit.

Westermarck, Edward. 1932. *Ethical Relativity.* New York: Harcourt, Brace, and Co.

Wilson, Richard A., ed. 1997. *Human Rights, Culture & Context: Anthropological Perspectives.* London: Pluto Press.

Wong, David. 1984. *Moral Relativity.* Berkeley: University of California Press.

5 | Groups and human rights

PETER JONES

Introduction

Human rights are rights possessed by human beings, and human beings are individual beings. An individualism that gives primary moral standing to individuals is therefore built into the very idea of human rights. However, the description "individualist" is often applied to human rights in a more far-reaching and pejorative sense. Human rights are sometimes said to manifest an atomistic conception of human life in which individuals are set apart from one another and channeled away from communal to more individualistic forms of life. Human rights, the charge goes, fail to recognize and to provide adequately for the social nature of human beings and the value of human community. The charge is not easily sustained (Howard 1995). Human rights are thoroughly social in both context and purpose and, rather than steering people away from communities, they aim to secure the freedoms and social arrangements that are essential for living a decent human life of any sort, including the most communitarian of communal forms of life.

There is, however, one aspect of the argument over the "individualism" of human rights that continues to divide the proponents of human rights as well as to attract the attention of the critics: the relationship between groups and human rights. There is continuing division over whether human rights can be group rights or whether they can be possessed only by individuals taken severally.[1] It is that question that I investigate in this chapter.

I shall use the terms "individual right" and "group right" to describe the *holder* of a right. So when we ask whether group rights can be human rights, I take the question to be whether some human rights can be held by groups rather than by persons individually. Nowadays, the term "group right" is often used to describe a right that a person holds qua group member.[2] That

---

[1] For examples of argument that human rights cannot be group rights, see Donnelly (2003, 23–27); Graff (1994); Griffin (2008); Miller (2002); Waldron (1993, 339–369). For examples of the contrary claim, see Felice (1996); Freeman (1995); Mello (2004); Van Dyke (1985).

[2] The rights that people possess as members of national, ethnic or cultural groups are now often described as "group rights" (e.g., Casals 2006) and Kymlicka's term "group-differentiated right"

is a quite different, and potentially misleading usage, since the rights people hold as group members can be, and most commonly are, rights they hold as individuals. For example, the rights people hold as members of sports clubs or gardening clubs or trade unions or universities or churches are commonly rights that they hold and exercise as individuals. The same applies to many "ascriptive" groups. The UN, for example, has declarations and conventions that provide specifically for the human rights of women, children, older persons, disabled persons, persons with mental illness, refugees and stateless persons. Once again, the great majority of the rights assigned by these declarations and conventions are assigned to individuals; the mere fact that they are assigned to particular categories of individual is no reason to label them "group" or "collective" rights (Felice 1996).

I shall understand human rights to be the rights that people have, or that they are assigned, in virtue of being human persons. Hence, while I draw my examples primarily from UN and other formal human rights documents, I do not treat those documents as definitive of whether a right is an authentic human right. I shall also understand human rights as primarily moral rather than legal rights, although that distinction will not be significant for much of what I argue.

Groups can be of various sorts: voluntary, involuntary, organized, unorganized, ascriptive, identity-based, and so on. None of those differences in type provides the essential test of whether a group is, or might be, a right-holder. I follow Joseph Raz's interest theory of rights according to which A has a right if he possesses an interest of sufficient moment to ground a duty for B (Raz 1986, 166). If we adopt that theory, the critical test of whether a group has a right will be whether it has an interest, qua group, of the required sort. That test may be contingently related to other features of a group, such as whether it is formally organized or has a strong sense of its own identity, but the ultimate test will be whether the group has an interest of the right sort rather than what sort of group it is. For example, according to the interest theory, it is perfectly possible for a linguistic group to have a group right, even though the group is in no way formally associated and even though its members value their language in a wholly instrumental fashion that has no significance for their identity.

---

is frequently abbreviated to "group right" (e.g., Miller 2002; Pogge 1997). But both sorts of right might be held by a group's members severally rather than collectively (Jones 2010; Kymlicka 1995, 46).

Groups and individual human rights

Before turning to the issue of group rights, I want to notice a number of ways in which individual human rights support people's group member-ships and facilitate group activity.

Individual human rights may seem divorced from people's group mem-berships simply because they are rights possessed by human beings gen-erally. By contrast, the rights that people possess as members of groups (other than as members of the human race) are "special" rights – rights that people have only if and because they belong to the relevant group. These special rights may therefore seem wholly disconnected from human rights. In fact, they are underwritten by the human right to freedom of association, which entitles people to belong or not to belong to groups as they see fit. There are so many groups that people may wish to belong to or to form, and so many shared activities in which they may want to engage, that is it difficult to know how a body of norms could provide for all of those possibilities other than by according individuals the right to freedom of association.

Human rights also protect people's group affiliations and identities by not being dependent upon them: people do not lose all or any of their human rights because of their group affiliations or identities. Article 2 of the UDHR provides that everyone is entitled to all of the rights and freedoms set out in the Declaration "without distinction of any kind, such as race, colour, sex, language, religion, political or other opinion, national or social ori-gin, property, birth or other status." That general prohibition on discrimin-ation reappears frequently in other UN and regional statements of human rights.

It is particularly important that we recognize that individual human rights can enable people to do things together that they cannot not do separately. Consider the freedoms that typically figure in catalogues of human rights, such as freedom of expression, freedom of religion and freedom of associ-ation. These freedoms are often considered the most individualist of rights since they accord individuals the freedom to choose and to act on their own choices. Yet they are also closely associated with collective behavior.

That is most obviously true in the case of freedom of association. One cannot associate on one's own; one necessarily associates with others, so that to associate is to join with others in some form of interpersonal rela-tion or shared activity. Freedom of association includes the freedom *not* to associate, so it can be used to avoid or to withdraw from relationships. Nevertheless, in its primary sense, the right is a right to associate with others as one wishes and the primary duty it imposes upon others, including governments, is the duty not to impede or prevent that association.

Freedom of expression can also enable collective conduct. It is possible to argue with oneself but normally debate and discussion are interpersonal rather than intrapersonal activities. Those who engage in debate and discussion therefore exercise their individual rights to do something together that they could not do singly.

If a right is a right to engage in a collective activity, can it be a genuinely individual right? If an activity is collective, the right to engage in it may seem necessarily to belong to the group of participants as a collectivity rather than to each participant separately. Again, that is not so. Two people who dance together do something that neither could do singly, but it does not follow that their right to dance together must be a collective right. Rather A has the right to dance with B if B is so willing, and B has the right to dance with A if A is so willing, so that, in dancing together, A and B jointly exercise their individual rights to dance with one another rather than a joint or collective right that they possess only as a duo. The same applies to the right to marry, the right to sing with others in a choir, and the right to participate with others in a street protest. In each of these cases, people *exercise* their rights to engage in a shared activity, but the rights they exercise are rights that they *possess* as individual persons.

The joint use of individual rights is particularly significant for freedom of religion. That is recognized explicitly in Article 18 of the UDHR, which states that everyone's right to freedom of thought, conscience and religion includes the freedom "either alone *or in community with others* and in public or private, to manifest his religion or belief in teaching, practice, worship and observance" (my emphasis; see also the ICCPR Article 18, the ECHR Article 9). It would be absurd if the right of freedom of religion did not include, for example, the right to engage in collective acts of worship – acts in which people can engage only "in community with others"; but, once again, the rights exercised in that collective act are frequently intelligible as the rights of the several individuals who participate in it.

Article 27 of the ICCPR uses the same phrase in providing for the rights of ethnic, religious and linguistic minorities: "In those States in which ethnic, religious or linguistic minorities exist, persons belonging to such minorities shall not be denied the right, *in community with the other members of their group*, to enjoy their own culture, to profess and practice their own religion, or to use their own language" (my emphasis). This time, there is no mention of the possibility that individuals might enjoy these rights "alone" as well as "in community with" others. That is misleading. Cultures and languages are necessary group phenomena, and religions almost always have a group dimension. Nevertheless, an individual may still enjoy aspects of these group phenomena alone: I may, in private and on my own, practice a craft that is peculiar to my culture, read a novel that is written in my native language, and pray in accordance with a religion I share with my fellows. My activities remain group-dependent since, if I were not a member of the group whose culture, language or religion I share, I would not have the wherewithal to do any of these things. Yet, in these instances, the activities themselves are not ones that I engage in "in community with" others. Very frequently, however, enjoying a culture, practicing a religion, and using a language will involve participating with others in group activity. I can participate in a communal form of life, I can engage in a collective act of worship, and I can use my language as a tool of communication only "in community with" others.

Groups and collective human rights

We should not suppose too readily therefore that group activity must signal the presence of a group right. There are, however, rights to collective goods that, if they are rights, are intelligible only as group rights. A clear example, strongly associated with human rights, is the right of a people to be self-determining. That right is asserted in the first articles of the UN's ICCCPR and ICESCR, and both Covenants go on to affirm that "by virtue of that right they [peoples] freely determine their political status and freely pursue their economic, social and cultural development."

Might we conceive a people's right to be self-determining as no more than the pooling together of several individuals' rights to be self-determining, just as we might understand the right to engage in a collective act of worship as the joint exercise of each participant's individual right to freedom of worship? This time that understanding of the right will not do. The right that is asserted in the UN's Covenants is the right of a people, *as a people*, to be self-determining and that is not the same as a set of individuals opting to exercise their individual rights of self-determination in a coordinated way. The right is the right of a group to determine the course of its life as a group, rather than an aggregation of individual rights that enable individuals to engage in a common activity.

If there were an individual right that a people should be self-determining, it would have to be the right of an individual that his or her people (presumably the people to which he or she belonged) should be self-determining.

The obvious objection to any such alleged right would be its utter dispro-
portionality: how could it be morally plausible that an individual, qua individual, should have a right over how an entire people should be treated?
Moreover, any such right would fly in the face of human rights thinking.
It is essential to that thinking that individual persons enjoy a fundamental
equality of moral standing and possess rights over the conduct of their own
lives. If one individual, entirely on his own, were to have a right relating to
the life of an entire people, he would, in effect, have rights over their lives,
which would be odds with others' equal standing and equal rights.

The right of a people to be self-determining must therefore be a group
right. Could it also be a human right? The answer depends very much on
how we understand the group that possesses the right.

Group rights have traditionally been understood as rights held by groups
conceived as unitary entities: just as the holder of an individual right is a
single unitary entity (an individual person), so the holder of a group right
has often been conceived as a single unitary entity, which we might think
of as a "group-individual" or "group-person." We might describe this way of
understanding group rights as the "corporate" conception, since it conceives
the right-holding group as a single corporate entity. The group is attributed
with a being and identity that is not translatable, without remainder, into
those of its members. The rights of the group are therefore conceived as
"its" rights rather than "their" rights.

This conception of group rights is both uncontroversial and readily intelligible in the case of legal group rights. Legal systems commonly
ascribe legal personality to organizations, such as business corporations,
so that those organizations can possess both standing and rights as "legal
persons." More controversially, some proponents of group rights suggest
that we should deploy the same corporate conception in our moral thinking (e.g. French 1984; Newman 2004, 2011). If we do, we shall conceive a
right-holding group as possessing a moral identity and a moral standing as
a group that is not reducible to those of its members. Moral standing is a
precondition of right-holding and the attribution of moral standing to the
group qua group means that it can hold rights as a group that are not rights
possessed by the several individuals who constitute its members. (Those
who reject the very idea of group rights typically suppose that group rights
must take this corporate form; e.g., Graff 1994; Hartney 1991.)

If that is how we conceive group rights, it is very difficult to see how they
could also be human rights, assuming that we continue to think of human
rights as the rights of (natural) human persons. On the corporate conception, a group right is held by an entity whose identity and moral status is

independent of those of its individual members and its rights are not to be understood as their rights. Thus John Rawls (1999), for example, having conceived right-holding peoples according to the corporate conception, goes on to treat peoples' rights as wholly separate from human rights.

We can, however, conceive group rights quite differently and in a way that is more consonant with human rights thinking. We might describe this alternative understanding of group rights as the "collective" conception, since it conceives group rights as rights held jointly by a collection of individuals. If we understand group rights in this way, we need not posit a group that possesses an identity and a standing that is separate from those of its members. The relevant group will be simply the group of individuals who jointly hold the right, but their right will remain an authentic group right since it is a right that they will hold jointly and not singly. People *possess*, as well as exercise, collective rights together. The conception here is not therefore one in which each individual holds a right as an individual, and in which individuals' rights are somehow aggregated to yield a collective right. On the contrary, collective rights are rights that individuals hold only in combination with others.[3]

In contrast with the corporate conception, the collective conception understands a group as, in Margaret Gilbert's phrase (1989, 2), a "plural subject" and accordingly conceives a group right as "their" right rather than "its" right. The moral standing that underwrites the collective right is not that of a group entity but simply that of the several individuals who make up the right-holding group, yet their right remains a genuine group right, since it is a right that they hold together as a group and not separately as individuals.

If we understand a group right according to this collective model, it becomes possible for a right to be both a group right and a human right. The standard objection to ascribing human rights to groups is that human rights are rights possessed only by human beings and only individual persons are human beings (e.g. Donnelly 2003, 23–27). But, if we understand group rights according to the collective conception, they will be rights held by individual persons; they will differ from individual human rights only in being held by individual persons jointly rather than severally.

So we can understand a people's right of self-determination as a right that is held jointly by the several individuals who make up the relevant people. An external power that imposes its will upon them will violate the

---

[3] For statements of the collective conception of groups, see Jones (1999); Miller (2001, 210–233); Raz (1986, 207–209).

right of the subjugated population to be self-determining, rather than the right of a group entity that is, for some reason, not fully intelligible as the body of individuals who actually constitute the people. A people's right of self-determination, so conceived, is readily intelligible as a collective human right.

Of course, not all collective rights will be human rights, just as not all individual rights are human rights. But there are several rights that, in addition to the right of popular self-determination, we can plausibly conceive as collective human rights. We have seen how Article 27 of the ICCPR secures for religious, linguistic and ethnic minorities the rights to profess and practice their own religion, to use their own language, and to enjoy their own culture.[4] We have also seen how the Article ascribes those rights to the members of minorities individually, even though individuals will commonly exercise their rights "in community with" others. But there are rights relating to religion, language and culture that make sense only as group rights.

The Vienna Declaration issued by the World Conference on Human Rights, 1993, called on governments "to counter intolerance and related violence based on religion or belief … including the desecration of religious sites, recognizing that every individual has the right to freedom of thought, conscience, expression and religion" (II.B.22). If someone desecrates a religion's sacred site, whose right does it violate? The most plausible answer is a collective right of the religion's adherents. Here the right is a right to one and the same thing for all adherents of the religion: the non-desecration of their sacred site. The unitary nature of the right's object differentiates the right from the rights of individuals to engage in a shared activity, such as a collective act of worship. All of the religion's adherents have the right to engage in a collective act of worship, but A's right is the right of A to engage in that act, B's right is the right of B to engage in that act, and so on. In that respect, the object of each individual's right is non-identical. But the sacred site cannot be disaggregated in that way, which is why it would be misplaced to attempt to disaggregate the right to its non-desecration into rights held severally and separately by the religion's adherents.

Consider now the European Charter for Regional or Minority Languages (1992). Amongst many objectives and principles that Parties to the Charter recognize is "the need for resolute action to promote regional or minority

[4] Although Article 27 refers only to minorities, the rights it enunciates are intended to be universal rather than unique to minorities. Its import is that, even if a group finds itself in a minority position in a state, its members are still entitled, like the majority population, to enjoy their culture, to profess and practice their religion and to use their own language.

languages in order to safeguard them" (Article 7.1.c). The Charter does not formulate that need as a right, but let's suppose that a minority whose language is under threat of erosion has a right that the society of which it is part should take steps to safeguard its language. Once again, that right makes sense only as a right possessed by the minority collectively rather than by its members severally. In this case, proportionality helps contribute to the case for the right being a collective right: it is most unlikely that the interest of a single individual in the maintenance of his language could justify the expenditure of resources required to achieve that goal (cf. Raz 1986, 187, 207–209). But we can amend the case to eliminate that sort of consideration. Rather than merely failing to support a minority's language, a government may set out deliberately to eradicate it. In that case, it seems no less appropriate to hold that the right the government violates is a collective right of the linguistic minority rather than a set of rights held separately by its individual members. The reason resides in the collective nature of the bad that the government visits on the minority.

The UN's Declaration on the Rights of Indigenous Peoples (DRIP) recognizes group rights more explicitly and more extensively than any other of its Declarations or Conventions. It ascribes some rights to indigenous peoples, some to indigenous individuals, and some to both; but it assigns the majority of the rights to indigenous peoples and rightly so insofar as they are rights that make sense only as group rights. These include the right of indigenous peoples to self-determination (Article 3) and other rights that stem from that general right, such as the right "to maintain and strengthen their distinct political, legal, economic, social and cultural institutions" (Article 5). They also include the right that their culture shall not be destroyed (Article 8), the right not to be forcibly removed from their lands and territories (Article 10), and the right to practice and revitalize their cultural traditions and customs (Article 11). Once again, the objects of the rights identify them as rights that indigenous people hold together and not separately.

The case of indigenous peoples does, however, raise the question of how far we can reasonably go in interpreting group rights as *collective* rights. There is no clear obstacle to interpreting all of the rights mentioned in the previous paragraph as collective rights, but DRIP also recognizes the historical injustices that indigenous peoples have suffered, such as the dispossession of their lands, territories and resources, and accords them a right of redress (Article 28). If group A wronged group B a century ago and if, as a consequence, B is now duty-bound to compensate A, it is difficult to explicate that state of affairs using the collective conception since the sets of wronging and wronged individuals a century ago (A1 and B1) are non-identical with their current heirs (A2 and B2). The idea of one group owing compensation to another makes more sense if we think of the relevant groups as transgenerational entities that have identities over and above that of any particular generation of members, and that, in turn, implies a corporate conception of groups A and B. The passage of time will then make no difference to the identities of perpetrator and victim. We might save the collective conception by substituting the idea of rectification for that of compensation: because A1 wronged B1, A2 now holds goods that ought to be held by B2. A2 should therefore restore to B2 goods that would have been theirs had A1 not wronged B1. The historical injustice is then corrected without any implication that the injustice concerns an A, that transcends A1 and A2, and a B that transcends B1 and B2.

Yet our thinking on peoples' territories is typically more corporate than collective in character. We think, for example, of the legitimate territory of France as a territory that belongs to France conceived as a transgenerational entity with an unchanging identity. We could think of it as belonging to the current population of French nationals, who, as they come into existence, inherit title from their forebears and, as they go out of existence, bequeath it to the next generation. French territory will then have not a single right-holder, France the corporate entity, but a multitude of ever-changing collective right-holders concatenated across time. But, insofar as we do not think in that way (and I cannot here consider whether we should), we cannot cast our thinking in terms of collective human rights. Moreover, while the idea of human rights can figure in argument that each people has a right to be self-determining and to have their territorial rights respected, that idea cannot determine for us the particular territory to which a people has a right.

Group threats to human rights

Conceptual reasons are not the only reasons why commentators often resist the ascription of rights to groups. Much of the resistance also stems from fear of the consequences of that ascription (Eisenberg and Spinner-Halev 2005; Okin 2002; Shachar 2001; Tamir 1999). A major practical purpose – perhaps *the* major purpose – of ascribing human rights to individuals is to provide them with safeguards against the abuse of power. Power-holders include groups, particularly groups that possess internal structures of authority. If we ascribe human rights to groups, such as the right of self-government, we may find ourselves enhancing the very power that human rights are supposed to keep in check. In enhancing a group's power, we may increase its capacity to oppress its own members; if we then upbraid the group for its oppressive conduct, it can respond by insisting that it is doing no more than exercising its human right to self-government. It is not surprising therefore that many proponents of human rights insist that we should ascribe human rights to the individual members of a group but not to the group itself.

How should we respond to this concern? The obvious answer is by being discriminating in the rights we attribute to groups. We do not ascribe to individuals the right to do just anything, nor should we to groups. There is no reason why, if we recognize some collective rights as human rights, we must slide ineluctably toward entitling a group to wrong its own members.

There is a logical feature of the collective conception of group rights that stands in the way of that slide. By common consent, an individual cannot hold a right against himself; he cannot be simultaneously the bearer of a right and the bearer of the duty that the right imposes. An individual's rights must be directed "outwards" toward others. The same logic applies to jointly held rights. A group of individuals who jointly hold a right cannot hold that right against themselves as a group, nor can any individual in the right-holding group jointly hold the right against herself. Thus group rights understood according to the collective model must, like individual rights, be externally directed. They will be rights directed at outsiders rather than rights targeted at members of the right-holding group. That is, indeed, how we would ordinarily understand the orientation of a people's rights to collective self-determination, or the right of a religious group not to have its sacred sites desecrated, or the right of a linguistic community not to suffer deliberate efforts to erode its language.

We shall see in a moment that it is not quite that straightforward, but there is here a significant contrast between the collective and corporate conceptions. On the corporate conception, a right-holding group has a being and a standing that is independent of its individual members and that makes it possible for the group as one entity to hold rights against its members conceived as other entities. A corporate right can therefore be directed inwardly toward the group's own members. That feature of the corporate model has done much to inspire fear and suspicion of group rights and hostility to the suggestion that groups might possess human rights. But, as we have seen, we have reason not to accept that groups corporately conceived can be the bearers of human rights.

Jettisoning the corporate for the collective conception of group rights does not, however, dispose entirely of the possibility of conflict between the power of a group and the human rights of its members. Since I have pressed the case for collective human rights, I want to notice that even the collective conception can be deployed in ways that are inimical to the human rights of a group's members. A moment ago I pointed out that, logically, collective rights can be directed only outwards, that is, only toward people who are external to the right-holding group. How, then, could collective rights ever constitute a threat to members of the right-holding group? In what follows I want to notice two possibilities: one arises from a possible asymmetry between group membership and collective right-holding; the other arises out of the interest theory of rights.

As a way of getting to grips with the first possibility, consider a set of individuals who agree to form a yacht-racing crew. We can say that each crew member has a duty to the others to play his full part in their shared endeavor and each is the object of a right held jointly by the others to play his due part. Now suppose that one member, Smith, fails to pull his weight and as a consequence the crew loses races it would otherwise have won. Smith infringes a collective right that the other members of the crew hold against him. That collective right remains "externally" directed since it is a right of which Smith himself is not a joint holder; rather, he bears the duty that stems from the joint right. It is possible therefore for someone to share group-membership with others but, within the group, to be the object of a collective right in which he does not share.

Now consider the same possibility in relation to a people's right of self-determination. In the ordinary run of cases, a people will hold that right against parties external to itself. But suppose that a member of a people turns traitor and conspires to undermine his people's right of self-determination either by delivering them into the hands of a foreign power or by imposing his own rule upon them. In that case, the conspirator violates a right held jointly by the rest of the people that he should not deny them their freedom to be self-determining. Here again we have an individual who shares a group-membership with the collective right-holders but who, in these circumstances, is the object of their right rather than one of its holders.

In both of these cases, we may find nothing untoward in the claim that the collective right makes upon the group-member. It is entirely reasonable for a yachting crew to require each member to play his due part and for a people to require each of their fellows not to subvert their collective freedom to be self-determining. But now consider another case.

A group distinguished by its common cultural heritage is split between a majority and a minority. The majority wants to continue with the group's inherited way of life; the minority wants to break away from it. The majority asserts its collective right to the group's inherited culture and protests that the dissent and deviance of the minority is subverting the way of life to which they are heir. They therefore claim the right to compel the minority to comply with the group's traditional mode of life, even though the minority wish not to live that form of life. Here again we have a collective right that is mobilized by some members of a group against others, but this time in a way that runs counter to rights that we would normally deem human rights.

Consider now a second possibility. As before, a cultural group is split between a traditionalist majority and a dissenting minority, but this time the majority responds not by asserting a collective right against the minority but by insisting that the minority has mistaken its interest. If the dissenters understood their interest correctly, they would see that it was identical with the majority's. They would also appreciate that, because of that coincidence of interest, they shared in the group's collective right to live its traditional mode of life. Thus, the benighted minority can be compelled to remain members of the group and to comply with its traditional norms all in the name of a collective right in which they allegedly share.

The possibility of "undesired" rights of this sort is not unique to collective rights. It arises from the interest theory of rights together with our ability to impute interests to people that depart from their own view of their interests. It is therefore a possibility that can arise in relation to individual rights. However, it is perhaps more likely to arise in group contexts since, if individuals share a group membership, that commonality can spawn the belief that the group's members possess a common interest, which grounds a collective right in which they all share, even though some in the group mistake what their common interest is. Rousseau is a celebrated example of a philosopher whose thought took that direction.

These possibilities are no more than logical possibilities. They show only that we cannot rely on the mere *concept* of a collective right to ensure that collective rights will never be invoked to the detriment of human rights. Substantively, we should deal with this issue by holding that individual human rights set the limits of legitimate collective claims, just as they limit other forms of power. Moreover, when a group claim comes up against an individual human right, we should not say that the individual right trumps a group right; rather we should say that, in these circumstances, the group has no right, since human rights set the boundaries of group entitlements. But, allowing that individual human rights must curtail the claims of groups in this way does not require us to set aside the idea of collective human rights. It requires only that we must ensure that individual and collective human rights taken together form a coherent and consistent set.

Conclusion

If, then, we conceive group rights collectively rather than corporately, it is open to us to claim some group rights as human rights. Vindicating that claim will require us to show that the interests at stake justify the claim of right and that the putative human right passes a suitable test of universality, insofar as universality is a necessary feature of human rights (cf. Cruft 2005; Donnelly 2007). Does it really matter whether a group right is a human right? Why not keep group rights separate from human rights in the way that they are separated in, for example, the African Charter on Human and Peoples' Rights? One answer is that, if, as I have argued, human rights can intelligibly and coherently take the form of collective rights, it would be odd to pretend otherwise. A second is that, insofar as collective rights are human rights, their bearers have the same moral identity as those who possess individual human rights; we make plain that the rights are not borne by an entity that is a categorically different, and potentially rivalrous, moral claimant. Finally, given the special moral and political significance that attaches to human rights, it seems arbitrary to insist that human rights can pertain only to goods to which individuals can have individual rights and never to goods to which they can hold rights only collectively.

References

Casals, Neus Torbisco. 2006. *Group Rights as Human Rights*. Dordrecht: Springer.

Cruft, Rowan. 2005. "Human Rights, Individualism and Cultural Diversity." *Critical Review of International Social and Political Philosophy* 8: 265–287.

Donnelly, Jack. 2003. *Universal Rights in Theory and Practice*, 2nd edn. Ithaca: Cornell University Press.

   2007. "The Relative Universality of Human Rights." *Human Rights Quarterly* 29: 281–306.

Eisenberg, Avigail and Jeff Spinner-Halev, eds. 2005. *Minorities within Minorities: Equality, Rights and Diversity*. Cambridge University Press.

Felice, William F. 1996. *Taking Suffering Seriously: The Importance of Collective Human Rights*. Albany: State University of New York Press.

Freeman, Michael. 1995. "Are there Collective Human Rights?" *Political Studies* 43: 25–40.

French, Peter. 1984. *Collective and Corporate Responsibility*. New York: Columbia University Press.

Gilbert, Margaret. 1989. *On Social Facts*. Princeton University Press.

Graff, James A. 1994. "Human Rights, Peoples, and the Right to Self-Determination." In Judith Baker, ed., *Group Rights*. Toronto University Press, pp. 186–214.

Griffin, James. 2008. *On Human Rights*. Oxford University Press.

Hartney, Michael. 1991. "Some Confusions Concerning Collective Rights." *Canadian Journal of Law and Jurisprudence* 4: 292–314.

Howard, Rhoda E. 1995. *Human Rights and the Search for Community*. Boulder: Westview Press.

Jones, Peter. 1999. "Group Rights and Group Oppression." *Journal of Political Philosophy* 7: 353–377.

  2010. "Cultures, Group Rights and Group-Differentiated Rights." In Maria Dimova-Cookson and Peter Stirk, eds., *Multiculturalism and Moral Conflict*. London: Routledge, pp. 38–57.

Kymlicka, Will. 1995. *Multicultural Citizenship*. Oxford: Clarendon Press.

Mello, Brian. 2004. "Recasting the Right to Self-Determination: Group Rights and Political Participation." *Social Theory and Practice* 30: 193–213.

Miller, David. 2002. "Group Rights, Human Rights and Citizenship." *European Journal of Philosophy* 10: 178–195.

Miller, Seumas. 2001. *Social Action: A Teleological Account*. Cambridge University Press.

Newman, Dwight G. 2004. "Collective Interests and Collective Rights." *American Journal of Jurisprudence* 49: 127–164.

Newman, Dwight G.. 2011. *Community and Collective Rights*. Oxford: Hart Publishing.

Okin, Susan Moller. 2002. "Mistresses of their own Destiny: Group Rights, Gender and Realistic Rights of Exit." *Ethics* 112: 205–230.

Pogge, Thomas W. 1997. "Group Rights and Ethnicity." In Ian Shapiro and Will Kymlicka, eds., *Ethnicity and Group Rights*. New York University Press, pp. 187–221.

Rawls, John. 1999. *The Law of Peoples*. Cambridge, MA: Harvard University Press.

Raz, Joseph. 1986. *The Morality of Freedom*. Oxford: Clarendon Press.

Shachar, Ayelet. 2001. *Multicultural Jurisdictions: Cultural Differences and Women's Rights*. Cambridge University Press.

Tamir, Yael. 1999. "Against Collective Rights." In Steven Lukes and Christian Joppke, eds., *Multicultural Questions*. Oxford University Press, pp. 158–180.

Van Dyke, Vernon. 1985. *Human Rights, Ethnicity and Discrimination*. Westport: Greenwood Press.

Waldron, Jeremy. 1993. *Liberal Rights*. Cambridge University Press.

Entangled: family, religion and human rights

AYELET SHACHAR

Introduction

The family sits at the besieged juncture of the private and the public, intimate relations and communal affiliations, contract and status, state and faith-based jurisdictions, raising hard questions for human rights scholars and activists. This chapter focuses on contemporary dilemmas that place minority religious women at the center of charged debates about diversity and equality. It explains the critical role these debates play in broader citizenship and membership, human rights and private ordering challenges that have emerged recently in neoliberal states, before turning to explore possible ideas for overcoming, or at least mitigating, the current impasse.

Informed by jurisprudence from the world of comparative constitutionalism, the geopolitical focus of my discussion will be on secularized societies in Europe and North America that have adopted a relatively sharp distinction between secular, state-centered legal institutions and other types of institutions (religious, voluntary associations, communal dispute resolution processes, subnational or transnational institutions). Harold Berman famously argued that "it was out of the explosive separation of the ecclesiastical and the secular polities that there emerged the modern Western legal science" (Berman 1977, 898). This transformation has been accompanied by the creation of a "special class of legal professionals (lawyers), themselves trained in a body of legal doctrine which had been systematized into a particular legal science or jurisprudence" (Ahdar and Aroney 2010, 7). This professionalization and secularization of Western legal science both resulted from and enabled the rise of the familiar constitutional structure of "separation of church and state," although there are significant variations even within this model, in terms of conceptual origins, comparative manifestations, institutional structures, and so on (Esposito and DeLong-Bas 2001; Hirschl 2010). Unlike post-colonial societies that have long permitted a degree of communal autonomy in regulating matters of marriage and divorce (Agnes 2001; Larson 2001; Ndulo 2011; Shachar 2008), or "constitutional theocracies" that officially treat religion as a state-sanctioned source of norm-making and interpretation in constitutional documents and family law codes (Esposito and DeLong-Bas 2001; Hirschl 2010), the human rights and family law challenges raised in stable, secularized, rule-of-law societies that have *rejected* the option of formal religious legal pluralism represent the most difficult test case on offer.

All over the world, arguments over the recognition that ought to be afforded to religious faiths and practices have risen to the forefront of public debate. This is illustrated by the recent veiling controversies across Europe, which reached the European Court of Human Rights on several occasions over the last decade (Howard 2011; Laborde 2008), and we may well see a new wave of controversy and litigation with the coming into force of face-covering laws and regulations. As if these charged debates over the boundaries of recognition (or, increasingly, restriction) of expression of religious-identity markers in the public sphere – what I will call the terms of *fair inclusion* – do not present enough of a hurdle, we are also starting to see a new type of challenge on the horizon: *privatized diversity*. Unlike fair inclusion, the latter pattern captures the growing pressures by more conservative elements within religious minority communities to promote a whole new kind of politics, which invites members of the faith community to turn to private, religious dispute-resolution processes in lieu of engagement with the ordinary institutions of the state and its human-enacted constitution (Hirschl and Shachar 2009). Whereas the quest for fair inclusion is centripetal, the pull of privatized diversity is *centrifugal*. In its extreme variants, it represents a call for insulation from the secular legal order as the general law of the land, and possibly also from international human rights standards, in effect asking members of minority communities to take the route of "private ordering." This new trend and its impact on gender equality and the human rights of women in the family – the topic of my inquiry here – bears potentially radical implications for how we conceive of the relationship today between secular and religious law, especially in societies committed to their rigid separation. It also makes the attempt (however difficult) to balance gender equality with religious freedom an ever more pressing mandate.

Two kinds of multicultural claims: fair inclusion and privatized diversity

Let me begin by distinguishing between the fair inclusion and privatized diversity claims. I address each in turn.

Fair inclusion

No state is an island. And no state can be regarded as a tabula rasa. Each society makes collective choices about its official language(s), public holidays and national symbols, which welcome some members more completely than others. Even the most open and democratic society will have certain traditions that reflect the norms and preferences of the majority community, in part because the institutions of that society have been largely shaped in their image (Kymlicka 1995). To provide but one example, consider the controversial *Lautsi* decision recently handed down by the Grand Chamber of the European Court, the secular system's "highest priests" entrusted with the power and responsibility to interpret the provisions of the European Convention of Human Rights (*Lautsi and Others* v. *Italy* 2011). In *Lautsi*, the Court rejected the human rights claim of a Finnish-born mother residing in Italy who objected to the display of religious symbols (crucifixes) in her sons' public school. Rather than requiring state schools to observe confessional neutrality, the court upheld the right of Italy to display the crucifix, an identity-laden symbol of the country's majority community, in the classrooms of public schools.[1] Using the margin of appreciation technique, Europe's highest human rights court held that it is up to each signatory state to determine whether or not to perpetuate this (majority) tradition. In effect, this meant that non-Christian children and those professing no religion will continue to be educated (literally) under the cross in Italian state schools.

The *Lautsi* decision, with its privileging of a majority symbol, exemplifies a core concern that fair-inclusion measures are designed to address. Will Kymlicka succinctly makes the point: "The state cannot help but give at least partial establishment to a culture" (Kymlicka 1995, 111). On this account, the adoption of fair-inclusion measures is required in order to overcome "burdens, barriers, stigmatizations, and exclusions" under laws and institutions that "purport to be neutral ... [but] are in fact implicitly tilted towards the needs, interests, and identities of the majority group" (Kymlicka and

---

[1] In an earlier decision in this case, the Italian *Consiglio di Stato* interpreted the crucifix as a religious symbol when it is affixed in a place of worship, but in a non-religious context like a school, it was defined it as an almost universal symbol (from the perspective of the majority) capable of reflecting various meanings and serving various purposes, including "values which are important for civil society, in particular the values which underpin our constitutional order, the foundation of our civil life. In that sense the crucifix can perform – even in a 'secular' perspective distinct from the religious perspective specific to it – a highly education symbolic function, irrespective of the religious professed by the pupils" (*Lautsi and Others* v. *Italy* 2011, para. 16).

Norman 2000, 4). Fair inclusion, in other words, is a leveling-up remedy designed to allow equal opportunities and extensive human rights protections for members of non-dominant minority cultures.

An illustration of the principle of fair inclusion in operation is found in the influential *Multani* case, decided by the Supreme Court of Canada (*Multani v. Marguerite Bourgeoys* 2006). This legal drama involved an 11-year-old, Gurjab Singh Multani, a Sikh immigrant enrolled in a French-speaking public school in Quebec. The Court considered whether the boy should be allowed to carry a *kirpan* (a ceremonial dagger) in accordance with his beliefs but in the face of potential safety hazards and an apparent conflict with the school board's prohibition on weapons and dangerous objects. Indeed, the very categorization of the *kirpan* – as either a prohibited weapon in a schoolyard (as the school board in Montreal claimed) or as an important religious symbol (the position of the student, his parents and the interveners on behalf of the Sikh community) – was at the heart of this legal dispute. The Court ruled that a decision to ban the *kirpan* universally was not the least drastic means to address the rather limited harm potential, especially when weighing the sincerity of the student's religious beliefs and the fact that the interference (the ban on the *kirpan*) was not trivial. The Court thus held in favor of Multani, offering a resounding statement of the fair-inclusion vision of human rights and equal citizenship:

The argument that the wearing of kirpans should be prohibited because the kirpan is a symbol of violence and because it sends the message that using force is necessary to assert rights and resolve conflict must fail. Not only is this assertion contradicted by the evidence regarding the symbolic nature of the kirpan, it is also disrespectful to believers in the Sikh religion and does not take into account Canadian values based on multiculturalism.

Translating this commitment into a social reality is, of course, a major challenge. But it typically begins by placing on various public and private institutions an obligation to create fair conditions of inclusion for those once excluded and marginalized (often under the color of state law) from full and equal membership in our shared public spaces and the realm of citizenship. Moving beyond the traditional anti-discrimination measures that focus on the removal of formal and official barriers, proponents of this vision of substantive equality before the law also advocate anti-subordination interpretations of our social relations and human rights protections (Balkin and Siegel 2003; Fiss 1976), envisioning "a heterogeneous public, in which persons stand forth with their differences acknowledged and respected" (Young 1990, 119). This implies challenging established power relations; demanding a foothold in shaping the "rules of the game"; gaining political representation; accessing, on fair terms, a given society's economy and symbolic rewards; and so forth (Fraser and Honneth 2003; Habermas 1995; Taylor 1994).

Privatized diversity

The bulk of the literature on citizenship, multiculturalism and human rights has focused on the aspirations of fair inclusion, while almost completely ignoring the challenges raised by privatized diversity, which refers to growing demands emanating from politicized and "retro-traditionalist" interpreters of religious identity (Moghadam 1994) seeking to institutionalize privatized diversity practices for their members, especially in the family law arena. A dramatic example of this trend is found in acrimonious debates bearing global resonance that broke out in Canada with regard to the possibility of utilizing religious laws through private ordering to resolve, in a binding fashion, a range of family law disputes among consenting parties. In their most extreme variants, these demands amount to a call for the secular state (through its manifold institutions and agencies) to adopt a hands-off approach, whereby faith-based arbitral tribunals provide unrestrained choice of forum and choice of law to the parties, and operate, as it were, in a completely unregulated and parallel domain of service provision that is insulated from or oblivious to the general law of the land. On this account, respect for religious freedom or cultural integrity does not require inclusion in the public sphere, but exclusion from it.

This potential storm-to-come must be addressed head on because privatized diversity mixes three inflammatory components in today's political environment: religion, gender, and the rise of a neoliberal state. The volatility of these issues is undisputed; they require a mere spark to ignite. In England, a scholarly lecture by none other than the Archbishop of Canterbury (the head of the Church of England/Anglican Church), contemplated the option of the legal system in England allowing Muslim communities "access to recognized authority acting for a religious group" (Williams 2008). The suggestion has provoked zealous criticism from across the political spectrum.

This response echoed a similarly divisive controversy in Canada that broke out following a community-based proposal to establish a private "Islamic Court of Justice" (or *darul-qada*) to resolve family law disputes among consenting adults according to faith-based principles. The envisioned tribunal (which ultimately never came into operation) would have permitted consenting parties not only to enter a non-state, out-of-court, dispute resolution process, but also to use choice-of-law provisions to apply religious norms to resolve family disputes, according to the "laws (*fiqh*) of any [Islamic] school, e.g. Shiah or Sunni (Hanafi, Shafi'i, Hambali, or Maliki)," potentially delimiting rights and protections that the involved women would have otherwise enjoyed under prevailing statutory and constitutional provisions. In addition, the tribunal would have brought to the fore the multitude of interpretative challenges associated with the idea of "recognizing Shari'a" in a secular state.[2] In the United States the dynamics have taken a different twist. We recently witnessed a slew of state legislatures passing amendments that "preempt" the use of religious principles in private dispute resolution, specifically singling out sharia law and international law as competing normative orders that must be avoided (Helfand 2011).

With this background in mind, we can now see more clearly why the Archbishop of Canterbury's lecture and the Shari'a tribunal debate in Canada provoked such uproar. These proposals were seen as challenging the normative and juridical authority, not to mention the legitimacy, of the secular state's asserted mandate to represent and regulate the interests and rights of *all* its citizens in their family-law affairs, as well as its liberal democratic telos to protect their rights more generally, irrespective of communal affiliation. In this respect, the turn to religious private ordering in the regulation of marriage and divorce raises profound questions concerning hierarchy and lexical order in the contexts of law and citizenship: which norms *should* prevail? And who, or what entity, ought to have the final word in resolving value-conflicts between equality and diversity, should they arise? The state clearly retains an interest in marriage and divorce for public policy reasons, such as the value of gender equality, the welfare of children, and the impact of the family's breakdown on third parties, to mention but a few. But it is no longer, if it ever has been, the only identity and norm-creating jurisdiction in town.

The narrative of gender and religion in the family has a long and complex history. The record is such that the state did not seize jurisdiction over marriage and divorce from the church until the late eighteenth century. (Once such control was seized, it took almost two additional centuries to remove persistent inequalities and legal disabilities that women suffered in the domestic sphere under color of state law and policy.) Among the conflicting claimants to sovereignty in the history of family law, it is therefore the state, not the church, that is the newcomer. Gaining the upper hand in regulating matters of the family was significant both politically and jurisdictionally. It

---

[2] For an excellent discussion of the complexities associated with "recognizing shari'a," see Bowen (2010). As Bowen explains, the suggestion that there is a "universal set of rules that constitute 'sharia law' … is a chimera. Not even Islamic legal systems, such as those in Pakistan or Bangladesh, enforce 'shari'a law'; they enforce statutes" (Bowen 2010, 435).

represented the solidification of power in the hands of secular authorities, a symbol of modern state-building. As historian Nancy Cott observes, "For as long as the past millennium in the Christian West, the exercise of formal power over marriage has been a prime means of exerting and manifesting public authority" (Cott 1995, 108).

Even today, the family remains a crucial nexus where both collective identity and gendered relations are reproduced (Cott 2000; Shachar 2001; Yuval-Davis and Anthias 1989). The stakes are particularly high for women. Marriage and divorce rules govern matters of status and property, as well as a woman's right to divorce, and remarry, and her legal relationship with her children. At the same time, it is a site that is vital for minority communities in maintaining their communal definition of membership boundaries. Religious minorities in secular societies are typically non-territorial entities; unlike certain national or linguistic communities (think of the Québécois in Canada, the Catalans in Spain, and so on), they have no semi-autonomous sub-unit in which they constitute a majority or have the power to define the public symbols that manifest, and in turn help preserve, their distinctive national or linguistic heritage. These minority communities are thus forced to find other ways to sustain their distinct traditions and ways of life. With no authority to issue formal documents of membership, to regulate mobility, or to raise revenues through mandatory taxes, religious family laws that define marriage, divorce and lineage have come to serve an important role in regulating membership boundaries. They demarcate a pool of individuals as endowed with the collective responsibility to maintain the group's values, practices and distinct ways of life (if they maintain their standing as members in that community). This is family law's demarcating function (Shachar 2001). As an analytical matter, secular and religious norms may lead to broadly similar results, coexist with one another despite tensions, point in different directions, or directly contradict one another. It is the latter option that is seen to pose the greatest challenge to the superiority of secular family law by its old adversary, religion.

The persistence of traditional norms in the family law arena is evidenced by the disproportionately high number of reservations to the ratification of the Convention on the Elimination of All Forms of Discrimination Against Women (CEDAW) that were demanded by signatory countries that have refused to accept its equality provisions in the family. CEDAW uniquely focuses on the elimination of discrimination against women in both the public and the private spheres.[3] Of its various provisions, Article

---

[3] Provisions of gender equality are also found in other international human rights frameworks, including the United Nations Charter, Article 2 of the Universal Declaration of Human Rights, and Article 26 of the International Covenant on Civil and Political Rights.

16 has drawn particular attention because it guarantees equality between women and men in all matters relating to marriage and family relations. As Rebecca Cook explains, reservations allow a state to ratify an international treaty without obligating itself to provisions it does not wish to undertake (Cook 1990, 650). Tellingly, CEDAW has been "ratified with reservations by more states than almost any other human rights treaty to date" (Riddle 2002, 605).

Caught in the web of secular and religious marriage norms and regulations

Family law thus serves as a case-book illustration of today's fraught gender and religion tensions.[4] Consider, for example, the situation of observant minority religious women who may wish – or feel bound – to follow the requirements of divorce according to their community of faith in addition to the rules of the state in order to remove *all* barriers to remarriage. Without the removal of such secular and religious barriers women's ability to build new families, if not their very membership status (or that of their children), may be adversely affected. This is particularly true for observant Jewish and Muslim women living in secular societies who have entered into the marital relationship through a religious ceremony – as permitted by law in many jurisdictions. For them, a civil divorce, which is all that a secular society committed to a separation of state and church can provide, is solely part of the story – it does not, and cannot, dissolve the religious aspect of the relationship. Failure to recognize their vulnerable "limping-divorce" status – namely, that of being legally divorced according to state law, though still married according to their faith tradition – may leave these women prey to abuse by recalcitrant husbands who are well aware of the adverse effect that this lack of coordination among these legal systems has on their wives, as these women fall between the cracks of the civil and religious jurisdictions.

For some religious minorities, family law comes close to serving the same core purposes that citizenship law does for the state, defining who holds a

---

[4] In the United States, these tensions also manifest themselves in debates that surround same-sex marriage, or the flare-up that was caused by the requirement that religious organizations provide their employees with insurance policies that grant contraceptives and other preventive health-care services for women, to mention but recent examples. These topics are beyond the scope of my analysis in this chapter.

legal affiliation to the community. It thus reinforces the link between past and future by identifying who is considered part of the tradition. This is why gaining control over the religious aspects of entry into (or exit from) marriage matters greatly to these communities; it is part of their membership demarcation and intergenerational project. At the same time, family law is also the area in which women have traditionally been placed at a disadvantage, in part, because of the recognition of female members' vital role in "reproducing the collective" – both literally and figuratively. Although this core contribution to the collective could, in theory, have empowered them, in most places and legal traditions (religious and secular alike), in practice it has often led to tight control and regulation of women, treating them, by law, as less than equal. Claims for private, religious-based dispute resolution processes inevitably intersect and interact with these complex historical (and in some cases, post-colonial) legacies, as well as with contemporary human rights concerns about power disparities and inequities within the family.

Of particular interest here are the hard-won equality guarantees afforded to women, children, sexual minorities, and other traditionally more vulnerable members of the family. These protections are relatively recent and the removal of structural and societal barriers to gender injustice in state law and practice has been preceded by fierce political struggle, and remains "uneven, and, in much of the world, still incomplete" (Htun and Weldon 2011, 148).

These tensions are only accentuated when privatized diversity trends are added to the picture. If faith-based dispute resolutions processes occur on the ground yet remain "illegible" in the eyes of the state, there is nothing to restrict the appetite of unofficial religious mediators, to whom the parties turn in trust, from extending their powers over the "full package" of rights and obligations between divorcing parties (and their children), even if the woman who had turned to the religious tribunal was seeking a more limited and specific service than what the secular state is, by definition, unable to grant her: the religious divorce decree. This potential for overextension is a major concern, as reported by Samia Bano in her research of the Shari'a councils in Britain. These councils routinely "re-litigated" property matters that were already settled by the civil courts, and even extended their reach to child custody disputes, which, by law, are not to be delegated to any non-state authority (Bano 2008). Another major source of unease is the lack of clarification regarding the relationship between religious private ordering and the public entitlements and protections that individuals hold as bearers of human rights and as citizens of a "free and democratic society," to draw upon the terminology of the Canadian Charter of Rights and Freedoms.

The standard legal response to the privatized diversity challenge is to seek shelter behind a formidable "wall of separation" between state and religion, even if this implies turning a blind eye to the concerns of religious women caught in the uncoordinated web of secular and religious marriage bonds. Alas, there is no guarantee that this strict separation approach will provide adequate protection to those individuals most vulnerable to the community's formal and informal pressures to accept "unofficial" dispute resolution forums in resolving family issues. Instead, it may thrust these tribunals and other privatized-diversity initiatives further underground, where no state regulation, coordination, or legal recourse is made available to those who may need it most.

It is therefore a grave mistake to assume that a legal ban on, or prohibition of, religious private ordering in family matters can simply make these matters – the "entanglement" of gender, religion and human rights – disappear. It may instead leave religious women in a more vulnerable position, whereby they will face increased pressures to turn to *un*authorized and *un*regulated, *un*official private religious dispute-resolution processes, without providing them the securities granted by the laws of the state, international human rights norms, and protected constitutional provisions.

This is a lose-lose resolution for both marginalized women and statist institutions that claim to protect *all* citizens and populations within their reach. But these difficulties do not lead me to conclude that the best response to these pressing challenges lies simply in restoring a belligerent model of strict separation that requires turning a blind eye to the religious concerns of women caught in the uncoordinated web of secular and religious marriage bonds. Instead, by placing these once-ignored agents at the center of analysis, I wish to explore the idea of permitting a degree of regulated interaction (as I will call it) between religious and secular sources of obligation, so long as the baseline of citizenship-guaranteed rights is strictly maintained.[5] From a human rights perspective, there is no justification for a secular state to abandon its governance responsibility toward its members, especially the vulnerable, simply because they may have contracted the marriage in another country, entered the relationship through a religious

---

[5] "Citizenship rights" here apply to anyone who resides on the territory, regardless of their formal membership status; they are defined expansively to include both domestic and international human rights protections.

ceremony in addition to the civil marriage, or because they have the opportunity to turn to mediation or arbitration by a non-state religious actor. Militating against such a result, we are better off pursuing new terms of engagement between the major players that have a stake in finding a viable path to accommodating diversity *with* equality, including the faith community, the state, the individual, and local and international human rights regimes – in ways that will acknowledge and benefit religious women as members of these intersecting (and potentially overlapping and conflicting) identity- and norm-creating jurisdictions.

This makes urgent the task of investigating the importance of state action (or *in*action) in shaping the context in which individuals "bargain in the shadow of the law" (Mnookin and Kornhauser 1979) – and to identify the legal system, or systems, under which the parties are, in effect, bargaining. Viewed from this perspective, privatized-diversity claims must be resisted if they place marginalized women and other potentially vulnerable members at jeopardy of losing the background protections, rights, and bargaining chips otherwise offered to them as equal citizens (a substantive restriction) or if they entail an unconstrained and unrestrained view of power and authority by private arbitration tribunals and other communal institutions that operate outside the official justice system (an institutional restraint).

The search for a new path: regulated interaction

Despite the understandable desire to "disentangle" law from religion by confining each to its appropriate sphere, the next step in my analysis is to investigate whether a carefully regulated recognition of multiple legal affiliations – and the subtle interactions among them – can permit devout women to benefit from the protections offered by the secular order, and to do so without abandoning the tenets of their faith. In other words, averting a punishing either/or dilemma: your culture or your rights (Shachar 2001).

Is it possible to find a more fruitful engagement that overcomes this predicament by placing the interests of women – as citizens, mothers, human rights bearers, members of the faith, to mention but a few of their multiple responsibilities and affiliations – at the center of the analysis? Arguably, the obligation to engage in just such renegotiation is pressing in light of growing demands to re-evaluate the relations between state and religion the world over. From the perspective of women caught in the web of overlapping and potentially competing systems of secular and divine law, the almost automatic rejection of any attempt to establish a forum for resolving standing disputes that address the religious dimension of their marriage might respect the protection-of-rights dimension of their lived experience but does little to address the cultural or religious affiliation issue. The latter may well be better addressed by attending to the removal of religious barriers to remarriage, which do not automatically flow from a civil release of the marriage bond. This is particularly true for observant women who have solemnized their marriage relationship according to the requirements of their religious tradition, and who may now wish – or feel bound – to receive the blessing of this tradition for the dissolution of that relationship.

In a world of increased mobility across borders, these pressures also acquire a transnational dimension. In Britain, for example, many Muslim families with roots in more than one country (e.g., UK and Pakistan) perceive a divorce or annulment decree that complies with the demands of the faith (as a non-territorial identity community), in addition to those of the secular state in which they reside, as somehow more "transferable" across different Muslim jurisdictions. In technical terms, this need not be the case – private international law norms are based on the laws of states, *not* of religions (Carroll 1997). But what matters here is the perception that an Islamic council dealing with the religious release from the marriage may provide a valuable legal service to its potential clientele, a service that the secular state – by virtue of its formal divorce from religion – simply cannot provide.

These multilayered and intersecting challenges cannot be fully captured by our existing legal categories (Shachar 2008, 2010). They require a new vocabulary and a fresh approach. In the space remaining I will briefly sketch the contours of such an approach – regulated interaction – by asking what is owed to those women whose legal dilemmas (at least in the family law arena) arise from the fact that their lives have *already* been affected by the interplay between overlapping systems of identification, authority and belief – in this case, religious and secular law. The Jewish test case of the *agunah* (pl: *agunot*), a woman whose marriage is functionally over, but whose husband refuses to issue or grant a writ of Jewish divorce (a *get*), will serve as an illustrative example. In contrast with privatized diversity, the alternative I develop invites both the state and the faith community to accommodate individuals who are already entangled in both secular and religious bonds. Many jurisdictions permit the solemnization of marriage by recognized religious, tribal or customary officials, allowing a degree of regulated interaction between state and non-state traditions at the point of entry into marriage. At least in theory, there is no restriction against envisioning some degree of coordination at the point of exit from such a relationship. This is already a reality in some jurisdictions. English law, for example, now permits collaboration between family courts and rabbinical tribunals (*beth din*, pl: *battei din*) in ensuring the removal of religious barriers to remarriage, as does the famous New York "*get* law" (State of New York 2012). Such engagement and coordination across the secular–religious divide is informed by a commitment to substantive (rather than merely formal) equality. It is designed to allow individuals with multiple belongings the same freedoms as other citizens, in this context, the right to be released from a dead marriage and to build a new family if they so wish. Taken to its logical conclusion, regulated interaction can be understood as a form of fair inclusion, taming and resisting the opposing centrifugal and harmful tendencies of privatized diversity.

The stirring motivation behind regulated interaction is to promote diversity *with* equality. This is not a prescription likely to be favored by advocates of privatized diversity who claim authority to define and enforce a "pure" or "authentic" manifestation of a distinct cultural or religious identity in face of real or imagined threats. Such self-proclaimed guardians of the faith wish to impose rigid readings of what are arguably more flexible and malleable traditions, and in the process stifle interpretative debates within the religious community itself about the potential for the adoption more gender-friendly readings of sacred texts and the tradition that evolved from them. The challenges for feminist and other equity-seeking religious interpreters are significant. Beyond gaining access to the historically male-dominated "temple of knowledge," they must work within the tradition's hermeneutic horizons so that their re-interpretive claims cannot be dismissed as "inauthentic." This path of change-from-within may take years to achieve, but the winds of change are already blowing through the world's major religious traditions. Nothing is, however, linear in our story. While women are challenging and changing the old ways, the tensions between minority communities and the state or the wider society frequently come to serve as a pretext to silence new voices from within the minority community. For those advocating privatized diversity, it is therefore convenient to portray the state as an external "enemy," a foreign intruder that offers nothing by way of truly recognizing or accommodating the special needs of the faithful. Such hyperbolic arguments, irrespective of whether falsifiable or not, then serve as a pretext for justifying or encouraging community members to "contracting out" of the secular state's legal order and regulatory control as part of an agenda to establish unofficial islands of jurisdictions that lie outside the governance of the secular order. No less significant, such pressures can also be utilized to "legitimize" rules and practices that breach the hard-earned rights of citizenship for women with respect to marriage, divorce, property, and a host of other issues. In the process, these pressures obscure a critical reality: that traditions are always contested, and that marginalized women hardly have a fair say in shaping these traditions.

Regulated interaction can intervene to break the cycle of silencing and radicalization that privatized diversity facilitates. Adherents of the faith are simultaneously citizens of the state and members of the larger family of humanity. Even religious communities that seek to build walls around their members find that diffusion of human rights ideas and resources is already occurring. Indeed, constructivist understandings of culture submit that such interactions are a major source for the rise of "retro" and more radical interpretations of the tradition that claim to purify it from the corrosive effects of the outside world (Benhabib 2002; Deveaux 2006; Moghadam 1994; Shachar 2001; Song 2007). Assuming that such direct and indirect influences are ongoing, there is "no neutral position for the state here: action and inaction both have consequences for the distribution of power and [authority] inside the cultural community" (Williams 2011, 71). Given that cultural and religious traditions are never as uncontested or as inflexible as advocates of privatized diversity would like us to believe, there is, inevitably, a need for minority communities to find creative answers to the ongoing challenges of interacting with the "modernist" pressures around them. For those *within* the community who reject the wholesale option of privatized diversity but wish to uphold the most precious aspect of personal status law from the perspective of their faith (namely, defining the community's membership boundaries and avoiding a breach of a strict prohibition), regulated interaction offers a viable alternative.

The secular system's standard solution – simply ignoring the problem, wishing it away – is no solution at all. It will fall straight into the hands of advocates of privatized diversity, affirming their desire to take over the void left by state inaction. Such a position effectively immunizes the wrongful behavior of more powerful parties. It has the perverse result of disempowering these women, or reinforcing their vulnerability, in the name of protecting their rights. In the deeply gendered world of intersecting religious and secular norms of family law, these more powerful parties are often husbands who may refuse to remove barriers to religious remarriage (as in the Jewish *get* situation) or may seek to retract a financial commitment undertaken as part of the religious marriage contract (as might be the case with deferred *mahr* in certain Islamic marriages), thus impairing the woman's ability to build a new family or to establish financial independence after divorce. The broader concern here is that while their multiple affiliations might offer religious women a significant source of meaning and value, the affiliations may also make them vulnerable to a double or triple disadvantage, especially in a legal and governance system that categorically denies cooperation between the women's overlapping sources of obligation.

Arguably, the regulated-interaction structure is permissible from the legal perspective of the secular order. Although it requires a departure from the formal and formidable image of erecting a "high wall" between state and religion, such an adaptation is justifiable if it promotes substantive equality and inclusion of those otherwise left outside the purview of standard judicial review and other rights-protecting mechanisms, all without demanding that judges or courts review the doctrinal aspects of a religion (something that they are barred from doing in countries that maintain a strict separation of state from religion).[6] Instead, the removal of *all* barriers to remarriage is the civil goal for which coordination with religious authorities is required.[7] Without this coordination, women of faith may be exposed to unfair extortion from their former husbands as they seek a religious divorce decree, even after a secular divorce has been negotiated or granted.

No less important, regulated interaction may also prove acceptable from the viewpoint of those elements within religious minorities that seek to preserve a degree of control over demarcating their membership boundaries and finding plausible ways for their members to navigate the worlds of secular and religious marriage and divorce proceedings, yet without intruding on the broader catalogue of rights that adherents of their faith hold as citizens and as members of the larger family of humanity. Instead of asking women caught in the knots of secular and religious marriage regulations to leave their cultural worlds behind, it is preferable to make these cultural worlds visible and "legible" to the legal system. The legislative

---

[6] In the United States, the recent *Hosana-Tabor Evangelical Lutheran Church and School* v. *EEOC* (2011) decision recognized the so-called "ministerial exception" barring a lawsuit against a religious organization by an employee seeking relief pursuant to federal civil anti-discrimination legislation (in that particular case, the Americans with Disabilities Act) in the name of protecting religious liberty. The Supreme Court recognized the societal interest in the enforcement of equality-enhancing employment discrimination statutes, but ruled that "so, too, is the interest of religious groups in choosing who will preach their beliefs, teach their faith and carry out their mission." In categorically barring the option of seeking relief by the individual alleging a civil harm by her church (here in the employment context), the Court has arguably given religious liberty precedence over equality.

[7] Canadian law, for example, recognizes this civil goal, which is incorporated in section 21.1 of the federal Divorce Act, RSC 1985, c 3 (2nd Supp). Ontario's Family Law Act, RSO 1990, c F.3, contains similar provisions in sections 2(4)–(6) and 54(4)–(7).

history of New York's "*get* law" confirms this observation; it was Agudath Israel of America, a national organization representing a broad coalition of Orthodox Jews under the leadership of rabbinic scholars, that spearheaded the efforts to reach out to the state legislature in an attempt to ensure such coordination that allowed Jewish men and women to have the religious barriers to remarriage removed as part of the civil divorce proceedings.

Briefly, let me demonstrate the potential benefits of such an approach, by focusing on the example of the *agunah*. In Jewish law, the plight of the *agunah* is recognized as one of the most agonizing challenges, and has been intensively discussed from antiquity to the present day. Although Jewish law (*Halakha*) is typically categorized by a non-hierarchical and pluralist hermeneutic discourse, proposed *Halakhic* solutions to the problem of the *agunah* "have met severe objections, frequently resulting in total rejection, accompanied by strong emotional reactions" (Westreich 2012, 331). No one doubts the importance of the matter. It is precisely this recognition that makes it so charged. The heightened sensitivity is the result of a unique combination of factors: the intersection of human rights and gender equality concerns in family affairs, which affects all members of society, along with the germaneness of marriage and divorce to defining the *Halakhic* boundaries of membership, as well as the subsuming of Jewish marriage and divorce bills under the command of *denim*. As Suzanne Last Stone powerfully demonstrates, the idea of separating certain aspects of law from religion has a long and established tradition not only from the familiar perspectives of European nation-state-building and Christian views conceptualizing church and state as separate entities, but also from within Jewish law (Stone 2008). For the purposes of our discussion, this opens up a political and jurisprudential space for the religious minority communities both to draw lines and to engage with the surrounding society's civil laws, offering a crucial path to *avoid* the privatized-diversity trap.

In Jewish law, matters of ritual and religious prohibition, under which marriage and divorce bills fall, permit no room (from the internal perspective of rabbinic Judaism) to "delegate" authority to civil courts to issue the religious divorce decree, the *get*. This structure allows, however, for state authorities to address "incidental" matters to the break-up of the relationship, such as property division, mutual support obligations between the spouses, child custody, and so on. Such a division of labor permits breaking up the (false) either/or choice between turning wholesale to state law or to religious law, allowing instead for a "retail" development of intersecting or joint-governance resolutions. This can help to address not only the plight of the Jewish *agunah*, but also to release Muslim women from the

Islamic marriage contract by Islamic religious authorities while leaving to the state the jurisdiction to address matters including child custody and spousal support.

Civil courts have in their arsenal plenty of resources, including an array of torts or contract-based remedies (where relevant) that can make a crucial difference in the lives of women caught in the knots, by taking into account the entangled dimensions of secular and religious family laws and traditions in shaping women's actual rights and bargaining positions. This is a path that civil courts in continental Europe have begun to develop by utilizing a range of causes of action and remedies in response to the harm caused to the anchored Jewish wife.[8] As Talia Einhorn explains, under Dutch law, the denial of the delivery of the *get* is regarded as a breach of a duty of care that the husband owes his wife. French courts, too, regard the refusal to deliver or accept the *get* as a civil delict, either on the grounds of *faute* (fault), or on the grounds of *abus de droit* (abuse of rights) or *abus de liberté* (abuse of freedom) (Einhorn 2000, 148–149). The Supreme Court of Canada has also proceeded in just such a direction. In *Bruker* v. *Marcovitz*, a landmark decision involving the interaction of a private-law agreement and a non-secular *get*, the Court explicitly rejected the simplistic your-culture-or-your-rights formula. Instead, it pursued a balance between competing values and admitted of a role for civil courts in spite of the religious dimensions of a dispute: "The fact that a dispute has a religious aspect does not by itself make it non-justiciable" (*Bruker* v. *Marcovitz* 2007, para. 41, paras. 3, 92). The Court held that a nuanced approach to such matters "is consistent with, not contrary to, public order … [It] harmonizes with Canada's approach to religious freedom, to equality rights, to divorce and remarriage generally, and has been judicially recognized internationally."

In the *Marcovitz* case, a Jewish husband made a contractual promise to remove religious barriers to his wife's remarriage in a negotiated, settled agreement, which was incorporated into the final divorce decree between the parties. This contractual obligation thus became part of the terms that enabled the civil divorce by a secular court. Once the husband had the secular divorce in hand, however, he failed to honor the agreement, claiming that he had undertaken a moral rather than legal obligation. The Supreme Court was not in a position to order specific performance, i.e., to force the

---

[8] In Israel, secular courts, recognizing their inability to grant the *get*, have also turned to private-law mechanisms in order to protect women from the inequities that burden *agunot*. These secular courts have had to approach this problem creatively because they cannot order specific performance of the religious divorce decree; as we have seen, this is something that requires the aid of a religious authority.

husband to implement a civil promise with a religious dimension. Instead, the judgment imposed monetary damages on the husband for the breach of the contractual promise in ways that harmed the wife personally and affected the public interest generally. What *Marcovitz* demonstrates is the possibility of employing a standard secular-legal recourse – damages for breach of contract, in this example – in response to specifically gendered harms that arise out of the intersection between multiple sources of authority and identity in the actual lives of women who are members of religious minority communities and larger, secular states as well.

The significance of the *Marcovitz* decision for our discussion lies in its recognition that both the secular and the religious aspects of divorce matter greatly to observant women if they are to enjoy gender equality, be able to articulate their religious identity, enter new families after divorce, and rely on contractual ordering just like any other citizen. This regulated-interaction framework offers us a vision in which the secular system may be called upon to provide remedies in order to protect the human rights of religious women and place justifiable obstacles in the path of husbands who might otherwise cherry-pick their religious and secular obligations as they see fit. This is a clear rejection of privatized diversity, offering instead a more nuanced and context-sensitive analysis that begins from the ground up. This requires identifying who is harmed and why, and then proceeding to find a remedy that matches, as much as possible, the need to recognize the (indirect) intersection of law and religion that contributed in the first place to the creation of the harm for which legal recourse is now sought.

As we have seen earlier, marriage and divorce rules play a crucial role in shaping and exerting the authority of secular authorities, as well as that of competing claimants seeking to exert power over this charged arena of social life and legal regulation. Despite persistent and at times oppressive attempts by the modern state to monopolize an exclusive power to regulate the family, other relations and values have retained a hefty influence in this significant realm of life. These issues are among the most complex and sensitive to address in today's diverse societies. Alas, the almost automatic response of insisting on the *dis*entanglement of state and church (or mosque, synagogue, and so forth) in regulating the family may not always work to the benefit of female religious citizens who are deeply attached to, and influenced by, both systems of law and identity. Their complex claim for inclusion in both the state and the group as full members draws upon their multilayered connections to both systems. Empowering the once voiceless has always been a central mission of human rights. To reach this goal, sometimes fresh ideas and innovative institutional designs are required in order to challenge settled conventions, including the very assumption that it is impossible to grant consideration to religious diversity and gender equality at the same time.

References

Agnes, Flavia. 2001. *Law and Gender Inequality: The Politics of Women's Rights in India*. Oxford: Oxford University Press.

Ahdar, Rex and Aroney, Nicholas. 2010. "The Topography of Shari'a in the Western Political Landscape." In Rex Ahdar and Nicholas Aroney, eds., *Shari'a in the West*. Oxford University Press, pp. 1–31.

Balkin, Jack M. and Siegel, Reva B. 2003. "The American Civil Rights Tradition: Anticlassification or Antisubordination." *Issues in Legal Scholarship* 2, Article 11.

Bano, Samia. 2008. "In Pursuit of Religious and Legal Diversity: A Response to the Archbishop of Canterbury and the 'Sharia Debate' in Britain." *Ecclesiastical Law Journal* 10, 283–309.

Benhabib, Seyla. 2002. *The Claims of Culture, Equality and Diversity in the Global Era*. Princeton University Press.

Berman, Harold J., 1977. "The Origins of Western Legal Science." *Harvard Law Review* 90, 894–943.

Bowen, John R. 2010. "How Could English Courts Recognize Sharia?" *University of St. Thomas Law Journal* 7, 411–435.

Bruker v. *Marcovitz*. 2007. Supreme Court of Canada. [2007] 3 S.C.R. 607, 2007 SCC 54 (Can.).

Carroll, Lucy. 1997. "Muslim Women and 'Islamic Divorce' in England." *Journal of Muslim Minority Affairs* 17, 97–115.

Cook, Rebecca J., 1990. "Reservations to the Convention on the Elimination of All Forms of Discrimination Against Women." *Virginia Journal of International Law* 30, 643–716.

Cott, Nancy F. 1995. "Giving Character to our Whole Civil Polity: Marriage and the Public Order in the Late Nineteenth Century." In Linda K. Kerber, Alice Kessler-Harris and Kathryn Kish Sklar, eds., *U.S. History as Women's History: New Feminist Essays*. Chapel Hill: University of North Carolina Press, pp. 107–122.

Cott, Nancy F.. 2000. *Public Vows: A History of Marriage and the Nation*. Cambridge, MA: Harvard University Press.

Deveaux, Monique. 2006. *Gender and Justice in Multicultural Liberal States*. Oxford University Press.

Einhorn, Talia. 2000. "Jewish Divorce in the International Arena." *Private Law in the International Arena*, 135–153.

Esposito, John L. and DeLong-Bas, Natana J. 2001. *Women in Muslim Family Law*, 2nd edn. Syracuse University Press.

Fiss, Owen. 1976. "Groups and the Equal Protection Clause." *Philosophy and Public Affairs* 5, 107–177.

Fraser, Nancy and Honneth, Axel. 2003. *Redistribution or Recognition? A Political-Philosophical Exchange.* London: Verso.

Habermas, Jürgen. 1995. "Multiculturalism and the Liberal State." *Stanford Law Review* 47, 849–853.

Helfand, Michael A. 2011. "Religious Arbitration and the New Multiculturalism: Negotiating Conflicting Legal Orders." *NYU Law Review* 86, 1231–1305.

Hirschl, Ran. 2010. *Constitutional Theocracy.* Cambridge, MA: Harvard University Press.

Hirschl, Ran and Shachar, Ayelet. 2009. "The New Wall of Separation: Permitting Diversity, Restricting Competition." *Cardozo Law Review* 30, 2535–2560.

Howard, Erica. 2011. *Law and the Wearing of Religious Symbols: European Bans on the Wearing of Religious Symbols in Education.* London: Routledge.

Htun, Mala and Weldon, Laurel. 2011. "State Power, Religion, and Women's Rights: A Comparative Analysis of Family Law." *Indiana Journal of Global Legal Studies* 18, 145–165.

Kymlicka, Will. 1995. *Multicultural Citizenship: A Liberal Theory of Minority Rights.* Oxford University Press.

Kymlicka, Will and Norman, Wayne. 2000. "Citizenship in Culturally Diverse Societies: Issues, Contexts, Concepts." In Will Kymlicka and Wayne Norman, eds., *Citizenship in Diverse Societies.* Oxford University Press, pp. 1–41.

Laborde, Cécile. 2008. *Critical Republicanism: The Hijab Controversy and Political Philosophy.* New York: Oxford University Press.

Larson, Gerald James. 2001. *Religion and Personal Law in Secular India: A Call to Judgment.* Bloomington: Indiana University Press.

Lautsi and Others v. *Italy.* 2011. Case of Lautsi and Others v. Italy, European Court of Human Rights, Grand Chamber. App. No. 30814/06, March 18.

Mnookin, Robert H. and Kornhauser, Lewis. 1979. "Bargaining in the Shadow of the Law: The Case of Divorce." *Yale Law Journal* 88, 950.

Moghadam, Valentine M., ed. 1994. *Identity Politics and Women: Cultural Reassertions and Feminism in International Perspectives.* Boulder: Westview Press.

Multani v. *Marguerite Bourgeoys (Comm'n scolaire).* 2006. Supreme Court of Canada. [2006] 1 S.C.R. 256 (Can).

Ndulo, Muna. 2011. "African Customary Law, Customs, and Women's Rights." *Indiana Journal of Global Legal Studies* 18, 87–120.

Riddle, Jennifer. 2002. "Making CEDAW Universal: A Critique of CEDAW's Reservation Regime under Article 28 and the Effectiveness of the Reporting Process." *George Washington International Law Review* 34, 605–638.

Shachar, Ayelet. 2001. *Multicultural Jurisdictions: Cultural Differences and Women's Rights.* Cambridge University Press.

2008. "Privatizing Diversity: A Cautionary Tale from Religious Arbitration in Family Law." *Theoretical Inquiries in Law* 9, 573–607.

2010. "State, Religion and the Family: The New Dilemmas of Multicultural Accommodation." In Rex Ahdar and Nicholas Aroney, eds., *Shari'a in the West.* Oxford University Press, pp. 115–133.

Song, Sarah. 2007. *Justice, Gender, and the Politics of Multiculturalism.* Cambridge University Press.

State of New York. 2012. Divorce (Religious Marriages) Act 2012.

Stone, Suzanne Last. 2008. "Religion and State: Models of Separation from within Jewish Law." *International Journal of Constitutional Law* 6:3–4, 631–661.

Taylor, Charles. 1994. *Multiculturalism: Examining the Politics of Recognition*, edited by Amy Gutmann. Princeton University Press.

Westreich, Avishalom. 2012. "The 'Gatekeepers' of Jewish Marriage Law: Marriage Annulment as a Test Case." *Journal of Law and Religion* 27, 329–357.

Williams, Rowan, Archbishop of Canterbury. 2008. "Archbishop's Lecture at the Royal Court of Justice, Civil and Religious Law in England: A Religious Perspective." February 7. Available at: www.archbishopofcanterbury.org/1575.

Williams, Susan H. 2011. "Democracy, Gender Equality, and Customary Law: Constitutionalizing Internal Cultural Disruption." *Indiana Journal of Global Legal Studies* 18, 65–85.

Young, Iris Marion. 1990. *Justice and the Politics of Difference.* Princeton University Press.

Yuval-Davis, Nira and Anthias, Floya. 1989. *Woman–Nation–State.* London: Macmillan.

7 | What does cultural difference require of human rights?

CLAUDIO CORRADETTI

Introduction

The contemporary right to freedom of thought together with all its further declinations into freedom of speech, religion, conscience and expression had one of its earliest historical recognitions at the end of the Wars of Religion with the Edict of Nantes (1598). In several respects one can say that the right to freedom of thought is virtually "co-original" with the end of the Wars of Religion. Following this thought further, one might think that human rights define the boundaries of our social coexistence and are inextricably connected to the "fact" of cultural pluralism.

By pursuing a critical-genealogical approach, I will first investigate the historical context within which the concept of human rights originated and then proceed to clarify the normative political significance of the notion of cultural diversity and pluralism. Pluralism is essential to the structure of the problem of justice within modern democracies. For example, it leads John Rawls in *Political Liberalism* (1993) to argue for a conception of political stability constructed on the basis of an overlapping consensus among "reasonable comprehensive doctrines." Drawing on this Rawlsian line of thought, I will attempt to clarify the notion of overlapping consensus, asking whether it can be taken as an *empirical fact* or as a *fact of political reason* and whether it is sufficient to political stability and what all this means for human rights and cultural pluralism.

Before I start let me explain how I define the critical-genealogical approach I have just referred to. In recent work, Honneth (2009, 43–53) clarifies the proper role of genealogical investigation within Critical Theory. He distinguishes between three distinct ideal types of enquiry:

1. "constructive";
2. "reconstructive";
3. "genealogical."

The first establishes a connection between social rationality and the validity of moral principles. The second interprets social reality to show the normative ideals that in fact regulate it. Finally, genealogical analysis asks

whether such normative (moral) ideals have been distorted in the process
of their empirical realization.

According to Honneth, Critical Theory requires the unification of all
these three models into a single paradigm since none of them, individually, suffices to provide an exhaustive account of the significance of "social
criticism." For instance, to pursue only the second reconstructive method
is to take for granted the normative validity of the reconstructed principles.
And to pursue only the first constructivist method is to take inadequate
attention of the facts of the existing social world. I understand the interconnection among these three approaches at the metacritical/constructiv-
ist level that Honneth leaves unspecified to originate from the conditions
of action-coordination exhibited by speech-acts. Speech-acts "disclose" a
possible world or value configuration and then "claim" for it truth or moral
validity on the basis of the specific function played by the speech-acts'
propositional content.[1] The critical-genealogical approach I take here proceeds from this understanding.

I will first explain how, within a truly democratic context, human rights
define "cultural pluralism," distinguishing it from cultural difference. Then
I will explain how human rights push certain commitments into a private
sphere while at the same time marking the boundary between public and
private spheres. Through this double movement, human rights, on the
one hand, disable certain cultural views from their inherent tendency to
conflict in the public sphere as comprehensive and exclusive explanations
of the good life while, on the other hand, enabling a plurality of cultural
perspectives to interact in the public sphere. From the recognition of such
function-duplicity it follows that human rights are ill-conceived as establishing only a private sphere of liberty, a view some liberals seem to hold,
or as an objectionable limit or constraint on the good of the community, a
view some communitarians seem to hold.

Our Western constitutional history, the historical root of the legal specification and embodiment of our political and civic liberties, is deeply
bound up with bloody historical struggles by religious movements to
achieve public recognition. The process has not been smooth and linear.
There have been forward-and-backward movements as both the public and private spheres have opened to a plurality of doctrines. From a

---

[1] Here I draw on the dimension of discourse exemplarity. Speech acts disclose exemplarily a
possible world or value configuration. The idea of exemplarity used here bears important
connections with the recently revived theory of the "signatura" (Agamben 2008, 35ff.) since it
mediates between the semiotic and the semantic domain.

genealogical perspective the progressive affirmation of the right to freedom of thought and conscience has generated a normative recognition of
cultural pluralism. The mere historical fact of pluralism has been given
normative significance. The tendency, notwithstanding various limited
concessions, has challenged the cardinal principle of state monism based
on "one faith, one law, one king" (*un roi, une loi, une foi*) or the principle
of "*cuius regio, eius religio*" of the Peace of Augsburg in 1555 then reaffirmed in 1648 with the Peace of Westphalia. Indeed, since Catherine de'
Medici's promulgation of the Edict of Toleration in 1562, Protestantism
(Huguenot) was recognized as an allowed practice, even if restricted
only to the private sphere or outside towns and finally, with the Edict of
Nantes of 1598, Huguenots were extended the liberty of worship. Also,
with the Treaty of Osnabruck, one of the treaty-components of the Peace
of Westphalia, a clear distinction was drawn between public and private
religious worships (*exercitium publicum* and *exercitium privatum*, respectively), granting toleration for minority faiths only within a non-public
space, either domestic or non-civic.

This halfway progression was followed by the English and American
"billing phase" of the seventeenth and the eighteenth centuries and culmi-
nated in the American and French "declaratory phase" of the eighteenth
century.[2] This latter period distinguished itself for having established a
strict connection between religious liberties and constitutional principles,
a combination lying at the root of our contemporary constitutional democratic models. This development frees public discourse over religious liberty
from arguments that presuppose, even if they don't make direct reference
to, particular religious doctrines. This is the genealogy of the freestanding
character of political liberalism emphasized by Rawls as part of the progress
of our liberal/democratic constitutional history.

And yet, notwithstanding this historical development, one can now
detect a clear functional shift in human rights away from the respect of
cultural liberties pursued in the name of equal liberty of thought and conscience and toward the recognition of equal liberty to communication as
a principle of political inclusion and self-determination. I argue that this
is both an adaptive and progressive manifestation of the never fully satisfied human impulse to actualize social-coordination through linguistic
action.

---

[2] For an alternative reading emphasizing the Reformist's basis of the American and French
declarations (as well as of the German *Staatsrechtslehre*) see Jellinek (1901 [1895]).

Pluralism

Let me now try to clarify the notion of pluralism from an analytical perspective. Given the historical and conceptual reconstructions reviewed above, what sense can we make of the distinction between cultural difference and relativism, on one side, and simple and reasonable pluralism, on the other? First of all, when one appeals to cultural difference and relativism as such it seems as if no commitment can be made to moral adjudication. To hold that there is cultural variety means simply to be committed to the idea that cultures, as normatively structured practices, *are* descriptively different. If, for example, I see that two cultures orient spatial objects in different ways, then I can appeal to the fact that there is a multiplicity of spatial categories organizing objects in different ways.

Of course, many cultural practices involve moral elements. Consider, for example, two cultures with different practices regarding child labor. The thought here is that there just are different social and normative categories for organizing practices involving work and children in different ways. But how would one identify the difference? From what perspective? On the one hand, to see an intelligible and articulable difference is to be able to see both cultural practices from a point of view that reaches each. On the other hand, to identify a practice at all, or two different forms of a practice, the point of view cannot be simply or purely neutral or descriptive. Practices are always empirically under-determined (Moody-Adams 2001, 93–106). So, descriptive cultural relativism faces a conceptual impasse. For any instance in which it's said to be true, we must, at least at the cognitive level, reject the thesis of empirical under-determination for the relevant practice. That's problematic. On the other hand, if we embrace the idea of empirical under-determination, then it seems that there is no possibility of identifying and articulating intelligibly the alleged difference (without invoking a normative perspective that ranges over the difference). In order to find a way out from this deadlock, what should be considered is a form of partial (in-)commensurability at the cognitive level that would admit differences without preventing understandability (Davidson 1984). The relevance of a partial form of (in-)commensurability would be considerable also as a way out from an impasse at the practical level, namely, in those attempts aimed at reconstructing an observed system of beliefs.

Assuming we have, by hypothesis, excluded descriptive relativism, we must consider normative and metaethical relativisms. Normative relativism is the view that moral and epistemic truths are always relative to some *x* (system of belief, etc.) that will determine also *how* (a relative) truth is to be conceived. So the very idea of truth is relative. Metaethical relativism would assume either that there is no truth at all (absolute metaethical relativism) or that only under ideal conditions is there the possibility of establishing parameters for the determination of truth – moral or cognitive. What is a possible response to these further relativist arguments? Here I can only limit myself to some cursory observations and notice how absolute forms of relativism at either the normative or metaethical level are self-contradictory. This certainly does not rule out a further variety of relativist approaches that have appealed, for instance, to internal expressivism (Harman 1982, 1996). Still, these approaches do not escape the problem of conflating what is *morally approvable* from an internal point of view with what is *morally required* according to a standard of morality.

Were normative or metaethical relativism true, in either their cognitive or moral version or both, there would be no possibility of intelligibly deliberating over and adjudicating social controversies through public procedures and within a system of mutual cooperation. Without some standards of truth or validity, moral argument arising out of cultural difference is reduced to dogmatic assertion or the assertion of power or privilege, leaving no toe-hold for human rights.

Once these different forms of relativism are proved to be inadequate candidates for explaining the relation between cultural difference and human rights, it is tempting to think attractive some sort of "monistic universalism" or even (mainly liberal) form of "pseudo-pluralism" according to which there is some abstract universal criterion by which truth or validity in moral argument might be assessed. But I do not think these paradigms advance a convincing thesis. A pure form of abstract universalism would be incapable of providing a convincing explanation for the legitimacy of different cultural claims. Or worse, it would ignore cultural difference as a relevant source of moral normativity. So abstract universalism is unattractive.

But rejecting abstract universalism does not mean rejecting the notion of "truth" or "validity" for the public domain. Indeed, as I have demonstrated on a different occasion, the defense of a cognitivist position for the practical domain does not require the endorsement of a rigid form of universalism, abstract or otherwise. It can accommodate, on the contrary, the defense of a certain pluralistic variation within a universalist picture (Corradetti 2009). A crucial role is played by the definition of the *extent* and the *degree of pluralism* that a specific form of universalism is capable of incorporating.

Let me recapitulate the stage achieved so far. What has been said is that the idea of absolute incommensurability among cognitive systems proves

to be untenable since, were one to face two totally incommensurable systems, it would be impossible even to recognize that a difference exists.
Additionally, I have insisted on the idea according to which even practical
systems of moral beliefs, were they proved to be totally incommensurable,
would result in not being comparable at all. I concluded, thus, that within
mutual terms of comparison, either a system of beliefs fulfills a standard
of morality or it does not. If it does, it is not simply valid, but it shows
also a specific instantiation of a validity criterion. The relation I have in
mind here is similar to the one suggested by structuralist phonology in the
token-type model. When transferred to social domains this means that disagreement among different views of the world does imply the fulfillment
of some background principles and particularly of the "principle of equal
communicative liberty." Such a principle underwrites cooperative social
systems by introducing the requirement of critical comparability within a
pluralist view. Pluralist universalism is the unavoidable prerequisite for the
construction of a system of mutual cooperation whose stability is entrusted
by public standards of reason.

Let's begin the formulation of the notion of pluralist universalism by
briefly introducing Rawls' concept of the fact of pluralism. A first question
to be answered concerns whether the fact of pluralism is to be intended
merely as a historical fact or as a normative statement.[3] Rawls invoked the
idea of the fact of pluralism to make the case for an overlapping consensus,
showing how different comprehensive doctrines are "reasonable" on the
basis of their de facto convergence on a set of normatively freestanding or
independent principles. Because these principles require openness toward
other doctrines or cultural forms the overlapping consensus is consensus
over a pluralist stance toward cultural or doctrinal difference. But this fact
of consensus does not yet provide support for pluralism itself except in a
very circular way; to be a reasonable doctrine *is* to be pluralist and pluralism *entails* reasonableness. Is there a way to avoid this circularity?

We need to look at the fact of pluralism as more than a mere "fact" of
"pluralism." To do so, I suggest we use a "critical-genealogical" method of
analysis and address both the normative and the historical-empirical side
of the notion. What I mean is that the fact of pluralism is a fact of institutional and political reason, that is, a fact strictly embedded into a normative design. As I have already introduced, there are precise historical

---

[3] Indeed, it is widely known how such alternatives have been at the center of one of the main
objections made by Habermas to Rawls along the well-known "family quarrel." See the
exchange between Habermas (1995) and Rawls (1995).

steps which can be detected at the root of a pluralist institutional picture. The perspective provided by the critical-genealogical approach suggested here consists in overcoming the strict opposition between the factual and the normative through a specific consideration of the kind of rationality embedded in institutional configurations. To maintain this perspective is to recognize that institutional facts, even if subject to criticism according to different standards and degrees of rationality, are never *merely contingent*, nor are they deprived of any normative content. In order to clarify this point let's reconsider Rawls' notion of the fact of pluralism on the basis of the distinction between two types of facts such as: "it rains today" and "all men are mortal" (White 2002, 475ff.). If the notion of the fact of pluralism were on par with "it rains today," then the discussion would be restricted only to pure contingency; on the contrary, were one to consider the fact of pluralism on par with the sentence "all men are mortal," one would be emphasizing that *necessarily* pluralism is a fact.

But what kind of necessity is shown by this latter statement? One cannot claim that the sort of necessity characterizing pluralism is the same as the one connoting "all men are mortal." As a matter of fact, in the latter case one refers to the physical and maybe metaphysical components of being human, whereas in the former the reference is made to the normative political necessity of pluralism within modern societies. The difference with traditional approaches to the normative, therefore, is that the critical-genealogical account attempts to ground normativity within a counterfactual view of historical occurrences. What is necessary is the normative political fulfillment of counterfactually established principles, whereas the same empirical institutional occurrence remains open to mere contingency. Let's reconsider for a moment the case of the emergence of pluralism within the public sphere. While the arising of pluralism is normatively attached to the counterfactual understanding of a non-exclusivist truth-role that can be assigned to any single doctrine, the empirical regulation of the interaction among different (comprehensive) doctrines remains a matter of historical (fortunate) contingency. The critical-genealogical method proposed here recognizes precisely this same (contingent) sequence of historical and institutional facts that have led to the end of the Wars of Religion and progressively contributed to the introduction of pluralism within the public arena.

I believe this is also how Rawls' notion of the fact of pluralism in §6 of *Political Liberalism* (1993) should be interpreted. Rawls argues that reasonable pluralism is to be taken as a necessary property of a society that aims to be truly democratic. Now, if his claim is that the variety of reasonable comprehensive doctrines is not a pure historical contingency but a necessity, then it's not clear how to distinguish pluralism *tout court* from reasonable pluralism. Let's recall the previously introduced logical requirement of moving from relativism to the idea of pluralist universalism in a context of mutual cooperation. The form of pluralism I sketched there is based – to a certain extent – upon an analogy between Davidson's view on partial (in-)commensurability within the epistemic domain and a similar notion extended into the practical domain (pluralism *tout court*). And within this context I applied the idea of the "token-type relation" to characterize the relation between contingent instances and universal principle(s). This means that not only it is always possible to understand what a system of beliefs signifies, but that it is also possible at least to try to understand such system as made up of different transcriptions of a shared principle (even if this, in fact, might turn out not to be the case). Now, within social systems of cooperation, a plurality of doctrines and cultural traditions can cooperate peacefully without being committed to a full system of justice as fairness, without being "reasonable" in Rawls' sense of being committed to fair terms of cooperation on the basis of a general condition of reciprocity. Rawlsian fair terms of cooperation might imply the overlapping of different doctrines on universal principles. But the reverse does not hold. That is, a plurality of doctrines and cultural traditions might cooperate subject to universal principles that do not come to Rawlsian fair terms of cooperation. Accordingly, in the next section, I will discuss the advantages of the kind of social cooperation derivable from the notion of pluralist universalism and explain why this approach leads to a much more inclusive theory than Rawls'. I will do so by showing how social cooperation is dependent upon the fulfillment of a condition of communicative coordination which paves the ground to the principle of equal liberty of communicative participation as a jus-generative principle for contemporary constitutional rights.

Pluralist universalism

Let's begin with the following question: can there be social coordination without communication? It might be answered that there are cases of animal species like bees that, strictly speaking, while not mastering a language but only a code, do show a high degree of social organization. But is this a form of intentional communication? That seems unlikely. Again, can one claim that the opposite is true? Namely that there is evidence of social organization without a language? Let's clarify this point by referring to Wittgenstein's example of a primitive form of language expressed under the command

"Slab!" What Wittgenstein wanted to show through such a language-game was that "Slab!" as an elliptical form for "Bring me a slab!" runs counter to the view of language as a mean for communicating thoughts (Wittgenstein 2009 [1953], §19). This point was also implicit in the well-known Fregean distinction between a sentence's *sense* (what a sentence communicates) and its *way* of expression (how it communicates). Since no clear separation can be drawn between these two aspects, it follows that language is not an instrument for communicating already structured thoughts. Thought and language are two co-dependent aspects of the same domain and communication does not amount to transferring one's thoughts into others' minds. If thought and language cannot be separated, then *no intentional social coordination can be admitted outside a communicative paradigm.*

Now, there is yet another horn of the dilemma that is particularly instructive for our case and this is the relation of language to reality. In his *Philosophical Investigations* (2009 [1953]), Wittgenstein claims not only that thinking is ineradicably discursive but also that language is not a mirror of reality. This implies that it is not at all true that there are predefined objects shaping our mind/language faculty as the Augustinian ostensive definition pretends to show (Wittgenstein 2009 [1953], §1); nor, *mutatis mutandis*, that it is possible to consider "private language" as a real hypothesis (Wittgenstein 2009 [1953], §261ff.). Let's develop this point further and show the possible interconnection between language and social praxis. The point I want to defend consists in demonstrating how Wittgenstein's idea of language embeds an analogy between the self-articulation of thoughts and the self-articulation of social arrangements within discourse practice. Which social functions can be mentioned for this view? One might think, for instance, of the performative or the critical functions in cases where it was crucial to emphasize either the institutional/constructive capacity of language or its emancipatory function; but, one might also highlight language's power-relation reiterative function, in cases where language is used in support of an existing status quo. So, whatever the stance taken toward social coordination, there can be no social coordination without linguistic communication. Social reality is organized on the same presupposition of a pragmatic use of language. It follows, from an evaluative perspective, that the social constructive function of language must be supplemented by the formulation of discourse moral/political validity. This point is what I introduce next by integrating Habermas' account of speech-acts theory with an extra layer of (exemplar-)validity claims.

Drawing from Searle's speech-acts theory (1969), Habermas makes the case of a professor asking one of his seminar students to bring a glass of water. Such a request can be criticized according to three validity-claims such as its truth-validity (there is no water tap nearby), its truthfulness (the professor's request aims at perlocutory effects by ridiculing his student) or, finally, according to its normative correctness (the professor is not entitled to treat his students as servants). Here Habermas reduces normativity to a "given normative context" (Habermas 2003 [1981], 140ff.). But if normativity were reducible merely to contexts then one would be unable to distinguish between a normatively correct behavior and a socially convergent practice, making it necessary to provide, first, an argument for the universal unavoidability of the pragmatic language presuppositions and rejoin only at a later stage such standards with contextual variation.

The argument I propose in this regard makes reference to the unavoidable presuppositions of speech-act theory and it treats respect for human rights as an unavoidable formal precondition necessary to the achievement of a normatively valid form of action-coordination (Corradetti 2009, 109ff.). More specifically, I consider how illocutive speech-acts aimed at reaching understanding raise two interconnected forms of normative validity: a commitment to the formal conditions of human rights and a commitment to an *exemplar* form of normative validity. The latter is a mediation of both formal universal validity and the appropriateness of contextually embedded practices. This double standard of normative validity lies at the core of my idea of "pluralist universalism." Action coordination through linguistic practice, indeed, commits subjects to the fulfillment of pragmatic presuppositions including the formal categories of human rights and cooperation organized around the most extensive system of liberties. Illocutive speech-acts, while showing a commitment to the most extensive system of liberty-rights, advance a *propositional* content specifying *how* such fulfillment is to be indexically realized. The indexical anticipation of a form of mutual coordination is what I see as a form of "exemplar universality." The proposal of a specific form of coordination-strategy (a specific form of exemplar universality), once criticized, can give place to a *dialectic* among communicative agents. In view of such dialectical dynamics of "identity of identity and difference," a reformulated notion of speech-act theory is capable of providing a normative account of what it means for a political community to realize action-coordination through the fulfillment of human rights presuppositions.

What remains to be explained is how reformulating the model of communicative action in accordance to a genealogical perspective leads to generation of constitutional rights from the principle of communicative action. As a matter of fact, under a historical perspective, "the principle of equal liberty of communication" represents the pragmatic presupposition for constitutional self-determination, so that the previously recognized right to profess one's own beliefs in private gets reconsidered as the most extensive liberty to political inclusion.[4] This "radial" interconnection justifies a *holistic* structure of human rights protection, that is to say, the enjoyment of a set of fundamental liberties within a constitutional process.

Our problem was to explain what pluralism requires from human rights once the weaker descriptive notion of cultural difference or relativism is proved to be conceptually inadequate. What I have argued is that pluralism is best understood in terms of the validity-claims of speech-act theory. This means that only when action-coordination depends on the fulfillment of the principle of communicative liberty it is possible to speak properly of "pluralist universalism." I also clarified how the Habermasian paradigm of communicative reason not only leads to the principle of communicative liberty but also when translated into constitutional configurations it takes the form of the right to freedom of thought, conscience, speech. These constitutionalized communicative liberties, nevertheless, acquire political significance only when seen as preconditions for public participation in the political arena, that is, only as political rights to socio-political self-determination.

What consequences does this view bear for a theory of justice? I defend a form of public reasoning not only at the root of the constitutional founding process but orienting also the interpretation of the "public sensitivity" – the Kantian *sensus communis* as I take it – by Constitutional or Supreme Courts. Additionally, according to the critical-genealogical reconstruction proposed here, the principle of equal communicative liberty introduces from the beginning certain normative checks into public reasoning. When seen in relation to the public sphere, the principle of equal liberty of communication provides a normative standard for evaluating the validity of public discourses, which can be formulated in the following way:

only those discourses, arguments, communicative interplays that do not contradict performatively the equal share of communicative liberty constitute valid reasoning.

---

[4] The principle of equal liberty of communication has important overlap with the "right to justification" recently defended by Forst (2010). Nevertheless, my defended principle is more inclusive since its fulfillment relies on a higher variety of speech-acts than Forst's critical justifications. Notwithstanding such differences, both models maintain a functional similarity differently from, for example, Griffin (2008). What these models primarily contribute to is the construction of favorable conditions for people's inclusion into public political life.

This formula suggests an alternative strategy to a supposedly neutral model of public reasoning by favoring a strategy of normative convergence. Normative convergence is normative because discourses are bound to the principle of communication and convergence is possible only if an argument that is exemplarily valid "for us" is provided. Normative convergence represents therefore the result of a common enterprise that constructs a self-interpretative narrative for our political community. One of the advantages of this model for the public sphere over Rawls' is that it does not characterize principles of justice, as Rawls does, as "not affected in any way by the particular comprehensive doctrines that may exist in society" (Rawls 1993, 141). On the contrary, on my view, the principles of justice, constructed out of public confrontation in a context faithful to human rights, are affected by the particular doctrines that may exist in society. In the normative-convergence model I suggest, discourse inclusivity is accompanied by a process of *normative bootstrap* on the basis of deliberative-dialectical interplay. Agents are obliged to comply with a duty of public acceptability rooted in the principle of equal liberty of communication. In their public communications they must respect of equality of treatment, inclusivity, non-coercion, the reciprocal exchange of views, and so on. These constraints exclude performatively contradictory arguments; that is their normative significance.

Conclusion

In conclusion, let me recapitulate the main arguments I have defended and add some final remarks about what pluralism requires of human rights. First, I have claimed that on the basis of a genealogical reconstruction one can detect in the Wars of Religion the historical roots of the political principle of equal liberty in communication. Also I have claimed that differently from its initial formulation based on the recognition of equality of men's faith and conscience, the contemporary constitutional right to freedom of thought and speech points to the recognition of political inclusivity and self-determination. Accordingly, I have reinterpreted the Habermasian model of communicative action along critical-genealogical lines and reconstructed the principle of equal liberty of communication as a constraint for normative convergence in the public realm. Such a model presents two advantages over Rawls' idea of the overlapping consensus: it is both more inclusive and uncontroversial. It is more inclusive since it does not define and limit reasonable comprehensive doctrines as those doctrines that accept an independently justified liberal theory of justice. So my model admits a wider range of diversity under the heading of pluralism. At the same time, my model is less controversial. It does not seek first a freestanding philosophical justification of principles of justice that are then merely shown to be legitimate or stable by reference to the idea of an overlapping consensus. Instead, by relying on the principle of communication my model generates (and fulfills) unavoidable constraints of performative (non-)contradiction that then underwrite normative convergence through rational deliberation within the socially rooted domain of the political public sphere. As a consequence, it considers public reason as grounded primarily within a maximally inclusive social sphere.

But even if maximally inclusive, the principle of equal liberty of communication excludes also a great deal of comprehensive arguments. While religious comprehensive doctrines could represent only one of the many epistemic sources for public discussion, they can neither exhaust the multiplicity of available sources at the public level nor avoid what Habermas has defined as the onus of "translation" of religious languages into a "generally accessible language" (in Mendieta and Vanantwerpen 2011, 25). An objection that could be moved to this latter point is that the onus of translation would frustrate the range of communication available at the public institutional level. To this it can be easily replied that the requirement of translatability does not necessarily exclude ritual and symbolic formulas making reference, for instance, to God as a way to enrich the elaboration of performative procedures. What cannot be admitted, instead, is that such formulas provide a normative justification for discourses aiming at being publicly defensible.

Let's consider the case of the veil for Muslim women. What would the suggested model have to say? While it cannot anticipate an outcome that depends on a public procedure of assessment, the view of public reasoning described here would nevertheless consider *only* those arguments that defend the veil as a publicly relevant expression of communicative freedom. The precise content of such arguments cannot be anticipated by the legislator since this would depend upon exemplarily contingent outcomes of a public deliberating body.

In conclusion, the answer to which human rights are necessitated by cultural difference is, first, that cultural difference is to be understood in terms of pluralism and, second, that pluralism is to be understood in the light of political inclusivity. This is precisely what I have referred to by reconstructing genealogically the normative significance of the principle of equal liberty of communication.

References

Agamben, Giorgio. 2008. "Teoria delle segnature." In *De Signatura Rerum. Sul metodo*. Turin: Bollati Boringhieri, pp. 35–81.

Arendt, Hannah. 1992. *Lectures on Kant's Political Philosophy*. University of Chicago Press.

Corradetti, Claudio. 2009. *Relativism and Human Rights: A Theory of Pluralistic Universalism*. Dordrecht: Springer.

Davidson, Donald. 1984. "On the Very Idea of a Conceptual Scheme." In *Inquiries into Truth and Interpretation*. Oxford: Clarendon Press, pp. 183–198.

Forst, Rainer. 2010. "The Justification of Human Rights and the Basic Right to Justification: A Reflexive Approach." *Ethics* 120:4, 711–740.

Griffin, James. 2008. *On Human Rights*. Oxford University Press.

Habermas, Jürgen. 1995. "Reconciliation Through the Public Use of Reason: Remarks on John Rawls's Political Liberalism." *The Journal of Philosophy* 92:3, 109–131.

   2003 [1981]. "Social Action, Purposive Activity, and Communication." In Maeve Cooke, ed., *On the Pragmatics of Communication*. Cambridge: Polity Press, pp. 105–182.

Harman, Gilbert. 1982. "Moral Relativism Defended." In Jack W. Meiland and Michael Krausz, eds., *Relativism: Cognitive and Moral*. University of Notre Dame Press, pp. 189–204.

   1996. "Moral Relativism." In Gilbert Harman and Judith J. Thomson, eds., *Moral Relativism and Moral Objectivity*. Oxford: Blackwell, pp. 1–64.

Honneth, Axel. 2009. "Reconstructive Social Criticism with a Genealogical Proviso: On the Idea of 'Critique' in the Frankfurt School." In *Pathologies of Reason*. New York: Columbia University Press, pp. 43–53.

Jellinek, Georg. 1901 [1895]. *The Declaration of the Rights of Man and the Citizen*. New York: Henry Holt.

Mendieta, Eduardo and Vanantwerpen, Jonathan, eds. 2011. *The Power of Religion in the Public Sphere*. New York: Columbia University Press.

Moody-Adams, Michele M. 2001. "The Empirical Underdetermination of Descriptive Cultural Relativism." In Paul K. Moser and Thomas L. Carson, eds., *Moral Relativism: A Reader*. New York: Oxford University Press, pp. 93–106.

Rawls, John. 1993. *Political Liberalism*. New York: Columbia University Press.

   1995. "Political Liberalism: Reply to Habermas." *Journal of Philosophy* 92:3, 132–180.

   1999. *The Law of Peoples*. Cambridge, MA: Harvard University Press.

Searle, John. 1969. *Speech Acts: An Essay in the Philosophy of Language*. Cambridge University Press.

White, Steven, K. 2002. "Pluralism, Platitudes, and Paradoxes: Fifty Years of Western Political Thought." *Political Theory* 30, 472–481.

Wittgenstein, Ludwig 2009 [1953]. *Philosophical Investigations*, edited and translated by Peter M.S. Hacker and Joachim Schulte. Oxford: Wiley-Blackwell.

PART III

What do human rights require of the global economy?

8 | What do human rights require of the global economy? Beyond a narrow legal view

ADAM MCBETH

Introduction

Economic activity, like any area of life, affects individual human beings, and therefore potentially impacts human rights, both positively and negatively. Direct impacts can be on a very small, individual basis, such as the improved livelihood one person receives as a result of his or her employment, or alternatively, the harm he or she suffers from poor work practices, discrimination or exposure to dangerous materials. They can also be on an enormous scale, such as when thousands of people are forcibly evicted to make way for a new infrastructure project, or when a waterway is severely polluted. Less directly, decisions and policies in the economic arena can affect human rights in a systemic manner, such as the impact on livelihoods of limiting or increasing market access for agricultural exports as a result of trade rules, or the impact of austerity measures required by international financial institutions as a lending condition.

Human rights as a concept holds that there are certain entitlements that are intrinsic to being human. These rights and their origins are chronicled extensively in other chapters in this volume. In the language of international human rights law, these intrinsic entitlements are said to derive from inherent human dignity (UDHR, Preamble paras. 1 and 5 and Article 1; United Nations Charter 1945, Preamble para. 2; World Conference on Human Rights, Preamble paras. 2 and 5 and Articles 11, 18, 20, 25 and 55). Any action that infringes those entitlements will therefore be illegitimate and amount to a breach of human rights, in the non-legal sense. Furthermore, the full realization of human rights for all humankind can require positive steps to be undertaken, at least where states are concerned, given the purpose of the state in governing for the benefit of its people.

The modern global economy poses challenges to a conception of human rights that channels all responsibility through the state, since much of the economic activity and the entities that drive it are themselves disconnected from the state and beyond the regulatory control of any one state. From the perspective of the individual whose rights are being infringed, the identity of the transgressor and the transgressor's relationship with the state is irrelevant. If a family is forcibly evicted from their home, it makes no difference to them whether the eviction was an action of their own government, of an international development agency, or of a private corporation, or some combination of forces; what matters is the deprivation of their home and the consequent impact on their livelihood, social interaction and other rights if they are forced to move. Therefore, in viewing human rights from the perspective of the rights-bearer, it is perfectly clear that human rights can be violated by the actions of all kinds of entities – state agents, international institutions, individuals and corporations alike.

When law is drawn into the equation, an obligation-holder must be identified in order to determine who is accountable for a particular infringement of an individual's human rights, and who must take responsibility to prevent such infringements. International human rights law has traditionally turned to the state as the obligation-holder. To the extent that any entity – an individual or a corporation, for instance – is within the regulatory control of a given state, the protection of human rights can be secured by requiring the state to put in place a regulatory regime that prohibits the harmful conduct, backed by the power of the state to investigate and punish the transgressor if a violation takes place. This is part of the state's duty under international human rights law to protect human rights.

The challenge to this approach posed by the global economy is that there are currently many commercial operations and economic development projects taking place that are beyond the regulatory control of any one state. This chapter therefore tackles a series of separate hard questions: at the general level, there is the hard question of how to seek accountability for human rights in the context of these operations that defy the control of a single state. A narrow, positivist reading of international human rights law would insist that any obligation must run through a state to have any validity in international law. A broader, purposive approach, however, can look beyond the state to protect human rights in other contexts. Looking at the roles of non-state actors under such a purposive approach leads to a series of entity-specific hard questions, relating to the appropriate method for protecting human rights for different types of actor. For instance, rule-making institutions have a different purpose to international institutions that engage directly in the community. Private entities such as corporations have a different purpose again compared to intergovernmental institutions of either species. The question of "what do human rights require of the global economy?" thus needs to be answered differently for these different entities.

Beyond a narrow view of international human rights law

The question of what human rights *law* requires of the global economy is fraught from the outset, because the answer will depend on one's conception of the scope of the international law on human rights.

An approach to international human rights law that looked only to binding international instruments would provide a heavily state-centric answer to this question, since treaties by their nature are directed to states. This limited, positivist approach would not recognize direct human rights obligations for corporations, or any other non-state actors for that matter. Rather, international human rights law would place obligations on states, and states in turn would be expected to regulate all actors within their territory or jurisdiction.

States are required to respect, protect and promote human rights within their territory and their jurisdiction (ICCPR 1966, Article 2(1); Maastricht Guidelines 1998). The duty to respect human rights is an obligation for states to refrain from actions, through the organs of the state, that would infringe the rights of individuals or groups. The duty to protect human rights extends beyond the state's own conduct to include an obligation to exercise the state's jurisdiction to ensure that one person or entity does not infringe the rights of another person. That includes an obligation to regulate to prevent conduct that would infringe human rights, and to investigate and punish any infringements that do occur. The duty to protect human rights is routinely exercised through states' municipal laws, usually without a "human rights" label: for instance, laws criminalizing homicide protect the right to life from infringement by other individuals; industrial relations laws protect labor rights from private exploitation; environmental laws protect the right to health; and so on.

In an economic context, the state's duty to protect human rights within its territory and jurisdiction means, at a minimum, that states are required to ensure the protection of human rights in the course of commerce, development projects and the like occurring within their borders. That would include requiring corporations, both domestic and foreign, to observe human rights standards in their business practices, through domestic legal channels such as labor laws. There is a strong argument that "jurisdiction" in this context goes beyond just territory, since states have the ability to regulate the operations of their nationals abroad (HRC 2004, para. 10). Thus a state where a multinational corporation is based, often called the "home state," could be said to have jurisdiction over that corporation even when it is operating in another country, because it could require the corporation to meet certain standards and impose punishments on the head office for failing to meet those standards. Prevailing state practice, however, holds that international human rights law *permits* home states to impose extraterritorial human rights duties on their corporations operating abroad, but does not *oblige* them to do so (Ruggie 2011, commentary to para. 2).

A different answer will emerge if a purposive view is taken of human rights obligations. Human rights are almost always expressed in treaties in terms of the entitlement of the individual or group, rather than emphasizing the obligation. This reflects an underlying presumption that human rights are pre-existing, that the instrument enunciating a certain right does not create that right; it merely gives form to the state's obligation to observe the right which derives from another source.

The development of the main human rights instruments early in the life of the United Nations lends weight to this view. The United Nations Charter assumes the pre-existence of human rights and that member states understood the content of the term (UN Charter 1945, Preamble para. 2, Articles 1, 55, 56), despite the fact that neither the precise obligations that flowed from those rights, nor the means for their enforcement, were elaborated in the Charter itself (Lauterpacht 1948, para. 6). The Universal Declaration of Human Rights then gave shape to the rights referred to in the Charter three years earlier, focusing almost exclusively on enumerating the rights that derive from human dignity, rather than codifying the corresponding obligations of states (or any other actor).[1]

On this view, human rights, deriving from inherent human dignity, exist independently of positive international law and in some respects operate to fetter the sovereignty of the state (Hannum 1995; Human Rights Council 2007, annex para. 1(b); Schwelb 1964, 36–47).[2] The role of international legal instruments is to give effect to human rights by articulating positive

---

[1] The UDHR only mentions state duties twice in its 30 articles: once in Article 16, when the family as "the natural and fundamental group unit of society" is declared to be "entitled to protection by society and the State"; and once in Article 22, according to which the realization of economic, social and cultural rights is to be achieved "in accordance with the organization and resources of each State."

[2] The deference paid to the UDHR as a source of legal norms, despite its format as a non-binding resolution declaring pre-existing norms, is evidence of this approach. While the UDHR was generally not considered to be legally binding, as a General Assembly resolution, at the time of its adoption in 1948, states have consistently treated it as a source of binding norms since that time. The most recent example is the fact that states' adherence to the UDHR is included in the Human Rights Council's Universal Periodic Review of states' human rights records, along with their adherence to the UN Charter and those human rights instruments to which the relevant state is a party: Human Rights Council (2007, annex, para. 1(b). Regarding the customary status of the UDHR, see Hannum (1995, 287); Schwelb (1964, 36–47).

obligations on states to respect, protect and promote human rights. To the extent that entities other than states are capable of infringing human rights, a purposive view of the law of human rights holds that such actors have an obligation, at a minimum, not to frustrate those rights (Clapham 2006, 546). In other words, if the rights are guaranteed as a matter of law, obligations can be determined by reference to the protection and realization of those rights for a particular actor, whether or not those obligations are articulated in an instrument of their own. The ability to enforce those obligations through existing mechanisms, however, is another matter.

Intergovernmental organizations

Intergovernmental organizations are in a special position with regard to human rights, because they are independent legal persons, and yet they are comprised entirely of member states and their decisions are made through the votes of government representatives. Intergovernmental organizations are therefore not caught directly by the obligations imposed on states by international human rights treaties; the International Monetary Fund (IMF) in particular has often made that point in decrying legal responsibility for human rights (Chaffour 2005, 10–3; Gianviti 2005, 118–138; Mudho 2002). On the other hand, state representatives who are participating in institutional decision-making in an intergovernmental organization carry with them the obligations of the states they represent. States cannot simply check their human rights obligations at the door when participating in the work of an international institution; they are obliged to consider what impact their actions will have on human rights and to ensure that human rights are respected, protected and promoted (Ruggie 2011, para. 9; UNHCHR 2002, para. 5).

While reminding governments of their human rights obligations when acting in international fora is an important part of ensuring that international institutions respect and promote human rights in their field of operation, it is not a practical means of accountability for violations. Unraveling the decisions or policies of an institution and trying to determine which of its member states supported that action and could be considered responsible for it is at best highly impractical, particularly in relation to the day-to-day operations that are implemented by institutional staff rather than big-picture policies voted on by state representatives. In most cases, pursuing accountability via member states is also undesirable, since it undermines the separate legal personality of the institution, and therefore

ignores the independent responsibility the institution has for the impact of
its operations on human rights. Proper and effective protection and promotion of human rights must look instead to the institution itself for human
rights accountability.

Rule-making institutions

There are essentially two categories of intergovernmental organization in
the global economy in terms of the way in which the organization affects
human rights. The first category is the rule-making organization, which
does not directly engage "on the ground" in any given community. The
effects of such an institution on human rights are the results of implementing the organization's policies, including the extent to which those policies
constrain governments in taking measures for the realization of human
rights. The most prominent example of this category is the World Trade
Organization (WTO). Criticisms of the WTO for real and imagined contributions to human rights abuses have dogged the institution since it came
into being (Garcia 1999; Howse 1999; Joseph 2011; Nichols 1996; Pogge
2008). Two particular types of criticism have persisted. The first type criti-
cizes WTO rules that constrain the policy space of states in issues with a
substantial connection with human rights. For example, the rules on patents in the Agreement on Trade-Related Aspects of Intellectual Property
Rights (TRIPs Agreement) have been criticized for the impact they have
on access to essential medicines in poor countries, which in turn affects
the right to life and the right to the highest attainable standard of health
(McBeth 2006). The second type of criticism is that certain values are prioritized in the WTO regime while others are neglected. For example, the
fact that protection of labor standards yields to the liberalization of trade
within WTO rules, and the constraints that such rules place on states' ability to regulate for the protection of labor rights in the context of trade, has
been a heated topic of debate since the inception of the WTO (Compa and
Diamond 1996; Howse and Trebilcock 1997; Weiss 1998).

   Of the first type, one example is the rules on patents in the Agreement on
Trade-Related Aspects of Intellectual Property Rights (TRIPs Agreement)
and the impact they have on access to essential medicines in poor countries,
which in turn affects the right to life and the right to the highest attainable standard of health. In short, the mandated terms of patent protection
and the restrictions on imports of generic copies prevent life-saving medicines, particularly for HIV/AIDS and tuberculosis, being offered at affordable prices to patients in impoverished countries, while exceptions such as

compulsory licenses issued by governments are of no use to countries without pharmaceutical manufacturing capacity – that is, almost all of the poorest countries (McBeth 2006). If a government wanted to provide affordable medicines by arranging imports of licenced generic copies, thereby fulfilling its obligations regarding the rights to life and health, WTO rules would have prevented it from doing so (at least before the amendments to the TRIPs Agreement to address this problem in 2003, which have such complicated conditions that they are almost never used).

The second type of criticism within the WTO context – that certain values are prioritized over others – is manifested in various ways. One commonly cited example is the treatment of labor standards. Any domestic regulation that treats the goods originating in one country differently to like products originating in another country is presumed to be disguised protectionism and therefore illegal under the WTO regime (Wolf 2001, 189). A number of exceptions to that general rule are enumerated in the General Agreement on Tariffs and Trade (GATT 1994, Article XX), but labor standards are not among them. A domestic law that sought to ban goods made with child labor, or goods made in conditions that violated international labor standards in some other respect, would almost certainly violate WTO rules, because it would discriminate between physically identical products according to the manner in which they were produced, rather than the inherent characteristics of the products themselves. In such a scenario, the importing state would be restrained from taking measures within its jurisdiction to protect labor rights abroad, due to the overriding obligations of non-discrimination in trade. The debate about the appropriate way to resolve this tension between trade principles and labor standards has persisted since the inception of the WTO itself (Compa and Diamond 1996; Howse and Trebilcock 1997; Weiss 1998). From a human rights perspective, the grievance is that the protection of labor rights yields to the pursuit of liberal trade. While that is not surprising within an institution dedicated to trade liberalization (Marrakesh Agreement 1994, preamble, paras. 3–4), the collective choice of states to prioritize trade values within an intergovernmental organization, and to constrain their ability to take measures for the protection of human rights in the process, creates problems for the realization of human rights.

Direct engagement institutions

The second category of intergovernmental organization in the context of the organization's effect on human rights is the category of organizations that have a degree of direct engagement in a given community, or engagement one step removed (such as financing a project carried out by another entity). For want of a better term, I call this category "direct engagement institutions" to distinguish them from institutions that set and enforce the rules but are not themselves active players in the global economy. Organizations in this category include international development banks, such as the World Bank[3] and regional institutions such as the Asian Development Bank. These organizations have a more localized effect on human rights because of their involvement in projects in the community, sometimes by funding a project directly and having substantial input in project design, and other times merely facilitating the project by providing funds or a guarantee for a project carried out by others. Because institutions of this sort are doing more than simply setting the rules by which others must operate – rather, they themselves are operating – the expectations upon them for the realization of human rights should be different than the expectations upon rule-making institutions. In other words, the human rights expectations should be determined at least in part by what the institution actually does and the way in which it impacts human rights, rather than being determined solely by the legal structure of the institution. For those institutions that sometimes resemble a rule-making institution and sometimes a direct engagement institution, depending on the function being considered, such as the IMF, it would follow that the expectations for the realization of human rights might differ according to the function.

To the extent that the projects of an intergovernmental organization are aimed at poverty reduction, and that they are successful in achieving that goal, they undoubtedly do a great deal of good from a human rights standpoint. For instance, a hydroelectric dam that brings affordable electricity to a region that previously lacked it would contribute to improved health-care, potential for refrigeration, greater potential for income-generating activities and all the improvements to livelihood that flow from that. Such beneficiaries may very significantly outnumber the people who are forced to relocate from their homes when the dam is built, or whose dependence on fisheries leaves them destitute when the watercourse is changed. However, human rights are not a matter of utilitarian calculus, whereby the good for the greater number outweighs the harm suffered by the few. In fact, human

---

[3] The World Bank is comprised of five agencies: the International Bank for Reconstruction and Development, the International Development Association, the International Finance Corporation, the Multilateral Investment Guarantee Agency and the International Centre for the Settlement of Investment Disputes. The first three of those could be considered "direct engagement institutions" as defined here.

rights demand the opposite approach: ensuring that minimum standards for the treatment of human beings, deriving from the inherent dignity of the human person, are accorded to people who find themselves on the wrong side of the utilitarian ledger.

In recognition of that need, most of the direct engagement institutions have developed policies since the 1990s to put in place safeguards for those who are negatively impacted by their operations, and have continually refined those policies over time. They included a number of matters that could be considered human rights issues, such as the policies relating to indigenous peoples, involuntary resettlement and forced labor and harmful child labor, as well as a range of issues that had been problem areas for previous projects but not directly human rights issues. The most recent revision of those standards in 2011 sought to incorporate the UN Special Representative's "Respect, Protect and Remedy" framework with regard to the human rights responsibilities of corporations, discussed below. To that end, the following overarching principle was added: "Business should respect human rights, which means to avoid infringing on the human rights of others and address adverse human rights impacts business may cause or contribute to" (International Finance Corporation 2012a, para. 3).

While the specific performance standards that follow remain somewhat piecemeal and do not incorporate all of the relevant standards emanating from international human rights law (McBeth 2009, 1133–1146; World Bank Compliance Advisor/Ombudsman 2003) the acknowledgment of a responsibility for private entities to respect human rights in the course of development projects is a significant step toward a consensus position on the human rights responsibilities of non-state actors in the global economy.

More commonly, development institutions address human rights issues through the paradigm of poverty reduction (for example, the World Bank and the IMF introduced a joint process known as Poverty Reduction Strategy Papers (PRSP) in 1999). There is a certain degree of overlap with human rights goals and a genuine attempt to identify and articulate the detriment that might be suffered by various groups as a result of a particular policy or projects, although human rights standards are not utilized. Where human rights and other paradigms that might serve similar aims diverge, though, is in the notion of rights, or legal entitlement. If a particular identified harm is a "social issue" or bears some other label, reasonable effort might be made to avoid that harm or to provide redress – such as relocating a family that has been forcibly evicted to a situation in which they are at least as well off as they were before the eviction (International Finance Corporation 2012b, paras. 3, 9, 19–29). However, if the harm does occur and the redress falls short, there is no presumption that individuals have been denied their intrinsic human entitlements; rather, the failing would be expressed as a shortcoming of the institution or its program partners in failing to adhere to institutional policy.

What do human rights require of an intergovernmental organization in the global economy?

Taking a purposive view of human rights obligations, intergovernmental organizations need to ensure that their actions do not infringe human rights and do not constrain the ability of governments to take action for the protection and promotion of human rights. A positivist perspective of international law would observe no documentary source for such an obligation; nowhere in the Articles of Agreement of the IMF or the WTO's Marrakesh Agreement, or the legal texts of any of the economic intergovernmental organizations is there any mention of a legal obligation to adhere to international human rights law in the organization's activities. However, if the obligations of states to respect, protect and promote human rights are not to be eviscerated when those same states cooperate to form an organization for economic purposes, the states' human rights obligations must endure and they must not be compromised by the operations of the institutions.

The appropriate recognition of human rights will take a different form for different types of organization, and in some cases, for different activities within the same organization. For rule-making institutions, the key is to ensure that the rules negotiated under the auspices of the organization and the way those rules are subsequently interpreted and enforced – for instance, by the dispute settlement panels and Appellate Body of the WTO – take account of human rights standards and the primary role that human rights are intended to play in the international legal system. In this context, it is relatively straightforward to identify organizational obligations as an extension of the universally acknowledged obligations of the member states.

For direct engagement institutions, additional steps are required. There needs to be an acknowledgment that human rights are entitlements of every person by virtue of being human, with the consequence that redress for the infringement of rights is available, and there is a mechanism that allows victims to assert their rights and seek a remedy for any violations. At present, engagement with human rights standards by institutions of this sort is generally ad hoc, covering only those rights that have repeatedly been problematic in past projects, and virtually always expressed as a goal or an institutional policy rather than a right. Accountability mechanisms exist in some of these institutions, but their mandate is limited to the enforcement of the institutional policies, which does not include the application of international human rights law (Darrow 2003, 225).

In summary, human rights require that actions taken in the name of an intergovernmental organization not only pursue the greatest good for the greatest number, but also respect the human rights of the lesser number, and recognize those rights as enforceable rights rather than merely desirable outcomes.

Corporations

The driving force for much of the debate about human rights in the global economy has been the conduct of multinational corporations. If a corporate enterprise based in one country causes significant harm to human rights in another country in which it operates, it would be reasonable to expect the enterprise to be held accountable for that harm. For example, when US-based mining giant Freeport-McMoRan was accused of involvement in human rights abuses in its mining operations in West Papua, Indonesia, including allegations of wrongful acquisition of lands from indigenous peoples (Andriyanto 2010), and complicity in extrajudicial killings of trade unionists by Indonesian police (Asian Human Rights Commission 2011), advocates for the victims sought to hold Freeport-McMoRan accountable.

The difficulty presented by the global economy to a scenario such as that is the fragmentation of responsibility. In a purely domestic setting, the state is expected to regulate corporations operating within its jurisdiction to prevent human rights violations and to punish them when they occur. In the global economy, however, the operations of a multinational enterprise are spread across multiple jurisdictions. In this example, the Freeport enterprise is based in the United States and operating in Indonesia. However, the company operating in Indonesia, PT Freeport Indonesia, is a distinct legal person from the US-based Freeport-McMoRan Corporation, and both are subject to the regulation of the state in which they are incorporated and in which they operate. International human rights law requires the US government to prevent abuses by its corporate nationals (at least) within its territory, and requires the Indonesian government to do the same. Thus the Indonesian government is obliged to protect the Indonesian people from harm committed by PT Freeport Indonesia, but has no practical ability to reach the parent company in the United States or any related entities in the enterprise. Relying purely on the traditional responsibility of the state to protect human rights within its territory and jurisdiction is therefore inadequate, as the regulatory reach of any given state does not match the global nature of the operations of many multinational enterprises.

In addition, in some cases, the host state is itself involved in the alleged human rights abuses, and in other cases they are unwilling to act because they are reliant on the investment of the multinational enterprise. Faced with intransigence from the host state, the question many ask is whether the enterprise should be allowed to get away with conduct abroad (particularly in the developing world) that would be unthinkable at home. And if the answer to that question is that it should not, the next question is *how* the enterprise should be held to account. It is here that the contemporary debate in international human rights law comes in, seeking an answer that provides practical accountability without relying exclusively on the host state.

The UN Special Representative

Within the United Nations, numerous initiatives have attempted to address the problem of accountability of globally operating enterprises within a state-based system of international human rights law, but none has yet been concluded to the point of implementation. In July 2005, at the request of the then Commission on Human Rights (UN Commission on Human Rights 2005), the United Nations Secretary-General appointed Professor John Ruggie to the post of Special Representative of the Secretary-General on the Issue of Human Rights and Transnational Corporations and Other Business Enterprises. The Special Representative has issued a report to the Human Rights Council[4] and the General Assembly every year of his mandate, which ended in 2011. In the 2008 report, the Special Representative proposed his "Protect, Respect and Remedy" framework (Ruggie 2008), and the 2011 report launched the "Guiding Principles" for the implementation of that framework (Ruggie 2011).

The "Protect, Respect and Remedy" framework emphasizes three aspects of human rights responsibility in the corporate context: first, the state's duty

---

[4] In March 2006, the UN General Assembly created the Human Rights Council, which replaced the former Commission on Human Rights. The Human Rights Council therefore inherited oversight of the Special Representative's mandate, which had been created by the Commission.

to protect human rights, including the obligation to regulate to ensure that business enterprises within their jurisdiction do not infringe human rights; second, the duty of corporations themselves to respect human rights, in that they should ensure that they do not violate human rights in the course of their operations; and third, the importance of access to a meaningful remedy when human rights are violated.

The state's duty to protect human rights was discussed earlier in this chapter. The Guiding Principles assert that "States are not generally required under international human rights law to regulate the extraterritorial activities of businesses domiciled in their territory and/or jurisdiction. Nor are they prohibited from doing so, provided there is a recognized jurisdictional basis" (Ruggie 2011, commentary to para. 2). To that end, the Guiding Principles give some fairly timid recommendations for states to regulate the activities of businesses based within their jurisdiction, emphasizing business certainty and state reputation rather than the efficacy of human rights protection (Ruggie 2011, paras. 1–6, especially commentary to paras. 2 and 3).

The second prong of the Special Representative's framework – that business enterprises have a duty to respect human rights – is the most significant aspect in terms of the development of the law. The duty to respect human rights includes a duty to refrain from causing or contributing to adverse human rights impacts, as well as a duty to "prevent or mitigate adverse human rights impacts that are directly linked to their operations, products or services by their business relationships, even if they have not contributed to those impacts" (Ruggie 2011, para. 13). The latter duty is a reference to the problem of diverse enterprises, or "supply chains," in which one company might be benefiting from or implicitly endorsing a human rights abuse, while not directly linked to the entity directly committing the harm. Common examples include gross violence committed by security contractors (especially in the mining sector), and manufacturing contractors using appalling working conditions, which are implicitly approved by the principal imposing prices and delivery times that would make proper labor standards impossible to observe. The supply chain issue has been a vexed one for those debating legal accountability for multinational enterprises, because the fragmentation of the chain makes it very difficult to identify and hold accountable the culpable corporations.[5]

---

[5] The Sub-Commission Norms, para. 1, addressed this by using the concept of the "sphere of activity and influence," within which business enterprises had the obligation to respect and promote human rights. The Special Representative was scathing of the "sphere of activity and influence" concept in his first annual report in 2006, despite the fact that the concept

The duty of a business enterprise to respect human rights – both directly and through its supply chains – is expressed in the Guiding Principles as a "responsibility"; the term "obligation" or even "duty" is only ever used in connection with states. The Special Representative appears to take a narrow, positivist view of human rights law in that respect. Nevertheless, the acknowledgment of a responsibility of business enterprises to respect human rights, separate from and in parallel to the state's human rights obligations, implicitly accepts that human rights can only be meaningfully protected if the duty to respect human rights applies to businesses as well as states; it is just the legal nature of the duty and the method of its enforcement that needs to be resolved. Indeed, there appears to be an emerging consensus accepting a duty to respect human rights on the part of corporations from quarters that were recently skeptical of such a concept. Prominent business organizations endorsed the business duty to respect when it was included in the Special Representative's 2008 report (IOE, ICC and BIAC 2008), while the resolution of the Human Rights Council that extended Ruggie's mandate as Special Representative following the 2008 report included a paragraph in its preamble, "[e]mphasizing that transnational corporations and other business enterprises have a responsibility to respect human rights" (Human Rights Council 2007, preamble, para. 5), treating that proposition as accepted fact.

The duty to respect human rights as articulated by the Special Representative encompasses the full range of human rights contained in the ICCPR, ICESCR, UDHR and the fundamental labor rights declared by the ILO, as well as the potential to include other standards that may be relevant in a particular context, such as the principles of international humanitarian law in a conflict zone (Ruggie 2011, para. 12). The source of the "responsibility," though, is never articulated. Is it an indirect derivative of the obligations on states contained in the corresponding treaties; a moral but not a legal obligation; or something else?[6] The Guiding Principles assert

had been adapted from Ruggie himself in the context of the Global Compact: Interim Report of the Special Representative of the Secretary-General on the Issue of Human Rights and Transnational Corporations and Other Business Enterprises, UN Doc E/CN.4/2006/97 (February 22, 2006), paras. 40 and 67. Without using the "sphere of activity and influence label" or the term "obligation," the Guiding Principles have now come full circle from the Special Representative's 2006 criticism.

[6] In his 2006 report, Interim Report of the Special Representative of the Secretary-General on the Issue of Human Rights and Transnational Corporations and Other Business Enterprises, UN Doc E/CN.4/2006/97 (February 22, 2006), para. 60, Ruggie criticized the Sub-Commission Norms for using state-based human rights treaties as the method of identifying the content of the relevant norms: "What the [Sub-Commission] Norms have done, in fact, is to take existing State-based human rights instruments and simply assert that many of their provisions are now binding on corporations as well. But that assertion itself has little authoritative basis in international law – hard, soft or otherwise."

that an enterprise's "responsibility to respect human rights is distinct from issues of legal liability and enforcement, which remain defined largely by national law provisions in relevant jurisdictions" (Ruggie 2011, commentary to para. 12). It would still be possible to have a legal obligation, even if there was no existing mechanism to enforce it: obligation is a matter of legal content, while enforcement is a matter of mechanics. Such a situation is hardly unknown in international law, including some instances when new mechanisms have been created to enforce pre-existing obligations, most famously in the trials of Nuremberg.

That brings us to the third prong of the Special Representative's framework: access to remedy. The Special Representative recognizes that access to a meaningful remedy for a violation and an avenue to assert such a claim is a vital requirement for the realization of human rights. Here, responsibility in the Guiding Principles is placed squarely on the state as part of its duty to protect human rights (Ruggie 2011, para. 25).

Accountability mechanisms

Once it is accepted that the realization of human rights requires corporations to be held responsible for their impact on human rights, the question turns to how that should be done. Primarily, the answer will be through existing channels of municipal law. Laws relating to labor standards, environmental standards, personal injury, land tenure and many other subjects can be invoked to hold corporations responsible. It is possible for home states to apply those laws extraterritorially to prevent corporations based in their own states from committing or assisting human rights abuses elsewhere, although that remains relatively rare.

On the other hand, international law contains the content of human rights norms, but not the forum for enforcing them. It is for this reason that so much attention has been given to the Alien Tort Claims Act (ATCA) of the United States. A 1789 provision, the ATCA potentially provides an opportunity to litigate breaches of international legal norms for which no international forum currently exists. There has been a series of cases arguing over what the precise human rights obligations of corporations are under the "law of nations" and precisely when the ATCA will grant US courts the jurisdiction to hear claims of the violation of such obligations (*Doe* v. *Unocal* 248 F 3d 915 (9th Cir 2001); *Presbyterian Church of Sudan* v. *Talisman Energy* 582 F 3d 244 (2nd Cir 2009); *Sosa* v. *Alvarez-Machain* 542 US 692 (2004)). To date, no case alleging human rights violations by a corporation has made it all the way to a merits decision in favor of the plaintiff, so the ATCA remains purely a theoretical enforcement avenue. At the time of writing, the US Supreme Court has agreed to hear argument on the scope of the ATCA in the context of corporate human rights obligations in the case of *Kiobel* v. *Royal Dutch/Shell*.[7] A discussion of the ATCA jurisprudence is beyond the scope of the present chapter. It serves here merely as an illustration of a potential enforcement mechanism that is disconnected from the body of law in which the norms can be identified.

Another avenue for human rights accountability in the context of multinational enterprises is the range of "soft law" mechanisms available in the international arena. They are labeled soft law because they lack coercive enforcement characteristic of court judgments. The OECD Guidelines on Multinational Enterprises are the best known example (OECD 2011), applying to all corporations operating in or based in OECD countries. The 2011 revision of the OECD Guidelines added a chapter dedicated to human rights standards, alongside other matters such as corruption, taxation and environmental protection, which enterprises must abide by in their transnational operations. Affected individuals may complain to the National Contact Point of a participating country if the standards are breached. The National Contact Point then mediates the dispute, but cannot impose remedies on an enterprise against its will.

There are also a number of sector-specific codes in place, such as the Voluntary Principles on Security and Human Rights (www.voluntaryprinciples.org/, as at 24 October 2011), which apply to the extractive industries. Such "soft law" regimes are necessarily limited to the sector they purport to cover. They are further limited in terms of their enforceability by the scope of the powers exercised by the body that oversees the regime. In some cases, enforcement comes as a result of contract law, for instance by embedding human rights standards in the loan agreement in the case of development finance. In others, the remedy will amount to an unenforceable recommendation.

A final possibility is that new mechanisms may be created to enforce human rights obligations against non-state actors. These could be domestic mechanisms implementing international standards, or expanded jurisdiction of an international mechanism that is currently state-focused, such

---

[7] The questions presented to the Supreme Court in *Kiobel* are: "(1) Whether the issue of corporate civil tort liability under the Alien Tort Statute, 28 U.S.C. § 1350, is a merits question or instead an issue of subject matter jurisdiction; and (2) whether corporations are immune from tort liability for violations of the law of nations such as torture, extrajudicial executions or genocide or may instead be sued in the same manner as any other private party defendant under the ATS for such egregious violations."

as the various regional human rights courts and commissions. Or (far less realistically, but theoretically possible), a new international forum could be established to hear and resolve disputes involving human rights violations by non-state actors.

Conclusion

Human rights derive from the inherent dignity of human beings, and the international law of human rights is intended to ensure the protection and realization of those rights in all aspects of life, including those aspects touched by the global economy. It has long been accepted that human rights are capable of being infringed by many different types of entity – the state, other individuals, corporations, institutions – but only some of those can realistically be held accountable through the state.

While the identity of the transgressor makes no difference from the perspective of the rights-holder, it makes the world of difference in identifying the corresponding obligation-holder and the scope of its legal responsibility. Violation by a state organ or by an entity within the jurisdiction of a single state is covered by traditional state obligations to respect and protect human rights. In the case of other entities, including multinational corporations and international institutions, human rights accountability has been problematic.

If human rights law is to achieve its intended purpose rather than retreat into legal formalism, it must be given effect in situations where the harm caused is not the act of a state. There is an emerging consensus that business has a responsibility to respect human rights, independent from the obligations of states, evidenced by the Special Representative's Guiding Principles and the IFC's Performance Standards, discussed above, among other developments.

The best way to answer the hard question of what human rights require of the global economy is to separate it into two limbs: a normative limb and an operational limb. From a normative perspective, there is a growing acceptance that human rights must be respected by everyone, resulting in a universal obligation to respect human rights, existing concurrently with the state's obligation to respect, protect and fulfill human rights within its territory and jurisdiction. From an operational perspective, however, there is no comprehensive system for enforcing such obligations, only a patchwork of methods with limited scope and force. We are therefore close to a consensus that all entities in the global economy must refrain from violating human rights in their operations, but, at present, the consequences for failing to do so are severely limited.

References

Agreement on Trade-Related Aspects of Intellectual Property Rights. Annex 1C to the *Marrakesh Agreement Establishing the World Trade Organization*, opened for signature April 15, 1994, 1869 UNTS 299 (entered into force January 1, 1995).

Alien Tort Claims Act. 28 U.S.C. § 1350 (1789).

Andriyanto, Heru. 2010. "Papua Tribe Files $32b Lawsuit Against Freeport." *Jakarta Globe*, March 8. Available at: www.thejakartaglobe.com/home/papua-tribe-fil es-32b-lawsuit-against-freeport/362747 (accessed November 4, 2011).

Asian Human Rights Commission. 2011. "Indonesia: Police in Timika Kill One Union Protestor and Injure others at Freeport." Urgent Appeal Case AHRC-UAC-204–2011, October 13. Available at: http://www.humanrights. asia/news/urgent-appeals/AHRC-UAC-204-2011#.TqwTqmwcjl4.gmail. (accessed November 4, 2011).

Chaffour, Jean-Pierre. 2005. "Institutional Accountability in pro-Human Rights Growth Policies: The IMF Perspective." Paper for Commission on Human Rights Social Forum, July 21, 2005. Available at: www2.ohchr.org/english/ issues/poverty/docs/3sfMrChauffourIMF.pdf (accessed November 10, 2011).

Clapham, Andrew. 2006. *Human Rights Obligations of Non-State Actors*. Oxford University Press.

Compa, Lance and Diamond, Stephen, eds. 1996. *Human Rights, Labor Rights and International Trade*. Philadelphia: University of Pennsylvania Press.

Darrow, Mac. 2003. *Between Light and Shadow: The World Bank, the International Monetary Fund and International Human Rights Law*. Oxford: Hart Publishing.

Doe v. *Unocal* 248 F 3d 915 (9th Cir 2001).

Garcia, Frank. 1999. "The Global Market and Human Rights: Trading Away the Human Rights Principle." *Brooklyn Journal of International Law* 25, 51–97.

General Agreement on Tariffs and Trade (GATT). Annex 1A to the *Marrakesh Agreement Establishing the World Trade Organization*, opened for signature April 15, 1994, 1867 UNTS 190 (entered into force January 1, 1995).

Gianviti, François. 2005. "Economic, Social, and Cultural Human Rights and the International Monetary Fund." In Philip Alston, ed., *Non-State Actors and Human Rights*. Oxford University Press, pp. 113–138.

Hannum, Hurst. 1995. "The Status of the Universal Declaration of Human Rights in National and International Law." *Georgia Journal of International and Comparative Law* 25, 287–397.

Howse, Robert. 1999. "The World Trade Organization and the Protection of Workers' Rights." *Journal of Small and Emerging Business Law* 3, 131–172.

Howse, Robert and Trebilcock, Michael. 1997. "The Free Trade – Fair Trade Debate: Trade, Labor and the Environment." In Jagdeep Bhandari and Alan Sykes, eds., *Economic Dimensions in International Law*. Cambridge University Press, pp. 186–247.

HRC (United Nations Human Rights Committee). 2004. *General Comment No. 31: The Nature of the General Legal Obligation imposed on States Parties to the Covenant*, CCPR/C/21/Rev.1/Add.13, May 26.

Human Rights Council. 2007. Resolution 5/1, "Institution Building of the United Nations Human Rights Council," UN doc A/HRC/RES/5/1 (June 18, 2007).

ICCPR (International Covenant on Civil and Political Rights) 1966. Opened for signature December 19, 1966, 999 U.N.T.S. 171 (entered into force March 23, 1976).

International Finance Corporation. 2012a. Performance Standard 1: Social and Environmental Assessment and Management Systems.

2012b. Performance Standard 5: Land Acquisition and Involuntary Resettlement.

International Organisation of Employers, International Chamber of Commerce, and Business and Industry Advisory Council to the OECD. 2008. *Joint Initial Views of the IOE, ICC and BIAC to the Eighth Session of the Human Rights Council on the Third Report of the Special Representative of the UN Secretary-General on Business and Human Rights*. Available at: www.biac.org/statements/investment/08–05_IOE-ICC-BIAC_letter_on_Human_Rights.pdf (accessed November 17, 2011).

Joseph, Sarah. 2011. *Blame it on the WTO? A Human Rights Critique*. Oxford University Press.

Lauterpacht, Hersch. 1948. Report to the International Law Association, *Human Rights, the Charter of the United Nations and the International Bill of the Rights of Man*, UN Doc. E/CN.4/89 (May 12, 1948).

Maastricht Guidelines on Violations of Economic, Social and Cultural Rights. 1998. *Human Rights Quarterly* 20, 691–705.

Marrakesh Agreement Establishing the World Trade Organization. 1994.

McBeth, Adam. 2006. "When Nobody Comes to the Party: Why Have No States Used the WTO Scheme for Compulsory Licensing of Essential Medicines?" *New Zealand Yearbook of International Law* 3, 69–100.

2009. "A Right by any other Name: The Evasive Engagement of International Financial Institutions with Human Rights." *George Washington International Law Review* 40, 1101–1156.

Mudho, Bernards. 2002. *Effects of Structural Adjustment Policies and Foreign Debt on the Full Enjoyment of Human Rights, Particularly Economic, Social and Cultural Rights*, report of the Independent Expert on the Effects of Structural Adjustment Policies and Foreign Debt, October 23, 2002, UN Doc. E/CN.4/2003/10.

Nichols, Philip. 1996. "Trade Without Values." *Northwest University Law Review* 90: 658–719.

OECD. 2011. *OECD Guidelines for Multinational Enterprises*.

Pogge, Thomas. 2008. *World Poverty and Human Rights: Cosmopolitan Responsibilities and Reforms*. Cambridge: Polity Press.

Presbyterian Church of Sudan v. Talisman Energy 582 F 3d 244 (2nd Cir 2009).

Ruggie, John. 2008. Report of the Special Representative of the Secretary-General on the Issue of Human Rights and Transnational Corporations and Other Business Enterprises, "Protect, Respect and Remedy: A Framework for Business and Human Rights," UN Doc. A/HRC/8/5 (April 7, 2008).

—— 2011. Report of the Special Representative of the Secretary-General on the Issue of Human Rights and Transnational Corporations and Other Business Enterprises, "Guiding Principles on Business and Human Rights: Implementing the United Nations 'Protect, Respect and Remedy' Framework," UN Doc. A/HRC/17/31 (March 21, 2011).

Schwelb, Egon. 1964. *Human Rights and the International Community: The Roots and Growth of the Universal Declaration of Human Rights, 1948–1963*. Chicago: Quadrangle Books.

Sosa v. Alvarez-Machain 542 US 692 (2004).

UNHCHR (United Nations High Commissioner for Human Rights). 2002. *Liberalization of Trade in Services and Human Rights*, UN Doc. E/CN.4/Sub.2/2002/9 (June 25, 2002).

United Nations. 1945. Charter of the United Nations.

—— 1990. *Draft United Nations Code of Conduct on Transnational Corporations*, UN Doc. E/1990/94 (1990 draft); UN Doc. E/1983/17/Rev.1, Annex II (1983 draft); 23 ILM 626.

United Nations Commission on Human Rights. 2005. *Human Rights Resolution 2005/69: Human Rights and Transnational Corporations and Other Business Enterprises*, UN ESCOR, 61st sess, 59th mtg, UN Doc. E/CN.4/RES/2005/69.

United Nations Sub-Commission on the Promotion and Protection of Human Rights. 2003. *Norms on the Responsibilities of Transnational Corporations and Other Business Enterprises with Regard to Human Rights*, UN Doc. E/CN.4/Sub.2/2003/12/Rev.2 (August 26, 2003).

Universal Declaration of Human Rights, G.A. Res. 217A (III), UN Doc. A/RES/217A (December 10, 1948).

Weiss, Friedl. 1998. "Internationally Recognized Labour Standards and Trade." In Friedl Weiss, ed., *International Economic Law with a Human Face*. The Hague: Kluwer, pp. 79–108.

Wolf, Martin. 2001. "What the World Needs from the Multilateral Trading System." In Gary Sampson, ed., *The Role of the World Trade Organization in Global Governance*. New York: United Nations University Press, pp. 183–208.

World Bank. 2011. www.worldbank.org (accessed November 15, 2011).

World Bank and IMF 2011. Poverty Reduction Strategy Papers, World Bank and IMF. Available at: www.imf.org/external/np/prsp/prsp.aspx (accessed November 15, 2011).

World Bank Compliance Advisor/Ombudsman. 2003. *Review of IFC's Safeguard Policies.*

World Conference on Human Rights. 1993. *Vienna Declaration and Programme of Action*, UN Doc. A/CONF.157/23 (July 12, 1993).

9 | Universal human rights in the global political economy

TONY EVANS

The post-World War II project for the protection of human rights, which features a growing body of international law and associated international institutions, is assumed to have changed the nature of sovereignty. While in the past is was accepted that how another state treated its citizens was of no concern to others, the creation of the international human rights regime meant that states could no longer claim legitimate sovereignty in the face of gross violations of human rights. In short, and according to this view, to past definitions of state sovereignty, which included the existence of a central government, the capacity to secure the borders of a particular territory and exclusive rights to the means of violence was added a good human rights record. The failure to embrace this addition brought the threat of delegitimization and exclusion from international society (Vincent 1986).

This model continues to inform the policies and practices of government and non-governmental organizations alike. However, the advent of new technology, particularly communications technology, has enabled the globalization of production, finance and exchange, creating social networks that challenge past understandings of community, sovereignty and authority. The increasing extent and intensity of networks for material exchange on a global scale is paralleled by networks for social exchange, heightening awareness of alternative social orders and ways of conceptualizing human rights, duty and dignity. Although research into globalization has exposed weaknesses in claims for the survival of an international order, solutions for questions of human rights continue to be sought in an international regime built upon notions of the state, sovereignty, and international law that remain "steadfastly unaffected" (Camilleri and Falk 1992, 1).

The hard question now facing the postwar project for the promotion and protection of human rights is "can the international human rights regime, and its associated normative foundations, be sustained in an increasingly globalized socioeconomic order?"

Human rights in global context

It is often acknowledged that the idea of human rights has a long and noble provenance, suggesting a dynamic discourse of challenge and counter-challenge, evolution, movement and process. However, the birth of the contemporary international human rights regime marks a period of stasis: a point of arrival in the history of humankind. While in the past the idea of human rights was seen as subversive – a threat *to* the dominant order – in the postwar era human rights assumed a central normative role *within* the dominant order (Stammers 1993). The move to achieve this was begun during postwar negotiations to create a new world order; an order that envisaged the full and unfettered engagement of the individual under global free market conditions (Evans 1996). Processes of deep reflection and critique that marked earlier times were replaced by a universal certainty that the idea of human rights was now mature and complete. All that remained was to create a corpus of international law in support of negative freedoms commensurate with free market activity. The popular model for the history of the modern human rights movement (idea-standard setting-implementation) reflects this approach.

This act of "closure" brought to an end the multifaceted discourse on human rights of previous periods. The language of law replaced that of philosophy and disputation. In place of the the rich debate characteristic of previous periods, the postwar idea of human rights became "driven by a totalitarian or totalizing impulse" that sought to transform all societies to "fit a particular blueprint" that offered a moral framework for building and strengthening the capitalist global political economy (Mutua 2002, 13). The postwar human rights regime can therefore be understood through its contribution to constructing global systems of production, finance and exchange that find in human rights the moral foundation for a particular kind of global, free market, economic order.

Although there was some resistance to establishing an international human rights regime built upon foundations developed by Hobbes, Locke and Kant, the postwar order was dominated by Western, capitalist states. In particular, socialist and less developed states sought to include economic and social rights on an equal basis as liberal civil and political rights. However, to include this set of rights in any legally binding agreement was seen as a threat to a set of values intended to legitimate free market individualism: an attempt to establish "socialism by treaty" (Eisenhower 1963; Kirkup and Evans 2009). The context of the Cold War did, however, provide capitalist states with a political rationale to give some attention to economic and social rights or risk driving many less-developed countries into alliances with the USSR. In response to this potential problem, capitalist economies sought to label economic and social rights "aspirations," to be honored when economic conditions permitted, rather than immediately, as demanded for civil and political rights. In this way, capitalist states sought to embrace economic and social rights through international law, while the politics of rights ensured only those rights that supported free markets were actively promoted (Evans 1996).

With the end of the Cold War, many believed that the promise of human rights as civil and political rights would be realized. The threat of nuclear war between East and West, which had dominated the international agenda since the end of World War II, often leaving human rights at the margins, was now gone. The disintegration of the Soviet Union was portrayed as providing the long-awaited opportunity to proclaim human rights as the "idea of our time." Within the space opened by the post-Cold War era, many assumed that civil society organizations would flourish, creating new social networks devoted to exposing human rights violations wherever they occurred and thus enabling international society to fulfill its promise to promote and protect human rights. In future, it was argued, states would develop and exercise an ethical foreign policy guided by the values found in the human rights regime (Committee 1998).

Human rights and world order

These expectations did not take full account of shifts in the global order, from a state system to one described by the term globalization. Globalization theory argues that the socioeconomic core and periphery cut across existing national boundaries, creating new patterns of economic growth and consumption over which the state has diminishing authority (Gill 1995). While in previous periods of history the state could adopt national strategies for ordering the national economy, including the nationalization of key industries, today the shift to globalization means that states "by and large play the role of agencies of the global economy, with the task of adjusting national economic policies and practices to the perceived exigencies of global economic liberalism" (Cox 1999, 12).

An ideology of modernity underpins the shift to a global economy, which rests upon the twin goals of economic growth and development, defined as global capital accumulation and consumption (Thomas 2000). The central means for achieving these goals is strategic planning at the global level, global management and the creation of global regimes and agreements. Ideological convergence has the effect of homogenizing and limiting the policy choices of governments. Global management requires adherence to rules that ensure all countries conform to a single development model so that the "hidden hand" of the market can operate efficiently. Consequently, responsibility for defining and implementing the rules for international action shift away from the state to international institutions and regimes (Chinkin 1998). Global governance replaces national government where policy bears on processes designed to further the smooth, efficient maintenance of the global economy.

The transformation of global politics and its consequences has been noted many times in the literature. Panitch, for example, argues that the primary function of the state is to create and manage a global order that supports the interests of global capital, not the rights and welfare of citizens (Panitch 1995). In the most recent stage of modernization, which is founded upon the goals of capitalist economic growth and development, globalization seeks to adapt all political and economic institutions as "instruments for achieving that goal" (Camilleri and Falk 1992, 4). All rules that govern the global order are thus shifted toward creating and maintaining market-orientated growth. While the power of capital has never been constrained within the state, under conditions of globalization the state assumes the central role of administering the capitalist global order. Capitalism may therefore be "fruitfully understood as a transnational social system which has encompassed the system of sovereign states as well as the seemingly discrete sphere of capitalist economy" (Rupert 2003).

In this view of globalization the maintenance of the global economy takes priority over the national economy. The state loses its role as the center of authority through which citizens express their preferences, including those preferences associated with economic and social well-being. The authority previously associated with the state is assumed by international institutions and organizations, where the tasks for rule creation and implementation are re-focused. While governments may continue to engage in international relations, governance is conducted by a group of formal and informal organizations, the "nébuleuse," charged with the task of providing and maintaining the conditions for capitalist expansion (Cox 1995). The move to gain legitimacy for rules that free global capital from all spatial and temporal constraints is significant because "all the noted texts [of international law], confer or hope to bestow a number of rights on transnational capital [but] … impose no corresponding duties" (Chimni 1999, 40). The link between government and the governed is therefore weakened, if not replaced, by new forms of governance related to the expansion of the global economy (Huysmans 1995). Over time, the decline in political participation, coupled with the maintenance of an order in which the governed are increasingly objectified, ensures that people become more accountable to remote centers of authority, rather than those centers being accountable to people.

A recent example of this is seen in the case of Portugal's 2011 economic crisis. Following the rejection of an austerity plan presented by Prime Minister Jose Socrates, new elections were called. During the campaign period, negotiations continued with the European Union and the International Monetary Fund. The outcome of these negotiations was an austerity plan that did not differ significantly from that rejected earlier. The election therefore did not offer voters alternative choices that connected popular will to political power, a principle that should be at the center of any democratic system. Rather, the electorate was asked to ratify decisions taken beyond the reach of their own national political system. Although the populace was urged to turn out to vote in the mood of national unity, and warned that not to participate negated the right to complain about what actions political leaders took, the turnout of 58 percent (the lowest since Portugal became a democracy) reflects an understanding that governments decide very little under conditions of globalization (Younge 2011). In this way, politics is no longer about alternative ways of living, but about who is best equipped to manage the "irresistible" and "inevitable" progress of globalization (Blair 1998), which is not presented as a political choice but as a "fact" (Clinton 1998). All that is left is "personality" politics that signal the "death of the citizen as the subject of politics, thus the death of politics as the forum for active citizens, and by implication the end of democracy" (Cox 1997, 64).

This raises important questions about changes in social and political identity. The social dynamics of globalization have caused a breakdown in the values that describe traditional ideas of identity within a specific community and the rights and duties that are embodied in community. As an integral component of the shift to globalization, human rights seek to establish an identity that pays no regard to traditional social mores or concepts of moral legitimacy. In place of claims of difference, defined by social rules and characteristics for expected behavior, human rights assert universal social attributes that are claimed to describe all societies (Lukes 1993). Consequently, there is an irresolvable tension between the normative demands of the emergent globalized world order and conformity to traditional ways of thinking, knowing and acting (Fraser 2000): a schizophrenic tendency that involves a breakdown in the relation between thought, emotion and behavior. As the UN Secretary-General Kofi Annan once noted, the crisis of identity makes us "vulnerable to a backlash from all the 'isms' of our post-cold-war world: protectionism, populism, nationalism, ethnic chauvinism, fanaticism, and terrorism" (Annan 1999).

A failed regime

Amnesty International's 2008 annual report asserts that little by way of substance has been achieved during the decades of the post-Cold War human rights regime. The report acknowledges the "progress" achieved in developing legally binding treaties and global and regional organizations for the protection of human rights, but concludes that "the fact remains that injustice, inequality and impunity are still the hallmark of our world today" (Amnesty International 2008). The report notes that while national and international leaders are prone to offer encouraging rhetoric to reassure publics that everything is being done to protect human rights, and never hesitate to associate themselves with human rights declarations and international law, political and economic interests take priority over all else. In the age of globalization, the report notes, the evolution of the formal machinery for the protection of human rights is rarely matched by a commitment to identify causes and undertake actions. Amnesty concludes, therefore, that "[w]orld leaders owe an apology for failing to deliver on promises of justice and equality in the Universal Declaration of Human Rights" (Amnesty International 2008).

Following over 60 years of painstaking work to develop law and global institutions for the promotion and protection of human rights for many this might seem a remarkable and misguided conclusion. However, given the transformation of the global political economy outlined earlier, it is perhaps unsurprising. Although human rights are often claimed as the idea of our time, a set of values that act as a guide for creating solidarity within global community, economic globalization is altering the context in which the postwar idea was created and implemented. What are the causes of this failure?

First, as globalization impacts upon the moral precepts that play upon individual and group identity, signifiers of the the past seem less relevant. Confidence in concepts like sovereignty, domestic jurisdiction, even central government, which in the past provided important icons for the construction of identity, are increasingly questioned. In the early decades of the twenty-first century, for example, capturing the essential character of sovereignty remains illusive and "subject to renegotiation by the play of political forces, moral attitudes, and prevailing perceptions" (Falk 2000, 70). For internal sovereignty, claims that the state and community coincide, and that the state therefore represents the people within its territory, overlooks the historic record of refugees, illegal aliens and excluded groups who do not attract the same status within the state. That domestic community is always in flux, and the range of authority that the community exercises is always unsettled, makes it difficult to define membership of the state (Weber 1985). Under conditions of globalization, complexity is further increased by the formation of new social networks possessed of loyalties that do not focus on the state but, rather, on membership of other communities, like transnational corporations, terrorist organizations and interest groups (Woodiwiss 1998). The earlier discussion on the consequences of globalization sought to show how the move from an international system, characterized by competing national economies, to a single global economy is indicative of compromised external sovereignty.

The definition of human rights that provides the foundation for the international human rights regime is not immune to these processes. Amnesty's claim that the international human rights regime has failed, even though much political and legal energy continues to be invested in its operation, suggests that existing dominant interests are served by its continuation. The "end of history" thesis, which proclaims that in human rights we have discovered a final truth, must surely be doubted in the face of transformative forces associated with economic globalization. Rather than leaving "humanity stuck at the door of liberalism, unable to go forward or imagine a post-liberal society" (Mutua 2002), globalization offers a field for struggle, resistance and contestation on the future of moral thinking.

International law and globalization

The focus on international law as the central institution for promoting and protecting human rights should also be interrogated. Summing up the historic movement of human rights from idea to international legal regime, Gearty offers a fourfold model. First, politicized exchanges on the nature of rights embrace a generality of rights talk that cannot be captured through the precise language of law. Debates on rights therefore include many areas of social and economic life, presenting difficult problems when creating legislation. Second, if legal technicalities can be solved, and legislation is eventually generated, the custodianship of human rights moves from the political to the legal sphere of authority. Third, the authority and high regard given to the law in liberal society, coupled with the centrality of negative freedoms associated with liberal ideology, provide a focus that attracts greater interest in rights claims. In effect, human rights law becomes the "basic" law of liberal society. Fourth, following Hobbes, Locke and Kant, who saw rights as an antecedent truth, Gearty notes that the legislation of human rights assumes the mantle of a supra-political idea and thus an idea beyond political critique. Through this process "our core or essential human rights are made up of a number of rights that people have which *precedes* politics or which are *above* politics" (Gearty 2006, 72).

In short, although the idea of human rights has its origins within the sociopolitical sphere, following the creation of international law the idea assumes the character of an unquestionable "settled norm" (Frost 1996). To adopt this view serves only to reinforce the argument that the final destiny of humankind is near. The argument that social, political and economic dynamics drive the social construction of ideas must therefore be rejected. Consequently, the "discovery" of human rights and subsequent expression of those claims through international law performs an act of "closure." No matter the dynamic of history, international human rights law is claimed as the expression of transcendental truths.

However, given the shift toward greater levels of globalization during recent decades, the conclusion that international law does, in fact, capture the abiding truths of human rights seems misguided. If the international no longer possesses the authority it was once imagined to possess, because power no longer resides exclusively within the state, the much vaunted "progress" in human rights seems misplaced. As Gearty notes, the "inability of this branch of international law to make itself felt on the ground is sometimes so complete that one is left wondering why it is called law at all" (Gearty 2006, 92).

Moreover, moral and ethical ideas associated with the dynamics of globalization have established guarantees for the primacy of economic growth and development by "declaring individual (and by extension, corporate) rights as inherent, inalienable, and universal" (Teeple 2005, 17), no matter the consequences for community, identity and the social welfare of many groups. Within this new order, human rights talk has become an ever-present aspect of global politics and international relations but only rarely are rights claims allowed to stand in the way of economic interests, no matter international human rights law.

Socioeconomic rights

Among the most important issues within struggles over human rights is the contested status of economic and social rights. As the reach of economic globalization offers the potential for creating a global society based upon mutual concern for political and economic security, the claim that economic and social rights are merely aspirations seems increasingly difficult to sustain. Equally difficult to sustain is a definition of development understood simply as industrialization, Westernization and economic growth, rather than in broader terms that include the necessary conditions to live a dignified and fulfilling life, welfare security, and political participation. As the UN Sub Commission report on human rights under conditions of globalization noted, the narrow approach to rights provides a rationale for corporate investment, which is for profit, rather than to assist in guaranteeing the fulfillment of civil, political, economic and social rights (Oloka-Onyango and Udagana 2000). Although the state's interest may include health, education, access to fresh water, nutrition and housing, these are not central to corporate interests. The assumption that globalization will inevitably encourage greater interest in achieving human rights thus overlooks the tension between contradictory rights claims. As the UNDP observed, "little in the current global order binds states and global actors to promoting human rights globally" (UNDP 2000).

According to many critics, globalization provides a socioeconomic context in which the protection of human rights, particularly social and economic rights, is less secure than in the past. This is because globalization structures the transfer of wealth from the poor to the rich, exacerbating existing inequalities within and between classes, rewarding capital at the expense of labor, and creating far more losers than winners (George 1999). Against this is the claim that globalization opens many more opportunities to initiate policies and programs for bringing down the 1.4 billion people currently living on less than $1.25 USD a day (World Bank 2005). However, following an extensive review of the major studies devoted to income inequality conducted over the last two decades, Anand concludes that attempts to decrease the gap between rich and poor has achieved, at best, patchy results (Anand 2008). Furthermore, what little success may have been achieved is largely as a result of economic growth in Asia. Many of the UN Millennium Development Goals, for example, are seriously behind schedule and may run into even greater difficulties during the current period of global economic crisis (World Bank 2005, 2009).

Following this, the foundational assumption that violations of human rights are always the responsibility of an individual perpetrator overlooks the possibility that the cause of many violations can be found in the socio-economic structures in which peoples must live their lives. Under the consensus on rights that support the practices of economic globalization, which find formal expression in international human rights law, just as rights reside with the individual so it follows that responsibility for violating rights also rests with the individual. Drawing on the Judeo-Christian notion of "sin," those who violate human rights are wholly responsible for their actions. Accordingly, the individual is free to act as he or she wills but remains accountable for all their actions, including violations of human rights (Galtung 1994). This approach is reflected in the Rome Statute, which created the International Criminal Court (UN 1998). It is rare to find an acknowledgment that the social, economic and political structures in which people conduct their daily existence have any significance when attempting to discover the causes of human rights violations. While there may be many examples of state leaders and officials violating human rights, many other violations flow from commercial and financial activity, largely conducted within the accepted normative structures of globalization (Ratner 2001). The global trade in shrimps offers a good example here (EJF 2003). Put simply, the notion of individual responsibility masks the potential for exploring structural violations of human rights, violations that are attributable to the emerging structures of economic globalization.

Structural causes of violations are confirmed by the report of the Sub-Commission on the Promotion and Protection of Human Rights, *The Realization of Economic, Social and Cultural Rights: Globalization and its Impact on the Full Enjoyment of Human Rights*. There is, the report states, a "new orthodoxy or ethos about the economic dimensions of globalization that exalts it above all other human values or phenomena, indeed even above the basic conditions of human beings themselves" (Oloka-Onyango and Udagana 2000). The report goes on to argue that the spread, depth and strength of this new ethical ethos acts to mask many of the causes of violations of human rights, particularly where economic restructuring, the move to the production of export goods, and financial liberalization are policy aims. While the report acknowledges that the creation of international institutions to support and promote economic globalization have benefited the material lives of some, little attention has been given to the negative effects that are also present, including violations of human rights.

To reinforce this point, it should be noted that the World Trade Organization's (WTO) founding instruments make only oblique reference to human rights. Although the rules of the WTO assume equality of bargaining power between members, the Sub-Commission report asserts that countries most vulnerable to trade related human rights violations possess the weakest voice. Furthermore, the rules of the WTO overlook the economic and political influence of powerful transnational enterprises, which control many of the most important global markets. The world trade in bananas offers an insight here (Chapman 2009). Within this context, so the report argues, the notion of free trade on which the rules are constructed is largely a fallacy. Consequently, the Sub-Commission's report concludes that the rules of the WTO are at best unfair and at worst prejudiced by omission. Rather than giving urgent attention to the human rights consequences that the conditions of globalization bring, the rules of the WTO reflect dominant corporate economic interests that continue to monopolize the arena of international trade (Taylor and Thomas 1999). Accordingly, the measures pursued by the WTO – as do those of the World Bank and the IMF – undermine the efforts of global human rights institutions, international human rights law, and the work of progressive advocates of socioeconomic rights. The silence over the relationship between trade liberalization and economic and social rights can therefore be explained in terms of dominant interests. Even when the linkage between the expansion of global trade and human rights is made to civil and political rights, "it is fraught with inconsistencies and national subjective interests" (Oloka-Onyango and Udagana 2000).

Moreover, programs for modernization are always aimed at particular types of development that do not necessarily benefit the socioeconomic needs of the people. Indeed, the human rights consequences of many development programs are known well before projects begin. The construction of dams to generate electricity and provide irrigation, for instance, does not necessarily generate jobs suitable for indigenous populations, overrides the democratic wishes of the people, "snuffs out separate cultural identities," degrades the environment and provides economic growth "where the benefits are seized by the rich" (UNDP 1995). Although modernization can lead to greater national wealth, this is often at the expense of violating the political, civil, social and economic rights of those already at the margins of society.

While globalization theory acknowledges that the development of a global economy is not a new phenomenon (Scholte 2000), the introduction of new technology, and in particular information and communication technology, which facilitates the organization of production and finance on a global scale, accelerates processes of change associated with social integration and disintegration, inclusion and exclusion. Access to these technologies has nurtured the formation of new transnational classes whose identities, loyalties and social bonds owe more to the global political economy than to geographically bound community, the state or national identity (van der Pijl 1998). These new global social formations present a challenge to the beliefs and values upon which traditional notions of community are built, including existing understandings of rights and duties.

On the other hand, this same technology is available to those who seek to mount resistance to forms of modernization that violate human rights, destroy the social and cultural fabric of people's lives, and bring immiseration to may millions of people.

The potential of these new networks inspires a move toward reconceptualizing existing forms of social and political organization within the context of a global community, rather than a community of independent sovereign states. Such a move would include a reconceptualization of human rights, taking account of voices from diverse social and political cultures, rather than doggedly asserting the norms associated with the past world order, which is seen as the product of a particular worldview and set of interests (Gill 2002). However, despite the many changes in the global political context that have taken place during the 60 years since the UDHR was created, proponents of the extant human rights regime continue to address the issue as though little has changed. In light of shifting relations of power, in particular the rise of Asian economic interests, this position may become untenable in the near future.

Resistance to globalization

There has already been some recognition of the need to reassess our current thinking on democracy and rights. One of the most well-known is the proposal to develop "international citizenship" designed to overcome the democratic deficit brought by the increasing authority of international institutions and corporate interests (Linklater 1992). This is necessary, it is argued, because while in the past national populations could hope to withhold their consent from decisions made by these institutions and organizations, today this is less the case, leaving state citizens unable to control their collective lives (Linklater 1998), as the earlier example of Portugal illustrates (Evans 2000).

The potential for resistance has not escaped the attention of those whose interests are closest to the center of economic globalization. To minimize the danger of destabilizing revolution springing from the ranks of what Cox

has referred to as "superfluous workers," the institutions of global governance have followed a twin track policy of "poor relief" and "riot control."
Humanitarian assistance (poor relief), which is the focus for the United
Nations and many international non-governmental organizations, domi-
nates the agenda aimed at redressing the wrongs people suffer as a consequence of economic globalization. In cases where this approach fails to
satisfy the disaffected, where social and political destabilization looms, "riot
control" is deployed in the form of police and military force, often with the
tacit consent of an international community that fears economic collapse
as a consequence of resistance. The violation of civil and political rights is
thus justified when the failure to acknowledge economic and social rights
causes social unrest. Taken together, this dual approach helps to "sustain
the emerging social structure of the world by minimizing the risk of chaos
in the bottom layer" (Cox 1997, 58).

Through this process, the "superfluous" are stigmatized for being responsible for all the ills in the world, including their own poverty, overpopula-
tion, pandemics, environmental degradation, drug trafficking, child labor,
terrorism, urban violence, populations movements and crime (Alves 2000).
The state of permanent fear that pervades those who can look forward to
a life of full employment stimulates the demand for ever more stringent
penalties for transgressions, no matter how minor, and increases levels of
intolerance that threaten to reverse decades of achievement to secure civil,
political, social and economic rights.

This is further emphasized when reflecting on the virtue of toleration.
Although toleration is often emphasized as a central virtue of the liberal
world order, it is not exercised when liberalism's core values themselves are
challenged (Evans 2011). Those who fail to embrace liberal values, including the idea of a society constructed upon individualism and a particular
conception of rights, are treated as outsiders. In accordance with liberal
principles, toleration of alternative social formations can be exercised only
in as far as action does not follow word. In this way, the move to a global political economy, which is legitimated by claims for individual human
rights and freedoms, has seen the creation of a regime for supporting particular interests rather than the rights of all. Although one objection to this
might be that some liberals do acknowledge the need to exercise toleration
of undemocratic liberal norms found in many cultural traditions, this raises
difficult questions about rights defined as possessions we all have by virtue
of being human.

Although this view benefits those whose interests lay in maintaining
order within the existing structures of globalization (Salmi 1993), because

it deflects attention from structural violations, it confuses the sites of violations with the causes of violations. Although this has been illustrated above during the discussion on the WTO, a further example is seen in the conditionalities imposed on borrowing countries by the World Bank (Brodnig 2005; Howse and Mutua 2000). Under conditions of globalization, the decisions of international financial institutions, international corporations and international organizations, which increasingly shape peoples lives, are more concerned with global planning than with local consequences (Giddens 1990). Democracy becomes little more than ritual as decision-making is decoupled from people's lives. But if the purpose of human rights is to guarantee the freedoms necessary for the individual to participate fully in economic, social and political life, it is necessary also to create and maintain an order that enables political participation in decisions beyond current state borders. However, the aim of the current human rights regime is to provide moral foundations for free market principles, principles that might be open to rejection in any system that moved toward democratizing the institutions of global governance.

The future for human rights

Where the global human rights regime brought "closure" to historic debates over what we mean by universal human rights, including the question of whether a society built on duty would produce a fairer and more egalitarian social order, economic globalization has created the conditions for further dialogue, discourse and renegotiation. If the claim that ethical and moral values are constructed within historical communities is apposite, then we should acknowledge the need to reignite debates over what we mean by human rights. At the least, we should interrogate the old categories of international political thought, investigate the construction of identity and community in a globalized order, and question existing distinctions between domestic and international politics, rights and duties. Indeed, the shift from an international order represented by discrete state communities to that of a global order represented by a complex of non-territorial socioeconomic relations offers an opportunity to develop a new normative order forged from what Parekh has referred to as a vague but unmistakable sense of a global community (Parekh 2005). To achieve this move would, however, require us to recognize that the ethical and moral dimensions peculiar to the past state-centric order may not fit with the new. In other words, the values and principles developed during the past period, in which the human rights regime was negotiated and agreed, may no longer be relevant to the present.

The conclusion that the human rights regime reflects a particular historic socioeconomic configuration, which is now in decline, leaves critics in the uncomfortable position of challenging one of the most totemic and emblematic symbols of what it means to be "civilized" in the postwar world. If human rights offers a site for contestation under conditions of globalization, it is necessary to develop an account that explains the (re-)emergence of social, political, economic and cultural critique of rights. In itself, this will not lead to rational answers or a program for action that will move us toward the conditions for human freedom, but it will provide the space for engaging in a discourse between the subjects of rights in response to the new dynamics of the current period (Chesterton 1998). To accept this view is to accept that the global human rights regime represents a particular view of rights and how to implement them, and that the contemporary global injunction to protect human rights is contingent upon historical contexts.

The motive for engaging in critiques of human rights is that we stand in a variety of relationships with others – sister, colleague, neighbor, business associate, friend, religious community, etc. – relationships that are regulated by particular norms describing particular rights and duties. To act morally is to recognize these norms and respect them. Although there may be little difficulty in accepting this formulation as a central characteristic of community, how we treat the "other" – those who we encounter outside our own recognizable community – presents a problem. Once encounters with the "other" become regular and frequent, a hallmark of globalization, the question of our moral responsibilities toward them arises. Can we treat them as we will, exploit them, and continue to engage in a global economy structured in ways that lead to the obliteration of existing traditions, communities and cultures (Parekh 2005)? While such contacts are not a new phenomenon, the intensity and reach of economic globalization exposes all communities to the politics of difference in ways that call for new reflections upon rights and duties. For example, under conditions of globalization, the very idea of the "other" in the context of national or regional community would seem to have less meaning than it did in the past.

Changes in world order since the creation of the global human rights regime, particularly the shift to ever greater levels of economic integration, which leaves no society untouched, provide a very different context in which rights talk is conducted today from that in the past. The global, regional and local institutions created for the protection of human rights were, and remain, largely built upon an understanding of rights that reflects a past period. The failure to grasp the idea of human rights as process, and to continue to cling to notions of rights that served in the past, acts as a barrier to taking up new moral challenges that cannot be solved through outmoded precepts. As the technology associated with globalization makes assessable knowledge that awakens us to the suffering of others, including those who suffer as a consequence of socioeconomic planning that supports the material well-being of wealthy communities, an opportunity arises for us to reconsider our moral responsibilities, including rights and duties. Where this will lead remains unclear, but it may see the development of new concerns, not for the individual as reflected in the Universal Declaration, but for communities as they struggle for survival in the face of private interests.

To take up this challenge there is a need to understand moral and ethical issues by constructing a radical and continuous dialogue about the central assumptions upon which societal norms and values are built. This should be an inclusive discourse, accessed by all moral agents with an interest in interrogating established moral precepts and institutional machinery designed to protect societal values. Our failure to take this path assumes that we have reached some end-point that permits us to say, with certainty, that human beings are a finished product, fully formed in every aspect, including our moral values. Instead, society is constantly undergoing change, refinement, reconstruction and transformation, making all our efforts to define our essential humanity tentative. What it means to be a rights bearing human being is socially constructed and reconstructed over the generations, which in the most recent formulation includes many ideas that are peculiar to the age, for example, the individual, choice and self-realization. While these ideas may have served during the past period there can be no certainty that such values will provide a secure foundation for notions of the moral life in a future world.

References

Alves, Jose A. Lindgren. 2000. "The Declaration of Human Rights in Postmodernity." *Human Rights Quarterly* 22:2, 478–500.

Amnesty International. 2008. Amnesty International Report 2008. London.

Anand, Sudhir. 2008. "What Do We Know About Global Income Inequality." *Journal of Economic Literature* 46:1, 57–94.

Annan, Kofi. 1999. Address to the World Economic Forum in Davos, January 31, 1999, edited by United Nations Secretary-General.

Blair, Tony. 1998. Speech at the WTO, May 19, 1998.

Brodnig, Gernot. 2005. "The World Bank and Human Rights: Mission Impossible?" Carr Centre for Human Rights Working Paper 21.

Camilleri, Joseph A. and Falk, Jim. 1992. *The End of Sovereignty? The Politics of a Shrinking and Fragmenting World.* Aldershot: Edward Elgar.

Chapman, Peter. 2009. *Bananas: How the United Fruit Company Shaped the World.* London: Canongate.

Chesterton, Simon. 1998. "Human Rights as Subjectivity: The Age of Rights and the Politics of Culture." *Millennium: Journal of International Studies* 27:1, 97–118.

Chimni, B.S. 1999. "Marxism and International Law." *Economic and Political Weekly* 34:6, 337–349.

Chinkin, Christine. 1998. "International Law and Human Rights." In T. Evans, ed., *Human Rights Fifty Years On: A Reappraisal.* Manchester University Press, pp. 105–126.

Clinton, Bill. 1998. Speech at the WTO.

Committee, F.A. 1998. *Foreign Policy and Human Rights.* London: House of Commons.

Cox, Robert. 1995. A Perspective on Globalization. In J.H. Mittelman, ed., *Globalization: Critical Reflections.* Boulder: Lynne Rienner, pp. 21–32.

   1997. "Democracy in Hard Times: Economic Globalization and the Limits to Liberal Democracy." In A. McGrew, ed., *The Transformation of Democracy.* Cambridge: Polity Press, pp. 49–72.

   1999. "Civil Society at the Turn of the Millennium: Prospects for an Alternative World Order." *Review of International Studies* 25:1, 3–28.

Eisenhower, Dwight D. 1963. *The White House Years: Mandate for Change – 1953–1956.* London: Heinemann.

EJF (Environmental Justice Foundation). 2003. *Smash & Grab: Conflict, Corruption and Human Rights Abuses in the Shrimp Farming Industry.* London: Environmental Justice Foundation.

Evans, Tony. 1996. *US Hegemony and the Project of Universal Human Rights.* Basingstoke: Macmillan.

   2000. "Citizenship and Human Rights in the Age of Globalization." *Alternatives* 25:4, 415–438.

   2011. *Human Rights in the Global Political Economy: Critical Processes.* London: Lynne Rienner.

Falk, Richard. 2000. *Human Rights Horizon: The Pursuit of Justice in a Globalizing World.* London: Routledge.

Fraser, Nancy. 2000. "Rethinking Recognition." *New Left Review* 3, 107–120.

Frost, Melvyn. 1996. *Ethics in International Relations: A Constitutive Theory.* Cambridge University Press.

Galtung, Johan. 1994. *Human Rights in Another Key.* Cambridge: Polity Press.

Gearty, Conor. 2006. *Can Human Rights Survive?* Cambridge University Press.

George, Susan. 1999. *The Lucano Report.* London: Pluto.

Giddens, Anthony. 1990. *Modernity and Self-Identity.* Cambridge: Polity Press.

Gill, Stephen. 1995. "Globalization, Market Civilisation, and Disciplinary Neoliberalism." *Millennium: Journal of International Studies* 24:3, 399–423.

2002. "Constitutionalizing Inequality and the Clash of Civilizations." *International Studies Review* 4:2, 47–65.

Howse, Robert and Mutua, Makau. 2000. *Protecting Human Rights in a Global Economy: Challenges for the World Trade Organization.* Montreal: Rights & Democracy.

Huysmans, Jef. 1995. "Post-Cold War Implosion and Globalization: Liberalism Running Past Itself." *Millennium: Journal of International Studies* 24:3, 471–487.

Kirkup, Alex and Evans, Tony. 2009. "The Myth of Western Opposition to Economic, Social, and Cultural Rights? A Reply to Whelan and Donnelly." *Human Rights Quarterly* 31:1, 221–238.

Linklater, Andrew. 1992. "What is a Good International Citizen?" In P. Keal, ed., *Ethics and Foreign Policy.* Canberra: Allen & Unwin, pp. 21–43.

1998. *The Transformation of Political Society.* Cambridge: Polity.

Lukes, Steven. 1993. "Five Fables About Human Rights." In Stephen Shute and Susan Hurley, eds., *On Human Rights: The Oxford Amnesty Lectures 1993.* New York: Basic Books, pp. 19–40.

Mutua, Makau. 2002. *Human Rights: A Political and Cultural Critique,* edited by B.B. Lockwood. Philadelphia: University of Pennsylvania Press.

Oloka-Onyango, J. and Udagana, Deepika. 2000. "The Realization of Economic, Social and Cultural Rights: Globalization and its Impact on the Full Enjoyment of Human Rights." Sub-Commission on the Promotion and Protection of Human Rights.

Panitch, Leo. 1995. "Rethinking the Role of the State." In J. Mittelman, ed., *Globalization: Critical Reflections.* Boulder: Lynne Rienner, pp. 83-116.

Parekh, Bhikhu. 2005. "Principles of a Global Ethic." In J. Eade and D. O'Byrne, eds., *Global Ethics and Civil Society.* Aldershot: Ashgate, pp. 15–33.

Ratner, Steven R. 2001. "Corporations and Human Rights: A Theory of Legal Responsibility." *Yale Law Journal* 111, 443–545.

Rupert, Mark. 2003. "Globalising Common Sense: A Marxian-Gramscian (Re)-Vision of the Politics of Governance and Resistance." *Review of International Studies* 29 (special issue), 181–198.

Salmi, J. 1993. *Violence and the Democratic State.* Oxford University Press.

Scholte, Jan Aart. 2000. *Globalization: A Critical Introduction.* Basingstoke: Palgrave.

Stammers, Neil. 1993. "Human Rights and Power." *Political Studies* XLI, 70–82.

Taylor, Annie and Thomas, Caroline, eds. 1999. *Global Trade and Global Social Issues.* London: Routledge.

Teeple, Gary. 2005. *The Riddle of Human Rights.* Canada: Garamond Press.

Thomas, Caroline. 2000. *Global Governance, Development and Human Security,* edited by C. Thomas. London: Pluto Press.

UN (United Nations). 1998. Rome Statute. UN Doc. A/Conf.183/9.

UNDP (United Nations Development Programme). 1995. Human Development Report 1995 – Gender and Human Development. Available at: http://hdr.undp.org/en/reports/global/hdr1995/.

2000. Human Development Report 2000 – Human Rights and Human Development. Oxford: United Nations Development Programme.

van der Pijl, Kees. 1998. Transnational Class and International Relations. London: Routledge.

Vincent, R.J. 1986. Human Rights and International Relations. Cambridge University Press.

Weber, Cynthia. 1985. Simulating Sovereignty. Cambridge University Press.

Woodiwiss, Anthony. 1998. Globalization, Human Rights and Labour Law in Pacific Asia. Cambridge University Press.

World Bank. 2005. Progress on the Millennium Development Goals: Reducing Poverty and Hunger. Available at: www.worldbank.org.

2009. World Bank Development Report 2009. Available at: www.worldbank.org.

Younge, Gary. 2011. "Ask Haitians whether Voters or Big Business Chose their Singing President." Guardian, July 4.

Human rights and global equal opportunity:
inclusion not provision

ANN E. CUDD

Introduction: equal opportunity and the challenge
of moral universalism

Political philosophers have long focused attention on the requirements of
a just domestic economic system, and one criterion consistently argued
for is equal opportunity in terms of education and employment. Roughly
speaking, the motivating intuition of the principle of equal opportunity is
that no one should be denied an important social opportunity on the basis
of a morally arbitrary feature about them. Although controversial or even
absurd when applied to some social opportunities, almost all agree that
there are some centrally important human activities that no one should be
denied access to within their society, such as equal opportunity to education or employment based on ability. Liberal societies typically codify this
in law, and social norms have come to reflect this principle of fairness and
equality.

Some philosophers have argued that the equal opportunity criterion
must be applied globally (Beitz 2001; Caney 2001; Moellendorf 2006; and
contra Boxill 1987; Brock 2009; Miller 2002). Taking only education and
employment into account, this would transform the global economic system, placing enormous restrictions on the deployment of capital and labor
and requiring a worldwide development of educational opportunities that
would massively reorient the deployment of resources. Thus, there is at
least prima facie reason to be skeptical about whether such a requirement
is feasible or desirable. But could it be justifiable to distinguish between the
domestic sphere and the global one on the principle of equality of opportunity? This question has particular normative edge for the cosmopolitan,
who holds that every person has global stature as the ultimate unit of moral
concern, and is therefore entitled to equal respect and consideration no
matter what her citizenship status or other affiliations happen to be, or even
the non-cosmopolitan who construes human rights as universal, applying equally to every human being. It would seem to violate the principle
of moral universalism to hold different criteria of justice for the domestic
and global economic systems. This chapter asks whether equal economic

opportunity is a requirement of justice of the global system, assuming that it is a requirement of the just domestic or national economic systems, and granting the normative force of moral universalism.

Thomas Pogge presses the challenge of moral universalism as follows. A moral conception such as a conception of social justice is universalistic if and only if:

A. It subjects all persons to the same system of fundamental moral principles;
B. These principles assign the same fundamental moral benefits (e.g., claims, liberties, power, and immunities) and burdens (e.g., duties and liabilities) to all; and
C. These fundamental moral benefits and burdens are formulated in general terms so as not to privilege or disadvantage certain persons or groups arbitrarily. (Pogge 2008, 98)

Universalism is clearly appealing, particularly to anyone who takes persons to be the fundamental units of moral value. There is some vagueness with regard to what it is to privilege or disadvantage persons or groups "arbitrarily," but it sets the burden of proof on any theory of social justice that would privilege or disadvantage any persons or groups in any way to say why it is not arbitrary. As a consistency test for such privilege or disadvantage that a conception of social justice would allow between societies, Pogge then poses two questions:

1. What fundamental claims do persons have on the global economic order and what fundamental responsibilities do these claims entail for those who impose it?
2. What fundamental moral claims do persons have on their national economic order and what fundamental responsibilities do these claims entail for those who impose it? (Pogge 2008, 98)

In short, he maintains that anyone who claims that there is a difference in the criteria of justice for the domestic and the global situation, that is, different answers to the two questions above, must give a rationale for the lack of the criterion in the global (domestic) case that does not apply in the domestic (global) one.

Moral universalism poses a challenge at some level for any scheme of global cooperation that claims to be just and takes there to be a difference between domestic and global requirements of human rights. Simon Caney draws out the implications of this challenge as an analogical argument for the principle of global equality of opportunity:

Underpinning our commitment to equality of opportunity is the deep conviction that it is unfair if someone enjoys worse opportunities because of his or her cultural identity. Thus we think that it is unfair if a person enjoys worse chances in life because of class or social status or ethnicity. This deep conviction implies, however, that we should also object if some people have worse opportunities because of their nationality or civic identity. (Caney 2001, 115)

He also provides an example: just as we should condemn racial apartheid within a country, so we should condemn the economic "apartheid" that prevents the global poor from reaching economic equality with the wealthy (Caney 2001, 116). Caney's analogical argument can thus be stated as follows:

1. It is unfair to have unequal opportunities because of cultural identity (presumably within a multicultural society).
2. This holds also for class, social status, ethnicity or race.
3. But cultural identity, class, social status, ethnicity or race are like nationality or civic identity.
4. Hence it is unfair to have unequal opportunities (globally) because of nationality or civic identity.

However, I think that it is worth considering whether all of the kinds of groupings that Caney lumps together here in premises 1, 2 and 3 (cultural identity, class, social status, ethnicity, race, nationality and civic identity) fall equally under the principle of equal opportunity. It seems to me that there are important differences between cultural identity and race, or class and race (to say nothing of gender). And these in turn are different from nationality. These groups differ by what they mean for persons' values and preferences, and by the degree to which one can escape being defined by or identifying with them. Furthermore, some of them group persons by cultural characteristics, some by economic ones; some such features are changeable for individuals, and some are not.

I disagree with Caney's analogy and with its implication that if one upholds the principle of equal opportunity domestically, then one must also uphold it globally. I will argue that a principle of equal opportunity holds by gender, race and some other social groupings, but not by nationality. On my view, domestic justice does not require equalizing the opportunity differences that arise from economic inequalities or cultural differences, provided that there is enough of the goods essential for autonomy provided to those who cannot secure them without assistance. Inequality in opportunity inevitably and, I shall argue, justifiably arises from our capitalist economy and from the fact that we are raised in families, even apart from individual differences in talents and interests. Analogously, inequalities in opportunities globally arise from economic trade and the fact that we live together in collectively self-determined nations, and erasing inequality at the cost of either curtailing international trade or national collective self-determination is not worthwhile. Nonetheless, a commitment to human rights, I shall argue, does require us to meet needs at a level that is likely to reduce inequality in opportunities as measured by income or capabilities. Naturally, such a discussion will require me to state carefully what is meant by both human rights and "equal opportunity."

Human rights and equal opportunity

I understand human rights to be universal in the sense of applying to every human being in every era or epoch, and to be ultimate, moral claims on the global institutional order (Pogge 2006). As ultimate moral claims, human rights override other moral claims.[1] There are many important moral claims, though, and that sets a high bar for a sub-set of moral claims that could plausibly override all others. For this reason, human rights must be in some sense the minimal demands that must be satisfied first, before all others. How is the minimum demand to be set? Pogge argues that it is empirically true that people have a concern for the interests of others, and that this concern is widely shared across persons and cultures. I am not sure that this is an empirical fact, but regardless of whether it is, it is surely a rather contingent one on which to ground universal, ultimate, moral claims. A better foundation, I believe, is a normative one, which we can arrive at by asking why human rights are important to us. They are important, I contend, because they guarantee that we are not deprived of whatever is necessary for a decent human life.[2] What makes a decent human life is empirically determined, contingent, and variable across time and place. But there are three broad categories of requirements that cut across time and place.

---

[1] There may be times when these human rights compete with each other for attention, given severe conditions and limitations on resources. I will not consider how these trade-offs should be made here. It suffices for my purposes to assert that human rights override all other rights.

[2] Stating this as a negative (i.e., not deprived, rather than the positive: provided with) may seem to set too minimal a level on human rights. But as Pogge argues, because of the way that we are globally interconnected and subjected to the coercive power of global institutions, negative duties are rather exacting in terms of how much is owed to the poor or those subjected to corrupt governments. A similar point can also be made about what it means for a person with a disability to be deprived of the necessities for a decent human life. One has a human right not to be so deprived by a social system that could be arranged so that one is not so deprived, but that does not mean that all handicaps can be overcome or that one has a right to compensation.

First, a decent human *life* requires basic subsistence: nutritious food, clean water, care during stages of dependency, health-care to some degree, and safe shelter. There are basic caloric and water requirements for life, but human rights extend beyond that to what is required to make it likely that persons will live out an average lifespan,[3] be able to choose a lifestyle that makes chronic diseases unlikely, and avoid acute diseases and parasites that modern public health-care has made readily avoidable. The kind and amount of food, shelter and health-care is relative to time and place, however, and is further elucidated by the next category of requirements.

Second, a *decent* human life requires, in Rawlsian terms, the bases for social respect so that one can interact among others as a moral equal, as a dignified person, a holder of human rights. Moral equality and dignity clearly do not require everything about persons or their resources and investments to be the same. Although no one's life could be decent if they were starving or subject to systematic violence and terror, the kind and amount of shelter, health-care and food required for respect varies widely by society and culture. One need not have a permanent structure to sleep in to be respected in one society, while in another that would be a minimal standard for respectable shelter. Beans and rice are perfectly acceptable daily food rations in some societies, while in others that would be inadequate to share with company. But everyone everywhere needs to be free from humiliation, discrimination and oppression on the basis of ascribed group identities, such as race, gender or caste. Inequalities or differences in the level of respect accorded to individuals based on these are unacceptable.

Third, a decent human life requires certain freedoms; a decent *human* life allows us the ability to be autonomous, to freely plan many aspects of our lives without having to request the permission of others, and to collectively determine laws by which our actions are to be mutually constrained. Minimal requirements for autonomy include basic freedom of movement, freedom to choose whom to marry (a freedom that is contingent on mutual interest[4] of the marrying parties), freedom of conscience, and a right to political participation. There are also minimal economic freedoms, such

---

[3] An "average lifespan" is a moving target, relative to time and place, but I think of a minimal demand as living at least long enough to see one's generation's grandchildren into maturity, so about 60–70 years. Most nations have achieved the "health transition" to life expectancies at or above this range, but the poorest ones, especially those in Africa, have not.

[4] A freedom that is contingent on "mutual interest" is not the same as a freedom contingent on permission. Mutual interest means that the parties seek each other's cooperation to do something together, and requires a two-way agreement and commitment, an exchange. Permission indicates one direction of assent from the permitter to the permittee, with no commitment or exchange.

as the freedom to own some private property and the freedom to choose one's occupation (again, contingent on mutual interests of others, such as employers, laborers, investors and consumers). Finally, to be autonomous one has to be educated to see the potential options open to one and the implications of one's choices. How much education one requires to have a decent human life is again relative to time and place; one must have a basic education to be able to choose from a variety of decent occupations and to be able to plan one's life and raise one's children well within the society in which one lives.

These broad categories are consistent with many lists of human rights, as well as conceptions of basic human needs and capabilities. However, like Gillian Brock's account of human needs (Brock 2009, 63–72), my account is minimalist in that I claim that only the minimum necessary for a decent human life rises to the level of a human right, which is a claim on the global institutional order that overrides all other claims.

Having established the three broad categories of minimal requirements for a decent human life – subsistence, respect and freedom – we can now consider the question of whether there is a human right to equal opportunity, and whether such a right, if it exists at all, is relative to one's society or whether its criteria apply globally. How could equal opportunity fit into the categories of human rights? Subsistence rights, as I conceive them, do not support a claim to equal opportunity once a minimal threshold has been reached. This is simply to say that a decent human life does not require an equal opportunity to gourmet food, luxurious shelter or copious water for long, hot showers. The human rights requirement of subsistence for a decent human life is much lower than that, and equality in these goods, as a matter of subsistence, is not required. Similarly, as a matter of freedom, we need not have equality in these goods. We can live perfectly autonomous, self-directed lives without the opportunity to achieve amounts of these goods equal to that of the wealthy.

The minimal requirements for respect as a human right offer a plausible ground for the claim that a decent human life requires equal opportunity for some achievements in life. Being excluded from participation in a competition is disrespectful if it is based on the ascribed social group status of potential competitors for three reasons. First, it sends the message that one's kind is unwelcome in society with members of other groups. Second, when the exclusion is from a highly sought or respected position, that exclusion sends the message that one's group is inferior to those that are included in the competition. Third, one's ascribed social group status is practically inescapable – it is involuntary and, at least practically speaking for most members of the groups, unchangeable. It is an identity that marks an individual for life. So, one cannot hope in the future to be considered welcome or of equal worth. Human rights require that one not be *categorically excluded* based on ascribed social group status.

Categorical exclusion is different from not qualifying for a good in a fair competition, because losing as a competitor is not dishonorable, though it is disappointing. But there is clearly no human right to be sheltered from disappointment. Competition of some sort is necessary in the case of scarce resources, but for socially valuable, scarce goods, competition must be based on individual ability or luck, not ascribed group status. One might ask whether all those denied the good on the basis of ability form an excluded group. While we could call this a group, it is an ad hoc one, and those who are not excluded but who are still denied the good are not thereby sent the message that they are unwelcome or that they are inferior because of a mark that they bear throughout life, across competitions for many or all socially valuable goods. Provided that there are other competitions and other ways for them to live a decent human life, losing in a competition is not a loss, at least not a serious loss, of respect. Furthermore, competitions based on ability for education or employment have social value in that they give persons incentive to strive and improve their abilities (Cudd 2007).

Fair competitions require an even playing field, and social group status can make a competition unfair even if one is not entirely excluded from the competition. Does one have a human right to a perfectly fair competition for education and employment? The minimal requirements of human rights provide slim grounds to justify requiring perfect fairness. If persons' rights to non-exclusion based on ascribed social group status are secured,[5] then the remaining disadvantage is due to past exclusion and its lingering effects on the ability to compete. Neither subsistence nor freedom would lead us to require perfect fairness in order to have an equal chance at competing; those requirements are for sufficiency, not equality. The question is, then, whether the demand for equal dignity and respect requires perfect fairness in competitions for education and employment. I think it does not. Many factors play a role, and in any given case it will be difficult to say which factor determines why someone achieves or fails. It may be that one fails for lack of interest, ability, experience, determination, effort, guile, or just plain luck. The fact that many will fail in any

---

[5] Securing freedom from categorical exclusion includes freedom from lingering prejudice or implicit bias, a condition that is, admittedly, difficult for a society to achieve. My position is that human rights requires this, however.

given competition means that no inference from the group to the individual's moral worth is licensed. Of course, human rights to subsistence or freedom in themselves can require mitigation of past and continuing social harms. But the level of provision required to uphold human rights for subsistence and freedom are sufficiency, not equality. Minimal human rights require some provision of educational and employment opportunities, and absolutely no exclusion from opportunity, but not provision of equal positive opportunities.

Being unwelcome in society and considered as unchangeably inferior to others is disrespectful in a way that makes a decent human life impossible, and thus is a denial of minimal human rights. Upholding human rights therefore requires that societies not allow persons to be excluded based on ascribed status, such as race, gender, caste or ethnicity. What about social class? Insofar as class indelibly, permanently, involuntarily marks its members, equal opportunity to erase that mark is required for a decent human life in the same way. In some societies at some times a person's class is readily determined from their dress, their manner of speaking, their gestures, and the like. In such societies class is handed down to one's children in the same way that one's race or caste is. Avoiding exclusion on the basis of class in such a society requires, first, that no one be excluded based on some perceivable mark of class, and, second, that every member of society be positively supplied the minimal amount of education necessary for living an autonomous life with many choices. Hence, adequate opportunity does not require the positive provision of equal educational opportunity, only the positive provision of adequate educational opportunity and avoidance of exclusion based on a mark.

Brock argues that equal opportunity as a principle of justice is very plausible when stated as a negative, that is, as something that one should not be deprived of. She writes: "it is unfair if some are significantly disadvantaged in life because of morally arbitrary features, so it is unfair if some have much worse prospects in life than others because of their race, ethnicity, class, and so on" (Brock 2009, 58). Stated as a negative, the principle says what should not be done to someone because of their identity – as I have argued, they should not be excluded from competition. Brock notes that the positive formulation of the equal opportunity principle is far less plausible, as it would state that everyone should be provided with equal advantages. But specifying what equal advantages as positive provisions are will either have to be done in terms of inputs – investments prior to the opportunity competition – or outcomes – proportions of persons in any given social group that achieve the opportunity.

Framed in terms of inputs, we will have to declare some point at which the inputs are sufficient to count as equality of opportunity. But we have already argued that human rights require sufficient inputs for a decent human life. The proposal here is that equal opportunity requires provision of some level of positive advantage. For opportunities in education and employment, equal advantages as inputs will be impossible and undesirable to achieve. Take education, for example. Suppose we give each person equal time with equally well prepared teachers and equal books, etc. That will disadvantage those who learn more slowly or start at a different level. Yet, it is arguably more fair to give more education to those who need it to get to a sufficient level of achievement to live a decent human life. Furthermore, if we give more and better education also to those who can achieve great levels of innovation, that is likely to benefit everyone in society. Individual talent and ability will determine how well inputs can be turned into outcomes, and it would be unfair and destructive to ask those with disabilities to do with less than what they need to achieve a decent human life or the talented to do with less than what they need to benefit everyone. So we need to look to the outcomes that will be produced by the opportunities.

Framed as outcomes, there is another problem that has been noted by both Bernard Boxill and Brock. Specifying the outcome that we ought to equalize in individuals' opportunities to achieve is hopelessly culturally relative. As Boxill puts it in the global case, "The root difficulty is that the world is made up of different societies with different cultures and different standards of success" (Boxill 1987, 148). Boxill does not think that this holds within societies, but in multicultural societies that strikes me as implausible. Just as Norwegians, Saudis and Argentinians are likely to have very different standards of success, so are Hispanic Americans, Orthodox Jewish Americans and Native Americans. Caney, on the other hand, denies that this is a problem even globally, and disputes Boxill's understanding of the global equal opportunity principle. Caney argues that the global equal opportunity principle should not be seen as requiring that there be equal opportunity for every occupation, but rather that it should hold that: "persons (of equal abilities and motivation) have equal opportunities to attain an equal number of positions of a commensurate standard of living" (Caney 2001, 120). But this conflates equal opportunity with economic equality, and we already saw that we cannot argue for economic equality from the three justifying criteria of human rights. Furthermore, as Brock argues, this way of specifying the positive ideal of equal opportunity runs into the problem of not being able to rule out all forms of discrimination that we want. For example, in a sexist society, if the wives of high status men of a society are able to secure the same capabilities through their men, then they are considered by Caney's criterion to have equal opportunity. But this is clearly not equal opportunity if they do not have the opportunity to achieve this status themselves. And as I have argued, the human rights criteria of respect demand security from categorical exclusion on the basis of gender.

Thus far I have argued that human rights demand only equality of opportunity understood as non-exclusion of ascribed social groups. Another argument for not extending equality of opportunity to erase all economic inequalities is that doing so would be too costly. Capitalism essentially creates inequalities because it distributes goods in markets, where trades take place because of different demands for goods and services. Inequality is created by a differential demand for certain goods, skills or services. People seek to discover and create goods, skills and services that are highly demanded because they are paid well for them. Instituting and maintaining economic equality would destroy capitalism. Admittedly, without capitalism there might be some happy coincidences between skills that are fun and interesting to exercise for the benefit of those who want or need them, or of goods that one creates because one needs them oneself, or services that are rewarding in themselves to provide, and the general need for them. People could be coerced by threat of punishment to work, but this would only bring forth the minimal efforts required to avoid punishment. Without the possibility of economic trade and differential reward, far fewer needed and wanted skills, goods and services would be developed. This would harm everyone severely, including the poor (Cudd in Cudd and Holmstrom 2011). Innovation and development of goods and services is clearly a morally acceptable justification for at least some inequality.

The principle of equal opportunity I have defended prohibits categorical exclusion of members of ascribed social groups from socially valuable opportunities. Human rights also demand that everyone be provided with what is required for a decent human life, and this demand requires that everyone, regardless of origin, be provided enough opportunities for education and employment to be able to live an autonomous and decent, respectable life. The human right to equal opportunity holds globally as it does domestically. It demands there be no exclusion in education based on an indelible mark that signals unwelcomeness or inferiority. Human rights also demand that there be some provision of opportunity – enough for one to secure a decent human life – but not to the point of equality. Yet, the standards for autonomy, decency and respectability are set within societies more than across them. So the number and kinds of opportunities that human rights require for persons are different in different societies.

I claim that this adheres to moral universalism, however, because in both cases the criterion for making a claim on the economic order – global or domestic – is what is minimally required for a decent human life. It is just that the opportunity requirements for a decent human life differ according to the society in which one lives.

The equality presumption

Egalitarians, and some who are willing to trade off equality for other values, will argue that equality has a moral presumption such that for any socially distributed good, an unequal distribution of the good will require a justification. This view, the "equality presumption," would put global equality of opportunity in a stronger position than the human-rights-as-sufficiency criteria justification that I have explored. Not only would economic opportunities have to be sufficient to allow a decent human life, but they would have to be equal unless an inequality could be justified. Darrel Moellendorf is an egalitarian who endorses global equality of opportunity, which he defines as follows: "Equality of opportunity in the global economic association, then, is directed towards ensuring that differences in initial wealth do not affect the opportunities of persons (of the morally relevant equal endowments) across a range of goods, including income, wealth, meaningful productive activity, leisure time, health, security, housing, education, and basic liberties" (Moellendorf 2006, 307). Thus, he presumes that any differences in opportunity in economic goods and basic liberties that are generated by differences in initial wealth are unjustifiable. But the equality presumption itself stands in need of justification. It is either question begging or we need to ask what is wrong with inequality such that it needs to be eliminated.

Charles Beitz explores several reasons for objecting to inequality that bear on this discussion (Beitz 2001).[6] First, inequality can lead to humiliation and be a denial of the agency of those who have less. Not just any inequality does this, but gross inequalities do. Setting aside absolute deprivation, which would not meet the standard of human rights, social standards about consumption determine the level of inequality that causes such humiliation. Beitz suggests that this is as true globally as it is domestically because people now compare their standard of living via media images. But this claim overstates the case for a global sense of one's standard of living. Surely it is the persons one sees and shares society with who matter more

---

[6] Beitz considers more objections to inequality than I consider relevant to this discussion.

for one's well-being than those across the globe.[7] Beitz is surely right when he claims that everyone values independent agency and the very poor do not have this. But to retreat to this claim is to argue that the problem is not inequality but rather absolute deprivation.

A second reason for objecting to inequality is that it abridges liberty. "Some inequalities are objectionable because they express social relations in which the advantaged exercise an unreasonably large degree of control over others" (Beitz 2001, 106). The wealthy have a much greater degree of control over what gets produced, what kinds of employment are offered, and over the environment and way of life of their community. This affects individuals' capacity to determine the course of their own lives. But does this lack justify the equality presumption or does objecting to it depend on the presumption? As we discussed with respect to human rights, a decent human life requires some good options in ways of life in order to be autonomous. What is clearly important is that one not be categorically excluded from any option based on one's social group status. But it does not require equality of numbers of options. No one has unilateral control over the options that their community provides. Everyone is dependent upon previous generations and one's fellows to determine the ways of life that are open to one. By encouraging more ways of life rather than truncating some in order to provide equality for all, we improve the number of opportunities open to all in the future. Again, sufficiency in provision of options, not equality, should rule.

Finally, inequality is objectionable because it undermines the fairness of processes such as competitions and bargains. This objection to inequality is powerful, because unfairness is always against justice, but contingent on the claim that the fairness of a process is corrupted. Yet it is important to be clear that it is the unfairness that is the problem. That is, for any given process, if it is unfair for any reason, including because of economic inequalities of the participants, then that unfairness is a reason for objecting to it. But this reason for objecting to inequality does not give a moral presumption to

---

[7] Empirical studies of this phenomenon are lacking, perhaps because the point seems rather obvious. In a special issue of *Oxford Development Studies* entitled "Missing Dimensions of Poverty Data," Diego Zavaleta Reyles (2007) takes up the issue of measuring shame and humiliation, prioritizing local or domestic comparisons of opportunity and wealth. A recent study by Kuziemko *et al.* (2011) suggests that people display "last-place aversion" rather than aversion to inequality overall. That is, persons who are relatively deprived in society will tend to oppose equality measures if it means that those who are even worse off will come up to their level.

equality in general; it merely provides a way of showing that the inequality is morally problematic in a given case.

Elizabeth Anderson argues that inequality is objectionable not in itself but only when it infringes on equal moral worth of persons (Anderson 1999). My view of the wrongness of opportunity inequality draws from her view. Nothing sends the message that one is of less moral worth than that one's gender, race or caste prevents one from entering into a relationship with anonymous others that others are permitted to engage in. When one is denied equal opportunity based on these grounds, one is actively prohibited because of that ascribed identity. Inequality of opportunity across cultures or borders is not this kind of categorical exclusion, but rather the lack of provision of opportunity. This sort of lack of opportunity is like being unable to engage in a trade because there is no one to trade with, while categorical exclusion is like being unable to trade with a trader who has a good but refuses to trade with one because of one's identity. While the former can be disappointing or depriving, the latter is humiliating. Although human rights to adequate subsistence, freedom and respect require that the global wealthy do more to provide economic opportunities to the global poor, equality is neither necessary for meeting human rights, nor would it be in the long-term interests of the poor to undermine the global economy and violate freedom to the degree necessary to provide economic equality.

Objections

I have argued that human rights requires equal opportunity only as a prohibition on categorical exclusion from educational or employment opportunities, and not as a demand for provision of equal resources. I have argued against the equality presumption that would underwrite a global equality of resource provision principle on the grounds that it would be too costly for everyone, including the global poor. This argument shows how I can respond to the global/domestic analogy objection that one's educational or employment opportunities should not depend on where one was born or what family one was born into.

This objection is best met by considering the values that we would have to sacrifice in order to equalize educational and employment opportunities across families and nations. Domestically, we grant families a degree of freedom from interference despite the inequalities that it creates because of the value of family life for human life. It is true that domestically we do some mitigation of this inequality in order to make sure that everyone has a good opportunity to have a meaningful life. But this is a sufficiency condition, not an equality guarantee. In the same way, national collective self-determination will create inequalities, but the value of self-determination for human life has to be counted as part of reason for not insisting on equality of opportunity. What the analogy between families and nations shows is that there are valuable trade-offs in those cases that show that equality of opportunity is not worth pursuing beyond sufficiency.

The analogy does not exist between ascribed group status and nationality. There are no valuable aspects to ascribed group status discrimination that prompt such a trade-off. While between families or between cultures there can be legitimate differences in values that make different opportunities inevitable and desirable, difference in the cases of ascribed social group status is only superiority or inferiority. Furthermore, while it is at least theoretically possible to change one's nationality, or deny one's family and start another one, it is not possible to change one's gender, race, caste or ethnicity.

It may be objected that my argument still shows that much should be done in the international case to improve opportunities. While I entirely agree that much should be done to relieve suffering of the poor, the argument shows that much should be done to meet needs in order *to satisfy human rights, not equalize provision of opportunities*, though that may be a by-product of achieving human rights. Opportunities can be provided by stimulating growth of poor economies, and need not be achieved by leveling down opportunities for the wealthy. Even if one grants that equality is a value in itself and that global equality of opportunity expressed as Caney or Moellendorf do in terms of equality of capabilities or standard of living is valuable, it is not the only value. Another value is growth of global opportunities, and pursuit of global equality of opportunity beyond the point of sufficiency is likely to thwart that.

Conclusion

The debate about global equality of opportunity has been based on a confusion about what constitutes the moral claim to equality of opportunity in the first instance. Opportunity equality is the right not to be categorically excluded from an opportunity. Any claim to have an opportunity created where none or few exist can only be justified by balancing it against other values. What human rights demand of the global economic system is that persons everywhere have sufficient means to meet their needs, that they have freedom to own personal property, and that they not be discriminated against because of their ascribed social group status.

On this view, equality of opportunity is an important principle of justice, is required by human rights, and applies globally. The principle demands that persons not be discriminated against in education and employment based on status. In much of the world this is a radical ideal, and will be resisted by many, including elites of poor countries, who are able because of their gender, ethnicity or caste to retain power over their fellow citizens. It will also be resisted by men in religions that deny women rights to equal status because of their gender. Equality of opportunity as a human right not to be categorically excluded requires us to see people as individuals with preferences, talents, resources and abilities and not as members of groups that we despise or disdain.

References

Anderson, Elizabeth. 1999. "What Is the Point of Equality?" *Ethics* 109, 287–337.

Beitz, Charles. 2001. "Does Global Inequality Matter?" *Metaphilosophy* 32, 95–112.

Boxill, Bernard. 1987. "Global Equality of Opportunity and National Integrity." *Social Philosophy and Policy* 2, 143–168.

Brock, Gillian. 2009. *Global Justice: A Cosmopolitan Account*. Oxford University Press.

Caney, Simon. 2001. "Cosmopolitan Justice and Equalizing Opportunities." *Metaphilosophy* 32, 113–134.

Cudd, Ann E. 2007. "Sporting Metaphors: Competition and the Ethos of Capitalism." *Journal of the Philosophy of Sport* 34, 52–67.

Cudd, Ann E. and Holmstrom, Nancy. 2011. *Capitalism For and Against: A Feminist Debate*. New York: Cambridge University Press.

Kuziemko, Ilyana, Buell, Ryan W., Reich, Taly and Norton, Michael I. 2011. "'Last-Place Aversion": Evidence and Redistributive Implications." NBER Working Paper No. 17234.

Miller, David. 2002. "Liberalism, Equal Opportunities and Cultural Commitments." In Paul Kelly, ed., *Multiculturalism Reconsidered*. Cambridge: Polity Press, pp. 45–61.

Moellendorf, Darrel. 2006. "Equal Opportunity Globalized?" *Canadian Journal of Law and Jurisprudence* 19, 301–318.

Pogge, Thomas. 2006. "Understanding Human Rights." In Ann E. Cudd, ed., *Introduction to Social and Political Philosophy*. Dubuque: Kendall Hunt Publishing, pp. 320–336.

    2008. *World Poverty and Human Rights*, 2nd edn. Cambridge: Polity Press.

Reyles, Diego Zavaleta. 2007. "The Ability to go about Without Shame: A Proposal for Internationally Comparable Indicators of Shame and Humiliation." *Oxford Development Studies* 35, 405–430.

PART IV

How do human rights relate to environmental policy?

11 | Human rights in a hostile climate

STEPHEN M. GARDINER

According to mainstream science, humanity faces a time of emerging global environmental crises. Massive increases in economic output and human population over the last two centuries or so are putting increasing pressure on natural systems, including those basic to the support of human and other forms of life, such as climate, fresh water, oceans and natural habitat. In this context, hard questions arise about how a human rights approach can help us to understand and act on these concerns.

This chapter investigates such questions through the example of global climate change. It makes three central claims. First, climate change and similar problems pose a profound ethical challenge to existing institutions and theories. Second, a human rights approach can play a role in addressing this challenge through its articulation, development and defense of a basic but often neglected ethical intuition. Nevertheless, third, there remains much to be done. In particular, early work tends to overplay the initial advantages of human rights as such, and underestimate the role played by specific conceptions of human rights that are much more controversial and ambitious. Moreover, current human rights paradigms are not directed to the central characteristics of the profound challenge. Given all this, a practical and theoretical reorientation is needed. This has implications for the evolving project of political philosophy on a global, intergenerational and ecological scale.

The ethical challenge

We live in incredible times. The world economy has more than quintupled since the middle of the last century, and is currently doubling every 20 years. Meanwhile, the human population has grown by more than 250 percent since 1950, and recently has been increasing by roughly a billion

This work was supported by a grant from the Netherlands Institute for Advanced Study in the Humanities and Social Sciences (NIAS), by a H.L.A. Hart Fellowship at the Oxford Centre for Ethics and the Philosophy of Law, and by a Visiting Fellowship at the Smith School for Energy and the Environment at Oxford University. I am also grateful to Simon Caney, Lauren Hartzell Nichols, Henry Shue and the editors for comments.

people every 12 years. This rapid expansion of the human footprint has eco-logical consequences for humans, animals and the rest of nature.

One prominent manifestation is human-induced global climate change. According to mainstream science, this is already occurring, with significant effects on humans and other forms of life. Nevertheless, the changes felt so far are modest by comparison to those projected for the future. If the science is correct, we are on the verge of a serious shift in global climate comparable in magnitude to an ice age (albeit to a hotter, rather than colder, world). Although the planet has been warmer in the past, this is not the past of human experience (for example, there were crocodiles at the poles). Moreover, whereas such dramatic shifts usually occur over hundreds of thousands, if not millions, of years, the changes we are set to inflict will play out over only a few centuries, and perhaps mere decades. In other words, we are very quickly creating what some scientists have termed a "different planet."

In the face of such a threat, one might expect societies to spring into action. Yet so far this has not occurred. Despite many fine speeches, inter-national reports, diplomatic conferences, accords and even a treaty, glo-bal emissions of the main greenhouse gas, carbon dioxide, are now up by more than 40 percent since 1990, and have increased substantially in most major countries. Moreover, recently, the short-term effects of the financial crisis aside, this growth has been accelerating at rates that seemed almost unimaginable two decades ago. Worst of all, international negotiations on new mitigation efforts seem entrenched in an ongoing cycle of procras-tination. In short, we are currently in the grip of a deep political inertia, characterized by repeated policy failure and apparent public indifference, on what the nations of the world have publicly declared to be "one of the greatest challenges of our time" (Copenhagen Accord 2009).[1]

In my view, central to the ongoing inertia is the fact that climate change poses a profound ethical challenge. It is genuinely global, strongly inter-generational, and occurs in a setting where our theories and institutions are weak. Each of these factors raises serious obstacles to ethical action in its own right. When they converge, they are mutually reinforcing, consti-tuting "a perfect moral storm" for ethically responsible behavior (Gardiner 2011a).

Climate change is a genuinely global problem because the spatial disper-sion of causes and effects means that agents can take the immediate benefits

---

[1] This Accord was signed by a group of countries that included the United States, European Union, China and India.

of their own emissions, but pass most of the costs onto others in different parts of the world. It is strongly intergenerational because the long time lags involved imply that current emitters can pass most of the costs – and especially the most serious – decades and centuries into the future. Climate change also brings together a set of issues – e.g., global justice, intergenerational ethics, scientific uncertainty, and our relationship with nature – where our general theoretical understanding is hardly robust, and which current institutions (e.g., market mechanisms, short-term democratic election cycles, realist international politics, and so on) seem ill-equipped to address. Indeed, both the problem and its urgency seem opaque (or even invisible) to many conventional ways of thinking and going on. Neither we nor our institutions can easily register the consequences of our behavior, the victims, the causal routes, and who should do what as a result.

If climate change is a perfect moral storm, this has practical implications. The first is that existing institutions and the theories that support them face a fundamental test of moral and political legitimacy (Gardiner 2011a, 2011b). If they fail to address the climate challenge – and problems of this type more generally – then they are at least subject to criticism (Robinson 2008, xix). If the failure is severe, then perhaps even rejection is warranted.

The second practical implication is that ours is not a neutral evaluative context. The global and intergenerational problems imply that the current generation of the affluent face strong temptations to ignore their ethical responsibilities. They hold significant power over the global poor, future generations and the rest of nature. No one can really stop them from taking benefits for themselves and passing on the costs to others; no one, that is, except themselves. There is room for hope here, since admitting that one is engaging in this kind of buck passing is morally uncomfortable, even when the admission is only to oneself and those similarly placed. However, this encouraging fact also implies that there is some incentive to disguise what is going on, with clever but shallow counter-arguments, flawed proposals and alternative framings. In short, ethical discourse itself is under threat from distorting influences. Unfortunately, there is plenty of evidence for this in the actual climate debate, where we have seen a succession of grand promises followed by empty agreements (Gardiner 2004, 2011a). Given this, arguments about climate change should be subject to extra scrutiny, and this includes theoretical arguments.

In summary, the climate problem has a specific shape (involving political inertia and a perfect moral storm), poses a test of moral and political legitimacy (to current institutions and theories), and occurs in a non-neutral evaluative setting (where there is a real threat of distortion). Understanding this is important if a human rights approach is to deal with the problem as it is.

Aspirations

If this is our situation, how might a human rights approach help? In my view, the most central answer is that human rights talk helps us to artic-ulate, develop and defend a fundamental ethical intuition: that there are some kinds of harms – i.e., violations of basic human rights – that should not be inflicted on others, and that institutions that systematically inflict such harms are ethically illegitimate.[2] The thought is that marshaling this intuition can make a central contribution to addressing the perfect moral storm and overcoming political inertia.

Recently, three more specific roles for a human rights approach have been suggested. The first is that of shifting the dominant discourse away from short-term geopolitical, and especially economic, thinking. Advocates claim that such a reframing is beneficial since these approaches miss much of the point of climate policy, and bring with them structural features that a human rights approach would reject.

On the one hand, in concrete terms, an economic approach is said to embed a system of value that strongly emphasizes consumption goods over other important values (such as life support, or historical and aesthetic val-ues), to exhibit a status quo bias toward the rich and the current generation (in valuing interests in economic terms and in employing standard dis-count rates for the future), and to license trade-offs between overall welfare and the interests of individuals that ought to be prohibited (Caney 2010, 169–172; ICHRP 2008, 17; Lawrence unpublished, 22).

On the other hand, methodologically, human rights enthusiasts reject the general holism of conventional economics (in its focus on maximiza-tion or optimization) and its resulting disregard for distribution (Caney 2010). Moreover, they draw attention to what they see as unmotivated and prejudicial departures from such disregard within economics. For example, they are skeptical about the usual rationales for temporal discounting, since these appear to discriminate against future generations (Caney 2009; Cowen and Parfit 1992; Gardiner 2011a, ch. 8).

---

[2] "Harm" is used in a very general way here.

By contrast, the human rights approach is said to be methodologically preferable because it is atomistic (having individual human beings as its focus), remains spatially and temporally neutral (rather than being biased toward the richer countries and the present), and has concern for distribution built in (ICHRP 2008, 20). It is also thought to be substantively superior because it prioritizes morally fundamental concerns (i.e., basic human rights) over more peripheral matters (e.g., the production of consumer goods), emphasizes the perspective of the victim, focuses on the most vulnerable, and disallows certain kinds of trade-off (Caney 2010). Finally, human rights are claimed to provide a better basis for policy, and to bring neglected issues into focus. For example, they are said to facilitate a new emphasis on adaptation, providing a "compass for policy" that encourages autonomous adaptation by demanding rights-specific information and responses (ICHRP 2008, 23–26).

The second possible role for a human rights approach is substantive. A human rights framing brings with it an existing legal structure that includes a set of statutes, rulings, regulations, norms, and so on. Moreover, these seem to deal with matters that are central to the climate problem, such as liability and enforcement, and to highlight issues that are largely hidden in the economic approach, such as causality, accountability and "harms to actual persons." For example, a human rights perspective might be thought to translate ethical demands into legal obligations, provide procedural guarantees, focus on concrete realities rather than abstract possibilities, and generate the mechanisms of accountability needed for viable policy (ICHRP 2008, 5–8, but see 64; cf. Rajamani 2010). Given all this, a human rights approach may provide not only a better goal for policy than conventional economics, but also the means of implementation.

The third possible role for a human rights approach is theoretical. The ethical intuition that a human rights approach serves to articulate, develop and defend has an important status. It is basic in at least three senses: first, satisfying it is a necessary condition for a minimally ethical policy; second, it serves as a foundation on which other things are built; and, third, it has priority over other ethical concerns.

These theoretical features suggest two practical virtues of a human rights approach to climate change. First, a human rights perspective may seem at least relatively uncontentious. For instance, a policy orientation based on human rights thresholds is said to provide "a platform for broad-based dialogue on burden sharing of a kind that has frequently lacked in climate change debates" because it "uses a language to which few will object," and is more "modest, achievable and fair" than other proposals (such as equal per capita shares, or greenhouse development rights) (ICHRP 2008, 7). Second, some advocates see the climate issue as a useful entry point for the wider human rights agenda. By providing "an invaluable opportunity to reappraise the most pressing needs of a highly inequitable global society," a human rights move in climate policy can help to "create the kind of international and social order that the framers of the Universal Declaration dreamed of" (Picolotti 2008, v; Robinson 2008, iv).

In conclusion, there are strong prima facie reasons to support a human rights approach to climate change and to global environmental crises more generally. The ethical intuition at stake is a central one, but is in danger of being overshadowed or ignored by contemporary policy discourse. A human rights approach promises to capture the theoretical importance of, and add depth to, that intuition, while also bringing institutional insights and precedents. In particular, it appears to reorient the theory and practice of climate policy in "shovel ready" ways that overcome the limitations of other approaches.

Such are the early aspirations of a human rights discourse for climate change. Let us turn now to the arguments for it.

The initial case

In an influential piece, Simon Caney argues for a human rights analysis of climate change, and claims that this argument "does not need to rely on controversial or ambitious conceptions of human rights" (Caney 2010, 166). According to Caney, human rights "designate the most fundamental moral requirements which individuals can claim of others" (Caney 2010, 165). He highlights four features of such rights (Caney 2010, 164–165). The first is *human dignity*: human rights are grounded in each person's humanity. The second is *universal protection*: "human rights represent the entitlements of *each and every individual* to certain minimal standards of treatment, and they generate obligations on all persons to respect these basic minimum standards." The third is *lexical priority*: human rights take general priority over other values, constraining their pursuit. The fourth is that human rights are *moral thresholds*. They represent levels below which individuals should not be permitted to sink. Summarizing, Caney states, "human rights specify minimum moral thresholds to which all individuals are entitled, simply in virtue of their humanity, and which override all other moral values" (Caney 2010, 165).

Caney's central argument for a human rights approach to climate change is that it jeopardizes three key human rights.[3] Appealing only to "the least contentious and most modest formulation of the human right in question" (Caney 2010, 166), he uses evidence from major scientific reports to argue that climate change endangers the enjoyment of rights to life, health and subsistence. For example, for the right to life, he points out that climate change is projected to result in an increased frequency of heatwaves and severe weather events (such as storm surges, flooding and landslides), both of which typically lead to direct loss of life (Caney 2010, 166–167 citing IPCC 2007). From this, he infers that climate change seriously threatens the enjoyment of the right to life. Using similar data for impacts on health and subsistence, he concludes that climate change also seriously threatens the enjoyment of these human rights. In short, generalizing, the basic strategy seems to be to argue:

1. There is a human right to X.
2. Enjoyment of X is seriously threatened by climate change.
3. Therefore, climate change seriously threatens the enjoyment of the human right to X.
4. Therefore, it is appropriate to analyze climate change in terms of its impact on human rights.

Call this "the Master Argument for Human Rights" (or simply "the master argument").[4]

At first glance, the master argument appears simple, straightforward and irresistible. In addition, the human rights framing looks exciting. For onc thing, it appears at least relatively uncontentious. When the rights themselves are characterized in the minimal way suggested by Caney, the approach seems to command a broad and overlapping political consensus across more substantive ethical doctrines. For another, it appears both refreshing and illuminating. As well as promising an escape from the tangled discourse of climate economics, the human rights concern offers a direct route through to the worry that, via the ongoing failures of international climate policy, existing institutions are at risk of failing a test of moral

---

[3] Caney also claims that a human rights approach has six major advantages over cost-benefit analysis. Roughly speaking, these are: (1) it limits the relevant impacts, (2) it makes costs irrelevant; (3) it requires compensation for harms; (4) it functions as a deontological constraint; (5) it constrains the distribution of duties; and (6) it provides a normative interpretation of the UNFCCC objective of avoiding "dangerous anthropogenic climate change." In what follows, I suggest problems with (1), (2), (4) and (6).

[4] Caney's pattern of reasoning is echoed in ICHRP (2008), Humphreys (2010) and a recent World Bank report (McInerney *et al.* 2011, ch. 2).

and political legitimacy. If current arrangements are failing to protect key human rights, then it seems clear that there is a case to answer.

Despite the initial appeal of the master argument, a human rights approach faces serious challenges. Some of these are familiar from other contexts, some are exacerbated here, and others are more novel. In the next three sections, I provide a brief overview of three such challenges, together with some examples of their policy relevance, paying particular attention to Caney's arguments.[5] Throughout, my aim is neither to defeat the human rights approach in general nor Caney's contribution, but rather – in keeping with the aims of this volume – to suggest where the hard questions are, on which further work needs to be done. My hunch is that answering such questions requires a normatively richer (and much more controversial) account of basic human rights that is reoriented to a very different setting. Such a re-envisioning of the content and role of human rights will be important for not only the climate, but also the wider and evolving project of political philosophy on a global, intergenerational and ecological scale.

Framing revisited

The first challenge is to the framing advantages of a human rights approach, and emerges from the internal limitations of the master argument. At its root is the gap between, on the one hand, the initial ethical insight it aims to articulate, and, on the other hand, how this insight is developed within both general and more specific conceptions of human rights. To see this gap, let us sketch three related problems.

The first is that the master argument seems to inherit much of its appeal from a more fundamental argument. This "vital interests" argument uses the same general strategy as the master argument, but to argue that climate change threatens vital human interests (rather than human rights). It claims:

1. There is a vital human interest in X;
2. Enjoyment of X is seriously threatened by climate change;
3. Therefore, climate change seriously threatens the enjoyment of the vital human interest in X;
4. Therefore, it is appropriate to analyze climate change in terms of its impact on vital human interests.

---

[5] For critical legal analysis see Bodansky (2010) and Lawrence (unpublished).

Taken by itself, the vital interests argument is highly plausible (Shue 1992, 393). However, it also appears to undercut the master argument, since it seems more fundamental, and more modest in its claims. Specifically, although vital interests might be conceptualized in terms of human rights, they may also be thought of in other – arguably more minimal – terms, such as (for example) basic human needs, security or capabilities. Given this, an independent argument for moving beyond vital interests to human rights is required.

One reason this matters is because many people's initial approval of the master argument may rest on an implicit endorsement of the vital interests argument rather than a robust human rights framework. For example, perhaps some have a common-sense conception of human rights that simply *equates* them with vital interests that deserve some kind of protection.[6] If so, they might resist tying their common-sense endorsement of the master argument to any more specific conception of human rights, such as one grounded in actual legal uses, political institutions or philosophical theories. If this is right, then the initial impression that the master argument establishes the *special* or independent relevance of existing human rights discourse to the climate case is illusory. Most of the underlying work is done by the vital interests argument, and so is compatible with a range of different normative frameworks.

The second problem emerges because both the master argument and the vital interests argument may be parasitic on a more general argument. Suppose that climate change threatens *all* important concerns (e.g., because it threatens systematic severe or catastrophic impacts). If "everything is affected," then it is not surprising that human rights are. Instead, the real task is to show the special relevance of human rights. Most importantly, there is a challenge from other ethical values. If everything important is affected by climate change, then one can run parallel arguments to the master argument for human rights for all manner of other values, including, for example, liberty, property, utility, community, and so on. If so, why not prioritize these framings of the climate problem instead?

This observation reveals several important facts about the master argument for human rights. First, much of the work is done by the severe threat posed by climate change rather than by the importance of rights per se.

---

[6] Some might object that this is sufficient for a human rights approach. However, this is not obvious. For example, note that this conception does not require that protection is *owed to the individuals whose interests are threatened*, which one might regard as a minimal condition for a human rights approach.

Second, the master argument for human rights is only one among many possible arguments for the relevance of core values, and alternative arguments are also likely to be plausible. Consider, for example, master arguments for liberty, community, security, and so on. Third, given this, the master argument for human rights does not by itself establish their *special* normative relevance. Instead, it is either silent on, or else simply assumes that relevance.[7] Note that the conclusion of the master argument is ambiguous on just this point. The "appropriate" in the claim "it is appropriate to analyze climate change in terms of its impact on human rights" might be read to assert only that human rights are one potential way to look at the climate problem (to be assessed against others), or it might be read more strongly as asserting that human rights are the pre-eminent consideration. Unfortunately, the former does not get us far beyond the "everything is affected" and vital interests arguments, whereas the latter simply asserts the primacy of a human rights approach. Either way, there is more work to be done.

The third, related, problem for the master argument for human rights is that, because it ignores other values, it offers only a partial ethical framing of the climate problem. In principle, this need not be a deep difficulty, so long as other values are also appropriately included. However, in practice, we must beware of the framing effects of beginning with the master argument.

To see this, consider one of Caney's own proposals. The basic commitment of international climate policy under the United Nations' Framework Convention on Climate Change is to avoid "dangerous anthropogenic interference with the climate system" (UNFCCC 1992). Historically, there has been some debate as to how the crucial concept – "dangerous climate change" – should be understood (Oppenheimer and Petsonk 2005). Caney proposes that it should be interpreted as climate change "that systematically undermines the widespread enjoyment of human rights" (Caney 2010, 172). In other words, he advocates for understanding the central objective of international climate law and policy in terms of human rights.

This proposal is bold and substantive. Still, the widespread undermining of human rights is only one of the ethical dimensions of climate change (as Caney acknowledges (2010, 173)); hence, if we follow his proposal, there is a real risk that the other ethical dimensions will recede from the policy agenda, or even become lost from view. This is a serious worry. Consider,

---

[7] Caney asserts "general" priority for human rights over other values; it is unclear whether he means simply to assume the special importance of human rights.

for example, ethical problems such as one country's unfair overexploitation of natural resources, or one generation's reckless use of generational power to pass severe costs onto the future, or our species' infliction of catastrophic damages on non-human animals and the rest of nature. In principle, these problems might persist even without jeopardizing key human rights, or human rights more generally. Yet if they did so, presumably we should not say that international climate policy had achieved its sole, or even central, ethical aim. Imagine, for instance, a future in which humans are able to enjoy their key human rights only because they devote almost all of their time, energy and resources to defending against severe climate change, and so have little left for anything else; or consider a world in which future generations have been bequeathed massive domes to live in on an otherwise desolate Earth. Should we really say that these are circumstances under which international climate policy has succeeded?[8]

In conclusion, the first challenge to a human rights approach to climate change is that the master argument has significant limitations both in terms of articulating the basic ethical intuition, and in differentiating it from (or integrating it with) other ethical concerns. One consequence is that, although the master argument may inspire those already committed (to the basic ethical intuition, a human rights analysis of it, and its primacy over other concerns), by itself it seems unlikely to either persuade or motivate a more agnostic audience. A second consequence is that, since the limitations can infect particular policy issues (such as the definition of dangerous climate change), even the converted must be careful not to overreach.

Substance revisited

The second challenge to a human rights approach involves its alleged substantive advantages. Even if we are persuaded by the importance of a

---

[8] One response would be to claim that the UNFCCC objective is at fault for being too narrow and anthropocentric. However, this is unclear. Even though the treaty states as its motivation the "protection of current and future generations of mankind," it has a broad understanding of what this involves, and this seems to move beyond ensuring key human rights. For example, appeals are made to "equity," "common but differentiated responsibilities," the "special needs" of developing countries, and the aim of promoting a supportive, open, sustainable and non-discriminatory international economic system. In addition, the treaty claims that its aims "should be achieved within a time-frame sufficient to allow ecosystems to adapt naturally to climate change … and to enable economic development to proceed in a sustainable manner."

A second response would be to argue that all this can be incorporated within an appropriately rich account of human rights. This promissory note is tempting, but no longer minimalist; in any case, it seems clear that much work remains to be done.

human rights approach, we should ask whether in its conventional forms it successfully picks out the commitments needed to address a problem like climate change, and whether it does so without relying on "controversial or ambitious conceptions" of human rights. In this section and the next, I argue that it does neither, in part because its usual components remain vulnerable to the perfect moral storm. Although this suggests that current human rights doctrine is not yet "shovel ready" for application to climate change, it does provide some sense of the development needed.

In this section, I note four problem areas. The first is the *identity* of the rights invoked. One strategy is to attempt a "bootstrapping" (or extrapolation) of existing non-environmental rights. The main advantage of this strategy is that such rights already have international standing in other contexts. However, one issue is that a very large number seem to be in play (Bell 2011, 101–102). For example, in addition to Caney's appeal to rights to life, health and subsistence, the early literature also invokes rights to adequate food, water, adequate housing (McInerney *et al.* 2011), "the right to take part in cultural life, the right to use and enjoy property, [and] the right to an adequate standard of living" (Malé Declaration 2007), the right to development and the right not to be forcibly evicted (Caney 2010, 80).

This proliferation raises a number of concerns. One is that people's lists vary, suggesting that they have different accounts of the problem to be solved. A second is that focusing on some rights rather than others can make serious differences to policy. A third concern is that an expansive plurality of rights may reintroduce a variant of the "everything is affected" problem at a lower level. A human rights approach is less impressive if it encourages a re-listing of every morally important consideration as a new right, and so simply defers difficult choices. More broadly, there becomes a point where one moves beyond "merely" extending existing rights to fit a new context into engaging in a covert reinvention of core values (Gardiner 2011b). At the moment, it remains an open question whether this will occur in the case of climate change (or the natural environment more generally), partly because little detailed work has been done to show how the bootstrapping of existing rights is supposed to work. Nevertheless, we should not simply assume in advance that bootstrapping will turn out to be adequate in a complex global, intergenerational and ecological setting.

One response to this last worry is to call for new, distinctively environmental rights. This "invention" strategy has strong supporters in both legal and philosophical circles. In the legal realm, the UN has declared that "[m]an has the fundamental right to freedom, equality and adequate conditions of life, in an environment of a quality that permits a life of dignity and well-being, and he bears a solemn responsibility to protect and improve the environment for present and future generations" (Stockholm Declaration 1972), and also spoken of "the fundamental right to an environment capable of supporting human society and the full enjoyment of human rights" (Malé Declaration 2007). Among political theorists, Caney suggests a human right "not to be exposed to dangerous climate change," Steve Vanderheiden proposes a "right to an adequate environment with a corollary that the right includes a claim to climate stability" and Tim Hayward promotes both a "right to an environment adequate for (human) health and well-being" and a "fundamental right of each individual to an equitable share of the planet's aggregate natural resources and environmental services that are available on a sustainable basis for human use" (Caney 2008, 539; 2006, 263; Vanderheiden 2008, 252; Hayward 2005, 29; 2007, 445).

The idea of new, distinctively environmental rights has some appeal. Still, one concern is that the various sources do not agree on the general shape or content of the relevant rights.[9] Another worry is that it is not obvious that the reductive, atomistic strategy of the rights approach will work. Why assume in advance that complex collective aims such as climate stability are reducible to rights that pertain to individuals? Clearly, more needs to be said.

The second problem area for a conventional human rights approach concerns the possibility of *conflict* between relevant rights. Just as rights may compete with other values, so distinct human rights (e.g., to life and to private property) may conflict with one another (Rajamani 2010). If so, a simple appeal to human rights does not resolve the issue.

The third area is the *role* of human rights. For example, one of the central features of human rights from Caney's point of view is that they make certain ethical concerns "nontradable," in the sense that they "override all other moral values," "constrain the pursuit of other moral and political ideals" and "condemn any trade-offs which would leave some below the minimum moral threshold" (Caney 2010, 165). On the face of it, this appears a strong requirement, and so hardly uncontroversial and minimalist. Even within contemporary human rights discourse it is common to accept a progression of concern for human rights that accompanies social development, and the suspension some provisions in situations of "emergency." In addition, such

---

[9] Another is that international institutions are reluctant to endorse new rights of these sorts. This is not a philosophical problem, except insofar as it casts doubt on the foundation in common law, or basic ethical intuition. However, it is a practical problem, especially for those who would claim that human rights provide a relatively uncontroversial basis for climate and global environmental policy.

compromises are highly relevant to climate ethics, since some claim that suspension is currently justified, given the extent of global poverty and the (alleged) priority of economic development. More generally, one cannot ignore the possibility that a broader human rights perspective may imply that climate change should take a back seat to more pressing threats, so that the master argument is too narrow to gain traction. Although many (including myself) would resist such arguments, the conceptual space they occupy cannot simply be assumed away, as if by definitional fiat.

The fourth problem area involves the *scope* of the relevant rights. Human rights initially appear very victim-centered. However, something needs to be said about who the duty-holders are and how far their responsibilities extend. In practice, this will determine much of the substance of a human rights approach.

To see why this might matter, consider another of Caney's claims: that it is vital to the human rights approach that "the threats to life, health, and subsistence … *are the products of the actions of other people,*" in the sense that "*if the impacts* of climate change were entirely the result of natural phenomena and *were not traceable to human causes*, then … *[those arguments] would not succeed*" (Caney 2010, 169, emphasis added). Hence, on Caney's view, something counts as a human rights problem if and only if human agency is responsible for it.

Understood literally, this causal claim suggests that the master argument is invalid. Climate change might threaten important human interests without thereby threatening the enjoyment of *rights* that protect those interests. In particular, if those rights only protect against some kinds of threats – e.g., those traceable to human causes – then rights need not be in play every time the relevant interests are threatened. In this case, for example, they would not be threatened by severe *natural* climate change. This is not Caney's own view, since he accepts an extremely generous (and controversial) interpretation of the causal claim.[10] However, the fact that it is

---

[10] In a footnote, he says: "Suppose that climate change were nonanthropogenic … but politicians could implement an effective program of adaptation and design institutions that would safeguard the vital interests of people in life, health and subsistence, but chose not to. They could then be said to violate the human rights of others to life, health, and subsistence because they would be acting in such a way as *to create* threats to life, health and subsistence" (2010, 176, n38, emphasis added). Hence, on Caney's view, if someone could protect the vital interests but chooses not to, they create the relevant threats. However, this is a very broad view of "creating" a threat, which others might resist, especially as part of a minimalist account of human rights. For example, we would not normally say that I *create* threats to famine victims in Africa just because I could assist them but choose not to. As Philippa Foot once said, refusing to aid the starving is not the same as deliberately sending them poisoned food (Foot 1967). This is so even if both are (very) morally wrong.

encouraged by the initial framing reinforces the impression that the master argument is much less powerful than it initially appears, and that more substantive and controversial conceptions of human rights are needed to do real work.

The main lessons of this section are that it is unclear whether a conventional human rights approach successfully picks out the commitments needed to address a problem like climate change, and whether it can do so without relying on "controversial or ambitious conceptions" of human rights. Most notably, it seems likely that much important work will be done internally, in the specific conception of human rights being invoked (rather than in the invocation of human rights as such), and that these internal matters can make a large difference to policy. Given this, it is not enough simply to invoke the language of human rights for climate change in the way that the master argument does. Even if one accepts that language, many – perhaps most – of the central issues remain to be addressed.

Theory revisited

Several of the preceding worries are familiar from other areas where human rights are deployed. This section takes up concerns that are more specific to climate change and global environmental problems more generally. In particular, we might ask: Is a human rights approach well-suited to addressing a perfect moral storm?

Presumably, the basic ethical intuition – that there are some kinds of harms that should not be inflicted on others, and that institutions that systematically inflict such harms are ethically illegitimate – remains highly relevant. Given this, it might be said, the internal difficulties of the human rights approach identified in earlier sections should not be too off-putting. Such an approach at least provides the right kind of framework within which to have the necessary discussions.

This position is attractive. Nevertheless, in the context of a perfect moral storm, where we are vulnerable to moral corruption, we must notice the obstacles to be overcome. In what follows, I shall (very briefly) point to three major worries that suggest that addressing the perfect storm requires at least a serious reorientation of much human rights discourse.

The first worry is that of merely *naming the problem*. Simply asserting that the perfect moral storm threatens human rights does not get us very far in addressing it. In particular, the bare statement does not tell us much about the principles, institutions and policies that we should employ to combat it.

To see why this might matter, consider, for example, a rival utilitarian approach that said simply, "allowing severe climate change is bad if it fails to maximize utility." Even if this is true in so far as it goes, it does not yet tell us much about what should be done, or how. Given this, a utilitarian political theory that contented itself with resting at this point would seem unduly complacent. If it also said that there might be many ways of dealing with the problem, none of which could be adequately discerned in advance, it could also be accused of being unduly opaque and perhaps also evasive. Importantly, these complaints would stick even if one had complete confidence in the initial diagnosis. A moral and political theory can be defective in ways other than being wrong at the first stage (Gardiner 2011a, ch. 7).

The parallel with human rights is that one might be confident that climate change is a human rights issue, and most fundamentally so, and yet still worry that existing appeals to human rights have other vices. For example, the difficulties of the previous section (e.g., deciding whether existing rights should be bootstrapped or new ones introduced, pinning down exactly which rights are most central, determining the scope of the relevant rights, identifying the relevant duty-bearers, and so on) might imply that the approach is opaque or even evasive at crucial points. If such matters are not addressed, one might worry that the approach has become unduly complacent; and recall that in a perfect moral storm, involving the threat of moral corruption for the current generation, complacency is a serious complaint.

The second major worry is that existing human rights paradigms go beyond mere complacency, to being *covertly biased* against the major victims of a perfect moral storm. The institutional advantages of the inherited legal paradigm are often mentioned. However, current institutions seem ill-suited to the climate problem in important ways.

First, they are typically highly reactive. For example, the paradigm legal forum for addressing human rights is judicial, and takes the form of remedial action once harm has been inflicted, victims identified, and causal routes explained. This paradigm is not a happy one in the climate case. Most notably, there are very long time lags involved. Greenhouse gas emissions, once made, can remain in the atmosphere for hundreds – even thousands – of years, affecting temperature and climate more generally. Hence, it will often be the case that harms do not occur, and specific victims cannot be identified, before the original emitters are dead and gone. Given this, the paradigm and much of its associated legal trappings will be inadequate to the intergenerational dimension of the problem and the severity of the harms involved. Remediation is likely to be too little, and much too late.[11]

Second, existing institutions focus on the wrong agents. Human rights law is largely concerned with the rights of individuals against their own states. Yet climate change is a profoundly global and intergenerational problem. Again, the intergenerational challenge is particularly notable. How does one hold earlier generations accountable for the harms they inflict on their successors? One concern is that existing human rights law provides no answer; another, even more serious one, is that this is the wrong question to be asking, and that something other than an accountability model is required.

The general lack of fit between existing human rights paradigms and the climate problem suggests that one serious threat posed by the current human rights discourse is that it facilitates only the inclusion of current victims of negative climate impacts in the political and policy discussion. In other words, it provides a limited avenue through which some existing (and early) victims of climate change in the current generation can try to pursue their claims. Such a focus hardly touches many of the main elements of the perfect moral storm, but is predictable within it.

The third major worry is that a human rights approach faces philosophical difficulties that provide a *convenient distraction* for those wishing to take advantage of a perfect moral storm. On the one hand, the moral paradigm for harm works best with readily identifiable and determinate agents, victims, impacts and causal pathways. Yet climate change and other genuinely global, intergenerational and ecological problems do not conform well to this paradigm (Gardiner 2011c; Jamieson 1992, 2010). For example, instead of specific individual agents and victims, much of the perfect moral storm is concerned with collectives, and especially generations. Moreover, climate impacts are not easily separated from other background social facts, and the causal pathways are complex and interdependent. In addition, there are vexed issues of identity. For example, according to the non-identity problem, we do not harm those whose existence depends on our polluting activities, so long as they have at least a minimally decent life (Meyer 2004; Parfit 1985).

On the other hand, there are also specific challenges to rights in this context. For example, some argue that it is incoherent to claim that future people have rights, since they do not yet exist (Beckerman and Pasek 2001);

---

[11] This complicates the typical claim that human rights "put a human face" on systemic impacts by highlighting their implications for actual people in actual places.

others insist that it would be rational for future people whose very existence depends on the continuation of polluting behavior to waive any rights violated by that behavior so long as their lives overall are worth living (Parfit 1985). Clearly these worries are important to the adequacy of a human rights approach. If future people lack rights – or would waive them even if they have them – then we cannot expect a rights approach to provide them robust protections in a perfect moral storm.

My claim is not that any of these philosophical difficulties constitute decisive reasons to reject either climate action or a human rights approach. (On the contrary, I am unmoved by most of them.) Instead, the point is that, if we ignore the limitations of the standard human rights approach, we are at risk of embracing a paradigm that does little to deal with many elements of the perfect moral storm – including the central element of intergenerational buck-passing. Given this, *even within a human rights approach there is a high risk of moral corruption.* We can sound appropriately ethical in our initial diagnosis and suggestion of remedies, when in fact these remedies are not adequate to the problem that confronts us.

How then might we move forward? The perfect storm analysis provides an agenda for the human rights approach in law and philosophy. Given its presence, and the challenge it poses to conventional institutions and theories, the human rights approach must resist complacency and seek to address the storm as it is. This would involve – at a minimum – addressing three major areas: risk, future generations, and the relationship with nature. It would also include a paradigm shift within the discourse from a reactive to a proactive stance, from an individual and short-term focus to one that incorporates a collective and intergenerational perspective, from an individual–state model of relationships to one that takes seriously individual–generation or generation–generation relations, and from a purely anthropocentric account to one that allows a place for the non-human and our relationship to nature.

This is a lot to ask. Moreover, presumably not all of it can take place within the human rights discourse considered merely as such; instead, wider theory will have to encroach. Nevertheless, the hard questions are worth asking. If our problem is the perfect moral storm, then making a human rights approach central may already sharply narrow the normative picture (e.g., in the "dangerous climate change" proposal). If this is not to facilitate continued buck-passing, then we must be alert to its internal and external limitations.

References

Beckerman, Wilfred and Pasek, Joanna. 2001. *Justice, Posterity and the Environment.* Oxford University Press

Bell, Derek. 2011. "Does Anthropogenic Climate Change Violate Human Rights?" *Critical Review of International Social and Political Philosophy* 14, 99–124.

Bodansky, Daniel. 2010. "Climate Change and Human Rights: Unpacking the Issues." *Georgia Journal of International and Comparative Law* 38, 511–524.

Caney, Simon. 2006. "Cosmopolitan Justice, Rights and Climate Change." *Canadian Journal of Law and Jurisprudence* 19, 255–278.

2008. "Human Rights, Climate Change, and Discounting." *Environmental Politics* 17, 536–555.

2009. "Climate Change and the Future: Discounting for Time, Wealth, and Risk." *Journal of Social Philosophy* 40, 163–186.

2010. "Climate Change, Human Rights and Moral Thresholds." In Stephen Humphreys, ed., *Human Rights and Climate Change.* Cambridge University Press. Reprinted in Stephen M. Gardiner, Simon Caney, Dale Jamieson and Henry Shue, eds., *Climate Ethics: Essential Readings.* New York: Oxford University Press, pp. 255–278. (Page references are to this version.)

Copenhagen Accord. 2009. Decision 2/ CP.15, "Copenhagen Accord," in FCCC/CP/2009/11/Add.1

Cowen, Tyler and Parfit, Derek. 1992. "Against the Social Discount Rate." In Peter Laslett and James Fiskin, eds., *Justice Between Age Groups and Generations.* New Haven: Yale University Press, pp. 144–161.

Foot, Philippa. 1967. "The Problem of Abortion and the Doctrine of the Double Effect." *Oxford Review* 5: 5–15.

Gardiner, Stephen M. 2004. "The Global Warming Tragedy and the Dangerous Illusion of the Kyoto Protocol." *Ethics and International Affairs* 18, 23–39.

2011a. *A Perfect Moral Storm: The Ethical Challenge of Climate Change.* New York: Oxford University Press.

2011b. "Rawls and Climate Change: Does Rawlsian Political Philosophy Pass the Global Test?" *Critical Review of International Social and Political Philosophy* 14: 125–151.

2011c. "Is No One Responsible for Global Environmental Tragedy? Climate Change as a Challenge to Our Ethical Concepts." In Denis Arnold, ed., *Ethics and Global Climate Change.* Cambridge University Press, pp. 38–59.

Hayward, Tim. 2005. *Constitutional Environmental Rights.* Oxford University Press.

2007. "Human Rights versus Emission Rights: Climate Justice and the Equitable Distribution of Ecological Space." *Ethics and International Affairs* 21, 431–450.

Humphreys, Stephen, ed. 2010. *Human Rights and Climate Change.* Cambridge University Press.

ICHRP (International Council on Human Rights Policy). 2008. *Climate Change and Human Rights: A Rough Guide*. Geneva: International Council on Human Rights.

IPCC (Intergovernmental Panel on Climate Change). 2007. *Climate Change 2007: The Physical Science Basis*. Cambridge University Press.

Jamieson, Dale. 1992. "Ethics, Public Policy and Global Warming." *Science, Technology, and Human Values* 17, 139–153.

2010. "Climate Change, Responsibility and Justice." *Science and Engineering Ethics* 16, 431–445.

Lawrence, Peter. Unpublished. "Human Rights, Future Generations and Climate Change: New Synergy or Costly Distraction?" Manuscript on file with author.

McInerney-Lankford, Siobhan, Darrow, Mac and Rajamani, Lavanya. 2011. *Human Rights and Climate Change: A Review of the International Legal Dimensions*. Washington, DC: World Bank.

Meyer, Lukas. 2004. "Historical Injustice and the Right of Return." *Theoretical Inquiries in Law* 5, 305–316.

Oppenheimer, Michael and Petsonk, Annie. 2005. "Article 2 of the UNFCCC: Historical Origins, Recent Interpretations." *Climatic Change* 73: 195–226.

Parfit, Derek. 1985. *Reasons and Persons*. Oxford University Press.

Picolotti, Romina. 2008. "Foreword." In ICHRP, *Climate Change and Human Rights: A Rough Guide*. Geneva: International Council on Human Rights, pp. v–vi.

Rajamani, Lavanya. 2010. "The Increasing Currency and Relevance of Rights-Based Perspectives in the International Negotiations on Climate Change." *Journal of Environmental Law* 22: 391–429.

Robinson, Mary. 2008. "Foreword." In ICHRP, *Climate Change and Human Rights: A Rough Guide*. Geneva: International Council on Human Rights, pp. iii–iv.

Shue, Henry. 1992. "The Unavoidability of Justice." In Andrew Hurrell and Benedict Kingsbury, eds., *The International Politics of the Environment*. Oxford University Press, pp. 373–97.

United Nations. 1972. Stockholm Declaration of the United Nations Conference on the Human Environment.

2007. Malé Declaration on the Human Dimension of Global Climate Change (November 14, 2007).

United Nations Framework Convention on Climate Change. 1992. Available at: http://unfccc.int/essential_background/convention/background/items/1349.php.

United Nations Office of the High Commissioner for Human Rights. 2009. *Report on the Relationship Between Climate Change and Human Rights*, UN Doc. A/HRC/10/61 (January 15, 2009).

Vanderheiden, Steve. 2008. *Atmospheric Justice: A Political Theory of Climate Change*. Oxford University Press.

12 | A human rights approach to energy, poverty and gender inequality

GAIL KARLSSON

Introduction

There are close to three billion people living with little or no access to modern energy sources for household and productive uses. They primarily use traditional biomass fuels from local woodlands and fields – firewood, dung, agricultural residues and charcoal. Recognizing the importance and magnitude of this problem, the UN General Assembly designated 2012 as the International Year of Sustainable Energy for All, and the UN Secretary-General has launched a global initiative on Sustainable Energy for All by 2030.

Is lack of adequate energy a human rights issue? Although the Universal Declaration of Human Rights includes the right to a standard of living that is adequate for health and well-being, energy is not specifically mentioned. Some level of energy access seems to be essential for basic subsistence, including fuel for cooking food and keeping warm. But is there a right to "modern" energy services, such as power for water pumping, agricultural production, food processing, lighting and communications?

In 1986, the UN member states expanded the list of human rights to include a right to development "by virtue of which every human person and all peoples are entitled to participate in, contribute to, and enjoy economic, social, cultural and political development" (United Nations General Assembly 1986). Possibly a right to energy would fall within this category, as a necessity for people's economic and social development.

Energy access is generally viewed in terms of technology and engineering, however, rather than human rights. Certainly, within governments, energy planners have little contact with ministries dealing with "softer" social equity issues. Applying a human rights perspective to energy access challenges helps us focus on the ways in which energy is essential for the fulfillment of basic human needs. It also highlights the links between energy, poverty and gender inequality.

One very important factor in the context of human rights and energy access is that due to culturally established gender roles in many developing countries, collecting firewood and other fuels in rural areas is generally

231

unpaid work performed by women. This unpaid work takes up large amounts of women's time, has adverse impacts on their health, and limits their opportunities for education and employment. It also contributes to their disproportionate poverty levels, especially when combined with scarcity of other necessary resources and lack of value placed on women's labor.

Extensive improvements in fuel supply chains and electricity grids are critical for meeting basic development needs. Yet women's distinct energy needs, especially in poor, rural areas, receive relatively little attention from governments. This both reflects, and reinforces, gender inequities and discrimination.

When governments and institutions actively affirm the equal human rights of men and women, this creates a strong moral and legal basis for incorporating women's perspectives into national and international energy policies and planning, thereby helping to promote women's economic and social empowerment and participation in decision-making. It also leads to improved results from actions aimed at reaching national goals on poverty alleviation, development and climate change. Achieving the United Nations goal of universal access to energy would definitely represent a key step in freeing up women's time and labor and enabling them to develop their full economic and political potential.

Women, themselves, can help their countries and communities move toward meeting this universal energy access goal by transforming their current energy roles into enterprises that produce and market more fuel-efficient and environmentally friendly energy technologies. Governments can support women in these efforts, including by adopting targeted policies that promote innovative financing and business development services accessible to women.

Links between human rights, environmental conditions, energy and poverty

The 1945 Universal Declaration of Human Rights attempted to set out a common vision acceptable to all countries in the post-World War II era. It incorporated the civil and political rights emphasized by democratic countries as well as the economic and social rights prioritized by the Soviet bloc. These economic and social rights set out in the Declaration include the right to a standard of living adequate for health and well-being, and this could be interpreted to require some basic level of energy usage.

Although many of our current environmental and energy-related concerns had not yet emerged at the time the Universal Declaration of Human Rights was adopted, the basic principles of the declaration allow for flexibility in defining basic rights and what is needed for an adequate standard of living. In 1972, the UN Conference on the Human Environment in Stockholm first focused international attention on the importance of healthy environmental conditions for human well-being, especially for people in poor countries who depend on the land and natural resources for fuel and other daily requirements. "Man has the fundamental right to freedom, equality and adequate conditions of life, in an environment of a quality that permits a life of dignity and well-being, and he bears a solemn responsibility to protect and improve the environment for present and future generations" (United Nations 1972).

The 1986 Declaration on the Right to Development referred to an explicit individual human right to economic development (United Nations General Assembly 1986). Because there is little opportunity for people to escape from subsistence-level lifestyles without significant energy resources, this right to development, if taken seriously, provides an even stronger basis for including increased access to energy as an essential element of basic economic human rights.

By 1992, the interconnection between the right to development and the need for environmental protection was the main focus of the UN Conference on Environment and Development in Rio de Janeiro (also known as the "Earth Summit"). Principle 1 of the Rio Declaration adopted at the Earth Summit states that: "Human beings are at the centre of concerns for sustainable development. They are entitled to a healthy and productive life in harmony with nature" (United Nations 1992a). The concept of sustainable development that emerged from the Earth Summit pulled together three interdependent and mutually reinforcing pillars: economic development, social development and environmental protection.

The goal of the Agenda 21 Plan of Action adopted at the Earth Summit was to support actions that promote people's livelihoods while also preserving the natural environment. Chapter 7, paragraph 1, noted that while the consumption patterns of industrialized countries were stressing the capacity of global ecosystems, developing countries needed more energy and economic development simply to overcome basic economic and social problems.

Recognizing the need for greater equity in income distribution and human development, Agenda 21 recommended focusing on the rights of women as a key element of an effective strategy for tackling poverty, development and environmental problems simultaneously (Chapter 3, paragraph 2). Women's roles were also emphasized in two of the three international conventions adopted at the Earth Summit, the Convention on Biological Diversity and the Convention to Combat Desertification. However, the UN Framework Convention on Climate Change did not explicitly recognize the importance of gender equity or women's participation. (In considering both mitigation and adaptation policies, climate change negotiators have preferred to focus on scientific and technological measures rather than "soft" policies that would address behavior and social differences (FAO 2006).)

In 2000, through the Millennium Declaration, the leaders of all the UN member states reaffirmed the principles of the UN Charter and the Universal Declaration of Human Rights and committed to protect social, cultural, economic and political rights for all, including the right to development. In Paragraph 6, the Millennium Declaration endorsed the fundamental value of solidarity: "global challenges must be managed in a way that distributes the costs and burdens fairly in accordance with basic principles of equity and social justice" (United Nations General Assembly 2000).

Although the Millennium Development Goals (MDGs) laid out in the Millennium Declaration include some targets for environmental sustainability, they do not directly address energy needs. Yet, strong arguments have been made that access to non-polluting energy sources is essential for meeting the goals on environmental sustainability, poverty reduction, health and education (Modi *et al.* 2006). Integrating rights to energy into the MDG framework is especially important for making progress toward eradicating extreme poverty.

In 2010, the International Energy Agency, UN Development Programme and UN Industrial Development Organization prepared a special report for the ten-year review of the MDGs that called for universal access to modern energy services. Noting the tremendous number of people who still rely on traditional biomass fuels for energy, the report concluded that: "the UN Millennium Development Goal of eradicating poverty by 2015 will not be achieved unless substantial progress is made on improving energy access" (IEA *et al.* 2010).

Based on the IEA report, and an April 2010 report from his Advisory Group on Energy and Climate Change (United Nations AGECC 2010), UN Secretary-General Ban Ki-moon called on the UN system and world leaders to commit to meeting the goal of universal access to clean, affordable energy by 2030 (Ban Ki-moon 2011). Over the next few years, it is possible that this international commitment to providing universal energy access could evolve into wider recognition of energy as a human right.

Energy, poverty and women's rights

Women represent a majority of the poorest people, largely due to current social and economic inequities and women's low levels of access to resources (United Nations Development Programme 1997). Poverty generally involves not only lack of income and assets, but also conditions of disempowerment and exclusion that severely limit people's opportunities for employment, ownership of property and political representation. "Energy poverty" has been defined as the absence of sufficient choice in accessing adequate, affordable, reliable, high quality, safe and environmentally benign energy services to support economic and human development (Reddy 2000).

The 1995 UNDP Human Development Report reported that: "Women still constitute 70% of the world's poor and two thirds of the world's illiterates. They occupy only 14% of managerial and administrative jobs, 10% of parliamentary seats and 6% of cabinet positions. In many legal systems, they are still unequal. They often work longer hours than men, but much of their work remains unvalued, unrecognized and unappreciated" (United Nations Development Programme 1995). The report further recommended investments in building women's capabilities, and empowering them to exercise their rights, as a way of contributing to economic growth and overall development.

In 2010, the Millennium Development Goal Summit found continued inadequacies in advancing gender equality and the empowerment of women (United Nations General Assembly 2010b). The outcome resolution called for action to ensure women's equal access to education, basic services, health-care, economic opportunities and decision-making, stressing that "investing in women and girls has a multiplier effect on productivity, efficiency and sustained economic growth" (United Nations General Assembly 2010a).

Women's poverty in developing countries is strongly linked to environmental degradation and inadequate energy resources, especially in areas where women must gather fuel and water from local sources to provide for their families' needs. Article 14 of the 1979 Convention on the Elimination of Discrimination against Women emphasized the needs of rural women and urged signatory governments to take actions to provide them with adequate living conditions, including electricity, water and sanitation. Chapter 24 of the Earth Summit's Agenda 21 outlined recommendations to reduce women's workloads, and to provide environmentally sound technologies, as well as improved fuel supplies. It also urged countries to take urgent action to "avert the ongoing rapid environmental and economic degradation in developing countries that generally affects the lives of women and children in rural areas suffering drought, desertification and deforestation" (United Nations 1992b).

The connection between women's poverty and environmental conditions was reiterated in the 1995 Beijing Platform of Action adopted by the Fourth World Conference on Women. "The deterioration of natural resources displaces communities, especially women, from income-generating activities, while greatly adding to unremunerated work" (United Nations 1995). Strategic Objective F.2 of the Beijing Platform for Action called on governments to support equal access for women to sustainable and affordable energy technologies (United Nations 1995).

The UN agencies have specifically acknowledged that: "Access to energy services is particularly important to women, given that energy services and technologies are not gender neutral. The lack of modern fuels and electricity reinforces gender inequalities" (UN-Energy 2005). Nevertheless, the energy poverty of women, especially in rural areas, still receives relatively little attention or funding from governments.

Energy policies that appear to be gender neutral may in fact be discriminatory. For example, many developing countries prioritize energy investments to promote industrial and commercial sectors rather than universal energy access (United Nations AGECC 2010). As a result, there is less energy available for household use, especially in rural areas. This has a disproportionate impact on women, due to their traditional roles in supplying the fuel needed for household cooking, heating and lighting.

Unpaid wood and biomass fuel collection can take up large amounts of women's time and labor (see Figure 12.1). It also makes women vulnerable to fuel scarcity caused by environmental degradation (including from climate change, industrial agriculture, and extractive or polluting industries). Women face risks of physical violence and injury when they have to travel far from home to find fuel and carry it back. At home, cooking over smoky fires causes serious respiratory diseases and other health problems, especially for women.

However, this unpaid women's work generally does not figure in national economic reports or energy sector planning, even when traditional biomass fuels, primarily collected by women, represent the majority of the country's energy resources. In Uganda, for example, biomass (mostly gathered by women) accounts for over 90 percent of the total energy consumed, and in Zambia wood fuel for use by households represents over 80 percent of the total energy supply (ENERGIA 2007).

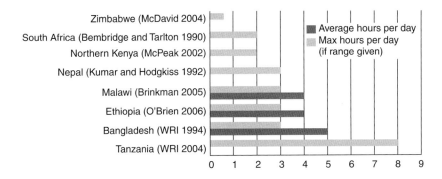

Figure 12.1 Selected data on time spent in wood collection. Source: Practical Action 2010 (reproduced with permission).

Meanwhile, without access to electricity or motorized power for pumps and processing equipment, women also have to carry water for household needs and food production, and grind grains for family meals using their own manual labor. These daily activities contribute to the constraints that limit employment options for women and educational opportunities for girls.

Incorporating a women's human rights perspective in energy policies

Applying a human rights based approach involves making respect for women's rights a specific objective of energy policies and actions, as well as a guiding principle for related decision-making and implementation processes. National affirmation of a human rights approach in government activities, including energy initiatives, can also change women's expectations of their governments. If access to electricity comes to be accepted as a right, then lack of access, or gender discrimination in delivery of services, can be viewed as a violation of government obligations.

Efforts to apply human rights principles in an energy context to benefit and empower women are usually more effective if there are already general government policies in place that promote gender equality. In Kenya, for example, the new Constitution adopted in 2010 includes a Bill of Rights, which states that men and women have the right to equal treatment and opportunities. This affects the policies and activities of government agencies, including the Ministry of Energy, and the operations of the national power companies.

In countries where there is resistance to gender equality, references to human rights covenants and principles can support the legitimacy of women's claims for basic services, and the obligations of governments to respond to those claims. The Convention to End Discrimination Against Women, for example, calls on signatories to take "all appropriate measures to eliminate discrimination against women in rural areas in order to ensure, on a basis of equality of men and women, that they participate in and benefit from rural development" (United Nations General Assembly 1979). Requirements for broad-based participation in decision-making and programming also help create frameworks for governments to take women's roles and rights seriously.

Gender equality in legal status and property rights is critical for women to be able to reach adequate standards of living for their health and well-being. In cases where women are subject to discrimination and exclusion under their country's political and legal systems, a human rights based approach to development would create a basis for viewing women as people whose rights must be respected. It would also provide a moral and legal basis for more participation of women in decision-making processes, and actions to change existing discriminatory norms, values, policies and practices. This might involve, for example, providing support for women's basic economic and social rights by reforming government policies that limit women's ability to own land, start businesses, obtain credit, or gain access to training and agricultural extension services.

With regard to energy policies and programs, a focus on rights helps to reveal existing injustices, and ensure that women benefit from energy services. With better services, and equal opportunities, women can make gains in education and incomes that improve not only their fulfillment of basic needs, but also their political power and representation.

However, understanding why and how to apply a human rights based approach to development can present significant challenges, especially for scientists and engineers who are more comfortable with technical planning than with social justice issues. It requires looking at the larger political and legal context and considering why certain people and communities lack basic rights, services and resources.

The ENERGIA International Network on Gender and Sustainable Energy has been working with governments and energy institutions to help them analyze the connections between gender equity, energy policies and development goals through gender audits. In Kenya, for example, an ENERGIA audit helped energy decision-makers identify and focus on the gender dimensions of their policies and decisions (see Table 12.1).

Table 12.1 Key issues in Kenya's energy policy and possible gender dimensions

Issue	Gender dimensions
1. Investment decisions The commercial and economic sectors receive the bulk of investment funding (for conventional energy sources, including grid electricity and petroleum fuels) compared to biomass and renewables	Policy determines which energy sectors receive attention and support. Poor women are unlikely to benefit from the large-scale commercial energy expansion programs, especially if the expansion programs do not support connections to households. Poor women derive their energy services from non-conventional energy sources including renewable energy. Support to local level, if focused on renewable energy, may provide women with both employment and new energy services.
2. Access to affordable clean energy	The rural poor including women do not have access to modern energy. Continued dependence on biomass for cooking and lighting disproportionately predispose women and children to health hazards of indoor air pollution, drudgery.
3. Energy pricing	Income disparities between men and women; men control household income; decisions about access to energy supply are male dominated. This means that energy pricing will impact men and women differently.
4. Infrastructure construction	Men benefit more than women in terms of employment opportunities. Also large-scale energy projects raise gender equality issues related to differentiated impact on women and men.
5. Community participation strategies	Men and women's concerns are not explicitly included in energy program implementation. Neither is gender approach emphasized during the pre-development Environmental Impact Assessment (EIA). Gender inequalities exist in various aspects of community participation.
6. Human resource planning	Women's specific contribution in energy decision-making is not explicitly recognized. Males at policy and technical and professional levels also dominate energy sector. For example in the renewable energy Department of Ministry of Energy, there is only one female professional against 20 men.
7. Energy related health hazards	Women and children are more exposed to biomass based indoor air pollution.
8. Access to electricity	Most rural women have no access to electricity. Even when connected through rural electrification, they lack finances to engage in income-generating enterprises.
9. Dwindling biomass energy supply	Biomass shortage increases drudgery for women. There are health implications on women walking long distances to collect firewood.

Source: Mbuthi *et al.* 2007.

Based on the recommendations made by the audit team, the Kenyan government considered ways to make gender issues more visible to energy managers, for example by establishing a database that includes gender-disaggregated data, and identifying criteria for assessing the impact of programs on men and women.

Similarly, in Botswana, an ENERGIA-sponsored audit showed that an apparently gender-neutral process for putting together the country's Draft Energy Policy did not include input from women, who are the major users and managers of domestic energy sources (Botswana Technology Centre 2006). Following the audit, the Botswana Power Corporation's rural electrification program adopted a gender-mainstreaming program for their rural electrification activities.

Energy access, women's rights and climate change solutions

The UN General Assembly's designation of 2012 as the International Year of Universal Energy Access, and the UN system's related global initiative, provide clear opportunities for promoting human rights and women's rights perspectives in international and national energy policies. This is particularly important as efforts to respond to climate change threats are likely to create new markets, investments and employment based on energy technologies with low greenhouse gas emissions, and women need to be included in these activities in order to take advantage of the increased economic development possibilities.

New cleaner energy market opportunities in developing countries can actually promote women's human rights and economic empowerment, if steps are taken to ensure that women as well as men are involved, and share the benefits. The report from world leaders attending the September 2010 UN Millennium Development Goals Review Summit particularly mentioned the importance of expanding opportunities for women and girls as agents of development, investing in rural infrastructure to reduce women's domestic burdens, and improving access to energy (United Nations General Assembly 2010a).

The recently formed Global Gender and Climate Alliance is playing a key role in pressing for attention to women's rights under the UN Framework Convention on Climate Change. The Alliance's workshops for national delegates attending convention meetings have led to more attention to gender disparities in climate negotiations, institutions and funding mechanisms. In November 2008, the Global Gender and Climate Alliance (which includes a number of UN agencies as well as civil society organizations) joined in the Manila Declaration for Global Action on Gender in Climate Change and Disaster Risk Reduction (GGCA 2008). The Declaration underscored the roles of women as vital agents of change, holders of valuable knowledge and skills, and potentially powerful leaders in climate change mitigation and adaptation. It also denounced the absence of a gender perspective in the global agreements on climate change, despite national, regional and international commitments, and legally binding instruments on gender equality.

Many women are already dealing with, and adapting to, climatic changes, and have valuable knowledge about local resources, as well as the energy needs and priorities of their communities. With appropriate training and incentives, women and women's groups can initiate energy access projects that reduce greenhouse gas emissions, support "green" economic development, and also contribute to the empowerment of women through energy entrepreneurship. If women's rights are not taken into account, however, the impacts of climate change, and related governmental responses, could instead reinforce existing gender inequities.

It particularly makes sense to promote women's engagement in producing and/or marketing low-emission cooking stoves (ones that are more fuel-efficient and produce less smoke), and other small-scale renewable energy technologies, through initiatives providing technical training, entrepreneurial skills and access to credit. For example, in India, the Self-Employed Women's Association (SEWA) has worked with the Solar Electric Light Company to develop a smokeless gas stove and, together with a partner organization, Mahila Housing Trust, is training women masons to construct and sell the stoves. In November 2011, the International Finance Corporation, a member of the World Bank Group, agreed to guarantee loans from local banks to SEWA members to finance sales of stoves, as well as solar lanterns, to more than 200,000 of its members. The aim is to test the potential for a financially self-sustaining business model engaging consumers, distributors and entrepreneurs at the lowest level of the economic pyramid (*The Hindu*, 2011). The project is expected to generate carbon credits by reducing greenhouse gas emissions, which can also generate some income for SEWA members.

In Uganda, Solar Sister is another women-focused energy enterprise that uses a woman-to-woman network of sales agents to distribute solar lanterns as replacements for candles and kerosene lanterns in areas without electricity. Solar Sister provides the lanterns to the agents, who sell them on consignment and keep a commission.

In off-grid areas, renewable energy options such as wind, solar and small hydro generators can be used to provide low-emission electricity or battery-charging services, and also empower women. For example, some of the Solar Sister lanterns also have battery-charging capacity, which provides possibilities for new small-scale business opportunities. In India, the non-profit Barefoot College teaches poor, illiterate women how to work in non-traditional occupations, including manufacturing and installing solar panels for electricity generation. The Grameen Shakti organization in Bangladesh also trains women as solar technicians and sales agents, and as renewable energy entrepreneurs, linking them up with various technical and financial services.

Renewable energy technologies can also provide motorized power for essential equipment such as water pumps and grain mills that relieve women in rural areas from domestic labor and free up their time for other types of productive activities. The Tanzania Traditional Energy Development and Environment Organization (TaTEDO) is one of the organizations in Africa facilitating the installation of village power systems called Multifunctional Platforms. They are based on a simple diesel engine mounted on a steel chassis, and interchangeable attachments can be used for a variety of tasks, including milling, grinding, water pumping, electricity generation, and battery charging. Women are trained to maintain and operate the machines, and manage sales of the services they provide. They also use the machines to support new income-generating activities.

In some cases, production of biogas and other biofuels from plant products and local agricultural waste materials may also allow women and communities to gain access to homegrown energy resources, as well as related social and economic development opportunities, while also reducing greenhouse gas emissions. For example, Nepal has undertaken a national program to promote biogas as a clean and convenient cooking fuel that can reduce women's time burdens and health risks. Due in part to a gender action plan facilitated by ENERGIA, this program is emphasizing the engagement of women as masons to construct the biogas systems, and as managers of biogas companies (Tamrakar and Manandhar 2009). Because the biogas systems help reduce the number of tons of firewood and liters of kerosene burned, and prevent large amounts of carbon dioxide from being released into the atmosphere, the program is also applying for greenhouse gas emission credits.

Conclusion

Without specific recognition of women's rights, and removal of gender-based barriers to economic development, women are less likely to be able to benefit from investments in clean energy technologies, new climate funds, and government energy policies. However, if women's human rights are respected and taken into account, energy access programs and investments will be more effective and comprehensive, and support better living conditions and economic opportunities for both men and women.

Given the flexibility of the UN's human rights principles, an international commitment to providing universal energy access could potentially evolve into recognition of energy as a human right. In any event, the UN Sustainable Energy for All initiative is likely to raise the expectations of individuals regarding the obligations of their governments in this regard. By incorporating a human rights perspective, the initiative can serve to ensure that the basic energy needs of women as well as men are addressed.

Besides being an essential factor for poverty alleviation and human development, energy policies and investments are also critical for effective climate change responses and overall environmental sustainability. In this context, adoption of low-carbon energy choices has a clear impact on everyone's human rights, as the risks of catastrophic climate changes threaten to undermine the economic, social and political rights of people across the entire planet.

References

Ban Ki-moon. 2011. Remarks to Young Future Energy Leaders. Abu Dhabi, United Arab Emirates. January 17, 2011.

Botswana Technology Centre. 2006. *Gender Audit of Energy Policies and Programmes: The Case for Botswana.*

ENERGIA. 2007. *Where Energy is Women's Business: National and Regional Reports from Africa, Asia, Latin America and the Pacific.* Leusden: ENERGIA.

FAO (UN Food and Agriculture Organization). 2006. *Gender: The Missing Component of the Response to Climate Change*. Rome: FAO.

GGCA. 2008. Manila Declaration for Global Action on Gender in Climate Change and Disaster Risk Reduction.

The Hindu, November 19, 2011. "SEWA to Provide Solar Lanterns and Energy-Efficient Stoves to its Members."

International Energy Agency, UN Development Programme and UN Industrial Development Organization. 2010. *Energy Poverty: How to Make Energy Access Universal*. OECD/IEA.

Mbuthi, P., Odongo, F., Machera, M. and Imitira, J. 2007. *Gender Audit of Energy Policy and Programmes in Kenya, Final Report*. Kenya Ministry of Energy, Practical Action East Africa, ENERGIA and East African Energy Technology Development Network.

Modi, V., McDade, S., Lallement, D. and Saghir, J. 2006. *Energy and the Millennium Development Goals*. New York: Energy Sector Management Assistance Programme, United Nations Development Programme, UN Millennium Project, and World Bank.

Practical Action. 2010. *Poor People's Energy Outlook*.

Reddy, A.K.N. 2000. "Energy and Social Issues." In *World Energy Assessment*. New York: UNDP/UNDESA/World Energy Council.

United Nations. 1972. *Report of the U.N. Conference on the Human Environment*. UN Doc. A/CONF.48/14. June 16, 1972.

   1992a. *Rio Declaration*. UN Doc. A/Conf.151/26, August 12, 1992.

   1992b, *Agenda 21*. UN Doc. A/Conf.151/26, August 12, 1992.

   1995. *Beijing Platform for Action*. UN Doc. A/Conf.177/20, October 17, 1995.

United Nations Advisory Group on Energy and Climate Change. 2010. *Energy for a Sustainable Future*, Summary Report and Recommendations, April 28, 2010. New York: UN.

United Nations Development Programme. 1995. *Human Development Report 1995*. New York: Oxford University Press.

   1997. *Energy After Rio: Prospects and Challenges*. New York: UNDP.

United Nations General Assembly. 1979. *Convention on the Elimination of All Forms of Discrimination against Women*. UN Doc. A/Res/34/180, December 18, 1979.

   1986. *Declaration on the Right to Development*. UN Doc. A/Res/41/128, December 4, 1986.

   2000. *Millennium Declaration*. UN Doc. A/Res/55/2, September 18, 2000.

   2010a. *Millennium Development Goals Summit Outcome Document*. UN Doc. A/Res/65/L.1, September 17, 2010

   2010b. *Keeping the Promise: United to Achieve the Millennium Development Goals*. UN Doc. A/65/L.1, September 17, 2010.

UN-Energy. 2005. *The Energy Challenge for Achieving the Millennium Development Goals*. New York: United Nations.

WRI (World Resources Institute). 1994. *World Resources 1994–95: People and the Environment*. Washington, DC: WRI.

   2004. *World Resources 2002–2004: Decisions for the Earth: Balance, Voice, and Power*. Washington, DC: WRI.

13 | Pollution wolves in scientific sheep's clothing: why environmental-risk assessors and policy-makers ignore the "hard issues" of the human rights of pollution victims

KRISTIN SHRADER-FRECHETTE

In 1998, seven-year-old Emily Pearson died of brain cancer. She was one of 16 children living in a four-block-area of Hammond, Indiana, of all of whom (mostly toddlers) were diagnosed with rare cancers, all clearly tied to ethylene-dichloride (EDC) and vinyl-chloride releases from nearby Keil Chemicals, owned by Ferro Corporation. In 1993, the year before Emily's diagnosis, the US Environmental Protection Agency said the local corporation was the nation's top emitter of EDC. It predicted the Hammond facility would cause scores of new, otherwise-avoidable local cancers. After many young children died, Ferro-Keil denied responsibility but admitted annually releasing 2,000,000,000 pounds (907,184,470 grams) of EDC – only a gram of which can be fatal for a child (Shrader-Frechette 2007a, 3–7).

Apart from whether Ferro-Keil actually caused all these deaths and injuries of Indiana children, did it violate their human rights by subjecting them to high doses of known carcinogens and neurotoxins? Why is recognizing the human rights of vulnerable groups, threatened by pollution, a hard question?

This chapter provides a first answer to both questions. In a four-part analysis, it first explains why these two issues constitute ethically "hard" questions. Second, it shows why they are scientifically hard and, third, why they are practically hard questions. The fourth section suggests how these hard questions can begin to be resolved. Three solutions include developing ethical theory regarding rights to life; requiring risk- and welfare-relevant regulatory science to follow specific methods; and adopting several human-rights proposals, already championed by medical and health groups. With regard to beginning to answer the "hard question" in ethical theory, the chapter discusses seven constraints, such as causing very high probability of death, that pollution cases must satisfy if they are to be said to involve genuine rights violations, and not merely some other injustices or regrettable harms. Because of this ethically hard question, it is difficult to specify the content of such pollution-related rights – a difficulty that this chapter begins to address by formulating the seven constraints. Because of

246

the scientifically hard question, it is difficult for laypeople to understand the nature of the harms against which the rights protect – a difficulty this chapter addresses by discussing scientific concepts such as statistical casualties and animal testing. Because of the practically hard question, it is difficult for polluters and governments to recognize these rights – a difficulty this chapter addresses by exposing polluters' financial conflicts of interest; their funding of misleading pollution-related science; their funding of PR agencies, lobbyists and campaign donations to promote misleading science; and their disincentive to fund pollution controls, given the risk–benefit asymmetry caused by the absence of pollution controls.

Why human rights to protection from deadly pollution are hard issues in ethical theory

To understand why the human rights of pollution victims constitute ethically difficult questions, consider the stance of Harvard University attorney Cass Sunstein, touted as an expert on environmental protection and named in 2009 by President Obama to head the White House Office of Information and Regulatory Affairs. Like many pro-industry and pro-market persons, Sunstein believes pollution protection is a matter of cost–benefit analysis, not human rights. Thus any pollution-related rights arguments are difficult for many to accept. Although roughly 600,000 Americans die each year of cancer, the US Office of Technology Assessment says up to 90 percent of these deaths are "environmentally induced and theoretically preventable" (Davis and Hoel 1990; Devesa *et al.* 1995; Epstein 2002, 2005; Landrigan 1992, 1996; Lashof *et al.* 1981, 3, 6ff; Lichternstein *et al.* 2002; NIH 2000; Schulte 2005; SEER 1998). Yet Sunstein claims that society overregulates pollutants. Why?

Cass Sunstein: technocratic, crude-utilitarian, rather than human-rights-based decision-making

Sunstein says society emotively and irrationally rejects risk decisions based only on cost–benefit analysis (CBA) and therefore overregulates, reducing manufacturing jobs, shrinking the economic pie, making people poorer, and thus causing unnecessary deaths. He claims every nation should become a "cost–benefit state," discount lay views of risk, and provide "a large role for technocrats" (Sunstein 2002, ix, 7). Arguing for societal decision-making based on "reason," on protecting the greatest number of lives for the fewest dollars, Sunstein seeks regulations based on the cheapest cost-per-life-saved – a CBA stance that presupposes all other ethical distinctions among risks are irrelevant. These distinctions include who is responsible for creating a risk, who benefits, or whether it is involuntarily imposed or voluntarily chosen. Instead, Sunstein's only criterion is cost-per-life-saved.

Because most of the public rejects the least-cost/most-lives-saved criterion for risk policy-making, Sunstein says laypeople irrationally demand regulation and are victims of "mass delusions" that "produce wasteful or even harmful laws and policies," especially because "it remains unproven that [pollution exposures such as] the contamination of Love Canal ever posed significant risks to anyone" (Sunstein 2002, 40). Rejecting any human rights against pollution, Sunstein argues the Clean Air Act must be judicially reviewed, to determine if it passes the CBA test (Sunstein 2002, 79). Otherwise, he says it should be dropped. Instead of human rights, he defends market-based economic rationality, defined in terms of willingness-to-pay (Sunstein 2002, 40). Repeatedly calling for "sound science," Sunstein uses almost no citations to scientific journals to support his claims about pollutants (Sunstein 2002, ch. 9). Instead he repeatedly cites non-scientific, corporate sources such as the American Enterprise Institute and the Reason Institute (Sunstein 2002, 5, 27).

By reducing ethical rationality to CBA, thereby ignoring merit, consent, human rights, justice and fairness, Sunstein accepts a highly reductionistic, crude-utilitarian view of pollution-related decision-making that arguably would harm the most vulnerable members of society – and that most utilitarians probably would reject insofar as it reduced overall welfare. According to his crude-utilitarian stance, the public is irrational in demanding money be spent to control environmental toxins that (he says) kill 60,000 people annually, but not demanding money be spent to encourage people to eat properly and exercise daily, which (Sunstein says) could save 300,000 people a year. Ignoring fairness, rights to know and to consent, Sunstein denies that people have human rights to choose whether or not to exercise, what to eat, and how to reduce such personal risks. He denies that people have rights to consent to deadly pollution risks from which they gain no benefit (Sunstein 2002, 8).

Even if his data about the relative size of personal and societal risks were accurate, Sunstein does not say why he thinks "rational" CBA justifies denying "companies should be required to do 'whatever they can' to reduce risks" they create; Sunstein redefines notions of blame and responsibility, assuming no obligation not to put innocent people at involuntary risk for the sake of personal gain; likewise, in arguing for free-market environmentalism, the cost–benefit state, and willingness-to-pay, he assumes children, minorities, poor people, and others should have to pay for clean air (Sunstein 2002, 65, 71, 72, 287). Why shouldn't those who polluted the air pay to clean it up? How can a poor child, growing up in south-side Chicago, have rights to equal protection and rights to life, if her ability to breathe clean air is based on willingness-to-pay?

Sunstein responds that regulators "are permitted to take distribution into account," that government is "entitled to consider who is helped and who is hurt" (Sunstein 2002, 74, ix). But human rights arguably require, not merely permit, taking account of distribution and harm. What would have happened to recognition of African-American human rights if governments merely followed Sunstein's crude-utilitarian ethics? Of course, arguably Sunstein's ethics arguably are not genuinely utilitarian, because ignoring human rights would cause massive societal disutility. To confront his attacks on human rights, ethical theorists face the hard task of countering claims about the alleged benefits of Sunstein's crude-utilitarian criteria for pollution regulation.

Alan Gewirth: misleading appeals to human rights not to be caused to get cancer

A second major reason human rights against life-threatening pollution are hard cases is that many theorists say they are prima facie rights – rights one possesses in the absence of compelling arguments to the contrary, rights that can be overridden *ultima facie* in specific cases. For instance, in 2011 Tokyo Electric overrode prima facie rights to protection against life-threatening pollution; after four core melts at its Fukushima Daiichi reactors, repeatedly it deliberately released deadly radiation, saying this was necessary to avoid a worse outcome, an explosion releasing even more radioactivity (Brumfiel 2011). As typically occurs, *ultima facie* considerations overrode pollution victims' prima facie rights not to be subjected to life-threatening emissions.

Alan Gewirth, however, argues that people have rights not to have cancer inflicted on them through pollution, that states should enforce these rights, and that human rights to the non-infliction of cancer (RNIC) are "absolute" or *ultima facie*; nevertheless, he admits RNIC may not apply in cases where (1) the probability of inflicted cancer is low, (2) knowledge of risk/harm is limited, or (3) there is no consent (Gewirth 1982). However, if RNIC does not always apply in cases like (1)–(3), arguably it is not an absolute or *ultima facie* right, merely a prima facie right. Thus the question of RNIC is ethically hard because either one must reformulate it precisely, so as to make it absolute – despite problems specifying different causal and medical constraints, and despite problems of how to precisely specify its *ultima facie* core, in different situations. Or, one must admit RNIC is merely a prima facie right, something that can be overridden – contrary to the needs of hundreds of thousands of cancer victims annually killed by pollution. These victims want relief, not a difficult ethical, scientific and legal debate over relief.

Derek Parfit: problems with collective responsibility and deterministic, not probabilistic, harms

A third major reason human rights to protection against life-threatening pollution are hard cases is that they typically involve collective responsibility and harms that occur not deterministically, but probabilistically – with some degree of likelihood, depending on the pollution dose, different individual susceptibility, and so on. Moral philosophers have difficult times dealing with collective responsibility, given problems with specifying relevant causal chains of harm and precise degrees of individual responsibility, especially for probabilistic harm. Why? Scientists often disagree about alternative causal factors and small probabilities. Moreover, although people are not responsible for trivial, unavoidable "harms" – such as interacting with others when one has the sniffles, at what point does a trivial harm become non-trivial?

Both difficulties (collective responsibility and probabilistic harm) are illustrated in the work of Derek Parfit. He argues, correctly, that one ought not follow "commonsense morality" and ignore acts – such as tens of thousands of agents, each releasing small amounts of deadly pollutants and causing imperceptible effects on large numbers of persons (Parfit 1984, 67–86). His conclusion is correct, but because his arguments are ethically questionable – hard to accept – he has no compelling case for responsibility for small harms. Although there is no time to assess Parfit's assumptions here, they arguably err in (1) taking pain as the paradigm instance of harm; (2) assuming pain predicates, like "at least as bad as," are transitive; (3) attempting to show that acts with allegedly imperceptible effects – such as multiple small pollution releases – are members of a set of acts together causing perceptible harm; (4) presupposing there is an easy, practical way of ascribing responsibility for individual acts when one deals only with total effects of sets of acts; (5) assuming it is easy to determine causal chains of harm; (6) using questionable notions of collective responsibility; (7) presupposing that allowing ourselves to be mistaken about pain lets us preserve transitivity and therefore collective responsibility; (8) employing unrealistic, deterministic, causal examples to support key points; and (9) ignoring both the privacy problem and the fact that acts have different probabilities of causing harm (Gruzalski 1986, 780–782; Parfit 1984, 78–79, 31; 1986, 847).

Thus, while Parfit's instincts are correct, his flawed assumptions and ignoring of probabilistic harms provide little help in arguing for pollution-related human rights (Shrader-Frechette 1987, 50–60).

What is the upshot of this quick survey of theoretical, ethical difficulties with claims that victims have human rights not to be harmed by deadly pollutants? Contrary to theorists like Sunstein, on May 2, 2011, doctors, nurses, faith and tribal leaders, social-justice advocates and affected citizens from 50 states convened in Washington, DC to send a powerful message: all people have human rights to breathe healthy air. Sponsored by groups such as the American Nurses Association and Physicians for Social Responsibility, these clean-air ambassadors call themselves "50 States United For Healthy Air" (50 States 2011). As their stance illustrates, pollution victims claim trumps, *ultima facie* human rights to protection against life-threatening pollutants.

Except perhaps for Alan Gewirth, however, philosophers recognize that, because there are no easy, exception-free definitions of such *ultima facie* human rights, protection against deadly pollutants relies on prima facie rights. Moral philosophers thus appear unable to provide a quick and easy solution to difficulties over pollution-related rights claims. Partly because they have not, traditional international law does not consider human rights to a healthy environment to be *jus cogens* rights. *Jus cogens* or "compelling law" human rights are those guaranteed by pre-emptory legal principles; they are norms that are binding on all international states, regardless of their consent. Including protections against slavery or torture, they are axiomatic and universally accepted norms that bind all nations under *jus gentium*, the law of nations. They also invalidate all international agreements in conflict with them, and they may be modified only by a subsequent norm with the same preemptory character (Third Foreign Relations Law 1987). Thus, while the international legal system recognizes and codifies human rights like those against torture, human rights against life-threatening pollution are not accepted; instead there are only modest levels of *ultima facie* recognition, usually through regulated economic activities, such as mandated pollution-control expenditures (Perez-Leiva 2011).

Why human rights to protection from deadly pollution are hard issues in scientific theory

Scientific problems also contribute to the difficulties associated with guaranteeing human rights to protection against life-threatening pollution. As already noted, pollution-related harms tend to be greatest as a result of small exposures to roughly 80,000 chemicals that together contribute to increased probability of death, often through cancer. Although the highest pollution levels are deterministically associated with immediate death, many probabilistic pollution threats remain unnoticed – discovered only through epidemiological testing or increased cancer rates.

Statistical casualties: threats to recognizing human rights to protection against deadly pollution

The complexity of pollutant threats also often leads them to be scientifically misunderstood, thus jeopardizing protection against them and making pollution-related rights "hard issues." They frequently are neither immediate nor obvious, particularly for low-dose exposures to multiple toxins. Blue-collar crimes like murder have direct, immediate impacts, therefore direct, immediate publicity, even if their perpetrators are unknown. White-collar crimes, like falsifying pesticide data or illegally releasing toxins, however, can cause more harm but often are less noticed because of their indirect, delayed, often unattributable effects. Consequently only rarely are they publicized and stopped. They are known mainly statistically, as spikes in curves that track numbers of deaths. The FBI collects no data on white-collar crime, and cancers do not wear tags saying they were caused by releases from Monsanto or Ferro Chemical.

Given no national health-tracking acts in most countries, including the United States, scientists cannot easily see case-clustered diseases and deaths surrounding polluting facilities. Even to discover that some area/occupation has higher rates of pollution-caused death or disease, they must perform costly studies. Yet to avoid damning data, polluters often try to keep relevant research from being done. Even when government has relevant evidence, often it is incomplete. Besides, pollution-related epidemiological studies typically reveal only "statistical casualties" – fatalities identified as population-level increases in percentages or numbers of deaths. Statistical casualties alone do not enable scientists to know which pollutants killed which people. They show only above-average percentages of death or disease. And when multiple (including non-pollution) factors cause diseases, like cancer, identifying pollution victims is difficult, partly because toxins may cause different symptoms in different people. Except at high doses, effects typically occur probabilistically, only in some people. Frequently pollutants are tasteless, odorless and unseen. As a result, people's senses may mislead them. They confuse aesthetics with environmental health – assuming that what looks healthy is healthy. Because air in most cities is not filled with coal soot, as it often was a century ago, people may not realize they are at risk from unseen threats like dioxins, PCBs and ionizing radiation – a complex chemical "soup" that makes it difficult to distinguish specific environmental causes of different diseases. Sometimes scientists cannot even find uncontaminated control groups – people – to use for testing.

Although almost all exposures are to combinations of hazards, virtually no data exist on effects of multiple exposures. Given different combinations of many different toxins – of the 80,000 human-made chemicals to which people are exposed – millions of combinations need to be tested. Yet only about 1 percent of all chemicals have been tested individually. Virtually no combinations have been tested. And most pollution victims do not have measurements of their various exposures, over time. Only costly individual testing reveals who has been harmed. For all these reasons, polluters often can deny that some chemical caused individuals' deaths or injuries. The result? Many pollution threats go unrecognized or are blamed on something else. As the US Centers for Disease Control, the International Commission on Radiological Protection, and most scientists confirm, illnesses occurring after years of exposure to low-level pollutants typically are not detectable – until it is too late. Cancers may be dormant, latent or unnoticed for 10 to 60 years – long after people remember what exposures they had. Instead low-level pollutants bioaccumulate until their effects are obvious, and people become ill or die.[1] They are like slow-acting "invisible bullets," harming people who often cannot even prove they were "shot" (Shrader-Frechette 2007a, 79–81).

Demanding human testing: threats to recognizing human rights to protection against deadly pollution

A second scientific reason – that human-rights claims to protection from pollution harms are hard – is that evidence for pollution harm often relies on animal testing not human-epidemiological studies. Scientists who reject animal evidence say causal inferences about harm require human-epidemiological data. For instance, although the US National Academy of Sciences (NAS) says children are not adequately protected by current pesticide standards (US National Research Council 1993), chemical-industry groups have used

---

[1] For instance, the International Commission on Radiological Protection's *Draft 2005 Recommendations* state that "any effect on IQ following in utero doses of a few tens of mGy would be undetectable and therefore of no practical significance" (2005, 33). The US Centers for Disease Control has similarly stated, "illnesses occurring after years of exposure to low-level toxins are not detectable" (1990, 7).

demands, for only human evidence, to reject the legally mandated, tenfold safety factor for children's pesticide-exposure standards (Lockwood 2004; Shrader-Frechette 2007b).

A key argument (against this more protective pesticide standard) was that despite abundant animal data showing pesticide harm, and despite children's known higher sensitivity to toxins, reliably confirming causal harm also requires human-epidemiological data. Scientific supporters of this argument include University of California geneticist Bruce Ames and many industry-funded scientists like Elizabeth Whelan, president of an industry "front group," the American Council on Science and Health (Ames and Gold 1989, 757; 1997; Gough 2005; Whelan 2005, 1994, 18–20).

On the scientific side, those who require human-epidemiological evidence for regulating pollutants typically ignore at least two problems that make human-epidemiological data almost always inferior to good animal data. These include (1) errors in gathering human-exposure data and (2) selection biases such as the healthy-worker survivor effect. Problem (1) occurs because most human exposures to pollutants must be estimated, after the fact, and not measured, as part of a deliberate experimental dose, because it is unethical to deliberately expose someone to a substance likely to be harmful. Problem (2) occurs because studies where doses are often measurable, as with workers exposed to occupational pollutants, typically have other biases, such as the fact that workers are healthier than the average member of the population – which includes the young, the aged, those too sick to work. Those who reject purely animal tests for pollutants likewise err because they (3) confuse the precision of exposure-disease relations – obtained through human testing – with the strength of such relations – obtained through animal experiments, although humans and other animals typically have the same responses to given pollutants. Likewise those who reject solely animal testing (4) reject classical accounts of scientific explanation – which rely on structural and molecular properties of toxins, not merely on evidence from particular species, collected in only one way. They also (5) erroneously privilege human-epidemiological data but ignore weight-of-evidence rules that require scientists to consider all available evidence and assess it. Scientists who require only human-epidemiological data likewise (6) demand infallible, rather than highly probable, scientific evidence, although all of science is based on the most likely evidence, not infallible evidence. In ignoring the fact that epidemiologists and toxicologists regard animal data as superior to human data, mainly because of problems (1) and (2) above, those who reject animal data (7) ignore past inductive evidence for using animal data, and they (8) ignore dominant scientific practices regarding using animal evidence for causal claims about humans (Cranor 2006, 250, 267; EPA SAB 2000; Finkel 1994, 20–22; Hattis and Silver 1994; Jasanoff 1995, 125; Richardson *et al.* 2004; Steenland *et al.* 1996; Weed 2005). After all, virtually all national and international agencies deem materials carcinogens or neurotoxins, based on animal studies, not human research, for the reasons already given. Animal studies can be done more quickly and cheaply, thus testing more generations than human studies, and scientists can better control the experimental conditions for non-human animals than for other animals. For all these reasons requiring purely human data about pollutants is scientifically misguided (Rall *et al.* 1987, 356).

On the ethical side, requirements for human epidemiological evidence also are misguided, for at least three reasons. *First*, they ignore classical bioethics prohibitions against experimenting on humans in ways that are likely to harm them. For instance, because it is ethically/legally questionable to dose humans with pesticides so as to obtain epidemiological data, these studies could/ought not be done. Consequently, demanding human data on pesticide and other pollutant harms begs the question against following bioethics, against rejecting the null hypothesis, and against protective regulation (Beauchamp and Childress 1989; Culver and Gert 1982; Daniels 1985; EPA SAB 2000; Veatch 1981). If it were right to demand only human data on pollutants, medical ethics would be reduced to a guinea-pig approach, doing nothing until dead bodies started to appear.

A *second* ethical problem with requiring only human data is that these data are impractical and expensive to obtain, given the large sample sizes and long time-frames required for human-epidemiological studies. These exorbitantly high transaction costs for human-epidemiological studies help explain why less than 1 percent of all hazardous substances have been tested epidemiologically. Instead government relies mainly on controlled laboratory testing of animals. A *third* ethical problem is that requiring only human evidence for pollutant harm ignores the classical ethics rule to protect the vulnerable. If human data were always needed, not animal data, then obtaining such scientific data – even if it were somehow ethical to do so – would place the heaviest evidentiary and health burdens on the most vulnerable potential victims of pollutants, namely children, minorities and low-income people. Thus, for all these scientific and ethical reasons, use of animal testing for pollution effects makes pollution-related, human-rights claims difficult to make (Shrader-Frechette 2007a, ch. 3, 2002).

Lack of symmetrical transparency: threats to recognizing human rights to protection against deadly pollution

A third reason that human-rights claims to protection from pollution harms are hard is that only federally funded science is subject to transparency requirements, encouraging obfuscation and manipulation of scientific data by others. Much science relevant to public and environmental health is done in the private sector and, largely because of the 1999 US Data Access Act and the 2001 US Data Quality Act, it is not subject to the same requirements of public data access and transparency as public or government-funded science – even when this private science assesses public-health threats, defends pollution permits, or supposedly supports industry's regulatory compliance. This public–private asymmetry constitutes a tilted scientific playing field and makes recognition of pollution-related human rights "hard issues" (Shrader-Frechette and Oreskes 2011).

Why human rights to protection from deadly pollution are hard issues practically speaking

For practical reasons, it likewise is difficult to secure practical recognition of human rights to protection against life-threatening pollutants. For one thing, special interests – typically companies that produce, use, or otherwise profit from dangerous pollutants – control most science relevant to pollution regulation and control. Recently the American Association for the Advancement of Science (AAAS) reported that roughly 75 percent of all US scientific work is funded by industry ($300 billion). About 25 percent is funded by government, some of which also goes to universities. Because more than half of government science funding is military, for every $6 that private interests spend on science, the US government spends about $1 for non-military science. AAAS estimates that for every $100 that industry spends on its science, environmental-health groups spend about $1. The result? Polluters often obtain the best science money can buy, what can be called "private-interest science" (Koizumi 2004a, 2005a, 2004b, 2005b; Shrader-Frechette 2007a).

Who actually performs private-interest science? Because polluters who claim their products or emissions are harmless would not be trusted, typically special interests pay others to do science that serves their interests. They buy "science" from front groups, think tanks, and "hire education." (Industry funds academic research that serves its corporate goals. Instead of standard university education, students and professors often are influenced by education whose content is partly driven by outside interests.) Outside interests often pay for private-interest science that typically uses incomplete data, contraindicated models, inadequately sensitive tests of pollution damage, and so on. Private interests also ghostwrite journal articles that are misleading, then pay scientists thousands of dollars to publish them under their own names, to try to give the results credibility. Several years ago, the World Health Organization (WHO), a UN group, reported on industry-funded, scientific front groups that spend billions of dollars annually to generate misleading, anti-regulatory, health-related research (WHO 2000). There are scores of such front groups, including The Global Climate Coalition, funded by the oil and automobile industries to oppose climate-change regulations. The Advancement of Sound Science Coalition, funded by the tobacco and chemical industries, argues for the health and safety of tobacco smoke, fast food, saccharin, pesticides and growth hormones in cattle (Beder 2002, 28–31, 237).

Special interests also mislead the public about pollutant threats by donating to charities, capturing them, then exercising important control over their public statements. The American Cancer Society (ACS) is a case in point. For instance, physicians say that, contrary to the chlorine warnings of the American Public Health Association, ACS and the chemical industry's Chlorine Institute have issued joint statements supporting continued use of organochlorine pesticides, despite their long history of causing cancer. Critics also say that because of hefty donations from polluting industries, ACS used press releases, crafted by agri-chemical-company experts, to downplay risks of food-borne pesticides. For years, the ACS refused to join the March of Dimes, American Heart Association and American Lung Association in supporting the US Clean Air Act. The ACS also contradicts the WHO, NAS, National Cancer Institute (NCI) and scientific consensus by calling risks from dietary pesticides, toxic-waste dumps and ionizing radiation "negligible" (Epstein 1999; Epstein *et al.* 2002; Shrader-Frechette 2007a).

One example of how scientists can be captured by corporate donors/polluters is toxicologist Edward Calabrese. For years, he has made significant money by doing private-interest science, and he testifies for companies accused of killing people – like Walter Allen – with their pollutants. Allen was a maintenance worker who for years was exposed to high occupational doses of ethylene oxide (ETO). After he died of brain cancer, in 1996 his widow and son sued the manufacturer for wrongful death and claimed Allen's exposure to ETO contributed to his brain cancer (*Allen* v.

Pennsylvania Engineering Corp 1996). Their lawsuit should have been an "easy win," especially because the International Agency for Research on Cancer had showed ETO is a potent carcinogen and genotoxin. Acting directly on the genes, it causes chromosomal and genetic damage in both humans and other mammals. Because of its small size, ETO directly penetrates cell DNA and crosses the blood–brain barrier (IARC 1994, 73).

The court, however, granted a judgment against the Allens and denied them a jury trial. Why? A key reason was that the judge relied on Calabrese's testimony and claimed ETO can cause human stomach cancer and leukemia but said there was no evidence that it could cause brain cancer (Cranor 2006, 18–20, 324–325). The Allen family lost its lawsuit mainly because the pretrial judge erroneously relied on the misleading testimony of the manufacturer's "expert," Edward Calabrese, who said brain-cancer-specific studies of ETO were required (*Allen* v. *Pennsylvania Engineering Corp* 2006). However, two facts precluded need for brain-cancer-specific ETO studies. (1) Because scientists agree that ETO is a "multisite mutagen," potent carcinogen, and potent genotoxin, they recognize it likely causes brain and other cancers. (2) Because of its small size, ETO can "cross the blood–brain barrier" and reach the brain/most other human-body targets (Cranor 2006, 325–326; IARC 1994). Although (1) and (2) eliminate evidentiary need for brain-cancer-specific studies to show ETO is a probable brain carcinogen, the judge instead relied on Calabrese's report (paid for by the industry) that ignored facts (1) and (2). Calabrese erroneously claimed that ETO's causing other cancers was "irrelevant" to whether it caused brain tumors (Calabrese 1993; Cranor 2008). Yet a PhD toxicologist (like Calabrese) arguably knows (or should know) that ETO is a multisite mutagen, able to cross the blood–brain barrier, thus able to cause brain cancer. In US National Science Foundation-funded research at the University of California, outside reviewers confirmed that Calabrese's Allen-case behavior was ethically questionable. They said Calabrese relies "on inadequate epidemiological data as well as misstatements" and that his report/testimony is "subjective … inconsistent … contrary to that of all national and international agencies … unsupported" (Cranor 2008, 118).

Of course, it is not difficult to secure practical recognition of human rights to protection against deadly pollutants, merely because some scientists appear to be "paid off" or because industry funds most science and, later, PR agencies and lobbyists to disseminate its pollution "science," or because polluters are major campaign donors. Practical recognition of pollution-related human rights also is difficult because pollution must "go" somewhere, few people want it, many pollution controls are expensive, and the industries who pay for the controls are neither those who mainly benefit from them, nor those who are mainly put at risk because of their absence: there is a risk–benefit asymmetry. Moreover, at least in English-speaking nations, workers are allowed to be subjected to dangerous levels of pollution in exchange for so-called "hazard pay" or a "compensating wage differential" (Shrader-Frechette 2002). Because these are all topics that the author has addressed elsewhere, they are not addressed here.

How to resolve the ethical-theory problem of recognizing pollution-related human rights

To address the theoretical ethical difficulties associated with recognition of human rights to protection against pollutants, moral philosophers with scientific and medical expertise need first to attempt to specify criteria for when particular violations of prima facie human rights to protection against deadly pollutants become *ultima facie* violations. That is, they need to specify a precise formulation of human rights to pollution protection, such that the precise rights-claims are as close to being *ultima facie* or absolute claims as possible. Although there is no space here to investigate many crucial law-related questions – such as whether rights (not to be harmed by pollution) are better treated as core rights or as derivative rights, whether the corresponding duties to protect such rights fall mainly on the national or international community, or whether strict-liability or market-share liability are better vehicles for rights enforcement (Lye and Muller 2004; Walker 2011), the beginning outlines – of the epistemic constraints on a formulation of such rights – is clear. For instance, one obvious first step would be to improve on Gewirth's formulation (discussed earlier) suggesting that such rights require – in order to protect genuine rights, and not merely to protect against regrettable harms or injustices (1) that the *probability* of harm be very high, (2) that there be *knowledge* of this high probability of harm, and (3) that the imposition of this harm be *involuntary* in the sense that victims have not consented to it (Gewirth 1982). In addition to developing these three constraints, I have argued for at least four additional constraints on any claims of rights violations, so as to distinguish them from other injustices or from regrettable harms. These four additional constraints are that specification of such a human right need not require that perpetrators have knowledge of the threat/harm, as Gewirth suggests, but instead only (4) that they have *culpable ignorance* of it, (5) that its imposition be *inequitable*,

(6) that its *severity*, not just probability, be great, and (7) that the threat be reasonably *immediate* (Shrader-Frechette 2007a).

Constraint (4) is important because philosophers at least since Aristotle have recognized that people are not responsible merely for what they know and fail to take account of, but also for what they should know, and fail to take account of. Arguably, at a minimum Edward Calabrese was guilty of culpable ignorance, if not worse, in failing to advise the court that ETO was a multisite threat and crossed the blood–brain barrier – when he testified against ETO victim Walter Allen. Constraint (5) is important because rights recognition requires equitable consideration of the interests of different persons. Equitable consideration is key because, like Ronald Dworkin, most moral philosophers argue that the characteristic, by virtue of which people have human rights, is procedural, not factual (Dworkin 1977). They believe human rights are procedural in the sense that they depend on recognizing the fundamental moral requirement of consistent and equal processes. According to this requirement, humans have rights not because they are rational or can exercise agency, but simply because they are human and all humans ought to be treated consistently or equally. Another way of formulating this procedural justification for human rights is to say that all humans (regardless of their factual characteristics) are equal subjects of "moral value." Although they may differ in intelligence or physical strength, they are equally deserving of respect or consideration precisely because they are human. As a result they have equal rights – that is, equal claims to have their basic interests or needs considered with equal respect.

Yet children, minorities and poor people do not receive equal consideration of their rights to life, thus rights to protection against life-threatening pollution. In general, children are at least ten times more sensitive to pollutants than adults; for some pollutants, like organophosphate pesticides, children's lethal doses are only 1 percent of that for adults (Spyker and Avery 1977). Thus, although cancer rates are increasing 1 percent annually for adults, they are increasing 40-percent higher – 1.4 percent annually – for children, a fact that signals a rights violation (Epstein 2002; SEER 1998; Shrader-Frechette 2007a). Children are thus "the canaries in the coal mines" of industrial emissions. The same is true for minorities and poor people, both of whom bear greater pollution levels, thus greater health harms such as cancer, than other people. Even after one controls for other variables – like crime, medical coverage and income – this inequality is only reduced, not eliminated (Institute of Medicine 1999). As the American Public Health Association (APHA 2005a) confirms, minorities and poor people are much more likely to receive higher exposures to pollutants (APHA 2005b, 2005c;

Shrader-Frechette 2002). Because APHA warns that government "policies and decisions" fail to reflect these three groups' (children, minorities, poor people) "particular need for special protection from pollutants," arguably their human rights are violated (APHA 2000; Shrader-Frechette 2007a).

Constraints (6) and (7) are important because defensible human rights against imposition of pollution cannot be directed at condemning every assault or potential risks suffered by every person. Rather, only some "official" and immediate assaults seriously threaten people's personal security because their harm exceeds certain thresholds. Toxins that cause only a simple cough, for instance, likely do not exceed this threshold. Pollution harms that cause statistically significant increases in deaths or serious/debilitating injuries, however, can rise to the level of human-rights violations because of their severity. All other things being equal, obviously thresholds for human-rights violations are different, depending on their severity for different rights, people, situations and circumstances involved. All other things being equal, human-rights threats of greater severity and immediacy have more stringent, more protective thresholds than threats whose severity and immediacy is lower. Likewise, the threshold for protecting children's rights to life is far more stringent than that for protecting rights of others. Children deserve more protection because they are less able to protect themselves. Using such agreed-upon moral principles (that are far too numerous to be listed here), as well as the techniques of deliberative democracy, people must carefully evaluate the case-specific threshold for human-rights violations (Dworkin 1977; Pogge 2002; Shrader-Frechette 2007a).

Moreover, a second way to improve ethical theory regarding human rights to protection against deadly pollutants is to develop the theory that human rights arguably ought to be fulfilled by the many people who have causal influence over their recognition, not just by state actors. All humans in a position to causally effect those rights must recognize them (Pogge 2002). What is recognized and fulfilled? People's basic needs and interests. Following the strong/weak-rights characterization of Dworkin, the most basic or strong human right is that to life, precisely what pollution threatens. To the degree that citizens have participated in, or derived benefits from, social institutions that have helped cause life-threatening pollution, I have argued elsewhere that they have prima facie duties either to stop their participation in these institutions or to compensate for it by helping to reform them and to make them more equitable in their consideration of interests. The basic argument is that because of both ethical and democratic responsibility, people have prima facie duties to compensate for life-threatening, rights-threatening pollution from which they unfairly benefit – as when they pay lower prices for gasoline because US corporations, in their drilling operations, violate Third-World persons' human rights – and that this compensation can take the form of helping to reform social institutions (Shrader-Frechette 2007a, chs 4–5).

Some of the institutional reforms needed include developing and publicizing ethical theories showing responsibility for speaking and acting against the free-market environmentalism, espoused by Cass Sunstein and others (Sagoff 2004). Other needed institutional reforms are developing ethical theories against consideration only of deterministic and individual harms, rather than also probabilistic and collective harms (Gruzalski 1986; Shrader-Frechette 1987). Obviously this responsibility differs, depending on factors such as the level of harm caused, the benefits gained, whether beneficiaries intend the harm, whether they bear culpable ignorance for it, whether they try to prevent it, and so on. Each person's level of ethical responsibility needs to be assessed on the basis of many such factors, case by case, situation by situation, since there is no single algorithm for handling so many differences among people (Feinberg 1970; Glover 1970; Shrader-Frechette 2007a).

How to resolve the scientific-theory problem of recognizing pollution-related human rights

Three of the many scientific-theory reforms needed, in order to assist recognition of human rights against imposition of deadly pollution, include developing mandatory scientific criteria (1) for avoiding private-interest manipulation of "science," especially in science used for regulatory purposes, and (2) for reliance on protective default rules, in situations of scientific and mathematical uncertainty that involve life-threatening pollution and potential regulations. Once (1) and (2) are accomplished, much of the obfuscation that surrounds concepts of statistical casualties and animal testing can be eliminated. In other words, because these two concepts (statistical casualties and animal testing) – and many others – create uncertainties for pollution-relevant science, they create obstacles to recognition of human rights regarding pollution. Instead of resolving all these uncertainties, on a case-by-case basis, scientists merely could argue for welfare-protective, rather than merely profits-protective, default rules to use in pollution-relevant and regulation-relevant science (Cranor 2006; McGarity and Wagner 2008; Michaels 2008; Shrader-Frechette 2007a).

A third scientific strategy for resolving some of the "hard" issues in recognizing pollution-related human rights would be to amend both the 1999 US Data Access and 2001 US Data Quality Acts – and analogous laws throughout the world – so that they also apply to private science, not just government-funded science. Also, the national academies of science in all nations and the US National Research Council could provide guidance for best practices regarding data access and transparency for private science affecting public health and the environment. For example, privately funded science used for public or regulatory purposes should be subject to the same transparency requirements as publicly funded science, and industry requests to protect data, under claims of confidential business interests, should be granted only when public health and safety are demonstrably not at stake (Shrader-Frechette and Oreskes 2011).

How to resolve the practical problems of recognizing pollution-related human rights

Some of the most practical things that citizens can do, to promote recognition of human rights to protection against deadly pollutants, include working with other groups that have made calls for recognition of these rights. As already mentioned, various groups of medical personnel, including physicians and nurses, already have made such calls, and citizens can join with their efforts. For instance, citizens could join with the APHA in its recommending a US constitutional amendment that guarantees all Americans rights not to be harmed by pollutants (APHA 2005a; Nichols 1997; Shrader-Frechette 2007a).

A second thing citizens can do, to promote protection of pollution-related human rights, is to lobby with groups, such as the American Association for the Advancement of Science and the US National Academy of Sciences, to argue for more government funding of pollution-relevant science. Currently most developed nations spend between 1.5 and 3 percent of GDP on research funding, and only Sweden exceeds 4 percent. Thus one goal might be to have all nations increase scientific-research funding to at least 4 percent. Another goal might be to have all nations spend less on military scientific research and development, and more on pollution-related research, especially in the United States. Currently the United States spends more than any other nation on military scientific research, roughly half of all its government research dollars (UN OECD 2008, 2010).

A third way to promote protection of human rights against life-threatening pollutants would be to work toward all scientific authors and front groups revealing their sources of funding. In this way, the massive expenditures of special interests would be revealed, and members of the public could more easily decide whether special interests were promoting reliable science about pollutants or merely "private-interest" science. After all, numerous authors have shown that knowing the funders of particular studies are the best way to predict the conclusions of those studies (Krimsky 2003).

Conclusion

Without the philosophical, scientific and practical work to help resolve the hard issues associated with recognition of human rights to protection against life-threatening pollutants, all humans will continue to be threatened. As previous citations reveal, most of us are dying from cancer, and most cancers are "environmentally induced and theoretically preventable." Long ago, children, minorities and poor people began to be the canaries in the coal mines of industrial pollution. Today, we are all the canaries, except that we are losing our ability to hear the warnings.

References

50 States United For Healthy Air. 2011. Oakland: Earthjustice. Available at: http://earthjustice.org/50states.

Allen v. *Pennsylvania Engineering Corp.* 1996. 102 V.3d 194, 195 (5th Cir.).

Ames, Bruce and Gold, Lois. 1989. "Pesticides, Risk, and Applesauce." *Science* 244, 755–757.

1997. "The Causes and Prevention of Cancer." *Environmental Health Perspectives* 105, Supplement 4, 865–874.

APHA (American Public Health Association). 2000. "The Precautionary Principle and Children's Health." Available at: www.apha.org/legislative/policy/Pols2000_rev.pdf (accessed February 18, 2006).

2005a. *Priority 2005 Issues: Fact Sheets, Health Disparities, Environmental Disparities, Racial/Ethnic Disparities*, 2005. Available at: www.apha.org/legislative/legislative/index.htm (accessed February 25, 2006).

2005b. "Human Rights in the Curricula for Health Professionals." Available at: www.apha.org/legislative/policy/policysearch/index.cfm?fuseaction=view&id=165, policy 9813 (accessed March 17, 2005).

2005c. "Public Health Code of Ethics." Available at: www.apha.org/codeofethics/ethics.htm (accessed February 25, 2006).

2005d. "APHA's Principles on Public Health and Human Rights." Available at: www.apha.org/wfpha?PrincPH1.htm (accessed March 17, 2005).

Beauchamp Thomas and Childress, James. 1989. *Principles of Biomedical Ethics*. Oxford University Press.

Beder, Sharon. 2002. *Global Spin*. White River Junction: Chelsea Green Publishers.

Brumfiel, Geoff. 2011. "Water Leak Stops at Fukushima, But Big Problems Remain." *Nature*, April. Available at: http://blogs.nature.com/news/thegreat-beyond/2011/04/water_stops_at-fukushima_but_b.html (accessed June 4, 2011).

Calabrese, Edward. 1993. *Did Occupational Exposure to ETO Cause Mr. Walter Allen's Brain Tumor?* 809 Unpublished Report, April 13, 1993.

Cranor, Carl. 2006. *Toxic Torts*. Cambridge University Press.

   2008. Personal communication regarding *Allen v. Pennsylvania Engineering*, Document 846 C, email to Kristin Shrader-Frechette; received November 24, 2008, at kshrader@nd.edu.

Culver, Charles and Gert, Bernard. 1982. *Philosophy in Medicine*. Oxford University Press.

Daniels, Norman. 1985. *Just Health Care*. Oxford University Press.

Davis, Devra and Hoel, David, eds. 1990. *Trends in Cancer Mortality in Industrial Countries*, Annals of the New York Academy of Sciences 609. New York Academy of Sciences.

Devesa, S., Blot, W., Stone, B., Miller, B., Tarone, R. and Fraumeni, J. 1995. "Recent Cancer Trends in the United States." *Journal of the National Cancer Institute* 87:3, 175–182.

Dworkin, Ronald. 1977. *Taking Rights Seriously*. Cambridge, MA: Harvard University Press.

EPA SAB (US Environmental Protection Agency Science Advisory Board). 2000. *Comments on the Use of Data from the Testing of Human Subjects*, EPA-SAB- EC-00–017.

Epstein, Samuel S. 1999. "American Cancer Society." *International Journal of Health Services* 29:3, 565–578.

   2002. "Reversing the Cancer Epidemic." *Tikkun* 17:3, 56–66.

   2005. *Cancer-Gate*. Amityville: Baywood.

Epstein, Samuel S., Ashford, Nicholas, Blackwelder, Brent, Castleman, Barry, Cohen, Gary, Goldsmith, Edward, Mazzocchi, Anthony and Young, Quentin. 2002. "The Crisis in U.S. and International Cancer Policy." *International Journal of Health Services* 32:4, 669–707.

Feinberg, Joel. 1970. *Doing and Deserving*. Princeton University Press.

Finkel, Adam. 1994. "Rodent Tests Continue to Save Human Lives." *Insight* 10, 20–22.

Gewirth, Alan. 1982. *Human Rights*. University of Chicago Press.

Glover, Jonathan. 1970. *Responsibility*. London: Routledge.

Gough, Michael. 2005. *"Environmental Cancer" Isn't What We Thought or Were Told*. Cato Institute website at www.cato.org/tetimony/ct-mg030697.html (accessed May 28, 2005).

Gruzalski, Bart. 1986. "Parfit's Impact on Utilitarianism." *Ethics* 98, 780–782.

Hattis, Dale and Silver, K. 1994. "Human Interindividual Variability – A Major Source of Uncertainty in Assessing Risks for Non-Cancer Health Effects." *Risk Analysis* 14, 421–431.

IARC (International Agency for Research on Cancer). 1994. *Some Industrial Chemicals: Ethylene Oxide CAS No.: 75–21-8.862*, Monograph 60. Available at: www.inchem.org/documents/iarc/863 vol60/m60–02.html (accessed November 24, 2008).

ICRP (International Commission on Radiological Protection) *Draft 2005 Recommendations*. Stockholm: ICRP.

Institute of Medicine. 1999. *The Unequal Burden of Cancer*. Washington, DC: National Academy Press.

Jasanoff, S. 1995. *Science at the Bar*. Cambridge, MA: Harvard University Press.

Koizumi, Kei. 2004a. *R&D Trends and Special Analyses, AAAS Report XXVIII*. Washington, DC: AAAS.

2004b. Remarks to the U.S. EPA Science Advisory Board.

2005a. *R&D Trends and Special Analyses, AAAS Report XXIX*. Washington, DC: AAAS.

2005b. Remarks to the U.S. EPA Science Advisory Board.

Krimsky, Sheldon. 2003. *Science in the Private Interest*. Savage: Rowman & Littlefield.

Landrigan, P.J. 1992. "Commentary: Environmental Disease – A Preventable Epidemic." *The American Journal of Public Health* 82:7, 941–943.

1996. "The Prevention of Occupational Cancer." *CA: A Cancer Journal for Clinicians* 46:4, 254–255.

Lashof, J.C., Banta, David, Gough, Michael, Fensterheim, Robert J. and Gelband, Helen, Health and Life Sciences Division of the US Office of Technology Assessment. 1981. *Assessment of Technologies for Determining Cancer Risks from the Environment*. Washington, DC: Office of Technology Assessment.

Lichternstein, Paul, Holm, Niels, Verkasalo, Pia, Iliadou, Anastasia, Kaprio, Jaakko, Koskenvuo, Markku, Pukkala, Eero, Skytthee, Axel and Hemminki, Kari. 2002. "Environmental and Heritable Factors in the Causation of Cancer." *New England Journal of Medicine* 343:2, 78–85.

Lockwood, Alan. 2004. "Human Testing of Pesticides." *American Journal of Public Health* 94, 1908–1916.

Lye, Geoff and Muller, Francesca. 2004. *Changing Landscape of Liability: A Director's Guide to Trends in Corporate Environmental, Social and Economic Liability*. Sustainability Limited.

McGarity, M.O. and Wagner, W.E. 2008. *Bending Science: How Special Interests Corrupt Public Health Research*. Cambridge, MA: Harvard University Press.

Michaels, David. 2008. *Doubt Is Their Product: How Industry's Assault on Science Threatens Your Health*. Oxford University Press.

Nichols, A.W. 1997. "Amending the United States Constitution to Include Environmental Rights." *The Nation's Health* 27:8, 18–19.

NIH (National Institutes of Health). 2000. *Cancer Rates and Risks*. Washington, DC: NIH and NCI. Available at: http://seer.cancer.gov/publications/raterisk/ (accessed May 28, 2005).

Parfit, Derek. 1984. *Reasons and Persons*. Oxford University Press.

1986. "Comments." *Ethics* 98.

Perez-Leiva, Manuel. 2011. "International Law and the Right to a Healthy Environment as a Jus Cogens Human Right." *International Conference of Information Systems for Business*, January 20, 2011. Available at: www.iet-wsn2010.org/7/International-Law-And-The-Right-To-A-Healthy-Environ ment-As-A-Jus-Cogens-Human-Right (accessed May 26, 2011).

Pogge, Thomas. 2002. *World Poverty and Human Rights*. Cambridge: Polity Press.

Rall, D.P., Hogan, M.D., Huff, J.E., Schwetz, B.A. and Tennant, R.W. 1987. "Alternatives to Using Human Experience in Assessing Health Risks." *Annual Review of Public Health* 8, 356.

Richardson, D., Wing, S., Steenland, K. and McKelvey, W. 2004. "Time-Related Aspects of the Healthy Worker Survivor Effect." *Annals of Epidemiology* 14, 633–639.

Sagoff, Mark. 2004. *Price, Principle, and the Environment*. Cambridge University Press.

Schulte, Paul. 2005. "Characterizing the Burden of Occupational Injury and Disease." *Journal of Occupational and Environmental Medicine* 47:6, 607–622.

SEER (Surveillance Epidemiology and End Results). 1998. *Cancer Statistics Review, 1973–1997*. Washington, DC: National Cancer Institute, National Institutes of Health.

Shrader-Frechette, Kristin. 1987. "Parfit and Mistakes in Moral Mathematics." *Ethics* 98:1, 50–60.

2002. *Environmental Justice*. New York: Oxford University Press.

2007a. *Taking Action, Saving Lives*. New York: Oxford University Press.

2007b. "EPA's 2006 Human-Subjects Rule for Pesticide Experiments." *Accountability in Research* 14, 211–254.

Shrader-Frechette, Kristin and Oreskes, Naomi. 2011. "Symmetrical Transparency in Science." *Science* 332:6030, 663–664.

Spyker, J.M. and Avery, D.L. 1977. "Neurobehavioral Effects of Prenatal Exposure to the Organophosphate Diazinon in Mice." *J. Toxicology and Environmental Health* 3:5–6, 989–1002.

Steenland, K., Deddens, J., Salvan, A. and Stayner, L. 1996. "Negative Bias in Exposure-Response Trends in Occupational Studies: Modeling the Healthy Worker Survivor Effect." *American Journal of Epidemiology* 143, 202–210.

Sunstein, Cass. 2002. *Risk and Reason*. New York: Cambridge University Press.

Third Foreign Relations Law of the United States, § 102 cmt. k (1987).

UN OECD. 2008. *Main Science and Technology Indicators*. Paris: OECD.

   2010. *Main Science and Technology Indicators*. Paris: OECD.

US Centers for Disease Control. 1990. *Mortality and Morbidity Weekly Report* 39, no. SS-2.

US National Research Council. 1993. *Pesticides in the Diets of Infants and Children*. Washington, DC: National Academy Press.

Veatch, Robert. 1981. *A Theory of Medical Ethics*. New York: Basic Books.

Walker, Angela. 2011. "The Hidden Flaw in Kiobel: Under the Alien Tort Statute, the Mens Rea Standard for Corporate Aiding and Abetting Is Knowledge." *Northwestern Journal of International Human Rights* 10:2, 119–145.

Weed, D. 2005. "Weight of Evidence." *Risk Analysis* 25, 1545–1557.

Whelan, Elizabeth. 1994. "Stop Banning Products at the Drop of a Rat." *Insight* 10, 18–20.

   2005. *Ratty Test Rationale*. American Council on Science and Health. Available at: www.acsh.org/healthissues/newsID.1035/healthissue_detail.asp (accessed November 29, 2005).

WHO (World Health Organization). 2000. *Tobacco Company Strategies to Undermine Tobacco Control Activities at the World Health Organization*. Report of the Committee of Experts on Tobacco Industry Documents. Geneva: World Health Organization.

PART V

Is there a human right to democracy?

14 | Is there a human right to democracy?

HILARY CHARLESWORTH

Introduction

An intriguing episode in the life of the now-defunct United Nations (UN) Commission on Human Rights was its adoption of a series of resolutions on human rights and democracy. In 1999 the Commission adopted a resolution entitled "Promotion of the right to democracy" (CHR Res. 1999/57), in anticipation of the new century and millennium. The resolution endorsed a "right to democratic governance" as including a range of civil and political rights such as those to freedom of expression, thought and association. It also included the rights of "universal and equal suffrage," free voting procedures, periodic and free elections and "the right of citizens to choose their governmental system through constitutional or other democratic means." The resolution was introduced by the United States and co-sponsored by almost all 53 members of the Commission. Cuba moved an amendment to the draft to delete the words "the right to" from the title of the resolution, on the grounds that no such right existed, but this failed to garner majority support. In the end, the resolution was adopted without a negative vote, but with China and Cuba abstaining.

This was the only occasion on which the Commission, the major UN forum for human rights development, endorsed a specific right to democracy. Later resolutions avoided this language and addressed the relationship between the concepts of human rights and democracy, which became a lightning rod for North–South tensions in the Commission. Some of the subsequent resolutions endorsed the process of democratization of states, focusing on democracy at the national level. They presented "free and fair elections [as] an essential feature of democracy" (e.g., CHR Res. 2001/41). These resolutions were typically supported by the United States, the United Kingdom and Canada as well as some developing states, while states such as China, Cuba, Saudi Arabia and Syria would abstain from voting. Another strand of resolutions, adopted within days of the others, countered this understanding by endorsing the "promotion of a democratic and equitable international order" (e.g., CHR Res. 2001/65). These resolutions avoided any reference to elections and emphasized the economic and social dimensions of democracy at the international level. In defin-ing democracy, they invoked many concepts favored by the global South, such as self-determination, permanent sovereignty over natural wealth and resources, the right to development, the principle of solidarity (which calls for the distribution of the costs of global challenges "in accordance with basic principles of equity and social justice"), and the right to a healthy environment. These resolutions would typically attract support from the abstainers on the North's resolution and negative votes from all Northern states on the Commission.

The UN Human Rights Council, which replaced the Commission in 2006, has adopted two resolutions, in 2008 (HRC Res. 8/5) and 2011 (HRC Res. 18/6), on the promotion of a democratic and equitable international order, in similar terms to those of the Commission earlier in the decade. Again, all members from the North on the Council voted against the resolutions. The success of these resolutions, and the absence of their Northern-sponsored counterparts, reflects the power of the South in the Council.

These UN debates illustrate some of the complexities of the question "is there a human right to democracy?" in international law. At the most general level, the question of whether there is a human right to democ-racy implicates the nature of international human rights law and its role in regulating international behavior. If the role of international law is to provide standards by which to criticize and influence the actions of states (Koskenniemi 2011), what standards does the notion of democracy imply? In what political spheres is democracy relevant: does it operate in similar ways on the local, the national and the international level? What does dem-ocracy require? Does it extend beyond the holding of national elections? Can it operate to redress economic inequalities? Second, the UN debates signal the North/South politics any reference to democracy attracts at the international level. For the South, the term has imperial overtones, signal-ing the imposition of alien forms of governance that respond to the dictates of the global financial institutions rather than local conditions. The idea of a human right to democracy implies that there are universal democratic standards that can be applied to all national contexts. This is controversial not only because of its whiff of colonialism, but also because of the respect international law traditionally accords to local constitutional arrangements. Third, the idea of democracy does not fit easily into the paradigm of a right that can be asserted by an individual against the state. It is rather more typ-ically associated with the area of institutional design. These issues combine to make the question of whether there is a human right to democracy a hard one.

The conceptual controversies are exacerbated by the tensions between the professional cultures involved in the discussion. The sensibilities and approach of the human rights movement contrast with democratic theories and practice: the former rest on universal claims about fundamental or natural values; while the claims of the latter category are "time-dependent and contingent" (Steiner 2008, 466). The different academic backgrounds of human rights scholars, who tend to be lawyers, and theorists of democracy, who tend to be political scientists, exacerbate the theoretical divide (Beetham 1998, 71).

In this chapter, I first describe the sketchy nature of international commitments to a human right to democracy. I then discuss debates among international lawyers about the place of democracy in the human rights canon and the content of such a right. I suggest that the controversy illustrates a tension between understandings of international human rights law as a political vocabulary for judging behavior and as universal standards that change behavior. I argue that, from the perspective of international law, there is no human right to democracy. It remains, however, an important political task to support an idea of democracy as resting on popular control of, and political equality in, collective decision-making.

The international law framework

The Universal Declaration of Human Rights, adopted in 1948, gave specificity to the broad commitments of the UN Charter to human rights and fundamental freedoms. The sub-committee of the UN Commission on Human Rights responsible for drafting the Declaration debated at length the best form of governance for the protection of human rights. Some delegates argued for explicit reference to multiple political parties, but Soviet resistance made this difficult (Morsink 1999, 59–61). The final outcome of the debate was Article 21 of the Declaration, which presents an election-focused notion of participation in government, strikingly without reference to the concept of democracy. Article 21 provides:

(1) Everyone has the right to take part in the government of his country, directly or through freely chosen representatives.
(2) Everyone has the right of equal access to public service in his country.
(3) The will of the people shall be the basis of the authority of government; this will shall be expressed in periodic and genuine elections that shall

be by universal and equal suffrage and shall be held by secret vote or by equivalent free voting procedures.

Steiner has pointed out that the drafting history of Article 21 "reflects concern by states on both sides of the Cold War divide to ensure that their own system of politics was not in instant violation of [the provision]" (Steiner 1988, 77; see also Morsink 1999, 61). The only explicit reference to democracy in the Universal Declaration is found in Article 29, which declares "the general welfare in a democratic society" as a possible limitation on the exercise of rights. This formula emerged from a fierce debate about whether this provision should include a reference to the "requirements of the democratic state." The Soviet Union argued strongly for this phrase, but it was resisted on the basis that it could be deployed to undermine the individual rights and freedoms set out in the Declaration: reference to the state in this context was regarded as antithetical to the idea that human rights were essentially claims against the state (Morsink 1999, 63–65).

The language of Article 21 of the Universal Declaration was incorporated into Article 25 of the International Covenant on Civil and Political Rights (ICCPR) in 1966 in a slightly altered form, but still avoiding the word "democracy" (Nowak 1993, 437).[1] Article 25 provides:

Every citizen shall have the right and the opportunity, without [discrimination] and without unreasonable restrictions:

(a) To take part in the conduct of public affairs, directly or through freely chosen representatives;
(b) To vote and to be elected at genuine periodic elections which shall be by universal and equal suffrage and shall be held by secret ballot, guaranteeing the free expression of the will of the electors;
(c) To have access, on general terms of equality, to public service in his country.

Article 25 is noteworthy as the only ICCPR right that is confined to citizens. It is less than a right to democracy, rather a right of political participation and to political accountability through elections. While they are expressed in individual terms, however, Article 25 (a) and (b) make full sense only in the context of a political society; to have meaning, they involve a collective enterprise. The tension between individual claims and the collective political context this creates has emerged in the

---

[1] The only references to democracy in the ICCPR are found in limitations clauses: Articles 14 (the right to a fair trial), 21 (the right to peaceful assembly) and 22 (the right to freedom of association) of the ICCPR allow restrictions on these rights if they are necessary "in a democratic society."

jurisprudence of the ICCPR's monitoring body, the UN Human Rights Committee.

An example is a case brought against Namibia by a minority community, the Rehoboth Basters, for (among other things) violating Article 25 (a) and (c) through merging the Baster community into regional electoral districts, which effectively reduced their voting power (*Diergaardt* v. *Namibia* 760/37). The Human Rights Committee found that these rights were individual rights that could not be asserted by the community as a whole (para. 10.8). A separate opinion by Martin Scheinin however criticized the Committee's insistence on the individual nature of Article 25 rights. He argued that:

> there are situations where article 25 calls for special arrangements for rights of participation to be enjoyed by members of minorities and, in particular, indigenous peoples. When such a situation arises, it is not sufficient under article 25 to afford individual members of such communities the individual right to vote in general elections. Some forms of local, regional or cultural autonomy may be called for in order to comply with the requirement of effective rights of participation.

The Human Rights Committee has rather optimistically described Article 25 as lying "at the core of democratic government based on the consent of the people" (General Comment 25 on Article 25, 1996). The Committee read the provision as implicitly holding elected representatives accountable for the exercise of public power. It also articulated a duty on states to ensure that the right to vote can be exercised, including positive steps to reduce barriers to political participation such as poverty and illiteracy. The General Comment however provided a thin legal articulation of the value of democracy. It was mainly concerned with the details of electoral practices, although it noted the significance of citizen participation in the conduct of public affairs through "public debate and dialogue with [political] representatives or through their capacity to organize themselves" (General Comment 25 on Article 25, 1996, para. 8). While the General Comment also emphasized the protection and promotion of freedom of expression, assembly and association as "essential conditions of the right to vote" (General Comment 25 on Article 25, 1996, para. 12), it did not elaborate the connections between these rights and democracy.

Another treaty provision that arguably supports a democratic ideal is common article 1 of the ICCPR and the International Covenant on Economic, Social and Cultural Rights of 1966, which proclaims the right to self-determination, including the right of a people to "freely determine their political status." The meaning of this phrase is open to debate. James

Crawford has argued that the right to self-determination does not necessarily mean the establishment of a form of government based on the idea
of "one vote, one value" (Crawford 2006, 333). He pointed to cases such as
Swaziland where the United Nations General Assembly sanctioned governance by traditional authorities (in Swaziland's case a hereditary monarchy)
because they had the support of the people. In the case of Fiji, the UN
approved the adoption of a constitution in 1970 that discriminated between
racial groups, giving preference to Indigenous Fijians over Fijians of Indian
ancestry (2006, 333). On the other hand, Crawford has noted that the minimum core of the right to self-determination must be government that has
the support of the relevant people and in this sense represent them (2006,
334). The link between self-determination and democracy was also emphasized by Martin Scheinin in the case of *Diergaardt v. Namibia*, referred to
above. He regarded Article 1 as affecting the interpretation of Article 25 of
the ICCPR, allowing group, rather than individual, interests to be taken
into account.

The most developed international account of human rights and democracy is found in regional human rights systems. For example the Statute
of the Council of Europe refers to the "basis of all genuine democracy" as
"devotion to the spiritual and moral values which are common heritage of
[European] people and the true source of individual freedom, political liberty and the rule of law." The Council adopted the European Convention on
Human Rights in 1950. While the Convention makes no reference to democracy, Article 3 of its First Protocol requires member states to "hold free
elections at reasonable intervals by secret ballot, under conditions which will
ensure the free expression of the opinion of the people in the choice of the
legislature." At the end of the Cold War in 1990 the European Community
adopted the Charter of Paris for a New Europe, which required EU members "to build, consolidate and strengthen democracy as the only system of
government of our nations." It further stipulated that "[d]emocratic government is based on the will of the people, expressed regularly through free
and fair elections." Europe's embrace of democracy rests on "respect for the
human person and the rule of law" and democracy is presented as "the best
safeguard of freedom of expression, tolerance of all groups of society, and
equality of opportunity for each person." With its "representative and pluralist character," democracy "entails accountability to the electorate, the obligation of public authorities to comply with the law and justice administered
impartially" as well as the rule of law.

The Americas have also articulated a specific commitment to democracy. Under the Charter of the Organization of American States (OAS),

OAS members pledge to "promote and consolidate representative democracy, with due respect for the principle of nonintervention." In 2001, the OAS General Assembly adopted the Inter-American Democratic Charter, endorsing a right to democracy. It states that "peoples of the Americas have a right to democracy and their governments have an obligation to promote and defend it" (Article 1). It defines the "essential elements" of representative democracy as including:

respect for human rights and fundamental freedoms, access to and the exercise of power in accordance with the rule of law, the holding of periodic, free, and fair elections based on secret balloting and universal suffrage as an expression of the sovereignty of the people, the pluralistic system of political parties and organizations, and the separation of powers and independence of the branches of government.

Article 7 provides in turn that:

Democracy is indispensable for the effective exercise of fundamental freedoms and human rights in their universality, indivisibility and interdependence, embodied in the respective constitutions of states and in inter-American and international human rights instruments.

The Democratic Charter asserts OAS power to suspend members whose democratic government have been overturned (Article 21).

Overall, then, at the global level, international law has endorsed an essentially institutional account of democracy, limited to participation in an electoral competition. It shies away from any substantive commitments to equality. Nevertheless international instruments present democracy and human rights as closely related: democracy is critical for the protection of human rights and respect for human rights is essential to democracy. The price of international agreement is vagueness on the human rights that are implicated. But there is some wariness about the idea of a right to democracy. The right has had a brief appearance in the UN Commission on Human Rights, as noted above, and its major articulation has been at the regional level in the Inter-American Democratic Charter.

A different angle on democracy has emerged in arguments that international institutions themselves need to adopt democratic practices. For example Secretary-General Boutros-Ghali contended that it is difficult to endorse democracy within states if the international system is itself undemocratic (Boutros-Ghali 1996). This has inspired challenges such as those to the permanent membership of the UN Security Council and the associated veto power and proposals for global peoples' assemblies that would give voice to civil society and transnational interest groups (Falk 2007). Both types of reform are animated by an idea of democracy based on broader participation in decision-making, but are not based on a human right to democracy.

Debates about a right to democracy

The assertion of a human right to democracy has divided international lawyers and is often presented at the outer edge of plausibility. As we have seen international instruments at the global level provide a rickety structure for such a right. Typically, proponents of such a right develop it with evidence of state practice while its critics fear that recognition of a right to democracy might understate the requirements for democracy, or be used as a platform for intervention.

International lawyers' long-standing wariness about explicitly endorsing democracy as an international norm dissipated after the ending of the Cold War as part of the more general global pause in contestation over democracy's value. In particular, international lawyers based in the United States began to articulate a right to democracy in international law. In an influential article written early in the post-Cold War euphoria, Thomas Franck identified an "emerging right to democratic governance" based on what appeared to be the renaissance of electoral democracies and the increase of election monitoring by international institutions (Franck 1992). He reflected on the contemporary tumult within the Soviet Union and the strong international reaction to the overthrow of President Aristide in Haiti in September 1991, observing a "cosmic, but unmysterious, change" in the preparedness of governments to argue for a democratic entitlement (Franck 1992, 47). Franck presented this development as almost entirely as the product of Western thinkers, such as Hume, Locke, Jefferson and Madison (Franck 1992, 49). His writing was infused with spiritual language, suggesting both the inevitability and moral value of the move to democratic governance; indeed Franck's article ended with the exhortation that "[t]he task is to perfect what has been so wondrously begun" (Franck 1992, 91). But Franck's account of the content of the right to democratic governance was limited: it was essentially a right to participation in elections, rather than to any particular political form.

International lawyers moved onto stronger claims about a human right to democracy. Thus Christina Cerna (1995), and Gregory Fox and Georg Nolte (1995), argued that the legitimacy of governments should be assessed by international rather than national criteria, that the international requirement is of democratic government and that individuals everywhere have a right to democratic government (see also Steiner 1988, 2008). Similarly, Steven Wheatley has argued that creating and sustaining democracy is an international legal obligation, enabling the international community to scrutinize the substance and processes of a state's political system (Wheatley 2005, ch. 3). He has also suggested that international law endorses a form of Habermas' deliberative democracy – a system that engages citizens in active deliberation and allows broad participation in politics, resulting in consensus positions – as opposed to what he terms "aggregative" democracy – a form of democracy that is focused on competitive elections (Wheatley 2005, 185–187; see also Wheatley 2010).

A bolder strand in international legal scholarship emerged through linking the concept of a right to democracy to national foreign policy agendas, particularly in the work of US international lawyers. For example, some adopted an explicitly liberal democratic political approach, such as Anne-Marie Slaughter (1995) and Fernando Tesón (1992), arguing that a fundamental distinction should be drawn between liberal democracies and non-liberal democracies in international law. For these scholars, undemocratic governments did not have the requisite sovereignty to enjoy full status in the international community and liberal democracies could be relied on largely to self-regulate. Michael Reisman developed the argument that a right to democracy could be discerned in international law to support "pro-democratic intervention" (Reisman 1994, 2000). He inverted the traditional notion of state sovereignty in international law to argue that the critical sovereignty protected in international law was not that of the ruler, but that of the people. This led him to conclude that if the people's preferences for government were usurped, international law would support intervention to remove the usurper. Fox and Roth articulated the idea of a "democratic entitlement" in international law, arguing that "measures to implement democratic rights, undertaken by foreign states collectively and/or individually, need not respect the sovereign prerogatives of governments that violate those rights" (Fox and Roth 2001, 336).

More cautious accounts of the connection between human rights and democracy came from international lawyers outside the United States. Thus James Crawford resisted the concept of a claim to democracy, largely on the basis of the lack of evidence of state practice. Third World scholars have suggested that the colonial-era distinction between civilized and uncivilized states is reproduced in the modern distinction between liberal democratic and illiberal undemocratic states (e.g., Chimni 2012, 301), providing a carapace for intervention rather than promoting human rights.

Susan Marks and Andrew Clapham have described the relationship of human rights and democracy as one of "mutual dependence," but not one that can be expressed in terms of a human right to democracy (Marks and Clapham 2005, 68). They chronicle problems of recognition of a right to democracy: the ambiguity of state practice supporting such a right; the troubling implications of a right to democracy in supporting "the imperial project of remaking the world to suit the most powerful"; the potential for such a right to conflate democracy with simply regular elections; and the implication that national politics is the primary site for democracy, marginalizing other arenas of collective decision-making, such as international and local arenas (Marks and Clapham 2005, 68–69). Marks and Clapham argue instead that while protection of human rights is essential to democracy, and democracy is necessary for protection of human rights, neither is sufficient to ensure the other. They prefer an account of democracy as "an argument, a critical tool, and a set of principles for political life in all its multifarious settings" (Marks and Clapham 2005, 70). In their view a commitment to democracy constitutes an ongoing challenge to ensure popular control and political equality. Henry Steiner takes a similar approach in depicting human rights and democracy as intertwined, as "two sides of the same coin," but resists the definition of a human right to democracy (Steiner 2008).

Few international lawyers have paid attention to the principles underpinning democracy or explained the democratic theories on which they rely. David Beetham's work has however been influential on some international legal accounts of democracy (e.g., Marks 2000). Beetham's formulation of the central commitment of democracy rests on two principles: popular control over collective decision-making and equality between citizens in exercising that control (Beetham 1998, 72). On Beetham's account, human rights are deeply implicated in democracy, but this is not enough to sustain a human right to democracy.

Conclusion

What would it mean to have a human right to democracy? Levitt and Merry argue that human rights ideas have impact if they are adopted locally, if they affect the consciousness of those who invoke them, and if they have some form of "institutional teeth" that leads to recognition of the claim (Levitt and Merry 2009, 457). They emphasize the paradox that human rights must have resonance with local cultures while also having their roots in universally applicable standards. These criteria for human rights suggest that there is not a human right to democracy; this would require local adoption, clarity about the elements of the right and some measures of accountability for its breach. While this concept is powerful as a rallying cry to support struggles for popular participation in politics, it has little institutional support internationally. The fact that there is scarce evidence for such a right at this stage does not however undermine the symbiotic relationship between the two concepts: human rights form central components of democracy and in turn democracy is critical to the protection of human rights.

This approach does not depend on regarding human rights as a question of law and democracy as a question of politics: in this sense, I differ from Steiner's assessment that the problem of a human right to democracy is one of incompatible categories, despite their parallel evolution and histories: for him human rights have a much richer texture and systematic quality reflected in legal principles; while democracy belongs in the realm of contestation and politics (Steiner 2008). This account does not acknowledge the intensely political function of human rights law. Its main value can be seen as the provision of an authoritative vocabulary of critique of institutional power and standards by which power can be held accountable (Koskenniemi 2011, 324). Indeed the dominance of legal discourse in the human rights field has obscured fundamental questions about the causes of human rights violations. It implies that breaches of the law can be remedied through legal institutions, when, as Evans argues, the breaches may be the product of particular economic and political arrangements (Evans 2005).

If we accept Marks and Clapham's approach to democracy as a critical tool, a challenge to ensuring popular control and political equality in collective decision-making, the international legal debate would change. It would take into account the evidence that international actors generally play a circumscribed role in promoting democracy, usually only supporting, rather than shaping, domestic democratic change (Carothers 2007). It would be less concerned with devising formulas for democracy, or associating democracy with a fixed set of institutions, and more engaged with fostering effective forms of communal debate. These might include supporting local institutions that enhance self-government and responding to social and economic inequalities as they affect the capacity to have access to political power (Marks 2000, 64–65). The idea of democracy as self-rule on the basis of equality between citizens also challenges the international consensus about the centrality of elections for the creation of democracy. Elections are often given priority by local people when an autocratic government has collapsed, although the legitimacy they bring has been uncertain and inconsistent (Carothers 2007, 21, 23). It also suggests that elections should not be rushed, particularly following a period of violent conflict, and that encouraging public conversations about major social issues should be a priority. Such a gradualist approach marked, for example, the South African transition in the 1990s (Carothers 2007, 25).

Understanding democracy as a complicated journey, rather than a destination (Marks 2000, 66), also undermines the popular notion of a "two-track" definition of democracy in states affected by conflict. The idea is that in especially fractured states, governance should aim at simply achieving stability; a fuller democratic structure is understood as a luxury available only to more stable states. The empirical basis of this "democratic sequencing" approach is weak: Carothers points out that it assumes that autocratic stabilizers will have an interest in developing the conditions for the less orderly atmosphere of democracy. The cases of China and Vietnam show that economic success is possible without the nurturing of democratic elements such as the rule of law (Carothers 2007, 15–16). And an independent judiciary will often be perceived as a threat to an autocratic government, as has occurred in Pakistan since 2007.

More fundamentally, a "two-track" approach implies that some peoples and their governments – those on the advanced track – embody the successful achievement of democracy, without recognizing that all democracies are imperfect and that the very nature of democracy is contestation. As Guillermo O'Donnell reminds us, democracy:

is and always will be in some kind of crisis: It is constantly redirecting its citizens' gaze from a more or less unsatisfactory present toward a future of still unfulfilled possibilities … [to] an always pending agenda that calls for the redress of social ills and further advances in the manifold matters which … most concern human welfare and dignity. (O'Donnell 2007, 5)

These characteristics underline the distinction between regarding human rights as legal standards and human rights as the yeast for social movements (Levitt and Merry 2009, 459). Assertion of a human right to democracy in international law is likely to reduce the promise of democracy to that of a checklist of institutional measures. A political goal of promoting self-rule between an equal citizenry relies rather on debate, discussion and experimentation.

References

Beetham, David. 1998. "Democracy and Human Rights: Civil, Political, Economic, Social and Cultural." In Janusz Symonides, ed., *Human Rights: New Dimensions and Challenges*. Aldershot: Ashgate, pp. 71–97.

Boutros-Ghali, Boutros. 1996. *An Agenda for Democratization*. New York: United Nations.

Carothers, Thomas. 2007. "The 'Sequencing' Fallacy." *Journal of Democracy* 18:1, 12–27.

Cerna, Christina. 1995. "Universal Democracy: An International Legal Right or the Pipe Dream of the West?" *New York University Journal of International Law and Politics* 27, 289–329.

Chimni, B.S. 2012. "Legitimating the International Rule of Law." In James Crawford and Martti Koskenniemi, eds., *The Cambridge Companion to International Law*. Cambridge University Press, pp. 290–308.

Crawford, James. 2006. *The Creation of States in International Law*, 2nd edn. Oxford University Press.

Evans, Tony. 2005. "International Human Rights Law as Power/Knowledge." *Human Rights Quarterly* 27, 1046–1068.

Falk, Richard. 2007. "What Comes After Westphalia: The Democratic Challenge." *Widener Law Review* 13, 243–253.

Fox, Gregory and Nolte, Georg. 1995. "Intolerant Democracies." *Harvard International Law Journal* 36, 1–70.

Fox, Gregory and Roth, Brad A. 2001. "Democracy and International Law." *Review of International Studies* 27, 327–352.

Franck, Thomas. 1992. "The Emerging Right to Democratic Governance." *American Journal of International Law* 86, 46–91.

Koskenniemi, Martti. 2011. "The Mystery of Legal Obligation." *International Theory* 3, 319–325.

Levitt, Peggy and Merry, Sally. 2009. "Vernacularization on the Ground: Local Uses of Global Women's Rights in Peru, China, India and the United States." *Global Networks* 9, 441–461.

Marks, Susan. 2000. *The Riddle of all Constitutions: International Law, Democracy, and the Critique of Ideology*. Oxford University Press.

Marks, Susan and Clapham, Andrew. 2005. *International Human Rights Lexicon*. Oxford University Press.

Morsink, Johannes. 1999. *The Universal Declaration of Human Rights: Origins, Drafting and Intent*. Philadelphia: Pennsylvania University Press.

Nowak, Manfred. 1993. *U.N. Covenant on Civil and Political Rights: CCPR Commentary*. Kehl am Rhein: N.P. Engel.

O'Donnell, Guillermo. 2007. "The Perpetual Crises of Democracy." *Journal of Democracy* 18, 5–11.

Reisman, W. Michael. 1994. "Humanitarian Intervention and Fledgling Democracies." *Fordham International Law Journal* 18:3, 794–805.

    2000. "Unilateral Action and the Transformations of the World Constitutive Process: The Special Problem of Humanitarian Intervention." *European Journal of International Law* 11:1, 3–18.

Slaughter, Anne-Marie. 1995. "International Law in a World of Liberal States." *European Journal of International Law* 6, 503–538.

Steiner, Henry J. 1988. "Political Participation as a Human Right." *Harvard Human Rights Yearbook* 1, 77–134.

2008. "Two Sides of the Same Coin? Democracy and International Human Rights." *Israel Law Review* 41, 445–476.

Tesón, Fernando R. 1992. "The Kantian Theory of International Law." *Columbia Law Review* 92:1, 53–102.

Wheatley, Steven. 2005. *Democracy, Minorities and International Law.* Cambridge University Press.

2010. *The Democratic Legitimacy of International Law.* Oxford: Hart Publishing.

15 | The human right to democracy and its global import

CAROL C. GOULD

Introduction

A human right to democracy is controversial, at least among political philosophers, if not on the streets of Tunisia, Egypt, Syria, and even Iran. Although the Universal Declaration of Human Rights specifies a right to take part in the government of one's country, including free elections with universal suffrage, in an article sometimes referred to as specifying a right to democracy, the term democracy is not explicitly mentioned there,[1] perhaps because of political concerns at the time of its drafting. Indeed, some philosophers have advanced influential arguments against recognizing such a human right, generally proceeding from within a Rawlsian framework of justice. In this chapter, I will begin by considering – and putting aside – some of the objections that have been lodged against recognizing democracy as a human right. Among these objections are (1) that if democracy were recognized as a human right, that would enable forcible intervention to impose it on countries that lack it, which would in turn involve interference with the internal affairs of the country involved; (2) relatedly, that requiring democracy would violate the premier human right of self-determination and would additionally not show an appropriate level of toleration for societies that are not fully liberal though presumably respectful of human rights (what Rawls calls "decent" societies); (3) and further, that it would involve a Western or liberal imposition on societies organized around a common good or social harmony conception; and (4) perhaps most problematically,

Earlier versions of this paper were presented at the Conference on Global Democracy, Center for Deliberative Democracy and Global Governance, Australian National University, Canberra, Australia, August 4–5, 2011, at the IVR World Congress, Special Workshop on Human Rights, Global Justice, and Democracy: Issues at their Intersection, Frankfurt, Germany, August 15, 2011, at the APA Eastern Division Meeting, Washington, DC, December 29, 2011, and at the Dept. of Philosophy, The University of Tennessee, Knoxville, February 24, 2012, and at For discussion at the Yale Political Theory Workshop, March 21, 2012. I would like to thank John Dryzek, Alistair Macleod, Pablo Gilabert, David Reidy, Cindy Holder, Andrew March and Joshua Keton for their helpful comments on earlier versions of the manuscript.

[1] Note that Article 29 does refer to the role of law in "meeting the just requirements of morality, public order and the general welfare in a democratic society."

that democracy requires equality, which is too demanding for some societies, and is not required by a minimal or less demanding list of human rights. I will not be able to consider all these objections in depth in this chapter, but will focus primarily on the last one, which has been advanced by Joshua Cohen (2006). In the ensuing part of this chapter, I will go on to indicate what is involved in the claim that democracy is a human right and provide some arguments to support that proposition, drawing on my own earlier writings on the justification of democracy (and of human rights). It will be seen that the conception of democracy advocated here goes considerably beyond its rather bare understanding in the recognized international human rights as a matter simply of the free and universal election of representatives (however important that may be).

In addition to these critical and constructive tasks (themselves sufficiently challenging), I want to focus especially on a further question in the second half of the chapter: namely, granting that democracy in the sense to be specified here should be recognized as human right, what are the implications for global governance that would follow from this recognition? Should we be supporting global democracy writ large or more modest forms of democracy across borders? I will here appeal to my previous work on two criteria for justifying democratic participation and deliberation and for determining their scope. These criteria have importantly different spheres of application. I have called them the *common activities* criterion and the *all-affected* (or *affectedness*) criterion. Both of these grounds for justifying democratic participation in turn raise interesting philosophical conundrums, which I can only point to here, and I will address these with some brief clarifications and arguments. The first criterion, which appeals to rights of democratic participation among the members of a political community (broadly construed), raises the problem of what I previously called the *constitutional circle*, in which rights agreed to in a democratic process of constitution making would already have to be constrained by rights (in my view, these are human rights) (Gould 2004, ch. 1, esp. 39–46).

The new case of global governance and the need for input into global policies by a broader public also raises an interesting conundrum. While affectedness can be reinterpreted to support democratic rights of input (though not full participation) by distant publics in global governance, is this sort of democratic input something that people can claim as a human right? If we choose to demarcate those affected by the degree to which their human rights are impacted by these decisions (as I in fact have previously suggested), we run the danger of a different kind of potential circularity, in which human rights fulfillment serves both as a criterion for being affected and as a ground for participation by those so affected. Moreover, to further complicate matters, some level of democratic or quasi-democratic participation may be required (or at least desirable) in the process of interpreting human rights themselves and certainly for giving them effect. But this could take us in the direction of a possibly vicious circle, in which some sort of democratic participation is required for interpreting and specifying the human rights, while at the same time these very rights serve to justify democratic participation. I suggest that these issues raise theoretical questions about a human right to democracy that have not been adequately explored by political philosophers, while the practical import of such a right for global governance contexts also needs to receive much more attention from political and social theorists.

Objections to a human right to democracy – are they viable?

The most sustained and prominent set of criticisms regarding democracy as a human right has been advanced by Joshua Cohen (2006) in his article "Is there a Human Right to Democracy?" Without reviewing his entire argument, we can note that – in large measure in accord with Rawls' approach – Cohen proposes that democracy is required by justice and entails a "demanding conception of equality," a conception that is more demanding than what human rights entail. Human rights, on his view, are a subset of what justice requires, and are "entitlements that establish the bases of membership" in a political society. Further, human rights are "part of an ideal of global public reason," serving as "a shared basis for political argument" among "adherents of conflicting religious and philosophical and ethical traditions" (Cohen 2006, 226).

Before considering these various claims, we can note that Cohen helpfully does not endorse one of the leading objections to democracy as a human right, namely, that recognizing it would support forcible intervention in other nation states. A consideration of this sort seems partly to have motivated Rawls' rather short list of human rights, which Rawls seems to believe would support such intervention in case they were violated. But there need be no direct connection between recognizing or criticizing human rights violations and intervening to stop such violations. It is a separate question what, if anything, should be done to help people recover their human rights, or what would be involved in putting institutions in place to fulfill them. Therefore, recognizing democratic participation as a human right would not entail that the United States or other powerful countries or alliances, or even the UN, would have the right or the duty to establish democracy globally through the use of force or other forms of intervention. The question of what duties the international community has in regard to protecting various human rights is an important question, but its legitimacy does not settle the issue of what rights should properly be included among the list of human rights. Although a right's being a human right surely establishes its importance, human rights also serve as goals for the development of institutions that can fulfill them, and as a basis for critique and for social and political changes short of intervention (Beitz 2001). (Of course, none of this implies that intervention is never justified, only that it is not entailed in the recognition of something as a human right.)

Accordingly, it should also be clear that human rights are not taken here as limited to the legally recognized list of international human rights. Rather, in the first place they are central normative or moral claims that call for the establishment of political (and economic and social institutions) that would realize them, along with legal instruments to assure their recognition and protection. They are also here broadly understood as fundamentally cosmopolitan in nature, though instrumentally often best assured through primary institutionalization within nation states, as well as at regional and more global levels.

Before proceeding to consider some of Cohen's own views regarding the meaning of democracy and human rights, I should perhaps clarify that I will be operating with a broader conception of democracy than is common in the literature, broader even than electoral democracy and certainly not requiring a particular structure of government. (I will discuss this broader significance later.) Cohen himself recognizes that democracy can (and indeed should) be used to refer to a democratic form of society (in addition to its political meaning), and in this sense is clearly committed to a general notion of equal respect for persons (or alternatively, in a different tradition, to equal consideration of their interests). It is therefore especially odd that Cohen takes this commitment to equality to militate against recognizing democracy as a human right. Surprisingly, he seems not to acknowledge that human rights entail a strong commitment to equality as well, indeed, perhaps even a stronger one than democracy does, or at least a more universal egalitarian commitment. This equality consists in the recognition that human rights can be claimed (equally!) by all humans. Indeed, the equality of these fundamental rights is one of their main normative functions, and speaks to their power in contemporary discourses. Thus, Cohen's crucial objection to democracy as too egalitarian to be a human right is mystifying. Moreover, once the equality aspect of human rights is recognized, it becomes impossible to accept the inequality of women or of other groups within a society as consistent with human rights, contrary to what seems implied by Cohen's view. (Again, it does not follow that a state should forcibly intervene in another society to impose egalitarian changes. Aside from not being effective, this is not necessarily the correct course of action.)

Equally puzzling is Cohen's reading of human rights as entitlements that establish the basis of membership in a political society. One of the strengths of human rights, which in fact served as a ground for introducing them into global politics, is that they apply to all humans everywhere, even to stateless persons, and to immigrants and refugees seeking membership in a given political society. Although nation-states were given the role of implementing them in the first place and these rights hold primarily against the members of one's own political society, the significance of human rights transcends state boundaries, as is increasingly evident in the contemporary world. Cohen takes the social and economic human rights (e.g., in regard to welfare) to show that they elaborate conditions of membership in a political society. But as the recent global justice literature has revealed, it is possible to take economic human rights as showing the need for more transnational forms of transfer or redistribution.

Finally, with regard to Cohen's claims regarding global public reason and toleration, we can recognize the importance of inter-cultural dialogue concerning the meaning of human rights without going along with the idea that it is acceptable for societies to allow systematic or structural forms of domination of some groups over others. The more cosmopolitan perspective of human rights counsels respect for the freedom and dignity of each person and respect for groups that are genuinely self-determining. Such self-determination requires that all members of a society be able to participate in these dialogues and cultural interpretations, and that we not take the word of the powerful for what the people as a whole want. In my view, the Arab Spring uprising of 2011 (whatever its ultimate outcome) has put definitively to rest the idea that only the global North is interested in human rights. And such groups as Women Living under Muslim Laws and various other progressive women's groups around the world have shown that it is essential to hear from historically oppressed and marginalized groups before accepting the notion – normally promulgated by elites – that people are satisfied living in conditions of unfreedom and inequality.

However, this sort of ringing endorsement of freedom and equality, and of democracy as a human right should not be understood as a proclamation of simple liberal democracy, as Cohen would see it. Indeed, I think that the notions of freedom, human rights, and democracy as well, need to be taken in more social and relational ways than they usually are. I will not be able to elaborate this claim in depth here, but I hope it will be evident that this social conception informs the justification of democracy as a human right.

Democracy as a human right

In the approach I have advanced in previous work, human rights specify the material, social and political conditions needed for the development of people's agency, where this agency is taken in the first place as human life activity and in a fuller sense as the development of capacities and the realization of long term projects over time (Gould 1988, chs 1 and 7; 2004, chs 1 and 9). This understanding sees human rights as part of an account of positive or effective freedom, which understands people to be equally agents. However, agency differs from the notions of it found in the work of such human rights theorists as James Griffin (2008) or Alan Gewirth (1982, 1996). I take it to be a more open conception, and also a more social or relational one, and I see this agency as emerging through social practices, including practices of reciprocity (at elementary or more complex levels). On my view, then, human rights should not be seen as protections of Kantian dignity or of a high-level purposiveness that would tend to exclude children or some people with disabilities from the protections in question. Moreover, given that individuals realize their projects or develop capacities in interaction with others, various forms of *common or joint activity* play a major role in my conception. (This is especially important for the case of democracy, as we shall see.)

Correlative to the distinction between basic agency and its development (whether in individual or social forms), is a distinction between basic human rights, as conditions for any human activity whatsoever, and non-basic – though still essential – ones, which are conditions needed for people's fuller flourishing. Note that this account also strives to mediate between an agency-based and an interest-based account, though it does not endorse the view of people as "bundles" of interests. The theory makes room not only for purposiveness and the development of capacities, but also for the realization of projects over time, and the importance of flourishing, here taken as importantly related to freedom in the positive sense. As a theory of positive or effective freedom, it is related to capability approaches, which have similar historical roots, without giving exclusive weight to these capabilities to the neglect of the fundamental capacity to choose, on the one hand, or of the realization of long-term projects, on the other.

The social practices that this theory highlights are much more basic than the sorts that Charles Beitz (2009) points to – in his case, practices regarding human rights in international relations. Beitz attempts to find a basis for human rights in those historically emergent practices and in the norms ingredient in them, but as a result his account remains highly particular and historically limited. I suggest that the relevant practices that lay the ground for the acceptance of human rights are more elementary ones, evident in both interpersonal and institutional contexts. They involve the practices of reciprocal recognition found in everyday experience, in which people implicitly or explicitly recognize the equal agency of others. These practices include not only the fundamental forms of communicative interactions, which Habermas (1994, 1998) has emphasized, but also the range of non-verbal interactions through which people reciprocally recognize each other, e.g., in ordinary greetings, or in Goffman-type "vehicular interactions," in which people reciprocally navigate their encounters with others, whether as pedestrians or drivers. Such practices of reciprocal recognition are far from sufficient to support the more robust acknowledgment of people's equality that is called for in full-fledged respect for universal human rights. But these elementary practices are nonetheless among the preconditions for the social and historical emergence of a more robust egalitarianism.

The full recognition of human rights is importantly supported by a normative argument that turns on a conception of justice as equal positive freedom, as equal rights to the conditions of self-transformation (whether the latter are individual or social). This argument proceeds from the equal (basic) agency of all to the requirement of access to conditions for people to develop capacities and realize projects. Since their basic agency is equal, and requires conditions for its development, no one of them has more of a claim to these conditions than do others. This asserts that they have prima facie equally valid claims of access – that is, in Feinberg's (1970) terms, equal rights – to these fundamental conditions of action. The conditions (which are specified in human rights) include the absence of constraints such as threats to bodily security, or restrictions on basic liberty (including freedom from domination), as well as the availability of enabling material and social conditions, such as means of subsistence and health-care, the provision of education, and support for crucial social relationships, e.g., in childcare, along with access to the means of cultural development. Thus an articulated account of both civil and political human rights and of economic, social and cultural ones is important, in my view.

Various democratic rights – e.g., freedom of expression and association – play an important role in protecting people's basic liberty and also their further flourishing. But beyond this, we can see the argument for democracy as itself a human right. Inasmuch as people are social beings, or what I have called "individuals-in-relations," engaging in common or joint activities with others can be seen as itself one of the prime conditions for their freedom. Common activities are here broadly understood to be activities oriented to shared goals. If none are to dominate others in these joint activities, they must have equal rights to participate in determining their course. This is a very general principle that pertains to joint activities of diverse sizes. In my view, when such common activities are institutionalized, they serve as arenas for democratic decision-making in a formal sense, and no longer remain merely casual or ad hoc. Democracy is thus a form of decision-making involving equal rights of participation among the members of a given community or institution. It is therefore broader in application than only to political societies, although the latter has been its prime context. Clearly, democracy is understood here more flexibly than as a political system defined by elections and majority rule (although there is much to commend those procedures), and the approach here does not take a stand between parliamentary or winner-takes-all systems of representation or between different sets of voting rules. It can countenance consensus decision-making and even certain consultative methods as democratic, providing the procedures respect equality among the participants.

It is evident that this is a quite expansive conception of democracy, one that supports the extension of democratic forms of decision-making to institutions beyond the political and also sees it as applying to all intensionally defined communities (that is, where people take themselves to be part of a community, or engaged in "common activities" defined by shared goals). The global import of this is that democratic participation is required not only within nation states, but also in the newer transnational or cross-border communities that are emerging with economic, technological and ecological globalization. This approach would also support democratic participation at the global level to the degree that the world came to be understood as a single political community. Indeed, this approach supports equal rights of participation for the members of any of these variously sized communities.

However, it is also clear that this justification for democracy, however wide-ranging, does not yet address what are perhaps the most important forms of democratic participation that are lacking globally and seem very much to be needed. The need for such new forms grows out of the impacts that decisions or policies by the institutions of global governance or by other powerful actors like nation states and corporations have on people who are distantly situated and not part of these institutions or communities. This problem, of impacts on distant others and of the democratic deficit involved in global governance, needs to be addressed with a different criterion for democratic participation, though one that has some deep connections to the first. I have previously proposed the relevance of the "all-affected" or affectedness criterion for such contexts, and have argued that this criterion needs to be further specified in order to avoid the implication that since everyone is distantly affected by many global policies therefore everyone would need to be able to participate in every decision and policy – clearly an unsupportable consequence. I have suggested instead that it is possible to demarcate those who are *importantly affected* in terms of an appeal to the *fulfillment of basic human rights*, and to propose that when people are thus affected in their ability to realize these basic rights, they should have significant input into the decision or policy in question, though not necessarily fully equal rights of participation, in contrast to the case of the "common activities" criterion discussed previously, where equal opportunities for participation are always required (Gould 2004, chs 7 and 9; 2009).

We now have the question of whether such affectedness serves to support a claim to a human right to democracy in this sense of having a say, or significant input, in cases where people at a distance are importantly affected by a given policy or decision. That is, does the human right to democratic participation pertain not only to the robust sense of equal rights of participation within communities (the "common activities" criterion) but also to rights of participation in decisions or policies of powerful institutions on the part of non-members (in accordance with the "affectedness" criterion)? On the one hand, one could argue that this latter sort of participation in decisions that affect the conditions for distant people's agency is in fact mandated, because of the importance of these conditions for people's agency, and because their rights of individual self-determination are to be respected. Insofar as human rights specify conditions needed by agents for their self-transformation, that is, are conditions for their positive freedom, democratic participation of those affected would indeed be needed to avoid domination or control by outsiders. On the other hand, in regard to many global policies, at least at present, people tend to be *differentially* affected, so that they would lack equal rights of participation, which seem to be required by the earlier argument for a human right to democracy. In the case of the needed contribution by distant others, it makes sense to limit democratic participation to what I have called significant input or "having a say," to distinguish it from the equal membership case. However, it should be remembered that many of those affected at a distance are in fact more seriously impacted by the decisions or policies in question than are the current powerful decision-makers themselves. For example, if Shell Oil decides on actions in Nigeria, it may in fact have more of an effect on Nigerians than on the policy-makers. So there is no necessary conclusion that they should have fewer opportunities to take part in the decision-making or to influence the outcome than do those currently holding the power to decide or to make policy.

I believe it is possible to argue for a human right to democracy in both the cases I have discussed – that of equal rights of participation for members of existing communities and institutions, and rights of democratic input into decisions that importantly affect one's fulfillment of basic human rights. In fact, both of these criteria as applied here can be seen to derive from a conception of positive freedom. The first one does so by virtue of the fact that participation in common activities is a condition for such freedom and that there should be equal rights of co-determination of these activities. The second case, of participation by those physically at a distance, also appeals to people's rights to have some control over their own activity and the conditions for it. If others are determining the possibilities for the agency of distantly situated groups of people, then these latter should have some say about it.[2] The forms of appropriate input will vary from consultation to representation within the decision procedures themselves. Nonetheless, to the degree that these distant others are affected by policies rather than standing in the relation of equal membership within a community, their participation is not yet subject to the robust requirements of the common activities criterion.

Interestingly, some recent theorists have sought to reinterpret rights of participation even in communal or standard democratic cases in differential ways depending on the various and differentiated impacts that policies have on people within the community, and have accordingly argued

---

[2] Note that being affected here need not always be negative. For example, even if the impact of a transnational corporation is held to benefit the affected people and the people are disposed to make the required transition, e.g., an agrarian society gaining important access to means of subsistence but in a way that impacts their traditional way of life, the argument here is that others ought not to make these decisions – including any trade-offs between basic rights – on behalf of those affected without their input and consent. Those affected would have a right to participate in the decision or policy in question and appropriate institutional arrangements are needed to facilitate this input. It is thus a matter of who makes the decision rather than which decision is the better one; the claim here is that those people affected in their basic rights need to be an essential part of the process.

for proportional rights of input or participation (Cavallero 2009). My own inclination is instead to retain the emphasis on equal participation for communities or for the members of institutions, and to add the possibility of differential participation for non-members whose interests and human rights fulfillment are foreseeably seriously affected by the decisions and policies of these communities and institutions. (This is particularly important in regard to global governance institutions.) However, it is important to remember that it may not always be the powerful decision-makers who have the most at stake in these various policies and plans.

Theoretical problems in the relation of democracy and human rights at the global level

In my book *Globalizing Democracy and Human Rights*, I articulated the problem that I called the *constitutional circle*, in which democratic or consensual processes of determining constitutional rights in a democracy themselves have to be constrained by rights (Gould 2009, 39–46). My proposal for avoiding that circle was to suggest that the rights that are recognized in this process are not in fact constituted by democratic choice but are recognized as those already ingredient in social life and that also give rise to the requirement of democracy in collective decision-making. I identify these fundamental rights with the valid claims that each makes on others for the conditions of self-transformation and see this sort of claiming as based on social processes of reciprocity and of care. Whereas reciprocal recognition may often take an instrumental or tit-for-tat form, more developed versions may come to involve mutual respect and explicitly shared aims. When the interdependence of persons is most fully realized, reciprocity can take the form of what I earlier called mutuality, which involves not only a recognition of equal agency but relational forms oriented to enhancement of the other (Gould 1983, 1993). This latter is of course more common in interpersonal relations, rather than in politics or economics or in institutional forms more generally.

When we move to the global level, however, new problems of potential circularity emerge, especially if we take impact on (or being affected in) one's possibilities for fulfilling human rights as a criterion for requiring democratic input into a given decision. This might seem problematic if it is also recognized that democracy is one of the human rights. And it would indeed be awkward (at best) to propose that what justifies democratic input is the effect of decisions on the possibilities of exercising democratic decision-making. Explaining why the approach I propose for input from distant others is not in fact circular in this way can also help clarify the significance of "affectedness" as a justification for democratic participation, as well as the role of impact on people's human rights, and the connection of both of these to the first criterion of co-determination of common activities.

If we examine the significance of "being affected" (in the specified sense of being importantly affected), we can see that it is in fact grounded in positive freedom, as are the human rights themselves, which in my view specify the conditions required if freedom is to be effective. Likewise, the requirement of democratic participation in determining common activities (the first criterion given above) has roots in this sort of positive or effective freedom, on my account. This suggests that the two criteria I have proposed – common activities and impact on distant others' human rights – share much of the same basis. In the affectedness case, the requirement for people to have a say follows from their need to have some control over the conditions of their life activity. The impact on human rights thus only provides a determinate, and in some cases a measurable, way of gauging whether decisions will significantly affect people's freedom. It is what triggers the need for democratic input, where these human rights are valuable by contributing to the more basic value of positive freedom. Thus I suggest that there is no circle at the level of justification.

Still, some might suggest that a circularity remains (though a less troubling one), if we claim that the human rights to be considered as affected by a given decision or policy include democracy among others. One way around this would be to clarify that impact only on the basic human rights of subsistence, security and fundamental liberty is what triggers the need for democratic input. In this case, democratic input would be instrumental to realizing these basic human rights, as distinct from impact on those conditions needed for its fuller flourishing (specified in the non-basic, though still essential, human rights). An alternative way of dismissing the circularity would be to distinguish among the two senses of democratic human rights characterized earlier, with the robust requirement of equal participation in common decisions characterized as Democracy1, and the input sense articulated in the second case as Democracy2. Even if the argument were made that impact of decisions or policies on the possibilities of fulfilling the human right to democracy (as Democracy1) is sufficient to trigger the requirement for input into these decisions, circularity would be avoided since the claim would then be that Democracy2 is required for the fulfillment of Democracy1.

Moreover, regarding the further potential circularity that there is a need for some (quasi-)democratic deliberation regarding the meaning of the various human rights themselves, we can observe that this is not a serious problem for my approach, since this sort of deliberation is not constitutive of the rights themselves and does not itself serve to justify them (as would be the case on some deliberativist views of democratic justification). Finally, it is worth emphasizing that despite the close connections I have indicated between the common activities criterion and the democratic input one, a difference between them remains with regard to whether strictly equal decision-making is required (at least in principle). The first criterion requires equal rights of participation. The second criterion – namely, affectedness – may admit of some differentiation, recognizing again that people at a distance may in fact be more affected by decisions than are the decision-makers. In that case, they should have a greater say, even though they are distantly situated in space. It is clear, then, that the "affectedness" principle cannot be satisfied by simply hearing from broader publics in a superficial or random way. It requires the development of procedures for systematically involving the affected people in the decisions or policies taken by powerful transnational actors or institutions of global governance. Thus, when taken in its relation to human rights and ultimately to people's positive freedom, this criterion can also be a highly demanding one, even though it does not necessarily incorporate the requirement for equal rights of participation by equal members as the more familiar communal criterion does.

Democratic input into global governance institutions

We can finally sketch some possible applications of this analysis to the difficult issue of how more democracy can be introduced into the various forms of transnational decision-making. I propose that there are four possible directions for moving toward democratic participation in those contexts, which I will briefly take note of in this final part and only in general terms. It is important to acknowledge that none of these are likely to be developed in the short term and also that their development will require considerable institutional innovation.

The fourfold strategy is as follows:

1. Democratic procedures need to be introduced into all (self-understood) communities and institutions, which are increasingly cross-border or

transnational, whether regional or global. This requirement follows from the common activities criterion discussed above, in view of the principle of equal positive freedom. I have suggested that members of these communities have equal rights to co-determine these institution-alized contexts, whether in politics, economics (e.g., in firms) or social life, and whether the relevant institutions are within or across borders. An additional benefit is that such widespread democratic procedures (formal or informal) would likely help to contribute to a democratic culture and to the evolution of what I earlier called the democratic per-sonality (Gould 2004, 283–306). The democratic procedures involved here would include equal opportunities for participation and deliber-ation where possible, along with forms of representation coupled with new forms of public input and deliberation, both online and off. A rele-vant principle is provided by the notion of subsidiarity, with decisions to be taken at the most local levels possible, but where the local does not necessarily have a geographical interpretation, but instead one of prox-imity and size (recognizing that many of the new communities will cross borders).

2. Proposals for a global democratic parliament, or Global People's Assembly, within the UN should be implemented. However, such a par-liament would only be significant if it had real authority. Moreover, a people's assembly does not yet amount to some sort of ultimate plan in my view, primarily because it leaves the "great powers" in place as they are currently. Nonetheless, to the degree that a set of global shared ends are emerging and coming to be recognized, this sort of global parlia-ment could also be seen to follow from the common activities criterion, as enunciated here.

3. There is a need to devise new forms of public input and new modes of transnational representation within the institutions of global govern-ance. This representation would have to go beyond giving NGOs a seat at the table; and the NGOs themselves must in any case become more rep-resentative. As with the first proposal, the public input called for can be increasingly enabled by the use of deliberative software and other forms of online interaction (e.g., in forums) and I have elsewhere suggested how these new formats can contribute to influence in decisions and poli-cies by a dispersed transnational public (Gould 2007). Representative deliberative polling is also a possible direction for innovation at the glo-bal level. However, such polling would need to go beyond sampling or merely soliciting opinions. If polling is to be effective, politicians would have to commit to taking the results of these deliberations as binding.

But we can see how these suggested directions could help to concretize the second criterion's requirement for gaining input on the part of those significantly affected by the policies of global governance institutions.

4. Finally, the least likely new direction in the short run, but worth considering for the longer term, would be the development of a system of delegate assemblies, based on principles of subsidiarity, with real power to determine global policies, for example, concerning regulatory matters and labor policies. These assemblies could be geographically based for some issues or could be functionally oriented, and would need to involve the election of delegates at higher levels. This alternate approach to representation (including in transnational contexts) would be designed to give ordinary and distantly situated people a say in accordance with the affectedness criterion, and if successful could serve as something of an antidote to the currently unresponsive and very powerful institutions of global governance. Delegate assemblies or people's assemblies are now being developed in southern Europe and in Latin America. Perhaps they could take different forms in other regions of the world. In any case, it may well be useful to think about constructing some of these alternate sources of democratic power, in addition to finding ways to make existing political communities and economic institutions, whether domestic or transnational, more deeply democratic and more responsive to the needs and the participation of distant others.

References

Cavallero, Eric. 2009. "Federative Global Democracy." *Metaphilosophy* 40:1, Special Issue on Global Democracy and Exclusion, edited by Ronald Tinnevelt and Helder de Schutter, 42–64.

Cohen, Joshua. 2006. "Is there a Human Right to Democracy?" In Christine Sypnowich, ed., *The Egalitarian Conscience: Essays in Honour of G.A. Cohen*. Oxford University Press, pp. 226–248.

Beitz, Charles. 2001. "Human Rights as a Common Concern." *American Political Science Review* 95:2, 269–282.

2009. *The Idea of Human Rights*. Oxford University Press.

Feinberg, Joel. 1970. "The Nature and Value of Rights." *Journal of Value Inquiry* 4, 243–257.

Gewirth, Alan. 1982. *Human Rights*. University of Chicago Press.

1996. *The Community of Rights*. University of Chicago Press.

Gould, Carol C. 1983. "Beyond Causality in the Social Sciences: Reciprocity as a Model of Non-Exploitative Social Relations." In R.S. Cohen and M.W. Wartofsky, eds., *Epistemology, Methodology and the Social Sciences: Boston*

Studies in the Philosophy of Science, vol. 71. Boston and Dordrecht: D. Reidel, pp. 53–88.

1988. *Rethinking Democracy.* Cambridge University Press.

1993. "Feminism and Democratic Community Revisited." In J. Chapman and I. Shapiro, eds., *Democratic Community: NOMOS XXXV.* New York University Press, pp. 396–413.

2004. *Globalizing Democracy and Human Rights.* Cambridge University Press.

2007. "Global Democratic Transformation and the Internet." In John R. Rowan, ed., *Technology, Science and Social Justice, Social Philosophy Today, Volume 22.* Charlottesville: Philosophy Documentation Center, pp. 73–88.

2009. "Structuring Global Democracy: Political Communities, Universal Human Rights, and Transnational Representation." *Metaphilosophy* 40:1, Special Issue on Global Democracy and Exclusion, edited by Ronald Tinnevelt and Helder de Schutter, 24–46.

Griffin, James. 2008. *On Human Rights.* Oxford University Press.

Habermas, Jürgen. 1994. "Human Rights and Popular Sovereignty: The Liberal and Republican Versions." *Ratio Juris* 7:1, 1–13.

1998. *The Inclusion of the Other: Studies in Political Theory*, edited by Ciaran Cronin and Pablo De Greiff. Cambridge, MA: MIT Press.

16 | An egalitarian argument for a human right to democracy

THOMAS CHRISTIANO

Introduction

Democracy is often defended on the grounds that it treats the members of society as equals by giving them an equal say in the process of collective decision-making. Yet the question remains of whether there is a human right to democracy or a right that ought to be realized in every society and that ought to receive the protection of the international community. What makes this a hard question is that it may seem that the human right to democracy is incompatible with the legitimate self-determination of peoples, at least when these peoples do not accept the egalitarianism at the heart of democracy (Cohen 2010). Elsewhere I have argued in favor of a human right to democracy by tying it instrumentally very closely with other human rights that are less controversial (Christiano 2011a). In this chapter I want to suggest that the traditional argument for democracy may provide the basis for a limited defense of a human right to democracy and that this argument holds even for those societies that do not accept the principle of equality.

The general argument is very simple. It proceeds in two steps, which correspond to the two dimensions of human rights as I conceive of them. In the first step I give a general argument for democratic institutions in domestic societies. In the second step I proceed from the traditional democratic premise that people have a right to a say in the institutions that have serious effects on their lives, to the thought that individuals ought to have a say in the process of the construction of international institutions and law. But in the absence of the possibility of meaningful global democracy it is a necessary condition of persons participating as equals in the shaping of the international environment that they have an equal say in the political institutions of their society that participate in creating international law and in diplomatic relations with other societies.

In this chapter I start by defining the notions of "human right" and "democracy." I then lay out some of the main considerations in favor of democracy generally and show how they apply first to the context of domestic political decision-making and then to the specific context of international law making. Then I present an argument to the effect that hierarchical societies interfere not only with the rights of their own citizens but also with the equal rights of all persons at least in the context of the making of international law. This sets the stage for a treatment of the objection from the legitimate self-determination of peoples. I conclude with some observations about the implications of a human right to democracy for how the international community ought to act toward non-democratic societies.

The human right to democracy: conceptual preliminaries

In this chapter, I will defend a set of jointly sufficient conditions, which are particularly salient for my argument. These are conditions for a moral human right to democracy and not a legal right human right. Two jointly sufficient formal conditions for a moral human right to x are: (1) there is strong moral justification for any state to establish, respect, protect and promote a legal or conventional right to x (or a set of legal and conventional rights that can be usefully summarized as a right to x) and (2) there is moral justification for the international community to respect, protect and promote the above legal or conventional right to x in all persons. By "international community" I mean states other than the one in question, international non-governmental organizations and international organizations.

The institutional structure constituted by conventional or legal rights has a strong moral justification when it is minimally necessary and sufficient for realizing very urgent moral goods (Sumner 1987, 144–145).[1] Without it, it is very unlikely that the very urgent moral goods will be realized; with it, it is very likely that the very urgent moral goods will be realized. An institution or action has a moral justification when it is morally desirable that it be constructed or undertaken in order to realize morally urgent goods.

I will not settle here for a definitive list or a basic account of the very urgent moral goods. Very urgent moral goods can include the protection of human dignity, the satisfaction of fundamental interests, natural rights or not being treated as a moral inferior. Here I will rely on the very urgent moral goods that constitute the basis for a traditional ground for democracy. These are the basic interests that ground democracy and the equality of persons.

---

[1] This account is close to Joseph Raz's interest theory of rights though it broadens the possible grounds of a right to include other morally very urgent goods that can be possessed by the right-holder (Raz 1986, ch. 7).

To be clear, this account does not require the existence of states or international institutions recognizing the right in question. In the absence of an international institution or even of a functioning state, one may still say that the human right to x exists since one is saying that the construction of institutions that include a conventional right to x is strongly morally justified. And I think one may even say that the right is violated or infringed by those who block the construction of these institutions or interfere with the proper functioning of those institutions.

The human right to democracy that I will argue for asserts that there is a strong moral justification for states to adopt or maintain the institutions of minimally egalitarian democracy and it is morally justified for the international community to respect, protect and promote the right of each person to participate in minimally egalitarian democratic decision-making concerning their society. By "minimally egalitarian democracy" I mean a democracy that has a formal or informal constitutional structure that ensures that persons are able to participate as equals in the collective decision-making of their political society. A paradigm instance of it can be more precisely characterized in terms of the following three conditions:

1. Persons have formally equal votes that are effective in the aggregate in determining who is in power, the normal result of which is a high level of participation of the populace in the electoral process.
2. Persons have equal opportunities to run for office, to determine the agenda of decision-making and equal opportunities to influence the processes of deliberation. Individuals are free to organize political parties and interest group associations without legal impediment or fear of serious violence and they are free to abandon their previous political associations. They have freedom of expression at least regarding political matters. In such a society there is normally robust competition among parties so that a variety of political parties have a significant presence in the legislature.
3. Such a society also acts in accordance with the rule of law and supports an independent judiciary that acts as a check on executive power.

This cluster of rights can be characterized simply as a right to participate as an equal in the collective decision-making of one's political society. I will refer to it here on out as a right to democracy.[2]

---

[2] I use the expression "paradigm instance of democracy" here because, though I think representative democracy is the main instance of what I have in mind, I want to leave room for some forms of democracy that are not representative but that are recognizably egalitarian (Webber 2009).

Such a society need not be fully just by any means nor need it live up fully to the ideals of democracy. For that reason I call it minimally egalitarian. Such a society may in effect limit some opportunities to participate due to inequalities of wealth. It might have a suboptimal system of representation. It need not be fully liberal since it may restrict non-political activities and violate liberal rights that are not connected to the democratic process. But it is not merely majoritarian with universal suffrage and elections. Minorities must have the protections of the rule of law, free association and expression as well as equal opportunities for organizing politically effective groups and there must be free and fair competition for power among a variety of groups that compete on an equal footing. Normally this will result in minorities having a significant place in the legislature.

This conception of a human right to x as entailing a strong moral justification for a legal or conventional right to x first at the state level and then a moral justification to protect and promote those rights at the international level is supported by four considerations. One, it implies that we are talking about rights because it supports a legal or conventional right to x in order to protect and promote the very urgent moral goods. The very urgent moral goods are sufficient to ground duties in each to protect the minimally egalitarian democratic rights of each. And the protection of the urgent moral goods justifies putting a brake on the pursuit of the common good. Two, the proposed conception implies that we are talking about universally held rights. Three, the rights are pre-institutional in the sense that they do not depend for their existence on actual institutions. Four, the moral structures of these rights correspond to the structure of moral justification that is common for many if not most of the human rights we observe in contemporary international human rights practice. Justifications impose upon states the moral duties to realize certain fundamental moral goods by instituting and protecting various legal rights and they impose on the international community the duties to help states do this (Beitz 2009).[3] If we can successfully show that there is strong moral justification for states to be minimally democratic and that the international community is morally justified in promoting and protecting democracy then we have an argument for a human right to democracy that fits within the mainstream concept of human rights.

---

[3] Unlike Beitz, I do not insist that these conditions are necessary for human rights and I do not insist on an interest theory of human rights.

Democracy at the domestic level

Democracy at the level of domestic political decision-making is, I argue, a realization of the central political value of treating persons publicly as equals in the context of serious conflicts of interest and disagreement among fallible and cognitively biased equal persons about how best to organize the society they share. When people disagree and collective decisions must be made, democracy is the way of making these decisions in which people can see that they are being treated as equals.

The argument for this thesis proceeds from the observation of certain basic facts in political societies of fallibility, pervasive disagreement, conflict of interest, and cognitive bias in persons and from the need for collective decision-making despite these facts. I argue that in the light of these facts there are certain fundamental interests that human beings share and that anyone can see that they share in the context of political society. The central importance of these interests and the idea that persons ought to be treated as equals in ways that are publicly evident to all point to democracy as the uniquely appropriate method for collective decision-making.

The facts of disagreement, conflict of interest and cognitive bias are apparent to all. There is disagreement on what the interests of persons in different parts of the society are. There is disagreement on how justly to accommodate these differing interests and on what the common good is. These disagreements arise from the fact that we are fallible beings with very limited understandings of the world we live in and we are beings with different and conflicting interests. In part our conflicting interests arise from the fact that persons are born into and live in very different sectors of the society. In part they arise from the fact that any society consists of a variety of differing cultures and traditions. Finally differences of interest arise from differences in gender, race and ethnic origin. We are cognitively biased as a consequence of the fact that we are embedded in different sectors of the society and different cultures and traditions within the society. Our judgments tend to reflect our own interests and the social backgrounds in which we live. As a consequence, we don't have very good understandings of the interests of others in other parts of the society even when we do understand our own interests. In this kind of context where there is a need for collective decision-making we have three very salient and important political interests that we seek to have protected: the interest in protecting against cognitive bias, the interest in being at home in the world and the interest in being recognized and affirmed as an equal.

The interest in correcting for cognitive bias is a politically salient interest because it arises in the context in which cooperation is needed but in which there is disagreement, cognitive bias and conflict of interest. When there is a need for cooperation on particular terms and where there is disagreement and conflict of interest, if one party can structure the cooperation on its own terms, the others will have reason to think that their interests will not be advanced even if all are acting conscientiously. This is because even conscientious agents have cognitive biases toward their own interests and backgrounds. And if they are allowed to structure common terms unfettered, the terms will express their interests and not those of others. Persons have interests in correcting for cognitive bias in the sense that they have interests in being able to make sure that the terms reflect their own interests as well. Correcting for cognitive bias does not ensure a fully impartial scheme of cooperation; it only ensures that all parties have the opportunity to make sure that the scheme of cooperation takes account of their interests. Having a say over the scheme of cooperation ensures that one can correct for cognitive bias at least in a way that is consistent with others having a say. When each has a say, each must appeal to others to get legislation and policy made. Consequently each must listen to the arguments of others and respond to those arguments. And each must make efforts to accommodate the views of others in compromise when disagreement cannot be overcome. These facts ensure that when one has a say one has an opportunity to influence outcomes, which opportunity ensures that one's views are heard and taken account of. As a consequence, the terms of cooperation must take into account the underlying interests of all persons.

The interest in being at home in the world is an interest in having one's world make sense to one's self both in the sense that one understands the social world one lives in and in the sense that it conforms to norms for social worlds that one holds. This interest is political in that it arises when there is a need for cooperation among very different persons, who have very different cultural and ideological backgrounds and whose interests conflict. When one person is able to impose terms of cooperation, the others are threatened with living in a world they do not understand and that doesn't conform to norms they hold. They are threatened with alienation. The interest in being at home in the world is secured to an extent compatible with others' similar interests being secured when each has a say in the process of collective decision-making. The interest is secured through the very same devices that the interest in correcting for cognitive bias is secured.

Finally the interest in being recognized and affirmed as an equal is a fundamental political interest that arises when there is arduous conflict of interest and disagreement. This interest cannot be fully vindicated until and unless equality is vindicated. The basic argument for the interest is that one has an interest in being recognized by other moral agents for what one is as a matter of basic political status. Not being afforded an equal say in collective decision-making implies that one is not recognized and affirmed as an equal because it is a clear setback to the fundamental interests in correcting for cognitive bias and being at home in the world. Furthermore not being afforded an equal say has the direct implication that one is being treated like others who are not given an equal vote: children and the insane. It suggests that one is not competent at the task.

The idea is that social justice requires that persons be treated publicly as equals or must be treated as equals in a way that is publicly clear to conscientious and informed persons. In my account, to be treated publicly as an equal is for it to be the case that one's interests are equally advanced in a publicly clear way. The interests described above are political interests in the sense that they are interests that people have in political environments marked by conflicts of interests, disagreement and cognitive bias. They are also public in the sense that even if people do not fully grasp the interests of others because of the diversity of their backgrounds, they do understand that each person has the political interests. They can see that each person is in a similar position with regard to these interests in the context of a diverse political society. And they see this because of and despite a great deal of disagreement about each other's more particular interests.

The only way to treat persons as equals in a publicly clear way in collective decision-making is to give each an equal say in the process. This is because the political interests are public ones and the way to advance them in a publicly clear egalitarian way is to ensure that each has a say in the collective decision-making that displays the equal advancement of each person's interests. We cannot appeal to equality in the outcome of collective decision-making because there is too much disagreement about what would constitute an equal outcome. We cannot even appeal to equality in the satisfaction of the interests in being at home or in correcting for cognitive bias since the extent of satisfaction of these are also subjects of disagreement. So in order to treat persons publicly as equals we must stand back from an equal outcome standard and give each person the means to advance their distinctive concerns and interests in collective decision-making. And we must distribute those means in a way that treats everyone as an equal (Christiano 2008, 46–130).

The above argument establishes the first of the two conditions for a human right to democracy. States have strong moral justifications for realizing the right to participate as an equal in collective decision-making, based on the very urgent moral good of realizing public equality among the members of the society. Democracy, I have argued, is necessary and reliable in realizing this good in the context of the modern state.

The right to have a say in international treaties and institutions

The second part in the argument for a human right to democracy comes in five steps. First, I observe that there is a significant and growing amount of interdependence of interests among persons in the international environment and there is a real and perceived need for collective action. Second, persons have fundamental political interests in being able to fashion the law and institutions that regulate the international environment. Third, I argue that persons have rights to participate as equals in the process of fashioning the global environment. Fourth, I assume here that global democracy is not a viable option. So, only if the states that participate in the making of international law are democratic can it be said that the process of making international law is one that respects the rights of persons to participate as equals in the collective decision-making. The final step argues that only when all states are democratic can the individuals within and across societies treat each other as equals in the process of making international law. This argument establishes the second of the two elements that are sufficient for asserting a human right to democracy.

The international environment and the need for cooperation

Flows of international trade, communications, international migration, and internationally spread environmental problems have pervasive effects on the lives of the various countries involved and the citizens in them. International cooperation between particular states is increasingly necessary and increasingly has an effect on the lives of particular persons.

Furthermore, international institutions and law play an increasingly significant role in regulating everyday life. From law that enables and constrains international trade to law that imposes burdens for the purpose of producing public goods to human rights law, international law is increasingly pervasive throughout much of the globe. International law increasingly takes on tasks that have been previously allotted to domestic institutions or at least directs the domestic institutions of states to do these things. For example, international law increasingly defines the property rights of persons either directly or indirectly because it requires states to define the property rights of their citizens in various ways to advance international trade or the protection of the environment.

Most important of all, there are certain morally mandatory aims that the international system must pursue. The aims of international peace and security, the protection of basic human rights, the mitigation of global environmental catastrophe, the alleviation of severe global poverty and the development of a decent system of international trade are generally recognized aims of the international system. Furthermore, all human beings have duties to contribute to the pursuit of these aims and so the international system must attempt to achieve them through the construction of international law and institutions.

Furthermore there is a great deal of disagreement about how to pursue the mandatory aims both in terms of the economics and politics as well as in terms of what the exact nature of the aim is and what a fair distribution of the burdens are. There is significant disagreement on the proper regulation of international trade and the appropriate demands that may be put on persons within political societies, on the level of provision of public goods and the appropriate price that should be paid for these as well as the fair distribution of those costs, on the exact character of human rights and on what may permissibly be done to protect those rights.

The interests in having a say

In the light of these politically salient facts, persons have important political interests in having a say over the creation of international law and institutions: the interest in correcting for cognitive bias, the interest in being at home in the world and the interest in being recognized and affirmed as an equal. These interests are very much like the interests people have in having a say in the domestic organizations of their societies. Let us look at how the relevant interests we discussed in the context of the justification of domestic democracy are present in the context of the international arena.

Differences between national political histories and intellectual and moral cultures and differences in economic and political structure may have the effect that there is a greater degree of disagreement and a greater degree of difference of interests among persons across different societies than within particular domestic societies. Differences of economic structure such as whether a society is predominantly agricultural or industrial, or differences in the size and structure of welfare state institutions and differences in the legal systems of property, contract and government regulation may all contribute to very strong differences in view and in interests about how to structure the system of international cooperation. And differences in political history will have an important impact here as well. As a result, in some instances the interests in correcting for cognitive bias, the interests in making the world a home and the interest in being recognized and affirmed as an equal may be even more at stake in the process of making international law than at the domestic level.

For example the three basic political interests may be more threatened in the international environment by the dominance of a particular state or grouping of states in the creation of schemes of cooperation. Powerful states may impose ideas that are suited to a particular intellectual culture and economic and political structure and not to all the societies affected by the scheme. And the interest in being at home in the world may also be more threatened when cooperative schemes are chosen by a particular grouping since the norms of a society with one intellectual history and culture and economic and political structure may be quite different from those of others. Persons from less powerful societies may properly see themselves as not being treated as equals.

This diversity of interests makes it important that not only different societies have a say in the making of international law and institutions but also that all the persons in those different societies have a say. This is because the societies are in no way unitary. They each have different sectors and different cultural groupings with distinctive interests and concerns. The various fundamental political interests attach to persons in different societies as much as to persons in our own society.

In the light of the recognized and objective need for cooperation and in light of the basic political interests at stake in the making of international law, only if persons may participate as equals in the process of making international law can it be said that they are being treated publicly as equals in the international realm. If some cannot participate as equals in the international realm, then there is a clear sense in which their basic political interests are being subordinated to those who have superior rights of participation. Such a system cannot be said to be publicly advancing the equal interests of all persons. The argument for this thesis runs parallel to the argument in the domestic case. And my sense is that this argument will run parallel for a variety of theoretical accounts of the grounds of democracy that treat equality as a fundamental principle (Cohen 2009; Dahl 1989; Rawls 1971, 223–228).

Democracy best realized through states

Because of the distinctive features of the international environment, the parallel is limited. The right to have a say in the making of international law is best realized through a process of negotiation between his or her state and other states when those states are democratic.

The argument for this is, first, that global democracy and global democratic institutions are at the moment and probably for the foreseeable future not feasible and for a variety of reasons not desirable. I have given three reasons for this skepticism about global democracy elsewhere (Christiano 2011b). But briefly, the worries are, one, such a system would not be obviously fair since it would at least purport to give persons an equal say over issues on which they may have very different stakes, even when one considers the totality of issues put together. Two, such a system of global majoritarianism would likely produce very large cases of persistent minorities and, three, there is not likely to be anytime soon the kind of global infrastructure of civil society necessary to make democracy work at that level.

The second part of this argument is that the modern state is by far the best mechanism developed over the last 500 or 600 years for accommodating the interests of large numbers of people and making political power accountable to large numbers of people. Though far from perfect there is nothing else like that in the offing in the international system. The best bet for a process of international law making that is reasonably responsive to persons' interests and egalitarian is by a process of fair negotiation among democratic states.

This idea involves two big parts. The first part is the idea of fair negotiation among political societies. If the process of international negotiation is reasonably fair in that it takes into account the interests of the members of different states and the stakes of different political societies in the process of bringing about agreements, the only thing left is to ensure that persons within states are represented equally. I do not have the space to go into an account of the nature of fairness in negotiation among political societies in this chapter.[4] The second is the idea of persons participating as equals in the decision-making in each particular society. And this requires some kind of democratic decision-making. The combination of these two requirements ensures that persons are treated publicly as equals in the process of making

---

[4] I am developing such an account in other work. See my "Fairness and Legitimacy in International Institutions" (Christiano unpublished).

international law.[5] My claim here is only that the requirement of democracy at the domestic level is a necessary condition of the process being egalitarian at the larger level.

This will require some kind of modification of the democratic state as we currently know it. It is currently structured so that the foreign policy establishment is the primary responsible in the making of international law. The foreign policy establishments of most states are quite secretive and aloof from their populations. This may have been defensible when the principal concerns of foreign policy were war making and alliances in preparation for war. But this must be modified given the new functions of international law or at least the greatly expanded functions of international law not having to do with war making and alliances. Hence, the foreign policy establishments will have to become more democratic than they have been.

The external effects of cooperation with hierarchical societies: complicity and subordination

In this section I argue that in the context of international law making: (1) cooperation with non-democracies in the creation and implementation of international law involves complicity on the part of citizens of democratic societies in the non-democratic decision-making of the non-democratic societies; (2) cooperation with these societies damages the democratic credentials of democratic societies and of international law as a whole. The non-democratic features of these societies cannot be contained within them; they have external effects that undermine the equality within other societies and within the context of international law making as a whole.

We face a dilemma: either democratic societies cooperate with non-democratic societies, in which case the whole system is non-democratic and there is some damage to the democratic character of the original democratic societies, or we insist as a matter of moral principle that all societies be democratic thus preserving democratic equality at the level of international

[5] Here I should briefly comment on the use of the expressions "participation as equals" and "public treatment of equals" that figures in my characterization of the process of making international law and institutions. I use the more abstract formulation because, strictly speaking, an equal say for all persons in the making of international law is not appropriate. Persons have quite different stakes in the making of international law and so it is not strictly just that they have an equal say over it. In my view the fair process of negotiation among states will take account of the differing stakes of persons in a way that treats them as equals. For an exposition and defense of the broader principle that persons ought to have a say in proportion to their stakes see Brighouse and Fleurbaey (2010).

law making. I want to argue that the solution to this dilemma must require, if democracy is indeed the right way to make decisions, that all societies be democratic.

To illustrate this argument, let us use an idealized example of inter-state negotiation among democratic and non-democratic states. Let us suppose that we have two states of equal size and that have roughly equal stakes in how a certain issue is resolved. Their populations have diverse interests and so there are competing and qualitatively distinct interests regarding the outcome of the negotiation. Now let us suppose that one state is democratic and the other is autocratic. And under the assumption that the democratic state has properly democratized its main foreign policy decisions we can think of this state's decisions in the negotiations as regulated by the population as a whole in which each has an equal say. At the same time the autocrat makes the autocratic state's decisions in negotiation. To the extent that we regard decisions as reflecting the interests of the decision-makers, we can see that the democratically made decisions will reflect the interests of a broad section of the society while the autocrat's decision will reflect her interests and those of her clique. And to the extent that we regard the interests as diverse, we can assume that the interests of the autocrat do not correspond with those of the rest of the population of her society or to those of the democratic society's population. The consequence of this is that the autocrat negotiates with the people of the other society to determine mutually agreeable arrangements that affect both their societies.

Now it seems to me that there is an intuitively clear sense in which the autocrat has much greater power over the results of these negotiations than any of the individuals in her own society and also over any individuals in the democratic society. It may be the case that the autocrat has the same power to determine an agreement as the whole of the people of the other state. But it seems that the consequence of this is that the autocrat has much more power over the outcome of the negotiation than any member of the other society. They have massively disproportionate influence over the negotiations and the subsequent arrangements.

To appreciate this, notice that the content of the agreements made between autocratic and democratic societies will be different for all involved than the content of the agreements made with the equal participation of all in the members of the now autocratic society. The reason for this is that the interests of the autocrat are different from those of the other members of her society.

But this difference in content affects not only the members of the autocrat's society but also those of the democratic society. Who the democratic society negotiates with determines what kinds of compromises are made and therefore what terms the members of the democratic society must live with. As a consequence the autocrat has an influence over the democratic society in the making of these negotiations. And that influence must be greater than the influence of any of the members of the democratic society. The reason for asserting this is that the autocrat has what amounts to a veto over at least the bilateral arrangements that the democratic and non-democratic societies create. The citizens of the democratic society do not individually have such veto power. They merely have the equal voting power in the collective decision-making of the democratic state, which has as a whole a kind of veto power over bilateral arrangements. But this looks like it gives the autocrat significantly more power than any citizen has.

There are really two external kinds of consequences of this situation that offend against democratic principles. The first is that the autocrat has much greater power over her own society than anyone else does. That one is obvious. But there is a further implication of this observation. It would appear that the citizens of the democratic society are complicit in imposing norms on the subjects of the other society without those persons having any say. They are in a sense colluding with the autocrat to create international law and policy that is imposed on the subjects of the autocrat. They are complicit in treating the subjects of the other society as unequals. Cooperation in this context implies that democratic citizens are required to treat the members of the other society in a way that violates their own egalitarian norms. They are not just watching and tolerating another society's treatment of its own subjects; they are participating in that treatment. The cooperation comes at a cost that involves the violation of the norms of equality by egalitarians. Let us call this the *complicity thesis*.

The second is that the autocrat has more power over the collective arrangements that the two societies make than any citizen in the democratic society. And to the extent that this affects the content of the arrangements even in the democratic society, the autocrat has more power over some aspects of the democratic society than any citizen of that society. Not only is a democratic society complicit in treating the subjects of an autocratic society as unequals, it is also allowing its own members to be treated as unequals by the autocrat. Since the autocrat has much more influence than any individual citizen of the democratic society over the arrangements that are agreed upon between the societies, the citizens of the democratic society seem to be giving vastly disproportionate power to the autocrat over their own lives at least with respect to international law and those parts of domestic law that are directed by international law.

Thus the inequality within the autocratic society is externalized in the context of the making of international law to an inequality between citizens of democratic societies and the autocrats in the non-democratic society. Inequality becomes an external effect of non-democratic societies when they cooperate in the making of international law. Let us call this the *subordination thesis*.

One way to see this is to think of a domestic society in which one group of people within the larger society gives all of its votes to a small elite in the group. The citizens outside the group have equal votes. First, the members of the group that do not have the votes would be less powerful. So, all those citizens who have equal votes would be in some sense complicit in the inequality since they would be participating in making collective decisions that are imposed on those who were deprived of the votes. And, second, all the members of the society outside the group would be at a disadvantage relative to the elites within the group as a consequence of the distribution of votes within the group. The elite in the group would have a great deal more voting power than any other member in the society including those outside the group.

To be sure, there is a sense in which the arrangements within the non-democratic society above do not diminish the voting power of the citizens in the democratic society. In a sense, the citizens of the democratic society would be confronting the veto power of the other society whether it was democratic or not, whether all the voting power was concentrated in the hands of the elite or not. But the inequality would matter a great deal for all that. The reason is that the concentration of voting power in one hand and the consequent inequality threatens the interests of the other citizens in a way that the equal distribution does not. In the case of two democratic societies, citizens of different groups in one society could find common cause with citizens of different groups in the other society. But when power is concentrated in one hand, this is far less likely.

So far I have used the case of cooperation with autocratic societies to make my point about the external effects of non-democracy. This has been for ease of analysis. But it seems clear to me that the same problems hold, though in lesser degrees, with cooperation between democratic societies and other societies that permit some participation on the part of citizens but not on the basis of equality. The fact of complicity will still hold since democratic citizens are in effect cooperating with elites in a way that deprives the citizens of the non-democratic country of an equal vote. And the subordination effect still occurs because the elites have more power than the citizens of the democratic society in the making of international law and in the making of domestic law to the extent that this is directed by international law.

I want to argue that complicity and subordination in the sense described above extend to the whole of the international system. If we suppose the analysis above is correct, what we face is the choice between an order in which all persons are treated as unequals and one in which everyone is treated as an equal. The complicity thesis extends to all those societies that have dealings with non-democratic societies. And when they act in a multilateral setting, the complicity spreads to all the societies that participate. Furthermore, the subordination thesis also applies for the most part to the whole of the globe. Every democratic society that cooperates with non-democratic societies accords a greater say to the elites of the non-democratic society than to the ordinary citizens of the democratic society. And in multilateral settings non-democratic decision-making is externalized to all the democratic societies. To be sure, inequality may not extend entirely to other hierarchical societies since their elites could be on an equal footing with the elites of the initial society. But as a general rule what we have is the universalization of the complicity and subordination theses in the system of international law making as a whole. The consequence of the universalization of these two theses is that the whole system for the making of international law is undemocratic when any society within the system is not democratic and all the participants in democratic societies participate in, and are victims of, this inequality.

There is a kind of impasse here. In the making of international law, to the extent that we base international law on state consent we face a difficult dilemma. Either we accept the making of international law with non-democratic states so that we participate in deeply unequal ways in making decisions in which we accept a much greater voice for autocrats or political elites than ordinary citizens, or we require democracy for every society. There is no way to escape this dilemma. But it seems to me that the two branches of this dilemma are not morally equal since we have a prior view that justice requires democracy. Hence, we must choose the principle that demands that democracy be realized in each and every society.

But this implies that the international community has a moral justification for promoting and protecting democracy in every state that is a member of that community.

The human right to democracy

We have now established the two conditions that are sufficient for the human right to democracy. We have seen that every society ought to realize democratic rights and we have seen that the international community has a genuine moral justification in trying to realize democracy in every society because only in this way can the international community itself make law for its members that is democratically legitimate and only in this way can democratic societies make law for themselves that is fully democratically legitimate. These are the two sufficient conditions for a human right to democracy that I described above.

A qualification to the argument

It is important to note that the second part of the argument on offer here advocates for democracy in a qualified way. Strictly speaking it may not provide an argument for a full-fledged democracy since it really only shows the necessity of democracy with regard to the process of making international law. Strictly speaking we can imagine a society that is hierarchical in the process of making domestic law but that is democratic in its contribution to the making of international law. The sphere of domestic law making may be cordoned off from the sphere international law making, on this view. One question is whether it is reasonable to say that the domestic and the international spheres can be cordoned off from each other. No doubt they cannot be entirely since the whole point of the concern for international law now is that it impinges on the domestic legal systems of member states. But the question is whether the interaction between them is sufficient for asserting that non-democratic decision-making in the domestic sphere also makes other states complicit in the inequality or whether it has the external effect of imposing inequality between the non-democratic society's elites and the citizens of other democratic societies.

I have argued elsewhere, though (Christiano 2011a), that the international community has important moral justification for promoting and protecting democracy in every society on the grounds that, one, democracy is a necessary and reliable mechanism for the protection of uncontroversial human rights such as the rights not to be tortured, disappeared, murdered or arbitrarily imprisoned by the state. These are rights all agree ought to be the concern of the international community. I have also argued that because democracies have a widely accepted tendency not to go to war with one another and because they tend to comply more readily with international agreements that the international community has further interests in promoting and protecting democracy. Thus, I believe that the qualified character of the argument I gave above in favor of a moral justification for the international community to promote and protect democracy can be supplemented by more unqualified arguments of the democratic peace and democratic cooperation.

Equality and self-determination

Some have objected that the human right to democracy interferes with the legitimate self-determination of peoples. On one conception of self-determination, a people is self-determining when (1) their political institutions accord with political ideals they share and that have survived their critical reflection and when (2) the political institutions are such that all the different groups in society are consulted in the making of decisions (Bernstein 2004; Cohen 2010, 357–358; Mandle 2006; Rawls 2001, 61; Reidy 2004).[6]

On Joshua Cohen's version of the argument (Cohen 2010), one must tolerate societies in which the members share political ideals (even if they are different from ours) and which are responsive to the persons in them. He claims that some societies share non-democratic political ideals because they reject egalitarian ideas. If there is a human right to democracy, he argues, then the international community is morally committed to protecting and promoting democracy. But if the international community is committed to protecting and promoting minimally egalitarian democracy, then it does not tolerate non-democratic societies, that is, it will not treat them as equal cooperating members of the international system. But non-toleration of non-democracies is a threat to their legitimate self-determination. Therefore, the idea that there is a human right to democracy is a threat to the legitimate self-determination of peoples.

Two brief replies are in order before I move on to my main point. I do not think that a human right to democracy limits a legitimate right to collective

[6] Cohen says that since "democratic ideas lack substantial resonance in the political culture, or the history and traditions of the country … the value of collective self-determination itself recommends resistance to the idea that the political society should be required to meet the standard expressed in a principle of equal basic liberties" (2010, 358). In contrast David Miller seems to think that liberal democracy is an important though not necessary condition of national self-determination (Miller 1995, 89–90).

self-determination. Legitimate collective self-determination usually implies, one, that the society respects uncontroversial and very urgent human rights and, two, considerations of legitimate self-determination require unanimity or near unanimity on the alternative to democracy. In the absence of near unanimity, it is unclear that many would argue against the need for democracy. In this respect the above conditions of near unanimity and broad participation are sufficient but not necessary conditions. In my initial reply then to the objection, the absence of minimally egalitarian democracy seems to imply the absence of legitimate collective self-determination. This is because, as I have argued extensively elsewhere, non-democratic societies tend to violate very urgent and uncontroversial human rights. Furthermore, the condition of unanimity is rarely (if ever) met in societies except if they are minimally egalitarian democracies. Indeed, in every region a majority seems to prefer democracy, at least in the modern world. And citizens within democracies do have near unanimity on their democratic structure (Gallup 2005). So it looks like in the case of societies that are non-democratic, neither condition of legitimate self-determination normally holds. Hence, these societies do not have legitimate collective self-determination.

But I think that there is some interest in briefly thinking about the kinds of pure cases of collective self-determination that Rawls and Cohen seem to have in mind. Suppose it is true that the society in question nearly unanimously accepts non-democratic rule. And let us set aside the issue of the human rights violations in these societies for the moment. Is the demand for democracy in this context defeated by the unanimity of persons in the society on non-democracy?

Consider two plausible political principles that might be invoked here in support of the right of collective self-determination that might defeat the demand for democracy in a particular society. The first principle is the *volenti* principle: that one does not do injustice voluntarily to oneself. This principle is often used to limit the impact of principles on persons. And if near unanimity for non-democracy holds in a society perhaps we can say that the people involved are not doing injustice. The second principle may attach to the human right to democracy as it does to many rights. Many rights come with normative powers that permit one to waive the right in question. If we have near unanimity, perhaps we can say that the members of the population of the non-democratic society are exercising the normative powers attached to their rights to democracy to waive the right to democracy.

Both of these alternatives are, strictly speaking, compatible with there being a human right to democracy even though they assert that under conditions of near unanimity on non-democracy, a particular society need not be democratic. Furthermore, both of these theoretical alternatives explain why the defenders of non-democratic societies maintain the condition of near unanimity. The absence of unanimity would undermine the use of either one of the two principles to support non-democratic regimes. Still, even if these ideas do not defeat a human right to democracy, they may defeat the universal demand for democracy. And it is this latter implication that I wish to explore here.

Toleration, complicity and subordination

In response to this admittedly remote possibility, I want to argue that even under circumstances of unanimity on non-democracy, the demand for democracy cannot be entirely defeated. This becomes clear in the context of international law making.

If unanimous or near unanimous agreement on non-democratic rule has the effect of waiving the right to democracy at least internally, we must try to figure out what implications it has regarding the external effects of non-democracy. I have listed two variants of this external effect: complicity of democrats in non-democratic rule and subordination of democratic citizens to non-democratic elites.

The subordination effect seems not to go away even if we do accept that the non-democratic subjects have assented to their non-democratic status. The fact remains that when non-democratic subjects assent to their non-democratic status, they in effect grant greater power to the elites in their society than is afforded ordinary democratic citizens over the making of international law. This is the case that is most analogous to the context in democratic societies in which some citizens give their votes to others. They in effect not only give the other more power than they themselves have they also give the other more power than other citizens have including those who have not consented to the arrangement. This is a straightforward instance of external effect. And what is clear is that it cannot be justified by appeal to the idea that the persons are unanimous among themselves that this is what they want to do and that they waive their rights only. In effect they damage the rights of others as well, others who have no intention of giving up their rights, and therefore they act in ways that violate the rights of others. So it seems to me that toleration of non-democracies does have the external effect of granting elites of non-democracies greater power than democratic citizens over international law and over those parts of the domestic law of a democratic society that is directed by international law.

Matters are not so clear when it comes to the complicity effect. On the face of it, it appears that the problem of complicity goes away if the purported victims of these actions have assented to them. They can say that they assented to this arrangement between themselves and the elites and so if democratic citizens make international law with those elites, the arrangement accords with what they have assented to. To the extent that democratic citizens are dealing with persons who are treated as less than equals, it is only because those persons have agreed that they do so. They have waived their rights and so there is no problem.

But there is a lingering worry here. Don't the democratic citizens also have to assent to this to make it fully legitimate? After all they too are participants in the relationship. Perhaps one can say that they do have to assent but that they should assent because the others have freely waived their rights. What can the democratic citizens complain of? They could complain that they wish to deal with equals. As stated, this may seem like too weak a complaint. But perhaps this complaint is weightier when we consider the reasons for the assent to non-democratic institutions. If the assent is grounded on what is, by hypothesis, a mistaken view about the nature of justice and democratic citizens do not want to treat others as inferiors just because they have a mistaken view of justice then perhaps the complaint is stronger. Democratic citizens can complain that they are drawn into an unjust arrangement merely because the others do not think it is unjust.

One way of deflecting the complicity problem in dealing with non-democratic societies is to say that democratic societies do not have to engage with the non-democratic societies if they do not want to. They need not consent to making any arrangements with non-democratic societies. They only risk complicity if they find the terms of an engagement sufficiently attractive. But this implies that in addition to the non-democratic subjects assenting to their non-democratic society, democratic citizens can choose to assent or not by choosing to cooperate or not with the non-democratic society. So, to say that democratic societies have complicity imposed upon them is misguided.

But this retort mistakes the nature of the international system. It treats it as if it were one of purely voluntary association where it is just a matter of states engaging with each other on a discretionary and mutually beneficial basis. But, though some agreements among states have this character, the international system cannot be thought of anymore as a system of pure voluntary association. There is, first of all, the necessity of cooperation in pursuit of morally mandatory aims. If non-democratic states are to be thought of as equal cooperating members of the international community, this implies that democratic states must engage in cooperation with them in pursuit of the morally mandatory aims. There is some choice over how to pursue these aims but all states must pursue them through cooperation. Second, there is the simple fact of significant transnational interdependence of interest which makes democratic states dependent on non-democratic states for essential resources, trade, financial interactions and so on. The modern democratic state cannot afford to adopt a posture of autarky with respect to many other states. Hence, it is a mistake to think that democratic states engage with non-democratic states on a purely discretionary basis. They are drawn into a complicity with inequality that they may not extricate themselves from.

Perhaps we can think of the situation as a conflict between toleration of non-democratic societies and the justice of democracy. Perhaps it is a conflict between two independent values that needs to be negotiated in some way. But it is not clear that this is what is going on here. For it is not clear that we can think of toleration as a genuine value here once we see that we are participating in the very injustice at issue and we are victims of the very injustice we are saying ought to be tolerated. Toleration as a principled moral posture makes some sense when we are confronted with discrete injustices that all the participants in some sense accept. But in this instance the injustice cannot be contained; we who regard it as an injustice are drawn into it. We participate in it, we may benefit from it in some respects and we may also be victims of it in some other respects. To tolerate implies that we tolerate our own injustice and that we tolerate others treating us unjustly.

It is certainly possible to tolerate a situation in which we participate in injustice and are being treated unjustly. But it seems that we can have no more than a pragmatic reason for such behavior. We can hope that our participation in this injustice will be short-lived and we can hope that our participation may even help to undermine the injustice in the long run. But we must think of ourselves in this context as participating in, benefiting from and being victimized by a complex of injustices.

To conclude this last section, I think the argument for toleration from self-determination fails because the purported self-determination of non-democratic societies actually has the external effect of making all others complicit in and subordinate to the non-democratic character of the non-democratic societies within the international system. It conflicts with democracy everywhere and so it cannot be thought to be limited only to those who accept the non-democratic norms. Unfortunately, in the contemporary international system we must decide between democracy and non-democracy. To compromise on the demand for democracy is to compromise ourselves and to undermine justice.

Conclusion

The severity of this view can be mitigated in a number of different ways. First, we might accept a weaker conception of collective self-determination and a correspondingly weaker conception of international toleration, both of which can be extended to non-democratic societies. We may think it is important for a variety of reasons for a society to arrive at democratic institutions on its own for the most part. Home-grown democratic institutions may be much more stable and satisfying than externally imposed ones. External intervention to impose democracy may not very likely succeed since the intervener's interests do not usually coincide fully with the supposed beneficiary's interests and the intervener is not accountable to the supposed beneficiary. In this respect we might have an instrumental argument for the weaker notion of collective self-determination as freedom from forcible or other forms of highly intrusive intervention. And we might have a correspondingly weaker notion of toleration as non-intervention (Gibbs 2009; Mill 2002 [1859]; Russett 2005). We might reserve the stronger notion of toleration for democratic societies, where this consists in treating the society with a full kind of equality in the international realm that implies unreserved cooperation.

There are a number of ways to act on the basis of a human right to democracy short of military or other highly intrusive intervention. We can offer non-essential assistance to societies only on condition that they take steps to democratize. We can limit cooperation, at least on non-essential goods, with the non-democratic society. We can step in, in a variety of ways, when an elite attempts to take over a democratic society by force or by fraud. We can offer assistance to societies struggling to achieve democratic institutions (Franck 1996).[7]

Finally, my arguments for the human right to democracy do not require perfect democracy or perfect justice. They defend minimally egalitarian democracy. Hence they do leave significant room for local variation among societies in terms of the kind of democratic system they adopt as well as

---

[7] For a frank and thorough and only partially positive assessment of election monitoring in the contemporary international arena see Kelley (2012).

the justice of the political system they create. They do not resolve all issues and allow for room in which significant disagreement can be expressed and different views can be realized. Minimally egalitarian democracy is compatible with consociational democracy, majoritarian democracy, presidential systems, parliamentary systems, proportional representation and single-member district representation as well as other non-representative forms of democracy. In this sense, the argument I have provided for democracy leaves substantial room for the self-determination of peoples. It does limit that room but so will any conception of human rights.

References

Beitz, Charles. 2009. *The Idea of Human Rights*. Oxford: Oxford University Press.

Bernstein, Allysa. 2004. "A Human Right to Democracy? Legitimacy and Intervention." In David Reidy and Rex Martin, eds., *Rawls's Law of Peoples*. Oxford: Blackwell, pp. 278–298.

Brighouse, Harry and Fleurbaey, Marc. 2010. "Democracy and Proportionality." *Journal of Political Philosophy* 18:2, 137–155.

Christiano, Thomas. 2008. *The Constitution of Equality: Democratic Authority and Its Limits*. Oxford University Press.

   2011a. "An Instrumental Argument for a Human Right to Democracy." *Philosophy and Public Affairs* 39:2, 142–176.

   2011b. "Democratic Legitimacy and International Institutions." In Samantha Besson and John Tasioulas, eds., *The Philosophy of International Law*. Oxford University Press, pp. 119–138.

   Unpublished. "Fairness and Legitimacy in International Institutions."

Cohen, Joshua. 2009. "Procedure and Substance in Deliberative Democracy." In *Philosophy, Politics, Democracy: Selected Essays*. Cambridge, MA: Harvard University Press, pp. 154–180.

   2010. "Is There A Human Right to Democracy?" In *The Arc of the Moral Universe and Other Essays*. Cambridge, MA: Harvard University Press, pp. 349–372.

Dahl, Robert. 1989. *Democracy and Its Critics*. New Haven: Yale University Press.

Franck, Thomas. 1996. *Fairness in International Law and Institutions*. Oxford University Press.

Gallup International Association. 2005. *Gallup International Voice of the People 2005 Survey*. Available at: http://dx.doi.org/10.3886/ICPSR04636.v1.

Gibbs, David N. 2009. *First Do No Harm: Humanitarian Intervention and the Destruction of Yugoslavia*. Nashville: Vanderbilt University Press.

Kelley, Judith. 2012. *Monitoring Democracy: When International Election Observation Works and Why It Often Fails*. Princeton University Press.

Mandle, Jon. 2006. *Global Justice*. Cambridge: Polity Press.

Mill, John Stuart. 2002 [1859]. "A Few Words on Non-Intervention." In Chris Brown, Terry Nardin and Nicolas Rengger, eds., *International Relations in Political Thought*. Cambridge University Press, pp. 486–493.

Miller, David. 1995. *On Nationality*. Oxford University Press.

Rawls, John. 1971. *A Theory of Justice*. Cambridge, MA: Harvard University Press.
    2001. *The Law of Peoples*. Cambridge, MA: Harvard University Press.

Raz, Joseph. 1986. *The Morality of Freedom*. Oxford University Press.

Reidy, David. 2004. "Political Authority and Human Rights." In David Reidy and Rex Martin, eds., *Rawls's Law of Peoples*. Oxford: Blackwell, pp. 169–188.

Russett, Bruce. 2005. "Bushwhacking the Democratic Peace." *International Studies Perspectives* 6:4, 395–408.

Sumner, L.W. 1987. *The Moral Foundation of Rights*. Oxford University Press.

Webber, Jeremy. 2009. "The Grammar of Customary Law." *McGill Law Journal* 54, 579–626.

PART VI

What are the limits of rights
enforcement?

17 | Is it ever reasonable for one state to invade another for humanitarian reasons? The "declaratory tradition" and the UN Charter

JULIE MERTUS

Introduction

This chapter considers the opportunities and limitations for the use of military force for humanitarian reasons under the UN Charter. In so doing, it employs what has come to be known as the "declaratory tradition" of international law and international ethics, a much underutilized tradition for analyzing hard choices in the global arena. The declaratory approach stands in contrast to the classical tradition of international law, which places states squarely at the center of the international order and decision-making. Although states do play a key role in the declaratory tradition, non-state actors are important as well. In fact, one might characterize the declaratory tradition as "the product of non-state aspirations to improve the substance of international order" (Simpson 2004). Although the roots of this tradition run deep, its contemporary practice emerged primarily after World War II when "in conference after conference and in numerous treaties, conventions, declarations, and the like, the states have, through their official representatives, set down principles to guide their own behavior and to provide standards by which that behavior can be judged" (Nardin and Mapel 1992).

According to Dorothy Jones, a pre-eminent scholar on the declaratory tradition, the endeavor to develop normative ethics to guide state behavior "has created a body of reflections and rules that is closer to moral philosophy than it is to positive law" (Jackson 2000, 183). Therefore, the declaratory tradition concerns itself not only with what international actors "shall" do (acknowledgments of actually existing practices warranting immediate recognition), but also with what they "ought" to do (declarations of intent regarding desired future conduct). The goal of the declaratory tradition is

---

This chapter draws from earlier work by the author on humanitarian intervention in Kosovo. See Julie Mertus, "Reconsidering the Legality of Humanitarian Intervention: Lessons from Kosovo." *William & Mary Law Review* 41:5 (2000), 1743, http://scholarship.law.wm.edu/wmlr/vol41/iss5/7.

aspirational, that is it endeavors "to change international society into a fundamentally different normative arrangement that is based on values that elevate non-state elements above the state, the elimination of poverty everywhere in the world, terms of trade that favor underdeveloped countries as a social class, elevation of human rights above sovereign rights" (Jackson 2000, 127). The resulting code of international conduct that has emerged on these hard questions is not concerned only with promoting certain types of action, but also with preventing behaviors that would disrupt the human rights system.

To take one illustration, human rights can be viewed as a standard of conduct in contemporary world politics and meeting the standard can be a goal that is pursued globally. However, knowing that the world is pluralistic, proponents of human rights in the declaratory tradition seek to do more than push for the universal application of human rights protections. They also examine the structures that support human rights to ensure that they are functioning in a transparent, fair and participatory manner; furthermore, the interrelationship and power dynamics between human rights claim-holders and duty-bearers are addressed.

In perhaps the most cited source on the declaratory tradition – "The Declaratory Tradition in Modern International Law" – Dorothy Jones lists nine principles that have been widely accepted by the nations of the world:

1. The sovereign equality of states;
2. The territorial integrity and political independence of states;
3. Equal rights and the self-determination of peoples;
4. Nonintervention in the internal affairs of states;
5. Peaceful settlement of disputes between states;
6. No threat or use of force;
7. Fulfillment in good faith of international obligations;
8. Cooperation with other states;
9. Respect for human rights (Jones 1992, 42–43).

The declaratory tradition insists that any attempt by international actors to engage in humanitarian intervention must somehow address and affirm these principles.

It is not enough just to assert moral claims based on these factors, the claims put forth must be grounded in law as well. Straying from the legal justification risks delegitimizing international law and dismantling the gains human rights advocates have made over the past decade. International law generally, and human rights law specifically, are most influential when communities perceive their terms as legitimate and fair (Alvarez 1991;

Franck 1995, 1990). Only human rights processes and bodies perceived as legitimate will be taken seriously, and only states perceived as legitimate can enforce human rights norms successfully (Reisman 1990, 866, 867). As Thomas Franck explained in the *Power of Legitimacy Among Nations*, the group to which a rule is addressed must perceive the rule as legitimate (Franck 1990, 1988, 705–706). Ad hoc justifications for the use of force, or the failure to use force, render the resulting actions or inactions indeterminate, and thus open to criticism as illegitimate (Franck 1990, 50–66).

Whenever a political leader declares numerous and conflicting justifications for intervention, the determinacy of rules on the use of force are undermined and the status of the entire field of international law suffers (Aoi 2011). At the same time, too much or the wrong kind of focus on the determinacy of rules alone does not necessarily comport with justice. Franck critiques "blind compliance" with simple "idiot rules" when the very simplicity of the rules leads to injustice, incoherence and absurdity upon consistent application. To be perceived as legitimate and fair, rules and their application must comport with notions of justice. In other words, a rule must be deemed just at both a substantive and a procedural level. If the principle of non-intervention becomes an oversimplified "idiot rule" that cannot be applied fairly to all circumstances, international leaders must articulate additional rules more in concert with principles of justice and fairness. At the very least, in order to be considered both legitimate and fair, the process by which decisions on intervention are made should be transparent, accountable and open to participation from interested groups.[1] In line with the declaratory tradition, states "are not to break or ignore their pledged word but are to carry out in good faith their obligations as members of the international community" (Jones 1992, 47).

This chapter is divided into two parts. It first outlines the explicit and implicit ways in which the UN Charter has made room for humanitarian intervention. This could be viewed as the answer to the simple question: "Is humanitarian intervention permitted by the UN Charter – or not so much?" An answer in the affirmative should spell an end to the matter, and then humanitarian intervention is not a hard question after all. But the law does not work in that way. Locating human rights and humanitarian issues in the law is just the beginning. The second part of this chapter focuses on shared understandings of when and how humanitarian intervention should be permitted – or not.

---

[1] Today these norms are recognized as essential elements of several areas of international law and practice. See Corten *et al.* (2010).

Humanitarian intervention under the UN Charter

At face value, the words of the UN Charter appear to disfavor intervention (Barnett 2011; Cooper 1986, 68, 69–70). Anti-interventionists point to the first part of Article 2(4) of the UN Charter, which plainly declares that states "shall refrain in their international relations from the threat or use of force against the territorial integrity or political independence of any state." This admonition is followed by Article 2(7), which sharply states that "[n]othing contained in the present Charter shall authorize the United Nations to intervene in matters which are essentially within the domestic jurisdiction of any state." The general prohibition on the use of force in Article 2(4) is supported by language in subsequent General Assembly resolutions (United Nations 1981).[2] Together, the Charter provisions and its subsequent interpretations appear to provide a nearly ironclad prohibition against intervention. The Charter's proscription against intervention, however, is not as strict as it may appear from a plain reading of these articles.

Lawful use of force expressly recognized by the UN Charter

The central focus for humanitarian intervention does not rest on the issue of "territorial integrity," but instead falls within the parameters set for the "use of force" by international law. The UN Charter recognizes three main exceptions to the prohibition on the use of force: (1) individual and collective self-defense; (3) UN-sanctioned intervention; and (3) regional military units.

First, states may act in self-defense. Specifically, Article 51 of the Charter preserves "the *inherent right* of individual or collective self-defense if an armed attack occurs against a Member of the United Nations, until the Security Council has taken the measures necessary to maintain international peace and security." The term "inherent right" also is significant because it refers to the customary right of self-defense that predates the Charter. Thus, "rather than artificially limiting a state's right of self-defense – it is better to conform to historically accepted criteria for the lawful use of force – including circumstances that exist outside the 'four corners' of the Charter" (US

---

[2] The 1965 Declaration on the Inadmissibility of Intervention in the Domestic Affairs of States and the Protection of Their Independence and Sovereignty provides that: no State has the right to intervene, directly or indirectly, for any reason whatsoever, in the internal or external affairs of any other State. Consequently, armed intervention and all other forms of interference or attempted threats against the personality of the State or against its political, economic and cultural elements, are condemned.

Army 2010). A case, therefore, can be made that states do not have to wait until an armed attack is launched to pre-empt an armed attack.

A second exception to the general ban on the use of force relates to Security Council enforcement actions under Chapter VII of the Charter. Under Article 24(1), the Security Council has "primary responsibility for the maintenance of international peace and security." Article 39 of the UN Charter provides that it is the Security Council that shall determine the existence of "any threat to the peace, breach of the peace, or act of aggression and shall make recommendations, or decide what measures shall be taken." In their landmark book *Legitimacy and Legality in International Law*, Jutta Brunnee and Stephen Toope explain the importance of these provisions read together: "[w]ithin the UN Charter framework, military force can be employed only on the basis of a decision of the Council which in current practice means that coalitions of UN Member States are authorized to use force" (Brunnee and Toope 2010).

The third explicit exception to the general prohibition on the use of force, is found in Chapter VIII of the Charter, through actions undertaken by "regional arrangements or agencies for dealing with such matters relating to the maintenance of international peace and security." Regional arrangements may undertake any action in this regard that is "consistent with the purposes and principles of the United Nations." Under this argument, the requirement of Security Council authorization would still apply, but the requirement itself would be based not on Chapter VIII, but on Chapter VII of the Charter. Many scholars contend that regional military organizations offer a viable alternative to a UN entity authorizing the use of force on humanitarian grounds (Badescu 2007, 2011; Bellamy 2009; Evans 2008).

Lawful use of force implicitly permitted under the UN Charter

At the outset, military action for humanitarian intervention appears to contradict the UN Charter's goal of promoting peaceful dispute settlement. The UN Charter is replete with references to peaceful cooperation in solving global problems. For example, Article 2(3) flatly declares that "[a]ll Members shall settle their international disputes by peaceful means in such a manner that international peace and security, and justice, are not endangered." The traditional methods of pacifistic settlement in international law are negotiation, inquiry, mediation, and conciliation. Through the use of these methods, international law encourages the use of any and all peaceful methods to avoid the use of force. However, peaceful methods do not always work, and therefore it is important to determine when, if ever, there exists a legal basis for military intervention on humanitarian grounds.

Four strong arguments can be made for the use of force being legal and/ or legitimate under the UN Charter: (1) intervention as action in line with contemporary conceptions of sovereignty; (2) intervention as promoting UN goals; (3) intervention as action mandated by human rights violations or other systemic problems; (4) intervention as steps taken by UN surrogates as a stopgap measure until a UN force can be created and deployed. These exceptions to the general non-intervention principle are discussed in turn below, with attention given to both an explanation of shared understandings of each principle and identification of "hard questions" that remain unanswered.

Use of force as not violating "territorial integrity" or "political independence"

The legal debate over humanitarian intervention has been posed as a tension between two contending principles: respect for the "territorial integrity" and "political independence" of states and the guarantees for human rights and "self-determination" (Szasz 1999). As such, the debate implicates two competing purposes for the United Nations: ensuring "national sovereignty and maintenance of peace" (Farer 1999, 185, 190; Thaker 2006). This framing of the issue, however, obfuscates the real questions at hand: who has the authority to use force and when does it arise? The principles of territorial integrity and human rights, however, need not conflict and instead may be regarded as complementary. Indeed, "territorial integrity" cannot exist without human rights, and the realization of human rights can support the integrity of a territory (Henkin 1991).[3]

The traditional notion of sovereignty upholds that "even scrutiny of international human rights without the permission of the sovereign could arguably constitute a violation of sovereignty by its 'invasion' of the sovereign's *domaine reserve*" (Krasner 1990; Reisman 1990, 869). Embracing this traditional concept of sovereignty, however, requires acceptance of a rigid conception of sovereignty that renders superfluous modern developments in international law concerning the interpretation of the core purposes of

---

[3] The main opponent to this view, Louis Henkin, counters: "Clearly it was the original intent of the Charter to forbid the use of force even to promote human rights … Human rights are indeed violated in every country … But the use of force remains itself a most serious – the most serious – violation of human rights" (Henkin 1991, 61).

the UN Charter. The traditional definition of sovereignty contradicts the modern understandings of both sovereignty and "territorial integrity."

An alternative understanding of sovereignty refers not only to state borders, but also to *political* sovereignty, that is the ability of people within those borders to affect choices regarding how they should be governed and by whom. Those who threaten that ability, be they internal or external in origin, can be said to violate the sovereignty of the people (Rosas 1993, 225). Accordingly, when another state intervenes to protect human rights in such circumstances, it is not violating a principle of sovereignty. Rather, it is liberating a principle of sovereignty (Reisman 1990, 872). The concept of political sovereignty represents one example of the emergence of the declaratory approach and the reconceptualization of classical norms of sovereignty.

This kind of intervention, which could be termed "self-determination assistance" (Paust 1999, 3), finds support in the numerous international instruments that recognize a right to self-determination, including Articles 1 and 55 of the UN Charter. The 1970 Declaration on Principles of International Law Concerning Friendly Relations and Cooperation Among States in Accordance with the Charter of the United Nations observes that "[e]very State has the duty to refrain from any forcible action which deprives peoples … of their right to self-determination" and that "[i]n their actions against, and resistance to, such forcible action in pursuit of the exercise of their right to self-determination, such peoples are entitled to seek and to receive support in accordance with the purposes and principles of the Charter." Under this theory, intervention is permissible when it is designed to support the sovereignty rights of the peoples.

Another modern understanding of sovereignty maintains a focus on state borders, but stresses the various ways in which recent globalization has eroded the classical definition of sovereignty, thereby widening the parameters of permissible use of force under the doctrine of humanitarian intervention (Amison 1993, 199, 203–204; Chesterman 2003). Globalization is marked by two interrelated tendencies: the restructuring of the world economy on a regional and global scale through the agency of transnational corporations and financial markets, and the rise of transnational social forces and transboundary networks concerned with environmental protection, human rights, and peace and human security. Especially in cases where the central focus for humanitarian intervention is not state-based, the source of legitimacy cannot rest on the issue of "territorial integrity," but instead, should lie within the parameters set for the "use of force" by international law. Hard questions that persist on the use of force include an identification of who has the authority to make decisions on when and how to use force.

Intervention consistent with the purposes of the United Nations

The central purposes of the UN are set forth in Article 1 of the UN Charter as follows:

- To maintain international peace and security;
- To develop friendly relations among nations based on respect for the principle of equal rights and self-determination of peoples, and to take other appropriate measures to strengthen universal peace;
- To achieve international co-operation in solving international problems of an economic, social, cultural, or humanitarian character, and in promoting and encouraging respect for human rights and for fundamental freedoms for all without distinction as to race, sex, language, or religion; and
- To be a center for harmonizing the actions of nations in the attainment of these common ends.

Humanitarian intervention furthers the most central purpose of the organization – namely, the maintenance of international peace and security. Indeed, international peace and security must mean more than the absence of an internationally recognized war; human rights violations short of all-out war also constitute major breaches of peace and security. Other central purposes of the United Nations, noted in Article 1 of the Charter, include developing respect for the principle of "equal rights and self-determination of peoples" and "encouraging respect for human rights and for fundamental freedoms for all without distinction as to race, sex, language or religion." These articles appear to confirm the view that people are rights-bearing entities and therefore states are the vehicles that should be held accountable for the protection of those rights (Sohn 1982, 12; Sohn and Buergenthal 1973). The prohibition on the use of force in Article 2(4) does not rule out intervention designed to promote these goals.

Where a government flouts respect for the principles of equal rights and self-determination and violates the most basic human rights and fundamental freedoms of individuals, intervention may be the only way to ensure that the central goals of the United Nations are upheld. Hard questions that arise include: is there adequate agreement on which goals of the UN should be prioritized? Must these goals be universal?

Intervention mandated under human rights provisions

A related argument contends that the UN Charter not only permits intervention on humanitarian grounds; it requires it in cases of gross and systemic human rights abuses (Bazyler 1987; Levitin 1986; Lillich 1974, 1969; McDougal and Reisman 1969).

Notably, Articles 55 and 56 of the UN Charter implore "[a]ll Members [to] pledge themselves to take joint … action in cooperation with the Organization for the achievement of … higher standards of living, full employment, and conditions of economic and social progress and development" and universal respect for, and "observance of, human rights and fundamental freedoms for all without distinction as to race, sex, language, or religion."

The trend in recent years has been toward the development and improvement of human rights monitoring and enforcement mechanisms (Stamatopoulou 1998).[4] If the target state is a party to any of the relevant human rights conventions, or if the human right can be said to be customary international law applicable to all states, humanitarian intervention can be grounded or categorized as a means of enforcing these obligations on behalf of the victims. Matters concerning genocide, crimes against humanity, and certain war crimes are subject to universal jurisdiction and responsibility (Chang 2011; King and Theofrastous 1999, 47, 53–54). The human rights grounds for intervention also are particularly strong where the group targeted for human rights violations is singled out because of its "race, sex, language or religion" – the groups explicitly mentioned in the UN Charter and reaffirmed as especially pertinent classifications in other international instruments (Donner 1994, 241, 248).

While the principle of "non-intervention" continues to be an influential counter-argument against military humanitarian intervention, in recent years, international human rights norms have begun to erode the position of non-intervention (Brown 2003, 31). Former UN Secretary-General Kofi Annan has proven a key figure in supporting the norm cascade in favor of intervention to preserve human life. The UN Charter, he explained, "was issued in the name of 'the people', not the governments to trample on human rights and human dignity" (Jentleson 2007, 280). Annan's statement upholds the human right to life above state sovereignty and suggests that intervention may be necessary if states fail to protect their own citizens. The 2001 International Commission on Intervention and State Sovereignty (ICISS) Report framed intervention as a responsibility in situations of

---

[4] This point, like many in this chapter, is not free from controversy. It suggests that individuals are third parties possessing rights under human rights treaties, thereby warranting state action for violations.

widespread human rights abuses, even while retaining a bias in favor of sovereignty:

[T]he responsibility to protect (R2P) its people from killing and other grave harm was the most basic and fundamental of all responsibilities that sovereignty imposes – and if a state cannot or will not protect its people from such harm, then coercive intervention for human protection purposes, including ultimately military intervention, by others in the international community may be warranted in extreme cases. (IDRC 2011)

One major benefit of R2P is that it "comprises more complex and subtle responses to mass atrocities than the use of force, ranging from prevention to post-conflict rebuilding to protecting civilians at risk" (Badescu and Weiss 2010). The responsibility to protect remains, however, an "emerging norm" and must be reinforced with more unified support and action from the international community in order to become customary law (Badescu and Weiss 2010). The legal stuff of humanitarian intervention, that is the rules stating when states may intervene, with force based on performance to date at home provides a useful guide. Hard questions that remain unanswered include: does the Charter provide room for a right to resist colonial occupation? Could anti-colonialist movements in two separate states support one another in their struggles? Are states responsible to do so?

Intervention as a stopgap measure

Diplomatic negotiations on the UN Charter led to a compromise between states and the UN. States would accept "an absolute obligation to refrain from unilateral resort to armed force" on the condition that the United Nations would "effectively safeguard international peace and security" (Verwey 1998, 180, 194). Article 43 of the Charter envisioned a system wherein states would make available to the Security Council, "on its call and in accordance with a special agreement or agreements, armed forces, assistance, and facilities … necessary for the purpose of maintaining international peace and security." These agreements were to be negotiated as soon as possible on the initiative of the Security Council. Article 106 of the Charter envisioned the creation of transitional security arrangements whereby signatories to the Charter could undertake joint action to maintain peace and security as stopgap measures until the signing of Article 43 agreements. However, negotiations on Article 43 mechanisms were effectively abandoned by 1950.

Attempts to revitalize the debate on standing UN militia have not garnered many adherents. Hard questions that must be answered include:

What would a standing military look like? How would the chain of command operate? Who would be responsible for establishing the legality of any UN military force? What test would be used to determine legality?

Limiting principles

The declaratory tradition in international ethics and law reminds us that our analysis of the rules on intervention does not stop with a reading of the UN Charter. Our obligation to our community and to the world writ large is also found in declared goals and ideals. These are declarations of "intent regarding future conduct rather than acknowledgements of actual practices" (Brunnee and Toope 2010, 273). With regard to humanitarian intervention, answers to hard questions are often not neatly found in the text of the Charter or in any subsequent interpretive document. Instead, the answers are cobbled together, serving as a yellow light urging military and political leaders to pause and think about the impact of their actions and to study whether and when the use of force is necessary.

The three main factors that must be weighed when determining the legitimacy of intervention in the name of humanitarianism include: humanitarian motives; humanitarian grounds for intervention; and humanitarian means of intervention.[5]

Humanitarian motives

For military intervention to be deemed "humanitarian," humanitarian motives must be among the concerns shaping the state action (Blanchet and Martine 2011; Perez 2011). For the state claiming humanitarian motivations, this means acting in a manner consistent with humanitarian law and refraining from military actions that could not be justified on humanitarian grounds. In the words of historian Quentin Skinner: "Even if the administration is not in fact motivated by any of the principles it professes, it will nonetheless be obliged to behave in such a way that its actions remain compatible with the claim that these principles genuinely motivated it" (quoted in Wheeler 2000, 288).

---

[5] "Humanitarian results" are often suggested as a requirement for intervention, and indeed a high degree of success is desirable. However, to claim "success" as a prerequisite is like requiring a top notch cake to be placed in the oven before the cook begins to mix the ingredients – it makes no sense and, thus, the results requirement will not be included here.

Claims advanced by humanitarian intervention advocates often are a result of normative change at the domestic level that places increasing pressure on political and military leaders for humanitarian intervention. A case for humanitarian intervention can be made when the human rights abuses are extreme and verifiable – that is, when the human rights abuses "shock the conscience." The case for intervention is particularly strong when the following criteria are met: moral outrage from domestic publics, shocked by television pictures of slaughter and suffering, demanding that "something be done" (Clarke 1999; Wilson and Brown 2009). In liberal democracies, media-driven support for humanitarian intervention is crucial in order for politicians to accept the political risk of military engagement.

One of the fundamental disagreements of pro-interventionists and anti-interventionists concerns the credibility of claims to a humanitarian motive. Aware that the humanitarian reasons for intervention may be one set of reasons among many, pro-interventionists often come to their support of military force reluctantly, asserting that it should be used as a last resort, and with appropriate legal safeguards to ensure that it is not misused against weak states by self-interested strong states.

Humanitarian grounds

Under one theory of justifiable intervention, governments that commit gross violations of human rights are said to forfeit any claims to the protections normally offered by sovereignty. If sovereignty is contingent upon compliance with international legal obligations, then gross violations of international human rights guarantees open the door for intervention. Under another theory of intervention, where a state is incapable of protecting the human rights of a political or ethno-national minority or is itself the perpetrator of violations against civilians, the use of force on human rights grounds stands as a legal option in international terms (Krylov 1994; Lillich 1967; Mertus 2001; Meyers 1997; Reisman 1971, 666–667; Smith 1998; Tesón 1997, 174). Both these arguments depend on the participation of the state in gross human rights violations and/or the failure of a state to stop such violations.

Scholars who support these arguments are divided over whether intervention ought to be triggered by evidence of the imminence of a humanitarian disaster or whether it should only be undertaken in response to actually existing humanitarian crises. In either case, as explained above, intervention that promotes central principles of the UN Charter is permissible. The

UN Charter not only permits intervention on humanitarian grounds; in some grave cases of gross and systemic human rights abuses, the Charter requires it. The argument that grounds for intervention exist is particularly strong when the following criteria are met: (1) the abuses threaten widespread loss of human life; (2) intervention would likely avert a disaster; (3) the ongoing nature of the problem threatens the peace and security of the region; and (4) there has been a good faith attempt to use diplomatic and peaceful means of settlement.

Humanitarian means

There is no need to come up with a new checklist of limitations for the means and methods of military intervention particularly with regard to humanitarian situations. Indeed, the laws of war already provide comprehensive restrictions. To be legitimate, the means of intervention must be consistent with international humanitarian law. In a nutshell, the means employed should be necessary to meet a legitimate objective, they should be proportionate to a legitimate military outcome, they should discriminate between civilian and non-civilian targets, and they should be appropriately related to the probability of success.

The most fundamental principle of the law of war is that combatants must be distinguished from non-combatants and military objectives distinguished from protected property or protected places, such as civilian property and cultural and religious property and places. To this end, the 1977 Protocol Additional to the Geneva Conventions of 1949 (Protocol I) provides that "the civilian population as such, as well as individual civilians, shall not be the object of attack." Protocol I specifically prohibits "[a]cts or threats of violence the primary purpose of which is to spread terror among the civilian population." In provisions that are considered customary international law, Protocol I protects civilians from "indiscriminate attacks."

In addition to limiting the choice of targets, humanitarian law limits the means of attack. Article 57 of Protocol I is of particular relevance because it requires military planners to "take all feasible precautions in the choice of means and methods of attack with a view to avoiding, and in any event to minimizing, incidental loss of civilian life, injury to civilians and damage to civilian objects." At all stages of their operations, interveners should consider whether their actions place non-combatants at increased risk. Military planners must provide effective advance warning of attacks that may affect the civilian population.

As embodied in Protocol I, the concept of proportionality requires an ends-oriented comparative assessment: "The loss of life and damage to property incidental to attacks must not be excessive in relation to the concrete and direct military advantage expected to be gained" (US Army 2010). If military planners are able to realize their goals without loss of civilian life, Protocol I suggests that they should change their course of action accordingly.

Conclusion

The declaratory tradition in international ethics and law is useful for exploring how the decision to intervene can be grounded firmly in the UN Charter and represented in aspirational goals. This, however, is not the end of the inquiry. For humanitarian intervention to be perceived as legitimate, further limiting principles must be applied to guard against its misapplication or exploitation.

In the colonial and Cold War periods, the doctrine of humanitarian intervention was at times misused by strong states as a pretext for vigilante activity and for the occupation of weaker and politically disobedient countries (Brownlie 1973, 139, 147–148; Schachter 1985, 291, 294). Today, more than ever before, only a few powerful states are in a position to use their economic and military power on behalf of human rights (Falk 1981, 85). Thus, the doctrine remains open to "cynical manipulation" (Ball 1983, 313–314). This need not be the case. As Brad Roth, a critic of US imperialism, observes:

Instead of asking the typical American question, "What should *we* be allowed to do to further justice abroad?" to which the answer might well be – "Everything we can" – one might be better to pose ... the question, "What should powerful foreign states be allowed to do in our troubled country in the name of furthering justice?" (Roth 2003, 232)

Drawing from the UN Charter itself, UN Security Council resolutions, and other international instruments, particularly those pertaining to humanitarian law, it is possible to identify workable criteria that limit the imperialist tendencies of the countries spearheading humanitarian intervention and to enhance their legitimacy (Butler 2011; Holzgrefe and Keohane 2003; Newman 2009; Wheeler 2000). Humanitarian intervention need not threaten world order. Rather, it can vindicate the fundamental principles upon which the United Nations was founded.

References

Alvarez, Jose. 1991. "The Quest for Legitimacy: An Examination of *The Power of Legitimacy Among Nations* by Thomas M. Franck." *New York University Journal of International Law & Politics* 24, 199.

Aoi, Chiyuki. 2011. *Legitimacy and the Use of Armed Force: Stability Missions in the Post-Cold War Era*. New York: Routledge.

Amison, Nancy D. 1993. "International Law and Non-Intervention: When Do Humanitarian Concerns Supersede Sovereignty?" *Fletcher Forum of World Affairs* 17:2, 199.

Badescu, Cristina G. 2007. "Authorizing Humanitarian Intervention: Hard Choices in Saving Strangers." *Canadian Journal of Political Science* 40:1, 51–78.

   2011. *Humanitarian Intervention and the Responsibility to Protect: Security and Human Rights*. New York: Routledge.

Badescu, Cristina G. and Weiss, Thomas G. 2010. "Misrepresenting R2P and Advancing Norms: An Alternative Spiral?" *International Studies Perspectives* 4:11, 354–374.

Ball, Milner S. 1983. "Ironies of Intervention." *Georgia Journal of International and Comparative Law* 13, 313.

Barnett, Michael. 2011. *Empire of Humanity: A History of Humanitarianism*. Ithaca: Cornell University Press.

Bazyler, Michael J. 1987. "Reexamining the Doctrine of Humanitarian Intervention in Light of the Atrocities in Kampuchea and Ethiopia." *Stanford Journal of International Law* 23, 547.

Bellamy, Alex J. 2009. *Responsibility to Protect: The Global Effort to End Mass Atrocities*. New York: Polity Press.

Blanchet, Karl and Martine, Boris. 2011. *Many Reasons to Intervene: French and British Approaches to Humanitarian Action*. New York: Columbia University Press.

Brown, Chris. 2003. "Selective Humanitarianism: In Defense of Inconsistency." In Deen K. Chatterjee and Don E. Scheid, eds., *Ethics and Foreign Intervention*. Cambridge University Press, p. 31.

Brownlie, Ian. 1973. "Thoughts on Kind-Hearted Gunmen." In Richard B. Lillich, ed., *Humanitarian Intervention And The United Nations*. Charlottesville: University of Virginia Press, pp. 147–148.

Brunnee, Jutta and Toope, Stephen. 2010. *Legitimacy and Legality in International Law*. New York: Cambridge University Press.

Butler, Karina Zofia. 2011. *A Critical Humanitarian Intervention Approach (Rethinking Peace and Conflict Studies)*. New York: Palgrave Macmillan.

Chang, Chih-Hann. 2011. *Ethical Foreign Policy? US Humanitarian Interventions*. Burlington: Ashgate.

Chesterman, Simon. 2003. "Hard Cases Make Bad Law: Law, Ethics, and Politics in Humanitarian Intervention." In Anthony F. Lang, Jr., ed., *Just Intervention*. Washington, DC: Georgetown University Press, pp. 46–61.

Clarke, John N. 1999. "Ethics and Humanitarian Intervention." *Global Society* 13:4, 489–510.

Cooper, Robin A. 1986. "The United Nations Charter and the Use of Force: Is Article 2(4) Still Workable?" *American Society of International Law Proceedings* 78, 68.

Corten, Oliver, Sutcliffe, Christopher, Jouannet, Emmanuelle and Simma, Bruno. 2010. *The Law Against War: The Prohibition of the Use of Force in Contemporary International Law.* Oxford: Hart Publishing, Ltd.

Donner, Laura A. 1994. "Gender Bias in Drafting International Discrimination Conventions: The 1979 Women's Convention Compared with the 1965 Racial Convention." *California Western International Law Journal* 24:2, 241.

Evans, Gareth. 2008. *The Responsibility to Protect: Ending Mass Atrocity Crimes Once and For All.* Washington, DC: Brookings Institute.

Falk, Richard. 1981. *Human Rights and State Sovereignty.* New York: Holmes & Meier Publishers.

Farer, Tom J. 1999. "An Inquiry into the Legitimacy of Humanitarian Intervention." In Lori Fisler Damrosch and David J. Scheffer, eds., *Law and Force in the New International Order.* Boulder: Westview Press, p. 185.

Franck, Thomas M. 1988. "Legitimacy in the International System." *American Journal of International Law* 82:4, 705.

1990. *The Power of Legitimacy Among Nations.* Oxford University Press.

1995. *Fairness in International Law and Institutions.* Oxford: Clarendon Press.

Henkin, Louis. 1991. *Right v. Might: International Law and the Use of Force.* New York: Council on Foreign Relations Press.

Holzgrefe, J.L. and Keohane, Robert O. 2003. *Humanitarian Intervention: Ethical, Legal and Political Dilemmas.* New York: Cambridge University Press.

IDRC (International Development Research Council). 2011. "The Responsibility to Protect," International Development Research Council. Available at: www.idrc.org/es/ev-28745-201-1-DO_TOPIC.html, (accessed October 7, 2011).

Jackson, Robert. 2000. *The Global Covenant: Human Conduct in a World of States.* Oxford University Press.

Jentleson, Bruce W. 2007. "Yet Again: Humanitarian Intervention and the Challenge of 'Never Again.'" In Chester A. Crocker, Fen Osler Hampson, and Pamela Aall, eds., *Leashing the Dogs of War: Conflict Management in a Divided World.* Washington, DC: United States Institute of Peace Press, p. 280.

Jones, Dorothy. 1992. "The Declaratory Tradition in Modern International Law." In Terry Nardin and David Marpel, eds., *Traditions of International Ethics.* Cambridge University Press, pp. 42–61.

King, Henry T. and Theofrastous, Theodore C. 1999. "From Nuremberg to Rome: A Step Backward for U.S. Foreign Policy." *Case Western Reserve Journal of International Law* 31:1, 47, 53–54.

Krasner, Stephen. 1990. *Sovereignty: Organized Hypocrisy*. Princeton University Press.

Krylov, Nicholai. 1994. "Humanitarian Intervention: Pros and Cons." *Loyola International and Comparative Law Journal* 17, 365–407.

Levitin, Michael J. 1986. "The Law of Force and the Force of Law: Grenada, the Falklands, and Humanitarian Intervention." *Harvard International Law Journal* 27, 621.

Lillich, Richard. 1967. "Forcible Self-Help by States to Protect Human Rights." *Iowa Law Review* 53, 325–351.

  1969. "Intervention to Protect Human Rights." *McGill Law Journal* 15, 132.

  1974. "Humanitarian Intervention: A Reply to Ian Brownlie and a Plea for Constructive Alternatives." In John Norton Moore, ed., *Law and Civil War in the Modern World*. Baltimore: Johns Hopkins University Press, p. 229.

McDougal, Myres S. and Reisman, W. Michael. 1969. "Response by Professors McDougal and Reisman." *International Law* 3, 438.

Mertus, Julie. 2000. "Reconsidering the Legality of Humanitarian Intervention: Lessons from Kosovo." *William & Mary Law Review* 41:5, 1743–1787.

  2001. "Legitimizing the Use of Force in Kosovo." *Ethics & International Affairs* 15:1, 133.

Meyers, Mitchell A. 1997. "A Defense of Unilateral or Multi-Lateral Intervention Where a Violation of International Human Rights Law by a State Constitutes an Implied Waiver of Sovereignty." *ILSA Journal of International and Comparative Law* 3, 895.

Nardin, Terry and Mapel, David R., eds. 1992. *Traditions of International Ethics*. New York: Cambridge University Press.

Newman, Michael. 2009. *Humanitarian Intervention: Confronting the Contradictions*. New York: Columbia University Press.

Paust, Jordan J. 1999. "NATO's Use of Force in Yugoslavia." *Transnational Law Exchange* 2, 3.

Perez, Ruth Elizabeth Prado. 2011. *Motives and Outcomes in Humanitarian Intervention: Are they Related?* Saarbrücken: VDM Verlag Dr. Müller.

Reisman, W. Michael. 1971. *Nullity and Revision*. New Haven: Yale University Press.

  1990. "Sovereignty and Human Rights in Contemporary International Law." *American Journal of International Law* 84:4, 866.

Rosas, Allan. 1993. "Internal Self-Determination." In Christian Tomuschat, ed., *Modern Law of Self-Determination*. Dordrecht: M. Nijhoff Publishers, pp. 225–252.

Roth, Brad. 2003. "Building the Law, Breaking It or Developing It?" In Michael Byers and Greg Nolte, eds., *United States Hegemony and the Foundations of International Law*. New York: Cambridge University Press, pp. 232–263.

Schachter, Oscar. 1985. "The Lawful Resort to Unilateral Use of Force." *Yale Journal of International Law* 10, 291.

Simpson, Gerry. 2004. "Dueling Agendas: International Relations and International Law (Again)." *Journal of International Law and International Relations* 1:1–2, 61–74.

Smith, Michael J. 1998. "Humanitarian Intervention: An Overview of the Ethical Issues, in Ethics and International Affairs." *Ethics & International Affairs* 12:1, 63–79.

Sohn, Louis B. 1982. "The New International Law: Protection of the Rights of Individuals Rather than States." *American University Law Review* 32:1, 12.

Sohn, Louis B. and Buergenthal, Thomas. 1973. *International Protection of Human Rights*. Indianapolis: Bobbs-Merrill.

Stamatopoulou, Elsa. 1998. "The Development of United Nations Mechanisms for the Protection and Promotion of Human Rights." *Washington and Lee Law Review* 55:3, 687.

Szasz, Paul. 1999. "The Irresistible Force of Self-determination Meets the Impregnable Fortress of Territorial Integrity: A Cautionary Fairy Tale About the Clash in Kosovo and Elsewhere," April 8, 1999, speech on file with author, the University of Georgia School of Law, Georgia Society of International & Comparative Law Banquet.

Tesón, Fernando R. 1997. *Humanitarian Intervention: An Inquiry into Law and Morality*, 2nd edn. New York: Transnational Publishers.

Thaker, Ramesh. 2006. *The United Nations, Peace and Security: From Collective Security to the Responsibility to Protect*. Cambridge University Press.

United Nations. 1981. Declaration on the Inadmissibility of Intervention and Interference in the Internal Affairs of States, December 9, 1981. Available at: www.un.org/documents/ga/res/36/a36r103.htm (accessed October 4, 2011).

US Army. 2010. *Operational Law Handbook*. Available at: www.loc.gov/rr/frd/Military_Law/pdf/operational-law-handbook_2010.pdf (accessed October 4, 2011).

Verwey, Wil D. 1998. "Humanitarian Intervention in the 1990s and Beyond: An International Law Perspective." In Nederveen Pieterse, ed., *World Orders in the Making: Humanitarian Intervention and Beyond*. New York: St. Martin's Press, p. 180.

Wheeler, Nicholas. 2000. *Saving Strangers: Humanitarian Intervention in International Society*. New York: Oxford University Press.

Wilson, Richard Ashby and Brown, Richard D. 2009. *Humanitarianism and Suffering: The Mobilization of Empathy*. New York: Cambridge University Press.

| Conflicting responsibilities to protect
human rights

LARRY MAY

Introduction

There are two conflicting goals of the emerging "Responsibility to Protect"
(hereafter "R2P") doctrine. The first is that states have the responsibility
to protect their own citizens from human rights abuses either domestically or internationally. The second is that states have a responsibility to aid
other states in developing the capacity to protect their own citizens from
human rights abuses. While it does not appear that these goals conflict, I
will argue that in some cases they do, or that they could. The most basic
reason for this, as this chapter will attempt to show, is that states have scarce
resources available for human rights protection. Most dramatically, if a
state has the responsibility to wage war to aid a weak state in defending
itself from aggression, then to do so it may be required to jeopardize the
protection of the human rights of its own citizens, most especially those
who would be called into military service to protect the rights of those in
other states, or those who would otherwise get welfare assistance from their
own state. I will argue that a state's soldiers and other citizens have human
rights that may, and sometimes should, be taken into account in deciding
whether to wage humanitarian war. I do not argue that the lives of soldiers
(or citizens needing welfare assistance) are an overriding concern, but only
that they should count. And if they do, there is a generally unrecognized
conflict of responsibilities concerning human rights. Especially in debates
about human rights, the lives and basic human rights of soldiers should not
be discounted.

This issue sits at the intersection of the set of concerns that reconciliation
addresses and the set of concerns that involve rebuilding, especially the part
of the R2P that concerns rebuilding. How returning troops are viewed is
one of the key considerations in achieving reconciliation after war ends.
People will not come to respect the rule of law if they believe that their sons
and daughters have been sacrificed unnecessarily or the lives of their fellow citizens disvalued vis-à-vis the lives of foreign nationals. Such considerations will haunt the *jus post bellum* reflections and make reconciliation
and rebuilding efforts all that much harder. The R2P is a noble doctrine but

in its practical effects there are problems and conflicts that need to be given more attention than they have so far.

The R2P doctrine has cosmopolitan ambitions but is locked in a world where states are still the dominant actors. Human rights are treated as rights that people have by virtue of being members of the world community, and states are assigned responsibilities to protect those rights. But states also continue to have strong special responsibilities to their own citizens. In a world of states, the responsibility to protect one's nationals is supreme; but in a cosmopolitan order the rights of a state's nationals do not have priority. In this sense, the special responsibility to one's nationals seems to conflict with the international community's general responsibility to its members, namely all humans. In this chapter I will explore this conflict in several different ways, especially as it relates to the emerging R2P doctrine.

The structure of this chapter is as follows. First, I will discuss some of the relevant portions of the R2P doctrine, as well as some of the commentary on the doctrine. Second, I will indicate why the use of force to support the R2P can be especially problematic. Third, I will discuss the special responsibilities of states to their own nationals and indicate why in a world of states this responsibility is thought to be supreme. Fourth, I will discuss a possible way to adjudicate the conflicting responsibilities of states by reference to the doctrine of human rights itself. Finally, I will take up several objections to my proposed solution to this problem of conflicting responsibilities to protect human rights.

Responsibility to protect and human rights

If human rights really are equal rights that each person has by virtue of being human, and if rights have correlative duties, then it would seem that it is the whole world that has the duty or responsibility to protect human rights wherever they are abused. And if states are to be the main enforcers of human rights in the world, then it also follows that states have a duty or responsibility to protect human rights from abuse anywhere in the world that abuse occurs. As has sometimes been mentioned, this idea is essentially Lockean. Actually Locke himself held only that everyone had a right, not necessarily a duty, to punish offenders of the law of nature. Here is his most famous discussion of this point:

And that all men may be restrained from invading other's rights, and from doing hurt to one another, and that the law of Nature be observed which willeth the peace and preservation of all mankind, the execution of the law of Nature is in that state put into every man's hands, whereby every one has a right to punish transgressions of that law to such a degree as may hinder its violation. (Locke1989 [1682], Second Treatise, Chapter 2, Paragraph 7)

Yet in the previous paragraph of this work, Locke had intimated that there is also a duty or responsibility here, when he said:

Everyone as he is bound to preserve himself, and not to quit his station willfully, so by the like reason, when his own preservation comes not in competition, ought he as much as he can to preserve the rest of mankind. (Locke 1989 [1682], Second Treatise, Chapter 2, Paragraph 6)

And so the Lockean position is often associated with the idea that everyone has a responsibility to go to the aid of those whose rights are being violated.

   Today, the Lockean position is exemplified in the doctrine of the "Right to Intervene" that was popularized by the founder of Doctors Without Borders, Bernard Kouchner (Evans 2008, 32). That doctrine, as is also true of Locke's, was aimed at establishing that states and other parties had the right to intervene to aid those whose rights were, or were about to be, abridged. But having a right of humanitarian intervention proved not to be sufficient to prod the states of the world into action to prevent massive human rights abuses. While rights generally are best understood to have correlative duties, the existence of a right does not call for any specific duty. If Locke provides the historical argument for the Right to Intervene, we must search a bit later in the history of political and legal thought for the historical argument for the R2P doctrine that came to replace Kouchner's doctrine.

   One of the clearest, and earliest, ancestors of the R2P doctrine is the eighteenth-century theorist, Emir de Vattel. Vattel spoke of "offices of humanity," the duties "which Nations mutually owe to one another." Vattel argued for the recognition of the principle that "every Nation should give its aid to further the advancement of other Nations and save them from disaster and ruin, so far as it can do so without running too great a risk" (Vattel 1916 [1758], 114). Specifically, Vattel spoke of a requirement that what we today call rogue states be confronted by the rest of the states of the world.

But if a Nation, by its accepted principles and uniform policy, shows clearly that it is in that malicious state of mind in which no right is sacred to it, the safety of the human race requires that it be put down. (Vattel 1916 [1758], 135)

In my view, this is the true ancestor of the R2P doctrine as it is emerging today, providing for an obligation of states to go to the aid of other states.

As Gareth Evans, one of the founders of the R2P, has written:

The responsibility to protect embraces three specific responsibilities:

A. *The responsibility to prevent*: to address both the root causes and direct causes of internal conflict and other man-made crises putting populations at risk.
B. *The responsibility to react*: to respond to situations of compelling need with appropriate measures, which may include coercive measures like sanctions and international prosecution, and in extreme cases military intervention.
C. *The responsibility to rebuild*: to provide, particularly after a military intervention, full assistance with recovery, reconstruction, and reconciliation, addressing the causes of the harm the intervention was designed to halt or avert. (Evans 2008, 41)

Notice that the R2P differs from the doctrine of humanitarian intervention in that the use of force is considered a last resort. But it is also of note that the first major report on the R2P was issued by the International Commission on Intervention and State Sovereignty, where "intervention" was the key consideration of the report (*The Responsibility to Protect* 2001).

The R2P is still highly controversial, even nearly ten years after it was first proposed amidst what was expected to be general approval in the international community. Today, many diplomats and state leaders are deeply suspicious of the R2P doctrine. As I have argued elsewhere, at least part of the controversy surrounding the principles of this doctrine is that war is sanctioned to protect human rights and yet war itself often involves massive violation of human rights (May 2008, ch. 13; 2010, ch. 12). War, after all, involves the intentional taking of human life. And since most soldiers are not themselves deserving of loss of life, it is a human rights violation that they are intentionally killed. If it is understood as a last resort, then its controversial aspect can be diminished, but there is still the worry that any intervention that employs state use of force could also involve human rights violations, as I will argue in the next section of this chapter.

State responsibility and the use of force

As we will see, it is the call for military intervention that has proved to be the most controversial, and the most difficult normatively, of the various provisions of the R2P. A state's responsibility to use military force to protect another state's nationals raises a host of problems. And similar, although not as strong, worries arise with other means to implement the R2P. In the case of organized violent force, human beings, both soldiers and civilians, will be killed or harmed, and thus have their own human rights violated. In the case of non-violent use of force, it is also highly likely that the human rights to liberty and property will be adversely affected. So, here is the problem: as a contingent matter, in order to secure the human rights of some people (non-nationals) the human rights of other people (nationals) are likely to be rendered insecure.

One does not have to be a pacifist in order to see that contingently the use of violence, or other forms of force, to secure rights involves a trade-off in that other rights are abridged. It could be argued that in a world of scarce resources, and all worlds are of that sort, the most innocent should be protected even if it means that the less innocent, and especially the guilty, will have their rights abridged. Surely, this is the rationale for incarcerating offenders and even those who merely display the tendency to be offenders. Hard choices often need to be made, and when they are made, surely it seems fair to favor the most innocent and disfavor those who are less innocent. And so even though it is true that human rights on both sides of a war will be abridged, the lives lost on the side of the aggressor should count as less than the rights of those who are on the side of the defenders. While I acknowledge the intuitive appeal of the above argument, it does not adequately resolve the problem I am addressing in this chapter.

I acknowledge that trade-offs concerning rights, even human rights, are not uncommon. But it is especially problematic for one state to abridge, or risk abridging, the special human rights of its own citizens so as to protect the general human rights of the citizens of another state. If it is a question of one or another, but not both, person's rights, it should be allowed that a state can choose to protect its own citizens first. Indeed, it is even worse if a state is the instrument of the abuse of rights of its own citizens, as happens when a state initiates war or other means of force that sends its citizens into harm's way so as to protect the citizens of another state. So, the main worry is that even initiating a just humanitarian war involves putting one's own citizens in harm's way, jeopardizing the human rights of one's own citizens in order to secure the protection of the human rights of non-citizens.

Of course, a cosmopolitan could argue that all people's human rights are on an equal level. And once this is acknowledged it is not irresponsible for a state to choose among people on the basis of innocence rather than on the basis of nationality. Indeed, to choose on the basis of nationality appears, at least prima facie, as if it is an unfair way to make such choices, since the rights in question are not a specific society's civil rights, but human rights of all people merely because they are indeed fellow humans. Of course, if the proposed humanitarian war will harm one's own innocent civilians, then it may be that one could prefer them to the innocent others who are non-nationals. But in the case of soldiers, especially the ones who volunteer for military service, preferring these nationals over innocent non-nationals seems to be ruled out by any doctrine that respects human rights.

Since I am not a cosmopolitan, I do not necessarily find the above argument compelling. When rights protection requires a state's resources, it does seem odd to me to disregard whether the person who is in need of protection is one of that state's nationals. Now, I do not think that such nationalistic considerations are always overriding, but I merely want initially to argue that it is plausible that a state be allowed to give some weight to the fact of nationality of the people whose rights are put in jeopardy. And I will then advance the more controversial claim that this is true even in the case of one's own citizen-soldiers.

There has been an excellent debate recently about relational norms, such as the norm that would favor those interests associated with people with whom one is close (Wellman 2000). But the case of human rights is an especially difficult case in this respect. For, as I said earlier, human rights are supposed to be rights that ignore all other features of the person except his or her humanity. So, the difficult question is whether or not considerations of nationality can affect how one should respond to issues concerning conflicting responsibilities to protect human rights. I do not believe that being a fellow national should have great weight, but I believe this factor can have some weight, as I shall attempt to show.

Let us start with cases where the responsibilities to protect human rights are in conflict between two groups and where there are the same rights for the same number of people, with one group being nationals and the other group not. As a tie-breaker, it is often thought to be uncontroversial that a lot of otherwise insignificant factors can be appealed to. In order to see this, think of such things as using "first come, first served" or "first past the post" as tie-breakers when everything else is equal, and where these factors when not tie-breaking considerations would normally be afforded very little, if any, weight. Or consider giving ability to pay a tie-breaking presumption – this is also normally thought to be uncontroversial in true tie-breaking cases. Given this consideration, something like nationality should easily be seen as a legitimate tie-breaker as well. Nationality at least has the advantage over these other tie-breakers that it can be given some moral rationale in its behalf.

Indeed, nationality is not merely a tie-breaker, but can have independent moral value. One's compatriots share values and solidarity that is valuable as the kind of motivational stimulus that makes one ready to go to the aid of one another. Given that human rights are most often protected by states, the additional motivation of nationalism is of value as a bulwark against the loss of human rights protection in an otherwise dangerous world. With global rights protection a difficulty, it is important that the one institution that remains active and strong, namely the state, is pressured to protect some rights, and the rights of its citizens certainly count as some rights. Indeed, the responsibility to protect one's own citizens is part of the R2P doctrine.

Of course it might be claimed that nationalist sentiments can actually make cosmopolitan protection of rights harder. When one state reserves its resources for protecting rights only for its own nationals, there is less available for the rest of the world where weaker states may not be able to protect the rights of its citizens. But there need not be an exclusive attention to the interests of a state's own citizens. Rather all I am arguing for at the moment is that a state can legitimately show favoritism toward its own nationals when there are conflicts among human rights. And I would be happy to add to this proposal that it is only justified for a state to favor its own citizens if the net protection of human rights in the world is not thereby adversely affected.

Human rights risks of the use of force

Going to war, or initiating other forms of force by one state against another, involves quite serious risks of human rights abridgement. Most attention is typically directed, and with good reason, to the increasing number of civilian casualties that are caused by modern wars of all sorts. When war is engaged in, even for seemingly very good reasons, such as to combat long-standing injustice or oppression, many civilians are likely to die. Civilian casualties are most likely for those who live in war zones, but with the increased use of long range missiles, people outside of battle zones can be killed or harmed in other ways as well. And this should give us pause in endorsing the waging of such a war. In addition, and much less discussed, all wars will involve abridgement of the human rights of soldiers. Indeed, war is all about the loss of life of soldiers, and such abridgement of human rights also seems to have some weight against even humanitarian war.

Of course if one voluntarily joins a military unit knowing that one's life or liberty will be threatened, and one's life or liberty is jeopardized, this is not necessarily a human rights curtailment. But if one is conscripted, or if one does not understand the risks one is facing when one volunteers, human rights curtailment is a distinct possibility. In violent use of force, the chief human rights abridgement risked is the right to life. In non-violent use of force, the chief human rights infringement risked is the right to liberty. The abridgements of these human rights may occur while fighting for a just cause, namely the liberation of an oppressed people. But the justness of the cause does not mean that the rights of those who serve in defense of that cause should always be overridden.

It may perhaps seem odd to speak of the loss of the lives of soldiers as involving human rights abridgement. The lives and liberties of soldiers are often thought to be discountable. Some think that soldiers have made themselves into "dangerous men" (Walzer 1977) who can be killed at will. Others argue that those who fight in wars without just cause make themselves liable to be killed (McMahan 2009). Here the idea, which I do not support, is that soldiers fighting in an unjust war are unavoidable casualties in the service of the side that has a just cause. To say the least this idea is controversial. But it would pale by comparison with the claim that the lives and liberties of soldiers fighting a just war should also be discounted. This discounting really only makes sense, in my view, if the soldiers volunteered and knew, or should have known, the true risks of such volunteering. For in that case there is something like a waiver of right. But even in these cases, not insignificant objections about whether anyone can truly waive a human right are hard to dismiss. Contrary to what many of the Just War adherents believed historically, war is not best understood on the analogy of a boxing match, where participants understand the risks and voluntarily consent to them, thereby waiving their rights.

Perhaps another objection is that even if soldiers' lives have value, and can be the subject of human rights abridgement, the lives of soldiers are less significant than are the lives of innocent civilians. Indeed, the principle of discrimination or distinction in the Just War tradition as well as in international law calls for the favoring of civilian lives over those of soldiers. The principle says that during war soldiers may be targeted for attack but civilians may not be directly targeted. For war is about the killing and wounding of soldiers, and can be difficult to conceptualize otherwise. So, unless one thinks that war is always immoral, there must be some sense to the idea that the lives of soldiers are less valued than those of civilians. If the lives of soldiers are less valued than the lives of civilians, and if there is a conflict of responsibilities to protect rights between soldiers and civilians, then it seems plausible to prefer the lives of civilians. And so if the conflict is between risking the lives of soldiers and stopping oppression against civilians, it seems to make sense to discount the lives of the soldiers.

One set of considerations that are relevant here involves not just the risk of loss of life of the solders but also the ancillary losses to the families of soldiers. The family members of soldiers are generally civilians, and their losses can be quite significant and not as easily discounted as would be the lives of the soldiers, which for centuries have been derisively described as mere "cannon fodder." This image is meant to explain why the killing of soldiers is not very important, given the nature of war. But it is not so easily argued that the maiming, both physical and mental, of male and female members of the military, is also the likely and justified result of war. Returning soldiers commit violence against family members and are often unable to hold meaningful employment because of the scars of combat. Such costs cannot easily be dismissed.

In addition, as I mentioned above, there are often real costs involved to the rest of the civilian population when its government decides to wage humanitarian war. Waging war today is enormously costly. And these costs must be paid for. While many Western states are often assumed to be able to bear these costs easily, recent history has proved difficult to assimilate to that assumption. Even the United States has found it difficult to wage wars in Iraq and Afghanistan while also keeping the benefits of its previously modest welfare system intact. And if a state pursues its war with the objective of producing as few casualties as possible, the costs of such war climbs very high indeed.

My view is that it is especially difficult to justify jeopardizing the lives of soldiers and the basic interests of civilians when we are talking not about wars of self-defense but wars undertaken for humanitarian reasons. In wars of self-defense, there are really three groups: the civilians who are nationals and whose lives are threatened by the invading army; the soldiers who are co-nationals and are trying to repel the invasion; and the soldiers who are part of the invading force. Discounting the lives of the invading force seems plausible, if it is, since these soldiers have no right to threaten the population of the state they are invading. But in humanitarian wars, the soldiers who are invading do have a putative right to invade, namely to stop the oppression of the civilian population. The lives of these soldiers cannot be discounted merely on the grounds that they lack the right to do what soldiers typically do, namely kill other soldiers and increasingly indirectly to kill civilians as well.

When soldiers are fighting for a just cause, and also one that is humanitarian in its motivation, their lives cannot be disvalued in any of the standard ways that soldiers' lives have been disvalued. This means that the loss of life or liberty of these soldiers must be seen as in conflict with the lives of those who they are attempting to rescue. At very least, what this means is that when the number of civilian lives to be saved is less than the number of soldiers' lives that are risked in the rescue there is a conflict that cannot be dismissed as inconsequential or confused. In any event, soldiers should not be required to risk their lives or liberty to help save the lives or liberty of smaller numbers of civilians who are not their co-nationals. If this is accepted, then it can be seen that the rights of soldiers can be legitimately appealed to in discussions of humanitarian interventions.

I should admit that I also have similarly argued, in another work, that sometimes the lives of soldiers should generally not be risked for rescuing the lives of co-nationals either (May 2011). Indeed, only in the most extreme situation, where the lives of many civilians are at stake and the risk to soldiers is considerably smaller, is there even the beginning of an argument for requiring soldiers to risk life and liberty for civilians, whether the civilians be co-nationals or not. In any event, we stand in need of an argument that supports the view that soldiers can be required to risk life and liberty for the liberation of smaller numbers of civilians who are not co-nationals. And if the numbers of civilians who are not co-nationals and the number of soldiers are roughly equal, the home state of the soldiers needs an argument for why we cannot favor the lives of these soldier nationals over the lives of civilian non-nationals.

Adjudicating conflicts involving human rights

There are several seemingly plausible strategies for resolving such conflicts as we have explored above, but each has its own distinctive problems as well. First, one can merely look to the greater number of rights that are in jeopardy. Second, one can look to the different moral character of the rights. Third, one can look to the character or circumstance of the right holder. And, fourth, one can look to the character of the act or the person that has caused rights to be put in jeopardy. I shall take up each of these in turn in this section of the chapter. What will emerge is a set of factors that should be considered, none of which is overriding. I will thus provide a loose adjudication procedure for solving some of the seemingly intractable problems of rights conflict.

The first and most obvious strategy is to regard all responsibilities to protect human rights as being equally important and then resolve conflicts by simply favoring the action that has the least number of human rights abridgements. This strategy is obviously simple to apply. In the case that has concerned us, where soldiers' lives and liberty are jeopardized to save the lives or liberty of civilians, we simply favor the sending of troops into humanitarian ventures where the projected loss of life or liberty of the soldiers is less than that of the civilians to be saved. There has been controversy over the years about whether the numbers should count when discussing human rights, but it seems to me that especially in otherwise intractable conflicts letting the numbers count surely is prima facie plausible.

One objection to this adjudicatory strategy is to point out that while all human rights of the same kind should be treated equally, there is little reason to think that a right to life should be weighed equally to a right to a fairly minor liberty. While it is true that all human rights are ultimately grounded in the same normative principles, such as the principle of equal respect for the dignity of all persons, such a principle does not call for treating all human rights as existing on the same level of importance. Indeed, some human rights seem much more central to the value of dignity than other human rights. One need only recall the debates over the years about how to regard the very long list of rights in the Universal Declaration of Human Rights, where there is both the right to life and the right to holidays with pay. Most authors who have considered this quandary have allowed that human rights can be at least divided into basic and non-basic ones, with the basic ones holding sway (Shue 1980). Such considerations make plausible a second adjudicatory strategy.

The second strategy is similar to the first, largely a consequentialist way of adjudicating conflicts among responsibilities to protect human rights, but where the character or type of right matters. Here we still adjudicate conflicts by favoring the act that has the projected least loss, giving greater weight to losses that concern more important human rights than to those that involve less important human rights. And we would assign weights to human rights in terms of how central the right is to the core normative consideration of human rights, the equal dignity of persons. In this respect, the right to life is very important but can be seen as not always the most important right, since in some cases remaining alive in an emaciated and pain-ridden existence may not be consistent with dignity. There are obvious problems with setting a hierarchy of rights, as well as figuring out how much weight to assign to rights at each level. But at least a rough adjudicatory process can be constructed that will solve some of the problems of the first strategy.

While it is relatively easy to see that some rights listed in the Universal Declaration of Human Rights, such as the right to paid vacations, are of less importance than other rights, such as the right to life, many of the cases of conflict are not so easily resolved. Indeed, many rights have increased or decreased value based on the context, such as the example of even the right to life of a person with low quality of life just mentioned. And because of the importance of context, it will be very difficult to construct a calculus, or anything close to such a decision-making metric, that will allow us easily to resolve conflicts among human rights. In this respect, one of the chief determiners of context is whether or not the agent has voluntarily placed himself or herself into a situation where his or her rights are likely to be abridged.

This brings up our third strategy, where an increasingly complex consequentialist solution to the problem of conflicts of responsibilities to protect human rights also considers the character or circumstances of the person whose rights are in jeopardy. As was discussed above, on many accounts the fact that the right-holder is innocent as opposed to not innocent will matter in terms of how rights are weighed in adjudicating conflicts. Those who are non-innocent may be regarded as having waived their rights, or, for those who disallow the waiver of *human* rights, as having less value because voluntarily jeopardized. Some others have argued that putting on a uniform allows for exceptions to be made to general prohibitions on not violating rights (Chou 2010). Innocence does seem to matter here, but the difficulty is to determine how much it matters. I do not think that non-innocence negates human rights, and allow that it does matter somewhat, but remain unsure how much innocence should count in conflicts about rights protection.

As I suggested above, entering war is not like entering a boxing ring. The likely consequences of entering a war to engage with an enemy are not nearly as clear as the likely consequences of volunteering to box with an opponent, despite their similarity in structure. And the dissimilarity is greatly increased if the soldier volunteers to join a military unit in peacetime, only to find that war breaks out subsequently but before his or her tour of duty has ended. And if innocence is based on whether the war in which a soldier fights is just or unjust, the voluntariness of entering a military unit is not determinative of whether or not the soldier should be considered innocent since the justness of the war, or battle, is normally outside of the voluntary control, or even knowledge, of the individual soldier.

This brings us to the fourth strategy for adjudicating conflicts of responsibilities to protect rights, looking to the character of the act or person that has caused the risk of rights abridgement, whether to self or others. If a state that is sending its soldiers into harm's way is itself innocent or non-innocent, the rights conflict might be adjudicated by decreasing the weight of the human rights claims of those in the non-innocent state or increasing the weight of the human rights claims of those in the innocent state. Unlike the other strategies this one looks backward rather than forward in time. What is crucial is the moral character of the act or actor who has caused the situation where human rights are in conflict. In the cases of war, someone might propose that the rights of the citizens of a state that is acting aggressively would not count as much as the rights of citizens of a state that is contemplating action based on humanitarian motivations.

The major problem with this fourth approach, especially the last factor where the aggressiveness of a state's war matters, is that it makes rights claims of citizens conditional on what their state has done. This attribution can sometimes be justified if the citizens have approved and voted for the government that merely does the bidding of those citizens. But if the state acts against the bidding of the citizenry, even seeking to oppress the citizenry, or a significant part thereof, it would be odd to taint the citizenry with the wrongs of their state. And this is even odder if the rights of the citizens are diminished by acts of the state that is causing the human rights problem in the first place. Such a strategy makes sense when the human rights conflict is generated by state action that is truly representative of the wishes of the citizenry. But in most situations we will be forced to look at consequentialist considerations in order to resolve human rights conflicts.

The lessons learned from the previous sections tell in favor of some kind of weighing of human rights claims, either in a modified consequentialist way that looks to the amount of good to be done by favoring or disfavoring a certain human rights claim, or in a non-consequentialist way that looks to the past situation that caused the conflict to develop. While weighing of human rights claims is problematic in some respects, it is preferable to other strategies that could adjudicate conflicts of responsibility to protect human rights. Mixing consequentialist and deontological categories is messy but often best represents the intuitions that give rise to the problem in the real world. In general, I have argued that such a mixing of normative theories is often a good strategy, and indeed a better strategy than trying to twist things in such a way that one or the other theoretical approach is pushed beyond its plausible borders (May 1996).

So, I propose that conflicts of responsibility to protect human rights of the sort addressed earlier in this chapter be adjudicated in most situations by preferring that action that causes the least human rights abridgement, considering the number of people affected, the strength of the rights in play, and the situation of the agents and their actions primarily in terms of their voluntariness. In some rare cases, it will be possible merely to look to the innocence or non-innocence of the parties. This will only be true where those who are suffering in some sense approved of the government knowing that there was a serious risk that their government would jeopardize just the rights that are now being jeopardized. In this way, a complex decision procedure can be constructed that will allow for the resolution of many cases of conflicting responsibilities to protect human rights when the question is whether humanitarian intervention should be conducted to end or prevent a human rights atrocity.

Throughout this chapter I have argued that there is a serious conflict of responsibility to protect human rights to life and liberty. On the one hand, human rights are jeopardized by oppression and mass atrocities. On the one hand, there is jeopardy for human rights to life and liberty of the soldiers who are ordered to engage in military operations to stop or prevent oppression and mass atrocity as well as the civilians who will bear the economic costs of the war. I have attempted to provide a strategy for resolving this conflict, but I have not backed away from thinking that my resolution, which takes seriously both sides of this conflict, will mean that fewer humanitarian interventions are justified than is normally thought. But in the end, the lives of soldiers, and their co-national civilian compatriots, should not be disvalued in the headlong rush to support humanitarian action.

References

Chou, Yvonne. 2010. "Uniform Exceptions and Rights Violations." *Social Theory and Practice* 36:1, 44–77.

Evans, Gareth. 2008. *The Responsibility to Protect*. Washington, DC: Brookings Institution Press.

Locke, John. 1989 [1682]. *Two Treatises of Government*, edited by Peter Laslett, Cambridge University Press.

May, Larry. 1996. "Integrity and Value Plurality." *Journal of Social Philosophy* 27:1, 123–139.

   2008. *Aggression and Crimes Against Peace*. New York: Cambridge University Press.

   2010. *Genocide: A Normative Account*. New York: Cambridge University Press.

2011. "Contingent Pacifism and the Moral Risks of Participation in War." *Public Affairs Quarterly* 25:2, 95–112.

McMahan, Jeff. 2009. *Killing in War*. Oxford University Press.

Shue, Henry. 1980. *Basic Rights*. Princeton University Press.

The Responsibility to Protect, Report of the International Commission on Intervention and State Sovereignty. 2001. Ottawa: The International Development Research Centre, December 2001.

Vattel, Emir de. 1916 [1758]. *Le Droit des Gens, ou Principes de la Loi Naturelle* (The Law of Nations or the Principles of Natural Law), translated by Charles G. Fenwick. Washington, DC: Carnegie Institution.

Walzer, Michael. 1977. *Just and Unjust Wars*. New York: Basic Books.

Wellman, Christopher Heath. 2000. "Relational Facts in Liberal Political Theory: Is There Magic in the Pronoun 'My?'" *Ethics* 110:3, 537–562.

19 | Searching for the hard questions about women's human rights

MARYSIA ZALEWSKI

> The problem comes in knowing which unanswerable questions to ask.
> (Haraway 1992, 316)

Introduction

Transitional times appear to offer hope for real change. They invoke a sense of movement and space that might be effectively exploited to slot into place gender demands traditionally thwarted by a range of political, cultural and institutional obstacles. In recent times the plethora of societies and nations in transition from conflict to post-conflict, from authoritarian regimes to democratic ones, from colonial authority to sovereignty, from under-developed to developing/developed have presented numerous chances to intervene. Rwanda, Afghanistan, Iraq, Timor Leste and, more recently, the "Arab Spring," are just a few of the places that have emerged on the international media-scape in this regard. In the contemporary globalized political environment dominated by neoliberal foreign policy agendas with accompanying "good intentions" (Žižek 2009), the spaces of political transition transpire as full of opportunities to activate neoliberalism's devout sense of authority and agency. What is the place of women's human rights in this grandiose international picture?

Under the pseudonym of Olympe de Gouges, Marie Gouze wrote prolifically (plays, works of prose and political pamphlets) on women's rights and the abolition of slavery. Owing to their disobedient content and force, these writings earned her another pseudonym, that of "woman-man" – an "unnatural" being (Hunt 2007, 171). Here is a comment from a contemporary of hers, French politician Pierre Chaumette:

Never forget that virago, that woman-man, the impudent Olympe de Gouges, who abandoned the cares of her household to get involved in politics and commit crimes. She died on the guillotine for having forgotten the virtues that suit her sex. (Quoted in Beckstrand 2002; Hunt 2007, 171)

Similar to her English counterpart Mary Wollstonecraft, de Gouges suffered egregious public vilification, though much worse for de Gouges as she lost her life for her audacious beliefs about women. She was executed in 1793. Her "crimes" included writing the "Declaration of the Rights of Woman" in 1791, in an early phase of the tumultuous, transitional time of the French Revolution. Olympe de Gouges' alleged amnesia about the duties of her sex finds echoes in more recent times, suggesting something very powerful and tenacious about the category and identity of woman.

I cannot accept them [lesbians] as Indonesian women … because lesbians have forgotten their fundamental duties to be mothers, giving birth and raising children. (Gayatri 1996, 86 quoted in Jauhola 2010, 30)

In phallogocentric society women get equality as long as they don't forget to stay women and don't become ambiguous. (MacCormack 2009, 144)

Questions about women and their entitlement to the apparent rights of humanity are clearly not new. But are such questions as hard now as when de Gouges was writing her polemical tracts?

Bringing women into the realm of the human has been a central philosophical and practical goal of women's human rights activities. The reasons for this, particularly post-1948, appear self-evident. The Universal Declaration of Human Rights (UDHR) promised a great deal, its affirmations of universal equality, rights and freedoms seemed to offer lucid and unambiguous entitlements – and hope – for all. The unilateral gendering of the 1948 Declaration has been increasingly viewed as linguistically inadequate and conceptually anachronistic, however adding women "in" has proved much more difficult than imagined. With theoretical hindsight and operational experience this difficulty is unsurprising, but that "adding women in" has transpired as inadvisable or even impossible is a problem to which hard questions are appropriate to ask.

In the second decade of the twenty-first century it is regularly and comfortably acknowledged that there is widespread acceptance of, and a "remarkable consensus" (Ackerly 2011, 3) on, the value of human rights in theory and practice. Such rights are widely regarded as "universal ethical standards that affirm the equality and dignity of all individuals" (Bumiller 2008, 132). And, in important addition to this, the requirement to include women under the banner of the "human" has garnered powerful rhetorical and legislative currency. How far this has been successful in securing the human rights of women recurs as a key question and is one I will consider in this chapter.

I begin by setting the "usual scene" in academic discourses on women and human rights. In this context I will introduce the example of Timor Leste. I then move to reflect on the failures of women's human rights as these failures are promising. Then I turn to reconsider the conjoined category central to this discussion "women/human." I then move to open a different tenor of questions, ones which fuse "identity," "the political" and "transition." This leads into a discussion about vampires and apes. Finally I offer some concluding thoughts.

Women's human rights: setting the usual scene

No matter how you cut it universal – whether common or communist – meant "man." (Ronell 2004, 5)

In this section I briefly set the usual scene in regard to the contemporary status and state of women's human rights. To do this I will draw on a defining moment and significant influence, the Fourth UN World Conference on Women held in Beijing in 1995.

The idea of women's human rights was initially established some 30 years after the UDHR when the United Nations adopted the Convention on the Elimination of All Forms of Discrimination Against Women (CEDAW) in 1979. Consequent to CEDAW, a series of policies, statements of intent, resolutions and declarations have been produced with the unequivocal objective of improving, developing and (more) effectively implementing women's human rights. These include: DEVAW (1993), UN Security Council Resolutions 1325, 1820, 1888, 1889 and 1960 (UN Security Council 2000, 2008, 2010a, 2009, 2010b) as well as Millennium Development Goal 3 (UNDP 2011). But it is the fourth and last United Nations World Conference on Women held in Beijing in 1995, together with the subsequent Beijing Platform for Action (1995), that figure as defining and significant temporal, conceptual and legislative markers of the state and promise of women's human rights. I will momentarily return to the Beijing Conference and the Platform[1] to open up questions about the current state of women's human rights.

Consequent to CEDAW, institutional recognition that women suffer unduly and unfairly because of the constructed character of gender became increasingly accepted. In this context, the concept of gender as

---

[1] Hereafter referred to as "Beijing" and/or the "Platform." A brief description of the Platform's 12 critical areas of action appears later in the chapter.

a social construction has proved crucial, an obvious point but one that regularly goes radically under-theorized (Zalewski 2010). Three decades after CEDAW, sensibilities about, and definitions of, gender abound in both UN documentation and in national legislative machineries on an impressively wide scale. Below I include part of a definition of gender taken from a report on *Sustaining Women's Gains in Rwanda* (Uwineza and Pearson 2009). This East African country, still marked by the pain of the 1994 genocide, is regularly touted as having achieved impressive gains for women given Rwanda stands as the first country in the world where women outnumber men in parliament. This is how gender is defined in the report:

The term "gender" refers to the socially constructed (as opposed to biologically determined) identities of men and women. Gender is not the same as "sex," and gender differences are not the same as sex differences. For instance, the ability of women to bear children is a sex, or biologically determined, difference from men, that women, in many societies, are responsible for food preparation and house-hold chores is a gender, or socially constructed, difference … World Bank literature notes that in any given society, gender shapes the definitions of acceptable respon-sibilities and functions for men and women in terms of "social and economic ac-tivities, access to resources and decision making authority." (Uwineza and Pearson 2009, 7)

This rendition holds and re-constitutes many currently familiar stories about what gender is (as a social construction separate from sex), along with an implicit but profound assumption that gender is both malleable and amenable to targeted intervention, most especially in the context of women's human rights (Stern and Zalewski 2009). And though there are a range of feminisms globally and historically, a central goal has coalesced around the achievement of transformational change in gendered practices and lives and not simply a "tinkering or tailoring" (Rees 2005). This posi-tions women's human rights as *revolutionary* given the ultimate objective is to eliminate gender-based inequities in *all* its forms. Even the most philo-sophically liberal of feminist theories in regard to rights and equality entail significant theories of, and expectations for, radical social change (Ackerly 2011). This is particularly evident in policies developed in relation to *gender mainstreaming*,[2] many of which have developed consequent to the UN's

---

[2] "Gender mainstreaming" is defined by the United Nations Economic and Social Council in 1997 as "a strategy for making women's as well as men's concerns and experiences an integral dimension of … the policies and programmes in all political, economic and societal spheres so that women and men benefit equally and inequality is not perpetuated." Available at: www. undp.org/women/mainstream/whatis.shtml (accessed November 6, 2011).

commitment to integrating women's human rights as an integral part of generic human rights activities. And it was at Beijing that this burgeoning commitment was explicitly translated into the language of gender main-streaming (Charlesworth 1994).

Given the stifling of women's life chances, the thwarting of opportuni-ties to thrive socially, personally and politically through cultural and episte-mological impositions of gender, it should not be surprising that demands for their rights and freedoms materialize as radical. The violences imposed through gender make radical transformation logical. To be sure, these forms of gender induced violence manifest very differently across the globe, but nevertheless demands for gender rights and equality are not benign as they often seem to appear, perhaps explaining why equality remains a "hard sell" (Sahgal 2008, 5). Yet since the 1990s the increasing activities and political and sociocultural impact of women's movements (Reilly 2007), alongside the ongoing overt acceptance of conceptual ideas about what gender is, what gender does and how it works (typically reflected in the definition of gen-der in the report mentioned earlier; see also the WHO definition (2011)), fueled the status, impact and reach of the Beijing Platform. To illustrate one effect of Beijing combined with the impact on and of women's organizing, we can briefly look at the example of Timor Leste.

Timor Leste

Timor Leste is a society that has witnessed numerous political transitions, each accompanied by social and cultural turmoil. Initially colonized by Portugal in the sixteenth century and then the Netherlands, Indonesia seized control in 1975. Subsequent to the relinquishing of control by Indonesia in 1999, Timor Leste became the first new sovereign state of the twenty-first century in 2002. In 2000 a Women's Congress was formed, explicitly inspired by the Beijing Platform's agenda. This transitional time was seized upon by the Women's Congress in order to install a specific set of gender demands, including: (1) gender mainstreaming in policy-making, (2) greater representation of women in politics; and (3) the mobilization of women's voices in civil society (Hall and True 2009, 160). That these three arenas were advanced with some success has been hailed as remarkable especially given the goals of gender rights and equality are more usually marginalized or traded off in the face of ostensibly larger and more impor-tant goals (Hall and True 2009, 160; UN Women 2011a). This "forgetting" of why gender matters is perhaps even more the case in politically tran-sitory moments when the "bigger picture" (typically democracy, security and the economy) tends to swiftly take its natural comfortable precedence. To be sure there were setbacks to the Congress's demands, and resistance was robust. There was particular fury over the issue of "quotas" for women political candidates, to which I will now briefly turn (see for a discussion of quotas, Towns 2010, 149–183).

The Women's Congress wanted to set a quota goal of at least 30 percent women in all decision-making bodies. The UN, though spearheading the move to democracy, was divided on this matter, with the head of the Electoral Affairs Division arguing that quotas would set unacceptable precedents ("we'll be having quotas for everyone's uncles and cousins"), whilst the head of the Department of Political Affairs of the UN is alleged to have (disparagingly) said that quotas "only happen in socialist countries" (Hall and True 2009, 168). Ultimately, a gender quota for women was opposed. Despite or because of this setback, women committed to advancing the equality agenda put even more energy into raising the profile and skills of women who wanted to stand for political office. The upshot was that women won 23 out of 87 seats in parliament (26 percent), placing Timor thirty-third in the world on this measure. Thus, as a result of the robust and energetic networking and campaigning skills of the women involved and despite resistance to formal quotas, notable success was achieved. What questions does this answer about women's human rights? That hard work and tireless commitment by women can, if there is some political and legislative room for maneuver, achieve great things? Surely true. That women can be politically astute and extremely capable? Surely also true. But what question might we ask about the rabid and confused reaction to the idea of quotas for women political representatives?

One of the reasons feminist-informed analysis claims that political quotas for women are defensible is because conventional cultural bias in favor of men installs a clear but camouflaged quota for men – as such men generally materialize as "natural" leaders. Hence for feminist scholars the overabundance of men in positions of political power is, at least partly, a result of entrenched gender favoritism. Redressing the consequent imbalance thus cannot solely rely on meritocratic legislative processes given they inevitably re-produce inequalities. Enforcing a specified quota for women in, for example, elections, is one way to help overcome implicit bias and ensure better representation of women. Yet the reaction to quotas for women in Timor Leste (not an untypical reaction) suggests that (implicit) quotas for men are (literally) unquestionable given the (epistemological) difficulty of seeing the bias that renders the work gender is doing invisible. What real difference will it make to increase women's political participation if gender is so poorly understood?

Women's political presence remains relatively high in Timor Leste though domestic violence remains virulent. However Timor Leste has been hailed as an example of gender equality: "Anyone looking for a model for the promotion of gender equality should look to Timor Leste" (Pandaya 2009). A photograph accompanying the newspaper article from which this quotation is drawn shows two female soldiers. The caption reads: "**Women power**: Two female members of the Timor Leste Army stand guard in Dili. In the young nation of Timor Leste, women are bring encouraged to take a more prominent position in society" (Pandaya 2009). The female soldiers are proffered as clear examples of gender equality. What would Pierre Chaumette have thought of these women? Perhaps that they too, like de Gouges, were "women-men." And they surely are "women-men" given the gender of "soldier" is masculine. To be "a soldier" is to be "a man," even if you are "a woman." Does the example of Timor Leste reveal what the hard questions about women's human rights are?

Failures of women's human rights

I want to further consider the state of women's human rights consequent to Beijing by briefly reflecting on a roundtable discussion hosted by UNESCO headquarters in 2009. This roundtable – "Beijing: 15 Years After" – was convened to explore "the progress made in the twelve critical areas of action of the *Beijing Platform for Action* adopted at the *Fourth World Conference on Women* in Beijing in 1995" (UNESCO 2009). Here is a brief explanatory note on the Platform's agenda, which crystallizes the series of demands for action made:

The Platform for Action is an agenda for women's empowerment. It aims at … removing all the obstacles to women's active participation in all spheres of public and private life through a full and equal share in economic, social, cultural and political decision-making … Equality between women and men is a matter of human rights and a condition for social justice and is also a necessary and fundamental prerequisite for equality, development and peace. (Beijing Platform 1995)

The atmosphere at the roundtable was jovial and positive. It was noted with pleasure by the Chairwoman that the room was unusually full, indeed full for the first time, indicating high levels of interest in issues of gender. Also noted was the fact that the Director General Elect of UNESCO was a woman, Mme Irina Bokova, the first female DG in the UN in all its 63 years. Despite these initial points of positivity it was also noted that the issues in regard to women globally were still very serious. In 2009 the burden of poverty, education, health-care, violence, armed conflict, lack of respect for human rights, gender inequalities, and discrimination all remained unresolved. It was judged that the agenda for women's human rights was unfinished and, despite many achievements on the way, a great deal more work had to be done. It was also acknowledged that gendered violence had become a global pandemic and, moreover, such violence was increasingly perceived as a security issue given the most dangerous places for women in the world also pose "the greatest threat to International peace and security" (Verveer 2009).

A few years later the situation appears little changed. Fewer than 10 percent of countries have female heads of state or government; fewer than 30 countries have reached the target of 30 percent of women in national parliaments (Ban Ki-moon 2011). Sexual violence appears endemic in conflict zones, the Democratic Republic of Congo for example. Indeed concern about sex- and gender-based violence (SGBV) has moved high up on the women's human rights agenda especially in the UN (UN Security Council 2008, 2010b). And to make the case for robust action copious details of violence against women are relentlessly supplied. The following list is a typical example.

- 20,000–50,000 women were raped during the Bosnian War in the early 1990s.
- 23,200–45,600 Kosovar Albanian women were believed to be raped during the Kosovo conflict.
- The Rwandan genocide memorial states that 500,000 women were raped during 100 days of conflict in 1994.
- In Sierra Leone 50,000–64,000 internally displaced women suffered sexual assault at the hands of combatants (IPU 2008; Ward and Marsh 2006).

The evidence about sex- and gender-based violence is overwhelming. So why is progress so slow?

At the local level answers to the question of slow progress include: inadequate resources (human and financial), inadequate political will and cultural resistance. At the more globalized institutional level, for example with the UN, such a monolithic instrument with its inevitable internal incoherencies on policy issues (as in the Timor Leste example) may well be too unwieldy to deliver effectively on gender demands. To counter these hurdles more initiatives continue to be introduced.

Recent initiatives to help further overcome the obstacles to progress in women's human rights include the Network of Men Leaders launched by UN Secretary General Ban Ki-moon on November 24, 2009, the tenth anniversary of the International Day for the Elimination of Violence against Women (UN 2011). Ban Ki-moon described the Network as a major new initiative that would bring together current and former politicians, activists, religious and community figures in order to combat what he called the global pandemic of violence against women (UN 2011). Emotive rhetoric and promises of extra resources bolstered his proposal. He called upon men and boys not to ignore or condone acts of sexual violence against women. He announced new grants for projects on the ground to be awarded by the UN Trust Fund in Support of Actions to Eliminate Violence against Women, managed by the UN Development Fund for Women, amounting to $10.5 million for 13 initiatives in 18 countries and territories. And he stressed that his commitment to this issue stemmed not just from his role as UN Secretary-General, but also in his role as a son, husband, father and grandfather. "Men," he claimed, "have a crucial role to play in ending such violence – as fathers, friends, decision makers, and community and opinion leaders" (UN 2011). To further consolidate efforts to more effectively obliterate the violations of gendered inequities, in July 2010 the UN General Assembly voted unanimously to the establishment of the UN Entity for Gender Equality and Empowerment, to be known as "UN Women" (UN Women 2011b). At least US$500 million has been recognized by member states as the minimum investment needed for UN Women: interestingly the same amount that the Jimmy Choo conglomerate has been sold for (Reuters 2011) – an oblique reminder of the very different manifestations of "feminine gender" that is "woman" across the globe.

Thus one range of responses to the question of slow progress has been to introduce more schemes, initiatives and programs, ones that promise to be more robust and institutionally coherent and hopefully to offer solutions to the tarnished promises and hopes of women's human rights. As such commitment at international and national levels is vigorous. Why then, are the day-to-day realities of women's lives so little changed (Valasek and Nelson 2006: i)?

A slightly different range of answers to the question "why is progress so slow and women's lives so little changed?" emerges when we look more closely at theoretical analyses. A significant amount of nuanced work has been produced to better understand what the obstacles are that inhibit dealing more effectively with the complexities around women's human rights. As such, theoretical knowledge about gender is profuse. A typical goal in this context centers on paying more attention to converting theoretically informed knowledge into effective practice/action. In other words, to better transmit and disseminate theory in order to increase the potential for effective dialogue and understanding as well as to better and more explicitly guide activism (Ackerly 2011).

However, consequent to recent feminist work, many scholars are less sanguine about the possibilities of more productively translating theory into practice to better secure women's human rights. This is particularly the case consequent to influential feminist scholarship that convincingly demonstrates a variety of ways feminist expositions of gender have been co-opted or desecrated (or both) by a range of governments, national and international organizations (Bumiller 2006; Eisenstein 2010; McRobbie 2009; Prügl 2009). This work invites a deeper reckoning into the conceptual and theoretical problematiques and opens up further layers of questioning regarding the putative blockages and hindrances to the effective operationalization of women's human rights. The paradox of the deep infiltration of ideas about gender accompanied by complex and attentive theorizing sits uncomfortably alongside ongoing and persistent evidence that gender inequities remain globally rampant. This begs harder and more vexing questions about the failures of women's human rights. To think about these I move to discuss two specific ways in which contemporary post-structurally inflected feminist social and political theory invites a different range of questions about women's human rights, focusing first on the category "women/human," and second on the idea of "the political."

Women/human

The human is a site of ambivalence, agonism, and, of course, exclusion (Lloyd 2007, 103).

Contemporary feminist social and political theories, at least those prevalent on the academic landscape, are heavily informed by post-structural philosophies broadly conceived. In the context of women's human rights this has significance in a range of ways; one is in the realm of *identity*. The emancipatory hope offered by the discovery of, and insistence on, the identity of woman – recognizing her as a distinct category – becomes precarious and even dangerous when thought through post-structurally. The feminized alignment of "woman" with "vulnerability" suggests that gendered "victim-saviour" and "protector-protected" stereotypes are constantly being re-installed through policies and legislations geared toward achieving women's human rights, though that this re-installment is inadvertent is usually claimed. How could placing women politically and legislatively center stage and demanding their lives be made better and be made free from gendered violence "inadvertently" recreate gender-laced violence? A post-structurally inclined response is that it is, in part, the very attachment to the identity of gender, an identity that tautologically transpires as injurious especially, it seems, for women, which (re-)produces itself as injury (Brown 1995; Stern and Zalewski 2009). And more than this, the attachment becomes fetishized, producing a form of Nietzschean *ressentiment* (Brown 1995; see also Hawkesworth 2006, 189–191). Here the pain, injury, guilt and revenge borne out of the discovery of injurious social formations become wedged in the very effects meant to be dismantled. In short, the theoretical attachment to gender-injury and the appeal to establishment sites of power and authority (often the state in the context of women's human rights, though the UN figures as hugely important) "reinstate[s] rather than transform[s] the terms of domination that generated them" (Hawkesworth 2006, 190). Here the apparently self-evident good of including women under the banner of the human starts to go awry. If the category of woman reproduces itself as injured, can incorporation into "human" dismantle this?

The human is a category that marks a luminous promise to transcend the rending trauma of the particular. (Haraway 1997, 214)

The human has generally been understood as emblematic of the binary "man-woman" presenting an image of universality and inclusivity (of all). Yet any unpacking of the idea of "the human" begins to illustrate its exclusions and subjugations. As Patricia MacCormack puts it, rather than offering ultimate evidence of wholeness, the human is acutely illustrative of the subjugation of all others identities and categories by a "dominant one" (2009, 135) – the dominant one being "white male." On this view, including "others" under the banner of human will necessarily prove, at a minimum, difficult and, as gestured toward earlier, potentially dangerous.

The political

A second way in which contemporary post-structurally informed feminist social and political theory is significant in the context of women's human rights is in the realm of *the political*. Overwhelmingly, as the earlier discussion illustrates, this has been understood as appertaining to the traditional realm of "doing" politics. Thus questions about appropriate legislation and the obstacles of translating political and legislative commitments into effective action become the obvious ones to ask. Thinking about "the political" more post-structurally and consequently reflecting on the construction of meanings and acknowledging their provisional status, leads to the asking of a different tenor of questions, ones that push thinking about categories such as women/human more forcefully into the realm of disturbing contestations over meanings, subjects and thought. This can become tricky as there is a powerful conventional draw to wonder whether "it would not be better to question less and act more, not reflect on abstract ideas like philosophical foundations and the like but continue to use the term [human rights] to do good things in a world in which goodness is in short supply" (Gearty 2006, 20). Yet it is not as if thinking (or questioning) are not forms of action in themselves, or if acting could proceed without thought or thinking. Thus to think about "the political" post-structurally I want to consider the idea of the human and the idea of transition together. Here we can work with the idea of "identity" and "the political" to stretch and conjoin questions about the "human" and "transition." Splicing these together offers interesting possibilities for re-thinking questions around women's human rights.

Despite its entrenchment in human rights discourse and generic warm acceptance, the "human" is a capricious category. Who or what might be included or excluded is never foreclosed. Yet despite this unpredictability, the magnetism of very traditional cultural configurations forcefully demarcates the form and shape of who might count as (a) human. There is clearly a sorry history here for women, as both masculinity and racial privilege regularly "shore up the notion of the human" (Butler 2004, 13). How is it, then, that women figure as human sometimes? What becomes apparent is that what has facilitated woman's intermittent legibility as human has, in large part, depended on acceptable and recognizable alignment with the expectations of her gender. To recall an earlier quotation, "in phallogocentric society women get equality as long as they don't forget to stay women and don't become ambiguous" (MacCormack 2009, 144). On this view, for women not "to forget to be women" they must live in ways which align enough with specific expectations related to sexuality and reproduction.

Yet the idea that women might only be awarded "human status" if they adhere correctly to conventional local/global gender expectations, especially in the realm of sexuality and reproduction, seems anachronistic, certainly in a Western dominated academic and legislative milieu. It also seriously unsettles the commonplace idea (as evidenced in the *Sustaining Women's Gains in Rwanda* report mentioned earlier (Uwineza and Pearson 2009)) that gender is separate from sex as closer theoretical attention reveals how gender is intimately tied to sexed bodies for women, which are in turn defined in relation to sexuality and reproduction. To try to unsettle this connection I want to return to the idea of transition but staying with the category of woman/human. My questions now focus less on the ways women are occluded or refused – the traditional focus of women's human rights discourse – but rather open up what other identity categories might be included within the rubric of human. This is not to move toward a decision about the truth of the human (as if we might finally get there), but to think again – if somewhat awry in Žižekian fashion – about women's place in the grand scheme of the realm of human rights by asking questions about "others" who appear both further away yet uncomfortably close to human-ness: vampires and apes.

Vampires and apes

Having no presence – the subject must be continually produced. (Haraway 1992)

There is no shortage of philosophical, literary, cultural and popular fascination around the idea of stretching imaginations about who or what might be included in/as the human.

And vampires, defined by their categorical ambiguity and troubling mobility (like lesbians) hold fascination for many (Haraway 1997, 215). The resurrection of vampire tales in contemporary popular culture indicates something of this allure, for example Stephenie Meyers' modern-day vampires in the highly popular series The Twilight Saga (2010). In this, the central (male) vampire character Edward Cullen valiantly struggles with his need to drain the life-blood of others to ensure his own survival. His anxiety is easily read as human/humane. Though a barely buried narrative of very traditional sexual mores seeps through this modern tale as Cullen's abstinence when it comes to human blood allows for "safe sex" in the confines of marriage – a sanitized take on the traditional idea of vampires as violently infecting wholesome life and lives (Haraway 1992, 215).

However, the transitional form of vampires offers significant challenges for thinking about women/human. Crossing with ease across borders and boundaries, defying gravity, materializing through walls or morphing into bats and wolves, these boundary transgressions simultaneously repel and fascinate. As the undead their alive vitriolic presence inverts and exceeds conventional (common) senses about reality – senses steeped in Enlightenment desires about knowledge, truth, agency and subjectivity and the boundaries constituted to secure these. These desires have found a solid place in the locus of "the human" posited as the bearer of knowledge and truth and the source of secure subjectivity and political agency. These foundational ideas have been faithfully reproduced in human rights discourses but they start to unravel when we think a little more deeply (if briefly here) about vampires.

How are vampires helpful for the discussion here? As oscillating hybrids, their constant melding of, and transiting between, form(s) can profoundly challenge conventional senses of unity and wholeness. Though fascinating, entities or subjects that are more and other than "one" are also culturally monstrous. This dual interest – fear and fascination – begins to offer a glimpse into the reasoning fueling the barely concealed horror invoked when women "forget." In other words, the sense of monstrousness attached to "fictional" hybrid subjects like vampires helps to make a little more sense of the deep apprehensiveness when women "forget" and become, for example, sexually/reproductively or otherwise ambiguous. Acting as a metaphor for empty subjects, the allusion toward the illusion of identity is beguilingly gestured toward in the lack of mirrored reflection for vampires. We can think more about this through another apocryphal story that has recently been re-visited cinematically – the "Planet of the Apes" genre.

The commercial and scientific traffic in monkeys and apes is a traffic in meanings, as well as in animal lives. (Haraway 1992, 1)

In the 2011 film *Rise of the Planet of the Apes* the origin of the metamorphosing of apes into speaking, thinking, acting ("human") beings[3] is revealed. In common with many early twenty-first century "blockbuster" movies, a sense of impending apocalyptic futures if humans do not change their ways in regard to people, animal and planetary exploitation is offered as a less than subtle warning (though one perhaps easily forgotten in the mesmerizing mire of CGI and motion capture technology). The central chimpanzee character (named Caesar) in *Rise of the Planet of the Apes* enacts a touching and recognizable range of emotions and human behaviors, feelings and struggles, as do his fellow apes. Compassion, hate, bitterness, loyalty, love, cunning, intelligence: just like "us." Interestingly, if not surprisingly, gender seems irrelevant and the gender regime of this new form of "humanity" is cinematically unremarkable and unquestionable. Action and agency are masculine marked with females (re)presenting as love/sex interest and reproducers. That apes might be perceived as "human," yet female agency and activity are consistently subsumed into the quagmire of invisible gender, is telling. But of what, is a hard question.

Picking back up on the specter of the absence of self invoked by the lack of mirrored reflection for vampires – this is differently depicted in *Rise of the Planet of the Apes*. There is a touching scene and something of a Lacanian "mirror moment" when Caesar looks at himself in the

---

[3] The main plot line of earlier films in the genre.

mirror. Having just rescued one of his "human-owners" from attack by another man, the ensuing fracas raises questions about Caesar's place in the world of humans. He looks at himself in a full size mirror. He appears disgusted with himself in his non-human-ness. He does not look like the others (the other humans). The pretend human heart of the film is exposed in this false moment. In our "looking at primates" we know they "look back" (Halberstam 2011, 35). In this scene the "looking back" seems once again to be stolen by white hu(man)ity. The chimera of self is differently presented in vampires. With vampires there is nothing to see gesturing toward the emptiness of self. With Caesar, the image of the "dominant one" (white male) is viscerally *not* reflected back. The racial inflection is stark.

Identity is infinitely incomplete – "becomings never become" (MacCormack 2009, 142). Thinking about this by asking about the transitional place of apes and vampires in the realm of the human helps to begin a re-thinking about the persistent thwarting of women's human rights in practice – or at least a re-thinking of what kinds of questions are useful to ask. They help us to remember that subjects are constituted rather than have essential form. This must surely invoke questions about insisting on rights for women. Women get equality if they don't forget to stay women. But women forget all the time, when they are lesbians for instance. Or when women act "unnaturally," like de Gouges, or when they forget to have children. Being a woman continues to mean something, often only remembered when women "forget" and someone realizes.

Concluding thoughts

Is there no way to stop the repetition of gendered logics? (Butler 2001, 414)

The questions we ask mirror the political and ontological commitments we already have, and the epistemological frames within which we work. The questions we ask reflect the limits of our imaginations and our senses of the relationship between theory, method and practice. They also reflect the limits of our philosophical courage.

The intimate and intricate ways gender works, in its racial and heteronormative manifestations, in its myriad of different ways across the globe – these complexities have been well theorized in academic literatures. The human rights machinery has eagerly swept up theoretical knowledge about gender in order to stem some of the gender-based violences done to women. The legislative breadth is impressive. The rhetorical commitment inspiring. The speed and urgency with which new initiatives are introduced is remarkable. Yet the problems remain profligate. A radical re-thinking of the kinds of questions asked is called for.

Perhaps Olympe de Gouges might have been successfully enjoined to remember the duties of her sex. The temporality invoked here suggests something has been forgotten that "was" and needs retrieving in the present. This is (non)sense as nothing past has been forgotten. Rather the normative terms of feminine gender have been sidestepped, evaded, ignored, refused. The violent response to de Gouges' refusal of her gender (at least this is one way her behavior was read) tells us something about the power of the category. It also tells us something about the emptiness of the category given such violent energy put into enforcing appropriate completion. "The problem comes in knowing which unanswerable questions to ask." Haraway's conundrum suggests the search for the hard questions about women's human rights is not over.

I stood on a hill and I saw the Old approaching, but it came as
the New.
It hobbled up on new crutches which no one had ever seen before
and stank of new smells of decay which no one had ever
smelt before. (Bertolt Brecht quoted in Edgerton 2008)

Transitional times offer flurries of hope for transformational change, though most often the grandiose importance of the "bigger picture" swiftly recoups center stage. This and the persistent failures around women's human rights suggests we might consider stopping asking the same questions over and over. What women might "become" shifts, but boundaries holding the category in place remain, if variably policed round the globe. It is the category that's the problem and the one that needs to be questioned, disturbed and even ignored. Perhaps the hardest question is, "is it time to give up the quest for women's human rights?"

When feminism is no longer ... secured by the categories of "women" or "gender" ... it is doing the most "moving" work. (Ahmed 2004, 176)

References

Ackerly, Brooke. 2011. "Human Rights Enjoyment in Theory and Activism." *Human Rights Review* 12:2, 221–239.

Ahmed, Sara. 2004. *The Cultural Politics of Emotion*. Edinburgh University Press.

Ban Ki-moon. 2011. "Remarks at Roundtable on Gender Equality and Democracy." Available at: www.un.org/apps/news/infocus/sgspeeches/print_full.asp?statID=1164 (accessed September 4, 2011).

Beckstrand, Lisa. 2002. "Olympe de Gouges: Feminine Sensibility and Political Posturing. (18th Century French Writer Marie Gouze)." *Intertexts*, June 14. Available at: www.highbeam.com/doc/1G1-93210406.html (accessed July 27, 2011).

Beijing Platform for Action. 1995. Declaration of the Fourth World Conference on Women. September 15, 1995, Beijing, China. Available at: www.un.org/womenwatch/daw/beijing/platform/plat1.htm (accessed September 4, 2011).

Brown, Wendy. 1995. *States of Injury*. Princeton University Press.

Bumiller, Kristin. 2006. "Freedom from Violence as a Human Right: Toward a Feminist Politics of Nonviolence." *Thomas Jefferson Law Review*. 28, 327–354.

2008. *An Abusive State: How Neoliberalism Appropriated the Feminist Movement Against Sexual Violence*. Durham, NC: Duke University Press.

Butler, Judith. 2001. "The End of Sexual Difference." In E. Bronfen and M. Kavka, eds., *Feminist Consequences: Theory for the New Century*. New York: Columbia University Press, pp. 414–434.

2004. *Undoing Gender*. New York: Routledge.

CEDAW (Convention on the Elimination of All Forms of Discrimination Against Women). 1979. Opened for signature December 18, 1979, 1249 U.N.T.S. 13 (entered into force September 3, 1981). Available at: www.un.org/womenwatch/daw/cedaw/ (accessed September 4, 2001).

Charlesworth, Hilary. 1994. "What are 'Women's International Human Rights'?" In Rebecca J. Cook, ed., *Human Rights of Women: National and International Perspectives*. Philadelphia: University of Pennsylvania Press, pp. 58–84.

DEVAW (Declaration on the Elimination of Violence Against Women). 1993. General Assembly Resolution 48/104, December 20 1993. Available at: www.genderandpeacekeeping.org/resources/5_DEVAW.pdf (accessed September 4, 2001).

Edgerton, David. 2008. *The Shock of the Old*. London: Profile Books.

Eisenstein, Hester. 2009. *Feminism Seduced: How Global Elites Use Women's Labor and Ideas to Exploit the World*. Boulder: Paradigm Publishers.

Eisenstein, Zillah. 2010. "Hillary is White." In Beverly Guy-Sheftall and Johnnetta Betsch Cole, eds., *Who Should Be First? Feminists Speak Out on the 2008 Presidential Campaign*. Albany: SUNY Press, pp. 79–83.

Gayatri, B.J.D. 1996. "Indonesian Lesbians Writing Their Own Script: Issues of Feminism and Sexuality." In Monika Reinfeder, ed., *Amazon to Zani: Toward a Global Lesbian Feminism*. London: Cassell, pp. 86–97.

Gearty, Conor. 2006. *Can Human Rights Survive?* Cambridge University Press.

Halberstam, Judith. 2011. *The Queer Art of Failure*. Durham, NC and London: Duke University Press.

Hall, Nina, and True, Jacqui. 2009. "Gender Mainstreaming in a Post-conflict State." In Bina D'Costa and Katrina Lee-Koo, eds., *Gender and Global Politics in the Asia-Pacific*. London: Palgrave Macmillan, pp. 159–174.

Haraway, Donna. 1992. *Primate Visions. Gender, Race, and Nature in the World of Modern Science*. London: Verso.

  1997. *Modest _Witness@Second_Millennium. FemaleMan_Meets_OncoMouse*. New York and London: Routledge

Hawkesworth, Mary. 2006. *Feminist Inquiry: From Political Conviction to Methodological Innovation*. New Brunswick: Rutgers University Press.

Hunt, Lynn. 2007. *Inventing Human Rights: A History*. New York: W.W. Norton & Company.

IPU (Inter-Parliamentary Union). 2008. "Sexual Violence Against Women and Children in Armed Conflict." Available at: www.ipu.org/splz-e/unga08/s2.pdf (accessed November 6, 2001).

Jauhola, Marjaana. 2010. "Building Back Better? – Negotiating Normative Boundaries of Gender Mainstreaming and Post-Tsunami Reconstruction in Nanggroe Aceh Darussalam, Indonesia." *Review of International Studies* 36, 29–50.

Lloyd, Moya. 2007. "(Women's) Human Rights: Paradoxes and Possibilities." *Review of International Studies* 33, 91–103.

MacCormack, Patricia. 2009. "Unnatural Alliances." In Chrysanthi Nigianni and Merl Storr, eds., *Deleuze and Queer Theory*. Edinburgh University Press, pp. 134–149.

McRobbie, Angela. 2009. *The Aftermath of Feminism: Gender, Culture and Social Change*. London: Sage.

Meyer, Stephenie. 2010. *The Twilight Saga Complete Collection*. London: Atom.

Pandaya. 2009. "Timor Leste's Women Struggle to Make Their Voices Heard." *The Jakarta Post*, September 14. Available at: www.thejakarta-post.com/news/2009/09/14/timor-leste%E2%80%99s-women-struggle-make-their-voices-heard.html (accessed November 6, 2011).

Prügl, Elisabeth. 2009. "Does Gender Mainstreaming Work? Feminist Engagements with the German Agricultural State." *International Feminist Journal of Politics* 11:2, 174–195.

Rees, Teresa. 2005. "Reflections on the Uneven Development of Gender Mainstreaming in Europe." *International Feminist Journal of Politics* 7:4, 555–574.

Reilly, Niamh. 2007. "Seeking Gender Justice in Post Conflict Transitions: Towards a Transformative Women's Human Rights Approach." *International Journal of Law in Context* 3:2, 155–172.

Reuters. 2011. "Labelux Buys Jimmy Choo for £500 Million – Sources." Available at: http://uk.reuters.com/article/2011/05/23/uk-jimmychoo-idUKTRE74L1OZ 20110523 (accessed September 5, 2011).

Rise of the Planet of the Apes. 2011. Director, Rupert Wyatt. Twentieth Century Fox Film Corporation.

Ronell, Avital. 2004. "The Deviant Payback: The Aims of Valerie Solanos." In Valerie Solanos, *SCUM Manifesto with an Introduction by Avital Ronell*. London: Verso, pp. 1–31.

Sahgal, Gita. 2008. "Gender, Human Rights and International Law." *The Conversations Project, School of Law, University of Westminster*. Available at: www.kent.ac.uk/clgs/news-and-events/Conversations/documents/FinalVersion.pdf (accessed September 4, 2011).

Stern, Maria and Zalewski, Marysia. 2009. "Feminist Fatigue(s): Reflections on Feminism and Familiar Fables of Militarization." *The Review of International Studies* 35:3, 611–630.

Towns, Ann, 2010. *Women and States: Norms and Hierarchies in International Society*. Cambridge University Press.

The Twilight Saga Triple Limited Edition Steelbook. 2010. Directed by Catherine Hardwick and Chris Weitz. New York: E1 Entertainment.

UN (United Nations). 1995. *Fourth World Conference on Women: Action for Equality, Development and Peace*, September 4–15, 1995, Beijing, China. Available at: www.un.org/womenwatch/daw/beijing/tue5.htm (accessed September 4, 2011).

    2011. "Network of Men Leaders." Available at: www.un.org/en/women/endviolence/network.shtml (accessed September 4, 2011).

UNDP (United Nations Development Programme). 2011. *Millennium Development Goal 3: Promote Gender Equality and Empower Women*. Available at: www.un.org/millenniumgoals/pdf/MDG_FS_3_EN.pdf (accessed September 4, 2011).

UNESCO (United Nations Educational, Scientific and Cultural Organization). 2009. "7th Forum – Beijing 15 Years After." Available at: www.unesco.org/new/en/unesco/themes/gender-equality/features/unesco-forum-on-gender-equality/7th-forum/ (accessed September 4, 2011).

UN Security Council. 2000. Resolution 1325. UN Doc. S/Res/1325 (2000). Available at: www.un.org/events/res_1325e.pdf (accessed November 6, 2011).

    2008. Resolution 1820, UN Doc. S/Res/1820 (2008). Available at: www.state.gov/documents/organization/106577.pdf (accessed November 6, 2011).

    2009. Resolution 1889, UN Doc. S/Res/1889 (2009). Available at: www.unifem.org/gender_issues/women_war_peace/unscr_1889.php (accessed November 6, 2011).

    2010a. Resolution 1888, UN Doc. S/Res/1888 (2009). Reissued for technical reasons on June 22, 2010. Available at: www.unifem.org/gender_issues/women_war_peace/unscr_1888.php (accessed November 6, 2011).

    2010b. Resolution 1960, UN Doc. S/Res/1960 (2010). Available at: www.makeeverywomancount.org/images/stories/documents/UN_UNSecurityCouncilResolution1960_2010.pdf (accessed November 6, 2011).

UN Women (United Nations Entity for Gender Equality and the Empowerment of Women). 2011a. "UN Women in Timor Leste." Available at: www. unifem-eseasia.org/Timor-Leste/index.html (accessed November 6, 2011).

  2011b. "About Us." Available at: www.unwomen.org/about-us/ (accessed September 4, 2011).

Uwineza, Peace and Pearson, Elizabeth. 2009. *Sustaining Women's Gains in Rwanda: The Influence of Indigenous Culture and Post-Genocide Politics*, edited by Elizabeth Powley. Washington, DC: The Institute of Inclusive Security and Hunt Alternatives Fund.

Valasek, Kristin and Nelson, Kaitlin. 2006. *Securing Equality, Engendering Peace: A Guide to Policy and Planning on Women, Peace and Security (UN SCR 1325)*. United Nations International Research and Training Institute for the Advancement of Women (INSTRAW).

Verveer, Melanne. 2009. "Remarks at UNESCO Gender Equality Roundtable: 'Beijing: 15 Years After.'" Available at: http://unesco.usmission.gov/ verveer-remarks-3.html (accessed September 4, 2011).

Ward, Jeanne and Marsh, Mendy. 2006. "Sexual Violence Against Women and Girls in War and Its Aftermath: Realities, Responses, and Required Resources." Available at: www.unfpa.org/emergencies/symposium06/docs/finalbrus-selsbriefingpaper.pdf (accessed November 6, 2011).

WHO (World Health Organization). 2011. "What do we mean by 'Sex' and 'Gender'?" Available at: www.who.int/gender/whatisgender/en/ (accessed September 14, 2011).

Zalewski, Marysia. 2010. "'I Don't Even Know What Gender is'. A Discussion of the Relationship between Gender Mainstreaming and Feminist Theory." *Review of International Studies* 36:1, 3–27.

Žižek, Slavoj. 2009. *Violence: Six Sideways Reflections*. London: Profile Books.

20 | Are human rights possible after conflict? Diary of a survivor

EVELYN AMONY AND ERIN BAINES

The challenges of protecting human rights after violent conflict are daunting. Often the very state institutions charged with protecting and promoting rights are the same ones that perpetrated crimes during the war, or must accommodate disarmed groups within new governance structures to move toward peace. Critical institutions to protect rights – the judiciary, the police, schools, hospitals and social welfare institutions – may have been destroyed and the economy and national treasury necessary to reconstruct them are empty. The rule of law exists mainly as an idea, and must be reconstructed to build social trust. Communities, families, have endured and fractured under the strain of violence, and must learn to live together again after so much loss. How is a survivor of mass violations of human rights to rebuild her life in such circumstances? How does her situated knowledge, as one who navigates such a complex and fraught terrain, provide further insights into the possibilities of realizing human rights after conflict?

Northern Uganda is the site of a decades-old conflict (1987–2008) between the Ugandan government and the Lord's Resistance Army (LRA). During this war – which now continues in the Democratic Republic of Congo, South Sudan and the Central African Republic – the LRA abducted over 60,000 children and youths, forcing them to fight, act as porters and become wives to commanders (Blattman and Annan 2010). The Ugandan government pursued multiple military strategies to crush the rebels, one of which was to forcibly displace up to 90 percent of the population into poorly protected camps (Dolan 2009). Both the LRA and Ugandan People's Defence Forces (UPDF) are responsible for inflicting grave atrocities on the civilian population, including rape, murder, lootings, arson, torture, beatings, forced enslavement and humiliation (Amnesty International 1999; Branch 2011; Human Rights Watch 2003).

Some names and places have been changed to protect the identity of the first author's relatives. We are grateful for the support of a research team to assist in the translation, proofreading and editing of the chapter, including earlier support from researchers in Canada and Uganda, but also withhold their names for privacy. Thank you all.

It was in this war that Evelyn grew up, avoiding soldiers by hiding, running and sleeping in *alup* (in the bush, and away from home at night). When she was 11, her luck ran out. She was abducted by the LRA and spent multiple years as a soldier and porter before being forced to marry Joseph Kony, the general and commander of the LRA. She bore three children – Bakita, Winnie and Grace, the last on a battlefield before she was captured by the Ugandan military and returned home to Gulu to be reunited with her mother and father. Winnie disappeared during the confusion of one battle. Evelyn does not know her fate, but she adopted Jane, an orphan of the war, in her memory and in hopes that if Winnie is alive, someone else is taking care of her in the same way. Later, Evelyn would have a fourth child, Cynthia.

Evelyn raises her daughters amid a fraught political climate. In 2005, the International Criminal Court (ICC) indicted high ranking LRA rebels. Joseph Kony, still at large at the time of writing, is a person of interest to the prosecutor for his reported war crimes. The ICC indictment is controversial among victims of the war for some believe it frustrated efforts to settle the war through peace talks or disarm commanders like Kony while the indictment stands (Allen 2006).

In 2009, Evelyn accepted a digital tape recorder from Erin and agreed to record her day-to-day life as part of a larger research project to document women's stories of the war. These were then translated by research assistants in Uganda, resulting in a written script. The experiences of survivors like Evelyn, who endured years of displacement, denial of education, humiliation and degradation, forced marriage and pregnancy, forced conscription and forced labor, "provide unique insights into the connections between individual life trajectories and collective forces and institutions beyond the individual" (Maynes *et al.* 2008).[1] Evelyn's life experiences since she returned "home" expose structures of power and exclusion (Collins 1998; Haraway 1988), even in a setting of post-conflict, and the contested and complex ways she attempts to remake her world. Evelyn begins each entry with the declarative statement, "I am Evelyn Amony," reclaiming the name she had lost for more than a decade, announcing to us who she is and of her right to tell her story.

---

[1] For one of the most profound studies of how people cope with war and the crisis it entails in everyday life, see Sverker Finnström (2008).

November 1, 2009

I am Evelyn Amony. I was reunited with my family in 2005 [after 11 years in captivity]. We had just arrived from the military barracks to the rehabilitation center [for formerly abducted youth] when a woman entered the room and asked us, "Who here is called Evelyn?" I replied, "When I was a girl, I was called Evelyn but in the bush I went by the name Betty."[2] She told me that I had a visitor. I asked her who it was. She told me my family had come to see me. We walked across the compound to the Visitors Room. My father had come with my brothers but I did not recognize a single one of them. I greeted them and just stared. They were also staring at me.

My father then asked me if I knew him and I told him that I did not. He asked me where I was born, and I told him it was Nyero. My father asked, "What is your father's name?" I told him, "My father's name is David O." He asked me, "What was your father doing when you were abducted?" I told him my father was a veterinary doctor. He then said to me, "I am your father. The person you are talking about is me." I began to cry. My father also started crying. I was confused. I did not recognize him or my brothers at all. I did not know that this man was my father. We were both crying as he begged me to stop. My brothers were the ones who told him that if he stopped crying I would also stop. We cried for almost an hour. I sat at his feet. I looked at my father.

Not long after, my mother arrived at the rehabilitation center for children. When she came, she started crying. I held her and consoled her to be still, to keep quiet. When she finally stopped crying, I started crying. I do not know what came to my mind but I could not stop from crying. We stayed together for two days before they had to return to the village. My health grew worse but I told no one. I feared if I told my parents that I was sick, they would cry.

My strength kept on deteriorating. I could not stand. It was as if I had been shot. I could not even hold the baby and I just crawled on my hands and knees if I had to go to the bathroom. I ate nothing, I only took water. In the night, I do not know how but I fell from the bed. People found me and decided to call the nurse. She called a driver and at one in the morning they took me to the hospital. I do not recall what happened next but when I woke up my mother was there.

I still refused to eat.[3] I thought that I would be killed. My mother bought fresh fish and prepared it for me in the hospital. I just looked at the food and refused to eat it. Instead I took porridge brought to me by my friends from the rehabilitation centre. I spent three days in the hospital. Then my mother said to me, "My daughter, I am the one who gave birth to you. Don't you want to eat what I have prepared? Please try eating it." I looked at my mother and thought, "This woman is the one

---

[2] A common self-protection strategy in Northern Uganda, people would give the LRA false names and villages of origin to protect their real identities and that of their families in case of future retaliations should the person escape. See Erin Baines and Emily Paddon (2012).

[3] She was convinced she was going to be poisoned, a common belief amongst the LRA abductees.

who gave birth to me. She is my mother. I did not separate from her and go to the bush of my own free will. God, if you want my mother to be the one to kill me, then let her do so." I started eating my mother's food.

November 2, 2009

I am Evelyn Amony. I woke up this morning and I swept my compound and then I swept my house. I began to wash utensils … I did what women do in the morning. I did this up to eight in the morning. At 8:30, I took my daughter Grace [who was suffering from a double ear infection] to the hospital. I found the doctor and she injected my daughter. I came back home and I began to wash clothes with Bakita. We were arranging things in the home. The good thing is that my young-est daughter Cynthia is used to her eldest sister Bakita and she can stay well with Bakita. Grace is in pain this week and I have to carry her, so it is good that Cynthia can stay with Bakita. I washed clothes and took millet to the grinding mill but when I reached the mill I found it was on fire and everyone rushed to put it out. This was at around one. I didn't get to grind the millet until four. My children felt so hungry. Grace said, "Mum don't you know that the doctor said that I should eat a lot of food. You do not want to cook." It was not that I did not want to cook. There was no flour and there is no way I could buy it. Where will I get the money from? That is what happened that day. My children really starved. After cooking I went to the hospital for Grace to be injected again. I came back at eight. There were so many people in that clinic. These are the things that happened today.

November 6, 2009

I am Evelyn Amony. I had left work and was on my way back home when some-thing shocking happened. Just as I reached Gulu Hospital, there was a dead man who had drunk a lot of this type of alcohol sold in jerry cans; men like him just praise that drink. He was from Bobi. That man's wife was also there with her six children. I was thinking about her, how would she cope with those six kids now her husband was dead? Just as I watched that woman weeping, another vehicle pulled into the hospital ferrying close to 30 women and men from Palaro. Some of them couldn't see very well; their eyes were almost popping out. Some could still talk, but some were no longer able to talk. Immediately, nine of them died there and then. When I saw those dead bodies, I went crazy. It reminded me of all the past things I saw happen in the bush. The only difference or good thing about it is that you don't see blood oozing out of someone's body. In a death by gunshot, someone bleeds to death, but for this one, death by alcohol poisoning, there was no blood. Some people's eyes had popped out of their head and it was so scary to see them.

I kept thinking about this as I walked home. The remainder of the day was so weird for me. I called my Dad as I was still walking home. I told him, "Dad, there is some kind of alcohol here in Gulu which is killing people. If you keep on drinking alcohol, just know that you will be running away from the responsibility of bringing up my children. You should have been the one to raise me and take care of me as a child, but I was abducted. In my place, you should care for my children." My Dad asked me, "Evelyn, why do you think that I am drinking alcohol? I don't drink!" I told him, "Only you know the truth if you are drinking or not. I can only remind you of your responsibilities." I warned him of what I had just seen, that it wasn't good to drink these days because the alcohol has been poisoned; very many people are dying.

The war disturbed people in Northern Uganda so seriously and later alcohol started killing so many people. I really don't know if that was what God planned for Northern Uganda to go through, and I wonder if the other countries also experience things like we do here. The pain of dying from these alcoholic drinks is even more painful than death in the war. You could see someone looking very well today but the next day you will hear that the person has died. It first started killing some women in Cereleno; the first woman to die was about 25 years old. After that, Yusuf's wife died and several others died. It started by killing so many women in the beginning and men used to make fun about it, saying that women have weak blood, their blood is afraid of alcohol, not knowing that it was the alcohol doing all that. So this is what was happening in Northern Uganda; alcohol is killing so many people just like the war killed very many too.

On one hand, the war led to loss of many lives and on the other hand, alcohol killed many. On the other hand, as people are returning home, land issues are bringing problems too. So I really don't know; it may be that God is just tired of the people of Northern Uganda. Talk about poverty, people are so poor up here in the north, this is how I see all these things happening here in the north. But I do believe that there is nothing that defeats God. I know that God is able (*Rubanga twero*) and he is in charge of everything.

November 20, 2009

I am Evelyn Amony. Today my daughter graduated to Primary One. This is an important day. Grace was proud to wear the gown, as she had accomplished her studies successfully. The only setback was that parents were showering their children with gifts and taking their pictures but as I had not saved for this occasion I could not do much. I bought biscuits and wrapped them very well, but when my daughter opened them, she exclaimed, "Mum, I thought you had bought me a dress!" I told her not to fancy other people's things but to be content with what she has or God would punish her. I told her the Ten Commandments caution you against admiring what isn't your own. I thought about the importance of education. I got lost in my thoughts wishing I had studied. There are so many times when I want to interact with someone directly but have to use an interpreter. Today I also had to go to Lacor Hospital to attend to two relatives: my brother's child, who is in a very critical situation, has been put on oxygen.[4]

---

[4] The burden of patient-care in hospital falls on the relatives of the patient. Evelyn must help bring food.

January 15, 2010

I am Evelyn Amony. In the morning, after praying, I walked to work. I cannot afford a *boda* [motorbike taxi], so I walk each day. I felt weak as I am fasting[5] and I didn't have breast milk to feed Cynthia. As I traveled home, I came across a man I knew from Primary School named Saki. We both looked at each other for a bit and then he said to me, "Evelyn, is it you?" I said, "I am she." He came and hugged me, saying, "I haven't seen you for over 20 years but I heard you came back." He insisted I sit down and we talked for a long time. I never thought I would see Saki again. He was a very good child and I liked him so much. We were happy to see each other. He reminded me of those days when we were growing up and of the names of all the different children we went to school with. He said he cried every time he saw my mother and that I resembled her and one of my sisters. He worried about what I was going through in the bush, saying he would imagine me walking in the hot sun and carrying heavy loads in the rain. I realized as he spoke that after I was abducted, my friends missed me. He asked me so many questions! Like how I lived in the bush and what that long journey by foot to Sudan was like. I laughed at some of his questions. He said, "I heard that you were Kony's wife, is it true?" I told him, "What you heard is what happened." He asked, "Evelyn, how were you able to stay with him?" I answered, "Whether you wanted to stay with him or not, you had to, I had no ability to refuse." I began to realize that there are people not related to me that care more about me than my very own brothers and sisters ...

February 2, 2010

I am Evelyn Amony. When I woke, I felt ill, as if I had flu, so I did not do the household chores the way I usually do. I walked to [my daughter's] School and joined a very long queue to meet the head teacher to talk about taking the children back to school. He said that I should return on Monday as he had not yet received the list of names of children that the NGO Sponsor Uganda will pay school fees for. So I went and picked up Jane's report card and as I was doing so, I ran into "Janet" [a former co-wife]. We talked for some time, discussing our children. Jane was thirty-seventh in her class but she passed to go to Primary Two. I then left and began walking to the office, but before long I ran into another woman who I stayed with in the bush called "Nancy."

She said, "Evelyn, I have been looking for you. I heard that you were sewing in [an international Evangelical NGO]. If possible, could you take me there to sew? Life is so hard because I am alone with the children and have no job." I told her, "I do not have the capacity to give you a job, and anyway I do not know what to tell you, because to find work you need to write application forms. What will those of us do who cannot write? When you go to look for a job they ask your education level, even if the job is mopping the floor. They might want someone who studied Senior Four onwards. It is hard for us to get jobs."

---

[5] For religious purposes.

After work, I borrowed money and left to buy school supplies for the children. I bought two books for Grace, three for Bakita, a dozen pencils and a pen. I then queued up in a very long line to buy paraffin. After this, I ran into "Ruby" – a staff member of a local aid organization. He said, "I have been looking for you. I went to your home but didn't find you. We want you to give you a job making tea for us and cleaning offices. You can live there with your children." I told him, "I already have a job." I then asked him about the Italian we had met together in Juba who promised she would build me a house when we came back from the peace talks. I told Ruby that I had identified a good piece of land and was ready to build, although it was not true. He said, "There is no problem. I will call the Italian woman and find out if the offer is still there or not." They always promise the same thing.

At home, Cynthia had fallen and hit her head. It was swollen and I had to carry her to soothe her until she finally fell asleep. While she slept, I sat outside the house with my sister, who had been discharged from the hospital. We sat together for some time. When the electricity came back on, we decided to shave the children's hair. Grace told us many stories and we laughed.

February 6, 2010

I am Evelyn Amony. I went to the salon very early in the morning to plait my hair. When I arrived, I began to organize the braids. The lady plaited my hair from morning up to half past two o'clock. I was worried because I knew today was the day for *cup* [a rotating fund], and when you arrive late you have to pay a fine. I went straight to the meeting where we give our *cup*. When I went, I began to talk to my *cup* group [composed of others who returned from the LRA] on how we can work to make our project grow. We waited for those who were late. When they came, I talked to them. I told them that we had to have one spirit so that our group may grow and prosper. I distributed a book to each and every member to keep a record of how much they had given.

I then went to Kabedopong to meet with another group [of formerly abducted women] we wanted to give advice to. On the way back I decided to branch and go to the rehabilitation centre as I heard that there were some mothers who had just escaped from the Congo and were back at the reception centre. We spoke [to them] for a long time about the conditions they went through. I asked them how my friends were and how *ladit* [Kony] was. They told me it was not easy in the Congo. That it was not the way it used to be in Sudan. "These days you have to struggle a lot." They said the only good thing is that there is always something to eat in the forest, like avocados, pawpaw and things like that. They just ate raw food like that. They told me this was better than when they were in Darfur because that place was very dry, without any water to drink and it was so dirty.

I was also able to see one of Kony's new children who had returned with them. The soldiers had found the child and brought her to the rehabilitation centre without the mother. She was a Teso girl from the Katakwi district. She was one of the children who was abducted when the soldiers went to Katakwi. I remember thinking that girl could not give birth [she was so young], but the baby was here and very healthy. Still, I think the girl must have lost her life.

After some time I walked back home. As I reached home I found my *cup* group was still continuing with the meeting so I rejoined them until people began to disperse to go to home. You know, I did not eat the whole day. I thought I would eat when I came home but we had a visitor and I gave what little food we had to the visitor. So I took tea and slept. This is what happened today. Thank you. I wish you luck and best wishes.

April 15, 2010

I am Evelyn Amony. As I was walking to office, the heel of my shoe broke. I walked slowly back home as it was so difficult to walk. I went inside and removed those shoes, picked another pair, cleaned them, put the spoilt ones inside the house and started walking to the office again. I walked for a bit and as I was crossing the road, I saw Grace. I was so pissed off when she told me that they had chased her from school [sent her home]. So I decided to walk her back to school. I was so angry. I went to the school and asked them why they chased my little girl out of school. I spoke to the sister of the school and said, "I want to know immediately, Sister. The way I see it is that you always chase her because of her ears, but Sister let me tell you that I wasn't the one who wanted Grace's ears to flow with pus like this (*ka mol kiti eni*); you will forgive me for her sick ears, but this is a result of the war. She does not hear well. What would you do if someone had stolen her on her way home? What would you tell me then sister?"

Tears started rolling down my cheeks and I later realized that all I said wasn't good. I told her that, "Sister, from today on, you should know that Grace's sick ear is not due to my carelessness or my wish, it was the result of the war."[6] Then the sister said that, "It is not like that, I know you have endured such problems, don't think that we enjoy chasing your daughter from school; when we chase her it is because she doesn't wear the right uniform." I wondered what uniform she meant. Indeed there was a time her sportswear was stolen and so she had to wear her school dress instead, but sincerely I had enough. I told the nun so much and said, "Today, I had to tell you I was not happy as you keep chasing my child away. If all I have said has broken your heart, forgive me."

I left immediately to walk to the office. When I arrived, "Lucy" [a forced wife to Kony] had come to visit and was waiting to speak to me. I was still so angry and had to calm down first. I went inside for a while then I returned and went out to the toilet. When I was just leaving the toilet, I met the *Mzee* [an elder man in office], who started yelling at me, "You people, you use this toilet but you don't clean it, you just leave it dirty." He talked to me as though I was a little child. I kept quiet and I waited for him to first finish all that he was saying. Grace responded to the *Mzee*.

[6] Grace was born during a battle, and Evelyn believes she has had chronic ear infections because of the loud noise of the bombs sounding at the time of her birth.

She said that, "You are not a respectful elder and you don't deserve respect." I told the *Mzee*, "Don't think that I am that stupid the way you think." Then he started saying, "My daughter, I did not complain for no reason, but my shoes are dirty, how?" I said, "From today onwards, if you see me as your daughter, just forget about it. I don't like elders who are not respectful. I also have my *Mzee* that is my father who is about your age but he is not as stupid as you." Then the *Mzee* said, "My daughter, I did not think the argument should go to this level."

Today was just a bad day for me right from the time I left home in the morning when my shoe broke. I just went back to the office to meet with Lucy and conversed about the past. I started remembering some of the things that happened in the past and that calmed my heart a bit and I went back inside as they were showing us how to photocopy. They showed us how to photocopy and soon it was time for lunch.

After lunch, I returned to Grace's school at 3:00 p.m. at the request of the sister. So I went and sat there in front of the office for a long time. The sister wasn't even there. I sat there for a long time, until 5:00 p.m., without seeing anyone so I just left and started walking back home. As I was walking back, I found "Nighty" [a forced wife to Kony] and we walked together. We reached the market and I discovered that the prices of vegetables had risen. I bought *boo* and continued walking to go home as it started to rain. I plucked the leaves of the *boo* and Bakita came and said that she wanted to be the one to cook it.

Michael [Evelyn's brother] called me to say that he wanted to borrow some money. I arrived at his home just as his wife's brothers were leaving together with his wife. They had refused to leave their sister with Michael [he was unable to give them money for brides wealth]. Michael then gave me some of the mangoes that his wife had brought. He told me that, this month, they won't pay them salary as when they are on holidays they will not work. So he wanted to borrow some money. I gave him 10,000 shillings and told him that was all I had. You know I did have more money with me, 100,000 shillings, but when I give him the money, he never returns it. I have to mind about the future of my children. The money just keeps quiet there where I have hidden it. I thought to myself, I am home alone struggling and now my brother wants me to help pay for him to get married.

His wife had cooked but hadn't even served him food. I told him that I wouldn't eat but suggested he let me go and warm his food, and I went and did so. He insisted I eat a bite but I told him, I won't eat. Still he insisted that I have a taste, so I ate a piece of meat and some soup and then left to go home. It was dark and since it had rained, I couldn't see the road properly and I kept falling along the way as it was very slippery. When I arrived home, Bakita had finished preparing the food.

I asked them where Cynthia was and they told me she was with "Mary" [a forced wife to Kony]. I went there and found her asleep. I chatted a bit with Mary and she told me how her son was also chased from school due to lack of school fees. I told her that I was incapable of assisting her. It was getting late so I told her I needed to get back home and sleep. I went and served food and ate. Bakita had cooked it very nicely.

Grace is on so much medication it is as though she is HIV positive, there are so many drugs and they are so big. She even asked me, "Mum, am I an HIV patient?" I asked her why she thought that, and she said that, "Our teacher said I was." I just kept quiet.

April 28, 2010

I am Evelyn Amony. This morning, Cynthia was very sick; she vomited a lot so I took her to the hospital. They hurried to assist her. What was making her so weak was vomiting, diarrhea and a very high fever. She was given an injection then they said that we had to spend the night there in order for her to get three more injections. We did not stay. I took her home and cooled her body with a damp cloth. Cynthia slept well through the night, but in the morning, she immediately started vomiting and passing loose stool again. I thought it was just flu but all along it was real sickness [malaria].

When we reached the local medical clinic there were many people waiting in a long line to be treated. When we returned home, I tried to cool the baby's body with a wet cloth but there was no change. It was as though we hadn't been to the hospital at all. My cousin bought some Painex and Cynthia's body started cooling slowly. Life was so hard because her fever was really high.

Finally, I went back to the hospital. One of the sisters came to see the child and started to suggest that maybe I didn't feed the baby properly. You know, those sisters don't have children and they just don't understand these things. Sometimes they think that the mother's weakness causes the child to be sick. She went and brought bananas and cakes for Cynthia, thinking she would eat them, but the baby just refused. She just looked at the food and didn't say a word. I told the sister, "I feed this child well, it's just today that she is sick." She took our photo with Cynthia and said that she would go to Paidha [an NGO, to try to get assistance].

May 7, 2010

I am Evelyn Amony. Today I went to the hospital to see my sister Harriet, who was admitted for treatment. When I saw her I was shocked; she had lost so much weight she no longer looked like a human being. She saw me and said, "My sister, now that you have come, I will survive." Harriet had waited too long to start taking the anti-retroviral drug medication; she refused for so long and now the sickness has affected her mind. It was so painful to see her; she was so thin. Tears rolled down my cheeks. I worried and thought how my sister had not grown up in the bush like me, but grown in town where she got AIDS (*two jonyo*). She should have been the one to teach us from the bush how to exercise good morals and prevent getting the disease. Instead I was the one to tell her to take the medication and to use it regularly the way the doctors had instructed. She told me that she got that disease long ago. Her husband was a soldier who had the disease, but she found it difficult to tell anyone at home to avoid people treating her as something terrible. So I feel that sometimes in this world it is very bad to be so hard hearted and at the same time so bad to be soft hearted. Then she asked me to give her some money to buy vitamins. "My sister, if only I had something to eat I would not be so sick. I have nothing to eat and I vomit." I told her not to mind and gave her the little money I had. I felt heartbroken.[7] As I left she told me not to forget her: "My sister, please remember me." I told her I would. Then I started walking back home. I walked slowly and the rain drizzled on the way.

May 16, 2010

I am Evelyn Amony. In the morning, I woke up and started washing clothes but Cynthia was sick and she kept crying. As I tried to wash the clothes, she vomited and had diarrhea seriously. Each time I tried to give her medicine, she would vomit up the drugs. Each time I breastfed, she would vomit again. It took me a long time to finish the laundry.

"Mary" came by and said we should go register to vote. I put Cynthia on my back and we walked to Gulu Public School where they took our photo and fingerprints for the voter card. You were expected to put all ten fingers on a certain thing and it would be scanned into a machine. I grew annoyed as the man registering us asked me to spell my name. I was pissed off. I told him that if he was literate, he should know how write and yet here he was asking for me to spell my name. He asked me three times, "How do you write the name Evelyn?" I wondered what was wrong with this man? Didn't he know that I didn't know how to write? That I never studied at school? Why did he ask me such questions?

I decided to let the issue go, but then the very same man asked me questions like, "Are you married? What is your husband's name?" There were many people listening who knew me. One boy whom I stayed with in the bush whispered that they were just looking for the name. I worried he would say Kony's name and gave him a bad look. I did not like what was happening, nor did I want anyone to say Kony's name: it was as if he was accusing me. So I just made up a name for my husband: Otukene Justine. When Mary finished registering we left. [...]

May 21, 2010

I am Evelyn Amony [...] When I was on my way home from work, I met some guy called Komakech who was with me during those days in the bush. He told me that he sees me suffering a lot all the time, walking about, and he sympathizes with me. He proposed that I live with him. He is a *boda* man [motorcycle taxi driver]. Then I asked him, "What kind of living do you mean?" He said, "Living in a house as husband and wife." I replied, "I am looking for a way to forget the bush, to forget my suffering, so let me first concentrate on what I am doing." Then he said that he is going to struggle hard so that no matter what, I become his wife. I told Komakech that I am living with no man and I love it like that. He just shut up. He is the guy who came to me one time, took my phone to be repaired, but never

---

[7] Harriet died a year later of AIDS-related complications. Evelyn assumed responsibility of raising her niece until she was relocated with the father's relatives; she continues to support the child by paying school fees and liaising with her teachers.

came back. He later told me that he feels very hurt when people call me and that was why he took the phone and never wanted to return it. He thinks that people keep disturbing me with those phone calls. Then I told him that he was just being big-headed, "Where did you get the right to stop me from talking on phone?" I demanded. "If you know that you are the one who bought me the phone, you would have the right to do that, but if you know that you are not the one who bought me that phone, why did you do that? Does it mean that if someone doesn't want you, you should take their things? Besides, I have three children and what else do you still want from me?" These are the things that I started telling him and I just continued walking to the office …

The hard questions

This chapter is a selection of excerpts from Evelyn's diary that poignantly illustrate the hard questions that confront the field of human rights in a post-conflict environment. Survivors in Northern Uganda live in settings of extreme structural violence. Evelyn's diaries highlight the challenges of living in poverty and inadequate access to state institutions, such as medical care, education and social welfare. Both Evelyn's mother and sister succumbed to HIV-related illnesses, and her daughter's chronic illness is considered by her teachers to resemble that of a disease that has a high prevalence in the Acholi sub-region. She and her daughters are hungry; "I did not eat the whole day," Evelyn tells us, and this is further complicated by illnesses like flu and malaria. The burden of an extended family falls on her shoulders; she is the eldest of eight children, and her father is a man who has lost access to his land and livelihood because of the war. Her mother is now dead. She must pay for the bride wealth of her brother to keep his family together. Evelyn continues to suffer humiliation and lack of dignity in multiple ways: she is unable to give her daughter her desired gift on graduation; her other daughter is chased from school for being sick; a co-worker accuses her of not knowing how to keep clean and when she goes to register to vote; she does not know what name to give for the father of her children. Humiliation extends to the NGOs she turns to in the absence of state protection, where "They always promise the same thing" but do not deliver on their promises. At the same time, Evelyn is the defender of her own rights to be respected as a human being: she invents a name for her children's father, she tells the NGO she already has a job and is not desperate for the one they offer, and she tells Komakech she does not need to marry him to take care of her and her children; she can do it herself. Her stories of suffering illuminate the ways she also "encounters, resists and deals with violence" to realize her right to be an autonomous person (Riaño-Alcalá 2006).

Evelyn faces reminders of the war and its impact on society everywhere; she understands the abuse of alcohol is related to the war and wonders if God is tired of them because so many have died. Evelyn fears stigma of those around her if they were to discover that her children are of one of the men responsible for so much suffering. She finds a new community and sense of belonging with others likewise excluded – her co-wives from those days in the bush. Yet in moments with those like Saki, she is reminded that not everyone hates her, that indeed she is loved and, in that, she finds hope. A large part of that hope is in her daughters and their future education, for which she struggles.

These everyday moments of moving on with life reveal the intersecting social, economic and political challenges facing the most vulnerable victims of war and the difficulty of realizing human rights after violent conflict. Evelyn's diaries illustrate a section of the enormous the gap between legal conventions, rules, regulations and mechanisms and the lived realities of the majority of war affected persons. If human rights are to be realized after violent conflict, practitioners must consider the grounded knowledge of people like Evelyn, in addition to pursuit of macro-approaches to democracy, justice and development. The indictment and possible prosecution of those most responsible for the war, including Kony, will never replace Evelyn's sense of belonging, provide a father for her children, find her missing daughter or bestow a sense of justice. Evelyn's day-to-day struggle to remake her world brings her closer to a sense of dignity and belonging, and is a profound reminder of the limits and limitlessness of what is possible after so much loss. It is precisely the memories, the losses and the struggles that bind her to a bitter past, that also restore hope, that drive Evelyn to continue to care for those she loves and that love her and to work to sever those ties that frustrate her life, that give local meaning to human rights. In this sense, the hard questions are the ones that consider how to protect human rights based on the knowledge, work and valuation of Evelyn's lived reality. In doing so, the realization of human rights are not only possible after conflict; they are being actively enacted by those who refuse to believe that anything less is acceptable.

References

Allen, Tim. 2006. *Trial Justice: The International Criminal Court and the Lord's Resistance Army*. London: Zed Books.

Amnesty International. 1999. *Breaking the Circle: Protecting Human Rights in the Northern War Zone*. New York.

Baines, Erin and Paddon, Emily. 2012. "This is How We Survived: Civilian Agency and Humanitarian Protection." *Security Dialogue* 43:4, 231–247.

Blattman, Christopher and Annan, Jeannie. 2010. "On the Nature and Causes of LRA Abduction: What the Abductees Say." In Tim Allen and Koen Vlassenroot, eds., *The Lord's Resistance Army: Myth and Reality*. London: Zed Press, pp. 132–155.

Branch, Adam. 2011. *Displacing Human Rights: War and Intervention in Northern Uganda*. Oxford University Press.

Collins, Patricia Hill. 1998. "The Social Construction of Black Feminist Thought." *Signs* 14:4, 745–773.

Dolan, Chris. 2009. *Social Torture: The Case of Northern Uganda, 1986–2006*. New York: Berghahn Books.

Finnström, Sverker. 2008. *Living with Bad Surroundings: War, History and Everyday Moments in Northern Uganda*. Durham, NC: Duke University Press.

Haraway, Donna. 1988. "Situated Knowledges: The Science Question in Feminism and the Privilege of Partial Perspective." *Feminist Studies* 14:3, 575–599.

Human Rights Watch. 2003. *Stolen Children: Abduction and Recruitment in Northern Uganda*. New York: Human Rights Watch.

Maynes, Mary Jo, Pierce, Jennifer L. and Laslett, Barbara. 2008. *Telling Stories: The Use of Personal Narratives in the Social Sciences and History*. Ithaca: Cornell University Press.

Riaño-Alcalá, Pilar. 2006. *Dwellers of Memory: Youth and Violence in Medellin, Colombia*. New Brunswick: Transaction Publishers.

PART VII

Are human rights progressive?

21 | Moral progress and human rights

ALLEN BUCHANAN

This chapter makes the case that the concept of human rights on which the modern international human rights enterprise is grounded is morally progressive. I first clarify the idea of moral progress. Next, I focus on what I take to be some of the most important improvements in thinking about justice and explain how they are connected to one another. Then, I show that the modern conception of human rights encompasses all of these improvements.

My account of moral-conceptual progress will be neutral on the crucial question of causal relations between changes in normative ideas and interests or other so-called "material" factors. What I will say is compatible with both the view that the moral-conceptual changes I describe played a major causal role in progressive institutional change (such as the abolition of slavery) *and* with the view that they were largely post-hoc responses to institutional change caused by realignments of interests, as well as with a range of more nuanced alternative views that allow complex reciprocal causality between normative beliefs and interests. It will also be compatible with a sensible rejection of the facile distinction between normative beliefs and interests on the basis of which the question of causality is usually framed.

My reflections on moral progress proceed from a liberal cosmopolitan point of view. The core idea of liberal cosmopolitanism, as I understand it, is that all people are of equal fundamental moral worth and that both domestic and global political institutions should reflect that equality. Liberal cosmopolitanism takes a number of forms. The kind of liberal cosmopolitanism I endorse is both moderate and pluralistic: it is compatible with the view that obligations among fellow citizens or co-nationals are more robust than those toward humankind generally and with the recognition that a proper acknowledgment of the fundamental moral equality of persons requires an appreciation of the diversity of human good. I do not attempt a bootstrapping argument for such a liberal cosmopolitan view here. For the most part I will assume, not argue, that the moral-conceptual changes regarding justice that I describe are improvements. Nevertheless, I believe

I thank Karen Knop and Emmanuel Adler for their comments on a draft of this chapter.

that once the nature of these changes is appreciated, the case for judging them to be progressive will be strong.

Before I proceed, a qualification is in order: the term "conceptual change" is misleading if it is taken to convey only cognitive change. The changes I describe include changes in moral beliefs but also more than that: they constitute remarkable alterations in our moral sentiments, in our commitments, and in how we perceive ourselves and one another. That is why, if they are moral improvements, they are moral improvements in us. Thus the label "moral-conceptual changes" seems doubly apt: the changes I will describe are changes in our moral concepts but also moral changes in us that depend on and are partly constituted by changes in our moral concepts.

Types of moral-conceptual progress

Better compliance versus better principles

One may distinguish, first of all, between improvement in compliance with what are assumed to be valid moral principles and improvement in the principles or rules themselves. Improvements of the latter type are not hard to find. For example, the very broad condemnation of torture is a very recent phenomenon. Throughout history torture, like slavery, was a widely accepted practice, thought to be a proper form of punishment and a permissible mode of revenge. Torture is now prohibited by international law and in most domestic legal systems. Government officials around the world overwhelmingly publicly disavow torture. When they use it they deny that they are doing so (sometimes by revising widely accepted understandings of what counts as torture). Similarly, aggressive war is now widely condemned, as is gratuitous infliction of pain on animals. (Relishing the public torture of cats is no longer thought to be an acceptable family pastime, as it was, for example, in eighteenth-century France.)

Changing conceptions of primary moral status

The contrast between improved compliance with moral principles and improved moral principles, though valuable, takes us only so far. It fails to capture the significance of some of the most striking instances of moral progress. This is especially true of improvements in our assumptions about who has primary moral status and why, and in our understanding of the implications of a being having basic moral status.

It is commonplace to observe that one important kind of moral progress is the practical recognition that some individuals have been arbitrarily denied what might be called primary moral status. The abolition of slavery is the most obvious example.[1] The recognition of gender equality is another. Widespread (though far from universal) acknowledgment that all persons, not just men or white people, have an equal primary moral status is a recent phenomenon and surely an important instance of moral progress.

The sum total of beings who have primary moral status might be called the primary moral community. There are different conceptions of what makes someone a member of the primary moral community and of what the implications of being a member of it are. My focus is on conceptions of primary moral status that are intimately connected with the idea of justice in two ways. First, there is the idea that *part* of what is involved in having primary moral status is being a subject of justice, that is, being the kind of being that can be treated justly or unjustly. Second, there is the idea that an especially serious form of injustice is to treat beings that have primary moral status as if they lacked it.

One major type of moral progress occurs when conceptions of who is included in the primary moral community undergo a significant and morally defensible expansion, as with the acknowledgment that African slaves are fully human. The beginning of a second, equally profound shift in conceptions of moral status may now be underway. Perhaps a greater percentage of the human population than ever before acknowledges that at least some non-human animals have moral status, though this still seems to be a minority view worldwide. It seems likely that if such a shift occurs on a large scale it will be unlike the recognition that all persons have the same primary moral status in one significant respect: the moral status accorded to non-human animals (or some of them) will be of an inferior sort. To the extent that this new moral status will be understood in terms of rights, non-human animals will be acknowledged to have a truncated set of rights, appropriate for their limited capacities.

The recognition that all persons have primary moral status is a reformist, rather than a revolutionary moral-conceptual change, because it consists of the removal of arbitrary restrictions on the class of beings thought to have primary moral status.[2] It is, nevertheless, a significant change in our

---

[1] The abolitionist movement in Britain began around 1787; by 1838 – in less than one lifetime – it had attained its primary goal, the abolition of slavery in the British Empire.

[2] J.B. Schneewind distinguishes between revolutionary and reformist changes in moral concepts. He cites Benthamism as a revolutionary change, on the grounds that it reconceived of the point of morality (Schneewind 1996).

conception of *the domain of justice*, in this sense: it expands our conception of the universe of beings to whom basic justice is owed. Later, I will distinguish another way in which our conception of the domain of justice can change, namely, through an expansion of our conception of the *territory* of justice, by which I mean roughly the subject matter of assessments of justice, the aspects of our world that can be judged to be just or unjust.

The concept of equal moral status by itself need not implicate rights. But as a matter of fact, some of the most significant expansions in conceptions of membership in the primary moral community have been conceived as expansions of the class of basic moral right-holders. I now want to argue that the membership expansions I have noted presuppose a much more profound moral-conceptual change: the adoption of what I call a *subject-centered*, or non-strategic conception of justice (Buchanan 1990). In my judgment, it is this moral-conceptual change that has a strong claim to being the most revolutionary kind of moral-conceptual progress that has yet been achieved.

The emergence of the subject-centered conception of justice

Before we can achieve an *expanded* conception of who has primary moral status, we must first have a conception of primary moral status. My contention is that the conception of primary moral status that has been extended to include persons previously excluded, such as African slaves, presupposes the rejection of Justice as Instrumental Reciprocity in favor of Subject-Centered Justice (Buchanan 1996a).

Justice as Instrumental Reciprocity is a view about what makes an individual a subject of justice, someone to whom justice is owed. At least in the liberal tradition broadly conceived, being owed justice includes having general moral rights. According to Justice as Instrumental Reciprocity, whether one is a subject of justice depends upon whether one has either or both of two *strategic properties*: the ability to make a net contribution to the good of others (in a given cooperative framework) and the ability to harm others.

Several prominent ancient ethical theorists either endorse or mention the negative version of Justice as Instrumental Reciprocity – the view that what makes a being a subject of justice is the ability to harm. For example, Epicurus says that non-human animals are not subjects of justice because they are weaker than us and hence we have no need to refrain from harming them in exchange for their not harming us (Epicurus [3rd century AD] 1987). Glaucon, in *The Republic*, endorses a similar view:

People say that injustice is by nature good to inflict but evil to suffer. Men taste both sides of it and learn that the evil of suffering it exceeds the good of inflicting it. Thus unable to flee the one and take the other therefore decide it pays to make a pact neither to commit nor to suffer injustice. (Plato [360 bce] 1921, 32: Bk II, sec. 359)

For both Epicurus and Glaucon the recognition of others as subjects of justice is the result of a strategic bargain among those of roughly equal power: we refrain from harming others on condition that they will not harm us. Only those with the capacity to harm are even eligible to be subjects of justice. Similarly, Hume speculates that creatures otherwise like us, but powerless to harm us, could at most hope to be treated charitably, but could not expect to be treated justly (Hume 1975 [1739], 190–191). Finally, Hobbes holds that what we call principles of justice are simply articles of peace adopted by rationally self-interested individuals to escape a situation in which each is subject to being harmed by the other (Hobbes 1958 [1660], 104–105). He makes it clear that this is a view according to which being a subject of justice is a matter of *power*: it is the rough equality of power among humans, in the sense of their ability to harm one another, that makes them subjects of justice. The most rigorous and sophisticated proponent of Justice as Instrumental Reciprocity in the positive version is David Gauthier. According to Gauthier, it is only to those capable of providing a net benefit to us that we owe obligations of justice (Gauthier 1986, 113–156).

What all versions of Justice as Instrumental Reciprocity have in common is this: they make one's having moral status depend upon whether one possesses the strategic properties of being able to benefit or harm. The explanation of the focus on strategic properties is simple: the recognition of moral status is seen to be the outcome of a rational bargain among self-interested individuals who are roughly equal in power.[3]

A conception of primary moral status that encompasses all people presupposes the rejection of Justice as Instrumental Reciprocity. This conception grounds the possession of moral status in our capacity for practical rationality or our common "humanity" or "dignity," not in our ability to harm or benefit others. Instead of grounding the status of being a subject of

---

[3] Justice as Instrumental Reciprocity, as defined above, is a thesis about the relationship between reciprocity as mutual liability to the exercise of power and being a right-holder, namely, that the former is necessary for the latter. Consequently, the rejection of Justice as Instrumental Reciprocity does not imply that reciprocity plays no important role in justice; on the contrary, it is compatible with the view that much of the domain of justice concerns relationships of reciprocity.

justice in power, this conception of justice explicitly denies the relevance of power to that status.

For those who have already embraced the subject-centered conception of justice it may be difficult to see Justice as Instrumental Reciprocity as a conception of *justice* at all, simply because it is central to our concept of justice that justice is contrasted with sheer power, not grounded in it. We may thus be prone to think that Justice as Instrumental Reciprocity is not a conception of justice in the normative sense, but rather a debunking explanation of justice discourse, predicated on the assumption that there is no such thing as justice – that the normative idea of it is inapplicable, given the reality of human life. This may be an instance where a conceptual change is so profound that it cannot even be understood, by those who embrace it, as a mere alteration in a pre-existing concept.

The emergence of a fully subject-centered conception of justice

The rejection of Justice as Instrumental Reciprocity, at least as it occurred in the abolitionist movement, was characterized by a profound ambiguity. Especially in the earlier phases of the struggle, most who advocated abolition did so on religious grounds. If we take them at their word, they were motivated to undertake the seemingly impossible task of ending the institution of chattel slavery because they thought it their duty as Christians. Similarly, many people today who are committed to the modern human rights enterprise view this as an important expression of their religious faith.

If the only reason that slaves ought to be freed was that they, too, are children of God, created in his image, then there would be a sense in which their right to freedom was *not* subject-centered: instead of being grounded in (non-strategic) properties of those who are said to have rights, for example, in their capacity for rational agency, it would be grounded, ultimately, in their relationship to something outside of themselves, namely, God.

Yet the appeal to the moral significance of the capacity for rational agency in effect rendered otiose the idea of our worth depending upon our relationship to God. Even if our common capacity for rational agency is a gift from God, the point is that if we have this capacity, then we have basic moral rights. In other words, it is the moral implications of having the capacity for rational agency that seems to count, not the origins of the capacity. The shift to what might be called a *fully* subject-centered conception of justice – the idea that primary moral status extends to all persons by virtue of something inherent in them, not on their power relative to others *or* their relationship to a higher being – is truly momentous. It may be difficult to imagine a more revolutionary moral-conceptual change.

The shift to a fully subject-centered conception of justice, understood as including the idea that moral status is a matter of having rights on one's own account, not derivatively upon one's power in relation to others or one's relation to God, is no longer limited, for some people, to a change in our conception of the moral status of human beings. A distinctive feature of contemporary animal rights discourse is that it is premised on the assumption that it is the way that animals are in themselves, independently of their usefulness to us or God's willing that we be compassionate toward them, that entitles them to be treated in certain ways.

The idea of disabilities rights as an expansion of the territory of justice

Along with the abolition of slavery, the acknowledgment of the equality of women, the condemnation of torture, and the realization that non-human animals have a moral status grounded in what they are like, the recognition of disabilities rights has a strong claim to be included in the list of accomplishments that count as moral progress. I now want to suggest that the idea of disabilities rights also can be understood as an implication of the shift to a subject-centered conception of justice. I also want to show that seeing the idea of disabilities rights in this way makes it clear how revolutionary that idea is. More specifically, I shall argue that the idea of disabilities rights, properly understood, is a clear rejection of a common understanding of what justice is about, an important expansion of the *territory* of justice, based on a revolutionary change in how we think about what makes one a subject of justice. I will then suggest that an important strand of contemporary thought about equal rights for women exemplifies the same revolutionary change.[4]

The idea that we have duties to those with disabilities is not new. The idea that we owe them duties of justice that are *both grounded in their primary moral status as persons and at the same time specific to their condition*, is. I noted earlier that the change in how we think about primary moral status that was marked by the emergence of an unambiguously subject-centered conception of justice expands the domain of justice in one important sense by including some individuals in the primary moral community who had previously been excluded. The idea of disabilities rights marks a different,

---

[4] This point is due to Karen Knop.

but equally significant, expansion by recognizing that everyone who has primary moral status has a right to access to effective participation in what might be called the dominant cooperative scheme (Buchanan *et al.* 2000, 258–303). This latter term encompasses the totality of the most important forms of social production, broadly conceived, as well as the more significant political and social institutions, whether they are concerned with production or not.

It is tempting to see disabilities rights as less revolutionary than they are. One might view them simply as a matter of removing obstacles to the effective exercise (or in Rawls' terms, the "fair worth") of the familiar civil and political rights that many people now think are required by a proper recognition of primary moral status. This reformist way of understanding disabilities rights ignores a crucial motivation of the struggle for disabilities rights, the conviction that persons with disabilities, because they are beings with the same primary moral status as the "abled," have a right to be effective participants in the dominant cooperative scheme, rather than being relegated to the condition of *dependence* that exclusion from the dominant cooperative scheme entails. Unless people have effective access to the dominant cooperative scheme of their society, they are likely to be seen by others as objects of charity and unfortunates to be pitied, rather than as subjects of justice and individuals with whom we can interact on equal terms.

Instead of thinking of justice as being concerned, in Rawls' terms, with the fair distribution of the burdens and benefits of social cooperation – which in effect takes all subjects' participation in the dominant cooperative scheme for granted – the idea of disabilities rights recognizes that access to effective participation in the dominant cooperative scheme is itself a question of justice.

A related progressive development can be seen in some contemporary feminist understandings of what equal rights for women entails. On these views, recognizing the equal primary moral status of women requires taking into account special barriers to access to effective participation in the dominant cooperative scheme that women face by virtue of their special situation. For example, it is argued that because women bear children, equal rights for women may require special social arrangements, such as legal rights to maternity leave.[5]

Of course, the idea of disabilities rights includes more than the notion that a proper recognition of primary moral status requires social efforts to enable all to be effective participants in the dominant cooperative

---

[5] This example is due to Karen Knop.

framework. For example, it also encompasses the insight that while individuals should be seen as whole individuals, not viewed as "the blind" or "the mobility-impaired," for example, there should also be a recognition that for many people with disabilities, their disabilities are implicated in their identities and in that sense are not viewed as misfortunes to be constantly lamented. In the next section I want to concentrate on a different element of the idea of disabilities rights that may not be so obvious, but that is important nonetheless. This is the idea, at which I have already hinted, that the features of the dominant cooperative framework that in part determine who has effective access to it are not fixed, but are to some extent a matter of human choice. In the next subsection I argue that the realization that institutions are human creations, not "natural," unalterable parameters of human existence, when taken along with the changes in our moral-conceptual framework I have already described, greatly expands the domain of justice. What I shall call *the institutionalist shift* is an important instance of moral progress, both in the sense that it is a precondition for even attempting to translate into practices the important moral-conceptual improvements I have already described and because it constitutes a morally valuable improvement in our understanding of ourselves and our responsibilities.

The institutionalist shift

The next transformation of our moral-conceptual framework I want to call attention to is a remarkable alteration in the way institutions are conceived. The point is not that we have now come to think of institutions generally as deliberately created, nor as being fully under our control – that would be delusional – but rather that we now understand that institutions are human creations and that it is sometimes possible to modify them and even to create new ones.

By an institution I mean, roughly, a relatively enduring pattern of organized behavior, proceeding according to norms, and usually featuring a division of labor in the form of recognized roles. Although I will not press the point here, one could well argue that the concept of an institution itself, as an abstract concept that can be instantiated by a wide range of entities, is itself a fairly recent innovation. Be that as it may, my chief point is that coming to think of institutions as being subject to human control, rather than as part of a fixed natural order, greatly augments the transformative potential of all of the changes in our moral-conceptual scheme I have already discussed.

First, when combined with the idea that all persons have a primary moral status that confers basic general moral rights, the notion that institutions can be altered by human choice expands our conception of duties of justice. If existing institutions violate the rights of some persons, then they should be altered, where this is possible, to make them more just, or replaced with better ones. This way of conceptualizing the impact of the realization that institutions are malleable underestimates its significance, however. The realization that institutions are malleable becomes important only when we also come to understand how powerful institutions are. An appreciation of the power of institutions, of their deep and pervasive effects on human well-being, when combined with the realization that we can alter them by design, opens up the possibility of an expanded conception of what is required by a proper public recognition of the primary moral status of all persons. In particular, the ground is prepared for expanding our conception of justice by using institutions to "perfect" what we previously regarded as imperfect duties, enlarging the universe of duties of justice to include robust positive duties (Buchanan 1996a, 1996b).

Redrawing the boundary between justice and charity

Duties to aid the needy were traditionally conceived as duties of charity, not justice. The distinction between justice and charity is typically drawn by three contrasts: the distinction between perfect and imperfect duties, the distinction between duties that may properly be enforced and those that may not, and the distinction between duties that are correlatives of rights and those that are not. First, duties of justice are said to be determinate in the sense that the obligation is specified, both with regard to what is required and with regard to the identity of who is the object of the duty. Imperfect duties are indeterminate in both respects: both the kind and the amount of aid rendered and the choice of the recipient are left to the discretion of the individual who has the duty. Second, where there is a duty of justice, there is a correlative right; with duties of charity there are no correlative rights. Third, duties of justice are said to be enforceable, but not so duties of charity; their fulfillment is supposed to be voluntary.

The three contrasts are thought to be related in the following way. If my duties of charity are imperfect, that is, indeterminate as to content and recipient, then it would seem to follow that no one has a right to anything in particular from me as a consequence of my having these duties. This same indeterminacy is thought to make enforcement of duties of charity inappropriate, on the assumption that only those duties whose content is determinate are suitable for enforcement, the idea being, presumably, that the use of coercion is morally problematic in any case and that clarity and predictability as to what is to be enforced is necessary for its legitimacy. The relationship between the three contrasts seems to be straightforward: it is the indeterminacy (i.e., imperfectness) of duties of charity that is their primary feature, the one that explains the other two. Indeterminacy implies both the lack of correlative rights and the inappropriateness of enforcement.

Institutions can "perfect" imperfect duties to aid those in need. The most obvious example is the modern welfare state. Ideally, at least, this rather new institution is designed to (1) identify the appropriate recipients of aid; (2) to coordinate efforts to render aid effectively and in forms that cannot be achieved by uncoordinated individual efforts; (3) to assign determinate duties for which individuals and groups can be held accountable in order to ensure that the needed aid is provided; and (4) to achieve a fair distribution of the costs of providing aid.

In the absence of institutions for collective beneficence, aid to others can only take the form of independent, uncoordinated, individual acts of charity. Since one individual cannot be expected to aid all of the poor, the idea that duties of aid are imperfect makes perfectly good sense, on the assumption of lack of institutional capacity (Buchanan 1984). But once an institution for perfecting imperfect duties of aid is available or can be created then the path is clear for extending the domain of justice into part of what had been the territory of charity. Once we see that institutions for specifying, fairly distributing and effectively enforcing positive duties can be created, it is hard to evade the conclusion that we have an obligation to lend our support to their creation.

Acknowledgment of positive rights

The forgoing account of an expansion of our conception of the domain of justice to include territory that we had previously regarded as belonging to charity is incomplete. It omits another crucial moral-conceptual change: the idea that a proper recognition of the primary moral status of all persons requires acknowledgment of not just negative, but also positive, rights, entitlements to the goods that are thought to be generally necessary (though not sufficient) for a decent human life. This is the idea that the same characteristics of persons that ground their negative rights also ground positive rights.

My aim here is not to provide a convincing argument for positive rights but only to indicate how the combination of a series of important changes in our moral-conceptual framework renders the idea that there are such rights coherent and makes it both salient and plausible.

The institutionalist shift I described earlier helps pave the way both for the idea that imperfect duties can be perfected and for the idea that proper recognition of primary moral status implies positive rights. The protection of negative rights, such as the right against theft of property and the right to physical security, requires institutions and creating and supporting institutions requires actions, not just refrainings. Furthermore, institutions that are powerful enough to provide effective protection for negative rights create threats of their own and to mitigate these threats positive rights, such as the right to legal counsel and other due process rights, are necessary. Finally, support for the institutions needed to protect negative rights and the positive rights needed to mitigate the risks of harm from institutions requires taxation. In consequence, the idea that redistribution of wealth need not be inimical to the protection of rights but instead necessary for it becomes plausible. Once we appreciate these implications of the protection of negative rights, it becomes harder to sustain the conviction that justice is restricted to negative rights.

If the same moral considerations that ground negative rights also create a presumption that there are some positive rights, then the expansion of our conception of justice to include some positive rights becomes more compelling. For example, if an important element of the justification for negative rights is that respect for them is generally necessary if people are to have the opportunity to live a decent human life, and if we realize that protection of negative rights alone is not sufficient to achieve this opportunity, then the idea that positive rights are required by a proper recognition of primary moral status can begin to take hold. If there are institutions that allow us to discharge these positive duties in a way that is both fair and not excessively costly to any individual, then it seems arbitrary to say that they, unlike negative duties, are mere duties, not correlatives of entitlements.

So far I have explicated several changes in our moral-conceptual framework that count as significant instances of moral progress, at least from a liberal cosmopolitan point of view, and that cannot be fully appreciated by invoking the simple contrast between improvement in principles and improvement in compliance with principles: (1) the expansion of the conception of the membership of the primary moral community to include some persons, such as African slaves, who were previously excluded from it; (2) the recognition that at least some non-human animals have a moral status that implies at the very least moral prohibitions on causing them gratuitous suffering; (3) the rejection of Justice as Instrumental Reciprocity in favor of a subject-centered conception of justice; (4) the recognition that the territory of justice includes the terms of access to the dominant cooperative scheme; (5) the realization that institutions are subject to alteration by human choice; (6) the recognition that, as institutional capacities develop, what had been a matter of charity can become a matter of justice; and (7) the expansion of our conception of the rights that primary moral status confers so as to include positive rights. I have also explored some connections among these shifts and made the case that the third and the fourth are the more fundamental changes and that therefore they might properly be called revolutionary rather than reformist. I now want to show that the modern conception of human rights encompasses *all* of these moral-conceptual changes and that understanding that this is so greatly strengthens the case for the human rights enterprise.

Before I proceed to that task, a word of caution is apropos. I am not arguing that all moral-conceptual progress flows from the shift to a subject-centered conception of justice, nor that every instance of moral progress can be described as an expansion of the domain of justice. I am arguing that the emergence of a subject-centered conception of justice is momentous and arguing that understanding its implications provides insights into some of the most significant instances of moral-conceptual change and that these changes all involve expansions in our understanding of the domain of justice.

The modern conception of human rights as embodying progressive changes in thinking about justice

By the modern conception of human rights (henceforth, for brevity, MCHR), I mean that conception of general moral rights that finds expression in the major human rights conventions as they have been interpreted and continue to evolve through a complex interplay of institutional processes in international human rights institutions, such as the Treaty Bodies for the major convenants and international courts, the European Court of Human Rights, domestic courts in various countries that have incorporated human rights law into their legal systems, and the public advocacy of human rights by national and transnational civil society organizations.

I have already indicated that the MCHR represents moral progress in the sense of improved principles, citing the prohibition on torture as an example. Focusing on this sort of change, however, underestimates the morally progressive character of the MCHR. Observing that the MCHR expresses the realization that all people have the same primary moral status and that the appeal to human rights is a powerful resource for ending egregious discrimination against those who have effectively been excluded from the primary moral community comes closer to appreciating how morally progressive the MCHR is.

To stop there, however, would still be to underestimate the extent to which the MCHR is morally progressive. The MCHR can plausibly be understood as incorporating the most fundamental moral-conceptual change I have thus far explored, the adoption of a subject-centered conception of justice. In the preambles of several of the major conventions the rights that follow are said to be grounded in the *inherent* dignity of the human individual and the notion that these are rights that we have only by virtue of our relationship to God or are ascribed only to those of roughly equal power is scrupulously avoided.[6] International legal human rights are understood to be rights that all individuals have, on their own account, not because their having them serves the interests of states.

In my judgment both those who praise the MCHR and those who are critical of it have failed to appreciate the distinctive aptness of the idea of human rights for helping to fill out some of the indeterminacy of the subject-centered conception of justice. The idea of human rights implies obligations, of course, but by utilizing the concept of a right, it adds something of distinctive value to the idea that we are obligated to treat all people in certain ways. Recourse to the idea of human *rights* makes it clear that the obligations in question are not simply obligations

[6] For example, consider the following: Preamble to the Universal Declaration of Human Rights (1948): "Whereas recognition of the inherent dignity and of the equal and inalienable rights of all members of the human family is the foundation of freedom, justice and peace in the world"; Preamble to the International Covenant on Civil and Political Rights (1966): "Considering that, in accordance with the principles proclaimed in the Charter of the United Nations, recognition of the inherent dignity and of the equal and inalienable rights of all members of the human family is the foundation of freedom, justice and peace in the world"; Preamble to the American Convention on Human Rights (1969): "Recognizing that the essential rights of man are not derived from one's being a national of a certain state, but are based upon attributes of the human personality, and that they therefore justify international protection in the form of a convention reinforcing or complementing the protection provided by the domestic law of the American states."

regarding people, that is, requirements for their treatment, but that these obligations are *owed to* people. Taken in the context of the MCHR's clear commitment to the subject-centered conception of justice, this means that we owe these obligations to people by virtue of what they are like, regardless of their power in relation to us and independently of any relationship to God – that they are entitled to be treated in certain ways, on their own account.

There is another crucial aspect of the power of the concept of a right to focus attention on the right-holder as a subject of obligations on her own account. If I violate a mere obligation regarding you, I have done something wrong; but if I violate an obligation owed to you, I wrong you, and it is to you that I owe apology or compensation or restitution. In this sense the idea of a right puts the individual toward whom the obligation is directed, rather than the obligation-holder, at center stage.

There is another advantage of the concept of a right, as it is employed in the MCHR, from the standpoint of giving more determinate content to the subject-centered conception of justice. At least for those rights that can be "wielded" by the right-holder (that is, invoked, exercised or waived), the concept of a right better expresses the idea that one important aspect of proper recognition of primary moral status is respect for rational agency. If your obligation regarding how I am to be treated is merely an obligation, not the correlative of my right, then there is a sense in which your acknowledgment of your obligation regarding me does nothing, in itself, to recognize me as a rational agent. If you have a mere obligation regarding me, how you are to treat me is determined solely by your obligation; I am, in an important sense, simply not in the picture, at least not as an agent who has preferences about how he is to be treated. The notion of human rights, so far as it includes rights that can be "wielded," is peculiarly appropriate for expressing both the shift to a subject-centered conception of justice and the realization that one central feature of the subject that grounds her primary moral status is her capacity for rational agency.

The institutionalist shift I described earlier is also clearly in evidence in the MCHR. The recognition that all people have the same primary moral status, to be acknowledged by protection of these rights, is proclaimed to have implications for how our institutions ought to be. Human institutions, including the most powerful one, the state, are regarded as alterable for the sake of human rights. States are said to be obligated to take appropriate measures, including the development of economic, political and legal institutions, in fulfillment of their duty to promote human rights.[7]

Very little is said in the preambles, beyond vague references to inherent dignity, about just which characteristics of the human subject are those that confer primary moral status and the rights that go along with it. Nor do the lists of rights themselves explicitly identify these characteristics. The content of the idea of the subject has to be inferred from the nature of the rights themselves.

It might be argued that whatever else it encompasses, the notion of dignity itself implies the capacity for rational agency; or one might make the stronger claim that the only way to make sense of the idea that inherent dignity grounds human rights is to understand "dignity" as referring solely to the value of rational agency, as James Griffin does (Griffin 2008). Without taking a stand on these issues, it is fair to say that many of the rights in the conventional lists of human rights, such as the right to choose whom to marry and the right to choose an occupation, not to mention the right of political participation, presuppose this capacity. To the extent that the human rights movement is the descendant of the abolitionist movement, and owes its conceptual framework in part to the tradition of natural rights, it would be surprising if the capacity for rational agency did not play a prominent role in the concept of the subject of rights the MCR operates with.

It is crucial to emphasize, however, that even a cursory inspection of the major conventions indicates that the concept of the subject they implicitly express is much richer than the concept of a rational agent. In particular, there is considerable emphasis on the fact that we are social beings. This

[7] Consider the following articles from some major conventions. Article 2 of the International Covenant on Civil and Political Rights (1966), "Where not already provided for by existing legislative or other measures, each State Party to the present Covenant undertakes to take the necessary steps, in accordance with its constitutional processes and with the provisions of the present Covenant, to adopt such legislative or other measures as may be necessary to give effect to the rights recognized in the present Covenant"; Article 2 of the International Covenant on Economic, Social and Cultural Rights (1966), "Each State Party to the present Covenant undertakes to take steps, individually and through international assistance and co-operation, especially economic and technical, to the maximum of its available resources, with a view to achieving progressively the full realization of the rights recognized in the present Covenant by all appropriate means, including particularly the adoption of legislative measures"; Article 3 of the Convention on the Elimination of All Forms of Discrimination Against Women (1979), "State Parties shall take in all fields, in particular in the political, social, economic and cultural fields, all appropriate measures, including legislation, to ensure the full development and advancement of women, for the purpose of guaranteeing them the exercise and enjoyment of human rights and fundamental freedoms on a basis of equality with men."

antidote to an overly abstract and individualistic understanding of the possessor human rights is perhaps most obvious in the International Covenant on Economic, Social, and Cultural Rights (1966), but it is present in the International Covenant on Civil and Political Rights (1966), the Universal Declaration of Human Rights (1948), the Convention on the Rights of the Child (1989), the Convention on the Elimination of All Forms of Discrimination Against Women (1979) and the International Convention on the Protection of the Rights of All Migrant Workers and Members of Their Families (1990) as well.[8]

The MCHR is also beginning to incorporate what I have described as one of the most significant implications of the idea that all people have an equal moral status, in the context of the shift to a subject-centered conception of justice: the recognition of disabilities rights and the awareness that equal rights for women must take into account their special needs and vulnerabilities (CEDAW 1979; CRPD 2006). I suggested earlier that the best understanding of disabilities rights includes the notion that a proper recognition of persons' equal primary moral status requires efforts to ensure that they have effective access to the dominant cooperative scheme. If this is the case, then its growing recognition of disabilities rights is one way in which the MCHR embodies progressive changes in how the territory of justice is conceived.

My conclusion, then, is that the modern conception of human rights incorporates and gives apt expression to the progressive moral-conceptual changes I have characterized in this chapter. This is not to suggest that justice, much less the whole of morality, is reducible to human rights or that moral progress consists solely or even mainly of improvements in how we think about justice. Nor is it to deny that wrong can be and has been done in the name of human rights. Nevertheless, the moral-conceptual improvements I have described are surely among the most significant that human beings have yet achieved. If this is so, then the case for the human rights enterprise is even stronger than most liberal cosmopolitans may have realized.

---

[8] For instance, the International Covenant on Civil and Political Rights (1966), Part I, Article 1, "the right of self-determination"; Part III, Article 18, "the freedom, either individually or in community with others, to manifest one's religion or belief," Article 21, "the right of peaceful assembly," Article 22, "the right to freedom of association with others," Article 23, "the right of men and women of marriageable age to marry and to found a family," and Article 27, "persons belonging to ethnic, religious or linguistic minority shall not be denied the right, in community with the other members of their group, to enjoy their own culture."

References

American Convention on Human Rights, "Pact of San Jose, Costa Rica." 1969. Opened for signature November 22, 1969 (entered into force July 18, 1978).

Buchanan, Allen. 1984. "The Right to a Decent Minimum of Health Care." *Philosophy & Public Affairs* 13, 55–78.

    1990. "Justice as Reciprocity Versus Subject-Centered Justice." *Philosophy & Public Affairs* 19, 227–252.

    1996a. "Charity, Justice, and the Idea of Moral Progress." In Jerome B. Schneewind, ed., *Giving: Western Ideas of Philanthropy*. Bloomington and Indianapolis: University of Indiana Press, pp. 98–116.

    1996b. "Toward a Theory of the Ethics of Bureaucratic Organizations." *Business Ethics Quarterly* 6, 419–440.

Buchanan, Allen, Brock, Dan W., Daniels, Norman and Wikler, Daniel. 2000. *From Chance to Choice: Genetics and Justice*. Cambridge University Press.

CEDAW (Convention on the Elimination of All Forms of Discrimination Against Women). 1979. Opened for signature December 18, 1979, 1249 U.N.T.S. 13 (entered into force September 3, 1981).

Convention on the Rights of the Child. 1989. Opened for signature November 20, 1989, 1577 U.N.T.S. 3 (entered into force September 2, 1990).

CPRD (Convention on the Rights of Persons with Disabilities). 2006. Opened for signature March 30, 2007, 2515 U.N.T.S. 3, UN Doc. A/RES/61/106 December 13, 2006

Epicurus. (3rd century AD) 1987. *Kurai Doxai (Key Doctrines) 32, 33*. In A.A. Long and David Sedley, eds., *The Hellenistic Philosophers*. Cambridge University Press, p. 127.

Gauthier, David. 1986. *Morals by Agreement*. Oxford University Press.

Griffin, James W. 2008. *On Human Rights: Completing the Incomplete Idea*. Oxford University Press.

Hobbes, Thomas. 1958 [1660]. *Leviathan*. Indianapolis: Liberal Arts Press.

Hume, David. 1975 [1739]. *A Treatise of Human Nature*, edited by L.A. Selby-Bigge, revised by P.H. Nidditch. 2nd edn. Oxford: Clarendon Press.

International Convention on the Protection of the Rights of All Migrant Workers and Members of Their Families. 1990. Opened for signature December 18, 1990, 2220 U.N.T.S. 3, UN Doc. A/RES/45/158 (entered into force July 1, 2003).

International Covenant on Civil and Political Rights. 1966. Opened for signature December 19, 1966, 999 U.N.T.S. 171 (entered into force March 23, 1976).

International Covenant on Economic, Social and Cultural Rights. 1966. Opened for signature December 16, 1966, 993 U.N.T.S. 3 (entered into force January 3, 1976).

Plato. (360 BCE) 1921. *The Republic*, translated by Benjamin Jowett. 3rd edn. Oxford: Clarendon Press.

Schneewind, Jerome B. 1996. "Philosophical Ideas of Charity." In Jerome B. Schneewind, ed., *Giving: Western Ideas of Philanthropy*. Bloomington and Indianapolis: University of Indiana Press, pp. 54–75.

Universal Declaration of Human Rights. 1948. G.A. Res. 217A (III), UN Doc. A/RES/217A (December 10, 1948).

MARK GOODALE

Introduction

To begin, let me provide an immediate opening to the chapter's principal claims. As the anthropology of the practice of human rights demonstrates, even in terms of an explicit understanding of "progress," it is very difficult to sustain empirically the conclusion that human rights has been a force for progress in the contemporary world. On the one hand, the postwar human rights project is intensely teleological; the movement toward a better, more advanced, more civilized future is implicit in the construction of "human rights" as the primary "symbol to all of victory over those who sought to achieve tyranny through aggressive war" (UNESCO 1949, 258–259).

To ask conceptually, that is, about whether or not human rights is progressive is to push right up against a tautology, since "human rights" and "progress" are mutually implied from the very beginning. But on the other hand, even if we were to devise a set of indicators in order to measure the impact of human rights in certain areas of concern – political freedom, torture, access to justice, etc. – we would immediately confront two problems. First, as Sally Engle Merry is documenting in her ongoing research on the use of quantitative indicators to measure human rights compliance (see, e.g., Merry 2009, 2012), there is a problematic degree of dissonance between the statistical techniques and assumptions that animate indicator research, and the multiplicity of processes that get radically condensed into "data." She argues that the broader impact of human rights – the kind of impact, that is, that would speak to the question of "progress" – is likely to prove statistically unmeasurable for purposes of the diverse group of constituencies involved in human rights enforcement and activism. And second, if we were to develop a set of qualitative indicators to assess the broader consequences of the globalization of human rights, particularly after the end of the Cold War, we would face the dilemma that our ability to make sweeping generalizations about something like "progress" would diminish the closer we examined the practices of human rights in context. This is a very anthropological dilemma and one that Melville Herskovits, a leading mid-twentieth-century anthropologist, made the basis of his – later, the discipline's official – rejection of a declaration of universal human rights during the drafting of what became the UDHR (American Anthropological Association 1947; see also Goodale 2009).

But if we leave aside, then, the simplistic and not-so-faintly unilineal evolutionist question of progress, there are other, much more productive, hard questions that can be put to human rights. The ways and means of human rights have become an indelible part of what might be described as "legacies of human experience" in the contemporary world; this much we can say with certainty. If we take a more modest critical approach to the presence of human rights within these legacies, we can then ask: How are human rights shaping modes of agency and what are the broader implications of these shifts? As I will show in this chapter, the logics of human rights have had the greatest consequences for the microdynamics of moral agency, those everyday moments that link normative cultures with purposive action. I will draw from the recent ethnography of human rights to flesh out the contours of this argument, since anthropologists, in particular, have found themselves – at first, serendipitously – on the frontlines (as both scholars and scholar-activists) of the emergence of human rights as an "archetypal language" of social and political change and as a globalizing moral grammar for addressing a range of contemporary vulnerabilities (see, e.g., Cowan *et al.* 2001; Goodale and Merry 2007). The cases I will survey reveal several patterns across the practice of human rights.

First, as ethnographic research from Bolivia shows, the mobilization of human rights discourse reorients moral relationships in ways that can create new lines of social disrupture and the possibility for conflict that didn't otherwise exist. Although it is in the nature of human rights practice to harness the constructive potential of struggle, particularly against institutional forms of oppression, the essentially neo-Kantain rigidity of human rights as a normative system makes it a blunt ethical tool that tends to reinterpret the nuances of social relations in terms of violations, victims and perpetrators (see also Hinton 2012).

Second, research from Malawi will illustrate the ways in which the increasing hegemony of human rights narrows the range of moral options available to people in conditions in crisis. The language of human rights exerts a power in part by excluding the possibility of other alternatives and denying the legitimacy of enduring conditions of normative pluralism.

Third, a case study from Chiapas reveals the unpredictable consequences of the essentially poetic nature of the practice of human rights as a new mode of moral agency. When Zapatista activists eagerly took up the idea of human rights within their ongoing struggle against the Mexican state, they vernacularized it not by simply translating it into cultural terms that could be mobilized according to a simple formula, but at its very conceptual foundations. The result was a folk theory of Zapatista human rights that had been shorn of many of the conceptual foundations of international human rights law.

And finally, a scholar's innovative study of conflicts within the World Bank over competing value systems demonstrates that the transformative potential of *any* mode of moral agency is limited by broader structural constraints – ideological, political, economic and so on. Although the age of human rights is not unique in this sense, it is important to understand how human rights can contribute to these structural constraints at the same time it comes to form part of the moral repertoire of everyday life.

So if these case studies are a useful reflection on part of the question – how has human rights shaped modes of moral agency? – what remains is a response – a brief one, alas – to the second part: what are the broader implications of these shifts? Pheng Cheah (2012) has recently argued that the project of human rights is riven by a fundamental dilemma, something he calls the dilemma of "sovereign self-making." He explains that from the early postwar to the present, the project of human rights has been a project for making humanity. "Human rights," in this sense, is a collective, if fraught, process of recognition, the recognition of what Cheah calls the "collective subject over itself." But when this project is made concrete, as it must be, the contradictions and inconsistencies that are a normal part of social and political life work to undermine the task itself. When states are required to use "all available resources" under international law to comply with treaty obligations, choices must be made and these choices inevitably lead to the instrumentalization of people and what might be called "selective diminishment."

The anthropology of human rights arrives at a similar conclusion through different means. The logics and language of human rights begin with a set of universal claims that offer people a novel normative framework that transcends the contingent circumstances of everyday life. And yet, the abstract universalism of human rights functions as a kind of moral mirage: it attracts people to it, but it gets fainter the closer the approach. Eventually, human rights discourse is grounded not in the pure form with which it appeared, but as a hybrid normativity that is the result of multiple processes of vernacularization and moral innovation. What is left, then, of the *progressive*, translocal project of making humanity? Even if research on the practice of human rights reveals it to be a process through which the project of humanity breaks down, fractures, with each moment that human rights becomes more resonant, more accessible, it also points to the emergence of new forms of moral practice and at least the suggestion of collective transformation.

Progress, intention and the limits of human rights

It is difficult to take up the question of human rights as a force for progress. On the one hand, the question itself is inseparable from the teleology of the postwar human rights project. As Eleanor Roosevelt – the chair of the commission that oversaw the preparation and drafting of what became the Universal Declaration of Human Rights (UDHR) – explained in a series of interviews and essays (see, e.g., Roosevelt 1948), the deeper intention behind what appeared to be a largely political and legal process was to forge an international symbol of a more advanced future in human relations. Beyond the obvious fact that the UDHR was not a binding international treaty, its real purpose was to point the way – for those who would follow – toward a different trajectory of social evolution, a different "arc of the moral universe" (as Martin Luther King, Jr. described it somewhat later) that inevitably bent toward conditions of peace, equality and global citizenship. This is what Roosevelt meant when she emphasized the "educational" mission of human rights in the postwar period. The success or failure of this mission would be measured by the extent to which what might be described as a "moral convergence" took place: did the globalizing project of human rights lead to a narrowing in conceptions of the person, the grounds for normative action, and ideologies of difference? If so, then the project of human rights would succeed and it would be a force for progress within its own terms.

And on the other hand, the question of human rights and progress is troubled by a framework introduced by the philosopher Richard Rorty. In a published (1993) version of a lecture he gave in the early 1990s as part of the Oxford Amnesty Lecture series, Rorty (to some, infamously) brought the destabilizing influence of a neo-pragmatism to bear on many of the foundational assumptions of contemporary human rights. But passing human rights through the neo-pragmatist crucible did not, as might be supposed, lead Rorty to a latter-day version of Bentham's classic rejection of natural/human rights as "nonsense on stilts." Instead, Rorty concluded that we should stop wringing our hands over the contested philosophical grounds of human rights and get on with the practical business of transforming the world in the image of a kind of multicultural humanism in which violations of human rights are precluded by new forms of transcultural empathy. Intriguingly, although he himself missed this historical interconnection, Rorty described the means through which a particular kind of liberal empathy should be globalized as "sentimental education," thereby gesturing toward the originary vision of Roosevelt herself. (He also apparently missed the echo of Flaubert, whose novel of sentimental education offers a devilishly different understanding of both "sentiment" and "education.")

Nevertheless, the troubling thrust of Rorty's argument is that the world would be unquestionably more peaceful if a culture of human rights were to take root – regardless of whether or not such a culture were consistent with prevailing philosophical opinion about the grounds of human nature, dignity, moral knowledge, and so on. The consequence, in other words, of an effective global campaign of sentimental education would be a form of progress in quite simple terms – the emergence of transhumanity and the sentimental impossibility of genocide. Indeed, the inspiration for Rorty's neo-pragmatist account of human rights is the work of Annette Baier, whose argument for a "progress of sentiments" (1991) suggests a process through which the relationship between similarity and difference is transformed once the transhuman is reconceived in terms of what the American novelist Walker Percy called (in his novel *The Moviegoers*) "the little way" – the ephemeral interlinkages of sentiment that connect us all well above the dubious claims of deep existential union that, as Rorty puts it, "instantiate … true humanity" (1993, 129). But if there is any value – not "truth," obviously – in Rorty's approach to human rights, then to question whether or not human rights has been a force for progress is to question the premise that the elimination of genocide from the earth would represent a tangible advance, not just for some, but for all.

And yet, I want to suggest that the invocation of genocide as a kind of human rights violation that is, for these purposes, good to think with – or, rather, feel with, to stay within Rorty's skepticism toward rationality – distracts us from examining more closely both the historicity of human rights and the more complicated ways in which the logics of human rights shape, and are shaped by, ethical practices within concrete moments of social and political struggle. In other words, for purposes of human rights, we must acknowledge that the question of progress is dialectically bound up with the historical circumstances of mass atrocity and human destruction, which create their own barriers to reflection and wonder. "Progress," in this sense, cannot be detached from the moments of greatest human tragedy, since as both a category for analysis, and as a teleology with real political and social purchase, it functions more like a mirror that reflects an antithetical image of the human condition as it has been, a simple opposition to the starkness of human suffering and the long grey line of vulnerability.

In this way, one cannot adequately take up the question of human rights as a force for progress at all, since both "human rights" and "progress" are – if my reading of "the last utopia" (Moyn 2010) is correct – simply different shadings of the same imaginary and not, as an alternative understanding might suggest, two concrete points on a spectrum of historical (or, perhaps, ethical) change. Of course, to argue that contemporary human rights is a particular kind of utopia – one that is represented, semiotically, by the dialectic of human tragedy and progress, among others – is not to argue that it is not, for this reason, consequential in ways that matter to an anthropologist; indeed, quite the contrary. But like Thomas More's island of Utopia – that Renaissance fantasy of the "Best State of a Public Weal" inspired by travelers' reports from the early stirrings of colonialism – this one too must be observed by looking backwards, as it were, from the vantage point of our disenchantments.

So if the question of human rights as a force for progress is an invitation into a rabbit hole that I decline, this does not mean that we should not ask questions about the ways in which human rights – as both an archetypal language of political and social change and moral logic for reinterpreting vulnerability – is shaping sentiment and offering new grounds for action. I want to approach this line of inquiry as a question of agency – specifically, moral agency. To explore the life of human rights in the contemporary world as a problem of moral agency is not without its hazards.

First, an anthropological account of agency, in particular, draws a distinction between intentionality-as-purposive action and intentionality-as-teleology (see, e.g., Desai 2010; Keane 2007). This means that to ask questions about the relationship between human rights and moral agency is to examine what might be described as the "microdynamics of moral action," the grounded contexts in which normativity mediates the constitution of the social. But to examine moral action from the inside out, as it were, tells us nothing about the course of a broader process of translocal moral development, that arc of the moral universe bending toward justice. For many human rights scholars and activists alike, human rights without this broader teleology is like human rights shorn of universality – unrecognizable, unacceptable, even dangerous.

Second, as I argue elsewhere (Goodale 2012, n.d.), recent ethnographic studies have revealed the practice of human rights to be a domain of moral agency that is marked by what the political theorist John Wall (2005) has called "moral creativity" – the fact that moral life, while shaped by the constraints of norms, ultimately must transcend them since moral practice is inextricably bound up with subject-making. But if the practice of human rights as a mode of moral agency is "poetic" in this sense – Wall's study revolves around a reconsideration of Ricoeur's poetics of the will – it is also essentially, and necessarily, unpredictable, since a "poetics of possibility" tells us nothing about the contexts of moral agency, or its consequences. That the practice of human rights is unpredictable at the basic level of moral agency presents any number of dilemmas for more programmatic visions of international law as a bridge toward a post-Westphalian future.

And finally, to leave the question of progress aside and take up, rather, the problem of human rights as a constitutive force within the microdynamics of the moral present, is to acknowledge obliquely the ultimate limitations of human rights – not *as* human rights, or even as international law in the post-Cold War world, but as a globalizing logic for moral, social and political transformation. If the anthropology of human rights has taught us anything, it is that the spaces in which international and transnational normativities are vernacularized are marked by contradictions and structural ambiguities – from the fora in which international law is debated and monitored (see, e.g., Merry 2009, 2012) to the village-level workshops around the world that serve as the leading-edge of transnational human rights activism and advocacy (see, e.g., Englund 2006; Goodale 2008). This is not to say, obviously, that the practice of human rights does not shape moral agency in ways that – for example – encourage resistance to oppression, lead to the formation of new political and social movements, or foster a reconsideration of gender relations. In fact, it is precisely the poetic character of the practice of human rights that offers at least the possibility of real transformation. But this same essential poiesis also functions as a limiting factor at the same time. This paradox is a striking feature of the recent ethnography of human rights, to which I now turn.

Moral agency in the age of human rights

Historians of rights tell us that we live in an "age of rights" (Henkin 1990) that is world-remaking (Glendon 2001). As Glendon explains, in her study of the forging of the modern human rights project from the tragedy of mid-century last, there was only one option then, only one possible vision, and that was to remake existing institutions of global governance, and to devise new ones, as a signal that the great powers, at least, would not tolerate future cataclysms of similar global scope and magnitude. But the strange attractors of the Cold War warped geopolitics in ways that remade a world in which genocide was not a central threat – although it continued to make its sinister appearance from Guatemala to Cambodia – but instead the threat was actually far greater: it was to the planet itself and all of its life-systems. This period of tense and increasingly absurd *Realpolitik* was one in which the cosmopolitan gestures of the late 1940s were largely forgotten, except by small groups of activists, international bureaucrats and intellectuals. Even the Cold War's greatest social leaders, like Martin Luther King, Jr., could only offer mere rhetorical gestures to human rights, since they were hemmed in by different forms of nationalism on one side, and Marxist-inflected visions of social transformation on the other (see, e.g., Jackson 2006). In his "Letter from a Birmingham Jail" (1963), King issued a world-historical plea to his fellow clergymen to leave their cultural prejudices behind and join him in the fight for equal "civil" and "constitutional" rights – that is, rights circumscribed by the contingent circumstance of US citizenship. Although he does invoke "God given rights" at one point in the letter (a strategic rhetorical device, given the audience), it is clear – as the broader civil rights movement in the United States demonstrated – that the fight was for dignity as equal American citizens, a narrowing compelled by the nature of US law itself, and not a struggle for rights as equal members of an abstract global polity.

But the end of the Cold War changed the warp of geopolitics yet again and created the conditions in which an "age of (human) rights" could finally flourish. And even as the threat of species-event destruction faded as the nuclear stockpiles of the United States and the countries of the former Soviet Union were slowly dismantled or effectively sequestered, the scourge of genocidal violence reappeared in its familiar forms from the former Yugoslavia to the Great Lakes region of Africa. At the same time, countries – primarily, but not exclusively, in the so-called developing world – were suddenly cut loose from the ideological constraints of the bipolar Cold War system. This opening also had economic implications, because as the more direct forms of financial colonialism of the postwar period faded, countries were left to either seek assistance from international financial institutions like the IMF and the World Bank, or to form partnerships with transnational NGOs, which promised to fulfill the functions of the state by providing social services and developing national infrastructures. In both cases, countries were confronted with demands to make human rights a cornerstone of national policy-making. For international financial institutions, "human rights" came bundled with the rest of the neoliberal agenda, which included a range of economic imperatives but also expectations for political and legal reform. And for the NGOs, those transnational agents of postwar development, the rise of human rights provided a way to transform the earlier project of knowledge transfer – symbolized best by the "Green Revolution" of the 1960s and 1970s – into a mission of moral transformation: development *as* a human right.

The result was that the logics and rhetorics – if not the institutions – of human rights took root at very deep levels in a very short period of time. Indeed, there were consequences to the fact that during the post-Cold War era the diffusion of human rights discourse was largely independent of either institutional developments within the UN human rights system, or the ratification and implementation of international human rights law within national legal regimes. This is not to say that the pace and scope of national ratification and implementation, in particular, did not quicken and widen during this time. But the real story is that the "curious grapevine" that Eleanor Roosevelt had envisioned 40 years before finally took shape in the form of grassroots activism, political debate and moral proselytization led by local-transnational partnerships connected within new networks and "global assemblages" (see, e.g., Ong and Collier 2004; Riles 2000).

More serendipitously than not, anthropologists found themselves caught up in these discursive shifts toward human rights at the local level in different regions and from different political and social vantage points. My own research is instructive. I arrived to Bolivia in the late 1990s prepared to conduct research in remote areas of the Bolivian *altiplano* on conflict resolution, access to law, and political and legal identity. I had expected to study the ways in which people living in small villages far from the centers of state power construct normative cultures that reflect local histories, social hierarchies and gender expectations. What I found, instead, was that the normative landscape of broad swaths of rural highland Bolivia had been transformed by the growing presence of a diverse collection of NGOs that had reinterpreted their work in terms of human rights (Goodale 2007, 2008).

Traditional lines of political power had been upended because the transactional demands of NGOs privileged younger, Spanish-speaking men with some experience of the city, the army, or the coca fields of the Chapare over older men who had spent decades moving up the ladder of positions of increasing responsibility. Younger men, sometimes in their first public position, suddenly found themselves invested with a new kind of moral authority, the ability to pass judgment on matters of public importance, and the responsibility to act decisively in moments of crisis. And because of the intense focus on women's rights in Bolivia during this time – as elsewhere, women's rights became a bridge across which other modes of human rights discourse passed into the public sphere (see, e.g., Merry 2006) – gender relations were rocked by the establishment of multi-purpose legal and psychological centers that were associated with the ratification at the national level of the Convention on the Elimination of All Forms of Discrimination Against Women (CEDAW).

In rural Bolivia, the consequences in practice were ambiguous: when newly morally empowered peasant women left their hamlets at the encouragement of human rights NGOs and government officials to pursue legal and psychological services in provincial capitals, their extended absences left young children vulnerable and caused new rifts with husbands, brothers and fathers (Goodale 2008). This, in turn, led to new conflicts between the women who had come to see themselves as bearers of "derechos humanos" and both other women – sisters, sisters-in-law, mothers – who had not undergone a similar shift in moral identity, and men, who had been transformed as a category into an oppositional presence in women's lives that clashed with local constructions of gender complementarity (best expressed in the common Quechua expression "tukuy ima qhariwarmi," or "everything is male-female"). After several years, legal services centers in rural areas were shuttered because of lack of funding, local opposition by town leaders, and, most importantly, the unwillingness of women from outlying hamlets to participate in what amounted to a wholesale restructuring of their lives.

All of this is not to say that a focus on the problems of domestic violence as a human rights violation did not lead to new forms of moral agency (for both women *and* men) and to the appearance of forms of social conflict that are perhaps a *sine qua non* of structural change. Indeed, during the ubiquitous rural *talleres*, or workshops, that were the primary mechanism through which the idea of human rights was rendered into normative terms that were meaningful for people, the message was clear: human rights was a new moral grammar for struggle, for conflict. But as this new language was taken up – as it must be – and utilized within the multiplicity of everyday life, it became dynamic and unpredictable. When the language of human rights was grounded within the realities of people's lives, it was transformed through a succession of smaller normative scales that became increasingly distant from the abstract conceptions of international law and human rights activism. In the end, the moral implications of human rights advocacy in rural Bolivia were not as sweeping or as totalizing as imagined. Instead, within the poetics of everyday moral life, itself embedded in conditions of normative pluralism, the language and moral logics of human rights were often rendered instrumental, to be used in carefully bracketed moments with uncertain consequences.

Ethnographic accounts of the practice of human rights from other parts of the world reveal it to be a mode of moral agency that is similarly marked by an ambiguous poetics. For example, Harri Englund's study (2006) of human rights activism in Malawi shows that the process of national ratification and implementation was an intensely political one that was shaped by ongoing conflicts among groups of elites, who were not shy about manipulating the language of human rights if it had strategic value in fights over political power and the control of natural resources. This manipulation of human rights at the national level affected the ways in which human rights was taken up by ordinary social actors. Englund's research confirmed Wilson's earlier observation that the ways and means of human rights, particularly in Africa, had become "archetypal," except that in the case of Malawi it was not the transition to democracy that was at issue, but the model for development that would guide the country's relationships with regional organizations like the African Union and international agencies like the World Bank and the IMF. As Englund explains, the rhetoric of human rights had become so dominant across the political spectrum that the struggle to institutionalize rights pushed aside other potential responses to the problem of chronic poverty in Malawi. The moral language of rights found its way into unlikely places. For example, schoolchildren refused to follow teachers' rules in the classroom on the basis that to do so would violate their human rights. The result, as Englund puts it in a startling phrase, was that the practice of human rights made Malawians "prisoners of freedom."

Shannon Speed (2008) spent several years observing the ways in which the hegemony of human rights discourse shaped the moral agency of Zapatista activists during the Chiapas rebellion and its aftermath. In many ways, as her research demonstrates, the rebellion itself would not have been possible without the active participation of legions of transnational human rights NGOs, which provided local activists the opportunity to rearticulate a series of centuries-old demands into the terms of indigenous rights-as-human rights following on the Mexican state's ratification of International Labor Organization Convention 169 – the so-called indigenous peoples' bill of rights – in 1990. (Mexico was the second country to ratify ILO 169 after Norway.) The rhetoric of human rights profoundly altered the normative grounds on which the primary village-level organizations, the *juntas de buen gobierno* (or "good governance councils"), interacted with the Mexican government. But as we have seen elsewhere, the mobilization of human rights discourse by Zapatista activists had similarly unpredictable consequences. When human rights were taken up within local forms of moral practice, their very conceptual foundations underwent a curious shift. Because of existing folk understandings of the relationship between norms and social and political agency, the Zapatistas did not accept certain core assumptions about human rights, including the notion of universality and the ontological implications of human rights as an embodied expression of what Isaiah Berlin (1958) described as "negative liberty." Instead, they constructed a normatively distinct version of human rights that was bounded by Zapatista cultural identity on the one hand, and, on the other, made the very existence of *Zapatista* human rights contingent upon their social and political efficacy. As Speed explains, the Zapatistas came to believe that their human rights existed only "in their exercise." The problematic implications of a contingent ontology of human rights would only become apparent much later as the rebellion matured.

Finally, Galit Sarfaty's recent research demonstrates that the ways in which human rights discourse shapes moral agency are themselves shaped by the wider ideological and geopolitical contexts in which the practice of human rights takes place. Moreover, her ethnographic study (2012) of what she calls "values in translation" within the World Bank shows the extent to which the logics of human rights are coming to influence moral practices within dominant global institutions at the very center of the Fergusonian "neoliberal world order." Sarfaty tracked the fortunes of a small group of World Bank employees who were intent on adding the moral calculations of human rights to the agenda of the Bank, which makes loans to countries that are often dependent on commitments to reform national political economies to bring them in line with prevailing market orthodoxy. The programs of the Bank have been traditionally guided by cost–benefit analyses and a flat model of economic reform and resource maximization, and the rank-and-file of the Bank has always been dominated, not surprisingly, by economists.

But in recent years, international lawyers and others with an interest in human rights have played a more active role within the Bank. As Sarfaty shows, this small cadre of Bank employees came into conflict with the structural imperatives of the Bank, which are codified in its governing charters, called "articles of agreement." For example, the branch of the Bank that focuses on the world's poorest countries – the International Development Association, or IDA – is guided by a simple formula: to "promote economic development, increase productivity *and thus* raise standards of living in the less-developed areas of the world" (emphasis mine; World Bank 2011). Because this formula is both simple (or simplistic) and also unambiguously stated – a particular kind of economic development leads to increased economic productivity, increased economic productivity necessarily leads to higher standards of living – it made it very difficult for human rights reformers within the Bank to offer policy alternatives that were not clearly related to "economic development." The result was that the attempt to translate the normative values of human rights into terms understandable to World Bank economists and policy-makers remained very much incipient; much of the clash over the competing, and unequally positioned, normative cultures took place informally, in hallways and outside of official policy-setting meetings. As Sarfaty's study thus shows us, the poetic unpredictability in the practice of human rights is the result of both wider social and political constraints and the microdynamics of moral practice.

Conclusion: the dilemma of humanity

Of the different contemporary domains of theory and practice, it is perhaps most appropriate that hard questions are put to the domains of human rights. In their multiple expressions – institutional, ethical, cultural, philosophical – human rights have become a particularly consequential hegemony. Although the story of the modern human rights project is older and more complicated than scholars like Samuel Moyn (2010) would have us believe (see Bass 2010), there is no question that the end of the Cold War, and the consolidation of what the anthropologist James Ferguson (2006) has called the "neoliberal world order," have created a conjuncture in which the logics of human rights have come to shape the ethics of the present in ways that go well beyond the modest imaginings of people like Eleanor Roosevelt, who could only hope that a "curious grapevine" would eventually allow human rights to "seep in even when governments are not so anxious for it" (quoted in Korey 1998).

Through his study of the role of human rights in the process of truth and reconciliation in early post-apartheid South Africa, Richard A. Wilson came to the realization that a "sea-change in global politics" had taken place in which human rights had become the only globalized "archetypal language of democratic transition" (2001, 1). It is not that the end of the Cold War meant that other normative languages were not available to social reformers and political actors around the world; from the different historical permutations of Marxism (including Maoism and Trotskyism) to religious doctrines that commit followers to specific forms of temporal action, the normative landscape remains contested, cluttered and marked by contradictions. It is that this normative pluralism has been fundamentally reconfigured through the emergence of human rights as the preeminent logic of institutional reform and political subject-making.

At the same time, the language of human rights in the vernacular has become a ubiquitous moral grammar for resisting vulnerability and responding to moral injury. As Jürgen Habermas has put it, "[n]otwithstanding their European origins … [i]n Asia, Africa, and South America, [human rights now] constitute the only language in which the opponents and victims of murderous regimes and civil wars can raise their voices against violence, repression, and persecution, against injuries to their human dignity" (2002, 153–154). Again, this is not to say that there are not other moral grammars readily available to "opponents and victims of murderous regimes and civil wars." But the formation of human rights over the last 20 years into something like the world's only "super-normativity" has created lines of hierarchy within the diversity of comparative ethical practice. Human rights exerts a centripetal force within a range of post-conflict processes and social and political struggles, pulling the moral imagination toward it and obscuring the possibility of other alternatives.

Nevertheless, the multiple logics of human rights remain contested, from the philosophical bases for the assertion of human dignity (Kohen 2012; Perry 2012), to the relationship between human rights and governance (Faulk 2012), to the ethical status of human rights as a legitimate object for critical scrutiny (Goodale 2012). The "contested status" (Sarat and Kearns 2002) of human rights comes into a particular kind of focus, and takes on a particular kind of urgency, in light of the "power and promise" (Kolodziej 2003) of human rights, the fact that the unfolding of the project of human rights – especially after the end of the Cold War – has taken place within a broader (largely neoliberal) narrative of human betterment, social development, and market democratization. This narrative is also vaguely utopian. There is nothing, as it were, beyond human rights. The realization of "a world made new" (Glendon 2001) in terms of human rights is not an intermediate step on the way to a Kantian world of perpetual peace. Rather, the language of human rights is the language for the "end of history" (Fukuyama 1992); it is the normative signpost marking the end of ideology and the emergence of human relations *as such*.

This makes it all the more necessary that the ways and means of human rights receive a heightened degree of attention at just this precise moment when the gap between the contested status of human rights and the power of human rights in the contemporary world is at the widest it has ever been. In this chapter, I examined one lingering dilemma that shadows this separation, namely, the relationship between human rights and progress. I began with the elemental question: Is human rights a force for progress? For Fukuyama among many other liberal theorists, and for the legions of activists all around the world, this is hardly a question worth asking at this point, since the very idea of human rights itself is – or has been, at least since it was reconceived from the ashes of World War II – a way of projecting a particular conception of progress by other means. But to ask the question, Is the human rights project a force for progress?, is also to ask a question that begs – and suggests an answer to – another, more problematic question: What is progress? Since I did not mean to take up this prior question at length – which one must, if one is to adequately examine the second – I instead reframed the problem of "progress" as a legitimate problem of agency and examined another – admittedly more obscure – question: How has the emergence of human rights as a hegemonic global normativity shaped agency?

I argued that the presence of human rights in its different forms has been most consequential to what might be described as "moral agency," the ways in which norms are deployed during moments of conflict, social disrupture and repair. This could be taken to be an essentially anthropological account of normativity and indeed it was to the anthropology of human rights that I turned as an empirical grounding for a broader set of reflections on moral agency in the age of human rights. What the ethnography of human rights practices in different parts of the world revealed is the fact that human rights have shaped what might be called "legacies of human experience" in ways that have introduced new lines of contradiction into processes of social change, political transition and economic reform. In other words, the inevitable processes through which human rights are "vernacularized," in Sally Engle Merry's (2006) formulation, is leading to a set of ambiguous judgments about the consequences of human rights for moral agency as purposive social action.

References

American Anthropological Association. 1947. "Statement on Human Rights." *American Anthropologist* 49:4, 539–543.

Baier, Annette. 1991. *A Progress of Sentiments: Reflections on Hume's Treatise.* Cambridge, MA: Harvard University Press.

Bass, Gary J. 2010. "The Old New Thing. Review of Samuel Moyn's *The Last Utopia*." *The New Republic*, November 11, 35–39.

Berlin, Isaiah. 1958. *Two Concepts of Liberty*. Oxford: Clarendon Press.

Cheah, Pheng. 2012. "Acceptable Uses of People." In Mark Goodale, ed., *Human Rights at the Crossroads*. Oxford University Press.

Cowan, Jane, Dembour, Marie-Bénédicte and Wilson, Richard A., eds. 2001. *Culture and Rights: Anthropological Perspectives*. Cambridge University Press.

Desai, Amit. 2010. "Dilemmas of Devotion: Religious Transformation and Agency in Hindu India." *Journal of the Royal Anthropological Institute* 16:2, 313–329.

Englund, Harri. 2006. *Prisoners of Freedom: Human Rights and the African Poor*. Berkeley: University of California Press.

Faulk, Karen. 2012. "Solidarity and Accountability: Rethinking Citizenship and Human Rights." In Mark Goodale, ed., *Human Rights at the Crossroads*. Oxford University Press.

Ferguson, James. 2006. *Global Shadows: Africa in the Neoliberal World Order*. Durham, NC: Duke University Press.

Fukuyama, Francis. 1992. *The End of History and the Last Man*. New York: Free Press.

Glendon, Mary Ann. 2001. *A World Made New: Eleanor Roosevelt and the University Declaration of Human Rights*. New York: Random House.

Goodale, Mark. 2007. "The Power of Right(s): Tracking Empires of Law and New Forms of Social Resistance in Bolivia (and Elsewhere)." In Mark Goodale and Sally Engle Merry, eds., *The Practice of Human Rights: Tracking Law Between the Global and the Local*. Cambridge University Press, pp. 130–162.

    2008. *Dilemmas of Modernity: Bolivian Encounters with Law and Liberalism*. Stanford University Press.

    2009. *Surrendering to Utopia: An Anthropology of Human Rights*. Stanford University Press.

    ed. 2012. *Human Rights at the Crossroads*. Oxford University Press.

    n.d. "Human Rights and Moral Creativity: Essays on Power, Agency, and Ethical Practice." Unpublished MS.

Goodale, Mark and Merry, Sally Engle, eds. 2007. *The Practice of Human Rights: Tracking Law Between the Global and the Local*. Cambridge University Press.

Habermas, Jürgen. 2002. *Religion and Rationality: Essays on Reason, God, and Modernity*. Cambridge, MA: MIT Press.

Hinton, Alexander Laban. 2012. "The Paradox of Perpetration: A View From the Cambodian Genocide." In Mark Goodale, ed., *Human Rights at the Crossroads*. Oxford University Press.

Henkin, Louis. 1990. *The Age of Rights*. New York: Columbia University Press.

Jackson, Thomas F. 2006. *From Civil Rights to Human Rights: Martin Luther King, Jr., and the Struggle for Economic Justice*. Philadelphia: University of Pennsylvania Press.

Keane, Webb. 2007. *Christian Moderns: Freedom and Fetish in the Mission Encounter.* Berkeley: University of California Press.

King, Jr., Martin Luther. 1963. "Letter from a Birmingham Jail." Available at: www.africa.upenn.edu/Articles_Gen/Letter_Birmingham.html (accessed November 3, 2011).

Kohen, Ari. 2012. "An Overlapping Consensus on Human Rights and Human Dignity." In Mark Goodale, ed., *Human Rights at the Crossroads.* Oxford University Press.

Kolodziej, Edward, ed. 2003. *A Force Profonde: The Power, Politics, and Promise of Human Rights.* Philadelphia: University of Pennsylvania Press.

Korey, William. 1998. *NGOs and the Universal Declaration on Human Rights: "A Curious Grapevine."* New York: St. Martin's Press.

Merry, Sally Engle. 2006. *Human Rights and Gender Violence: Translating International Law into Local Justice.* University of Chicago Press.

   2009. "Measuring the World: Indicators, Human Rights, and Global Governance." *Proceedings of the Annual Meeting of the American Society of International Law* 103, 239–243.

   2012. "Human Rights Monitoring and the Question of Indicators." In Mark Goodale, ed., *Human Rights at the Crossroads.* Oxford University Press.

Moyn, Samuel. 2010. *The Last Utopia: Human Rights in History.* Cambridge, MA: Belknap Press of Harvard University Press.

Ong, Aihwa and Collier, Stephen, eds. 2004. *Global Assemblages: Technology, Politics, and Ethics as Anthropological Problems.* Malden: Blackwell.

Perry, Michael. 2012. "Why Act Towards One Another 'In a Spirit of Brotherhood'? The Grounds of Human Rights." In Mark Goodale, ed., *Human Rights at the Crossroads.* Oxford University Press.

Riles, Annelise. 2000. *The Network Inside Out.* Ann Arbor: University of Michigan Press.

Roosevelt, Eleanor. 1948. "The Promise of Human Rights." *Foreign Affairs* 26, 470–477.

Rorty, Richard. 1993. "Human Rights, Rationality, and Sentimentality." In Stephen Shute and Susan Hurley, eds., *On Human Rights: The Oxford Amnesty Lectures.* New York: Basic Books, pp. 67–83.

Sarat, Austin and Kearns, Thomas, eds. 2002. *Human Rights: Concepts, Contests, Contingencies.* Ann Arbor: University of Michigan Press.

Sarfaty, Galit. 2012. *Values in Translation: Human Rights and the Culture of the World Bank.* Stanford University Press.

Speed, Shannon. 2008. *Rights in Rebellion: Indigenous Struggle and Human Rights in Chiapas.* Stanford University Press.

UNESCO. 1949. *Human Rights: Comments and Interpretations.* New York: Columbia University Press.

Wall, John. 2005. *Moral Creativity: Paul Ricoeur and the Poetics of Possibility.* Oxford University Press.

Wilson, Richard A. 2001. *The Politics of Truth and Reconciliation in South Africa: Legitimizing the Post-Apartheid State.* Cambridge University Press.

World Bank. 2011. "International Development Association, Articles of Agreement." Available at: http://go.worldbank.org/7XO4MV27T0 (accessed November 3, 2011).

LAURA PARISI

Introduction

At the time of its official adoption in the UN system in 1997, gender main-streaming was hailed as "progressive" by many transnational feminists because it was seen as a way to move beyond the biological sex binary of male/female, which had resulted in "just add women and stir" approaches to human rights, development and security. In tandem with the discursive shift from "sex" to "gender"[1] in the 1993 UN Vienna Declaration on Human Rights and 1995 Beijing Platform for Action, gender mainstreaming approaches seek to take into account the ideological power and circulation of gender. As applied to human rights, gender mainstreaming approaches are, in theory, attentive to how gender shapes and impacts our experiences and achievement of rights.

Gender mainstreaming is defined as:

the process of assessing the implications for women and men of any planned action, including legislation, policies or programmes, in all areas and at all levels. It is a strategy for making women's as well as men's concerns and experiences an inte-gral dimension of the design, implementation, monitoring and evaluation of pol-icies and programmes in all political, economic and societal spheres so that women and men benefit equally and inequality is not perpetuated. The ultimate goal is to achieve gender equality. (OSAGI 2002)

Jahan (1995, 13) identifies two dominant models of gender mainstream-ing: integrationist and agenda-setting or transformative. Integrationist refers to adding gender equality concerns and perspectives into existing frameworks whereas transformative (or agenda-setting) refers to deep institutional and transformational change that prioritizes gender equality and women's concerns.

Feminist arguments in favor of a transformative model of gender mainstreaming derive from critiques of the liberal conception of formal

---

[1] Defined as the "two sexes, male and female, in the context of society." The definition is not unproblematic for many feminists, as I will discuss further below.

"equality" in the UDHR and other international human rights laws and norms. Liberal feminists have long embraced the idea of formal equality in the public sphere, arguing that women should have full equality with men on the basis of their same abilities and rational capacities to fully exercise the requirements of citizenship. This argument results in the integration of women in the public spheres while leaving both public institutions and the private sphere intact. However, other feminists (Bunch 1990; Charlesworth 1995; Friedman 2006; Sullivan 1995) have argued for a more transformative notion of gender equality that is not based on androcentric conceptions of human rights in the public sphere. The public sphere has historically been gendered as a masculine space; hence, the idea that "women's rights are human rights," coined by Charlotte Bunch (1990), seeks to highlight how formal legal equality in the public sphere contributes to the false appearance of the state as non-gendered and fuels the state's complicity in facilitating gender hierarchies in the private sphere. Emphasis on the public sphere as the proper realm of human rights de-politicizes women's experiences in the private, as states are discouraged by international law to intervene in the private sphere given the primacy placed on the sanctity of the family and the right to privacy (Sullivan 1995, 127). The result is that states are held accountable only for the human rights abuses they perpetrate and not for the conduct of individuals in the private sphere, where most gender-based violence occurs.

Gender mainstreaming approaches to human rights render visible the relationship between the public and private spheres, and offer a potentially transformative and progressive path through actively seeking to understand how gender, as well as race, class, sexuality, age, religion, ability, etc., impact people's ability to access and achieve rights that go beyond the legal equality strategy and framework (Jahan 1995). Since 1995, gender mainstreaming initiatives have been adopted at all levels of governance, producing what Kardam (2004) calls a "global gender equality regime." Unsurprisingly, gender mainstreaming practices have been subject to particular scrutiny by feminist scholars and policy-makers alike (Charlesworth 2005; Daly 2005; Kouvo 2005; Meier and Celis 2011; Moser and Moser 2005; Parisi 2011; Parpart 2009; Prügl and Lustgarten 2007; Subrahmanian 2007; Tiessen 2007; True 2009; True and Parisi 2013; Walby 2005). Yet, many questions about gender mainstreaming human rights as a path to achieving gender equality remain. This chapter examines the idea of "progressiveness" with regards to gender mainstreaming human rights by considering the following: how should feminists evaluate claims about the value of gender mainstreaming human rights in light of the dominant narrative of human rights as a process of "progressive realization?" Given the understanding of "progressiveness" as a transformative practice in the gender mainstreaming human rights discourse, what are the implications for achieving gender equality?

Progressive realization

The notion of progressive realization of rights takes its clearest form in Article 2 of the UN International Covenant for Economic, Social, and Cultural Rights (ICESCR), which emphasizes the state duty to realize rights to "the maximum of its available resources." There is no mention of progressive realization in the ICCPR, as if legislative measures are sufficient for the protection and fulfillment of civil and political liberties and state-allocated resources are not needed. Yet, one could argue that legal provisions are a progressively realized process requiring resources from the state and other institutions – a process that feminists fighting for suffrage, equal pay, reproductive rights, etc. know all too well. Perhaps it is unsurprising, then, that the 1979 UN Convention on the Elimination of All Forms of Discrimination (CEDAW) uses more strident language demanding immediate, rather than progressively realized, action by state parties to fulfill, protect and respect women's human rights.

Despite the demands articulated in CEDAW, the notion of progressively realizing rights has become normalized in human rights literature, policy and practice to the extent that it is a "given." Since feminists have long challenged other gendered givens in the same human rights discourse that produced, sustained and legitimized the idea of progressive realization (Peterson 1990), it is important to assess the implications of gender mainstreaming human rights as a progressively realized process. For example, the principle of non-discrimination ought to be immediately realized, and indeed exists prior to any formulation of specific rights. Diane Elson argues that states always have an immediate obligation to ensure "that there will be no discrimination in the exercise of rights" and suggests that this requires states to prioritize women's equality in the progressive realization of rights (2006, 15).

Yet, in making trade-offs, progressive realization of rights requires justification of which rights will be fulfilled for which people and in which order, and this inevitably invites discriminatory practices, particularly in a system that many feminists regard as already androcentric and patriarchal.[2] Gender mainstreaming frameworks potentially provide a way to evaluate

---

[2] For a dissenting view see Howard-Hassmann (2011).

the process of progressive realization and to make normative claims about state duties to fulfill and protect the human rights of women.

Gender mainstreaming and quantitative approaches to measuring progressive realization

The concept of progressive realization assumes that human rights achievement and/or regression can be tracked over time, and a variety of concepts and indicators have been developed to measure human rights achievement and enjoyment (Ackerly and Cruz 2011; Cingranelli and Richards 2010; Fukuda-Parr *et al.* 2009; Green 2001; Hertel and Minkler 2007; Landman 2004; Landman and Carvalho 2010). In the gender mainstreaming literature there is a parallel debate around evaluation – how do we know when an organization, law, policy or program has been effectively mainstreamed? (Charlesworth 2005; de Waal 2006; Howard 2002; Jahan 1995; Meier and Celis 2011; Moser 2005; Moser and Moser 2005;). Even though feminists have argued for the collection of sex-disaggregated data in order to assess "progress" in achieving gender equality, these debates prompt consideration of whether or not gender is being effectively mainstreamed into human rights measures designed to track progressive realization.

However, when considering quantitative measures designed to capture the achievement of gender equality rights there are several types of measures to consider: those which measure process, like gender budgeting (Elson 2003, 2006); those which measure outcomes, like the right to education (women's literacy rates), the right to work (women's labor force participation), etc. (Apodaca 1998); and those I suggest are a combination of process and outcomes, like electoral reform that adopts legally mandated gender quotas (process), which in turn result in higher percentages of women elected to parliaments (outcome) (Bauer 2008). In addition, there are measures that quantify states' legal codification of gender equality rights, such as suffrage rights (Poe *et al.* 1997), or whether a country has ratified CEDAW (Kenworthy and Malami 1999).

The analysis usually takes the form of looking at the rate by which women are catching up with men on various indicators, since on almost all indictors of human rights and human development (except for life expectancy and infant mortality rates), women lag behind men. The UNDP's Gender Development Index (GDI),[3] which was revised into the Gender Inequality Index (GII) in

---

[3] The GDI was introduced in 1995 and was comprised of the following indicators: male and female life expectancy (years); male and female literacy rates (percent); male and female gross

2010, has typically used a ratio measure in which 0 indicates equality between men and women on selected indicators, and 1 indicates the widest gender inequality.[4] Though some may argue that the GDI indicators are more properly thought of as human development indicators, the recent theoretical and policy shift to human rights based approaches in development blurs earlier distinctions between human rights and human development (Cornwall and Molyneux 2006). As well, the GDI uses outcome variables that are often used in the human rights literature to capture the achievement of social and economic rights. Finally, the UN Office the Special Advisor on Gender Issues (OSAGI), in its definition of gender equality, makes the link between human rights and human development explicit by stating that "equality between women and men is seen both as a human rights issue and as a precondition for, and indicator of, sustainable people-centered development" (Women Watch n.d., paragraph 1).

Because the UNDP updated the GDI every year until 2010, when it introduced GII, it was possible to track over time the progressive realization of socioeconomic rights of women vis-à-vis men.[5] As the GDI retains the male experience as the primary benchmark to measure the achievement of social and economic rights of women, this implies that women are discriminated against in the sense that they have not achieved the same rights as men (Parisi 2009). Although the GDI appears to be underpinned by an integrationist form of gender mainstreaming, the question still remains: what are we mainstreaming when we mainstream gender (Eveline and Bacchi 2005)? First, in countries that have low human development and achievement of human rights, having a high GDI score may obscure the fact that many men are disenfranchised as well. Having equally poor rights achievement on human rights indicators is not the type of equality that feminists are seeking to achieve. Second, and related to the first point, it is difficult to tell if movement toward gender equality on the GDI is the result of men "equalizing down" to women (Elson 2006).

Third, as I have argued elsewhere, these types of measures are more appropriately thought of as capturing sex inequalities rather than gender inequalities as they reflect only the material differences between men and

---

school enrollment rates (percent); and male and female estimated share of earned income (percent). The complementary measure, the Gender Empowerment Measure (GEM) includes: percentage of total seats held in parliament by women; female legislators, senior officials and managers (percentage of total); female professional and technical workers (percentage of total); and ratio of estimated female to male earned income.

[4] Although the indicator has been revised recently, its importance in terms of policy-making at the global level was significant, and used to justify policies directed at achieving gender equality.

[5] Some years are not directly comparable due to changes in the measure of the GDI.

women rather than the "ideological dimensions of gender oppression that privileges and normalizes a particular understanding of such rights" (Parisi 2009, 415–416). As Baden and Goetz (1997, 7) suggest, these types of measures obscure how power relations are gendered and reinforce patterns of inequality, and also delink the feminist goal of transforming gender relations from the analysis of gender inequality. While this type of disaggregated data is useful as a starting point for tracking progressive realization of rights for women and men and identifying where gaps in achievement exist, if the data is not "harnessed to understanding of gender relations, [it] is analytically impoverished" (Jackson 2002, 499). For example, Charlesworth (2005) documents that in many general comments produced by various UN human rights committees, accounting for progress in gender mainstreaming human rights is an exercise that does not often go beyond focusing on counting how many women were/are affected by the issue at hand. Krook and True (2010, 19) note that this type of data collection on women's human rights achievements and violations may be used to identify "changes to policy-making processes, but not necessarily patterns of gender inequality, as intended by many advocates." Gender mainstreamed human rights indicators cannot be an end in themselves for tracking progressive realization of rights; rather, these indicators provide a basis for feminist analysis of the social, economic, cultural and political reasons that influence the progression or retrogression of these indicators. As the definition of gender equality put forth by OSAGI[6] indicates, it is necessary to take into account the different lived realities of women and men, and that these experiences produce different sets of needs and interests, which require a transformation and expansion of the idea of human rights.

The new GII includes a reproductive health dimension that works as partial solution to this problem, as well as a mix of sex disaggregated data (labor force participation rates, percent of population with secondary education). The GII,[7] in attempting to take into account the needs and priorities of women, and to draw attention to the roles that women play in society,

---

[6] Gender equality "refers to the equal rights, responsibilities and opportunities of women and men and girls and boys. Equality does not mean that women and men will become the same but that women's and men's rights, responsibilities and opportunities will not depend on whether they are born male or female. Gender equality implies that the interests, needs and priorities of both women and men are taken into consideration, recognizing the diversity of different groups of women and men. Gender equality is not a women's issue but should concern and fully engage men as well as women. Equality between women and men is seen both as a human rights issue and as a precondition for, and indicator of, sustainable people-centered development" (OSAGI 2002).

[7] This indicator also uses the same ratio measure that the previous GDI used, with 0 indicating gender equality and 1 indicating the widest gender inequality.

basically categorizes all women as mothers by using maternal mortality rates and adolescent[8] fertility rates as a measure of reproductive health. However, even though the indicator is not using a specific measure of legally realized reproductive rights, in my view the indicator is still capturing rights for several reasons. First, as previously noted, outcome data for social and economic rights is frequently used as a measure of rights achievement in a variety of areas. As such, the UNDP positions reproductive health as a gendered dimension and reflection of both the right to life and health. Second, CEDAW (Article 12) and the Beijing Platform for Action are clear in their articulations that women do have a right to reproductive health. Feminists have strategically adopted the language around reproductive health in the absence of being able to explicitly name abortion (and also access to contraception) as a right in these documents, and the idea of reproductive health can be interpreted as including access to abortion and other reproductive rights, because without reproductive rights it difficult to achieve reproductive health. Both maternal mortality rates and adolescent fertility rates can be read as proxies for the legal right to contraception and abortion, since the maternal mortality rate definition includes death from the termination of pregnancies (WHO 2012), and both the right to contraception (or family planning) and abortions play a key role in the reduction of maternal mortality rates and adolescent fertility rates.

However, while the new indicator on reproductive health attempts to gender mainstream what women's experience of living healthy lives might require, it does so in a gender essentialist and biological determinist way that unilaterally equates women with motherhood, an identity that has historically served to justify the denial of rights to women. The indicator can be read as a way to track progressive realization of conditions that enable women to exercise their "traditional roles" more fully, reifying and leaving gender relations relatively intact. I am not contesting that many women embrace their roles as mothers, but this is not the only role in society that they play. There are many other health concerns related to the right to life and the right to health that women have which vary tremendously across gender identity, class, race, place, etc. In addition, the emphasis on pregnancy in both the adolescent fertility rate and maternal mortality rates indicators implicitly privileges procreative heterosexual sex, leaving little room for the inclusion of women's health issues attached to a variety of sexual practices that are not necessarily motivated by procreation. Thus, there is

[8] Girls ages 15–19. This indicator is a bit curious because in the majority of the countries in the world, children are legally adults at the age of 18.

a very narrow conceptualization in these variables of which women count when calculating levels of gender inequality.

The other three components of the GII, labor force participation, political representation in national parliaments, and attainment of secondary level education, raise different concerns with gender mainstreaming human rights indicators. First, like the now defunct GDI, the three variables are based on the male-as-norm principle, and capture only gender parity not gender equality. That participation in national parliaments is seen as the ultimate expression of the right to political participation for women should be questioned, particularly when the quality and experience of participation for women in national parliaments varies (Bauer 2008), and women may actually more fully exercise their right to political participation and decision-making in sub-national political bodies or even in local community based organizations (Sacchet 2008). Sacchet's research on quota systems in Latin America shows that despite the low parliamentary representation of women in the Brazilian legislature, Brazil has some of the most progressive gender equality legislation in the region. She argues that Brazilian culture and political institutions make it difficult for women to participate in formal politics, so Brazilian women have developed a well-organized women's movement that has been highly visible and influential in promoting social change. A variable aimed at capturing the different interests and needs of women and men would not take the ultimate expression of male citizenship as a given for women. A similar argument can be made with the education indicator in that it obscures the many ways in which educational experiences are gendered, potentially unequal, and may also serve to reinforce traditional gender roles in cases where education is used to train girls to be better mothers, etc. (Kabeer 2005; Unterhalter and North 2011). Though both the political participation and educational attainment indicators track progressive realization of gender parity in access, they cannot account for discriminatory practices that happen within these institutions.

Second, all three variables reinforce the notion that progressive realization of rights occurs only in the public sphere, reinforcing the dichotomy between the private and public spheres that feminists have contested. The reinforcement of this dichotomy cannot take into account how the achievement of these rights in the public sphere affects women's lives in the so-called private sphere. Labor force participation rates, as a measurement of the right to work, are very problematic in this regard. Lourdes Benería (2003), among others, has argued that emphasis on paid employment obscures, invisibilizes and devalues unpaid and caring labor that many women do in the private sphere, despite the economic value it contributes to the global economy. There is no evidence to suggest, when looking at time-use studies, that women's unpaid labor significantly decreases when entering into the paid labor force (Hawkesworth 2006).

Women's association with private sphere activities also serves to devalue their labor in the public sphere based on their construction as supplemental wage earner to the male head of the household. Therefore, certain areas of the labor force are feminized, low paying and part-time, and may also be comprised of jobs that violate labor rights laws, etc. In addition, there is some mixed evidence to suggest that as women's labor force participation increases, so does domestic violence (Blanco and Villa 2008; Krishnan *et al.* 2010). Thus, it cannot be automatically assumed that an increase in women's participation in the labor force is indeed a measure of progressive realization of rights for women.

Gender mainstreaming process

What are the alternatives to gender mainstreaming output indicators commonly used to measure the progressive realization of human rights? Diane Elson suggests that focusing on processes, such as gender budgeting, may be more able to capture what is happening in terms of resource allocation to realize rights, and allows us uncover hidden gendered assumptions in both policy-making and budgets. This idea involves tracking inputs in relation to outputs, and ties directly to the core precept of progressive realization that states have the duty to realize rights at the maximum amount of their available resources. In addition, gender budgeting provides a way to track processes of discriminatory trade-offs and priorities in resource allocation and so allows us to track whose rights are being progressively realized through this process. For Elson, gender budgeting is not a technocratic process that results in the creation of separate or equal budgets for men and women (which would approximate the integrationist form of gender mainstreaming). Rather, she argues that gender budgeting initiatives should be guided by a reflexive feminist approach by asking: "What impact does this fiscal measure have on gender equality? Does it reduce it, increase it, or leave it unchanged?" (Elson 2003, 3).

Put in rights based language and in accordance with the definition of gender mainstreaming provided earlier in the chapter, gender budgeting as an indicator would require analyzing the impacts policies and fiscal measures have on the progressive realization of rights for both women and men, and would also require that spending and resource allocation equally serve the needs and priorities of women and men, with an eye toward reducing gender inequality (Elson 2003). The emphasis on process shifts the concept of gender from a noun to a verb, and would "view gendering as an incomplete and partial process in which bodies and politics are always becoming meaningful" (Eveline and Bacchi 2005, 502). The emphasis on "gender as an embodied process" potentially gives us a way to track progressive realization of women's human rights as a dynamic, discursively and materially contested process – one that is ongoing and perhaps non-linear, due to the social construction of both gender and human rights, and the meanings attached to these concepts. This politics takes us beyond the static nature of binary, quantifiable indicators as evidence of progressively realized gender mainstreamed human rights. Yet, while it may be possible to track over time processes like the gender budgeting initiatives within particular countries, it may be difficult to track these processes comparatively across countries, since no standardization for GBIs currently exists.

Further considerations

What the above discussion suggests is that what needs to be developed further to evaluate gender mainstreamed and progressively realized rights are measures that link inputs (processes) to outputs (outcome/benchmark indictors). Yet, as measures of progressive realization of rights for women, both types of rights indicators (outputs and inputs) suffer from two additional problems. First, the measures are unable to conceptually deal with and track progressive realization of rights within the categories of women and men,[9] because the indicators homogenize these groups and obscure the ways that gender, race, ethnicity, class, sexuality, age, nation, ability, and so on intersect to create inequalities within and across groups. This is partly due to unavailable data, but it is also partly a reflection of the silo effect of the human rights treaty system in the United Nations, in which claimants can identify only one form of discrimination, such as race or sex, but not multiple and intersecting ones (Lambert 2004). This same problem exists in many domestic legal systems as well. In recent years, feminists (Kuokkanen 2012; Parisi 2011) have increasingly argued for the need of intersectional frameworks to more fully understand rights violations and achievement. Intersectional approaches start from the analytical premise that people's identities, i.e., gender, race, class, sexuality, nation, etc., are not mutually exclusive or additive, but rather multiple, layered and interrelated and, as such, produce unique and specific experiences that are not easily

---

[9] These categories themselves are contested, as I discuss below.

essentialized (AWID 2004, 1–2). This idea is reflected in the OSAGI definition of gender equality, which guides the application of gender mainstreaming. Intersectional approaches go beyond simplistic binary gender-based analysis, which examines only one relationship of power, to highlight how social categories "gain meaning and power by reinforcing and referencing each other" (Bunjun *et al.* 2006, 8). It may be possible, however, to approach gender budgeting with a more intersectional analysis.

Second, though both types of measures can serve to monitor progressive realization of rights for women, neither measure can capture the idea of human rights enjoyment. On the surface of it, this issue may seem unrelated to the idea of gender mainstreaming human rights and how to measure progressive realization. However, much of the women's human rights literature focuses on rights as a means to women's empowerment, although the concept of women's empowerment is a contested term in the feminist literature and operates in a variety of discursive ways in international organizations and NGOs (Cornwall and Brock 2005; Eyben and Napier-Moore 2009; Kabeer 1999; Mosedale 2005). Indeed, in the GII women's achievement of some secondary school level education and women's participation in national parliaments are seen to make up the "empowerment" dimension of the GII. Implicit in both the rights and empowerment discussion is the assumption that as women's rights achievement increases so does women's empowerment; the fullest institutional embodiment of this relationship is the newly constituted United Nations Entity for Gender Equality and Women's Empowerment (more commonly referred to as UN Women).

If rights are assumed to be an important component of empowerment then presumably we can also track the progressive realization of women's empowerment. However, the relationship is more complicated than this. Empowerment implies the exercise and enjoyment of rights, since most definitions of women's empowerment focus on the idea of the expansion of choice and agency. But as Mosedale (2005) observes, providing the material resources and legal conditions for empowerment does not mean that women are in fact empowered since there is no guarantee that women can and will exercise their rights. Furthermore, the idea of enjoyment of rights and related empowerment has a wholly subjective component that can never be captured by a quantitative or a process indicator, even if it has been gender mainstreamed. The exercise of the rights that are deemed progressively realized by benchmark indicators cannot capture the quality of the right exercised. For example, women's participation in the labor force statistics do not reveal whether the exercise of that right is meaningful and fulfilling. Rather, the labor performed could be harmful and/or unfulfilling, resulting in disempowerment rather than empowerment. Similar parallels can be drawn with education indicators. Thus, where progressive realization of rights is actually taking place is in women's subjectivities and how they come to understand, claim, exercise, value and enjoy such rights. The implication of this argument is that the progressive realization of rights for women as currently measured and understood can provide the conditions for women's empowerment and the eradication of gender inequality, but does not constitute realization of rights in and of itself. As Ackerly asserts, "the realization of rights is in their *enjoyment*; a formal recognition of an entitlement unrealized for individual, social, political, or economic reasons is not the enjoyment of the right" (2011, 225, emphasis in the original). Following this logic, and going beyond the issue of formal recognition, I would suggest that a formal accounting of these entitlements also does not constitute the realization of rights.

Progressiveness: as in moving forward or transformative

The earlier discussion inevitably points to the disjuncture between the concept of gender mainstreaming human rights as a transformative practice, and the measures we have available to track progressive realization. In this section, I further consider the idea of "progressiveness" in relation to the concept of gender. Specifically, I consider this idea as one that guides our understanding of gender mainstreaming human rights as a step toward achieving gender equality. As the inclusion of "gender" rather than "sex" in the Beijing Platform for Action (BPFA 1995) and subsequent international law such as the Rome Statute that established the ICC, was hailed as a significant feminist moment, it is worth examining how the concept of "gender" is rendered in the definition and practice of gender mainstreaming and the implications of this for realizing human rights.

Many feminist scholars have commented on the problematic ways that terms such as sex, gender and gender equality circulate in global and other levels of governance (Baden and Goetz, 1997; Charlesworth 2005; Eveline and Bacchi 2005; Kouvo 2005; Smyth 2007; Squires 2005; Zalewski 2010). A full rendering of this feminist debate goes well beyond the scope of this chapter, but several points are worth noting here. The first point involves the definition of gender in international documents and treaties. The Beijing Platform for Action defines gender as the "two sexes, male and female, in the context of society" (BPFA 1995). This definition has proved to be highly problematic on a number of fronts as it has resulted in conceptual confusion that has produced a myriad of ways in which gender has been deployed in the process of gender mainstreaming human rights. Ironically the feminist strategy of shifting from the anti-discrimination language contained in CEDAW to the idea that women's rights are human rights and the widespread adoption of this mantra in the UN system (Waylen 2008) have in part contributed to some unintended consequences with regards to gender mainstreaming human rights.

The definition of gender in the BPFA allows for some notion of the socially constructed aspects of gender (which is often defined as socio-cultural interpretation of sex) yet still retains a binary notion of biological sex (i.e., "the two sexes"). This definition is the result of a political compromise in the document to appease the fears of the more conservative actors that the term gender would be employed to disrupt the "natural" order of human relations, and indeed possibly abolish the whole concept of human itself (Baden and Goetz 1997; West 1999). In practice, this definition has served to collapse and map the notion of gender onto sex, wherein femininity is equated with women, and masculinity is equated with men. The binary in the definition precludes any analysis of the dynamic and relational aspects of gender, as the sex binary (defined as male and female) renders gender as highly essentialist and exclusionary. The definition of gender is further buttressed by the strong liberal gender equality discourse that permeates the BPFA, despite a weak attempt at acknowledging diversity and attendant multiple discriminations (Chan-Tiberghien 2004; Otto 1996). This binary and essentialist conceptualization of gender and gender equality translates into a gender mainstreamed human rights framework that remains entrenched in the integrationist mode, rather than a transformational mode, as called for by many feminists.

This has the reductionist effect of usurping the analytic power of gender by normalizing and reifying gender difference on the basis of biological sex, which is often thought to be a more empirical and therefore countable category, even though many feminists argue that the biological sex binary is also socially constructed (Kinsella 2003, 296). Through this discursive mapping in women's equality documents such as CEDAW and the BPFA, issues of gender (in)equality become framed as solely between men and women (Jauhola 2010), with men always represented as the advantaged group (Connell 2005, 1806). In these discourses, men become an unmarked and undifferentiated category that casts them as both "the problem" and as the "power holders." The operationalization of gender (in)equality in these documents and policies also rests on an assumption that the categories of "woman," "man," "femininity" and "masculinity" are knowable, static (even as they vary across cultures[10]) and uncontested. The insistence on two genders precludes the possibility of claiming any other gender identity, and, as a result, people are understood to have only one gender, never the other, or both (Jauhola 2010, 31). A transformationalist approach to gender mainstreaming human rights would utilize a relational, fluid and dynamic approach to gender analysis that would transcend this false binary by being able to take into account all those who are feminized, including many men who are marginalized on the basis of sexuality, race, ethnicity and class. This marginalization occurs on the basis of men's inability to achieve "hegemonic masculinities," which refers to how "certain ways of being a man" are more culturally valued and accepted than others (Cornwall 1997, 12). The inability to achieve hegemonic masculinity suggests that many men are unable to achieve rights even in a patriarchal system that potentially favors them and may even afford them male privilege in certain contexts.

On the flip side, it is important to recognize and analyze how women can be masculinized, in ways that potentially advantage them over marginalized men in the achievement of rights. bell hooks (1984) argues that patriarchal systems can accommodate the granting of power to and inclusion of women of the dominant race in order to maintain race and class privilege. This means that some women's rights are progressively realized much faster than other women's and some men's, but are not realized to the fullest extent of those who have achieved hegemonic masculinity, since women can never achieve this. This path of course does nothing to change gender or racial relations that produce inequalities in the first place, since the expansion of power to achieve rights by women is largely contingent on maintaining the patriarchal order. That there are sanctions for contesting the essentialist gender binary can also be seen in the perceived transgressions of queer and lesbian women and queer and gay men. Although gender and sexual identity vary tremendously within GLBTQI communities, people who designate themselves as part of these communities are often seen as threat to both the hegemonic masculinities and femininities that constitute the heteronormative patriarchal order of mainstream human rights.

This example clearly illustrates the lack of progress that an integrationist and essentialist version of gender mainstreamed human rights produces, returning to an earlier point about intersectionality as part of a transformative process of gender mainstreaming human rights. In no international

[10] Many post-colonial feminist scholars (Grewal 2005; Kapur 2005) have rightfully noted that there is a hierarchy of femininities and masculinities that position the cultural construction of gender identities in the global North as superior to those in the global South.

human rights document, gender mainstreamed or otherwise, are the rights to gender identity and sexuality fully expressed.[11] Rather, what we see are inconsistent and unevenly applied interpretations across human rights bodies and documents. For example, in 1994 the UN Human Rights Committee ruled, in response to a case involving criminalization of same-sex acts of men in Australia, that "sex" as outlined in the ICCPR should be understood to include sexual orientation, particularly where the right to privacy and freedom from discrimination are concerned, and it has routinely criticized countries on their discrimination against the LGBTQI community (O'Flaherty and Fisher 2008, 216). However, other human rights conventions, such as the ICESCR and the CRC, have used "other status" in the non-discrimination clauses to cover sexual orientation and sometimes gender identity. The BPFA is more explicit in its declaration by asserting that "the human rights of women include their right to have control over and decide freely and responsibly on matters related to their sexuality" (1995, paragraph 96), yet the BPFA is also not legally binding in the same ways as human rights conventions.

Ironically, the collapse of gender onto sex binaries can also serve to de-politicize gender in ways that are antithetical to the transformative, and even the integrationist, intent behind gender mainstreaming human rights. This is often referred to as the "everywhere/nowhere" problem in which organizations and institutions, through cross-cutting gender mainstreaming initiatives, change their language from "women" to "gender" and adopt gender mainstreaming language precisely as a way to de-politicize gender inequalities (Charlesworth 2005; Daly 2005; Tiessen 2007). Adopting the language but not the intent of gender mainstreaming in this way is purely symbolic, and the refusal to meaningfully engage with gender relations can actually maintain or exacerbate existing gender inequalities, either within organizations themselves or through programming outputs (Clisby 2005; Tiessen 2007; Wallace 1998).

Conclusions

As the analysis above reveals, the answer to the central question posed in this chapter – is gender mainstreaming rights a progressive path toward gender equality? – is complicated. If progressive in this context means "linear,"

---

[11] The majority of the world's 190 countries also do not recognize the right to sexuality and/or gender identity/expression.

then the integrationist model of gender mainstreaming human rights, in its very limited form, might be viewed as a path to formal gender equality, in which gendered barriers to access and opportunity are removed without changing existing structures and ideologies. The appeal of this model is that presumably it is easy to tell whether or not women's human rights are being realized, and undoubtedly women's human rights achievement has progressed on some indicators.

However, if we understand progressive to mean "forward-thinking" or transformational, then gender mainstreaming human rights, at this juncture, remains an elusive goal to some degree, even as some states have rescinded reservations to CEDAW, established women's ministries, and adopted new constitutions with detailed gender equality provisions. Yet, following Joachim (2010), I have suggested that following the gender equality frame advocated by many feminist human rights activists, policy-makers and scholars encompasses more than formal equality rights as guaranteed by the state. This is not to take away from the very important role and meaning that human rights discourse has for social justice movements, including feminist movements. But to achieve the kind of societal transformation and gender equality that is at the heart of gender mainstreaming strategies, we need to look beyond the state as the arbiter of rights. Gender mainstreaming analysis gives us the discursive and analytic tools to also consider the ways in which other, non-state, actors such as community-based organizations and non-governmental organizations play a more substantive role in people's everyday lives to actually achieve rights. Finally, individuals and communities themselves are adopting action-oriented perspectives on rights and generating new conceptions of human rights that contest and expand the range of valid conceptualizations of rights, and as such are potential contributors to the dismantling of gendered, racialized, classed and sexualized hierarchies and inequalities (Ackerly 2001; Nyamu-Musembi 2005).

References

Ackerly, Brooke. 2001. "Women's Human Rights Activists as Cross-Cultural Theorists." *International Journal of Feminist Politics* 3:3, 311–346.

2011. "Human Rights Enjoyment in Theory and in Activism." *Human Rights Review* 12, 221–239.

Ackerly, Brooke and Cruz, Miguel. 2011. "Hearing the Voice of the People: Human Rights as if People Mattered." *New Political Science* 33:1, 1–22.

Apodaca, Clair. 1998. "Measuring Women's Economic and Social Rights Achievement." *Human Rights Quarterly* 20:1, 139–172.

AWID. 2004. "Intersectionality: A Tool for Gender and Economic Justice." *Women's Rights and Economic Change (Facts & Issues #9)*. Toronto: Association for Women's Rights in Development. Available at: www.awid.org/publications/primers/intersectionality_en.pdf.

Baden, Sally and Goetz, Anne Marie. 1997. "Who Needs [Sex] When You Can Have [Gender]?" *Feminist Review* 56:1, 3–25.

Bauer, Gretchen. 2008. "Fifty/Fifty by 2020: Electoral Gender Quotas for Parliament in East and Southern Africa." *International Journal of Feminist Politics* 10:3, 348–368.

Benería, Lourdes. 2003. *Gender, Development, and Globalization: Economics as If All People Mattered*. New York and London: Routledge.

Blanco, Lorenzo and Villa, Sandra M. 2008. "Sources of Crime in the State of Veracruz: The Role of Female Labor Force Participation and Wage Inequality." *Feminist Economics* 14:3, 51–75.

BPFA (Beijing Platform for Action). 1995. Declaration of the Fourth World Conference on Women. September 15, 1995, Beijing, China.

Bunch, Charlotte. 1990. "Women's Rights as Human Rights: Towards a Re-Vision of Human Rights." *Human Rights Quarterly* 12:4, 486–498.

Bunjun, Bénita, Lee, Jo-Anne, Lenon, Suzanne, Martin, Lise, Torres, Sara and Waller, Marie-Katherine. 2006. *Intersectional Feminist Frameworks: An Emerging Vision*. Ottawa: Canadian Research Institute for the Advancement of Women.

CEDAW (Convention on the Elimination of All Forms of Discrimination Against Women). 1979. Opened for signature December 18, 1979, 1249 U.N.T.S. 13 (entered into force September 3, 1981).

Chan-Tiberghien, J. 2004. "Gender-Skepticism or Gender-Boom? Poststructural Feminisms, Transnational Feminisms, and the World Conference Against Racism." *International Feminist Journal of Politics* 6:3, 454–484.

Charlesworth, Hilary. 1995. "Human Rights as Men's Rights." In J. Peters and A. Wolper, eds., *Women's Rights, Human Rights: International Feminist Perspectives*. London and New York: Routledge, pp. 103–113.

　　2005. "Not Waving but Drowning: Gender Mainstreaming and Human Rights in the United Nations." *Harvard Human Rights Journal* 18, 1–18.

Cingranelli, David L. and Richards, David L. 2010. "The Cingranelli and Richards (CIRI) Human Rights Data Project." *Human Rights Quarterly* 32, 395–418.

Clisby, Suzanne. 2005. "Gender Mainstreaming or Just More Male-Streaming?" *Gender & Development* 13:2, 23–35.

Connell, R.W. 2005. "Change Among the Gatekeepers: Men, Masculinities, and Gender Equality in the Global Arena." *Signs* 30:3, 1801–1825.

Cornwall, Andrea. 1997. "Men, Masculinity, and 'Gender in Development.'" *Gender & Development* 5:2, 8–13.

Cornwall, A. and Brock, K. 2005. "What Do Buzzwords Do for Development Policy? A Critical Look at 'Participation,' 'Empowerment' and 'Poverty Reduction.'" *Third World Quarterly* 26:7, 1043–1060.

Cornwall, Andrea and Molyneux, M. 2006. "The Politics of Rights – Dilemmas for Feminist Praxis: An Introduction." *Third World Quarterly* 27:7, 1175–1191.

Daly, Mary. 2005. "Gender Mainstreaming in Theory and Practice." *Social Politics: International Studies in Gender, State, and Society* 12:3, 433–450.

De Waal, Maretha. 2006. "Evaluating Gender Mainstreaming in Development Projects." *Development in Practice* 16:2, 209–214.

Elson, Diane. 2003. "Gender Mainstreaming and Gender Budgeting." Paper presented at the Gender and Equality and Europe's Future Conference, Brussels, March 4, 2003. Available at: http://ec.europa.eu/education/programmes/llp/jm/more/confgender03/elson.pdf.

  2006. *Budgeting for Women's Rights; Monitoring Government Budgets for Compliance with CEDAW*. New York: UNIFEM.

Eveline, Joan and Bacchi, Carol. 2005. "What Are We Mainstreaming When We Mainstream Gender?" *International Feminist Journal of Politics* 7:4, 486–512.

Eyben, Rosalind and Napier-Moore, Rebecca. 2009. "Choosing Words with Care? Shifting Meanings of Women's Empowerment in International Development." *Third World Quarterly* 30:2, 285–300.

Friedman, Elisabeth Jay. 2006. "Bringing Women to International Human Rights." *Peace Review: A Journal of Social Justice* 18, 479–484.

Fukuda-Parr, Sakiko, Lawson-Remer, Terra and Randolph, Susan. 2009. "An Index of Economic and Social Rights Fulfillment: Concept and Methodology." *Journal of Human Rights* 8:3, 195–221.

Green, Maria. 2001. "What We Talk About When We Talk About Indicators: Current Approaches to Human Rights Measurement." *Human Rights Quarterly* 23:4, 1062–1097.

Grewal, Inderpal. 2005. *Transnational America: Feminism, Diasporas, Neoliberalisms*. Durham, NC and London: Duke University Press.

Hawkesworth, Mary E. 2006. *Globalization and Feminist Activism*. Lanham: Rowman & Littlefield.

Hertel, Shareen and Minkler, Lanse, eds. 2007. *Economic Rights: Conceptual, Measurement, and Policy Issues*. Cambridge University Press.

hooks, bell. 1984. *Feminist Theory: From Margin to Center*. Boston: South End Press.

Howard, Patricia L. 2002. "Beyond the 'Grim Resisters': Towards More Effective Gender Mainstreaming through Stakeholder Participation." *Development in Practice* 12:2, 164–176.

Howard-Hassmann, Rhoda E. 2011. "Universal Human Rights Since 1970: The Centrality of Autonomy and Agency." *Journal of Human Rights* 10:4, 433–449.

Jackson, Cecile. 2002. "Disciplining Gender?" *World Development* 30:3, 497–509.

Jahan, Rounaq. 1995. "The Elusive Agenda: Mainstreaming Women in Development." In Ann Leonard and Martha Chen, eds., *Seeds 2: Supporting Women's Work Around the World*. New York: The Feminist Press, pp. 214–218.

Jauhola, Marjaana. 2010. "Building Back Better? – Negotiating Normative Boundaries of Gender Mainstreaming and Post-Tsunami Reconstruction in Nanggroe Aceh Darussalam, Indonesia." *Review of International Studies* 36, 29–50.

Joachim, Jutta. 2010. "Women's Rights as Human Rights." In Robert E. Denemark, ed., *The International Studies Encyclopedia, Vol. IX*. Oxford: Wiley-Blackwell Publishers, pp. 7570–7589.

Kabeer, N. 1999. "Resources, Agency, Achievements: Reflections On the Measurement of Women's Empowerment." *Development and Change* 30, 435–464.

    2005. "Gender Equality and Women's Empowerment: A Critical Analysis of the Third Millennium Development Goal 1." *Gender & Development* 13:1, 13–24.

Kapur, Ratna. 2005. *Erotic Justice: Law and the Politics of Postcolonialism*. London: Glasshouse Press.

Kardam, Nüket. 2004. "The Emerging Global Gender Equality Regime from Neoliberal and Constructivist Perspectives in International Relations." *International Feminist Journal of Politics* 6:1, 85–109.

Kenworthy, Lane and Malami, Melissa. 1999. "Gender Inequality in Political Representation: A Worldwide Comparative Analysis." *Social Forces* 78:1, 235–269.

Kinsella, Helen. 2003. "For a Careful Reading: The Conservatism of Gender Constructivism." *Review of International Studies* 5, 287–302.

Kouvo, Sari. 2005. "The United Nations and Gender Mainstreaming: Limits and Possibilities." In Doris Buss and Ambreena Manji, eds., *International Law: Modern Feminist Approaches*. Oxford and Portland: Hart Publishing, pp. 237–252.

Krishnan, Suneeta, Rocca, Corinne H., Hubbard, Alan E., Subbiah, Kalyani, Edmeades, Jeffrey and Padian, Nancy S. 2010. "Do Changes in Spousal Employment Status Lead to Domestic Violence? Insights From a Prospective Study in Bangalore, India." *Social Science and Medicine* 70, 136–143.

Krook, Mona Lena and True, Jacqui. 2010. "Rethinking the Life Cycles of International Norms: The United Nations and the Global Promotion of Gender Equality." *European Journal of International Relations* 18:1, 103–127.

Kuokkanen, Rauna. 2012. "Self-Determination and Indigenous Women's Rights at the Intersection of International Human Rights." *Human Rights Quarterly* 34, 225–250.

Lambert, Caroline. 2004. "Partial Sites and Partial Sightings: Women and the UN Treaty System." In Sharon Pickering and Caroline Lambert, eds., *Global Issues, Women and Justice*. Sydney Institute of Criminology, pp. 136–178.

Landman, Todd. 2004. "Measuring Human Rights: Principle, Practice, and Policy." *Human Rights Quarterly* 26:4, 906–931.

Landman, Todd and Carvalho, Edzia. 2010. *Measuring Human Rights.* New York: Taylor & Francis.

Meier, Petra and Celis, Karen. 2011. "Sowing the Seeds of its Own Failure: Implementing the Concept of Gender Mainstreaming." *Social Politics* 18:4, 469–489.

Mosedale, Sarah. 2005. "Assessing Women's Empowerment: Towards a Conceptual Framework." *Journal of International Development* 17:2, 243–257.

Moser, Caroline. 2005. "Has Gender Mainstreaming Failed?" *International Feminist Journal of Politics* 7:4, 576–590.

Moser, Caroline and Moser, Annalise. 2005. "Gender Mainstreaming Since Beijing: A Review of the Success and Limitations in International Institutions." *Gender and Development* 13:2, 11–22.

Nyamu-Musembi, Celestine. 2005. "Toward An Actor-Oriented Perspective on Human Rights." In Naila Kabeer, ed., *Inclusive Citizenship: Meanings and Expressions.* London and New York: Zed Books, pp. 31–49.

O'Flaherty, Michael and Fisher, John. 2008. "Sexual Orientation, Gender Identity and International Human Rights Law: Contextualising the Yogyakarta Principles." *Human Rights Law Review* 8:2, 207–408.

OSAGI (Office of the Special Advisor on Gender Issues and the Advancement of Women). 2002. *Gender Mainstreaming: An Overview.* New York: United Nations. Available at: www.un.org/womenwatch/osagi/pdf/e65237.pdf.

Otto, D. 1996. "Holding Up Half the Sky, But for Whose Benefit? A Critical Analysis of the Fourth World Conference on Women." *Australian Feminist Law Journal* 6, 7–28.

Parisi, Laura. 2009. "The Numbers Do(n't) Always Add Up: Dilemmas in Using Quantitative Research Methods in Feminist IR Scholarship." *Politics and Gender* 5:3, 410–419.

  2011. "Reclaiming Spaces of Resistance: Women's Human Rights and Global Restructuring." In Marianne H. Marchand and Anne Sisson Runyan, eds., *Gender and Global Restructuring: Sightings, Sites, and Resistances*, 2nd edn.. London and New York: Routledge, pp. 201–222.

Parpart, Jane. 2009. "Fine Words, Failed Policies: Gender Mainstreaming in an Insecure and Unequal World." In Jacqueline Leckie, ed., *Development in an Insecure and Gendered World: The Relevance of the Millennium Development Goals.* London and Burlington: Ashgate Publishers, pp. 51–70.

Peterson, V. Spike. 1990. "Whose Rights? A Critique of the 'Givens' in Human Rights Discourse." *Alternatives* 15:3, 303–344.

Poe, Steven C., Wendel-Blunt, Dierdre and Ho, Karl. 1997. "Global Patterns in the Achievement of Women's Human Rights to Equality." *Human Rights Quarterly* 19:4, 813–835.

Prügl, Elisabeth and Lustgarten, Audrey. 2007. "Mainstreaming Gender in International Organizations." In Jane S. Jaquette and Gale Summerfield, eds., *Women and Gender Equity in Development Theory and Practice: Institutions,*

Resources, and Mobilization. Durham, NC and London: Duke University Press, pp. 53–70.

Rounaq, Jahan. 1995. *The Elusive Agenda: Mainstreaming Women in Development*. London and New York: Zed Books.

Sacchet, Teresa. 2008. "Beyond Numbers: The Impact of Gender Quotas in Latin America." *International Journal of Feminist Politics* 10:3, 369–386.

Smyth, Ines. 2007. "Talking of Gender: Words and Meanings in Development Organisations." *Development in Practice* 17:4–5, 582–588.

Squires, Judith. 2005. "Is Mainstreaming Transformative? Theorizing Mainstreaming in the Context of Diversity and Deliberation." *Social Politics* 12:3, 366–388.

Subrahmanian, Ramya. 2007. "Making Sense of Gender in Shifting Institutional Contexts: Some Reflections on Gender Mainstreaming." In Andrea Cornwall, Elizabeth Harrison and Ann Whiteheads, eds., *Feminisms in Development: Contradictions, Contestations, and Challenges*. London and New York: Zed Books, pp. 89–94.

Sullivan, Donna. 1995. "The Public/Private Distinction in International Human Rights Law." In J. Peters and A. Wolper, eds., *Women's Rights, Human Rights: International Feminist Perspectives*. London and New York: Routledge, pp. 126–134.

Tiessen, Rebecca. 2007. *Everywhere/Nowhere: Gender Mainstreaming in Development Agencies*. Bloomfield: Kumarian Press.

True, Jacqui. 2009. "Gender Mainstreaming in International Institutions." In L.J. Shepherd, ed., *Gender Matters in Global Politics*. New York: Routledge, pp. 189–203.

True, Jacqui and Parisi, Laura. 2013. "Gender Mainstreaming Strategies in International Governance." In Gülay Caglar, Elisabeth Prügl and Susanne Zwingel, eds., *Feminist Strategies in International Governance*. London and New York: Routledge, pp. 37–56.

Unterhalter, Elaine and North, Amy. 2011. "Girls' Schooling, Gender Equity, and the Global Education and Development Agenda: Conceptual Disconnections, Political Struggles, and the Difficulties of Practice." *Feminist Formation* 23:3, 1–22.

Walby, Sylvia. 2005. "Gender Mainstreaming: Productive Tensions in Theory and Practice." *Social Politics: International Studies in Gender, State, and Society* 12:3, 321–343.

Wallace, Tina. 1998. "Institutionalizing Gender in UK NGOs." *Development in Practice* 8:2, 159–172.

Waylen, Georgina. 2008. "Transforming Global Governance: Challenges and Opportunities." In Shirin M. Rai and Georgina Waylen, eds., *Global Governance: Feminist Perspectives*. New York: Palgrave Macmillan, pp. 254–275.

West, Lois. 1999. "The United Nations Women's Conferences and Feminist Politics." In Mary K. Meyer and Elisabeth Prügl, eds., *Gender Politics in Global Governance*. Lanham: Rowman & Littlefield, pp. 177–193.

WHO (World Health Organization). 2012. "Maternal Mortality Ratio (per 100,00 live births)." Available at: www.who.int/healthinfo/statistics/indmaternalmortality/en/index.html (accessed May 15, 2012).

Zalewski, Marysia. 2010. "'I Don't Even Know What Gender Is': A Discussion of the Connections Between Gender, Gender Mainstreaming and Feminist Theory." *Review of International Studies* 36, 3–27.

Afterword: rights, practice, reality and hope: hard questions about human rights

CINDY HOLDER AND DAVID REIDY

When we set out to put together this volume, we conceived of it as organized around a series of hard questions about human rights, increasingly familiar to both scholars and practitioners, about, for example, the universality of human rights, the permissibility and wisdom of using force to secure human rights, and whether human rights can play a useful role in addressing harms to groups or to the environment. However, as the chapters began to come in, a different set of hard questions began to push to the surface, and not just the long-standing problems of state-centrism or the legacies of empire and colonization. Rather, there were general and abstract questions that seemed to bubble up and possibly constitute a deep structure running beneath and between many chapters. These general questions were not driving the specific questions that our contributors identified and grappled with, but they were key parts in explaining the special difficulty of those specific questions our contributors take up. We now see the chapters collected in this volume as contributing to academic and practical understanding of not only the questions they explicitly address – e.g., Is there a human right to democracy? Is global climate change a human rights issues? Can groups as such have human rights? – but also to three more general and abstract, but nevertheless crucial, questions. In what follows, we briefly discuss these questions and indicate how they relate to the specific issues and chapters that constitute the surface structure of this volume. We leave you, the reader, then with not only the hard questions identifiable from our Table of Contents, but with also a further set of hard questions – questions that the challenges taken up in and insights offered by the chapter in this volume push to the surface and that cannot be profitably addressed without further multi-disciplinary thinking about human rights in theory and practice in the twenty-first century.

What are people doing when they appeal to human rights?

One of the most basic questions running just beneath the surface of the chapters in this volume is: what are people doing when they appeal to a human right? At the minimum they are saying that some outcome or performance or good is morally appropriate to a human being. But in using the language of rights they are doing more. They are saying that something is morally appropriate because of human beings' *rights*. What does using the language of rights add to a normative expectation? And does it add something distinctive when the rights are ascribed to a person qua human being?

Hilary Charlesworth's contribution to this volume illustrates the significance of this question of what it is that's invoked in an appeal to human rights. In Charlesworth's discussion of the human right to democracy we see how different answers to the question of what a right to democracy implies may produce different answers as to whether what's appealed to is a human right at all. This happens, in part, because differing answers make the appeal to human rights part of different normative and political conversations. For example, to invoke international legal obligations and entitlements is to engage in a discussion of how international law constrains states in their treatment of individuals and in their relations with other states. That is a different normative conversation than that engaged by invoking universally justifiable moral rights. In this regard, Charlesworth's discussion of hard questions with respect to the right to democracy is directly related to Julie Mertus's discussion of hard questions regarding the responsibility to protect. In both of these issue areas part of what makes the hard questions hard is ambiguity about what, exactly, is required for states and other international actors to count as respecting human rights.

In his chapter on human rights and progressiveness Allen Buchanan suggests that what is distinctively valuable about the concept of a human *right* is its conferral of a special kind of status associated with claiming. This suggestion is congruent with observations about the potential value for human rights advocacy of highlighting the narratives and experiences of survivors and victims in transitions from conflict and in relation to non-state armed groups (Parker 2011; Staub 2006). However to emphasize the conferral of standing as a central element of what rights language adds is potentially in tension with theoretical treatments that emphasize establishing duties and elevating individual interests over those of collectivities (Tasioulas 2010). Emphasizing standing, especially standing as a claimant, further seems to exacerbate worries about cultural specificity as standing and claiming seem to valorize and reward specific character traits and specific forms of social relationship (Nickel 2007).

A focus on rights-holding as a distinctive type of standing further poses the question: standing in relation to whom? In his discussion of social and economic rights in this volume Tony Evans raises the possibility that the standing conferred by human rights is contingent on participation in global systems of production, finance and exchange; and Evans asks what this contingency means for human rights' potential to serve as a basis of normative critique. Part of the problem he identifies is that the conceptual structure by which human rights confer the capacity to assert claims makes it inevitable that some sources of harms or wrongs will be foreclosed as potential grounds for claims. Another aspect of the problem concerns whether and to what extent the practical value of human rights as a source of normative expectations depends on their being able to serve as a source of claims. For example, is there still value in using the language of human rights when the source of harm or wrong is not an actor, but a structure? Can there be claims against the logic of global capital playing itself out in a local context? Who would be the addressee of such claims? Is there practical value in the status of claimant when the harms or wrongs originate with actors whose liabilities and susceptibility to claims are ambiguous or difficult to enforce?

In his contribution Adam McBeth grapples with the problem of how to apply the international legal constraints associated with human rights to non-state actors such as intergovernmental organizations (IGOs) and corporations. McBeth takes it to be uncontroversial that human rights are direct and immediate sources of moral and legal constraints on the activities of non-state actors; the question is how to hold such actors accountable for respecting (or failing to respect) these constraints. However many theorists have argued that the claims human rights establish are defined by and contingent on participation in the structures of a state (Fox-Decent and Criddle 2009; Raz 2010). The capacity of human rights to function as rights seems to require definition in relation to a set of institutions; but defining rights in relation to a set of institutions channels and constrains the type of claimants and claims that can be effectively pursued. Ann Cudd grapples with exactly this challenge in her contribution to this volume as she seeks to develop a conceptual framework for understanding the right to a decent life that takes structural and institutional contexts seriously without arbitrarily limiting the duties that human rights establish to state officials and compatriots.

In part, this is the familiar problem of how the concept of a "right" structures and constrains who can be imagined as human and what can be important to them as human beings. In her contribution to this volume Marysia Zalewski brings out a less familiar but equally important part of the problem: how conceptions of "humanity" structure and constrain what can be imagined as following from rights. Feminist scholars have long noted how certain constructions of the human exclude the interests and priorities of "othered" people, including women, from specifications of what human rights protect (Charlesworth and Chinkin 1993; Chinkin 1999). Zalewski describes how conceptions of human and non-human, natural and monstrous play into and populate those constructions, limiting who can claim rights in part by limiting what can be conceived of as a plausible rights claim. Zalewski's observations about "natural" and "monstrous" women also apply to "natural" and "monstrous" men, "natural" and "monstrous" children – "natural" and "monstrous" exemplars of any human type.

In his contribution to this volume Chris Brown argues that appeal to some notion of human nature is inevitable when deploying the concept of a human right, so that the relevant question is not whether to generate human rights out of a conception of human nature but how to do so without undermining or betraying such rights' normative function. However, Larry May's contribution on the human rights of soldiers illustrates how, in addition to conceptions of femininity and masculinity and normal and monstrous, conceptions of heroism and cowardice and of innocence in the sense of unknowingness may limit the range of what can be imagined as a human rights abuse. The problem that May brings out is how judgments about the extent to which an action is mandated by reasons of humanity are framed by empirical assumptions about what is possible and inevitable in human relationships and social organization.

Do various human rights actually reference the same kind of norm?

Another important question lying beneath the surface of and making difficult the issues discussed in this volume concerns the kind of norm(s) human rights appeal to or express. More specifically, do the human rights most commonly appealed to actually reference the same kind of norm? Marie-Bénédicte Dembour (2010) describes four conceptions of rights in the academic literature: human rights as given, human rights as agreed upon, human rights as fought for and human rights as a discursive practice. All of these conceptions appear in this volume. But what is the connection between them? Is there any connection at all? Is there a core conception of human rights informing the contributions to this volume?

Added to this divergence in theoretical conceptions is the gap between how rights are academically theorized and how human rights are put to use. Ariadna Estévez (2011) describes three features of the way people use human rights concepts in social and political life that have become a focus of research by political sociologists: human rights as an axis of collective action; human rights as a site at which people participate in constructing the discourses to which they're subject; and human rights as a source of transformations in concepts of citizenship in response to global migration.

The diversity of theoretical conceptions and practical usages of human rights renders especially difficult many of the issues discussed in this volume, for it is not always clear how consistently to bring all to bear on any particular issue or to maintain consistency across issues. Consider the human right to democracy. Carol Gould, Hilary Charlesworth and Thomas Christiano arguably each emphasize and draw on different conceptions and usages of the right. And these differences reappear in the discussions of other human rights by other contributors. Gould offers persuasive reasons for thinking that democratic participation is a fundamentally important normative claim that can be appropriately be characterized as the basis of a right. Yet the human right to democratic participation as she describes it seems to function very differently, as a source of constraints and as a source of obligations, than does, for example, the human right to cultural difference described by Claudio Corradetti in his contribution. The objects of these rights – democracy on the one hand, institutions that respect cultural difference on the other – differ in very fundamental ways and these differences lead to differently structured normative implications, even different sorts of normative claims.

But the diversity of theoretical conceptions and practical usages need not entail any inconsistency and may simply point up the need for a more complex and integrated understanding of human rights. Consider Gail Karlsson's contribution to this volume. She offers several concrete examples in which different conceptions and uses of human rights – as claims against institutional actors, as vehicles of collective action, as descriptions of morally compelling interests of individuals, as discursive practices expressing or facilitating shared understandings – are mutually reinforcing and pull in the same direction. In Karlsson's examples state actors give impetus and support, both institutional and discursive, to projects that engage concrete problems people face in the context of a specific community or the performance of specific tasks, as part of an overall goal to reduce energy poverty. This integration of aspects of rights that are often in conceptual tension with one another is due in large part to the various participants in the projects – state actors, NGOs, local people – assuming that the institutional, collective action, individual interests and discursive aspects of human rights are integrated, mutually supporting and responsive to shared understandings, and organizing their participation accordingly. Was this assumption encouraged and facilitated by the use of human rights concepts? Or were human rights concepts simply convenient and strategically useful labels?

Mark Goodale's chapter suggests that no unified set of practices or single (even if complex) normative conception lies behind the diverse appeals to human rights made around the world and discussed in this volume. If he is right, then human rights may best be conceived of as what evolutionary biologists call "a good trick": apt for a variety of things that beings with a particular constitution are well-served by doing such that it becomes ubiquitous (Nelson 2008). But what is it about human rights that makes them so useful? And can they continue to be useful when the normative purposes for which they are deployed vary so widely?

How do human rights impact the lives of actual people?

Perhaps the most important question raised by and making difficult the studies in this volume is this: How do human rights impact the lives of actual people? The empirical literature on this question is mixed. There is some evidence that rhetorical affirmation of human rights treaties is positively correlated with minimum thresholds of respect for human rights within states (Keck and Sikkink 1998; Sikkink 2011; Simmons 2009). But there is also evidence that accession to human rights treaties is used as a tool to delay implementation of reforms and avoid changes to practices (Hathaway 2002; Neumayer 2005). Studies of the use of human rights concepts by NGOs and social justice movements indicate that sometimes such concepts are effective tools for improving the lives of people, but sometimes such concepts are ineffectual for improving the lives of people, and sometimes human rights concepts actually undermine the goal of improving lives (Engle 2011; Grugel and Piper 2009; Kennedy 2002). Whether the use of human rights concepts contributes positively seems to depend on the specific issues that are the basis of a group's work, the specific population a group serves or targets, and the group's goals with respect to those issues and populations (Engle 2011; Grugel and Piper 2009). Often it is ambiguous whether being able to effectively use human rights concepts and being able to effectively impact lives are both effects of some underlying feature of an NGO or social justice movement in relation to the social and political structures with which they engage.

Part of the difficulty in determining how human rights impact the lives of actual people is an absence of sustained and explicit discussion of methodological questions in human rights scholarship (Coomans *et al.* 2009; Gready 2009). Laura Parisi's chapter in this volume brings out the significance of methodological choices for the translation of theory into practice. For Parisi, the complexity of identifying what would constitute progress in relation to women's human rights is in part due to the difficulty of unpacking the implications of what at first seems a very simple theoretical insight: to genuinely respect the human rights of women requires more than treating them as men with special needs. Parisi's overview of the challenges NGOs and IGOs face in their attempts to incorporate that insight in their practice provides a very effective demonstration of how the complex intellectual and social constructions that produce theoretical insights can be part of the framework that generates difficult choices and unexpected effects in practice.

Another, perhaps more significant, part of the difficulty in telling how human rights impact lives is the level of analysis at which this question is discussed. Kristin Shrader-Frechette's chapter brings out the extent to which the level of analysis at which judgments about whether human rights protections are adequate has important impacts on the conclusions reached. For example, considered at the level of aggregated statistics, the impact of permitting industrial practices that increase levels of carcinogenic chemicals in the food supply may not appear as a violation of a state's human rights obligations. However, considered at the level of the individuals whose propensity to develop cancers is impacted by ingesting these chemicals, states do seem to have obligations not to permit practices that increase carcinogenic chemicals in food. This shift in the level at which phenomena are described is a valuable tool for a resistance strategy that Balakrishnan Rajagopal (2003) describes as "international law from below." In this strategy social movements and grassroots organizations use human rights and other international legal concepts to put a name to their claims and priorities and leverage a response. By taking the power to name and give content to human rights into their own hands, social movements and grassroots organizations diffuse control over human rights discourse, and so diffuse control over what counts as a proper candidate for the normative expectations that human rights generate.

However, this diffusion of control will have a built-in limit so long as the normative force of human rights concepts depends on association with international human rights regimes. For although international human rights regimes are not limited to treaties between states, a state-based treaty system is where those regimes originate, and a state-based international political system is the context within which international human rights concepts do their normative work. Consequently, there is an inherent tension between the project of diffusing power over how human rights concepts are defined and applied and the reality of how those concepts' normative force is generated. The political system within which international human rights structure normative expectations and empower individuals is organized around and for the sake of state-based relationships. Presence within international human rights regimes is always structured by and defined in relation to a state, even and especially when rights are claimed against a non-state actor.

Ayelet Shachar's discussion of human rights, multiculturalism and personal status illustrates the challenge of making rights that are state-centric in this sense of being defined and structured in relation to a state work and work equally for actual people. Actual individuals' relationships and vulnerabilities are structured by states, and so extracting state institutions from communally defined standing and claims is not a real option. But those relationships and vulnerabilities are neither entirely defined by nor exhausted by the states that exercise jurisdiction over them. This general fact about human lives becomes more visible and more challenging for human rights as the structures within which people live establish increasingly complex and transnational connections between them. Thomas Christiano, in his contribution on the human right to democracy, notes the ways that individuals' relationships and vulnerabilities in one jurisdiction are impacted by how relationships and vulnerabilities are structured in other jurisdictions by other states. International institutions are part of the context that defines and empowers states. International political and legal institutions also define and empower communities and individuals directly. And so international institutions, too, must be part of the equation if the goal is to think clearly about human rights.

Human rights and hope for something better

So what, exactly, are people doing when they appeal to a human right? Are they always, or even often, doing the same thing? The contribution by Evelyn Amony and Erin Baines provides one possibility for a unifying concern behind the wide range of conceptions and practices that go under the name of human rights: belief in the possibility that things can be, in some enduring or stable sense, better. One of the most striking things about Evelyn Amony's diary entries is that she has made them at all. The day-to-day demands of Amony's life are overwhelming; and yet she takes on the further task of diarizing. This commitment to documenting, to naming, to exposing life as it is and actions as they have been experienced is a central component of human rights practice. It is also a central avenue of theoretical critique. For example, one of the problems that Peter Jones grapples with in his contribution to this volume is whether it is possible to secure the most important interests of persons without ascribing human rights to groups. A parallel question regards whether the language of human rights captures in the right way the harms and wrongs we hope, in some enduring or stable way, to eliminate. In his chapter Stephen Gardiner asks not only whether the language of human rights adequately captures what goes wrong in failures to address climate change, but whether that language can and does generate the right kind of response. In this he asks a general and pressing question about the purpose of using human rights language. Is it enough to document and to name? Should appeals to human rights also indicate a path of action?

The centrality of documenting and exposing in human rights practice and theory only makes sense on the assumption that something better is not only possible but proximate. This does not imply that what this something better consists in must be definitively articulated by human rights practice and theory, or that such practice and theory must in itself be able to bring about something better. Nor does it imply that this something better is singular or unitary. Just as there is an ineliminable diversity to the "we" who hope for something better, there is an ineliminable particularity to our hopes, a point Neil Walker explores at some length in his discussion of the necessary universality and particularity of human rights. But there is also an ineliminable universality to human rights, as Rex Martin aims to vindicate, and this arguably expresses something universal about what it is we hope for, even if what it is we hope for is conditioned by various facts of modernity. At the end of the day, there is an element of faith in human rights practice and theory: faith that documenting and exposing life and what has been experienced, chronicling the distances between our diverse lives and our particular hopes, can make a positive difference. One of the hardest questions for human rights is whether, in existing theories and practices, academics and advocates are vindicating that faith.

References

Charlesworth, Hilary and Chinkin, Christine. 1993. "The Gender of *Jus Cogens*." *Human Rights Quarterly* 15:1, 63–76.

Chinkin, Christine. 1999. "Gender Inequality and International Human Rights Law." In Andrew Hurrell and Ngaire Woods, eds., *Inequality, Globalization, and World Politics*. Oxford University Press, pp. 95–121.

Coomans, Fons, Grünfeld, Fred and Kamminga, Menno T., eds. 2009. *Methods of Human Rights Research*. Cambridge: Intersentia Publishing.

Dembour, Marie-Bénédicte. 2010. "What Are Human Rights? Four Schools of Thought." *Human Rights Quarterly* 32:1, 1–20.

Engle, Sally Merry. 2011. "Measuring the World: Indicators, Human Rights, and Global Governance." *Current Anthropology* 52, Supplement 3, S83–S95.

Estévez, Ariadna. 2011. "Human Rights in Contemporary Political Sociology: The Primacy of Social Subjects." *Human Rights Quarterly* 33:4, 1142–1162.

Fox-Decent, Evan and Criddle, Evan. 2009. "The Fiduciary Constitution of Human Rights." *Legal Theory* 15, 301–336.

Gready, Paul. 2009. "Reasons to Be Cautious about Evidence and Evaluation: Rights-based Approaches to Development and the Emerging Culture of Evaluation." *Journal of Human Rights Practice* 1:3, 380–401.

Grugel, Jean and Piper, Nicola. 2009. "Do Rights Promote Development?" *Global Social Policy* 9:1, 79–98.

Hathaway, Oona A. 2002. "Do Human Rights Treaties Make a Difference?" *Yale Law Journal* 111:8, 1935–2042.

Keck, Margaret and Sikkink, Kathryn. 1998. *Activists Beyond Borders: Advocacy Networks in International Politics*. Ithaca: Cornell University Press.

Kennedy, David. 2002. "The International Human Rights Movement: Part of the Problem?" *Harvard Human Rights Journal* 15, 101–125.

Nelson, Lynn H. 2008. "The Descent of Evolutionary Explanations: Darwinian Vestiges in the Social Sciences." In S.P. Turner and P.A. Roth, eds., *The Blackwell Guide to the Philosophy of the Social Sciences*. New York: Blackwell, pp. 258–290.

Neumayer, Eric. 2005. "Do International Human Rights Treaties Improve Respect for Human Rights?" *Journal of Conflict Resolution* 49:6, 925–953.

Nickel, James W. 2007. *Making Sense of Human Rights*. New York: Blackwell.

Parker, Tom. 2011. "Redressing the Balance: How Human Rights Defenders Can Use Victim Narratives to Confront the Violence of Armed Groups." Human Rights Quarterly 33:4, 1122–1141.

Rajagopal, Balakrishnan. 2003. *International Law from Below: Development, Social Movements and Third World Resistance*. Cambridge University Press.

Raz, Joseph. 2010. "Human Rights in the Emerging World Order." *Transnational Legal Theory* 1, 31–47.

Sikkink, Kathryn. 2011. *The Justice Cascade: How Human Rights Prosecutions are Changing World Politics*. New York: W.W. Norton.

Simmons, Beth A. 2009. *Mobilizing for Human Rights: International Law in Domestic Politics*. Cambridge University Press.

Staub, Ervin. 2006. "Reconciliation after Genocide, Mass Killing, or Intractable Conflict: Understanding the Roots of Violence, Psychological Recovery, and Steps toward a General Theory." *Political Psychology* 27:6, 867–894.

Tasioulas, John. 2010. "Taking Rights out of Human Rights." *Ethics* 120:4, 647–678.

Index